Russia

EUROPEAN NATIONS

RUSSIA
A REFERENCE GUIDE
FROM THE RENAISSANCE TO THE PRESENT

Mauricio Borrero

Facts On File, Inc.

Russia: A Reference Guide from the Renaissance to the Present

Copyright © 2004 by Mauricio Borrero

Facts On File, Inc.
132 West 31st Street
New York NY 10001

Library of Congress Cataloging-in-Publication Data
Borrero, Mauricio
    Russia: a reference guide from the Renaissance to the present / Mauricio Borrero.
      p. cm. — (European nations series)
    Includes bibliographical references and index.
     ISBN 0-8160-4454-6
    1. Russia—History—Dictionaries. 2. Soviet Union—History—Dictionaries. 3. Russia
(Federation)—History—Dictionaries. I. Title. II. Series.
    DK36.B59 2004
    947′.003—dc22
                                                  2003060547

Facts On File books are available at special discounts when purchased in bulk quantities for businesses, associations, institutions, or sales promotions. Please call our Special Sales Department in New York at (212) 967-8800 or (800) 322-8755.

You can find Facts On File on the World Wide Web at http://www.factsonfile.com

Text design by David C. Strelecky
Cover design by Semadar Megged
Maps by Jeremy Eagle © Facts On File, Inc.

Printed in the United States of America

VB FOF 10 9 8 7 6 5 4 3 2 1

This book is printed on acid-free paper.

CONTENTS

FOREWORD

This series was inspired by the need of high school and college students to have a concise and readily available history series focusing on the evolution of the major European powers and other influential European states in the modern age—from the Renaissance to the present. Written in accessible language, the projected volumes include all of the major European countries: France, Germany, Great Britain, Italy, and Russia, as well as other states such as Spain, Portugal, Austria, and Hungary that have made important intellectual, political, cultural, and religious contributions to Europe and the world. The format has been designed to facilitate usage and includes a short introduction by the author of each volume, a specialist in its history, providing an overview of the importance of the particular country in the modern period. This is followed by a narrative history of each nation from the time of the Renaissance to the present. The core of the volume consists of an A–Z dictionary of people, events, and places, providing coverage of intellectual, political, diplomatic, cultural, social, religious, and economic developments. Next, a chronology details key events in each nation's development over the past several centuries. Finally, the end matter includes a selected bibliography of readily available works, maps, and an index to the material within the volume.

—Frank J. Coppa, General Editor
St. John's University

ACKNOWLEDGMENTS

I wish to thank my colleague Frank Coppa, editor of the European Nations series, for suggesting that I write this book. I also wish to thank Owen Lancer, editor at Facts On File, for patiently and expertly guiding the manuscript through its publication. At St. John's University, Anna Marie Mannuzza, Jacek Niedzwiecki, John-Emery Konecsni, and Teresa Purpura assisted with clerical and research matters. Research was conducted at the Slavic and Baltic Division of the New York Public Library, the Flushing Branch of the Queens Borough Public Library, and the Russian State Library in Moscow. I am grateful to their staffs for their bibliographic assistance. As always, my wife and children provided the support, space, and tolerance necessary to complete the manuscript.

A NOTE ABOUT TRANSLITERATION AND DATES

In transliterating terms from the Russian Cyrillic alphabet, I have followed a modified version of the standard Library of Congress system. For the sake of readability, last names ending in *ii* have been changed to *y* (thus *Dostoevsky* and not *Dostoevskii*, *Lunacharsky* and not *Lunacharskii*). Other last names have been rendered in forms already familiar to English-language readers (*Yeltsin* and *Yevtushenko* instead of *Eltsin* and *Evtushenko*, but *Esenin* instead of *Yesenin*). A similar approach has been used for first names ending in *ii* (*Yuri* and *Vasili*, but *Dmitrii*, *Anatolii* and *Grigorii*). The Russian "soft sign" has been omitted throughout the text (thus, *streltsy* and *Kazan* instead of *strel'tsy* and *Kazan'*).

From 1700 until February 1918, Russia followed the Julian calendar instead of the Gregorian calendar used in the West. The Julian (Old Style) calendar lagged 11 days behind the Gregorian (New Style) calendar in the 18th century, 12 in the 19th century, and 13 in the 20th century. Throughout the text, I have tried to render dates according to the Gregorian calendar.

INTRODUCTION

The inclusion of Russia in the present reference series on European nations from the Renaissance to the present reflects the belief that Russia is indeed a European nation, an assumption that many readers may take for granted but which has been debated for centuries. For while there may be important nuances in terms of how other present and former nations represented in this series, such as Great Britain, Austria-Hungary, Italy, France, Germany, Spain, and Portugal, have defined their relationship to the idea of Europe, their membership in the family of European nations has never been questioned to the extent that it has with regard to Russia. Stretching from the Baltic Sea to the Pacific Ocean across the vast Eurasian landmass, Russia has developed over the centuries at the periphery of the geographical, political, and cultural construct that we call Europe—sometimes welcome in the European family of nations, sometimes not. From the earliest accounts of European travelers to the Muscovite court to present-day discussions about Russia's future after communism, Western observers have debated the extent to which Russia is a part of Europe or something different. To be sure, Russians themselves have questioned their own identity with equal, if not greater, intensity and persistence. The mid-19th century intellectual debates between Russian Slavophiles and Westernizers were but one instance of a questioning that goes back to the early modern period and forward to the present day.

The idea that Russia is not European begins with the perception of a different historical development. Those seeking to place Russia outside of the European tradition can point to a different historical development marked by a heritage shaped by allegiance to Byzantine Christianity, two to three centuries of Mongol rule, and the absence of a Renaissance. In fact, the subtitle of the European Nations series, "from the Renaissance to the present," seems least applicable to a nation that was beginning to shake off dependence on Asian foreign rule roughly at the same time that western Europe was challenging the received wisdom of its medieval civilization. They also can point to the development in subsequent centuries of an autocracy based on a social foundation of serfdom that grew more rather than less restrictive as western European serfdom was beginning to recede. Finally, they can point to the absence of a strong capitalist tradition based on an independent, politically assertive middle class, and as a clincher they can point to the unique experience of Soviet communism in the 20th century.

At times, however, the differences between Russia and its European neighbors seem quantitative rather than qualitative, a product of the huge disparities in size between the two. None of the other European monarchs made as extensive claims to autocratic powers and for as long as the Russian czars. While cultural and class differences between rulers and ruled were common to all European states, nowhere did the gap appear as vast as it did in Russia, especially after the reign of Peter the Great. None of the many 20th-century dictatorships that appeared on the European political scene was as ruthless and remained in place for as long as the communist dictatorship ushered in by the Russian Revolution of 1917. Seen under this light, Russia is but a magnified extension of Europe, a view that is more in line with the true nature of the ambiguous geographical boundary that divides Europe from Asia. And yet after centuries of close interaction, one is hard-pressed to find clear dividing lines between Russia and Europe.

Just as one cannot think of Russia without Europe, it is untenable to think of Europe without Russia. What is European literature without the contributions of Pushkin, Tolstoy, Dostoevsky, or Chekhov, and what is Western music without the contributions of Tchaikovsky, Stravinsky, or Shostakovich? And even though Russia has been and continues to be portrayed as a threat to the West, in the case of Napoleon and Hitler it has also twice helped to save Europe from threats created by its own body politic.

The attempt to assess Russia's place in European and world history continues to this day, a decade or so after the end of the Soviet Union, as shown by two recent English-language interpretive works. Working within the paradigm that divides Russia from Europe, Marshall Poe argues that for the past five centuries up to the abrupt end of Soviet communism in 1991, Russian political and intellectual elites have created a "Russian moment in world history," distinguished by their ability to advance a modernizing agenda in non-European ways. Working with less broad brushstrokes, Steven Marks also begins with the Russian elites' search for alternatives to European or Western models of modernity. He then seeks to elucidate, in a book of the same title, how Russia shaped the modern world through political and cultural contributions ranging from the refining of terrorism as a revolutionary weapon and the development of mass-based dictatorships to the introduction of new forms of intellectual and cultural creativity in literature, ballet, and the arts.

The present volume seeks to introduce a general audience to the richness of the Russian historical tradition, with its villains and saints, militaries victories and defeats, as well as the improbable heights and absolute depths in human relationships that are evident throughout its history. In this volume's historical dictionary, readers will indeed learn about art, anti-Semitism, ballet, and Bolshevism (to borrow a page from the subtitle of Marks's stimulating book), well-known components—for better or for worse—of Russian history. From Yalta to Yashin and *zapovedniks* to Zubatov, they will also learn about smaller but equally important and fascinating Russian contributions to international diplomacy, world soccer, environmentalism, and methods of police surveillance.

—Mauricio Borrero
St. John's University, New York

HISTORY OF RUSSIA

KIEVAN RUS

882–1240

The origins of the people who call themselves Russians and of the polity that we know as Russia remain somewhat obscure, but we can sketch the basic outlines of those early centuries. It is generally accepted that the ancestors of the Slavs, from which the Russians descend, first appeared in the sixth century during the "great migration of peoples," moving eastward from the Carpathians into the area of the Dnieper River basin. The Dnieper River Slav settlements became part of an important trading route linking Scandinavia with Constantinople, capital of the Byzantine Empire. By the ninth century, a number of trading towns had developed in the area, and through a series of frequent wars they tried to seize nearby territory.

It is at this point that the Varangians (Norsemen or Vikings) made their appearance in the old historical chronicles that remain as one of the few primary sources of early Russian history. Regardless of their warrior image elsewhere in Europe, it seems that in the Dnieper River basin the Varangians were primarily interested in trade. Moving up and down the rivers of western Russia, the Varangians eventually linked Scandinavia and northern Europe to the Black Sea and Constantinople at a time when the Muslim conquests of the eighth century had reduced European trade in the Mediterranean Sea. The details surrounding the appearance of the Varangians have been debated by historians through the centuries, with much of the debate centering around the question of whether the Varangians gradually settled in the Dnieper River basin or whether they were invited by the local population to serve as a ruling class. At the center of this debate is the semilegendary figure of Rurik, whom the sources record as having conquered the city of Novgorod in 862.

Although little is known about Rurik, there is agreement that the reign of Oleg (r. 882–913), a relative of Rurik, is an important marker in the development of the political entity that came to be known as Kievan Rus. Oleg first succeeded Rurik as ruler of Novgorod, then moved southward, establishing himself at Kiev, a city on the Dnieper River. One of the main achievements of Oleg's reign was territorial expansion. He began the process of bringing the East Slavic tribes near Kiev under control, which his successors would continue. Another important achievement was the establishment of close trade relations with

Byzantium. In 907, Oleg led a military expedition to attack the city of Constantinople. Four years later, Kiev received favorable trade terms from the Byzantines.

Oleg was succeeded by his son Igor (r. 913–945), who continued the main themes of Oleg's reign. In 941, Igor led another campaign against Constantinople, but this time it was unsuccessful, and as a result Kievan traders lost their previous trade privileges with the Byzantines. Igor also tried to spread Kievan authority over neighboring Slavic tribes and, like Oleg, faced their frequent rebellions. He was killed collecting tribute from the Drevliane, one of the Slavic tribes the Kievans attempted to control.

Igor died when his son was an infant, so his widow, Olga (r. 945–962), led the Kievan state as regent. She was the first woman to serve as ruler of Russia. Olga began her years in power by wiping out much of the Drevliane, the tribe that had killed her husband. She is perhaps best remembered in Russian history for her conversion to Christianity around the year 955. As the first member of the ruling family to accept Christianity, she helped prepare the way for the conversion of the entire country. Olga died in 969 and was later proclaimed a saint by the Russian Orthodox Church.

In 962, Igor and Olga's son, Sviatoslav (r. 962–972) attained majority and became ruler of Kiev. From 964 to 967 he expanded Kievan rule to the east and the north, defeating nearby Slavic tribes as well as the Volga Bulgars and Khazars. As a result of these campaigns the Volga River route to the Caspian Sea came under Kievan control. Sviatoslav was less successful in his second major campaign in the region of the Balkans. In 967 his troops reached the Danube River valley. Although he fought and defeated the Bulgarians in several campaigns over the following years, by 971 he had been defeated by the Byzantines and forced out of the Balkans.

Sviatoslav's death led to a civil war among his sons, a problem that would recur throughout early Russian history because of the absence of an accepted means of succession. After an eight-year-long period of conflict, his youngest son, Vladimir (r. 980–1015) emerged victorious. In hindsight the central achievement of Vladimir's reign was his conversion to Orthodox Christianity in 988 and its adoption as the religion of the Kievan state. Orthodox Christianity became the basis for much of early Russian art and culture. It linked Kievan Russia to the highly advanced society of Byzantium. At the same time it hampered ties between Russia and the rest of Europe, where Western Christianity, with its center at Rome, held sway. The formal break between the Eastern and Western Churches that took place in 1054 heightened Russia's isolation from the peoples of central and western Europe, which looked to Rome. The Russian Church was led by a metropolitan bishop located at Kiev. These bishops were appointed by the patriarch at Constantinople and most of the early metropolitan bishops were Greek rather than Russian. The continued expansion of Kievan boundaries during Vladimir's reign has received less attention but was also an important feature. Vladimir restored Kievan authority westward over areas lost to Poland during the recent civil war. He also extended Kievan authority northward to reach the Baltic Sea.

Vladimir's death in 1015 and the uncertainty over his succession again triggered a period of conflict among his sons. After four years, Yaroslav (r. 1019–54)
defeated his brothers but then had to split control of Kievan territory with one
brother until 1036. Despite these tumultuous beginnings, Yaroslav, already
known as "the Wise" during his lifetime, presided over a reign generally considered the peak of Kievan history. Geographically Kievan Russia extended
from the Black Sea to the Baltic Sea and westward to the Carpathians. Ties with
central and western Europe were strengthened in a series of marriage alliances.
Yaroslav's sister married the king of Poland, and three of his daughters married
foreign monarchs: the kings of Hungary, Norway, and Poland. Yaroslav administered a decisive defeat to the Pechenegs in 1037, the warlike nomads who
lived between the Kievan state and the Black Sea and who had posed a threat
to Kiev for over a century. For a brief time afterward, Kievan Rus was free from
the threats of steppe nomads.

Kiev emerged as an important cultural center and one of the important cities
of Europe during Yaroslav's reign. New churches, schools, and libraries were
built. The Kievan era also marks the beginning of a distinctive Russian tradition
in art and architecture that at first was strongly influenced by Byzantine traditions and focused on religious themes. An early example of these were the St.
Sophia cathedrals constructed in Kiev and Novgorod. Another important component of early Russian art was the development of a tradition of icons, religious pictures painted on wooden panels that were placed both in churches and
in private homes.

The Kievan economy was based on both trade and agriculture. Although historians disagree on the relative weight of each in Kievan economic life, the bulk
of the population was engaged in agriculture. Trade tended to be dominated by
the princes, their retinues, and wealthy merchants. At its height the Kievan
state included both steppe and forest regions. Trade between northern centers
like Novgorod and southern cities like Kiev probably involved exchanging grain
and cattle from the south for furs and timber from the north. Kievan Rus also
had a lively and important trading relationship with the Byzantine Empire. The
grand prince of Kiev gathered tribute from the regions under his control. Each
spring he led a trading expedition down the Dnieper River and across the Black
Sea to Byzantium. Private merchants from all over Kievan Rus traveled along
under the prince's protection. The Kievans traded raw materials such as furs for
finished goods like weapons and luxuries such as spices and jewelry.

There were two regional types of farming. In the steppe, where land was
abundant and easy to cultivate, farmers moved frequently as fields wore out.
The basic crop was wheat. In the zones farther north, farmers got new land only
by laboriously clearing away the forest. Thus they were more settled, alternately
using a part of their land or letting it rest fallow. The basic crops were rye, bar-
ley, and oats.

In cultural matters, with the conversion of the population to Christianity in
988 and the diffusion of the Cyrillic alphabet initially developed by the Orthodox missionaries Cyril and Methodius to aid them in translating the Bible for
the conversion of the Southern and Western Slavs, Kievan Rus acquired a writ-

ten language known as Old Church Slavonic. A Kievan literature in the form of religious documents now appeared using Old Church Slavonic, the language of church services. A secular literature of poetry and historical chronicles in Old Church Slavonic developed as well. There are two important early texts from this period. The 12th-century *Primary Russian Chronicle,* despite a long and rich controversy about its origins, stands as the basic document recording the history of Kievan Rus. A copy of the *Chronicle* made by the monk Lavrentii in 1377 has survived to the present. The other text is the *Tale of Igor,* an epic poem that is perhaps the most famous literary product of the Kievan era. Written by an unknown author, it describes the defeat of Kievan forces at the hands of the Polovtsy nomads of the steppe in 1185.

The population of the Kievan state was divided into a number of social classes. Though most people were peasants, the population ranged from powerful princes to slaves. The top level of Kievan society consisted of the prince and his family, supposedly descended from the Varangian Rurik. The growth of the princely family made this a numerically substantial group. Just below the prince's family stood members of the *druzhina,* which made up the prince's aristocratic retinue. They were known as *muzhi.* Other aristocrats included dignitaries whose power and prestige were based on their regional prominence. They stood on the same level as the *muzhi.* During the Kievan era this difference between aristocratic groups gradually faded. Both aristocrats by virtue of serving the prince and aristocrats by virtue of their local power merged into a single noble group known as boyars.

In the middle of society, two groups of free citizens existed in the cities and the countryside. Historians refer to both groups as a social class called the *liudi.* In urban centers this middle class consisted of merchants and small entrepreneurs such as carpenters and tanners. This class of free citizens was a significant part of the population in a society partly based on commerce. Merchants engaged in long-distance trade with Europe and Byzantium traveled together for safety. This cooperation led in turn to the formation of merchant guilds in Kiev similar to those in western and central Europe. In the countryside, there was also a group of middle-class landowners, possessing small estates but without the privileges of boyars.

At the bottom of the social scale were laborers with varying degrees of subordination, who made up the majority of the population. In rural areas, these laborers were called *smerdy;* although historians are not certain about their legal status, it seems that at this early stage of Kievan history most of them were not yet serfs tied to the land. Beneath the *smerdy* were two groups tied down by firm obligations. Slaves, known as *kholopy,* were usually prisoners of war or formerly free laborers who had been penalized for violating the law. On the other hand, *zakupy* were indentured servants, held in a form of temporary servitude until they had discharged a debt.

In hindsight the reign of Yaroslav the Wise was probably the peak of Kievan Rus; Yaroslav's death in 1054 traditionally marks the beginning of its gradual decline. Kiev was also divided by internal conflicts that often resulted from the lack of an accepted principle of succession and the practice of giving lands to the descendants of a ruling prince. Yaroslav's death was followed by almost three decades of intermittent strife among his sons for control of Kiev. The Cumans in the east and Teutonic Knights, Lithuanians, Swedes, and Magyars, or Hungarians, from the north also began to threaten Kiev. One common response by Kievans was to flee toward the forest of the northeast, establishing towns that would later pick up the torch of emerging Russian culture as Kiev declined.

Kiev's decline was also linked to broader changes that affected the hereto profitable trade route from the Baltic to the Black Sea, especially the creation of new maritime trade routes to the Black Sea from Venice or the overland route to Constantinople by way of Bohemia. The city of Constantinople itself, to which Kiev's economic and cultural fortunes had been linked, began to decline in the 11th century, and in 1204 it was conquered by Latin Crusaders who held it for the next half-century.

As Kiev declined, three other areas of Rus increased in importance: the north, the northeast, and the west. These areas had always maintained some independence from Kiev, because they were remote, had separate economies, and in large part resented paying tribute to Kiev. In fact, many aspects of Kiev society had shown differences based on geography.

To the north, Novgorod had always been a challenger to Kiev. In the early 12th century, it became an independent polity, adopting an oligarchic republican system centered on its *veche*, an assembly that some scholars have seen as the prototype of a parliamentary system, but was in actuality controlled by a small group of boyars. As Kiev's power declined, Novgorod took over Rus trade around the Baltic, focusing on new growing trade with German merchants who displaced the earlier Varangian influence in the region. In Novgorod, the Hanseatic League, an association of merchants in Germany and Germans abroad played an increasing role in the town's commercial life until 1478, when Ivan III of Moscow captured Novgorod and expelled the Hanseatic merchants who were living there.

To the northeast a number of principalities arose, such as Vladimir, Rostov, and Suzdal to challenge Novgorod and more distant Kiev. The city of Moscow, founded in 1147 by Yuri Dolgorukii, a son of Vladimir Monomakh, was a relative latecomer to the roll of 12th-century Russian cities, but it was destined to play an immense role in shaping Russian history in later centuries. To the west, the territory of Galicia also gained in importance, especially with the development of a land trade route to the East. Its location, bordering Poland, Hungary, and the Russian towns, gave it important strategic advantages but also exposed it to threats from many sides. In its politics and religion, Galicia reflected its Western exposure, with a system in which the prince's powers were limited by the boyars and a greater Roman Catholic influence than elsewhere in Kievan Rus, where Eastern Orthodoxy dominated.

MONGOL CONQUEST AND RULE

1240–1480

By the early decades of the 13th century the lands of Kievan Rus emerged as a distinct cultural and political entity that was primarily agricultural, but with important commercial connections to the Baltic and Black Seas. While the ruler of Kiev held preeminent status, the Kievan territories were bound by a relatively decentralized political structure built around princes charged with defending their lands and administering justice aided by a council of independent landowners. A common Slavic language and adherence to Eastern Orthodox Christianity, which also linked them to the Byzantine world, further unified the lands of Kievan Rus.

This world was shattered between 1237 and 1240 by the arrival of the Mongols, a new and more ruthless group of invaders who would conquer and control most of the Russian lands for the next 250 to 300 years. Led by Batu Khan, a grandson of the great conqueror Chinggis Khan (Genghis Khan), Mongol armies first appeared on the eastern banks of the Volga in 1236, after conquering China, Central Asia, Iran, and Transcaucasia over the previous three decades. Already the ruler of the steppes north of the Aral Sea and Lake Balkhash, Batu Khan had his armies penetrating further west and within four years had conquered the Volga Bulgarians and the politically fragmented Russian principalities with the exception of Novgorod, capturing the great city of Kiev in December 1240.

On the eastern banks of the Volga, with its capital at Sarai, near modern-day Astrakhan, Batu Khan established the Mongol state generally known as the Golden Horde. From Sarai the Mongols ruled the Russian principalities through a system of tribute. After about a century, the Mongol grip on its vassal states began to weaken. During the 14th century, the western and southern Russian principalities fell under the sway of the newly established Grand Duchy of Lithuania.

Within the territory still held by the Golden Horde, the small principality of Moscow absorbed many of its neighbors until it felt strong enough to challenge the Horde. In 1380 the Muscovite prince Dmitrii Donskoi led a coalition of Russian princes to defeat the Tatars at the Battle of Kulikovo. The defeat was mostly a harbinger of future changes, because it was not for another hundred years that Moscow was able to fully shake off its tributary burdens. In 1480, Ivan III formally proclaimed that Moscow would not pay tribute, a claim endorsed by the Battle of the Ugra River. Although the Mongols continued to raid Russian territories through the late 16th century, their power declined as a result of internal divisions. During the 15th century, the Golden Horde disintegrated into a number of khanates (Astrakhan, Crimea, Kazan, and Siberia). With the exception of Crimea, they fell to the growing power of Muscovy during the 16th and early 17th centuries.

Concurrent with the decline of Mongol power the principality of Moscow, previously a minor player in the world of Russian principalities, began its rise toward supremacy. The two processes were interrelated. The town of Moscow was probably established by Iurii Dolgorukii in 1147 within the territories of the principality of Vladimir/Suzdal, and not far from Novgorod. For much of the 12th and 13th centuries it was eclipsed by both.

As with other cities, the Mongols destroyed Moscow in 1237. Toward the end of the century, the youngest son of Alexander Nevsky, Daniel, became the ruler of Moscow, holding it an appanage. Daniel concentrated on building his small principality and extending it along the Moscow River, and he inherited more property from a childless ruler nearby. Daniel's son, Iurii, who succeeded him in 1303, increased the appanage still further and turned to fight the prince of Tver, Moscow's rival city, with Michael as its prince.

Iurii married a sister of the khan of the Golden Horde (she became Orthodox), and received an appointment as grand prince. Iurii went against Tver again, but his wife was taken prisoner and died. The prince of Tver had to go to Sarai, where he was executed, and Iurii was reaffirmed as grand prince. The families of Iurii and Michael continued fighting and killing each other for about 20 years, leading to a Mongol army destroying Tver, with help from Moscow's army.

In 1328 Yuri's younger brother Ivan Kalita, prince of Moscow, was named grand prince, a position he held until his death in 1341. Ivan's nickname *Kalita* (Moneybags) refers to his skill at collecting tribute for the Mongols from other Russian princes. He used the money he kept from the tribute to purchase more land: entire appanages from bankrupt rulers, and separate villages. He added Vladimir to his rule, keeping the capital in Moscow. In addition, Ivan persuaded the new metropolitan of the Russian Church to move to Moscow. Moscow became the new spiritual center of Russia, and the connections between the church leadership and the grand princes were to become ever stronger. In fact, a new metropolitan, Alexis, helped to advise one of Ivan's sons as grand prince. Ivan's son Simeon the Proud (who called himself prince of all Russia) had told his heirs to follow Alexis's advice. Simeon's brother (Ivan's son) Ivan the Meek took over but left affairs largely in Alexis's hands. Metropolitan Alexis even traveled to Sarai to deal with the Golden Horde, where things were falling apart because of a civil war that produced 20 rulers in 20 years.

Ivan II's death brought a contest for the new ruler, between Ivan's son Dmitrii and a relative Dmitrii from Suzdal. The people of Moscow rallied behind their own boy and behind the principle of direct succession from father to son. The new grand prince, Dmitrii, reigned for three decades, until 1389. Continuing the growth of Muscovite territory, continued fighting with Tver and Lithua-nia (with Muscovite victories), victories over Ryazan and the Bulgars. But Dmitrii's claim to fame is his victorious war with the Golden Horde itself. There were a series of preliminary clashes, with a victory for Moscow in 1378, after which point the Mongols decided they had to deal with Moscow firmly. They made an alliance with Lithuania and took 200,000 troops to the Don River area, meeting the Lithuanians for a joint invasion.

Dmitrii took the initiative, crossing the Don with about 150,000 soldiers to take on the Mongols before the Lithuanians arrived. They fought on September 8, 1380, in an area with lots of streams, so that the Mongol cavalry could-n't fight as usual. Known as the Battle of Kulikovo field, the Mongols were completely routed by the Muscovite-led armies. Hearing of the Mongol defeat, their Lithuanian allies decided to turn back. After more than a century of uncontested Mongol military supremacy, Dmitrii Donskoi's army had broken the image of Mongol invincibility. The prince of Moscow was seen as the cham-pion of the Russians. Although not all the Russian princes supported Dmitrii, and some even tried to support Mongols against him, the Battle of Kulikovo was a turning point. It did not, however, mean the end of Mongol rule. Two years later the Mongols sacked Moscow and Dmitrii had to spend years rebuild-ing. Dmitrii's son Vasili (Basil) became grand prince without any challenge. Vasili I (r. 1389–1425) continued adding to Muscovy's territory by purchase and war. He continued the struggle against the Lithuanians and maintained fairly good relations with the Horde (often sending gifts), while Mongol troops attacked the Moscow region in 1408 but could not take the city itself.

Vasili's death in 1425 brought the only war of succession in Moscow. Fought between Vasili's son Vasili II and Vasili II's uncle Prince Iurii and later his sons, this war represented a reaction against the growing power of the princes of Moscow. Finally Vasili II prevailed in 1448. After Vasili and his rival were blinded, the former became known as Vasili the Blind and ruled until 1462. During this reign the Mongol state began to fragment, leading to the establishment of three separate khanates in Crimea (1430), Kazan (1436), and Astrakhan (1466).

These years also coincided with the final push of Ottoman Turkish power in the region, primarily directed against the Byzantine Empire but also against other neighboring powers. As Byzantium itself was threatened, Byzantine lead-ers turned to Europe for help against the Turks, and as part of the deal, in 1439 the Byzantine clergy had to sign an agreement recognizing the supremacy of the pope in Rome. The Russian metropolitan had been at these talks in Flo-rence, and when he returned to Moscow, he read a prayer for the pope. He was then arrested, imprisoned, and later escaped. The Moscow bishops elected a new metropolitan. When the Turks captured Byzantium itself 1453, this left a vacuum in the Orthodox world. The people of Muscovy saw themselves as the new leaders of Orthodoxy, and in these years the ideology of Moscow as the Third Rome, after Rome and Constantinople, gained currency in the Muscovite world.

MUSCOVITE RUSSIA

1480–1689

Ivan III, later known as Ivan the Great (r. 1462–1505), is often considered to have started the true Muscovite Russia. A ruler at age 22, after already assisting his blind father as coruler, Ivan III took over Novgorod and Tver, finished the process of forming single rule over Russia, and stopped paying tribute to the Mongols. This latter event is often considered as marking the end of Mongol rule in Russia, even though Mongol armies continued to threaten Russian cities for the next century. Ivan III is best known, however, by his renunciation of any further allegiance to the Golden Horde in 1480. The stage was set for a military confrontation between the two. Playing on the diplomatic rivalries of the day, the Mongol Khan tried to get help from Polish and Lithuanian forces, while Ivan got help from the khan of Crimea. At the Battle of the Ugra River, the Mongols retreated, seeking to go back and defend their capital Sarai from Russian and Turkish forces.

With this victory in hand, Ivan III considered himself rightful heir to all the former Kievan lands, which he saw as his patrimony, and in 1493 he assumed the title sovereign of all Russia. The only challenge to Moscow's claims to the lands of the former Kievan Rus was Lithuania, which had taken over parts of the western and southwestern Kievan territories, but in 1503 Lithuania recognized Ivan's right to these territories. He further consolidated his claims to the Orthodox mantle by marrying a Byzantine princess, Zoe (Sophia), the niece of the last Byzantine emperor. Ivan added the Byzantine two-headed eagle to his family's crest and developed a court ceremony based on the Byzantine model. Modeling himself on the Byzantine emperor, he adopted the title of czar, the Russian form of the word *caesar*. The Muscovite state encouraged legends about Christianity coming to Russia through the apostles, about Muscovite princes descending from Roman emperors, and more lastingly about Moscow as the new Third Rome.

Ivan was succeeded by his son Vasili III (r. 1505–33), who annexed all remaining appanages, continued fights against Lithuania for more land, and advanced Muscovy's borders at the expense of the Crimean khanate. Looking beyond the traditional borders of Russian diplomacy, Vasili also established diplomatic relations with the Holy Roman Empire, Suleiman I the Magnificent's Ottoman Empire, and even the court of Babar, Mogul ruler of India. He also continued his father's policies of considering the boyars exclusive servitors of Moscow. Service to the Muscovite prince was required; service to any other prince was considered equivalent to treason and a valid reason to take over that individual's lands.

Although the Mongol threat had subsided after 1480, it did not completely disappear. In 1521 the khan of the Crimean Tatars engineered the downfall of the pro-Muscovite khan of Kazan, and then, with the support of Lithuania, attacked Moscow, devastating large areas of the principality. Disaster threatened as several princes conspired with the Mongols to attempt separation of their lands from Muscovy. Vasili stifled the conspiracy, but discontent lingered on in the higher circles of the aristocracy, particularly after the czar divorced his first wife, a daughter of an old boyar family, in 1525, on the grounds that she was incapable of bearing him children. Before the discontent was entirely stilled, Vasili died suddenly in 1533, instructing his second wife, Elena, to begin a regency working with the boyar Duma, until their son Ivan came of age.

Thus, by 1533, the Muscovite state had emerged as a significant power in eastern Europe. Its religious claim to being the Third Rome went hand in hand with its military and political strength. Meanwhile great changes had taken place within Russia itself. The independent appanage states that had proliferated in the final years of Kievan Rus and during the early decades of Mongol rule had been brought under control by Moscow. A new group of nobles, the service gentry, based upon land grants from the czar, existed side by side with the traditional boyar class. More ominously for the future development of Muscovite and Russian society, the peasantry was increasingly hemmed by restrictions imposed by the state, which would almost a century later lead to the formal institutionalization of serfdom, a feature of Russian society that would survive until 1861.

The infant son of Vasili, Ivan IV (r. 1533–84), would come to dominate 16th-century Russian history and, known as Ivan the Terrible, leave a large imprint on the Russian historical consciousness. A complex and violent individual, Ivan brought major changes to Russian life. Like rulers elsewhere in Europe at this time, he solidified the power of his monarchy by striking brutally at high-ranking members of his country's aristocracy. His attacks on the boyars and his establishment of a personal tool of repression, the *oprichnina*, made Russia's ruler more of an autocrat than ever before. The *oprichnina*'s seven-year reign of terror (1565–72) left a trail of death and destruction before ending with Ivan's destruction of the very own vehicles of that terror, an experience that observers would later notice paralleled Joseph Stalin's own terror campaign of the 1930s.

Ivan displayed equally grand ambitions toward the outside world. His attacks on the khanates opened the way for Russian expansion eastward and southward, and individuals such as the Stroganovs soon pushed forward into Siberia. On the other hand, Ivan was far less successful in his attempts to expand Muscovite power toward the Baltic, embroiling his country in the long Livonian War (1558–82).

The reign of Ivan's oldest surviving son, Feodor (Theodore) (r. 1584–98), gave Muscovy some much-needed internal peace. Physically weak and extremely

Ivan IV the Terrible
(Library of Congress)

limited in intelligence and ability but well meaning and very religious, the new czar relied entirely on his advisers. Fortunately, these advisers, especially Boris Godunov, performed their task fairly well. In an important ecclesiastical and diplomatic victory that raised the prestige of the Russian Orthodox Church, Boris Godunov got permission from the Byzantine patriarch to elevate the status of the leader of the Russian Church from metropolitan to patriarch. Boris's historical legacy would be tainted by his, apparently unfounded, association in the murder of the nine-year-old prince Dmitrii of Uglich in 1591. Dmitrii, the only other surviving male heir for Ivan IV, was found with his throat slit, and many thought Boris Godunov was implicated, perhaps in an attempt to rid himself of someone who could challenge his power. Some historians have discounted this theory, arguing that Dmitrii was the son of Ivan the Terrible's seventh wife at a time when church law allowed only three wives, and therefore Dmitrii's claim to the throne was questionable. A formal commission absolved Boris Godunov of the crime, but the implication would come back to haunt him and Russia in the following decade.

Even if Boris did not murder Dmitrii, he made every other effort to take power. Coming from a Mongol gentry family, which had been converted to Orthodoxy and Russified, and virtually illiterate, Boris Godunov showed uncanny intelligence and abilities in palace intrigue, diplomacy, and statecraft. He capitalized on his proximity to Feodor, who was married to Boris's sister, Irina. In the course of several years, Boris defeated his rivals and became the effective ruler of Muscovy by about 1588. He acquired enormous personal wealth, an ever-growing official title, the formal right to conduct foreign relations on behalf of Muscovy, and a separate court, imitating that of the czar, where foreign ambassadors had to pay their respects after going to Feodor.

When Feodor I died in 1598 without an heir, Boris Godunov was ready to take the throne. His reign (1598–1605), however, was not a smooth transfer of power but the prelude to an extremely complex period of internal instability, known as the Time of Troubles (Smutnoe vremia), which lasted until 1613. Historians have generally divided the Time of Troubles into three overlapping phases: dynastic, social, and national. The dynastic phase was defined by internal struggles over the issue of succession to the throne of Muscovy. The social phase was marked by revolts that resulted from the growing rigidity of the Muscovite state and its attempt to limit the freedom of movement of its peoples, particularly the peasants. The national phase was connected to the rivalries that had developed in the preceding century between Muscovy and its two western neighbors, Poland and Sweden, both of whom invaded and controlled Russian territories during these years.

The crisis of the Time of Troubles ended with the establishment of a new dynasty—the Romanov—that would rule Russia until 1917. The first three Romanov czars, Michael, Aleksei, and Feodor III, have generally been portrayed as relatively weak, certainly when compared to their successor, Peter I. But recent research suggests that at least Michael and Aleksei actually had some talent for governing and restored a measure of stability to Muscovy after the debacle of the Time of Troubles.

Czar Michael (r. 1613–45) was only 16 when he was crowned. According to most sources, the *zemskii sobor* (Assembly of the land) that elected Michael stayed active in Moscow for about ten years, serving as advisers and supporters. Michael also appointed his own advisers but especially relied on his father, Filaret, once he returned from being imprisoned by the Poles. Filaret, who had been metropolitan, became patriarch of the Orthodox Church. Filaret exercised a great deal of power, even arranging to receive the title great sovereign (along with Michael) and setting up his own court. Filaret died in 1633, at almost 80 years old. Michael took over a country devastated by continuous wars, drought, and famine. During his reign, Muscovy managed to find some kind of peace with Sweden and Poland (even though Muscovy had to give up some land).

Although he tried a number of measures to raise money for the drained treasury, by the time he died at the age of 47, the treasury was fairly empty.

Aleksei (Alexis) I (r. 1645–76) succeeded his father, Michael, at the age of 16. He was known as the Quietest One (Tishiaishii) by many, including the great 19th-century historian Vasili Kliuchevsky, who called Aleksei "the kindest man, a glorious Russian soul." To many, Aleksei was the epitome of Muscovite culture as well as one of the pioneers of the new Russian interest in the West. The historical image of Aleksei is that of an attractive person, sensitive, considerate of others, an absolute ruler, but not a despot. Brought up in Muscovite religious tradition, he continued to be a dedicated, well-informed churchgoer throughout his life. At the same time he developed an interest in the West and Western culture, especially in European military technologies, but also architecture as well as the theater (new to Russia).

As a ruler, however, Aleksei is considered to have been somewhat weak, depending on not always trustworthy relatives. His reign was certainly not a quiet one. In foreign affairs, Russia continued to grow in strength, acquiring much of Ukraine and successfully defending its acquisition from outside challenges. Contacts with the West became much stronger than before, setting the stage for the emergence of someone like his son Peter. Domestically, Aleksei's reign witnessed periodic peasant rebellions, urban riots, a religious schism, and the legal definition of the peasantry as serfs.

Aleksei depended heavily on advisers, mostly his own or his wife's relatives. His advisers tried to raise money by such means as an increase in the salt tax and selling tobacco, to which the church objected. And some of Aleksei's appointees were corrupt. In May 1648, riots broke out in Moscow, with crowds insisting that the czar kill some of his worst advisers. His closest relatives managed to escape. Soon riots broke out in other towns, including Novgorod and Pskov.

Later, in 1656, the government tried to ease fiscal matters by debasing the current money—adding copper to silver coins. This did not work well then, just as it did not in other countries at other times. It led to inflation, more financial troubles, and a copper coin riot in 1662. But the greatest rebellion took place in 1670–71, led by Stenka Razin. Razin was the commander of a band of Cossacks in the Don region. He had raided Persia and other areas in the south. In the spring of 1670, he led his army on a more ambitious venture, moving up the Volga and proclaiming freedom from officials and landlords. Peasants murdered their landlords and welcomed Razin. The rebel army reached Simbirsk with about 200,000 troops. But regular Muscovite troops, probably better trained, won the battle there. Razin escaped, but in 1671 he was taken by cossacks and given to Muscovite officials for a public execution.

Perhaps one of the factors leading to peasant rebellions was the Law Code of 1649. The new code, or *ulozhenie,* was supposed to help regulate governmental, economic, and social affairs, to help prevent another Time of Troubles. The *zemskii sobor* appointed a commission to read all the old law codes and rewrite them; the new code was approved in 1649. But the new code also contained the final statement enserfing the peasantry by stipulating that peasants who had fled the land had to be returned to their former landlords; that peasants could no longer leave their lands at all, abolishing the St. George's Day exception; that all peasants and their children would be considered as serfs; and imposing heavy fines on those who sheltered runaway peasants. Although there was an important link between serfs and the land they worked, by the end of the century enough loopholes had crept into the system that serfs could be bought, sold, and willed to others—very much as slaves.

Aleksei's reign also witnessed a schism within the Russian Orthodox Church. Although there were deep-rooted issues related to the relationship between church and state, and between the church leadership and the, mostly peasant, congregation, the immediate cause behind the schism of the 1660s was the set of reforms introduced by the ambitious Patriarch Nikon. Over the centuries changes had come into the practice and theology of the Russian Orthodox Church. Nikon wanted to bring the Russian Orthodox Church in line with earlier Byzantine practices. Thus, his reforms centered around issues such as how to cross oneself (Nikon wanted to use three fingers as in the Greek Church), the return to pure Greek texts, and the spelling of the word *Jesus*. Nikon's opponents maintained that since the church possessed revealed truth, such changes amounted to heresy. Even though Nikon overreached when arguing that the church leadership should take precedence over secular leadership and was deposed during the Church Council of 1666–67 and subsequently exiled, the church adopted his reforms. Those who opposed them broke off into various sects, most notably the Old Believers and other sectarian groups. One of the Old Believer leaders was Archpriest Avvakum, who was imprisoned and burned at the stake in 1682. Prior to his death, Avvakum composed his autobiography, a moving account of his own faith and one of the early gems of Russian literature. Both Old Belief and sectarianism were movements with a strong popular base, and the church lost a lot of popular support and vitality after the schism. Peter the Great's reforms of the church leadership, including the abolition of the Patriarchate, would further weaken the church as an institution.

Aleksei died in 1676, at the age of 47 like his father, and was succeeded by his son Feodor (r. 1676–82), who was 14 at the time. Although well educated, Feodor was in poor health, and most of his short reign was characterized by fighting between relatives of his father's two wives. One important change, however, was the final abolition of the system of *mestnichestvo* (precedence) in 1682, shortly before Feodor's death. The system had become so cumbersome with its attempts to keep track of all family records of any kind of service, privileges, and so on, and it did not reflect current conditions—that advancement relied as much on favoritism and increasingly on talent as on one's record of past service. In addition, *mestnichestvo* made military assignments increasingly impossible to adjust according to ability. A Muscovite army consisted of five regiments: the big or main regiment, the right arm, the left arm, the forward regiment, and the rear guard. In the honor of command, the main regiment came first, then the right wing; the advance and rear guards were considered equal; then the left wing. Mestnichestvo made the calculations of who took command over which wing very difficult and had little to do with ability, so that a talented man whose family ranked low could not become a commander. Sometimes for important campaigns, the government would issue a temporary exemption from *mestnichestvo,* and sometimes generals would keep high-ranking but unable commanders back in Moscow "for advice," but the system was still cumbersome and unworkable. A similar system existed for the civil service. Most of the family records of service were burned when the system was abolished.

Feodor died childless in 1682, and for about seven years there was constant infighting about which of Feodor's half brothers (Peter or Ivan) would take over, under the direction of Ivan's full sister Sophia. Peter's father, Aleksei, had been married twice, first to Maria Miloslavskaia and then to Natalia Naryshkina. With Maria he had 13 children, but only two sons, Feodor and Ivan, survived. Peter was the first son of the second marriage. Feodor took over after Aleksei's death in 1676, then died without an heir in 1682. Without an acknowledged heir, it came to a question of which son would rule, and the families of the two wives competed for the throne. Peter's mother's side gained an early victory, and Peter was proclaimed czar in April 1682, with his mother as regent.

But a month later, the Miloslavskii family led a rebellion of the *streltsy* (the military caste of musketeers) regiments in Moscow. Probably the true leader of the rebellion was Aleksei's daughter Sophia, Peter's half sister. Members of Peter's mother's family were murdered, and Peter witnessed some of the murders. The *streltsy* requested that Ivan be declared senior czar, with Peter as junior czar, and then made Sophia regent. The *streltsy,* influenced by Old Believers, tried to pressure for more changes, but they were put down.

From 1682 to 1689, Sophia really ruled Muscovy—Ivan was mentally and physically incapable of ruling, and Peter was kept away from affairs of state. Sophia relied on Prince Vasili Golitsyn, a strong and relatively enlightened adviser, who liberalized the penal code and arranged a lasting peace treaty with Poland. That treaty, however, brought war with the Crimean Tartars, backed by Turkey. Golitsyn led the army to war against the Tartars but suffered disastrous defeats.

Sophia wanted to rule by herself in her own right and in 1689 encouraged the *streltsy* to try another coup, but they refused. Hearing about this, Peter escaped from the village of Preobrazhenskoe (near Moscow) to the Holy Trinity–St. Sergius Monastery. The patriarch, most boyars and the gentry, and the Western-oriented units of the military (and even some *streltsy*) rallied behind Peter. Sophia was left without strong support. She left without a fight and was sent to a convent; Golitsyn and other prominent boyars and supporters of Sophia were exiled; a few inciters of the *streltsy* were executed.

IMPERIAL RUSSIA

1689–1917

In August 1689, Peter won acknowledgment as the effective ruler of Russia, but Ivan retained his position as co-czar. Only 17, Peter left most of the government in the hands of his mother, Natalia and her associates, who preferred Muscovite traditions to the Western styles. Natalia had Peter marry a Russian woman who, she hoped, would lead him away from his fascination with Europe, but her ploy failed. Natalia died in 1694, and Peter took over the direction of the government at the age of 22. Thus began a reign that, like that of Ivan the Terrible, would leave a deep imprint on Russian history.

Almost seven feet tall, strong, and restless, Peter wanted to be personally involved in all kinds of state affairs—diplomacy, administration, justice, commerce, education, and finance. He valued expert advice but wanted to decide matters for himself. He was a successful military and naval commander, starting his training from the bottom up—serving in the ranks and learning the use of each weapon before promoting himself. He prided himself on his ability to make almost anything by hand, from a ship to a pair of shoes. More than any czar before him, Peter traveled around Russia to learn about his country. He also frequently visited Moscow's foreign quarter, established under his father's reign, to learn trades and obtain information about a Western European world that fascinated him. In 1697–98, true to form, he traveled to Western Europe in his celebrated Grand Embassy, where he spent time in the Netherlands working, not quite incognito, as the laborer Peter Mikhailovich.

Peter also had a violent temper and a habit of holding drunken parties that were wild even by the standards of the times. He admired Ivan the Terrible and was capable of similar cruelty (including a willingness to assist in the death of his own son), but he never descended to the paranoid depths of the 16th-century czar. The war games he started as a child in Preobrazhenskoe ended up becoming the first two guard regiments: the Preobrazhensky and the Semenovsky (another nearby village), which would later provide the backbone in his own struggle to modernize the Russian army against the power of the *streltsy*.

As ruler Peter brought rapid and intensive change to Russia. The Great Northern War (1700–1721) with Sweden over supremacy in the eastern Baltic region dominated most of his reign, and the victorious conclusion of this war marked

Peter I the Great
(Library of Congress)

Russia's emergence as a great European power. While Peter was a fervent believer in Westernization, many of his initial reforms were also guided by the need to mobilize the Russian population for military success. The process of borrowing from the West, already under way in previous reigns, increased enormously, spurred on by the czar himself. At the same time, through a series of reforms, Peter expanded the authority and influence of the Russian government over its own population. The church was subordinated to the state, and the gentry were placed under an obligation to provide either civilian or military service.

Like Ivan the Terrible, Peter has been accused of murdering his own son, Alexis, whom he believed to be guilty of conspiring against him and the state.

In assessing Peter's role in this affair, historians have written about Peter's personal problems with Alexis, tempered with his belief in the law and the importance of loyalty to the state above all else, without exception. After Alexis's death, Peter was without a mature, healthy son to assume the throne. On February 5, 1722, Peter issued a decree doing away with the traditional order of succession, but he did not indicate who should take the throne. Legend has it that as Peter was dying, in January 1725, he took a pen and started to write: "give all to . . ." but could not finish.

Government officials (mostly the Senate and high-ranking nobles) assembled to decide the succession, and most, especially the Guards regiments, supported Catherine, the emperor's second wife. From this moment, until the overthrow of Paul I in 1801, the Imperial Guards regiments forced decisions about rulers, making the Russian 18th century the century of palace revolutions.

Thus, between 1725 and 1762, Russia went through a period of political instability. Peter had changed the law of succession, allowing the czar to name his or her own successor. This had the unintended effect of allowing outsiders to interfere (often violently) to determine who the next czar would be. The rulers of this period were generally weak. The imperial guards at St. Petersburg frequently intervened to change rulers, and imperial favorites often dominated policy. Yet this "instability" at the top should not be allowed to obscure important developments that affected the country at large: Westernization continued to spread to more people and broader areas of Russian life.

In social terms, the main trend of this period was the process by which the gentry gradually freed itself from the obligation to do state service. At the same time, the peasants found themselves under heavier burdens of taxation and other restrictions. One of Peter's most crucial legacies was the widening of differences between the peasant villages and the outside world. Differences between the upper classes and the peasantry were already quite pronounced before Peter (mostly because of serfdom). Peter increased the differences. The classes looked different, talked differently, ate different foods, and thought differently. While the peasants remained loyal to traditional dress, customs, and religious practices, the nobility and government officials were increasingly exposed to Western-style education, fashions, and secularized culture.

After Peter's reign, the one justification for the system of serfdom was eliminated. Serfdom was based on the assumption of service state; peasants served landlords, landlords served the czar, and the czar served God and his people. Peter had reinforced the idea of service for all. But after his death, his successors revoked the requirements of service for the gentry.

Catherine I, a former Lithuanian peasant girl and the mother of Peter's illegitimate children, reigned from 1725 to 1727. She left the government in the hands of her adviser, Aleksandr Menshikov, who was arrogant and corrupt. Menshikov demoted the Senate to a mere college and created instead the Supreme Privy Council—a kind of kitchen cabinet of favorites. Catherine died in May 1727, probably as a result of heavy drinking, which accelerated after Peter's death.

Supposedly before her death, Catherine had signed a document that left the crown to her grandson Peter (Alexis's son), then to his descendants, and then to Catherine's two daughters, Anna and her descendants, and then Elizabeth and her descendants. (Catherine's signature might have been forged.) Until Peter was old enough to take over, the Supreme Privy Council would rule for him.

Peter II, grandson of Peter the Great, ruled from 1727 to 1730. He was 11 years old when he took the throne. That fall, he orchestrated the arrest of his grandmother's favorite, Menshikov, who had been instrumental in causing his father Alexis's death. Peter then moved the court back to Moscow from St. Petersburg. But Peter also died young, at the age of 14, after an attack of small-pox (supposedly on the day scheduled for his wedding, marrying a daughter of the Dolgorukys), and the male branch of the Romanov dynasty died out.

Peter was succeeded by Anna, the daughter of Peter's half brother, Ivan V, who had spent most of her adult life in the German duchy of Kurland, as wife to the duke. Her reign has long been presented as a period of cruel, misguided rule by individual Germans and by a "German party" in Russia. And in truth, Anna brought with her a band of favorites, whom she placed in positions of responsibility. She also tended to patronize Germans as well as other foreigners and distrusted the Russian nobility.

Anna herself had no interest in managing the affairs of the Russian state. So she relied on a number of favorites to rule. Some were quite capable, such as Ostermann, who was in charge of foreign affairs, and Andrei Munnich, head of the army. Others, however, such as her lover Ernst-Johann Biren were incompetent. Biren, also known as Biron, became the most hated figure of the regime and a symbol of her reign. The term *Bironovshchina* is applied to this period—meaning Bironism, a period of police persecution and political terror, which led to the execution of several thousand people and the exile of some 20,000 to 30,000 to Siberia. Many of the victims were Old Believers rather than political opponents of Anna or Biron. By the standards of the age the cruelty of Biron and his associates was not exceptional. Nevertheless, the persecutions of Anna's reign compare unfavorably to the more relaxed era of her eventual successor, Elizabeth.

Anna's death in 1740 triggered yet another succession crisis, as she had no children. Anna named her sister's grandson as her successor, an infant who would reign as Ivan VI (r. 1740–41). Ivan was an infant, so the key question was, who would be the power behind the throne. A struggle among Anna's German advisers ensued during which Anna's favorite, Biron, was ousted by Munnich, who in short order found himself overthrown by Ostermann.

At this point, the Imperial Guards intervened once again. With an assist from the French ambassador, they ousted the entire German Party and gave power to Elizabeth (1709–62), second daughter of Peter the Great and his second wife, Catherine. The unfortunate Ivan VI was confined to the Schlusserberg fortress, outside St. Petersburg, where he spent his entire life until he was killed in 1764, during another power struggle soon after Catherine the Great became empress.

Elizabeth has received a better press from historians than Anna. She, too, allowed power to fall into the hands of imperial favorites, but whereas Anna had installed a German clique, Elizabeth surrounded herself with Russian officers. Her reign has often been interpreted as a return to Russianness after the interval of pro-German rulers. This is not quite accurate since Elizabeth's successor, her nephew Peter III, could be considered a Prussianophile. On the other hand, Peter's wife, the German princess and future Catherine II, embraced Russia and its traditions and did not distinguish herself by pro-German leanings. Nevertheless, the replacement of Germans by Russians in the imperial circles under Elizabeth had some connection with the increasing interest of the Russian court in French society and culture. The move toward adopting the mannerisms of French culture among the nobility continued under Catherine, after the brief reign of Peter III.

Under Elizabeth, favorites continued to rule Russia. This group was slightly more distinguished in its political legacy than Anna's circle. The closest figure to the monarch was Alexis Razumovsky, whom Elizabeth married in a secret and morganatic wedding. Razumovsky was of simple Cossack origin, from the Ukraine. Known as a wonderful singer, he was brought to the court to perform. Elizabeth fell in love with him, and her attachment lasted until her death. However, Razumovsky had a negligible impact on state matters (unlike Biron). A more influential set of court favorites were the Shuvalovs (Peter and Alexander, and their cousin Ivan). Ivan left behind an almost unique reputation for integrity and kindness, for refusing honors and rewards, and for the promotion of cultural enlightenment in Russia. He founded the University of Moscow, Russia's first permanent university, in 1755. Peter Shuvalov, on the other hand, intervened in every kind of state business. He was very able but also shamelessly corrupt. He is largely responsible for the disastrous financial policies that characterized Elizabeth's reign. This was a time of extravagant expenditures, best symbolized perhaps by the construction of the Winter Palace in St. Petersburg.

The reign of Peter III was brief and unhappy. Another grandson of Peter the Great, Peter had been raised in the German duchy of Holstein-Gottorp. He was first brought up with the view of succeeding to the Swedish throne, since his father was a son of the sister of King Charles XII of Sweden. But as early as 1742 Elizabeth had designated him as her successor. Although he lived in Russia from the age of 14, he never adjusted to the country. By all accounts he was extremely limited mentally, as well as crude and violent in his behavior.

His reign of only a few months was an active one and best known in the long run for the law that abolished the compulsory state service of the gentry, instituted by Peter the Great. That law of 1762 was the final stage of a process that began with Peter's reforms. Under Peter's policy, the gentry in its entirety was affected and there was no limit to how long they should serve. In 1736, this service was limited to 25 years (the nobility had asked for 20). Moreover, one son in each noble family could be exempted from service to manage the family estates. Following the publication of this law and for the next few decades, many members of the gentry left state service to return to their landholdings. Not surprisingly, many nobles found a way to have their 25-year period of service counted from the time they were eight or 10 years old. Finally, in 1762, compulsory service was abolished. From now on members of the gentry no longer had to serve the state. They could even serve foreign governments, if they so desired.

The law of 1762 has received much attention from historians. To many older historians, such as the nineteenth-century historian Vasili Kliuchevsky, the law undermined the idea of service as the basic structure of Russian society as it had developed in the past centuries. If the serfs served the landlords to enable the landlords to serve the state, then the abolition of gentry service should have been followed by the abolition of serfdom. Yet, it would be another 99 years, before this happened. Other historians have emphasized a different interpretation, arguing that the law of 1762 had positive results, it allowed the gaining of independence from the state by at least one class of Russian society. This was Russia's first crucial step on the road to liberalism. Moreover, they argue that the freedom of the nobility contributed to the growth of a rich gentry culture and, beyond that, to the emergence of the Russian intelligentsia.

The peasants of course saw things differently. While the status of the gentry had been improving in the decades after Peter the Great, their own status deteriorated rapidly. On the other hand, the state granted all sorts of privileges to the gentry (not compelled to serve, a special gentry bank with low-interest loans, admission to cadet school and arise through the ranks without serving as soldiers, nearly complete financial and legal control over serfs). On the other hand, it increasingly limited the peasant's few remaining freedoms (they could not sign legal or financial documents, could be sold or sent to Siberia at will, could not volunteer for the military, with the administration of virtually all justice in the hands of an often corrupt provincial bureaucracy or their landlord). The demand for freedom of the peasants to follow the freedom of the gentry was voiced frequently in the peasant uprisings that soon followed, most notably the great Pugachev Rebellion of 1773–74.

Despite the benefits that the law of 1762 brought to the nobility in general, Peter III had made too many enemies in his brief reign. One was his wife, the future Catherine II, whom he mistreated and neglected in favor of other women. Another group of enemies came from the Imperial Guard, whom Peter III had threatened to disband. Catherine, who arrived in Russia in 1745, proved to be a far more savvy politician than her husband. In the midsummer of 1762, she seized upon the growing dissatisfaction with Peter and led the palace guards in yet another revolution. Peter was easily deposed and shortly thereafter killed, perhaps as a result of an argument with one of the leaders of the insurrection, Grigorii Orlov.

Catherine's coup also affected her son, Paul (born 1754). Rather than making Paul the successor and ruling in his name, she became empress. At the time, the coup of 1762 seemed like just one more of the many palace revolutions that had marked the 18th century. It was not clear how long a foreign empress would manage to hold on to the throne. As it turned out, this was just the beginning of a long and celebrated reign.

Catherine II brought Russia a period of stability in the monarchy, spectacular success in foreign policy, and continuing Westernization. Reigning for over 30 years, Catherine ended the era of palace revolts and court favorites that had prevailed since 1725. She directed policy herself and attained remarkable results, notably in expanding Russian territory. Poland was thrice partitioned,

Catherine II the Great
(Library of Congress)

with most of its land going to Russia. Russia defeated Turkey twice, taking territory that expanded Catherine's empire to the Black Sea.

Catherine had a deep interest in the reformist ideas of the French Enlightenment. However, the harsh conditions of Russian life and her need to safeguard her place on the throne set limits to her ability to implement reform. Her reign brought increased restrictions on Russia's peasantry and increased privileges for the nobility. Western ideas continued to enter Russia. With the outbreak of the French Revolution in 1789, however, Catherine felt it necessary to prevent new trends in Europe from affecting Russian life.

Catherine was succeeded by her son, Paul. The most important political developments at the close of the century took place in foreign policy. The most important political developments at the close of the century took place in the area of relations with Revolutionary France, where Napoleon Bonaparte had embarked on a process of territorial expansion. Under the direction of Paul, Russia followed an inconsistent course of action concerning France. Russia took the lead in forming a European alliance against France, then deserted its allies and went over to the French side. At home Paul's policies seemed just as erratic, and his attacks on the nobility created powerful enemies and led to his overthrow and murder in 1801 in a palace revolution led by Counts Nikita Panin and Peter Pahlen.

Paul was succeeded by his son Alexander, whom Catherine had groomed as her possible successor, educating him in the ideals of the French Enlightenment that she held so dear. Two developments made Alexander I's reign a crucial one in Russian history. First, success in defeating Napoleon in 1812 and leading the westward advance against France made Russia the most powerful and respected country on the continent. Only a century after Peter the Great had led Russia into the European diplomatic community, Alexander brought Russia to its peak of prestige and influence.

The other development saw Alexander as the first czar to address seriously the twin problems of serfdom and autocracy. In the end, however, Alexander made only minor changes in the system of serfdom. He feared noble opposition and the social disruption that sweeping change would bring. Similarly, he stopped short of political reforms that would infringe on his rights of autocrat. Yet the issue of reform would not disappear, as attested by the Decembrist conspiracy of 1825. Its participants are considered the first in a line of revolutionists who drew their inspiration from the political systems of Western Europe.

Between 1825 and 1855 Russia was ruled by a committed conservative. Nicholas I sought to preserve the existing order at home and in the rest of Europe. Serfdom and autocracy remained untouched. Russia's political and military influence played a vital role limiting the effect of the 1848 revolutions in central Europe. Only with the calamity of the Crimean War did Russia's international prestige fall sharply. Within Russia, however, lively debates broke out in the 1840s. Slavophiles and Westernizers sparred over the nature of Russia's past and the proper course for its future.

Nicholas died in the midst of the Crimean War, and it was up to his son Alexander II to extricate Russia from the war and address the problems that the war had brought to the surface. The reign of Alexander II brought rapid and intensive change to Russian life. Events moved in marked contrast to the immobility during the era of Nicholas I. The czar himself took the lead in one sweeping reform: the emancipation of the serfs in 1861. Meanwhile, disappointment over the limits of change led to the development of a widespread radical movement calling for change from below. Populism, with its call for peasant revolution, became a permanent part of Russian political life.

In international affairs, Russia found its role sharply diminished. The rise of a powerful Germany was one sign of Russia's declining role in Europe. So too was the way in which Britain and Austria blocked Russian expansion in the Balkans. Meanwhile in Central Asia and the Far East, Russian territory and Russian influence expanded notably.

Alexander III (r. 1881–94) came to power following the assassination of his father at the hands of the revolutionary terrorists of the People's Will. He made his primary goals the repression of revolutionary groups and the preservation of order. The dominant force of his reign was political and social reaction. He tried to stabilize the countryside by returning power to the gentry and curbing the rights of the *zemstvo*, rural institutions of self-government, established by the Great Reforms of his father. Most other reforms of the 1860s were also curtailed. A policy of Russification of non-Russian groups also aimed at maintaining a stable, conservative order.

And yet, Alexander III was also concerned with promoting industrial growth to maintain Russia's status as a great power. Paradoxically, this industrial growth promoted social and political change of the kind that so worried the czar and his government. In foreign affairs, the key event was the end of Russia's alliance with Germany, followed by a new link to France, surprising many observers who could not picture reactionary Russia allied to republican France.

Buffeted by government repression and increasingly convinced that terrorism was an ideological dead end, some revolutionaries turned to Marxist ideals to question the foundations of Russian society and provide a revolutionary alternative to the agrarian socialist vision that had long dominated debate in radical circles.

At the turn of the 20th century, the new czar, Nicholas II (r. 1894–1917) and his government struggled against growing problems at home and abroad. Nicholas tried to maintain the existing political and social order but faced increasing opposition. Like those of his father's government, the policies of Nicholas II produced deep changes that eventually contributed to the destabilization of the imperial order. Under the guidance of Minister of Finance Sergei Witte, Russia followed a policy of rapid industrialization that was certain to shake the whole system.

A nationwide revolution exploded as a result of the military disasters and strains on the home front of the Russo-Japanese War of 1904–5. The revolution reached its peak in the final months of 1905. Faced with a threat to the monarchy itself, Nicholas reluctantly issued the October Manifesto, which seemed to pledge a constitution and a representative body, or Duma. Between 1906 and 1914, Russians economic development continued and the country moved haltingly toward a constitutional monarchy. One of Nicholas II's few able ministers, Peter Stolypin, showed that imaginative land reforms could be instituted in the countryside.

Nonetheless, Russia's future remained uncertain. The monarchy resisted political change, while radicals were committed to the overthrow of the existing system. In international affairs, Russia was increasingly involved in a dangerous rivalry with Austria in the Balkans that, in conjunction with a system of rival European alliances, led to the outbreak of a continent-wide war in August 1914, later known as World War I.

The war brought irreversible change to Russia. The most significant development was the unmanageable strain that the conflict put on the political, social, and economic system. On the battlefield, Russia suffered an early and catastrophic defeat at the hands of the Germans at Tannenberg. This set a pattern for consistent Russian defeats in encounters with German forces. In the political sphere, the war was marked by the failure of the monarchy and its ministers to direct the military effort adequately. Meanwhile the major institution to gain prestige during the war was the Duma.

By the close of 1916, the country was in a severe crisis. For the average Russian, especially in the cities, every day brought shortages of food and fuel. For soldiers near or at the front, the war seemed a futile effort directed by inept military and political leaders. The monarchy in particular found itself discredited by the war. Nicholas II, never a popular monarch and who in 1915 moved to the front to be in personal command of his troops, was increasingly seen as weak, incompetent, and under the influence of his domineering wife and the monk Grigorii Rasputin. In December 1916, a group of noblemen, including a cousin of the czar, took matters into their own hands and assassinated Rasputin, the symbol to many Russians of the monarchy's corruption and decay. But the assassination failed to stem the disintegration of authority that had set in during the war. A harsh winter, ongoing military setbacks, and mounting food shortages by the first months of 1917 produced a social upheaval of unprecedented consequences.

THE SOVIET UNION

1917–1991

Russia experienced two revolutions in 1917, a relatively spontaneous one in February (March by the Western calendar) that resulted in the abdication of Czar Nicholas II and an organized seizure of power in October (November by the Western calendar) that brought the small Bolshevik Party to power, inaugurating the Soviet era that lasted until 1991.

In February, the accumulated tensions of the Great War and the widespread perception of the government's incompetence and corruption led to a popular uprising that overthrew the monarchy. A Provisional Government drawn from members of the Fourth Duma attempted to rule Russia until a popularly elected Constituent Assembly could convene to decide on more permanent political arrangements. From the start the authority of the Provisional Government was tempered by the power of the Petrograd Soviet of Workers' and Soldiers' Deputies, which drew its inspiration from the short-lived soviets of the 1905 Revolution and which claimed to speak for the downtrodden masses of the Russian Empire. In an arrangement later known as "dual power," the Soviet agreed not to challenge the Provisional Government's claim to power without actually supporting it.

During the following months the country's problems only increased as the Provisional Government failed to establish its authority. Alexander Kerensky, a lawyer of moderate socialist sympathies, emerged as the main figure in the government, but his own deep commitment to Russia's continued participation in the war further undermined the popularity of the Provisional Government and opened the way to a more radical alternative, and a second revolution.

The revolutionary process found a much more decisive leader in Vladimir Lenin, the leader of the Bolshevik faction of the Russian Social Democratic Labor Party. As in 1905, the 1917 February Revolution took Lenin by surprise, but this time he was prepared to seize this historical opportunity. While the Petrograd Soviet and members of his own Bolshevik Party were initially willing to cooperate with the Provisional Government, Lenin argued for an immediate revolution that would transfer power to the soviets, as representative institutions of Russia's working masses. Eager to create mischief for Russia, the German government provided the famous "sealed train" that transported Lenin and his retinue to Finland, from where he reached Petrograd (as St. Petersburg had been renamed during the war) in April 1917. His "April Theses," calling for the overthrow of the Provisional Government and transferring full power to the Petrograd Soviet, revealed his strategy for the coming months. Also benefiting from Lenin's consistent condemnation of the war, to which the Provisional Government still remained committed, the Bolsheviks gained popularity among workers and soldiers. His calls for revolution resulted in the "July Days," a premature attempt to overthrow the Provisional Government, which Lenin felt compelled to support despite misgivings about its timing. In the ensuing anti-Bolshevik backlash, Lenin fled to Finland. After the instrumental role played by workers in defeating the Kornilov mutiny in late August, Lenin renewed his calls for an uprising, returning secretly to Petrograd in mid-October. Despite significant internal opposition, he convinced his party to support an immediate

Bolsheviks on the street during the Russian Revolution, 1918 *(Library of Congress)*

insurrection to coincide with the forthcoming Second Congress of Soviets. Lenin's analysis proved correct, as the Provisional Government fell without much resistance.

The October Revolution that followed turned out to be a turning point in the modern history of Russia. The Bolsheviks claiming to represent the workers, soldiers, and peasants, overthrew the Provisional Government, set out to transform Russia, and promoted revolution throughout the industrialized world. In the first months following the October Revolution, Lenin and the Bolsheviks strengthened their hold on power and removed Russia from the war. The radicalism of the new regime became obvious as it shut down the elected Constituent Assembly on its first day of meetings, attacked the church, and established a secret police.

The formation of an anti-Bolshevik Volunteer (White) Army in southern Russia in December 1917 signaled the beginning of a bloody civil war that lasted for the next three years. At its weakest moment, the borders of Bolshevik-controlled Russia coincided roughly with those of 15th-century Muscovy, before it began its territorial expansion. Surrounded by White forces and their foreign allies, isolated from other socialists who felt the revolution was premature, and mired in a deep economic crisis of industrial production and severe food shortages the Bolsheviks revealed dictatorial underpinnings of their plans for the country: internal opposition within the party was restricted, other socialists like the Mensheviks and Socialist Revolutionaries (SRs) were persecuted, and a new ruthless secret police—the Cheka—was established to root out enemies of the revolution. On August 30, 1918, an SR terrorist, Fanny Kaplan, wounded Lenin in an assassination attempt. In response, the Cheka unleashed its Red Terror, which was met by an equally fierce terror campaign by anti-Bolshevik forces in the countryside. In 1919, the Bolshevik Party was renamed the Communist Party of the Soviet Union, and the Third International was established to coordinate and guide the efforts of other loyal communist parties. Anti-Bolshevik peasant rebellions, riots, strikes, and demonstrations were common during the civil war, culminating in the March 1921 rebellion at the Kronstadt naval base, an erstwhile hotbed of pro-Bolshevik radicalism. Under great pressure from Lenin, that same month the Communist Party approved a degree of free trade and small manufacturing while retaining control of the "commanding heights" of the economy, a less radical program known as the New Economic Policy, which remained in place until the late 1920s.

The New Economic Policy signaled a relaxation of the wartime dictatorship, but a controversy that would last through most of the decade raged within the Communist Party over whether it should be continued or replaced by a government-directed program of rapid growth that would be truer to Communist ideals. Another bitterly contested issue concerned whether to attempt to spread the revolution to other countries or to concentrate on the construction of a new socialist order in Russia. With Lenin alive these issues did not always come to the surface, but his illness triggered a brutal struggle inside the party. In January 1922, his health declining, Lenin retired to the town of Gorki, not far from Moscow. In May 1922 he suffered the first of three strokes, the second in December 1922, which partially paralyzed him, and the third in March 1923, which took away the power of speech. The writings of his last years reflect his growing disillusionment with the bureaucratization of the party *(Better Fewer, but Better)* and the shortcomings of its main leaders ("Last Testament"), and most notably the rude personal style of Stalin, the general secretary of the party. Lenin died on January 21, 1924. In a bizarre final twist for a confirmed atheist, his remains were embalmed and placed on Red Square in a specially designed mausoleum, which became a place of state-sponsored pilgrimage during the remainder of the Soviet period and still stands after the dissolution of the Soviet Union.

Following Lenin's death in 1924, Joseph Stalin consolidated his power within the party bureaucracy, outmaneuvering his more intellectually nimble but less politically astute colleagues by making full use of his considerable administrative and political skills and patronage opportunities. He countered Leon Trotsky's internationalist preferences with the slogan "socialism in one country," which appealed to the party's more nationalist rank and file. But he also borrowed from Trotsky's program of rapid industrialization and abandoned the more moderate program of the New Economic Policy advocated by the Party's other leading theoretician, Nikolai Bukharin. In rapid succession Stalin and his allies removed his main rivals—Trotsky, Grigorii Zinoviev, Lev Kamenev, and Bukharin—from their respective power bases. Stalin emerged as the leader of a devoted and ambitious group of younger Bolsheviks that included Sergei Kirov, Grigorii Ordzhonikidze, Viacheslav Molotov, Lazar Kaganovich, and Kliment Voroshilov. Together they helped Stalin ram through a program of rapid industrialization and enforced collectivization of peasant villages—a Second Revolution—that was arguably far more extensive in its impact than the original October Revolution. Peasant resistance to what amounted to a "second enserfment" was fierce and the government's enforcement of the policy brutal, leading to the deaths of at least 10 million and the deportation of millions more.

In the late 1920s the Soviet Union underwent three sweeping changes that together combined to form a "second" revolution, of perhaps greater long-term impact than the ones in 1917. In industry, the government instituted a system of five-year plans aimed at turning the Soviet Union into an advanced industrial country in the shortest possible time. Agriculture was collectivized in a brutal manner that ended a short period of peasant landownership. The Communist Party spread its control into the lives of most citizens, a process that also saw the steady growth of the country's internal security apparatus, the dimensions of which would soon become apparent during the campaign of mass state terror of the 1930s, an even more turbulent decade than the preceding one. Known as the Great Purge, the campaign was first directed against the party and state bureaucracy. The show trials of 1936–38 of prominent old Bolsheviks, which drew international attention, were accompanied by an even more devastating terror conducted across the various localities of the Soviet Union. A secret purge of the army led to the execution of about half the officer corps. Although exact numbers are difficult to obtain, one estimate holds that the Soviet Union suffered about 29 million "excess deaths" from terror and famine in the 1930s.

In foreign policy, Soviet diplomacy became increasingly preoccupied with the threat of German aggression after Hitler came to power in 1933. In 1934 the

Soviet Union joined the League of Nations and pursued unsuccessfully a policy of collective security against Germany for the next five years. Frustrated by the failure of negotiations with Great Britain and France, Stalin directed his diplomats to negotiate a nonaggression pact with Nazi Germany, which became a reality in August 1939, to the surprise of the world and many Communist faithful. The Soviet Union gained territories in eastern Poland and annexed the Baltic republics, while it supplied Germany with raw materials, mostly oil, for the next two years until Hitler ordered the invasion of the USSR in June 1941.

Stalin's performance as a World War II leader has been the subject of extensive debate. He has been faulted for ignoring various signals that Hitler was

Joseph Stalin (right) with Viacheslav Molotov *(Library of Congress)*

going to break the nonaggression pact and attack the Soviet Union and hence for the disastrous casualties and territorial losses the Soviets suffered during the first weeks of World War II. After a puzzling weeklong absence, Stalin reappeared and throughout the next four years rallied the country to victory. He relaxed the tenor of Soviet domestic politics somewhat, especially in the area of religion, allowing greater freedom to the Orthodox Church and identifying the Soviet struggle with age-old Russian nationalist themes. In foreign policy, he forged an alliance with the United States and Great Britain that survived until victory was achieved, and he held his own in negotiations with Allied leaders Franklin D. Roosevelt of the United States and British Prime Minister Winston Churchill. Through clever diplomacy and the sheer might of the Soviet war machine, Stalin created a bloc of satellite nations of Eastern Europe that survived until 1989.

By 1945, Stalin found himself at the peak of his power, the undisputed ruler of a country that had borne extremely heavy losses and emerged from the war devastated but an undisputed superpower. The opening to the West and the liberalization that some had expected quickly gave way to a cold war, exacerbated by the development of atomic weapons, which the Soviet Union first produced in 1949. The years between 1945 and 1953 remain among the least studied of Stalin's rule. His increasing paranoia and secretiveness shaped the behavior of his associates, who feared a return to the purges of the 1930s. The alleged conspiracy uncovered in January 1953, known as the Doctors' Plot, foreshadowed to many the beginning of a mass purge, particularly targeting Soviet Jews.

Soviet relations with the outside world were also affected by the acquisition of a bloc of satellites in Eastern Europe and by the successful Communist revolution in China of 1949. Friction with the United States arose over the future of Eastern Europe and Germany. The more restrictive regime at home became evident with a crackdown on the intellectual community and the establishment of a new five-year plan.

Stalin's death from a cerebral hemorrhage on March 5, 1953, was met with relief and joy in some quarters and with tears in others from those who had come to believe the mythology of the "Little Father." His body was placed next to Lenin's in the Red Square mausoleum, in keeping with the personality cult he had crafted. Stalin's death was followed by a power struggle among the Soviet political elite, of which the Ukrainian party leader Nikita Khrushchev was now a prominent member. By December 1953, Lavrenty Beria, Stalin's feared police chief, had been quietly executed six months after his dramatic arrest at a Kremlin meeting. Georgii Malenkov, initially considered the most likely successor to Stalin, remained prime minister but had relinquished the more influential post of first secretary of the Communist party, the position given to Khrushchev in September 1953. The two coexisted uneasily until February 1955, when Malenkov was forced to resign, although he stayed on as a member of the Presidium, as the Politburo was known from 1946 to 1964.

By 1956, Khrushchev had emerged as the unchallenged leader of the Soviet Union. With his ally, Nikolai Bulganin, as prime minister, Khrushchev became the long-term successor to Stalin, although he had one more challenge to survive. In June 1957, Malenkov, Molotov, Kaganovich, and other old-guard Stalinists, including Bulganin, later dubbed the "anti-Party group," engineered a vote in the Presidium to dismiss Khrushchev. With the help of war hero Marshal Georgii Zhukov, Khrushchev responded by calling an emergency meeting of the Central Committee that overturned the Presidium's decision. Malenkov, Molotov and Kaganovich were banished to minor positions in such outlying regions as Kazakhstan, Mongolia, and the Urals. Many consider the fact that they were not executed for their defeat as one of the most significant of Khrushchev's departures from the Stalinist practices of the previous decades.

More difficult for the Soviet leadership and the Soviet people to address was the nature of Stalin's legacy in a polity he had mostly created. The next decade witnessed Khrushchev's de-Stalinization campaigns begun by the Secret Speech of 1956 that denounced the most extreme excesses of Stalin's rule, but not its foundations, the removal of Stalin's body from the Lenin mausoleum in 1961 to be interred along with other Soviet heroes in the Kremlin wall, followed by the partial re-Stalinization of the Brezhnev years (1964–1982). Only three decades later in the late 1980s, under then-Secretary General Mikhail Gorbachev's glasnost (openness) campaign, did a free and candid discussion of all aspects of Stalin's rule become possible. Even then, many older Soviets remained uncomfortable in discussing Stalin's era, while a die-hard minority longed for his "firm hand" as the antidote to the troubles Russia faced in the 1990s.

Aside from his dramatic denunciation of the Stalin personality cult, as leader Krushchev became known for erratic policies and impetuous bureaucratic reorganizations. In domestic politics he allowed a limited degree of latitude to Soviet writers and artists (which his successors were later to try to rescind), while trying to shift the balance of Soviet industrial policy a little away from its relentless concentration on heavy industry in favor of consumer goods production. In international politics he sought to divide and delude the Western bloc by alternate bouts of peaceful coexistence and violent threats including "ultimatums" over Berlin, unrestrained testing of nuclear weapons, encouragement of wars of "national liberation," and stationing medium-range missiles on Cuba to threaten the United States, on the one hand, and the acceptance of the partial test-ban treaty with the United States in 1963, on the other. The penalty for these swings of policy was the alienation of the doctrinally rigid in the Communist bloc, especially the Chinese, led by Mao Zedong, the successive acceptance of Polish national communism under Władysław Gomułka and armed suppression of revolution in Hungary in 1956, loss of control over the Communist parties of Western Europe in the name of polycentrism, and, finally, his overthrow in 1964 by the other members of the CPSU leadership. The failure of his grandiose attempts to solve chronic Soviet food shortages by wholesale ploughing up of the "Virgin Lands" of Soviet Asia eased their task in overthrowing him. In October 1964, while resting in the Crimea, Khrushchev was removed from office by his Politburo colleagues and replaced as party secretary by Leonid Brezhnev.

The party officials who deposed Khrushchev deliberately set out to govern the Soviet Union in a collective fashion. Even though a single figure, Leonid Brezhnev, eventually dominated the system, the era from 1964 to his death in

November 1982 was marked by caution and stability. In domestic policy, the Brezhnev years were guided by the policy of "stability of cadres." The unpredictable bureaucratic maneuvers of the Khrushchev years gave way to a stable conservative party that successfully resisted threats to its control as with the derailment of the 1965 "Kosygin reform," which would have injected some measure of market mechanism into the Soviet command economy, Stalin's arbitrary terror, which had affected party and nonparty members alike, gave way to a more selective persecution of the small group of political and religious dissidents through job harassment and the disturbing use of "psychoprisons," condemned by the international community. The period of postwar growth gradually ended, as the economy stalled and corruption spread through the system.

In foreign policy, Brezhnev is generally associated with two major developments: the articulation and implementation of the Brezhnev Doctrine with regard to the Soviet satellites and the policy of détente with the West. The Brezhnev Doctrine, used to justify the invasion of Czechoslovakia in August 1968, gave the Soviet Union and its allies the right to intervene in Soviet socialist states if they judged socialism was under threat. Brezhnev was more personally associated with the relaxation of relations with the West, beginning with the normalization of relations with West Germany in 1970, through summit meetings in Moscow and Vladivostok with U.S. President Richard Nixon, and culminating with the Helsinki Agreement of 1975, generally seen as favorable to Soviet interests. Détente in Europe, however, did not mean an end to the cold war, as the two superpowers jockeyed for influence in the Third World. During these years the Soviet Union extended its influences to places like Angola, Ethiopia, and North Vietnam, in addition to providing crucial subsidies to the Castro regime in Cuba. After 1976, as U.S. Presidents Jimmy Carter and Ronald Reagan pursued less conciliatory policies, U.S.-Soviet relations rapidly deteriorated over issues of human rights, the Soviet invasion of Afghanistan in 1979, the rise of the Solidarity trade union in Poland in 1980–81, and the Reagan administration's desire to place missiles in Western Europe.

Brezhnev's final five years in office were marked by ill health and his inability to perform basic duties of leadership, punctuated by numerous Kremlin-level intrigues over the impending succession. Brezhnev died from a heart attack on November 10, 1982, three days after standing for long hours on Red Square watching the traditional parade celebrating the anniversary of the October Revolution. The most significant development of this period was the nation's deepening economic crisis. Evident in both agriculture and industry, Soviet economic problems made the country increasingly dependent on Western countries like the United States for technology and even for food. Paradoxically, the Brezhnev years produced a massive expansion of Soviet military strength, including a large, modern navy. During this period, Soviet diplomatic contacts and influence likewise grew, notably in Africa and the Middle East. A significant development within the Soviet Union was the emergence of a dissident community that included world-famous writers and scientists. Thus, criticism of the Soviet system became louder and more widely heard than at any time since the 1920s.

The decade following the death of Brezhnev can be divided into three remarkably different periods. Between 1982 and 1985, the Soviet Union remained under ineffective leaders incapable of pursuing a policy of change even as the nation's problems worsened. Economic decline and continuing tension with the United States were the two most obvious difficulties. Beginning in 1985, the Soviet Union acquired a new kind of leader who brought extraordinary change. Mikhail Gorbachev overturned what had seemed permanent features in the Soviet system in both domestic and foreign affairs. Finally, from 1989 to 1991, the changes that Gorbachev had encouraged among the Soviet citizenry

Nikita Khrushchev (right) and Leonid Brezhnev attending a session of the Supreme Soviet, Moscow, 1961 *(Library of Congress)*

gathered greater speed, quickly leaving the government in a defensive position, as the Soviet Union threatened to unravel. At the same time, dramatic changes developed from below. As Gorbachev loosened political controls, vast numbers of Soviet citizens took on active and unprecedented political roles. The growth of non-Communist and nationalist political parties was one sign of this political awakening, as was the emergence of mass public demonstrations and, in the extreme case, armed ethnic rebellions.

Gorbachev began his term by placing reformist allies, such as Alexander Yakovlev, Eduard Shevardnadze, and Nikolai Ryzhkov, in key positions, by signaling his commitment to a more open political culture by recalling the dissident physicist Andrei Sakharov from internal exile, and in more traditional Soviet fashion, by seeking to improve labor discipline through a widely unpopular campaign to reduce alcohol consumption. The more ambitious agenda of perestroika (restructuring) and glasnost (openness), for which he is widely known, met with mixed and unexpected results. Economic reforms consisting of moderate attempts to move toward a limited market economy met with resistance in the Communist Party and government bureaucracy, leading to inflation, shortages, and declining production by 1990. Political change, on the other hand, quickly surpassed what Gorbachev had originally envisioned. In rapid succession, an astonished Soviet public saw the Communist Party lose its leading role in the economy, a deep reevaluation of hitherto taboo topics in Soviet history such as the dark aspects of Stalin's rule, relatively open elections for a new Congress of People's Deputies, the reemergence of a thriving, creative artistic and intellectual climate, and democratic elections in the 15 Soviet constituent republics that brought democratic and nationalist movements into positions of power.

In Western eyes, Gorbachev was the most successful in foreign policy, where he overcame the initial suspicions of U.S. leaders to become a full partner in dismantling key components of the cold war apparatus. He reversed the disastrous occupation of Afghanistan, withdrawing all Soviet forces by early 1989. After spurring Eastern European Communist governments to reform themselves, he refrained from interfering in the remarkable revolutionary events of 1989, best symbolized by the dismantling of the Berlin Wall, thus ensuring a mostly peaceful transition away from communism in the region. The following year Soviet forces withdrew from Eastern Europe and the Soviet Union agreed to the once unthinkable reunification of Germany. Finally, in July 1991 the two superpowers signed the START I treaty, which sharply reduced their nuclear arsenals. For his pivotal role in the peaceful transformation of Eastern Europe and the Soviet-American relationship, Gorbachev received the 1990 Nobel Peace Prize.

Ultimately, the goal to reform the Soviet Union was doomed by the growth of nationalism in most of its 15 constituent republics. Beginning with the Nagorno-Karabakh crisis between Armenia and Azerbaijan in 1988, a full range of nationalist issues from autonomy to full independence surfaced in the non-Russian borderlands. When a crackdown came in Georgia and Lithuania in the spring of 1991, it was too late to stop the nationalist tide. With the democratic election of Boris Yeltsin, his former ally turned nemesis, as president of the Russian Republic, Gorbachev's power as leader of the Soviet Union rapidly dimin-

This cartoon shows Soviet leader Mikhail S. Gorbachev looking in dismay at a massive stone hammer and sickle, now shattered into many parts. Gorbachev found himself faced with reforming the remnants of the former Soviet power. *(Library of Congress)*

ished. By 1991, with the economy in shambles and a vibrant democratic political culture taking shape, the preservation of the union was at the top of his agenda. His proposed treaty for a new Union of Sovereign States would have significantly altered the nature of the Soviet Union, making it a more truly federal and voluntary union, but it was never signed because other, more pressing events intervened.

On August 19, 1991, a conservative Communist backlash took place in Moscow while Gorbachev was on vacation in Crimea. Headed by men whom Gorbachev had placed in power over the previous year, the attempted coup was poorly planned and executed. Within days, street protests, army defections, and Yeltsin's heroic leadership combined to defeat the "August putsch," as it became known. Freed from house arrest, Gorbachev returned to Moscow to a changed country and promptly resigned as general secretary of the Communist Party. He continued to seek a new federal union, but the Soviet Union was rapidly losing its member republics with all but Russia and Kazakhstan declaring independence by October 1991. His power rapidly declining, Gorbachev was unable to stop the leaders from the Russian Federation, Ukraine, and Belarus from formally dissolving the Soviet Union in December 1991. He resigned as Soviet president on December 25 and retired to private life.

The 1990s brought the unexpected dissolution of the Soviet Union into its 15 constituent republics. Russia reconstituted itself as the Russian Federation, a democratic parliamentary republic under the leadership of a popularly elected president, Boris Yeltsin. The Communist Party was temporarily routed, although by 1993 it had become an important force in parliament, obstructing Yeltsin's attempts to dismantle the old state-dominated economy. For average citizens, the 1990s were a traumatic decade, as the safety network of pensions, health care, and other social benefits from the Soviet system was dismantled, leaving them vulnerable to the vagaries of a new economy. This was not the capitalist market economy that Western advisers had optimistically assumed would take root in Russia, but rather a "wild capitalism" dominated by a few oligarchs who were able to take advantage of the opportunities offered in the transition between one system to another. Yeltsin was reelected president in 1996, but his increasing poor health quickly led to speculation about his successor. In the following years he played an astute game of politics, shuffling his cabinet, frequently changing prime ministers, until finally settling on Vladimir Putin, a relatively unknown young bureaucrat with a background in the internal security apparatus (KGB). Putin easily won election in 2000 and began the difficult task of continuing the transition of Russia away from decades of communism.

With Putin as president, the wild ride of the 1990s seemed to be over, and Russians prepared for a relatively more stable period. Many of the features that had emerged after the fall of the Soviet Union were still in place. Business tycoons, or oligarchs as they were known in Russian, continued to control important segments of the Russian economy, and even though they attempted to exert political influence as in the Yeltsin years, the Putin government followed a more selective policy toward them, favoring some while harassing or persecuting others. The Chechen problem continued to fester, draining the nation's resources and political capital in a bloody war with no apparent immediate solution. On several occasions Chechens brought the war into Russia through spectacular terrorist acts such as the seizure of a Moscow theater in the fall of 2003.

On the other hand, the Russian economy seemed to find a more firm footing after the debacle of 1998 and was aided by growing oil revenues. Signs of greater prosperity were still visible mostly in cities such as Moscow and St. Petersburg, but the bulk of the country had still not emerged from the spectacular decline that had accompanied the dissolution of the Soviet Union. In international affairs, Russia continued to chart its own course, no longer the superpower it had been during the cold war but still a great power claiming strategic interests beyond its borders. In the summer of 2003, the city of St. Petersburg, hometown of President Putin and long neglected during Soviet times, celebrated its 300th anniversary in a grand fashion. As Putin's term came to an end and the nation prepared for presidential elections in 2004, Russia continued to move away from the legacy of communism, even if the direction or final destination of this transition remained unclear.

HISTORICAL DICTIONARY
A–Z

A

Abkhazia

An autonomous republic within the Republic of Georgia whose 1994 declaration of independence has not been recognized by neighboring countries, Abkhazia is a region of about 3,300 square miles situated between the main Caucasian range and the Black Sea, with a subtropical climate along its coastline. A principality ruled by Ottoman Turkey since 1578, Abkhazia fell under Russian rule in 1810. After the abolition of the principality in 1864 and uprisings against Russian rule, the large majority of ethnic Abkhazians emigrated to Turkey. Another wave of Abkhazian migrants followed, after the conclusion of the RUSSO-TURKISH WAR OF 1877–78. Under Soviet rule, an Abkhazian Soviet Socialist Republic was established in 1921, but then was made part of the Georgian Soviet Socialist Republic in December 1921. In December 1922, both Abkhazia and Georgia were made part of the Transcaucasian Soviet Federated Socialist Republic, which existed until 1936. With the dissolution of the Transcaucasian SFSR, Abkhazia was again placed under Georgian jurisdiction. During Joseph STALIN's rule, Soviet authorities in Georgia followed a policy of enforced cultural assimilation and suppression of Abkhazian culture that was significantly relaxed after 1953. In 1978, the Abkhazians petitioned to secede from the Georgian SSR and join the Russian Soviet Federated Socialist Republic, but their request was not approved. With the unraveling and dissolution of the Soviet Union in the early 1990s, the tensions between Abkhazians and Georgians came to the surface. A declaration of independence from Georgia by the Abkhazian legislature in 1990 was reversed by ethnic Georgian deputies, and this eventually led to the outbreak of armed conflict in 1992. By 1993 Abkhazian forces had managed to capture the regional capital of Sukhumi, on the Black Sea, and drive out Georgian troops. Russia arranged for a cease-fire in 1994 through the establishment of a peacekeeping force sponsored by the Commonwealth of Independent States (CIS), composed of most of the former Soviet republics. The 1994 Abkhazian declaration of independence was followed in 1996 by CIS economic sanctions.

Abramov, Feodor Aleksandrovich (1920–1983)
writer

A writer known for his advocacy of peasants and rural themes, Abramov was in the forefront of the "VILLAGE PROSE" movement that played an important role in Soviet literature from the 1950s to the 1970s. Abramov was born in the town of Verkhola in Archangel Province to a peasant family. He enrolled in the philology faculty of Leningrad State University, but his studies were interrupted by military service during World War II. He graduated in 1951 and taught at his alma mater until 1960, serving as chairman of the department of Soviet literature. Abramov's concern for peasants and his critiques of the government's representation of village life led to reprimands from the Union of Soviet Writers and his expulsion from the staff of the literary journal *Neva*. In 1958 Abramov published his first novel, *Brothers and Sisters*, set in a northern Russian village during World War II. This novel proved to be the first of a four-novel saga about the travails of Russian peasants in the period after the war, collectively published as *The Pryaslins*. The other novels in the tetralogy are *Two Winters and Three Summers* (1968), *Paths and Crossroads* (1973), which was awarded the 1975 USSR literature prize, and *The House* (1978).

Abramtsevo

Located about two hours from MOSCOW, Abramtsevo is a village and estate that was the spiritual home of the Arts and Crafts movement that flourished in late 19th-century Russia under the name Style Moderne. Originally built in 1771, the main house was home to the Slavophile philosopher Sergei AKSAKOV, between the 1840s and 1860s, during which time the main outlines of the Slavophile movement to which he belonged took shape. Nikolai GOGOL worked here shortly before his death on the ill-fated second volume to his masterpiece *Dead Souls,* before he burned the manuscript. Ivan TURGENEV was also a frequent visitor. In 1870, Savva Mamontov, a railway magnate and patron of the arts, purchased the estate. For the next two decades, under his family's patronage, Abramtsevo became a living workshop of Russian culture, favoring the rediscovery of native Russian traditions of art. Abramtsevo became a kind of artists' retreat where painters, potters, singers, and theater directors commented on one another's work. Workshop products like furniture and ceramics were sold at the Abramtsevo shop in Moscow, established in 1880. Late-19th-century artists such as Ilia REPIN, Mikhail VRUBEL, and Valentin Serov left their mark on the estate. Repin's family portraits hang in the main house, while Vrubel's ceramic-tiled fireplace was made in the ceramic studio next door. The remarkable Abramtsevo Church on the estate grounds was built to recall the glories of medieval Russian architecture, and inside features icons by Repin, Vasnetsov, and Polenov. Abramtsevo now belongs to the ACADEMY OF SCIENCES and has been turned into a museum.

Academy of Sciences

The leading institution for scientific and scholarly research in Russia, the Academy of Sciences was founded on the basis of a decree of Peter the Great of January 1724. It opened its doors the following year in St. Petersburg. Construction for more permanent headquarters began in 1738 under the direction of the renowned architect Giacomo Quarenghi. For most of the 18th century the academy was staffed by foreign scholars, mostly Germans, invited by the government. One notable exception was the renowned Russian scientist Mikhail LOMONOSOV, who was elected to the academy in 1745. During the 19th century, the academy was gradually "Russified," although it continued to attract and invite scholars from abroad. The status and composition of the academy did not change much in the first decade after the 1917 Revolutions. In 1927, however, as part of a larger cultural offensive, it was renamed the USSR Academy of Sciences and brought in line with the demands of the COMMUNIST PARTY and the Soviet state. In 1934, the academy was relocated from Leningrad (formerly St. Petersburg) to MOSCOW. By 1987, toward the end of the Soviet period, the academy contained 250 research institutes and over 60,000 full-time researchers, concentrated mostly in the natural sciences. Over 300 scholars had the privileged status of "academician," while about twice as many were "corresponding members" of the academy. In addition, all the union republics except the RSFSR had their own mini-academies of science. About 90 percent of research was carried on outside the academy system. Most of this was of an applied character and much of it was related to weapons systems and done in secret facilities in the defense-production ministries. With the dissolution of the Soviet Union, the academy was renamed the Russian Academy of Sciences.

Adashev, Aleksei Feodorovich (unknown–1561)
government official

An influential government adviser in the early decades of the reign of IVAN IV (the Terrible), Adashev became one of the first casualties of the setbacks in the LIVONIAN WAR (1558–83), which drained valuable resources during the remainder of Ivan's rule. Adashev came from a noble family from Kostroma, which was linked to prominent Moscow boyars. He entered government service in the 1540s and became one of the leading advocates of policies that reformed the central government, strengthening it with regards to the boyar aristocracy. Adashev was involved in the preparation of the 1550 Law Code (Sudebnik), military and financial reforms, and the abolition of the system of *kormlenie* (feeding) that farmed tax collection to local administrators. Supporter of an active foreign policy in relation to the Tatar khanates, Adashev directed diplomatic preparation of the annexation of KAZAN and ASTRAKHAN khanates, and directed the engineering work during the siege of Kazan in 1552. He was one of the officials who laid the diplomatic groundwork for the Livonian War, which would occupy most of Ivan's reign and deplete much of Muscovy's reserves. In 1559, he negotiated a truce with Livonia, albeit on unfavorable terms for Russia. Adashev's opposition to the continuation of the Livonian War and to the growing influence of the Zakharin clan, relatives of the czar's wife, were the main reasons behind his downfall. In late 1560, he was arrested and jailed in Iurev (Tartu), where he died the following year. His brother, Daniil Feodorovich, was also an influential commander who participated in the capture of Kazan and, in 1553–54, helped suppress an insurrection in the Volga region. After a successful campaign against the Turks along the Black Sea, he was appointed artillery commander during the Livonian War. He was imprisoned with his brother and died in either 1562 or 1563.

Adrianople, Treaty of (1829)

Signed on September 14, 1829, the Treaty of Adrianople, also known as the Treaty of Edirne, marked the end of the RUSSO-TURKISH WAR of 1828–1829. Signed by Aleksei Orlov and Feodor Pahlen on the Russian side, the treaty gave Russia control of the Danube estuary and opened the Dardanelles to all commercial vessels. In the Caucasus, the Treaty of Adrianople confirmed Russian wartime conquests along the eastern coast of the Black Sea and placed the region of Guria under direct Russian rule. The Treaty of Adrianople also marked the beginning of the loosening of the Ottoman Empire's control over the Balkan Peninsula in southeastern Europe. Turkey was to demilitarize the right bank of the Danube River and withdraw its troops from the principalities of Moldavia and Wallachia. Moldavia, Wallachia, and Serbia were granted special status within the Ottoman Empire, while Greece was granted full independence. By the terms of the treaty, Russia was to occupy the principalities of Moldavia and Wallachia until Turkey paid its war indemnities to Russia and to Russian citizens who had suffered losses during the war.

Afanasiev, Alexandr Nikolaevich (1826–1871)

ethnographer and folklorist

Afanasiev was born into the large family of an attorney in Voronezh province, central Russia. After completing his secondary education studies in 1844, he passed the difficult entrance examinations to Moscow University and enrolled in the law faculty. Upon graduation he secured a position in the archival department of the Ministry of Foreign Affairs in Moscow. His real interests lay not in jurisprudence but in folklore and in collecting. It is said that he collected one of the finest private libraries of its day in MOSCOW. In 1860 he journeyed to the West, visiting Germany, Italy, France, Switzerland, and England. Back in Russia, he was arrested in 1862 and expelled from his job two years later for his alleged contacts with an associate of the revolutionary activist and London exile, Aleksandr HERZEN. He found new employment with the Moscow Municipal Court but died of consumption seven years later, an early end to a remarkably productive life.

Afanasiev's legacy, like that of the Brothers Grimm in Germany, is as a compiler of a vast amount of Russian folktales. He compiled and classified more than 1,000 tales recorded by

Vladimir DAL earlier in the century and supplemented them with tales from popular chapbooks and from the collection of the Russian Geographical Society. His reputation rests on two highly acclaimed works. *Russian Folk Tales* was a monumental and comprehensive collection of diverse material ranging from animal tales to longer tales of fantastic heroes, which he worked on for 15 years. The second, *Russian Folk Legends,* was banned by the censor on the insistence of the clergy. Initially published in London in 1860, it came out in Russia only in 1914. A third work, *Frivolous Tales,* a bibliographical rarity including tales that satirized priests and nobles, was also banned and published in Russian only in Geneva. Afanasiev was active in other fields, writing for progressive journals, publishing a multivolume work on Slavic views of nature, as well as other works on Russian satirical periodicals, folklore, and literature.

Afghanistan

Russia's initial involvement in Afghanistan in the 19th century was colored by the larger rivalry with Great Britain known as "The Great Game." While seeking to counter growing Russian influence in the region and increase their own, the British fought three mostly unsuccessful wars with the Afghan rulers (1839–42, 1878–80, 1921). On the other hand, Russia first established a fixed boundary between Afghanistan and its newly conquered territories around BUKHARA, Tashkent, and SAMARKAND, and promised to respect Afghanistan's territorial integrity in 1873. In 1885, however, Russian forces seized the Panjdeh Oasis, a piece of Afghan territory north of the Oxus River. After some fighting the Russians retained Pandjeh and promised once again to respect Afghanistan's territorial integrity. Ten years later, the northern border between Afghanistan and Russia was fixed through diplomatic negotiations. In 1907, as relations between Great Britain and Russia improved, both sides signed the Convention of St. Petersburg declaring Afghanistan outside Russia's sphere of influence.

After World War I, the Russian Revolution temporarily dampened Russia's interest in the region, while in 1921 Afghanistan regained control of its foreign affairs as a result of the Third Afghan War.

In the 1950s the Soviet Union again began to display interest in Afghanistan, in the context of the cold war and as part of its broader involvement in the Third World. In 1955, Prince Mohammad Daoud, prime minister of Afghanistan, turned to the Soviet Union for military aid, after his request to buy military equipment was turned down by the United States. A period of close relations between Afghanistan and the Soviet Union began in 1956. In 1965, the Afghan Communist Party was secretly formed, later gaining representation in the national parliament during the first nationwide elections held in Afghanistan. In 1973, Daoud, who had been removed as prime minister in 1964, overthrew King Zahir Shah in a military coup with the support of the Afghan Communist Party. He abolished the monarchy and declared himself president of the new Republic of Afghanistan. Five years later in 1978 the Afghan Communist Party, led by Nur Mohammed Taraki, seized power in a bloody coup in which Daoud was killed, and which was followed by a campaign of mass arrests. A guerrilla resistance movement, known as the Mujahideen, quickly took shape in the countryside. Later that year Afghanistan signed a treaty of friendship with the Soviet Union.

On December 24, 1979, with growing resistance to the Afghan Communists and with the Communists themselves in a virtual civil war, the Soviet Union took the fateful decision of intervening directly in Afghan politics by invading the country. The Soviet invasion of Afghanistan marked a crucial turning point in the diplomatic history of the cold war as well as in Soviet domestic politics. In foreign policy it triggered a new round of tensions with the West, after the détente of the 1970s, leading directly to a U.S.-led grain embargo of the Soviet Union and a boycott of the 1980 Olympics held in MOSCOW. The Soviet Union's inability to defeat the guerrilla resistance exposed its weaknesses as a superpower and contributed to the growing disenchantment with the government in the final decade of Soviet power. Close to 50,000 Soviet soldiers were killed in the war that lasted a decade, until the Soviet Union fully withdrew its troops in February 1989. The Soviets continued to support the Communist government led by Najibullah, but it was a losing battle. In 1992, the Mujahideen entered the capital city, Kabul, and established an Islamic state. Four years later, as the victorious guerrilla coalition fragmented, a more radical Islamic group known as the Taliban seized power in Kabul, which it held until 2001. Throughout the 1990s Russia continued to support regional chiefs or warlords in the northern parts of Afghanistan in opposition to Islamic governments.

"agit-trains"

Common name (Russian, *agitpoezd*) for the agitation trains—there were also agitation steamers— widely used by the BOLSHEVIKS for organizational and propaganda work during the Russian civil war. In czarist times trains with religious information were dispatched to the countryside, but it was the Bolsheviks who developed their propaganda and creative potential to a far greater degree. Most trains and steamers were equipped with a bookshop, printing press, meeting room, and film projector. They also had a radio transmitter-receiver to receive the latest information from MOSCOW. The first agit-train, named after V. I. LENIN, left Moscow toward KAZAN in August 1918, and later traveled to Ukraine, Belorussia, and Lithuania. Other trains with prominent Soviet officials on board followed. The *October Revolution*, with the future Soviet president Mikhail Kalinin on board, made over 12 trips to central Russia, Ukraine, the northern Caucasus, and Siberia in 1919–20. The *Krasnyi Vostok* (Red East) operated in Turkestan in March 1920, the *Sovetskii Kavkaz* (Soviet Caucasus) worked in the northern Caucasus and Azerbaijan from July to October 1920, and the *Krasnyi Kazak* (Red Cossack) traveled through the Don and Kuban regions from April to July 1920. Several agit-steamers operated during these years, the most notable being the *Krasnaia Zvezda* (Red Star), which sailed with Lenin's wife, Nadezhda KRUP-SKAYA, on board along the VOLGA and Kama Rivers from July 1919 to the fall of 1921. Of all the activities the agit-trains performed, the showing of agitation films (*agitki*) to a largely illiterate population probably had the most impact. Over 2 million people attended the cinema screenings shown on board. At a time of weak links between the center and provinces, these trains and steamers proved immensely valuable in bringing news of Soviet power to the countryside, strengthening local party organs, and mobilizing people and material aid for the fronts.

Aitmatov, Chingiz Torekulovich
(1928–)
writer

A bilingual writer, writing in his native Kirgiz (Kyrgyz) and Russian, Aitmatov first established his reputation in the BREZHNEV era and played an important liberalizing role in the literary politics of the GORBACHEV years. Born in the mountain village of Sheker in Kirgizia, Aitmatov completed only six years of school before becoming secretary of his village's soviet and a tax collector at the age of 14. He graduated in 1953 from veterinary school and worked on an experimental farm, but literature was already pulling him in another direction. He first published in 1952, became first secretary of the Union of Kyrgyz writers in 1964, and was elected to the Kyrgyz Academy of Sciences in 1974. He achieved Soviet and international prominence through his story *Dzamilia* in 1958, which chronicles the struggle of a Kyrgyz woman to choose her husband herself rather than follow tradition and have him presented to her. His collection of short stories, *Tales of the Mountains and Steppes* (1962), introduced local myths and values. He was elected deputy to the USSR Supreme Soviet in 1966. The following year he was elected to the executive board of the USSR Union of Writers and was awarded the Soviet state prize for literature (1968). The relationship of modernity to tradition remained a central theme of his work, but in later works, such as *The Day Lasts More than a Hundred Years* (1980), he linked them to broader themes like space travel, science fiction, and a more direct treatment of his characters' Stalinist past. In the late 1980s as a member of the editorial board of *Novyi Mir* (New World) and editor in chief of *Inostrannaya literatura* (Foreign Literature) he played an important role in bringing previously suppressed Soviet and foreign literature to Soviet readers at a crucial juncture in the development of Mikhail Gorbachev's glasnost (openness) campaign. He was elected to the landmark Congress of People's Deputies (1989), as well as to its Supreme Soviet. Gorbachev made him a member of his Presidential Council in March 1990 and appointed him ambassador to Luxembourg in 1990–91.

Akademgorodok

The third-largest research and educational center in contemporary Russia, Akademgorodok is a town of close to 100,000 inhabitants, located in the vicinity of the city of Novosibirsk in south-central Siberia. The town, a planned community, derives its name from the Russian term for "academic town" and was established in a scenic location on the northeast edge of the Novosibirsk Reservoir formed from the damming of the OB River. Founded in 1958, Akademgorodok has since been the seat of the Siberian branch of the Russian (USSR) ACADEMY OF SCIENCES, and numerous research organizations and institutions. In 1959, Novosibirsk State University was established within the city limits. Established on the initiative of the COMMUNIST PARTY and the USSR Academy of Sciences with the goal of decentralizing scientific research while contributing to the overall development of Siberia, Akademgorodok quickly staked out an important place in Soviet intellectual life. The town's distance from the more closely regulated world

of Moscow, 1,800 miles away to the west, allowed its scholars greater latitude in pursuing alternative research paths. The relatively open political and scholarly environment of Akademgorodok was sharply curtailed after 1968, as part of the overall conservative backlash that followed the WARSAW PACT invasion of Czechoslovakia. Nevertheless, Akademgorodok continued to contribute to Soviet intellectual and scientific life in the 1970s and 1980s. Two influential advisers to Mikhail GORBACHEV in the late Soviet period, the sociologist Tatiana Zaslavskaya and the economist Abel Aganbegyan, came from the Akademgorodok scholarly environment.

Akhmadulina, Bella Akhatovna (1937–   )
poet

A member of the group of young poets that included Yevgenii YEVTUSHENKO and Andrei Voznesensky, who formed part of a short-lived literary renaissance in the early 1960s, Akhmadulina became, like them, a leading literary celebrity in the GORBACHEV era. Born in Moscow of Italian-Tatar background, Akhmadulina graduated from the Gorky Institute of Literature. Her poems, lyrical and personal, drew from the Acmeist tradition begun by Anna AKHMATOVA, Osip MANDELSTAM, and Nikolai GUMILEV. Although a volume of her poetry, *Struna,* appeared in 1962, she was published sporadically in the intervening years, especially after the conservative reaction that set in during the BREZHNEV era. At one time married to Yevtushenko, she was awarded the state prize for poetry in 1989. She traveled widely but, although respected as an important Russian poet, never achieved the same public impact as her early colleagues.

Akhmatova, Anna Andreevna (1889–1966)
poet

Born Anna Gorenko near ODESSA of Ukrainian parentage, Akhmatova survived personal tribulations and political persecution in the Stalin years to become one of the great 20th-century Russian poets. Educated in Tsarskoe Selo (Pushkin), near St. Petersburg, and Kiev, she married the poet Nikolai GUMILEV in 1910 (they divorced in 1918). With Gumilev and Osip MANDELSTAM, she started the Acmeist movement, advocating clarity and concreteness as a response to the diffuseness and mysticism of the reigning Symbolist poets. First published in 1912, over the next decade she established her reputation among the intelligentsia with a lyrical poetry of spiritual undertones that was intimate, yet detached. The first four decades of Soviet power brought Akhmatova personal suffering (Gumilev was executed in 1921 and her son, Lev Gumilev, spent 14 years in labor camps) and ostracism by Soviet cultural authorities. She earned a living from translations, all the while writing masterful poems such as *Rekviem* (Requiem, 1935–40) that would not be published in Russia until after her death. A brief respite from official censure in 1940 saw the publication of 20 new poems, "Selections from Six Books." She experienced the siege of LENIN-GRAD before being evacuated to Tashkent, where she wrote her most avant-garde poem: "The Way of All Earth." After the war, she and Mikhail ZOSHCHENKO became the main targets of Andrei ZHDANOV's vicious xenophobic cultural campaign, and in 1946 she was expelled from the Writers' Union. Akhmatova entered a final period of great creativity and international recognition after 1956 with her son's return from the camps and the temporary relaxation of cultural norms after Stalin's death in 1953. During this last decade she published translations of Yiddish poems by Jewish poets shot in the anti-Semitic campaigns of 1952, as well as two of her own collections, *Poems* and *Poems, 1909–60*. In 1962, she finally completed her masterpiece, *Poema bez geroya (Poem without a Hero)*, begun in 1940. International recognition in the form of an honorary doctorate from Oxford University, the Italian Literary Prize, and translations of her work came in the 1960s and 1970s. At the time of her death in Domodedovo, near Moscow, Akhmatova had

succeeded in her goal to give witness to a "cruel age," becoming in the process a voice of Russia's conscience.

Akhmed (unknown–1481)
(also Akhmat)
Mongol ruler

As khan (r. 1459–81) of the GOLDEN HORDE, Akhmed tried to reassert control over the increasingly powerful Muscovite state. In 1472 Akhmed, having concluded an agreement with the king of Poland-Lithuania, Casimir IV, attacked Russian territory but was unsuccessful. In 1476, he sent an emissary to the grand prince of Moscow, IVAN III, demanding tribute, but was categorically refused. This set the stage for the Battle of the UGRA RIVER, 150 miles to the southwest of Moscow, which took place in 1480 between Muscovite and Mongol forces. Akhmed arrived at the southern bank of the river, prepared for a decisive confrontation. However, faced with the failure of expected Polish-Lithuanian reinforcements, distracted by Ivan's ally, the Crimean khan Mengli-Girei, to arrive, and with reports of domestic problems near his capital of SARAI, Akhmed chose to withdraw. His retreat marks the formal end of Muscovite subservience to the Mongols, even though this had been in progress for several decades and even though military confrontations between the two sides continued for almost another century. Akhmed was killed the following year by one of his subordinates, the khan of Tiumen, Ibak.

Aksakov family
writers

The Aksakov family produced two generations of influential intellectuals who made important contributions to the development of SLAVOPHILE thought in mid–19th century Russia. The elder Aksakov, Sergei Timofeevich Aksakov (1791–1859), made his name as a novelist who specialized in rural themes, and is considered one of the founders of Russian realism. From 1827 to 1832

Sergei Timofeevich Aksakov *(Library of Congress)*

he worked as a censor in MOSCOW. Retired from the civil service in 1843 he settled on the family estate in ABRAMTSEVO, where he wrote the autobiographical trilogy, *Family Chronicle* (1856), *The Years of Childhood of Bagrov the Grandson* (1858), and *Reminiscences* (1856). In *Family Chronicle* he realistically portrayed an 18th-century Russian squire's family (based on his own family's history) and conditions in Bashkiria, then being colonized by Russia. Other works dwelled on rural themes and the issue of Russian identity.

Two of his sons became prominent intellectuals and representatives of the Slavophile movement. Konstantin Sergeevich Aksakov (1817–60) was a historian, literary critic, and writer. He finished Moscow University in 1835 and joined the seminal Stankevich Circle, influenced by Hegel.

In the 1840s he joined the circle led by Aleksei Stepanovich Khomiakov and was influential in developing the important Slavophile concept of *sobornost'* (togetherness) as a distinctive trait differentiating Russia from the individualistic West.

Konstantin's younger brother, Ivan Sergeevich Aksakov (1823–86), was a brilliant orator and publicist, publisher, and editor of several newspapers, many of which were suppressed by the government. During the 1840s Ivan Aksakov worked as a civil servant in Moscow, Kaluga, ASTRAKHAN, Bessarabia, and Yaroslavl provinces. Commissioned by the Russian Geographic Society to study trade in the Ukraine, he published *Issledovanie o torgovle na ukrainskikh iarmarkakh (Researches on trade in Ukrainian fairs)* (1858). In 1855 he served in the volunteer militia that fought in the CRIMEAN WAR. After his brother's death he assumed a more prominent role in the Slavophile movement, especially as president of the Moscow Slavic Committee (1861–86). During the RUSSO-TURKISH WAR OF 1877–78, he reached the height of his influence as leading spokesman for the widespread public call for the liberation of the Balkan Slavs. In the 1870s and 1880s, Ivan Aksakov became involved in banking and was the chairman of the council of the Moscow Mutual Credit Society. But it was as an editor of publications with strong Slavophile views such as *Moskovskii sbornik* (1840s–50s), the journal *Russkaia beseda,* the newspapers *Parus* and *Den'* (1861–65), and *Moskva* (1867–68) that he made his mark. By 1880, as editor of the newspaper *Rus'* (1880–86), he had assumed openly anti-Semitic positions, writing against "the worldwide Jewish conspiracy."

Aksenov, Vasili Petrovich (1932–   )
writer

The son of Evgeniia GINZBURG, Aksenov became a leading novelist in the Soviet Union and abroad after he emigrated in 1980. He was born in KAZAN, Tatarstan, where his father was chair of the local soviet. His parents were put in the GULAG, and he was raised by his grandmother. At the age of 16 he was reunited with his mother in the town of Magadan, where she was now living in internal exile. Aksenov later entered the Leningrad Medical Institute, from which he graduated in 1956, after which he worked as a doctor in the Soviet Union until 1960. His first two novels, *Kollegi* (Colleagues, 1960) and *Zvesdny bilet* (Ticket to the stars, 1961), became instant bestsellers and established his reputation as a bold young writer. Other works such as *Apelsiny iz Marokko* (Oranges from Morocco) (1963) and *Na poputi k lune* (Halfway to the Moon) (1966) followed in the same vein. His early works appealed to an increasingly restless and assertive young generation, interested in the West, by making their concerns central and recording their slang. The latter, in particular, brought the unwelcome attention of cultural authorities, who saw in it only foul language. Aksenov tried to promote young writers by publishing a literary almanac, *Metropol* (1979), despite official prohibition. In trouble with the Soviet authorities and unable to publish his work, he emigrated to the United States in 1980, where he has taught at various universities. He continued to write prolifically and two important works, *The Burn* (1980) and *The Island of Crimea* (1981), belong to this period. *The Burn* paints a negative portrait of Soviet society through the adventures of five men with the same name. *The Island of Crimea* is a historical fantasy based on the fiction that Crimea is an island and not a peninsula, where, like Taiwan, the Whites have established over the decades a capitalist society, only a stone throw from the Communist mainland. Although he still lives in the United States, Aksenov revisited the Soviet Union in 1989, and his work was republished there from 1990.

Alaska

Russia's main North American colony, Alaska belonged to Russia from the mid-18th century until 1867, when it was purchased by the United States. Russian interest in Alaska dates back to the late 17th century following the conquest of Siberia, although precise knowledge of its geography was sketchy; in a 1701 map, it appears as an island. Beginning with the first expeditions of Vitus BERING and A. Chirikov in 1728–29, Russian explorers began to chart the Alaskan coastline, although it is customary to date the Russian discovery of Alaska from the expedition of 1741. For the next half-century, more than 80 exploratory and commercial expeditions sailed to America, most notably those led by the merchant G. I. Shelikov, who founded the first Russian settlement on Kodiak Island in 1784. Excessive competition among small trading companies, the rapid exhaustion of fur stocks in the area, and the threat of English penetration, especially after Cook's 1778 expedition, convinced Shelikov of the need to create permanent Russian settlements and an exclusive trading company in Alaska. The latter aim was realized with the foundation of the RUSSIAN AMERICAN COMPANY in 1799, which was given a monopoly on all trade and minerals located on the northwestern coast of America from 55 degrees north latitude to the Bering Strait and on the Aleutians, Kuriles, and other islands. The company also received the right to claim lands not occupied by other powers. The center of the Russian settlement was transferred from Kodiak Island to the town of Novo-Arkhangelsk.

Under its first and most able governor, Aleksandr BARANOV (1746–1819), Russian Alaska made important strides as a colony with settlers, schools, a library, shops, a shipbuilding yard, and active barter with the native populations. But the basic wealth of the colony was based on the rapacious exploitation of natural riches, most notably furs, and the use of Native Americans as forced labor for these enterprises. For several decades the Russian American Company acted with vigor, sponsoring 12 round-the-world expeditions between 1804 and 1840, maintaining regular communications between Alaska and Russia, and making port calls in California, Hawaii, and China. Russian explorers also expanded scientific knowledge of the region through expeditions like that of A. Kasherarov around Cape Barrow in 1838 and L. Zagoskin around the Yukon Basin in 1842–44.

Russian hegemony in the area did not last long, as English and American ships engaged in a profitable contraband trade. Under pressure from their governments, Russia gradually gave up its claims to a complete trade monopoly, granting both the United States and Great Britain favorable terms for navigation and trade in 1824–25. The relative economic weakness of the Russian-American Company and of Russia in general was complemented by a growing sense of military vulnerability in Russian Alaska. During the CRI-MEAN WAR of 1853–56, British forces threatened Russian Alaska, much as they did the Russian White Sea area. After the Crimean War, unable to provide for the defense of Russian settlements in North America, Russian government circles floated the possibility of selling Alaska to either Great Britain or the United States. Given its ongoing rivalry with Great Britain, the Russians preferred to sell to the United States, also hoping for American diplomatic support for their campaign to revise the Treaty of Paris, which had ended the Crimean War. In March 1867, Alaska was sold to the United States for $7.2 million (less than 11 million rubles), a purchase much criticized in American circles but that began to pay off handsomely with the discovery of the Klondike gold deposits soon after.

Aleichem, Sholem (1859–1916)
writer

One of the most creative and prolific Yiddish-language writers, Aleichem was a highly popular author whose short stories and plays captured the troubles and aspirations of the Jewish diaspora with affection and gentle humor. Aleichem was born Sholem (Solomon) Rabinowitz in the town of Pereyaslav near Kiev in the Ukraine. The product of a traditional Jewish education and the Russian state school system, Aleichem started writing at the age of 17. In 1877 he first worked as a tutor for the daughter of a Jewish landowner in Kiev, but he was dismissed after three years when his employer discovered that tutor and pupil were

romantically involved. Serving as a village rabbi, he devoted himself to writing, and his first Yiddish works were published in 1883. That same year he married his former pupil and, with all presumably forgiven, returned to the estate of his now father-in-law, who left him as executor of the estate after his death. Financially comfortable, Aleichem moved to Kiev in 1887 and entered the world of business, while continuing to publish stories. During these years he also contributed to the Yiddish Folk Library series. In 1890, however, after several financial losses he settled briefly in Paris. Before returning to Kiev in 1893, he also lived in Vienna and Czernowitz (Chernovtsy) in the western Ukraine. His well-known works *Tevya the Dairyman* and *Menachem Mendel* were written during these highly productive years in Kiev, when he also wrote for the Jewish and Russian press. After the 1905 POGROMS, he emigrated to the United States, settling in New York City. In 1908, while on a lecture tour of Russia, he fell seriously ill. Although in poor health, he continued to write and publish; *Motel Ben Pasey the Chazan* and *The Flood* belong to these years. The outbreak of World War I found him in Copenhagen, Denmark, with his family, but he eventually returned to New York, where he published his autobiography, *From the Marketplace*. He died in New York in May 1916. Aleichem was much beloved for his portraits of simple Jewish folk in small Russian towns, and his funeral was attended by more than three hundred thousand people and he was eulogized in the halls of the U.S. Congress. Beginning with *Stempenyu* in 1913, his works were regularly translated into English. As the inspiration for the popular musical comedy *Fiddler on the Roof* (1964), drawn from the stories about the resilient optimist Tevye, his work gained a new international public.

Alekhine, Aleksandr Aleksandrovich (1892–1946)
chess player

One of the most inventive, brilliant, egotistical, and eccentric players in the history of chess, Alekhine was born in MOSCOW to a nobleman and the daughter of a wealthy industrialist. He learned chess from his mother and at the age of 15 was already playing in tournaments. Three years later, in 1910, he took seventh place in his first international tournament, which was played in Hamburg. A chess master since the age of 16, he won the rank of grand master in 1913, at the age of 21. In 1921, one year after winning the Russian championship, Alekhine emigrated to France and eventually became a French citizen. Although a lawyer by training, educated at the Imperial Law School of St. Petersburg and the University of Paris (Sorbonne), Alekhine never practiced law, devoting himself instead to the full-time pursuit of his chess career.

In 1927 he became world chess champion by defeating the legendary Cuban grand master José Raúl Capablanca, with whom he developed an intense personal rivalry based on personal differences as much as playing styles. He held his title until 1935, when he was defeated by the Dutch player Max Euwe, during which time he refused to grant Capablanca a rematch in opposition to the desires of most of the chess-playing world, who longed to see the two chess giants play each other. Alekhine defeated Euwe two years later to regain his title, the first deposed champion to do so in the modern history of chess, which he held until his death in 1946. Always a showman, he established world records in 1925 and 1933 for winning simultaneous games while blindfolded.

As during his World War I years, when he either served with the Russian Red Cross and was decorated for bravery or played chess in an Austrian prisoner-of-war camp, accounts of his World War II years were shrouded in confusion, much of it caused by Alekhine himself. He claimed to have spent most of the war in Lisbon but was also reputed to have played in Germany and other occupied countries and to have written anti-Semitic articles. Although he initially denied authorship, he later alleged that the Nazis had inserted the anti-Semitic material into his chess articles. Nevertheless, he was roundly condemned by the chess world and public opinion for his collaboration. Still the world champion,

he was on the verge of arranging a championship match with the emerging star, Mikhail BOTVINNIK, when he died in a Portuguese hotel alone and penniless. The autopsy later revealed he had choked on a piece of meat. In 1956, the International Chess Federation arranged for his remains to be interred in the Montparnasse Cemetery in Paris.

Aleksandrov, Grigorii Vasilievich (1903–1983)
film director

The director of some of the most popular Soviet comedies of the 1930s, Aleksandrov, born Grigorii Mormonenko, started his career as an assistant costumer and stage designer in the Ekaterinburg Opera Theater. After the October Revolution, he held various jobs in several governmental art departments, while taking courses for a diploma in film direction. In 1921 he joined the Proletkult Workers Theater as an actor, where he met Sergei EISENSTEIN, an important influence on his career. He assisted Eisenstein in some of his early classic films, such as *Strike!* (1924), *Battleship Potemkin* (1924), *October* (1929), and *The General Line* (1929). From 1929 to 1932, he joined Eisenstein and his cameraman Eduard Tisse and traveled to the United States and Mexico. With the exception of Eisenstein's unfinished *Que Viva Mexico!,* the trip did not produce any lasting results. Back in the Soviet Union, he began an artistic partnership with his wife, the actress Liubov ORLOVA, and the composer Isaak Dunaevsky, which resulted in three highly successful and popular comedies: *The Happy-go-lucky Guys* (1934), which was greatly acclaimed at the Venice Film Festival, *Circus,* and *Volga, Volga.* Orlova's outstanding comedic talents, Dunaevsky's music, and Aleksandrov's directorial expertise combined to produce light but highly entertaining comedies that are integral parts of the Soviet film canon. Aleksandrov's films from the late 1930s and 1940s suffered from increasing political pressures. Even the best of these, *Meeting on the Elba,* which won the 1950 Stalin Prize, are essentially propaganda works.

Aleksandrov taught at the State Institute for Cinematography from 1950 to 1957. In 1983, he made the loving, well-received documentary, *Liubov Orlova,* about his wife, who died in 1975. Aleksandrov died in Moscow.

Alekseev, Mikhail Vasilievich
(1857–1918)
general

One of the most accomplished and hard-working czarist generals during World War I, Alekseev played an important role during the brief rule of the Provisional Government in 1917 and organized the beginnings of military resistance to the Bolshevik government. Born in TVER into the family of a military captain, Alekseev attended a military cadet school and the Moscow Military Academy, from which he graduated as a commissioned infantry officer in 1876. A year later he fought as a junior officer in the RUSSO-TURKISH WAR OF 1877–78. Promoted to captain in 1887, he attended the General Staff Academy in Moscow and graduated with honors in 1890. For the next 14 years he served in the headquarters staff in various organizational and instructional capacities. During the RUSSO-JAPANESE WAR of 1904–5, he first served with the Second Army in Manchuria as director of operations with the rank of major general, before being appointed to the main administration of the General Staff. In the years leading up to World War I, his career continued to develop smoothly; he became chief of staff of the Kiev military district in 1908 and commander of the Thirteenth Army Corps in 1912, and chief of staff of the southwestern front in August 1914, with promotions to lieutenant general and infantry general along the way. With NICHOLAS II as commander in chief of the army in September (August) 1915, Alekseev became chief of staff with the rank of full general and effective control over the army's entire military effort.

Following the czar's abdication in March 1917, the newly installed Provisional Government appointed Alekseev commander in chief, a position he held until the summer, when his disagreement with the wisdom of the June offensive advocated by Alexander KERENSKY, the minister of war and driving force of the Provisional Government, led to his dismissal. Nevertheless, Alekseev remained loyal to the Provisional Government and supported Kerensky in his showdown with General Lars KORNILOV in August 1917. With Kerensky as commander in chief, Alekseev agreed to return as chief of staff, but his frustration with the government's inability to support the reinforcement of army discipline precipitated his resignation in October 1917.

Alekseev was detained briefly after the October Revolution but managed to join the rapidly growing anti-Bolshevik movement in the Don region in southern Russia. Despite personal disagreements with other generals, such as Kornilov, Alekseev was instrumental in organizing the Volunteer Army that led the White resistance to the Bolsheviks during the civil war, which lasted until 1921. In September 1918 he was elected to the "Ufa Directorate," a provisional, anti-Bolshevik government organized by former members of the constituent assembly. Shortly afterward, however, he died of a heart attack in the town of Ekaterinodar.

Aleksei (ca. 1295–1378)
ecclesiastical leader and regent

A direct descendant of Prince ALEXANDER NEVSKY, Aleksei was an ecclesiastical leader who strengthened the Russian Orthodox Church and also greatly contributed to the continuing emergence of MOSCOW as the preeminent Russian principality during the second century of Mongol rule. Aleksei was born in Moscow to a prominent boyar family. By the middle of the 14th century, Aleksei was widely respected as a leader in Moscow, and following the death of Grand Prince Simeon the Proud (r. 1341–53) Aleksei was named regent to Simeon's younger brother, who reigned as IVAN II. In 1354 Aleksei was appointed metropolitan of Moscow, at the time the highest position in the Russian Orthodox Church. Following Ivan's death in 1359, a struggle for succession ensued between the supporters of Ivan's nine-year-old son Dmitrii and the supporters of Prince Dmitrii of Suzdal. The young Dmitrii, who would later be known as DMITRII DONSKOI won out, in great part due to the assistance provided by Aleksei. In return, Aleksei continued to serve as regent until Dmitrii came of age. As regent, he continued the expansionist policies of previous Muscovite rulers, even as Moscow deferred to the Mongol rulers in the city of SARAI. Moscow's struggle with the principality of TVER, supported by Lithuania, came to a head during Aleksei's second regency. As metropolitan, Aleksei identified the interests of Moscow with those of the church. Aleksei was canonized by the Russian Orthodox Church in 1448, and his feast day is celebrated on October 5.

Aleksei Mikhailovich (1629–1676)
czar

The son of Michael ROMANOV, founder of the ROMANOV DYNASTY, and father of the future PETER I the Great, Aleksei (Alexis) became czar in 1645. His long, eventful reign saw important social changes as well as Muscovy's continued territorial expansion. Known for his great piety as "the quietest one" (*tishiaishchii*), despite his impulsiveness and angry outbursts, Aleksei also provided the foundation for the great opening to the West, for which his son Peter is better known. Among the initial achievements of his reign is the Ulozhenie (Law Code) of 1649, the first systematized set of Muscovite laws since 1550, which would remain in place until 1835. The Ulozhenie, however, also provided the final legal confirmation for the enserfment of the peasantry, which had been developing in stages over the previous centuries. During his reign Aleksei relied, not always wisely, on advisers such as Boris Morozov, his tutor, and Prince Miloslavskii, his father-in-law; the latter was especially resented for his greed and corruption. The government's attempts to raise revenue through new taxes led to riots in 1648 in MOSCOW and other cities, while in 1662 its plan to debase the silver currency with copper led to the Copper Riots. His reign also witnessed Stenka

RAZIN's rebellion in 1670–71, later celebrated in folk song and stories. In the spring of 1670 RAZIN, a Don Cossack, led a band of soldiers that reached 200,000 at its peak, gaining followers as they marched up the Volga River proclaiming freedom from officials and landowners, while massacring many of them. Poorly organized, the rebels were defeated by better-trained Muscovite troops in 1671. Muscovy's territory grew considerably during Aleksei's reign as a result of the incorporation of Ukrainian lands to the east of the Dnieper River provided by the Treaty of Andrusovo (1667) with Poland, as well as the continued advances of Cossack explorers and freebooters in Siberia. Russian religious practices and politics were decisively affected first by the reforms begun by Patriarch NIKON in the 1650s, then by the schism of 1666–67 that resulted from the church's condemnation of those who rejected the reforms. In addition to wars with Poland and Sweden, other events of note that took place under Aleksei were the establishment of a foreigners' quarter in Moscow, the reorganization of the Muscovite army along Western European lines, the first postal service connecting Moscow with Berlin and Amsterdam, and the first theatrical performances in Moscow. Aleksei married twice, setting in motion a period of almost a century of contested and complicated successions between the two families of his wives—the Miloslavskiis and the Naryshkins—that was aggravated by Peter's decision in 1722 to change succession laws and give the reigning ruler the right to name his or her successor.

Alexander I (1777–1825)
(Aleksandr Pavlovich)
emperor

Known as the "enigmatic czar," Alexander came to the throne in 1801 as a result of the palace revolt that resulted in the death of his father, PAUL I. From his early years he was caught in the personal rivalry between his grandmother, CATHERINE II, and his father, Paul. From Catherine he received a solid humanitarian education through a Swiss tutor, himself influenced by

Rousseau; from Paul he learned to admire military discipline and the aesthetics of the parade ground. The contradictions that shaped his internal life reflected themselves in the trajectory of his own reign: a reformist first half followed by a second half of almost reactionary mysticism. The first decade of Alexander's reign witnessed a number of important reforms and new policies: the establishment of ministries and a Council of State, the foundation of a state school system and four universities, the relaxation of censorship, and the granting of a constitution to Poland. Conscious of the need to tackle the issue of serfdom, he allowed for the manumission of serfs by their landlords and liberated the serfs in the Baltic provinces, albeit without land.

In foreign policy he alternated alliances with England and Napoleon's France, trying to avoid war with France. The key event of Alexander's reign was the French invasion of 1812, known in Russian history as the Patriotic War. Alexander left the military details of Russia's defense to his generals, but refused to negotiate with Napoleon even when MOSCOW had fallen to the invaders. Having outlasted Napoleon, Alexander marched with his troops to Paris and was a central figure at the Congress of Vienna (1814–15), where he inspired the Holy Alliance. During his reign, Russia continued to add to its territory, acquiring through conquest or annexation Finland, Bessarabia, and large parts of the Caucasus.

The second half of Alexander's reign was dominated by two conservative advisers, Count Aleksei ARAKCHEEV and Prince Aleksandr GOLITSYN. Golitsyn, founder of the Russian Bible Society, had introduced Alexander to Bible study and accompanied him on the personal mystical quest that came to dominate the czar's life. Arakcheev convinced Alexander to establish military colonies, where soldiers and their families would combine military training with agriculture. Under Arakcheev's general supervision the colonies quickly became examples of the worst aspects of barracks life and serfdom and bred protests and uprisings. Discontent over the abandonment of the czar's earlier reformist course was especially evident among young aristocrats and junior army officers, some of whom formed secret societies whose goals ranged from discussion to conspiracies.

Toward the end of his life, Alexander withdrew into seclusion and died unexpectedly in Taganrog, a port on the Sea of Azov, on November 19, 1825. The coda to his death was the Decembrist revolt of December 14, 1825. Alexander's marriage to the German princess Elizabeth of Baden, known in Russian as Elizaveta Alekseevna, produced no children. By the succession law, the throne was to pass to his younger brother Constantine, but Constantine had secretly renounced his rights in 1820 in favor of the third brother, the future NICHOLAS I. Public confusion over the right heir provided an opening for the two secret societies that had been plotting a rebellion, which they carried out, without success, on the day that Nicholas was to be proclaimed emperor.

Alexander II (1818–1881)
(Aleksandr Nikolaevich)
emperor

Known as the "Czar-Liberator" for abolishing serfdom in 1861 and assisting in Bulgaria's independence from Turkey in 1878, Alexander was the eldest son of NICHOLAS I. Unlike his father he received the education considered appropriate for an heir to the throne. His tutor was the poet Zhukovsky, and he traveled widely throughout the Russian Empire and Europe. He assumed the throne in 1855 in the final stages of the CRIMEAN WAR and committed himself to reforming the empire, despite his own conservative instincts. Through the next decade in particular, his government set in motion a number of reforms that attempted to transform and modernize Russia, a time that is known as the period of the GREAT REFORMS. The centerpiece to the reforms was the emancipation of the serfs. After much discussion and consultation, the EMANCIPATION ACT OF 1861 freed privately owned serfs but required them to purchase the land they received. Other categories of peasants were freed in 1863 and 1866. Other important reforms provided for institutions of local government (ZEMSTVO), an elementary school system, an independent judiciary, and, in 1874, an army based on universal military service. Expectations of more far-reaching reforms had run high, especially among peasants and students, leading to disturbances in the countryside and the formation of the first revolutionary groups in urban centers.

After the stinging defeat in the Crimea, Alexander's foreign policy adhered to the principle of noninterference. The one exception was Russia's defense of Bulgarian interests in the RUSSO-TURKISH WAR OF 1877–78 that resulted in the independence of Bulgaria. At home, his government put down the POLISH REBELLION OF 1863 and secured a victory in the 35-year-long war to conquer the northern Caucasus. His reign also witnessed the conquest of most of Central Asia, an area that became known as Russian Turkestan.

The final years of his reign were dominated by a concern with terrorism, as Populist revolutionaries, notably the PEOPLE'S WILL, decided that a few selective assassinations could advance their cause. Alexander, who had already survived an assassination attempt in 1866, was condemned to death by the People's Will and escaped several more attempts, including an attack on the dining room of the Winter Palace. Convinced that new reforms were needed, Alexander appointed Count Loris-Melikov to pursue a twin program of suppressing terrorism while promoting reforms. But on March 1, 1881, after having indicated his support for a plan to introduce a representative assembly, he was killed when members of the People's Will lobbed a bomb at his carriage.

Alexander III (1845–1894)
(Aleksandr Aleksandrovich)
emperor

Second son of ALEXANDER II, Alexander became the heir to the throne after the death in 1865 of his older brother, Nikolai. A strong, honest, but

Alexander III *(Library of Congress)*

narrow-minded man, Alexander was given a broader education once he became heir but remained profoundly influenced by his tutor Konstantin POBEDONOSTSEV, a reactionary jurist who would later become procurator of the Holy Synod. Thrust on the throne by his father's assassination, he pursued politically reactionary policies designed to end the threats of terrorism and revolution. Convinced of the need to dismantle his father's reformist legacy, Alexander III began his reign by issuing the Temporary Regulations that gave officials the power to search, prosecute, and exile anyone deemed to be a threat to state security. He also pursued a policy of Russification of non-Russian nationalities, often by restricting the use of national languages. Deeply anti-Semitic, he approved special restrictions on Jews, whom he identified as disloyal and linked to the revolutionary movement. A wave of POGROMS took place in 1881, resulting in significant Jewish emigration that would increase through the next two decades.

With the goal of strengthening Russia, his government promoted significant industrialization that brought mixed results: economic development and the growth of an industrial working class that in time became influenced by the socialist message of revolution. His finance ministers, the most notable of whom was Sergei WITTE, followed protectionist policies that favored the development of heavy industry and the construction of railways. Among the latter, a major achievement was the construction of the TRANS-SIBERIAN RAILROAD, begun in 1891 and completed in 1903, which opened up vast areas of Siberia to peasant colonization and facilitated the movement of Russian troops to the Pacific Ocean. He unabashedly promoted the interests of the gentry through the creation of the State Gentry Bank in 1885, as well as by creating the office of Land Captains in rural districts to control the activities of the ZEMSTVOS his father had created and that Alexander III suspected of liberal sympathies.

In foreign policy, he continued his father's policy of nonintervention in European affairs, but toward the end of his reign there was an important shift in Russia's alliances. Stung by Wilhelm II's refusal to renew the Reinsurance Treaty between Germany and Russia, Alexander's government pursued a rapprochement with France, despite the czar's distaste for its republican regime, which resulted in the Franco-Russian alliance of 1894.

The FAMINE of 1891–92 damaged the government's image significantly, as it was blamed for squeezing the peasantry for revenue and then for failing to respond with assistance once the famine started. The 1890s witnessed a gradual renewal of revolutionary opposition, but it was the czar's son Nicholas who would have to deal

with its consequences, as Alexander died suddenly of a stroke in November 1894.

Alexander Nevsky (1219?–1263)
grand prince

Alexander Nevsky was born in 1219, the second son of Yaroslav, grand prince of Vladimir. He became prince of NOVGOROD in 1236. As prince of Novgorod, in 1240 he vanquished the Swedes on the river Neva (the source of his name "Nevsky," which was not used in his lifetime), and he defeated the Teutonic Knights in 1242 at the famous battle on the frozen ice of Lake Chud (Peipus). He successfully defended Russia against the Lithuanians and was confirmed as grand prince in 1252 by the khan of the GOLDEN HORDE. Subsequent glorification as a Russian hero has entangled fact and legend in our knowledge and assessment of his career. The defeat of the Teutonic Knights soon came to be seen as a triumph of Orthodoxy over Catholic aggression inspired by the pope. Early in the reign of Ivan the Terrible, the Orthodox Church canonized Alexander. Peter the Great paid tribute to the warrior-saint by ordering the construction of the Alexander Nevsky Lavra monastery on the supposed site of this victory over the Swedes in 1240. Peter also instituted a military decoration in his name, which was abolished in 1917 but revived by STALIN in 1942. The empress ELIZABETH encouraged the cult of Alexander by commissioning a massive silver shrine for the relics of the saint, which was made in the St. Petersburg Mint, between 1750 and 1753. Perhaps best known to contemporary audiences is the film *Alexander Nevsky* by Sergei EISENTSEIN, with a powerful musical score by Sergei PROKOFIEV. Released in 1941, it reinforced Alexander's heroic image and his role as the symbol of Russian resistance to the German invasion. Recently some historians have questioned the degree to which Russian principalities were threatened from the west, the real number of German casualties at Lake Chud, and whether the victory was an important turning point. Likewise, Alexander's decision to cooperate with the Tatars resulted in his being given the title grand prince of Vladimir, which had been previously held by his brother Andrei, who had rebelled against Tatar rule.

Alexandra Feodorovna (1872–1918)
empress

The German-born wife of the last Russian czar, NICHOLAS II, Alexandra contributed to the political isolation of the crown in the final years before its collapse in February 1917. She was christened Victoria Alix Helena Louise Beatrice, the daughter of the grand duke of Hesse-Harmstadt and the granddaughter of England's Queen Victoria, in whose household she was partly brought up. In 1894, she married the future Nicholas II and, following tradition for foreign spouses, adopted the Russian name Alexandra Feodorovna after being admitted to the Russian Orthodox Church. She gave birth to four daughters Olga (1894), Tatiana (1897), Maria (1898), and Anastasia (1901), before the birth of Aleksei, the heir to the throne, in 1904. Gravely worried about the health of Aleksei, who suffered from hemophilia, she was receptive to the healing powers that the sinister monk Grigorii RASPUTIN claimed to have. From 1905 until his assassination in 1916, Rasputin had a great influence on Alexandra and, through her, on the politics of the court, especially after 1915, when Nicholas II stationed himself at the front to lead the Russian armies during World War I, leaving Alexandra in charge in ST. PETERSBURG. Although wrongly suspected of pro-German sympathies because of her birth, Alexandra did have a highly negative impact on Russian politics during the war through her access to the czar and her support of incompetent or repressive prime ministers such as Sturmer and Goremykin. A staunch defender of the autocratic prerogatives of the czar, she advised Nicholas II to resist any type of accommodation with the DUMA, the parliament established in 1905. With the collapse of the monarchy after the February Revolution, she joined Nicholas and the rest of her family in house arrest, first in the imperial palace at Tsarskoe Selo and eventually in Ekaterinburg in the Ural Mountains. There, she was executed with Nicholas and her children by local Bolshevik officials on orders from LENIN on the night of July 17, 1918.

Allilueva, Svetlana Iosifovna (1926–   )
writer, daughter of Joseph Stalin

The daughter of Joseph STALIN and his second wife, Nadezhda Allilueva, Svetlana Allilueva astonished the world when she defected to the West in 1967. Allilueva's privileged life as the daughter of a leading COMMUNIST PARTY member received a first shock in 1932 when her mother committed suicide. Although her father's favorite, she was troubled by the courtlike atmosphere of her surroundings. By the 1960s, with her father's controversial legacy still at the center of Soviet politics, she had become increasingly uncomfortable in her native country. The death of her second husband, the Indian Communist Bradegh Singh, provided the opportunity for a change when she was allowed to accompany his ashes back home. Allilueva first settled in Princeton, New Jersey, and in three successive works, *Twenty Letters to a Friend* (1967), *Svetlana, the Story of Stalin's Daughter* (1967), and *Only One Year* (1969), she provided vivid accounts of the Stalin household and the Kremlin court at a time when these topics were still wrapped in secrecy. Her life in the West as a "celebrity defector" was turbulent and peripatetic. A third marriage, to the American architect William Peters, was short-lived but led to the birth of her daughter, Olga, in 1971. With Olga, she moved to England in 1982, where her daughter attended boarding school in Cambridge. In 1984, she confounded public opinion by returning to the Soviet Union with her daughter. Soviet authorities, uncomfortable with her presence in Moscow, convinced her to live in her father's hometown of Gori in Georgia, where she had trouble getting along with her Georgian relatives. Out of place in her homeland, with a daughter who spoke little Russian, she was allowed to emigrate again in November 1986, settling first in the United States, before moving to the United Kingdom, where she still lives.

Amalrik, Andrei Alekseevich
(1938–1980)
writer

A historian by training, Amalrik became an influential member of the Soviet dissident community. He was born in Moscow, where his father worked as a historian. His critical plays and essays, circulated clandestinely in *samizdat,* led to his expulsion from Moscow University in 1963. Two years later he was arrested and sent to Siberian exile on the charge of "parasitism," a Soviet-era legal term that made those without a full-time job liable to prosecution. Back in Moscow in 1968, his exile experience provided the material for his underground book *Involuntary Journey to Siberia* (1970). He was arrested again in 1970, a year after the publication in the West of what became his best-known work, *Will the Soviet Union Survive until 1984?* Playing on the title of George Orwell's *1984,* Amalrik raised questions about the durability of the Soviet system that were vigorously debated among dissidents in the 1970s, even though at the time it seemed almost inconceivable that the Soviet Union could collapse. (As is turned out, Amalrik was off by only seven years.) Amalrik was sentenced to three years in the GULAG and a further three years in exile. He was released in 1976 after repeated international protests and allowed to emigrate to Paris. He died in an automobile accident in Spain while traveling to Madrid to attend the 1980 International Conference on Human Rights, where the Soviet record on human rights was a prominently featured topic of discussion.

Amur River

The eighth-longest river of the world, the Amur River flows 2,744 miles from its headwaters until reaching the Tatar Strait that separates mainland Russia from the northwestern end of Sakhalin Island. The Amur is formed by the junction of the Shilka and Argun Rivers in eastern Siberia and flows southeast for about 1,000 miles, forming the border between Russia and China, before making a sharp turn to the northeast into Russian territory and emptying into the Tatar Strait near the city of Nikolayevsk-na-Amur (Nikolayevsk-on-the Amur). The Amur is navigable throughout its entire course, but it is closed to navigation during the winter months. Although the modern history of the Amur River and its basin has often been written in terms of the competing interests of Russia and China in the region, the Amur also holds great significance for the Gilyaks (Nivkhi), one of the indigenous people of the region who historically populated the river's mouth.

Russian explorers first reached the Amur region and charted the river in the 17th century, at which time they clashed with China. The Treaty of NERCHINSK (1689) settled the boundary between the two countries, leaving most of the Amur basin under Chinese control. By the mid-19th century the importance of the Amur River and basin for Russia's presence in eastern Siberia had increased significantly at a time when Chinese power in the region was declining. With the appointment of Count Nikolai Muraviev—later known as Muraviev-Amursky in recognition of his contributions to Russian power—as governor-general of Eastern Siberia, Russia advanced its interests in the region more aggressively. In 1858 Russia received the left bank of the Amur, and two years later China ceded the adjoining Ussuri River under the terms of the Treaty of Peking.

anarchism

A political philosophy that holds the source of oppression in human societies to derive from compulsory laws and states and government, anarchism advocates the creation of a stateless society through revolutionary action. Tracing its roots to the French Revolution, anarchism played an influential role in the development of the Russian revolutionary movement in the 19th and early 20th centuries. Russia also produced two of the leading theorists of modern anarchism, Mikhail BAKUNIN (1814–76) and Petr KROPOTKIN (1842–1921), both of whom came from prominent Russian noble families and both of whom spent most of their adult lives in exile. Their writings influenced the Russian revolutionary movement as well as the anarchist movement beyond Russia. In his writings, Bakunin emphasized the collectivist roots of anarchism and called for spontaneous mass rebellion as the means for achieving the anarchists' goals. Bakunin's belief that violence was an acceptable tool to achieve anarchist goals influenced the Russian POPULIST movement as it turned to terrorism in the late 1870s, while his profound suspicions of the dictatorial elements inherent in Karl Marx's socialism created divisions among the members of the First International that hastened its collapse in 1881. A geologist by training, Kropotkin developed a philosophy that rejected violence and envisioned anarchism as a scientifically based ethical philosophy. In some respects, Leo TOLSTOY's religious-based nonviolence also has anarchist undertones.

A home-grown anarchist movement developed in Russia after the 1905 Revolution. Most of its members saw themselves as "anarcho-communists," in the tradition of Kropotkin, but a significant element, the "anarcho-syndicalists" took advantage of Russia's growing industrialization to develop roots among trade unions. A third orientation known as "maximalists," linked initially to the Socialist Revolutionary Party, resorted to terrorism like its Populist predecessors from the 1870s. During the 1917 Revolution, anarchists opposed the Provisional Government and worked (albeit uneasily) with BOLSHEVIKS under the ideological umbrella of the soviets. Anarchists also gained support among sailors, particularly those of the Kronstadt naval base. After the October Revolution the Bolsheviks cracked down on the anarchist movement in leading Russian cities in the spring of 1918. A

rural anarchist base was established in Ukraine in the peasant movement led by the guerrilla leader Nestor MAKHNO. Although the KRONSTADT REBELLION of 1921 had broader ideological underpinnings, anarchist influence among the sailors helped them fashion their anti-Bolshevik but pro-Soviet message. The final public demonstration of anarchist feeling in Soviet Russia came during the funeral of KROPOTKIN in February 1921, for which jailed anarchists were given a one-day reprieve, in itself a sign of the political defeat of the movement.

Andropov, Yuri Vladimirovich (1914–1984)
Soviet ruler

Andropov succeeded Leonid BREZHNEV as general secretary of the COMMUNIST PARTY in November 1982. In poor health for most of his brief tenure, his main legacy was the promotion of Mikhail GORBACHEV to the inner circles of Soviet power. Andropov was born in Stavropol province in southern Russia to the family of a railway worker. After joining the KOMSOMOL (Communist Youth League) in 1930, he held numerous jobs while ascending through the Komsomol apparatus, until becoming a full Communist Party member in 1939. In the 1940s he worked in Karelia, recently annexed from Finland, where he met the Finnish Communist Otto Kuusinen, who served as his mentor at this stage. As Soviet ambassador to Hungary, he was instrumental in coordinating the suppression of the 1956 Hungarian Revolution and installing the pro-Soviet János Kádár in power. Back in Moscow, he continued to rise in the Communist Party, joining its Central Committee in 1961 and serving as Central Committee secretary from 1962 to 1967. In 1967 he was appointed director of the KGB (secret police), a move that was widely seen as an attempt by the party's ideological guardian, Mikhail SUSLOV, to remove a talented rival, since there was tacit agreement that the party secretary could not come from the ranks of the security service. Andropov's KGB gained notoriety for its ruthless, but selective, use of workplace harassment, forced emigration, and confinement to psychiatric hospitals to suppress dissent. Outside the Soviet Union, the KGB was also linked to terrorist acts, such as the attempt on the life of Pope John Paul II and the death of a Bulgarian dissident with the poisoned tip of an umbrella. Suslov's death in early 1982 allowed Andropov, a Politburo member since 1973, to leave the KGB and prepare his challenge to succeed Brezhnev. After Brezhnev's death in November 1982, he outmaneuvered Konstantin CHERNENKO to become general secretary of the party. Andropov's regime will best be remembered for its tentative domestic reforms, heightened tensions with the West, and his poor health, which kept him on dialysis for most of his time in power. The unsuccessful campaign to halt the deployment of NATO Pershing and Cruise missiles in Europe and the disaster of the Korean passenger airliner shot after entering Soviet air space were major diplomatic setbacks. His domestic reform program amounted to little more than a renewed emphasis on old-style party discipline to combat corruption and absenteeism. His most important legacy, however, is his promotion of reform-minded politicians, including Gorbachev, to carry out the next stage of reforms of the troubled Soviet system.

Anna Ivanovna (1693–1740)
empress

The daughter of Ivan V and niece of PETER I the Great, Anna was the widowed duchess of Kurland at the time of her election as empress in 1730. One of several possible successors to the throne after the death of PETER II marked the end of the male Romanov line, Anne was chosen by the influential Supreme Privy Council, an advisory body of nobles and de facto rulers of Russia since 1726, contingent on her accepting important restrictions on her power. Historians have seen this as a tentative step toward a type of monarchical constitutionalism closer to Western European practices. The restrictions on autocracy

Anna Ivanovna *(Hulton/Archive)*

proved to be short-lived, however, as Anna, now empress, took advantage of divisions within the gentry, promptly tore up the agreement, exiled or executed the members of the council, and reassumed full autocratic powers. Her reign has long been portrayed unfavorably as dominated by unpopular German advisers, most notably Ernst-Johann BIRON, her lover from Kurland. Unwilling and unfit to involve herself in matters of state, she delegated power to Biron, whose rule was long remembered as a time of great cruelty, police terror, persecution of Old Believers, and the exile of almost 30,000 people to Siberia.

During her reign many of the obligations and limitations that Peter the Great had placed on the gentry were rolled back, a process that was followed by her successors. The cadet school for the gentry opened in St. Petersburg in 1731 allowed its graduates to become officers without serving in the lower ranks. That same year,

Peter's provision that provided for single-male inheritance was repealed, a victory for gentry members who would be otherwise forced to turn to government service for a living. In 1736, gentry service—previously a lifetime obligation—was reduced to 25 years and exempted one son from service so that he could tend to the family estate. In 1762 PETER III abolished all compulsory gentry service. Anna's reign witnessed the continued deterioration of the status and conditions of Russia's enserfed peasantry. They were now forbidden to own property, establish factories, or enter into contracts with the government. Russia continued to expand its borders by finally subjugating the Bashkirs in the lower Volga region, obtaining a loyalty oath from the Kazakhs, and promoting Vitus BERING's second Arctic expedition, which reached ALASKA in 1741. To the west, Russia continued to embroil itself in European affairs, allying itself with Austria against France in the War of the Polish Succession (1733–35) and against the Ottoman Empire (1736–39). Childless at death, she appointed her niece's infant son, who reigned as IVAN VI, as her successor, but within nine months he was overthrown, jailed, and succeeded by ELIZABETH, Peter the Great's younger daughter.

anthems

For the first two decades of Soviet rule, the anthem of Russia was the "Internationale," the theme song of the international socialist movement. In 1944 it was replaced by a more martial and nationalist anthem, which began with the words "Indestructible union of free republics." The words to this Soviet anthem were written by G. El-Registan and Sergei Mikhalkov, the latter the father of two well-known film directors from the late Soviet era, Andrei Konchalovsky and Nikita MIKHALKOV. The music was by Aleksandr V. Aleksandrov. This anthem continued, with some revisions in 1977, through the rest of the Soviet period. With the dissolution of the Soviet Union, it became necessary to adopt a new anthem for the newly independent Russian Fed-

eration. The choice for a new anthem was the melody of the "Patriotic Song," an unfinished work by the 19th-century composer Mikhail Ivanovich GLINKA, which was most likely written in 1833. The anthem remained wordless until President Vladimir PUTIN held a competition to provide new words to the national anthem.

anti-Party group

The name applied to the group of old-guard Communists in the Politburo (then known as Presidium) who attempted unsuccessfully to remove Nikita KHRUSHCHEV as first secretary (general secretary) of the COMMUNIST PARTY in June 1957. The leaders of the "anti-Party" group—Georgi MALENKOV, Lazar KAGANOVICH, Vyacheslav MOLOTOV, Nikolai BULGANIN, and Kliment Voroshilov—had all occupied prominent positions under STALIN, and behind their ritual declarations of party unity were watching with alarm the growing concentration of power in Khrushchev's hands and his ongoing de-Stalinization campaign. The name given to their conspiracy arose from the fact that they all represented government ministries and opposed the transfer of power back to the party, where Khrushchev had his power base. In June 1957, they struck by forming a majority within the Presidium in support of Khrushchev's removal as party first secretary. Khrushchev outmaneuvered them by calling for an emergency plenary meeting of the Central Committee, which voted to expel three of the main conspirators (Malenkov, Kaganovich, and Molotov) from the Presidium and Central Committee. Bulganin, serving as prime minister at the time, was reprimanded after a confession of guilt and removed from the Presidium a year later. Voroshilov, official head of state of the Soviet Union, remained in this purely ceremonial post until 1960 in great part owing to his long-term association with Khrushchev. As further punishment, anti-Party group members were demoted to minor posts in remote areas. Malenkov was sent to Kazakhstan to manage a hydroelectric plant, Kaganovich to an asbestos factory in the Urals, Bulganin to the Stavropol region economic council, and Molotov to Ulan Bator as Soviet ambassador to Mongolia. Observers remarked that the relatively lenient treatment of the anti-Party group for its attempt to take power was further sign of the move away from the harshness of Stalin-era politics, when they most likely would have been executed.

anti-Semitism

Discrimination against Jews on a popular and official level became a more distinctive feature of Russian life after the annexation of former Polish territories in the late 18th century as a result of the POLISH PARTITIONS. In these former Polish provinces, now located to the west and south-west of the Russian Empire, also known as the PALE OF SETTLEMENT, to which Jewish residents were restricted, anti-Semitism had deep popular roots. In most places it was an urban phenomenon, but in Ukraine it also had strong rural roots. Under Russian rule, there was official discrimination against Jews with regard to place of residence (they were limited to the Pale of Settlement), landownership, education, and state service. The implementation of these policies varied, with some relaxation under the reformist era of ALEXANDER II. During more reactionary periods, especially the reigns of ALEXANDER III and NICHOLAS II, the government was not reluctant to divert popular discontent toward anti-Semitism. After 1881, the government tolerated and sometimes encouraged the waves of anti-Semitic riots known as POGROMS that were a frequent feature of life in the Pale of Settlement up through the 1905 Revolution. Russian Jews responded through massive emigration, and large numbers of them moved to the United States and, in lesser numbers, to Argentina. The infamous forgery known as the Protocols of the Elders of Zion, composed in semiofficial Russian circles, belongs to this dark period. Similarly, the imperial court saw the formation of anti-Semitic thug groups such as the BLACK HUNDREDS as a positive development. The BEILIS AFFAIR of 1911–13, in which a

Jewish workman was unjustly accused of ritual murder and barely acquitted, was the Russian equivalent of the French Dreyfus affair. Anti-Semitic violence flared up again during the turbulent years of the Russian Revolution and civil war at a time of general lawlessness, particularly in Ukraine, which witnessed some of the heaviest fighting between revolutionaries and Ukrainian nationalists.

While the new Soviet government condemned anti-Semitism as a leftover from the czarist past, popular anti-Semitism continued throughout the 1920s, focusing on what was perceived as a large Jewish representation in the COMMUNIST PARTY. As discontent with the Communist Party grew, so did anti-Semitism. Official anti-Semitism, however, did not reemerge until the mid-1930s, when most prominent Jewish leaders disappeared from the party and government apparatus. Yiddish language schools, which had flourished after the revolution, were closed in 1938 as part of a Russifying tendency that also affected other non-Russian nationalities. Official anti-Semitism increased in the period after World War II through STALIN's death in 1953. The campaign against "rootless cosmopolitans" launched in 1949 was largely an anti-Semitic campaign, during which prominent Jewish writers and many scholars were arrested and subsequently shot. The famous Jewish Theater of Moscow and all Yiddish newspapers but one were suppressed. This anti-Semitic policy culminated in the so-called DOCTORS' PLOT of January 1953, when rumors surfaced of the impending deportation to Siberia of all Soviet Jews. Stalin's death in March 1953 brought about a relaxation and Jewish intellectuals were posthumously rehabilitated, but both official and popular anti-Semitism continued. In the BREZHNEV years, Soviet Jews began to press for the right to emigrate, and the issue of Jewish emigration became tied to Soviet-American relations. Only in the late 1980s did the Soviet government relax restrictions on travel and large numbers of Soviet Jews emigrated to Israel and the United States. With the demise of the Soviet Union, the 1990s also witnessed a resurgence of Jewish culture and religion, especially in large urban centers such as Moscow.

Antonov Uprising (1919–1921)

The Antonov uprising of 1919–21 in Tambov province was one of the most brutal and extensive of a series of peasant rebellions that shook the foundations of the new Soviet state in the closing months of the Russian civil war. Its leader, Aleksandr Stepanovich Antonov (1885?–1922), had been a member of the Socialist Revolutionary Party since 1905. Arrested by the czarist police after the 1905 Revolution and sentenced to a 12-year term in Siberia, Antonov returned to Tambov province soon after the February Revolution and became chief of the local militia in the town of Kirsanov. One of the most overpopulated and poverty-stricken provinces of European Russia, the Tambov region was a stronghold of the peasant-leaning Socialist Revolutionary Party. By 1918 the anti-Bolshevik armed peasant bands, also known as Greens, who had found shelter in the region's wooded backlands, broke out into open revolt as the Bolshevik government began to enforce a policy of forced grain requisitioning (*prodrazverstka*). Antonov went underground in August 1920 and provided military leadership while the Socialist Revolutionary Party provided political leadership through the Unions of the Toiling Peasantry, headed by the Provincial Committee, which exercised civil authority. By January 1921, Antonov's troops consisted of some 50,000 men, mainly peasants and deserters from the Red Army. Close to 2,000 Bolshevik officials were killed in clashes with Antonov's armies and merciless peasant violence was met with equally ruthless Red Terror. A desire to isolate Antonov's peasant base of support played an important role in the debates that led up to the adoption of the New Economic Policy in March 1921, particularly the plank that replaced grain requisitioning with a food tax. This change and a year of campaigns by regular Red Army detachments under Mikhail TUKHACHEVSKY and Ieronim Uborevich

eventually defeated the Antonovshchina, as Antonov's movement became widely known. With the bulk of his army routed by August 1921, Antonov again went into hiding with a small group of followers. He was labeled a bandit by the Soviet government, and the Soviet press reported that he and his brother, Dmitrii, were killed in July 1922 in a confrontation with troops from the Tambov branch of the secret police.

Apraksin, Feodor Matveevich (1661–1728)
admiral

A lifelong friend of PETER I the Great, Apraksin is generally credited as the creator of the Russian navy. He had been close to Peter since 1682, when he helped him train the Preobrazhenskoe "play" regiments that would later become Peter's personal guard. In 1700, as head of the Admiralty and governor of the recently acquired territory of Azov on the Black Sea, Apraksin was placed in charge of shipbuilding and the construction of naval installations. During the Great Northern War (1700–1721) he served with distinction, first repealing a Swedish attempt to take St. Petersburg (1708), for which he was made count, and then leading the Russian navy to its first victory at the Battle of Hango (1714), which ended Swedish naval domination in the Baltic Sea. In 1721 he headed the Russian side in the negotiations that led to the Treaty of Nystadt with Sweden to end the Great Northern War. In the war with Persia of 1722–23, Apraksin commanded the Caspian Sea flotilla, and from 1723 to 1726, served as commander of the Baltic fleet. Prone to financial troubles, he was tried three times for embezzlement and each time was punished with heavy fines. After Peter's death, Apraksin was one of the six members of the Supreme Privy Council, composed of Peter's close advisers, which for four years served as Russia's de facto ruling oligarchy. He did not live to see the council's selection of ANNA IVANOVNA as empress and her reassertion of imperial authority over oligarchical rule in 1730. Apraksin's older brother, Petr Matveevich (1659–1728), was also a close adviser to Peter the Great. As governor of KAZAN (1708–13), he directed the incorporation of the Kalmyks of the Caspian Sea area into Russia. Accused of complicity with Peter's son Alexis in the alleged plot against his father, Apraksin was acquitted but was asked to serve on the council that sentenced Alexis to death.

Arakcheev, Aleksei Andreevich
(1769–1834)
general and statesman

A conservative, disciplinarian adviser to Emperors PAUL I and ALEXANDER I, Arakcheev is most renowned for the notorious and failed experiment of the "military colonies," implemented during Alexander's reign. In 1792, Arakcheev first impressed the future Paul I, Catherine the Great's son, as an exacting drillmaster and joined the garrison at Gachina, Paul's favorite residence. Under Arakcheev and Paul, Gachina resembled Prussian-style military camp. In 1796, Paul, now emperor, rewarded Arakcheev with an estate at Gruzino and made him governor of St. Petersburg. Their professional relationship was a stormy one. In 1798, Paul dismissed Arakcheev, appointed him inspector general of artillery, only to dismiss him again in 1799. The new emperor, Alexander I, reappointed him to the same position in 1803. Although he had not distinguished himself during the Napoleonic Wars, Arakcheev served as minister of war (1808–10). If the first part of Alexander's reign is associated with the failed liberal reformism of Mikhail SPERANSKII, the second part belongs to Arakcheev. From 1815 he was virtually the most powerful man in Russia after the czar, especially during his frequent trips abroad. He convinced Alexander of the need to establish "military colonies" on a nationwide basis, modeled after Arakcheev's own Gruzino estate, featuring uniformed soldier-peasants subjected to regimented work details, welfare services, and individual punishment books to track offenses. By the early 1820s close to 750,000 peasants were part of these military colonies. With the death of Alexander I in 1825, Arak-

cheev lost his political influence, and the military colonies were dissolved during NICHOLAS I's reign because of corruption and their extreme unpopularity among peasants. Arakcheev's health deteriorated dramatically after his serfs killed his mistress in September 1825, but he lived for almost another decade.

Archangel (Arkhangelsk)

Although remotely located and icebound during the winter months, the city of Archangel was the main Russian seaport from its founding in 1584 until the emergence of ST. PETERSBURG in 1703. Archangel is located on the Northern Dvina River, about 30 miles from where it empties into the White Sea. The city's growth was directly connected to the arrival of the English explorer Richard Chancellor in 1553 and the establishment of commercial relations between England and Russia two years later. Initially known as Novo-Kholmogory and renamed Arkhangelsk in 1613 in honor of the Archangel Michael, it grew up around a 12th-century monastery, benefiting from its monopoly on Muscovite trade with England. During IVAN IV's reign of terror, his political police, the *oprichnina* drew financial sustenance for its terror campaigns from its control of the valuable route connecting Archangel with central Russia. Until 1702 Archangel was the administrative center for Russia's northern territories, but its importance as a northern trade route diminished considerably over the next two centuries after the foundation of St. Petersburg. The completion of a rail link with MOSCOW in the late 19th century helped revive its trade. Archangel again drew attention during the Russian civil war when British and American troops occupied the city in 1918–19, initially to prevent Germany from seizing war matériel, but later—particularly in the case of the British—to assist in the effort to overthrow the BOLSHEVIKS. In this they supported the short-lived anti-Bolshevik government set up by the elderly former populist revolutionary Nikolai CHAIKOVSKY. The city's geographical location again proved important during World War II, when, with Leningrad (St. Petersburg) besieged, it served together with Murmansk as a staging point for Allied convoys. During the Soviet period, the city of Archangel was the seat of Archangel Oblast, an area of lowland coniferous forests that covers approximately 228,600 square miles. The famous SOLOVETSKII MONASTERY is situated on islands in the White Sea. Beginning in the 17th century and more recently from the 1920s to the 1950s, the area and the monastery itself was used for banishment of political or religious offenders. In the mid-1990s the city's population was 443,571, and it remains the center of an important timber-producing region.

Armand, Inessa Teodorovna
(1874–1920)
(born Steffen)

Bolshevik revolutionary

Long-rumored to have been LENIN's lover, Armand played an important role in advancing women's issues in the first years of the Russian Revolution. Left orphaned in Paris at an early age, Armand was sent to live with her aunt, a governess with the wealthy Armand family, living in the town of Pushkino. She married one of the family's sons, and after his death one of her husband's brothers. A mother of five, she started developing an interest in social and feminist issues after working with a school for peasant children and the Moscow Society for the Improvement of Women. She wanted to run Sunday schools for poor women and publish a newspaper, but the authorities were opposed. In 1903 she joined the Social Democratic Party, participated in the 1905 Revolution, and after several arrests was exiled to the ARCHANGEL region in the north, near the White Sea. She escaped and eventually reached Paris, where she first met Lenin. Armand translated Lenin's writings into French, served as a contact with the French Socialist Party, and became a devoted BOLSHEVIK. After a brief return to Russia that ended in another arrest, she left Russia in 1913 and spent World War I in Switzerland. After the FEBRUARY REVOLUTION, Armand returned with Lenin and

other Bolsheviks on the "sealed train" that arrived in Petrograd's Finland Station in April 1917. Loyal to Lenin, she did not always agree with him, as in the vote on the BREST-LITOVSK treaty with Germany, which she, along with the Left Communists, opposed. In the first years of the revolution, she occupied a number of posts, most importantly as director of ZHENOTDEL (the women's section of the Central Committee of the Communist Party). She organized the first conference of International Women Communists in Moscow in 1920. It met at the same time as the Second Congress of the Comintern. She died from cholera contracted while on holiday in the Caucasus, and is buried outside the Kremlin wall.

Ashinov, Nikolai Ivanovich
(1856–unknown)

adventurer

Ashinov was a semiliterate Terek COSSACK who convinced Russian nationalist and religious circles to support his plans to create a Russian colony in Ethiopia. After an early youth working the caravan trade in Persia and Turkey, Ashinov joined a group called the Brotherhood of Free Cossacks and fought as a volunteer in the RUSSO-TURKISH WAR OF 1877–78. An early attempt to obtain land for colonization for his Cossacks proved unsuccessful, but Ashinov made important contacts in ST. PETERSBURG. Ashinov then hatched a scheme to travel to Ethiopia to find land for his Free Cossacks with funds allegedly obtained by swindling the British embassy in Constantinople. He reached Ethiopia in 1886 and was received by Emperor Johannes, who promised land to the Cossacks and sent gifts to the czar. In 1887, Ashinov traveled to Paris, gained access to Russophile French nationalist circles, and bought 20,000 rifles, which he transported to Africa and stored near the French colony of Obok. On Emperor Johannes's insistence Ashinov returned to Russia with two Ethiopian monks in time for the celebrations for the 900th anniversary of Russia's conversion to Christianity. Although Foreign Minister N. K. GIERS objected to the whole enterprise,

ALEXANDER III formally received the Ethiopians after some delay—a reception that triggered the formation of a national fund-raising campaign to finance an "Orthodox mission" to Ethiopia and "reunite" the two churches. An expedition of about 200 Cossacks, their families, and a few priests set sail in December 1888, recovered Ashinov's guns, and occupied the Egyptian fort of Sagallo, claiming sovereign rights. After the embarrassed Russian government disavowed the expedition, the French colonial authorities bombarded the Russians, dislodged them from Sagallo, and dispatched them home. Alexander III exiled Ashinov for three years to Saratov Province, but he escaped to Paris in November 1890, where he tried unsuccessfully to press claims from the Sagallo affair. Expelled by the French, he traveled to London and sent a personal appeal to the czar. Ashinov returned to Russia in 1891 on the czar's orders. He was sentenced to ten years' exile in Chernigov, where he was living prosperously as late as 1906, after which time his trail vanishes.

Astrakhan

Located on the VOLGA RIVER, near the Caspian Sea, Astrakhan has long been a major port and trading center. First probably settled by the Mongols in the 13th century, Astrakhan became the center of the Khanate of Astrakhan, one of the successor khanates to the GOLDEN HORDE when it fragmented in the late 14th century. In 1395, Tamerlane's invading army destroyed the city. Later rebuilt, Astrakhan was conquered again by the troops of IVAN IV "the Terrible" in 1556 and permanently annexed to Russia. The conquest of Astrakhan opened the entire Volga River to Russian traffic and gave Russia access to the Caspian Sea. In the 1580s a fortress, or kremlin, was built that dominates the old city to this day. In 1705–6, in the first part of the reign of PETER I the Great, Astrakhan was the site of a blood revolt by the *streltsy* (musketeers) who had also opposed Peter in MOSCOW. Later in his reign, Astrakhan served as the base for his campaign of 1722–23 against Persia. In the 19th and 20th centuries,

Astrakhan was overshadowed by the emergence of Baku as a major oil-producing center and port. Nevertheless, in Soviet times Astrakhan retained some importance as a center of shipbuilding and fish processing, most notably of caviar. By the 1990s its population was around 650,000. With the dissolution of the Soviet Union, BAKU became the capital of the newly independent Republic of Azerbaijan and Astrakhan regained some of its previous importance to Russia.

Atlasov, Vladimir Vasilievich (1635–1711)
explorer

Born to a peasant family in the northern town of Velikii Ustiug, Atlasov was a COSSACK whose efforts in opening up the large Kamchatka peninsula on the Pacific Ocean to Russian conquest and colonization later earned him the name "Yermak of Kamchatka" by the poet Alexander PUSHKIN, in reference to the reputed first Russian explorer and conqueror of Siberia. Atlasov's family moved to Siberia when he was a boy. He later entered government service. His first major appointment came in 1695, when he was named commander in chief of the fort at Anadyrsk, the base for Russian activities on the shores of what is now the Bering Sea. Hearing rumors of a great peninsula to the south, in 1697 Atlasov organized an expedition of 120 men— Russians and Yukagir allies—to explore the territory and claim it for Russia. Despite fierce resistance from the indigenous Kamchadals and Koryaks fighting on skis and dogsleds, the Russian expedition marched down the western side of Kamchatka, crisscrossed the peninsula to the Pacific Ocean, and—more important for Russian colonizing activities in Siberia—imposed tribute on the native population. Near the southern tip of the peninsula, Atlasov's party learned of the existence of several islands (now known as the Kuriles) inhabited by the Ainu people, believed to be the original inhabitants of Japan, and of the existence of even larger islands to the south of the Kurils (Japan). There was also a prisoner named Denbei, a mysterious survivor of a shipwreck who identified himself as a subject of Hondo, a name often used for the island of Honshu, the largest of the Japanese islands. After founding Verkhnekamchatsk on the banks of the Kamchatka River, Atlasov returned to Anadyrsk in 1699. He sent Denbei to ST. PETERSBURG to be presented to Czar PETER I. In St. Petersburg, Denbei was placed at the center of a Japanese language school but died four years later. Atlasov himself traveled to Moscow to report on his discoveries of a land rich in furs and was rewarded with an appointment as commandant of Kamchatka. His good fortune changed quickly when on his return to Kamchatka, his party attacked and robbed a Russian caravan returning from China, for which he was imprisoned until 1707. While in prison, Kamchatka and its native population fell victim to the abuses of leaderless Russians and Cossacks. Atlasov was released and charged with restoring discipline, which he did with great savagery, earning him the enmity of his former associates. In 1711, during another Cossack mutiny, he was assassinated in his sleep. One of the Kuril Islands was later named Atlasov Island.

August Coup (1991)

A short-lived and unsuccessful attempt by the more conservative members of Mikhail GORBACHEV's government to undo the reforms of the late 1980s in the hope of preserving the Soviet Union and the communist system that they felt was in danger by 1991. Following a series of high-level appointments in late 1990, conservative politicians had gained ground within Gorbachev's inner circle. The spark that launched the coup was the proposed signing of a new union treaty scheduled for August 20, 1991, which would have altered the nature of the Soviet Union by transferring many powers to the constituent republics of the union. The leaders of the coup included Gennady Yanaev, vice president of the Soviet Union; Boris Pugo, minister of the interior; Valentin Pavlov, prime minister of the government; Vladimir Kriuchkov, head of the KGB; and Dmitrii Yazov, minister of defense.

With Gorbachev on vacation in Crimea the plotters moved on August 18, 1991, and formed an eight-member State Emergency Committee. The coup was accepted by the bulk of the COMMUNIST PARTY as well as the right-wing and nationalist politicians who had emerged in the last years of Gorbachev's rule. Opposing it were Boris YELTSIN, president of the Russian Republic with headquarters in Moscow, and the mayor of ST. PETERSBURG, Anatoli Sobchak. On August 19, troops loyal to the plotters occupied most of Moscow but met resistance at the seat of the Russian parliament, known as the Russian White House. There, Yeltsin made his signature appeal to resist the coup by climbing atop of an armored vehicle. Poorly organized and unwilling to use the full force available to them, the coup leaders soon lost their nerve. Enough members of the army remained loyal to Gorbachev or to Yeltsin, who quickly emerged as the leader of the resistance to the coup. By August 21, the coup had fizzled, and Gorbachev was released from house arrest. The failure of the coup led to a backlash against the Communist Party and accelerated the disintegration of the Soviet Union. On August 24, 1991, Gorbachev resigned as secretary-general of the Communist Party, and following Yeltsin's lead in the Russian Republic, he soon suspended the Communist Party's activities throughout the Soviet Union. By September 1991, the Soviet government had recognized the independence of the three Baltic republics—Estonia, Latvia and Lithuania. On December 8, 1991, the Russian Republic, Ukraine, and Belorussia (Belarus) agreed to formally disband the Soviet Union and form a new Commonwealth of Independent States. As other Soviet republics moved to declare their independence in the following weeks, Gorbachev was left a president without a state, until he himself resigned as president of the Soviet Union on December 25, 1991.

Avvakum Petrovich (1620?–1682)
religious leader

Avvakum was one of the most forceful and articulate opponents of the religious reforms proposed by Patriarch NIKON, as well as one of the founders of the OLD BELIEVER (Old Ritualist) sect that broke away from the Russian Orthodox Church during the Great Schism of 1666–67. At the age of 23, Avvakum followed his father's path and became a village priest in the NIZHNII-NOVGOROD region. While in Moscow in 1646–47, he became associated with the circle of pious zealots and acquainted with the devout czar ALEKSEI MIKHAILOVICH. After a short stay in Iurevich Povolskii in 1652, he returned to Moscow and became priest at the Kazan Cathedral. His strong words against the reforms proposed by Patriarch Nikon earned him a banishment in 1653, with his family, to Tobolsk, in western Siberia, and later to Dauriia. In 1663, Czar Aleksei, trying to bring Avvakum back into the official church, recalled him to Moscow, but Avvakum did not recant his previous statements, instead accusing Nikon of heresy. Although Avvakum's pronouncements against Nikon gained him the support of some prominent boyars, such as F. P. Morozov, Avvakum was again banished in 1664, this time to Mezen. Two years later he was recalled to Moscow, an anathema was pronounced against him, and in 1667 he was sent off to Pustozerskii prison. Here, over a span of 15 years, Avvakum did not cease his struggle with the church and wrote his most important works, *The Book of Conversations* (*Kniga besed*), *The Book of Learning* (*Kniga tolkovanii*), and *The Life of Archpriest Avvakum by Himself* (*Zhitie*). Avvakum's popularity was so great that even prison guards helped distribute his works. Finally, by czarist decree, Avvakum and his closest associates were burned at the stake on June 14, 1682. Conservative, almost fanatical in his views, Avvakum exercised an immmense influence on the Old Believer movement. He was also an outstanding writer, and his autobiography in particular is a remarkable work of early Russian literature. Here, he takes the traditional form of the lives of the saints and through sharp, lively writing transforms it into a captivating autobiographical narrative.

Azev, Evno Fishelevich (1869–1918) (Evgenii Filippovich)
terrorist and double agent

A founder of the Socialist Revolutionary Party, Azev was perhaps the most notorious and highly paid of many police agents in the revolutionary movement. His family, impoverished Jewish tailors from Grodno province, moved to Rostov-on-Don in 1874. Sought by the police for revolutionary activities, in 1892 Azev stole 800 rubles and fled to Germany, where he pursued studies in electrical engineering while becoming an informer for the czarist police (Okhrana). Back in Moscow in 1899, he became a member of the Northern Union, which in 1901 joined its southern counterpart to form the Party of Socialist Revolutionaries (PSR). A founding member of the party's Central Committee, Azev also was a part of its terrorist Fighting Organization, which for security reasons was an autonomous arm of the PSR. In 1903, Azev became the director of the Fighting Organization after the capture of its leader, Grigorii Gershuni. In this capacity, Azev masterminded the assassinations in 1904 of the interior minister, Vyacheslav Plehve, and in 1905 of the czar's uncle and governor-general of Moscow, Grand Duke Sergei Aleksandrovich, both hated enemies of the revolutionary movement. These two assassinations overshadow the extent to which Azev succeeded in sabotaging the party's terrorist activities. Working for Sergei ZUBATOV, the controversial chief of the Moscow Okhrana, Azev provided police with lists of participants at underground PSR congresses as well as active party members. In 1908, seven members of the group were hanged after his denunciations. He was unmasked to a great scandal by Vladimir L. Burtsev, a journalist and self-appointed hunter of police agents in 1908. Sentenced to death in absentia by the Central Committee of the Socialist Revolutionary Party, Azev fled to Berlin, where he reportedly worked at the stock exchange under an assumed name. He was arrested and interned by the German police in 1915 but released in December 1917.

B

Babel, Isaak Emanuilovich
(1894–1940)
writer

A gifted Jewish writer whose short stories about the Russian Revolution have survived as sensitive and succinct examples of Russian and Jewish life in a time of upheaval. Babel was born in ODESSA and grew up speaking Yiddish in the city's large Jewish quarter. After graduating from the commercial school in Nikolaev, Ukraine, in 1915, he turned to writing short stories. His early career benefited greatly from a meeting with Maxim GORKY, whom he greatly admired and who helped publish his first stories. During the revolution and civil war, Babel found himself caught in the turmoil of the times, finally joining Semyon BUDENNYI's First Red Cavalry as a journalist. The civil war experiences later formed the basis of his masterful collection of short stories, *Red Cavalry*, first published in 1926, which portrayed with great realism and subtlety the life of Cossack soldiers. After the civil war, Babel worked as a journalist in Leningrad and Tbilisi, Georgia. Another set of short stories, *Odessa Tales*, was published in 1931. Here Babel reached further back into his past to focus on life in his hometown, particularly the Jewish underworld. As the tenor of Soviet literary politics became ever more restrictive in the 1930s, Babel found himself increasingly isolated. At the 1934 Writers' Congress, which pronounced socialist realism as the official Soviet literary form, he made his famous declaration that he would now be practicing the "literature of silence." Babel was arrested in May 1939 and accused of being a French spy, but the more likely reason was his friendship with the wife of the recently disgraced secret police chief, Nikolai YEZHOV. For decades there was confusion about the date of his death, but a later commission of inquiry established that he was executed on January 27, 1940. In 1957 Babel was posthumously rehabilitated and his works were reissued in the Soviet Union. Previously unknown details about his arrest and captivity became known in the late 1980s and 1990s, leading to a renewed interest and appreciation of his work. A more tangible result of this was the republication of his *1920 Diary* (1997), which served as the basis of many of the stories in *Red Cavalry*.

Babi Yar

One of the many ravines in the city of KIEV that was the site of one of the most heinous atrocities of World War II when the Germans occupied the city for two years. On September 29–30, 1941 over 33,000 Jews were rounded up and machine-gunned to death at the edge of the ravine. The chilling number of casualties led one historian to calculate that, in two days, Jews were killed at Babi Yar at a greater rate than in the gas chambers of Auschwitz at their peak. Estimates of the total number of Jews killed at Babi Yar during the German occupation range from 100,000 to 150,000. In the 1960s, the massacre at Babi Yar became one of the focal points in the de-Stalinization debates of the early 1960s, affecting the careers of three prominent cultural figures. The massacre was first publicly memorialized in Yevgenii Yevtushenko's powerful poem *Babi Yar*, published in 1961. Describing the horror of the massacre of innocent Jews, Yevtushenko raised the then taboo topic of Russian ANTI-SEMITISM by condemning anti-Semitism in general, whether Fascist or Communist in origin. Loudly criticized by conservatives for insulting Soviet wartime heroism, Yevtushenko was praised by liberals for his courage in broaching a tangled and difficult topic. As KHRUSHCHEV's support for de-Stalinization wavered in later 1962, the topic of Babi Yar remained a flashpoint for larger political battles and now settled on a controversy over Dmitrii SHOSTAKOVICH's new 13th Symphony, scheduled to be premiered at a gathering of party officials and intellectuals. The party's ideological guardians condemned the symphony's first movement, a clear tribute to Yevtushenko's *Babi Yar*, and many musicians were hesitant to perform it, fearing reprisals. After another controversial performance, future performances of the symphony were canceled, to many a symbol of a growing conservatism in Soviet political life. Preceding the other two was the novel *Babi Yar*, by Anatolii KUZNETSOV, a young Soviet writer of great promise and a recent graduate of the elite Gorky Literary Institute. Although the Soviet authorities censored the novel heavily and it remained unpublished in the Soviet Union, the events Kuznetsov described served as the basis for Yevtushenko's poem. Kuznetsov continued to write for several years and remained quite popular with Soviet youth, but disillusioned over growing censorship, he sought political asylum while traveling in London in 1969. His novel was later published in the West.

Badmaev, Petr Aleksandrovich
(1851–1919)
medical practitioner

A Buriat by birth, Badmaev was a practitioner of Tibetan medicine with excellent political connections in the courts of ALEXANDER III and NICHOLAS II. Badmaev's father was a prosperous cattle farmer of Buriat stock. After early schooling in Irkutsk, near Lake Baikal, Badmaev entered the Faculty of Oriental Languages at St. Petersburg University. Here he developed the interests that would provide his entrée into the

upper reaches of imperial society: Russian foreign policy in East Asia and traditional Tibetan medicine. The future Alexander III served as Badmaev's godfather when he converted to Russian Orthodoxy, and Badmaev used Alexander's name for his patronymic. From 1875 to 1893, Badmaev worked in the Asiatic Department of the Ministry of Foreign Affairs. In 1893, in a memorandum sent to the finance minister, Sergei WITTE, he outlined what became known as the Badmaev Plan, a project that called for railroad construction and commercial trading companies to extend Russian influence in Mongolia and as far as Tibet. Badmaev argued that the extension of the TRANS-SIBERIAN RAILROAD through Kiakhta and Peking to the Russian port of Vladivostok would provide Russia with the opportunity to promote rebellion among dissatisfied Chinese subjects, such as the Mongolians and Tibetans, who would appeal to the Russians for help. Badmaev's fellow Buriat Mongols of the Transbaikal region, who as Buddhists had long-standing religious and commercial interests in Mongolia and Tibet, would play a pivotal role as agents of Russian imperialism. With Russia's support of China after the Treaty of Alliance of 1896, the Badmaev plan lost its rationale, and the Trans-Siberian Railroad was completed through Manchuria. Badmaev achieved greater influence at the court of Nicholas II through his knowledge of Tibetan traditional medicine, at a time when there was great interest in things Oriental and exotic. The czar was known to have an interest in Badmaev's herbal cures, as well as the Siberian monk Grigorii RASPUTIN, who appeared in St. Petersburg in 1903. Badmaev's friendship with Rasputin developed slowly, but by World War I, they were very close. Badmaev's medical practice served as a conduit for individuals seeking government appointments in the final years of the empire. Badmaev was in frequent contact with Anna Vyrubova, a confidante of Empress ALEXANDRA. Badmaev remained in Petrograd after the FEBRUARY REVOLUTION but later was arrested by sailors from the Baltic Fleet as he was trying to flee to Finland with Vyrubova and the adventurer Manasevich-Manuilov. Sent back to Petrograd, he died in 1919.

Bagration, Petr Ivanovich (1765–1812)
general

A talented student and associate of SUVOROV and KUTUZOV, Bagration was a hero of the War of 1812. Bagration was born in Kizliar to a princely Georgian family. He entered Russian service in 1782 and until 1792 performed military service in the Caucasus Musketeer Regiment, and later in the Kiev Chasseurs and Sofia Carabineer regiments, rising rapidly from the rank of sergeant to lieutenant colonel. During the various wars that preceded Napoleon's invasion of Russia in 1812, Bagration fought with distinction. In 1798, he was promoted to colonel and given command of the Sixth Chasseurs Regiment; the following year he was further promoted to major general. Bagration commanded the vanguard in Suvorov's Italian and Swiss campaigns of 1799; his troops played an important role in the battles of Adda and Trebbia, and at Novi. He also fought heroically and with distinction at St. Goddard during Suvorov's remarkable escape maneuver. In the campaigns of 1805–7, Bagration commanded the Russian army vanguard and fought with distinction in the Battles of Shoengraben, Eylau, and Friedland. He fought in the RUSSO-SWEDISH WAR of 1808–9 and headed the Aland expedition of 1809, after which he was promoted to infantry general. In the RUSSO-TURKISH WAR of 1806–12, he commanded the Moldavian army from July 1809 to March 1810, the Podolsk army from March 1811, and from March 1812 he commanded the Second Western Army. This was the army he commanded during the War of 1812. In March 1812 his troops skillfully eluded a stronger French force and joined BARCLAY DE TOLLY's First Western Army outside of Smolensk, not before causing heavy losses to the French army in rearguard battles at Mir, Romanov, and Saltanovka. Bagration commanded the Russian army's left flank at the Battle of BORODINO in September 1812. Seriously wounded, he died a month later in the village of Sima in Vladimir province, near Moscow. In 1839 his remains were transferred to the Borodino field.

Baikonur Cosmodrome

Also known as Tyuratam, the Baikonur Cosmodrome, located in south central Kazakhstan, is the oldest space launch facility in the world. From its foundation in the late 1950s, the Baikonur Cosmodrome served as the center of the Soviet space program until the dissolution of the Soviet Union in 1991, after which it has continued to operate under the sponsorship of the Commonwealth of Independent States. All the various projects of the Soviet and (since 1991) Russian space program—lunar, planetary, and geostationary—have been launched from Baikonur. Since the early Soviet space program was clouded in secrecy, there has been some confusion as to the exact location of the cosmodrome, as it is not located near the town of Baikonur itself, but rather about 400 kilometers to the southwest near the railhead at Tyuratam. In the decades since the 1950s, the Soviet government also built the town of Leninsk with apartments, schools, and offices for the staff that works at the cosmodrome. The dissolution of the Soviet Union raised the difficult question of the ownership of the cosmodrome, with Kazakhstan claiming ownership, while most of the staff were Russian. After protracted negotiations an agreement was reached in March 1996, according to which Russia would lease the space center for 20 years at a cost of $115 million in annual rent, with an option to extend the lease for another 10 years.

Bakhtin, Mikhail Mikhailovich (1895–1975)
literary theorist

A literary theorist whose influence spread worldwide after his death, Bakhtin spent most of his active professional life in obscurity, in trouble with Soviet literary authorities, writing under various pseudonyms. Bakhtin was born in the provincial town of Orel, to the south of Moscow. He attended St. Petersburg University until 1918 when he began teaching high school in Vitebsk, in present-day Belarus. In the early years of the Russian Revolution Vitebsk was a center of great intellectual creativity, and Bakhtin was deeply involved in organizing lectures and debates. Turning to ethics and aesthetics, Bakhtin focused on the semantics of literary texts, as opposed to the Formalists, who valued the technical construction of the text. He returned to St. Petersburg in 1924, the year the city was renamed Leningrad. With growing restrictions on intellectual work during the 1920s, Bakhtin published under a pseudonym works that criticized Sigmund Freud, Karl Marx, and the Russian Formalists with whom he had been arguing since his years in Vitebsk. A pioneering work on DOSTOEVSKY, *Problems of Dostoevsky's Poetics,* in which he developed the notion of "polyphony," or several balanced authorial voices, as the key to understanding Dostoevsky's work, was published in 1929 under Bakhtin's own name shortly before his arrest. Arrested on charges of belonging to a counterrevolutionary religious organization, Bakhtin was soon released and exiled to northern Kazakhstan. In 1945 he moved to Saransk in the Mordovian Autonomous Republic, where he taught at the Mordovian Teachers Training College until 1972, when he was given permission to return to Moscow. During these years he continued to write books on literary criticism, none of which was published. It was only in 1963, with the publication of a second edition of his work on Dostoevsky, that Bakhtin gradually gained the recognition his work deserved, first among Soviet scholars and later, especially after his death, in the West. In *Rabelais and His World* (1965) and *Voprosy literatury i estetiki* (1975, republished in English translation as *The Dialogic Imagination* [1981]), Bakhtin further developed the notions of polyphony, in which language served as a dynamic rather than static construct, and dialogism, a term that captured Bakhtin's understanding that texts are

shaped by the relationship between the author and the reader and the social context that surrounds them.

Bakikhanov, Abbas-Kuli-Aga (1794–1847)
(pseudonym: Kudsi)
scholar

An Azerbaijani scholar and writer, Bakikhanov was born in the village of Amiradzhani, near Baku, to a family of local rulers. In 1819 he served as a translator of Eastern languages in Tbilisi. He participated in the Russian wars with Persia and Turkey of 1826–29, and in the Russo-Persian peace negotiations at Turkmanchai. He was a widely educated man who knew several languages, as well as Eastern philosophy and literature. A strong advocate of cultural closeness between Azerbaijan and Russia, Bakikhanov was in contact with leading cultural figures of his day, such as A. S. GRIBOEDOV, A. A. Bestuzhev-Marlinski, M. F. Akhundov, Kh. Abovian, and A. Chavchavadze. True to his social background, he wrote in favor of the preservation of feudal privileges, but he also condemned punitive measures against rebellious peasants in the Kubinskii province in 1837. In 1841, he completed a work on the history of northern Azerbaijan from earliest times until 1813, entitled *Giulistan-Iram* (*Flower of Paradise*), which marked an important step in the development of Azerbaijani historiography. Although he focused primarily on the actions of rulers through the centuries, Bakikhanov drew from a wide range of Eastern and Caucasian sources and devoted extensive coverage to issues in the history of Azerbaijan and Dagestan. Bakikhanov himself translated his book into Russian from its Farsi original. His work was not published in its entirety until Soviet times, first in Russian (1926), later in Azerbaijani (1951). He also wrote a number of other literary and scientific works on pedagogy and philosophy; on the phonetics, morphology, and syntax of the Farsi language; and on astronomy and geography. In his work "The Secret

[Mystery] of Angels," he presented the foundations of Copernican thought to the Islamic world.

Baku

A city of about 1.1 million inhabitants located on the southwestern shore of the Caspian Sea, Baku (Baky in the Azeri language) is the present-day capital of the Republic of Azerbaijan. Annexed by the Russian Empire in 1806, it became an important urban center and port and the center of the Russian and Soviet oil industry until the dissolution of the Soviet Union in 1991. The earliest recorded mentions of the city date to ninth and 10th centuries, at which time it was already known for its oil resources. In 1509 Baku became a part of the Persian Safavid Empire, and the site of one of the strongest fortresses in the Caucasus region. The Ottoman Empire briefly held Baku from the 1580s until 1604 when the troops of the Persian shah Abbas I recaptured the city.

Russian interest in Baku dates to the reign of PETER I the Great and in 1723 during the RUSSO-PERSIAN WAR of 1722–23 Russian troops captured the city, which they held until 1735, when it was returned to Persia after the Treaty of Gandjeh. Baku became part of the Russian Empire on a more permanent basis in 1806 during the Russo-Persian War of 1804–13. In the 1870s Baku entered a period of sustained economic growth sparked by the development of the Russian oil industry, a process in which foreign investment by prominent Western business families such as the Rothschilds and the Nobels played a central role. By 1901 Baku accounted for 95 percent of Russia's oil production and close to 50 percent of the world's oil production. Oil production declined in the next two decades, as Baku suffered from the overall political turbulence that spread across the Russian empire. During the 1905 Revolution, Baku was the site of a large pogrom against its Armenian minority. In the summers of 1913–14 and again in the winter of 1916–17 general strikes swept through the city as the power of the Russian monarchy waned. After the October Revolution, a Soviet government known as the Baku Commune briefly held power in Baku between April and August 1918, when an anti-Bolshevik government that lasted until 1920 was established with British support. In September 1920 Baku hosted the Congress of the Peoples of the East that brought together nearly 2,000 Communist delegates from across Asia as part of the Bolshevik government's attempt to spread its revolution throughout the continent. Baku served as the capital of the Azerbaijan Soviet Socialist Republic from 1920 to 1922, when the three Caucasian republics of Armenia, Azerbaijan, and Georgia were brought together into one political unit named the Transcaucasian Federation. In 1937 the Transcaucasian Federation was dismantled and Baku restored to its status of capital of the Azerbaijan S.S.R. In the late 1980s Baku was at the forefront of the nationalist turmoil that contributed to the end of the Soviet Union. In February 1988 dozens of Armenians were killed during a three-day riot in the town of Sumgait north of Baku. In April 1990 Soviet troops fired on nationalist demonstrators in Baku. When Azerbaijan declared its independence from the Soviet Union in 1991 Baku became its capital. With the strategic maneuvering that took place in the 1990s over the construction of oil pipelines to transport oil from the Caspian basin fields, Baku regained some of the luster of the pre-Soviet era.

Bakunin, Mikhail Aleksandrovich (1814–1876)
revolutionary

Born to a prominent aristocratic landowning family, Bakunin turned away from a life of privilege and embraced the cause of revolutionary ANARCHISM. Bakunin was educated at a military school in St. Petersburg and later became an officer in the Imperial Guard, before resigning his commission. He was an early participant in the intellectual discussions of the seminal Stankevich Circle of Moscow University students formed in the 1830s. Bakunin left Russia in 1840, after rejecting the Hegelian ideas of the

Mikhail Bakunin *(Hulton/Archive)*

Stankevich Circle for an anarchism that embraced and romanticized the creative possibilities of violent destruction. During the pan-European revolutionary upheavals of 1848–49, Bakunin attended a Pan-Slav congress in Prague and later surfaced at the revolutionary barricades in Dresden. He was arrested and condemned to death, but instead was deported to Russia, where the authorities exiled him to Siberia. In prison, he wrote an ambiguously worded confession to Czar NICHOLAS I. In 1861, after escaping from Siberia by way of Japan, he arrived in England, where he resumed his revolutionary activism, briefly collaborating with Aleksandr HERZEN in the latter's influential émigré journal, *Kolokol* (The Bell). As Bakunin developed an anarchist platform that openly advocated social revolution, his views gained support among young Russian radicals, impa-

tient with the progress of government reforms and dissatisfied over the terms of the 1861 emancipation of the serfs. In 1869 he founded the Social Democratic Alliance to advance his anarchist views. With Karl Marx, Bakunin was one of the founders of the First International in 1872. However, constant conflict with Marx over personal and ideological issues soon resulted in Bakunin's expulsion from the socialist movement. His close association with Sergei NECHAEV, a controversial revolutionary later accused of murdering one of his colleagues, harmed Bakunin's reputation somewhat. Nevertheless, his ideas remained influential through the 1870s, especially among the expatriate students who, upon their return to Russia, formed the core of the populist crusade, known as the "Go to the People" movement of 1873–74 that sought, without success, to convince the peasantry about the virtues of revolution.

In his best-known writings such as *Statism and Anarchy* (1873), Bakunin defended the view that man is a natural rebel. He challenged revolutionaries to unleash the potential for revolt, especially found among peasants, whom he idealized. He consistently, and presciently, opposed the dictatorial potential of the state socialism advocated by Marx and his followers. Instead, he advocated an international federation of autonomous communities, where voluntary associations of workers would engage in productive work, freed from the oppression inherent in any form of government or organized authority.

Bakunin spent his final years in Switzerland and died in Bern. His famous treatise *God and the State* was published posthumously in 1882. His ideas, perhaps less suited for the emerging industrial societies of western Europe, found unexpectedly strong support among anarchist peasant communities in Spain and Italy.

Balanchine, George (1904–1983)
choreographer and dancer

Born Georgii Melitonovich Balanchivadze to a talented Georgian family of musicians in St. Petersburg, Balanchine went on to become one of the most prolific and important creators of twentieth-century ballets. His father was the Georgian composer Meliton Balanchivadze (1862–1937), and his brother, Andrei (born 1906), became an important composer in Soviet Georgia. From 1914 to 1921, Balanchine studied at the Imperial Ballet School (later known as the Kirov), then studied music at the Petrograd Conservatory, graduating in 1924. His early experiments in choreography antagonized the ballet establishment and, while on tour in Europe with the Soviet State Dancers in 1924, he joined DIAGHILEV's Ballets Russes, becoming its choreographer until Diaghilev's death in 1929. Among the 10 ballets he choreographed for Diaghilev were Stravinsky's *Le Chant du rossignol* (1925), Sauguet's *La Chatte* (1927), STRAVINSKY's *Apollo* (1928), and PROKOFIEV's *Prodigal Son* (1929). Balanchine came to the United States in 1933 on the invitation of Lincoln Kirstein, an author and prominent figure in the world of American dance and theater, to found the School of American Ballet. He also became director of the Metropolitan Opera House, a post he held until 1937. Beginning with TCHAIKOVSKY's *Serenade* (1934), he began a prolific and outstanding career that lasted half a century and is almost synonymous with the history of American ballet itself. Although he drew from a wide range of composers, he returned frequently to the classical Russian training of his youth, preserving and transforming it in his distinctive neoclassical style. His collaborations with Stravinsky, dating back to the 1920s, resulted in some of the masterpieces of Balanchine's canon: *Orphée* (1948), *Agon* (1958), and *Monumentum pro Gesualdo* (1960). In 1946, he again joined forces with Kirstein to found the company that two years later would become the New York City Ballet which went on to become one of the great ballet companies in the West. He choreographed over 100 ballets for the company, including his signature *The Nutcracker* and *Don Quixote*. Balanchine also choreographed Broadway shows and ballet scenes for films. In 1962 and 1972, he returned to the Soviet Union to great acclaim, touring with the New York City Ballet.

Banzarov, Dorzhi (1822?–1855)
scholar

Born to a Buriat COSSACK family in the Transbaikal region (currently the Dzhidinskii aimak of the Buriat Republic), Banzarov became the first Buriat scholar of renown within the broader scientific community of the Russian Empire. In 1846, he graduated from Kazan University, where he studied with the noted scholar O. M. Kovalevskii. In 1847–48, he conducted research at the Asiatic Museum in St. Petersburg, where he befriended a number of leading Orientalist scholars. From 1850 to 1855, he served as a bureaucrat based in Irkutsk, and during his travels in Siberia, he became acquainted with many Decembrist exiles. One of them, N. A. Bestuzhev, painted his portrait. Banzarov's scholarly legacy consists of 15 printed works and three manuscripts. His main work, *Chernaia vera, ili shamanstvo u mongolov* (*Black Faith, or Shamanism among the Mongols*), published in 1846, was the first scholarly work in Russia about shamanism. Banzarov argued that shamanism was the ancient religious cult of Mongols, which arose independently of other religions. This work and his specialized articles on historical philosophy and epigraphic problems is distinguished by the care with which he studied Mongol literary relics and is a model of philological investigation. In 1947, the Buriat Pedagogical Institute in Ulan-Ude was renamed in his honor. His collected works were published in Moscow in 1955.

Baranov, Aleksandr Andreevich (1747?–1819)
administrator

As the first, and most able, governor of Russia's Alaskan territories, Baranov provided the foundations for a thriving colony with settlers, schools, libraries, a shipbuilding yard, and wide-ranging commercial links that were not followed by his successors. Baranov was born in Kargopol and from a young age worked for a Moscow merchant. In 1780, he moved to Siberia, settling in Irkutsk, where he managed glass factories and vodka distilleries and prospered in the fur trade, establishing a commercial network with branches in Moscow, Petersburg, and Siberia. In 1790, he was appointed by the RUSSIAN AMERICAN COMPANY to his post in ALASKA. Thanks to his energy and administrative talents, Baranov significantly increased the trade links between the Russian settlements of North America with California, the Hawaiian Islands, and China. During his rule, he directed the establishment of new settlements, outfitted a series of expeditions to explore regions of the Pacific Coast, and laid the foundations of a shipbuilding industry. But the basic wealth of the colony was based on the rapacious exploitation of natural riches, most notably furs, and the use of Native Americans as forced labor for these enterprises. For several decades the Russian American Company acted with great vigor, sponsoring 12 round-the-world expeditions between 1804 and 1840, maintaining regular communications between Alaska and Russia, and making port calls in California, Hawaii, and China, a legacy of Baranov's original enterprising energy. Finally relieved of his post, after repeated requests, Baranov headed for home in early 1819. Sailing into the Indian Ocean, he died on April 12, 1819, and was buried at sea. An island in the Alexander I Archipelago in Alaska Bay was named after Baranov. In 1867, almost half a century after his departure, the Russian government, unable to pay for the cost of defending a remote colony from the inroads made by British and American commercial interests, sold the colony to the United States.

Barclay de Tolly, Prince Mikhail Bogdanovich (1761–1818)

military officer

A distinguished officer in the war of 1812 against Napoleonic France, Barclay de Tolly was born in Livonia, into a Baltic family of Scottish descent. He first fought for the Russian army in the Turkish War of 1788–89, then in campaigns against Sweden in 1790 and Poland in 1792 and 1794, at the time of the second and third POLISH PARTITIONS. Following the war with Sweden that

brought Finland into the Russian Empire in 1809, Barclay was made governor-general of Finland. In 1810, he was appointed minister of war by ALEXANDER I, even though many in the czar's circle were suspicious of him because of his foreign blood. At the time of Napoleon's invasion in June 1812, Barclay de Tolly was made commander in chief of the Army of the West. He became known for his controversial tactic of continual retreat "into the depths of Russia," a tactic opposed by the equally able General Peter Ivanovich BAGRATION that further inflamed the suspicions of the Russian national party. The French capture of Smolensk in August 1812 resulted in his dismissal and the appointment of Marshal Mikhail KUTUZOV as commander in chief, just before the Battle of BORODINO. More politically savvy than Barclay de Tolly, Kutuzov continued the strategy of retreat, surrendering Moscow in the process, until the tide of war turned in Russia's favor and Napoleon was forced to begin his disastrous westward retreat. Following Kutuzov's death in April 1813 and the defeats suffered in Germany by his successor, Petr Wittgenstein, Barclay was reappointed commander in chief in May 1813. He took part in the invasion of France in 1814 and was promoted to field marshal.

Baryshnikov, Mikhail Nikolaevich (1948–)

dancer, actor

A Soviet-born ballet dancer of worldwide renown whose career reached new heights after his defection in 1974. Baryshnikov was born in Riga, Latvia, and lived through personal traumas at home: his mother's suicide and his father's rejection of Baryshnikov's chosen career. He began his ballet studies in Riga, before moving to Leningrad in 1964 to finish his studies. In 1967 he joined the famous Kirov Ballet, quickly becoming one of its preeminent soloists and later its principal dancer. With the Kirov, Baryshnikov first developed an international reputation for technical virtuosity in classical ballets, but later company that initially served as the vehicle for Morris's works, but which later performed the works of prominent American and German choreographers. His engaging stage personality also served him well in cinema, where he reached broader audiences in films such as *The Turning Point* (1978) and *White Nights* (1985), in which he appeared with the American dancer Gregory Hines, and television (*Sex and the City*).

Basil the Blessed, Saint
(unknown–1550)
priest and saint

One of the most famous and beloved of Russian saints, Saint Basil the Blessed is best known for the impressive cathedral on Moscow's RED SQUARE that bears his name. The details of his life are sketchy, although much has been handed down through sayings and legends. Saint Basil is said to have begun his religious life as a nomad, believing that through wandering he could become one with God. He is also said to have marched into Moscow and punished dishonest merchants, much in the way that Christ denounced the moneylenders in the Jerusalem Temple. Basil's life is often contrasted to that of Ivan the Terrible, who reigned during the last decades of his life. Although Basil died in 1550, before the worst excesses of Ivan's reign took place, Basil gained a reputation for openly reproaching Ivan's penchant for cruelty. Eventually he was buried in the recently built church of Our Lady of Kazan, which Ivan built to celebrate his victory over the khanate of KAZAN. In the 17th century, however, it was renamed Saint Basil's Cathedral, by which name it is still known.

"Basmachi"

A popular anticommunist resistance movement in the region of Turkestan (Russian Central Asia), at its strongest the Basmachi fought the Red Army from 1918 until 1923. The term "basmachi" originally referred to bandits or brigands, but by 1918 groups of fighters began to organize

Mikhail Baryshnikov *(Hulton/Archive)*

he expanded his repertoire to include newly choreographed ballets such as *Hamlet* (1970) and *The Creation of the World* (1971). In 1974, while touring Canada with the Bolshoi Ballet, Baryshnikov defected to the West. He settled in New York City, dancing mostly with the American Ballet Theater and the New York City Ballet. From 1980 to 1989 he served as artistic director of the American Ballet Theater. Working with leading choreographers such as George BALANCHINE (then in the twilight of his career), Twyla Tharp, and Jerome Robbins, Baryshnikov continued his broad range of performances, from classical ballets to modern dance. In 1990 he joined the choreographer Mark Morris to found the White Oak Dance Project, a modern dance in reaction to the growing Sovietization of the area and restrictions on Islamic religion and traditions. Initially, the movement was predominantly anti-Bolshevik and anti-Russian. The anti-Bolshevik autonomous government in Kokand employed some of the Basmachi as their military force, and after the suppression of the government by the BOLSHEVIKS, many of its adherents, including the prime minister, Mustafa Chokaev (1890–1941), fled to the Basmachi and organized them as guerrillas. The movement spread throughout the rural areas of Turkestan and at times reduced the Soviet authorities to the main cities and railways. In 1920, the movement acquired a more distinct Islamic profile in response to the strict enforcement of labor and military conscription and the Soviet government's attack on Muslim religious institutions. The Basmachi received a new shot of energy when the former war minister of the Ottoman Empire, Enver Pasha, joined the movement in November 1921. Shortly afterward the Bukharan government also joined the cause, but the impact was short-lived. Enver Pasha was killed in 1922, and the Red Army offensives led first by FRUNZE and then BUDENNYI gradually overcame Basmachi resistance. More significantly, the Soviet government relaxed many of the restrictions on Islamic practices that had sparked the initial opposition to its rule. By 1924, remnants of Basmachi bands were limited to the mountainous areas where they were intermittently active until the early 1930s and again during World War II.

Batu Khan (1208?–1255)

Mongol conqueror

Batu—the second son of Juchi, oldest son of Genghis (Chinggis) Khan—led the Mongol armies that conquered Russia between 1237 and 1241. After the death of his father in 1227, Batu became the head of his territories, which included lands from the Irtysh River to the Ural Mountains. In 1236, the long-planned Mongol invasion of Russia was launched with Batu as its

commander. The political states to the west of the Urals fell in rapid succession: the Volga Bulgar khanate in autumn 1237, the principality of Ryazan in December 1237, and the principality of Vladimir-Suzdal in February 1238. He then turned southward, capturing Pereiaslavl and Chernigov in 1239, and after a siege of 10 days, the great city of Kiev in December 1240. The following spring, Batu's troops crossed into eastern Europe, then turned southward, reaching the Adriatic coast in the winter of 1241–42. News of the death of Great Khan Ugedei compelled Batu to suspend his campaigns and return to the Mongol capital of Karakorum to be present at the election of a successor. He refused to recognize the election of Ugedei's son Guyuk as great khan. Guyuk died in 1248, while preparing a campaign against Batu. Despite Batu's seniority he was not elected great khan, the honor passing instead to a cousin and friend, Mongka. Although a nominal subject of the great khan, the Mongol Empire was now really broken into two parts, with Batu the ruler of its western part, known as the GOLDEN HORDE by Russian and Western historians. Under Batu the Golden Horde controlled vast territories from the Irtysh to the Dunai River. His older brother ruled territories to the east (northeast of the Aral Sea), known as the White Horde and subject to Batu. The Russian principalities, as vassal states, were required to pay tribute. He established his capital on the eastern banks of the Volga at Sarai-Batu (Old Sarai), along a rich commercial trade route, near ASTRAKHAN.

Bazhenov, Vasili Ivanovich (1737–1799)

architect

An immensely talented but unlucky architect, Bazhenov was born in Kaluga province, near Moscow, to a family of modest means. His father, a sexton in the Moscow Kremlin, arranged for the precocious Bazhenov to study with two important late baroque architects, Ukhtomsky and Chevakinsky. He entered the Academy of

Arts in St. Petersburg in 1758 and two years later apprenticed with Bartolomeo RASTRELLI. From 1761 to 1765, he studied in Paris and Italy, and was honored with election to the academies of Rome, Florence, and Bologna. Back in St. Petersburg he sought, without success, an appointment as professor at the Academy of Arts; he would have to wait almost two decades, until 1784, to be elected to the academy. Bazhenov's work, distinguished by lavish use of columns and curves, added a "Russian" touch of Muscovite and baroque to the neoclassicist fashion of the late 18th century. Although he was admired and influential, few of his projects were built as designed. His reputation rests largely on plans for the reconstruction of the Moscow Kremlin, which by the time of CATHERINE II's coronation in 1762 had fallen into alarming disrepair, and for a new imperial palace in Tsaritsyno, to the south of Moscow. Together with Matvei Fedorovich Kazakov (1738–1813), Bazhenov worked on extensive and grandiose plans for the Kremlin begun in 1767 but abandoned after 1774 for unexplained, possibly financial, reasons. Bazhenov's plans for Tsaritsyno (1776–85) featured a unique Gothic style well before the Gothic revival in western Europe. The project was also abandoned after 10 years of extensive work; Kazakov later built a more modest version of Bazhenov's palace. The failure of the Kremlin and Tsaritsyno projects and Bazhenov's role as a leading Freemason contributed to his fall from favor in the mid-1780s. He survived on private commissions, the most important of which led to the building of the Pashkov House (1784–86), situated on a hill across from the southwest side of the Kremlin, today the Old Building of the Russian State (former Lenin) Library.

Beard Tax

A tax on beards that resulted from PETER I the Great's 1698 decree ordering all Russians, except clergy and peasants, to shave. Peter considered that beards were a symbol of all that was backward and non-European about Muscovite society. For most Orthodox Russians, however, the beard was a fundamental symbol of religious belief and self-respect, an ornament given by God, worn by the prophets, the apostles, and Jesus himself. Priests refused to bless beardless men, considering them shameful, unclean, and beyond the pale of Christendom. Attitudes toward beards, however, were beginning to change in 17th-century Moscow with the arrival of merchants, soldiers, and engineers from Europe, where beardless faces had long been fashionable. Peter's father, Czar ALEKSEI, had already relaxed restrictions on shaving, but few Muscovites had actually shaved their beards off before Peter's decree. Peter's attack on beards began in September 1698, on his return from the GRAND EMBASSY, when he assembled his grandees and surprised them by proceeding to shave their beards with his own barber's razor. A few exceptions were made, including the patriarch, but in the next few months the practice was enshrined in a decree that exempted only clergy and peasants from shaving. Peter's officials were empowered to shave on the spot anyone they encountered. As Peter's initial antibeard zeal waned, eventually those who wished to keep their beards could do so, providing they paid an annual beard tax. The amount paid ranged from two kopeks for peasants to 900 rubles for wealthy merchants. The taxpayer then received a bronze medallion with a picture of a beard and the words *den'gi vziaty* (tax paid) inscribed on it, which was to be worn on a chain round the neck. Some Russians, like the traditionalist OLD BELIEVERS, wore their medallion like a badge of honor, but over time the decree was widely ignored and tax payments evaded, although it was reissued several times and beards were not allowed in state service until the 19th century.

Beilis Affair (1911–1913)

A judicial process that exposed and inflamed feelings of ANTI-SEMITISM feelings in Russia. On March 20, 1911, the body of Andrusha Iushchinsky, a 13-year-old member of a gang of thieves, was found in a cave in Kiev. Coming close to the Easter season, local leaflets brought up the usual anti-Semitic canard of Jewish ritual murders of Christian boys. The rightist, anti-Semitic national press, concerned with discussions in the State DUMA about easing legal and residential restrictions against Jews, disseminated the charges and exacerbated anti-Semitic feelings. Rightist forces in Kiev contributed to the mood by calling for a POGROM and the expulsion of all Jews from the city. Although Kiev detectives soon concluded that fellow gang members had probably murdered Iushchinsky, the Ministry of Justice opened proceedings in July 1911 against Menachem Mendel Beilis, a Jewish dispatcher at a Kiev brickworks owned by a wealthy Jewish businessman. To the government's credit, the frequent calls for a pogrom against Kiev's Jewish community were averted, thanks to the efforts of the prime minister, V. M. Kokovtsev. Nevertheless, prosecution of the Beilis case took more than two years, attracting worldwide attention and exposing the government's almost desperate drive to establish Beilis's guilt, despite evidence to the contrary. The bureaucracy's desire to have Beilis found guilty was demonstrated by the pressure applied to lawyers and judges, harassment of newspapers reporting the case, and the Ministry of Justice's frantic search for an "expert" to testify that Jews did use Christian blood in certain rituals around Passover. In October 1913, after a trial and retrial, Beilis was finally acquitted, although in its verdict the court still did not rule out the possibility that unknown Jews were guilty of the murder. Beilis subsequently emigrated to the United States, where he died in 1934. Like the Dreyfus affair in France, the Beilis affair exposed the depth of anti-Semitic feeling in Russian official and rightist political circles.

Belinsky, Vissarion Grigorievich
(1811–1848)
literary critic

The foremost literary critic of the 1830s and 1840s, Belinsky shaped the course of Russian lit-

erature in the next half century through his belief that literature needed to convey a social purpose. An ardent Westernizer in the intellectual debates with the Slavophiles, Belinsky was born in Sveaborg, Finland, the son of a medical army officer, and grew up in the province of Penza, to the southeast of Moscow. In 1829 he entered the University of Moscow and two years later began publishing poetry and literary reviews. Authorship of *Dmitrii Kalinin,* a play that criticized SERFDOM, led to his expulsion from the university in 1832. Belinsky turned to journalism, publishing in some of the leading journals of the day such as *Moscow Observer, Notes of the Fatherland,* and *The Contemporary.* After recovering from poor health in the Caucasus, he returned to Moscow and edited *Moscow Observer* from 1838 to 1839. In 1839 he moved to St. Petersburg to become editor of the influential journal *Notes of the Fatherland,* a position he held until 1846. During these years Belinsky consolidated his reputation as a leading representative of the radical intelligentsia and strong defender of the "Westernizer" position in the seminal intellectual debates of the 1840s with the Slavophiles. Approaching art and literature from a utilitarian perspective influenced by Hegel and German romanticism, Belinsky argued that they should aim for the transformation of society rather than emphasize purely aesthetic principles. For the next half century after his death, Belinsky's views provided the foundation for the dominant strain of Russian art and literature. As a critic and editor, Belinsky's voice was instrumental in consolidating the reputations of Alexander PUSHKIN and Mikhail LERMONTOV and in advancing the careers of future literary giants such as Ivan TURGENEV, Fyodor DOSTOEVSKY, and Nikolai GOGOL. His correspondence with the latter was an important milestone in Russian intellectual history, particularly the famous "Letter to Gogol" of July 2, 1847, in which he attacked Gogol's defense of religion, the church, and state authorities as a betrayal of the common good. Published by Gogol soon after, czarist authorities quickly moved to ban its circulation. Nevertheless, the letter was widely distributed through clandestine channels and became essential reading for Russian liberals. Marriage to Maria Orlova produced a son and a daughter. Generally in poor health, Belinsky went abroad in 1847 to recover from tuberculosis. He returned to St. Petersburg in November 1847 and worked briefly for the journal *The Contemporary* as its review editor. His health never fully recovered, however, and he died of consumption in June 1848.

Bely, Andrei (1880–1934)
writer

A writer of dazzling, complex poetry, prose, and literary criticism who emerged as a major spokesman of the younger generation that helped shape Russia's Silver Age. Born Boris Nikolaevich Bugaev, Bely was the son of a well-known mathematician and dean of the faculty of science at Moscow University, from where he also received a degree in mathematics. His early work, in which he attempted to create the effect of musical compositions, was impressive in its virtuosity but difficult and somewhat contrived. Bely's talents were first recognized by a broader audience with the publication of his first novel, *The Silver Dove* (1909), about a sect that follows a RASPUTIN-like figure. Influenced by GOGOL, the novel combines the fantastic and the irrational, a style that Bely would develop throughout his work. His next novel, *Petersburg* (1913), is perhaps his best-known work. Here Bely plays with long-standing Russian literary themes such as the antinomy between East and West and the generational split between "fathers and sons," all in the context of terrorism and revolution of the early 20th century. Immensely talented and quick-witted, he dabbled in the many intellectual currents of the time such as Symbolism, Mysticism, and FUTURISM, frustrating many by what they perceived as his intellectual fickleness. A good friend of the poet Aleksandr BLOK, together they admired the work of the philosopher Vladimir SOLOVIEV. Attracted by the spiritual and mystical teachings of Rudolf Steiner,

Bely traveled to Switzerland to study with him, but they soon fell out and Bely returned to Russia in 1916. After the OCTOBER REVOLUTION he left Russia again but returned in 1923 and he continued to publish. His *Recollections of Alexander Blok* (1922) was an incisive account of the great poet and the Symbolist movement in general. Three other volumes of "Recollections," published between 1931 and 1934, re-create in Bely's usual style, often laced with humor, the remarkable early-20th-century world of Russian letters and culture. A man who frequently changed intellectual allegiances, after his final return to Russia Bely sought to imbue his writings with Marxism.

Berdiaev, Nikolai Aleksandrovich (1874–1948)
philosopher

Born in Kiev into a noble family, Berdiaev became one of the leading representatives of a group of early-20th-century intellectuals who moved from a materialist Marxist to a spiritualist Christian outlook. Berdiaev first studied law at Kiev University. Early involvement in revolutionary activities led to a brief term of exile in the northern region of Vologda in 1898. Released, he traveled to Germany for further studies. He returned to St. Petersburg in 1904 and became coeditor with Sergei BULGAKOV of *Voprosy zhizni* (*Problems of Life*), a philosophy journal. Berdiaev's work, often defined as personalism or Christian existentialism, stressed the value of individual liberty and freedom, which he considered to be the precondition of all true existence. His nonacademic approach to philosophy, and his colorful style, relying on aphorisms, account for the great popularity his work enjoyed. He himself considered his nonacademic approach to philosophy a virtue. After the OCTOBER REVOLUTION, Berdiaev taught at the private Academy of Spiritual Culture in Moscow until 1922, when, together with a large group of prominent intellectuals, he was expelled from Soviet Russia. After a short stay in Berlin, he settled near Paris in 1925, married, and became very active in the Russian émigré community as an author, editor, and publisher. Berdiaev was one of the founders of the influential YMCA Press in Paris, which published most of the prominent Russian émigré authors throughout the Soviet era. During the 1930s his reputation grew in the West, a result of his prolific writings on philosophy and books like *The Origins of Russian Communism* and *On Slavery and Freedom of Man.* During World War II, he supported the Soviet government and even took a Soviet passport, but he never returned to his homeland. He received an honorary doctorate from Oxford University in 1947, and at the time of his death in Paris he was the best-known living Russian philosopher.

Beria, Lavrenty Pavlovich (1899–1953)
Soviet official

One of the most sinister and feared officials in Joseph STALIN's close circle, Beria ruled as people's commissar for internal affairs and head of the Soviet internal security empire from 1939 until 1953. Beria was born in Georgia, a member of the Mingrelian ethnic minority. He joined the BOLSHEVIK Party in 1917 and, after the civil war, worked as the director of the Transcaucasian branches of the secret police (Cheka) and its successor, the OGPU. As first secretary of the COMMUNIST PARTY in Transcaucasia from 1932 to 1938, he ruled as virtual dictator. In 1938, Stalin brought him to Moscow and named him commissar of internal affairs (NKVD), successor to Nikolai YEZHOV, who had implemented the main stages of the Great Purge. As commissar, Beria oversaw the execution of Yezhov and many of his associates, organized the mass deportations of non-Russian nationalities in Soviet areas occupied by the Germans during World War II, and administered as a personal empire the vast network of slave labor camps known as the GULAG. In 1941 he was appointed deputy prime minister in charge of security affairs, a position he held until 1953. Beria is most closely identified with the unparalleled repressive police state that characterized the Stalin regime, especially in

Lavrenty Beria *(Library of Congress)*

its last decade. He survived Stalin by only a few months. Fearful of the immense power and information he had amassed in his career with the secret police, KHRUSHCHEV and MALENKOV agreed long enough to direct his arrest in July 1953 on trumped-up charges of "criminal anti-party and anti-state activities." He was executed in December 1953. Sadistic and known for his lecherous pursuit of young women, Beria occupies a prominent place in the gallery of 20th-century political thugs. Relief over his execution, and his personal cowardice in defeat, makes it hard to assess the extent to which he truly believed in some of the more liberal policies he advocated in the second half of 1953.

Bering, Vitus Jonassen (1681–1741)
explorer and navigator

Danish by birth, Bering entered the Russian navy as a sub-lieutenant in 1704 and served in the Baltic and Azov fleets until 1724. In 1725, shortly before PETER I the Great's death, he was appointed commander of the First Kamchatka Expedition (1725–30), whose secret mission was to discover whether Siberia was joined to North America. In July 1728, the vessel *Saint Gavriil* sailed under Bering's command from the Kamchatka peninsula, in a northeastern direction. The expedition established that a strait divided the two continents and gathered important information about eastern Siberia. Ironically, this question had already been answered in 1648 by Semyon DEZHNEV, a Cossack, who had sailed from the mouth of the Kolyma River on the Arctic around northeastern Siberia, and through the strait that now carries Bering's name. His report, however, lay unread in a Siberian archive until 1736. In 1733, a second Kamchatka expedition was formed, again under Bering's leadership. Its mission was broader. In addition to the vexing question of the link between Asia and North America, its members were to map the Arctic Ocean coastline, study the region of the Far East and the northern Pacific, and sail to Japan from Kamchatka. After unusual delays in preparing the expedition, the *Saint Peter,* commanded by Bering, and the *Saint Paul,* commanded by his assistant Chirikov, left the port of Okhotsk toward Kamchatka in September 1740, where Bering founded the town of Petropavlovsk-on-Kamchatka. After wintering in the region, the ships set sail again toward the east, but on June 20, 1741, they lost contact with each other. On July 16, one and a half days after Chirikov, Bering reached the coast of ALASKA. On the return trip he discovered the Shumaginskii islands and part of the Aleutians. After a difficult journey home, the *Saint Peter* did not reach Kamchatka but instead sailed toward what is now Bering Island, where the expedition planned to winter. Already in very poor physical condition, Bering died on the island.

Berlin, Congress of (1878)

An international meeting held in the German capital in June–July 1878 that is regarded as a major setback for Russian diplomacy. The Congress of Berlin was convened to revise the Treaty of SAN STEFANO, which had ended the RUSSO-TURKISH WAR OF 1877–78 but aroused concerns among European powers about its provisions. With the German chancellor Otto von Bismarck acting as its chairman and attended by senior European statesmen such as British prime minister Benjamin Disraeli, the congress met from June 13 to July 13, 1878. Russia was represented by its long-standing foreign minister, Aleksandr GORCHAKOV, by then almost 80 years old. Negotiations resulted in the Treaty of Berlin, signed on August 24, 1878, which maintained a few of the provisions of the Treaty of San Stefano but altered it in several important ways. Serbia, Montenegro, and Romania retained the independence from the Ottoman Empire that had been previously awarded to them. Russia was allowed to keep the territories it had gained in the Caucasus, as well as southern Bessarabia. On the other hand, the borders of the new state of Bulgaria were drastically reduced. The Bulgarian territories located north of the Balkan Mountains, roughly one-third of the Bulgarian state created at San Stefano, became an autonomous state. The territory known as Eastern Rumelia, located to the south of the Balkan Mountains, remained under Ottoman rule, albeit under a special status, until 1885, when it was added to the autonomous Bulgarian lands to create a new independent Bulgaria. The Macedonian lands granted to Bulgaria at San Stefano remained under Turkish rule and would become a source of contention during the Balkan wars of the early 20th century as the Ottoman Empire further disintegrated. The Congress of Berlin also ratified Austria-Hungary's occupation of Bosnia-Herzegovina, without giving it the right to annex the former Ottoman province.

Bezborodko, Aleksandr Andreevich (1747–1799)
statesman

Of Ukrainian Cossack background, Bezborodko became an influential official and diplomat during the reign of CATHERINE II the Great. He first began his government service in 1765 in the chancellery of governor-general of the Ukraine, P. A. Rumiantsev. Ten years later, he was appointed secretary to Catherine and, as such, prepared her manifestos and other documents until 1792. From the late 1780s to 1792, he reported daily to Catherine. A member of the College of Foreign Affairs since 1780, Bezborodko was in charge of Russian foreign policy from 1784 to 1796. During this time he participated in the preparation and negotiations of the most important moments of late 18th-century Russian foreign policy: Turkish recognition of the Russian annexation of the Crimea (1783), the favorable Jassy Treaty with Turkey (1791), and the third partition of Poland (1795). Although important by his rank, Bezborodko was more of an executor of the course laid down by Catherine, rather than an inventive diplomat. He retained his position in the college after Catherine's death and, in 1797, obtained the rank of chancellor and the title of enlightened prince. He was a major landowner in the south and used his important position to obtain huge latifundia in the southern Ukraine.

Biron, Ernst Johann (1690–1772)
(Ernst Johann Buhren)
official

A favorite of Empress ANNA (1730–40), Biron was born to a noble family in the province of Kurland. As of 1718 he was attached to the court of the future empress, traveling with her to St. Petersburg in 1730 when she was chosen to succeed PETER II, who had died childless. Biron was made a count in 1730, and although his official duties were only those of high chamberlain, he is generally considered to have been the true power behind the throne during Anna's reign. In 1737 she arranged for him to be elected duke of Kurland, and shortly before her death, in October 1740, named him regent to the infant IVAN VI, her successor. Biron's fortunes changed soon after Anna's death. Regent for only one month,

he was overthrown in November 1740 by his enemy Burkhard Munnich, a German military specialist who had come to Russia during the reign of PETER I the Great and risen to a position of great influence. Ivan's mother, Anna Leopoldovna, who herself would be overthrown a year later by ELIZABETH, became regent. Biron was charged with attempting to seize the throne and sentenced to death, but the sentence was commuted to exile, which he first served in Pelyi and then in Yaroslavl. Elizabeth's successor, PETER III, allowed Biron to return to St. Petersburg in 1762, and CATHERINE II subsequently restored him to the duchy of Kurland, which he passed on to his son in 1769, a few years before his death. Evaluations of Biron have long been colored by the pejorative term *Bironovshchina* (the time of Biron), with its connotations of arbitrary, repressive rule by a German clique. This interpretation took shape fairly quickly during Elizabeth's reign (1741–62), when it was used to consolidate her power and was later propagated by nationalist Russian and Soviet historians who highlighted the issues of anti-German feeling. Recent Russian scholarship shows that although they were perhaps in more visible positions, the proportion of foreigners in institutions like the army actually fell during Anna's reign.

Black Hundreds

A generic and pejorative term applied to a number of ultrarightist populist organizations in the first decade of the 20th century, of which the most prominent was the Union of the Russian People. Other organizations that fell within the purview of the Black Hundreds are the Russian Assembly, the Union of Russian Men, the Russian Monarchist Union, and the Union of the Archangel Michael. Most of these organizations appeared in the aftermath of the 1905 Revolution as a reaction of political forces that defined themselves as patriotic to the events of that year. Although their members came from various social backgrounds, they were united by a profound distaste for Jews and Poles and the intelligentsia, all of whom they considered to be responsible for the spread of "foreign" revolutionary socialist and liberal ideas among the Russian people. While endorsing better conditions for workers and peasants, they also shared a yearning for the old ideals of autocracy and nationalism bound together by Russian Orthodoxy. Their public activities ranged from popular demonstrations where crowds would carry icons and portraits of the royal family, while they sang patriotic songs, to organized pogroms against Jews, as well as intimidation of radical university students and other revolutionary "sympathizers." The Black Hundreds found support within small sectors of the police, the officer corps, the Russian Orthodox Church, the landed nobility, and the lower middle classes, but their actual membership was far below the millions they claimed at the time. The Union of the Russian People stood out from the others, partly for the leadership provided by a St. Petersburg physician, A. I. Dubrovin, and partly because of some positive public references to the group on the part of NICHOLAS II. With the victory of the OCTOBER REVOLUTION in 1917, the Black Hundreds disappeared from Russian public life; Dubrovin was executed by the Bolsheviks in 1918.

Blok, Aleksandr Aleksandrovich (1880–1921)

poet

Born in St. Petersburg, Blok was brought up in the family of his maternal grandparents after his parents separated. A published poet since 1903, he graduated in 1906 from St. Petersburg University with a degree in philology. Soon after, he married the daughter of the noted chemist Dmitrii MENDELEEV. His early views were those of the liberal gentry, shaped by the intellectual influence of Vladimir SOLOVIEV and the Russian countryside near Moscow. Shy and reclusive, he nevertheless became one of the most popular poets of the Silver Age, capturing the mood of the moment with poems that combined the feelings of a populist, penitent noble with the apoc-

alyptic imagery of Symbolism. Beyond his poetry he participated in public life, writing articles that explored the cultural gap between the intelligentsia and the masses, which had long bedeviled most attempts at wide-ranging social change. In 1917 he took part in the Muraviev Commission, which investigated czarist leaders after the FEBRUARY REVOLUTION. He welcomed the revolution but characteristically interpreted it as a symbolic historical moment with apocalyptic connotations. His most lasting literary legacy is the remarkable poem *The Twelve,* which scandalized both sides of the revolutionary divide with its haunting imagery comparing 12 Red Guards with the 12 apostles as they move through Petrograd following a fleeting vision of Christ. It remains the most artistically significant, contemporary literary celebration of the 1917 Revolution. Just before his death at an early age, he protested against the increasingly oppressive atmosphere under communist rule.

Bloody Sunday

A massacre of demonstrators at the Winter Palace in St. Petersburg that marks the beginning of the 1905 Revolution. The background to the events of Blood Sunday deal with the activities of the Assembly of St. Petersburg Factory Workers, a group led by Father GAPON, an activist priest with links to the city police. Gapon had organized a group of workers in the spirit of the ideals of "police socialism," inspired by Sergei ZUBATOV. The group, however, had been infiltrated by Social Democratic revolutionaries who pressed a more radical agenda than Gapon was willing to follow, organizing a strike at the Putilov plant that quickly spread to other parts of the city. Whether driven to prove his credentials with his workers or because he sympathized with their demands, Gapon agreed to organize a march to the czar's palace to petition for basic economic and political reforms. On Sunday, January 9, 1905 (O.S.) a procession of workers and families marched to the palace, where they were met by troops of cavalry and mounted police who ordered them to disperse. When they refused, the soldiers shot at the crowd, killing about 800 demonstrators and wounding even more. A wave of indignation swept the country and united opposition to the czar. An unprecedented number of factories across Russia went on strike, students also struck, and educated society and intellectuals of all stripes condemned the intolerance and cruelty of the regime. NICHOLAS II, who had inherited the informal title of *batiushka* (little father) accorded by the common people and peasants to their ruler, now became *Nikolai krovavyi*, (Bloody Nicholas). Unnerved by the extent and intensity of the opposition, a few weeks later Nicholas II agreed to the creation of an elected State DUMA (parliament) with an advisory role, but these and other concessions were deemed insufficient, and what became the 1905 Revolution took on its own dynamic.

bogatyr

From a term that means "hero" or "warrior," a *bogatyr* (pl. *bogatyri*) was one of a group of heroes who appear in traditional folktales or legends (*bylini*) that have been transmitted orally since the era of KIEVAN RUS. Many of the legends about *bogatyri* are set in the time of VLADIMIR I, who converted Russia to Christianity. Stories about the *bogatyri* helped bridge the myths of pre-Christian Russia with those of the new Christian era. In some accounts *bogatyri* were heroic champions, almost demigods, who traveled the countryside on horseback to search out evil, as depicted in the well-known painting *Bogatyr*, by Viktor Vasnetsov (1898). In other accounts they are represented as holy warriors, defending Holy Russia from invaders, especially the Mongols. One of the best known of the *bogatyri* was ILYA MUROMETS, the subject of a poem of the same name written in 1795 by Nikolai KARAMZIN.

Bolsheviks

Members of one of the two factions of the Marxist-based Russian Social Democratic Labor Party that took shape after the 1903 party congress in

London. Relying on a procedural vote taken at the congress, the faction led by Vladimir LENIN won a majority and became known as "Bolsheviks," from the Russian word for *majority*, while the other faction became known as "Mensheviks," from the term for *minority*. The divisions within the Russian Marxist movement had been brewing for close to a decade centered on the nature of the revolutionary party and its organization. The Bolsheviks advocated a centralized and disciplined party of professional revolutionaries; the Mensheviks wanted a loosely organized mass party. There were also important ideological distinctions based on different interpretations of Marxism. Led by Georgi PLEKHANOV, the founder of Russian Marxism, the Mensheviks followed a strict adherence to the tenets of Marxism, arguing that before Russia could move to a period of socialist and proletarian rule, it needed to experience capitalism with a bourgeois regime. The Bolsheviks believed that Russia's unique experience, its incomplete capitalist development, and its weak bourgeoisie allowed for a different path to socialism. In his famous pamphlet *What Is to Be Done?* (1905), Lenin advanced a theory of revolution that called for an alliance of workers and peasants to overthrow the czarist government and establish a transitional dictatorship of the proletariat and peasantry. While significant, these differences were not always clear-cut, and many revolutionaries, such as Leon TROTSKY, moved from one faction to another, even after 1912, when Bolsheviks and Mensheviks officially became separate parties. On the eve of the FEBRUARY REVOLUTION, the Bolsheviks were still few, united in their opposition to Russia's continued participation in World War I. With Lenin's return to Russia from exile in April 1917, the Bolsheviks emerged as the most consistent opponents of the Petrograd Soviet's policy of "dual power," or collaboration with the Provisional Government, calling instead for an immediate transfer of power to the Soviets, or councils of worker and soldier deputies, and an end to the war. During the course of 1917, as the Provisional Government lost its initial support, the Bolsheviks gained majorities in most of the soviets that had sprung up around the country, especially the Petrograd Soviet. On October 25, 1917 (O.S.), they took power in Petrograd in the name of the soviets and, once victorious, proceeded to establish a new revolutionary government. Initially they had the support of the Left Socialist Revolutionaries but lost it in March 1918, when Soviet Russia signed a separate peace with Germany. In 1919 the Bolshevik Party changed its name to the COMMUNIST PARTY to maximize the break with the other socialist parties that had wavered in their support of the Bolshevik Revolution. Throughout the 1920s and 1930s, the term "Bolshevik" remained in usage, especially in connection to the Communist Party members who had joined the party before 1919. Known as Old Bolsheviks, these party members bore the brunt of STALIN's purges and terror of the 1930s. Nevertheless, the official name continued to be Communist Party (Bolshevik) until 1952, when it became the Communist Party of the Soviet Union (CPSU).

Bonch-Bruevich, Vladimir Dmitrievich (1873–1955)
ethnographer and revolutionary

A close associate of LENIN, Bonch-Bruevich was also a recognized ethnographer and expert on Russian religious sectarianism. The son of a land surveyor, Bonch-Bruevich became interested in revolutionary activity from an early age and was banished from Moscow in 1889. Four years later he returned to Moscow and joined Marxist study circles, becoming a member of the Social Democratic Party in 1895. In 1896 he enrolled in the faculty of natural sciences at the University of Zurich, from which time he developed a close working relationship and friendship with Lenin. In 1903 Bonch-Bruevich joined the Bolshevik faction. Bonch-Bruevich's talents were many. As an editor, he was involved in various legal and illegal Bolshevik publishing efforts from 1905 through the 1917 Revolutions. At one time or another, he worked on the most important Social Democratic or Bolshevik newspapers, *Vpered, Zhizn i znanie, Zvezda, Pravda, Rabochii i soldat,* and

Izvestia, the latter the newspaper of the Petrograd Soviet in 1917. After the October Revolution, he organized the Soviet publishing industry. Well versed in military matters, Bonch-Bruevich served as commander of the Smolny district in Petrograd during the October Revolution and as a member of the committee for the revolutionary defense of Petrograd. He was also the founding chairman of the Petrograd Commission for the Struggle against Counterrevolution, later known as the Cheka. As an administrator, Bonch-Bruevich served as executive secretary of Lenin's government and organized the transfer of the Soviet government from Petrograd to Moscow in March 1918. Bonch-Bruevich's interest in ethnography and religious sects dated from an 1899 trip to Canada with a group of religious sectarians known as DUKHOBORS. In 1913 he interviewed RASPUTIN and wrote a report absolving him of the charge of sectarianism, allowing him to continue in public life. A lifelong admirer of Leo TOLSTOY, he founded and directed the Lesnye Polyany state farm (1920–29), its name adapted from Tolstoy's famous home. From 1925 to 1939, he edited the publication of Tolstoy's collected works. In 1933 he was appointed director of the State Literary Museum, and in 1945 he became the director of the Museum of History of Religion and Atheism in Leningrad, a post he occupied until the year of his death.

His wife, Vera Mikailovna, was also a revolutionary and played a key role in organizing Soviet health care. His brother, Mikhail Dmitrievich (1870–1956), a specialist on geodesy and cartography, was an officer in the Imperial Army who, in October 1917, became one of the first czarist officers to join the Red Army. During the civil war, he occupied important posts in Bolshevik headquarters and eventually attained the rank of general.

Bondarchuk, Sergei Feodorovich (1920–1994)
actor and film director

A Ukrainian actor and film director, Sergei Bondarchuk is perhaps best remembered for his lavish eight-hour-long version of Leo TOLSTOY's *War and Peace* (1967), which he directed and in which he played the central role. Bondarchuk was born in ODESSA and studied at the School of Theater in the town of Rostov-on-Don. He served in the army during World War II. He made his film debut in the cinematic version of Mikhail BULGAKOV's novel *The Young Guard* (1948), but it was his performance in the biographical film *Taras Shevchenko* that brought Bondarchuk to the attention of the film world. Other films followed in the mid-1950s, such as *The Grasshopper* (1955) and *Othello* (1956). Already established as one of the leading young actors of Soviet film, Bondarchuk made an impressive directorial debut with *Destiny of a Man*, based on Mikhail SHOLOKOV's short story about a Soviet war prisoner. The topic was still considered politically sensitive, in light of Joseph STALIN's harsh treatment of Soviet POWs after World War II, and thus was a test of the relative political openness of late 1950s Russia. An honest treatment of a difficult topic, *Destiny of a Man* was internationally recognized at various film festivals and won the first prize at the First Moscow International Film Festival, held in 1959. His reputation as a director secured, Bondarchuk was chosen to direct *War and Peace* (1966–67), a project that was meant to serve as a Soviet cultural statement and received generous funding (about $100 million) from the Soviet government. Epic in scope and execution (20,000 extras alone were used in filming the Battle of BORODINO), the film was artistically less creative than Bondarchuk's previous work, but nevertheless was very popular with Soviet film audiences. It also led to *Waterloo* (1970), an Italian-Soviet collaboration and thematic sequel to *War and Peace*. In 1971 he was appointed secretary of the Union of Soviet Filmmakers, a highly important post in the world of Soviet film, which he held until May 1986. By that time Bondarchuk had become one of the many symbols of corrupt or coopted leadership in the various branches of arts, letters, and the Soviet professional world. At the Filmmakers' Union Congress of May 1986 a new

leadership led by Elem KLIMOV, taking their cues from Mikhail GORBACHEV's early pronouncements about glasnost (openness), ousted the old leadership, Bondarchuk included, and made film one of the more creative arts of the late 1980s. Also in 1986, Bondarchuk released his last film *Boris Godunov*, based on Aleksandr PUSHKIN's novel. Shortly before his death, in a gesture of reconciliation before his death, Bondarchuk was named vice president of the union he had once headed.

Boris and Gleb (unknown–1015)
saints and princes

The youngest sons of VLADIMIR I THE GREAT, grand prince of Kiev, Boris and Gleb were killed in battle and canonized by the Orthodox Church, becoming Russia's first national saints. Little is known about their early lives, except that they were born to the same mother, a Bulgarian woman, one of Vladimir's many concubines. Upon reaching adulthood, around the years 987–89, Boris became prince of Rostov and Gleb prince of Murom. During the power struggle that followed Vladimir's death in 1015, they were killed by their half brother Sviatopolk, hence known as "the Damned," who himself was defeated and killed by another half brother, Yaroslav "the Wise" in 1019. In 1072 they were canonized as "Protectors of the Land of Rus" by the (Russian) church.

Over the centuries, as saints and martyrs, Boris and Gleb came to occupy an important place in the emerging popular and religious mythology of KIEVAN RUS and Muscovy, and their fate was given various interpretive twists. The earliest account of their deaths, the 12th-century *Primary Chronicle*, stresses that both Boris and Gleb were aware of Sviatopolk's plans to kill them and chose to submit to their fate rather than fight back. Here, Boris and Gleb accept their suffering in a Christ-like manner to save Kiev from internal divisions. Later interpretations added a more explicitly political component by emphasizing that the lesson to be learned from their martyrdom was that younger princes needed to subordinate themselves to older ones in the name of national unity. Other accounts focus on the pagan roots of the cult of Boris and Gleb and the legends that grew around them in an agrarian nation that had only recently been officially converted to Christianity under the reign of Vladimir. In this version, Saint Boris was a smith who forged the first plow with the help of Saint Gleb, using 12 golden hammers and tongs that weighed over 400 pounds.

Borodino, Battle of (1812)

Generally regarded as one of the deadliest European battles of the 19th century, the Battle of Borodino was fought on September 7, 1812, on the outskirts of Moscow during the Napoleonic Wars. Following Napoleon's invasion of Russia of June 1812, the Russian armies had retreated eastward, but by the late summer, following the Russian defeat at the Battle of Smolensk, there was increasing pressure on ALEXANDER I to confront Napoleon's armies before they reached Moscow. Alexander relieved BARCLAY DE TOLLY of command and replaced him with Mikhail KUTUZOV, a 67-year-old general. Kutuzov chose to build earthworks on the road to Borodino, a village located about 75 miles to the southwest of Moscow, and gathered an army of about 125,000 soldiers. Napoleon's army, numbering about 130,000 soldiers, reached Borodino on September 6, 1812. The following day a fierce battle ensued that resulted in about 40,000 casualties for the Russians and close to 58,000 for Napoleon and his allies. Thousands of officers, including Prince Petr BAGRATION, were among the casualties on both sides. By nightfall, even though the Russians had only retreated slightly, Kutuzov ordered the army to withdraw to the southwest, leaving Moscow open for Napoleon to enter. One week later, on September 14, 1812, Napoleon entered the city and took residence in the Kremlin, expecting that Alexander I would soon sue for peace. Instead he faced Alexander's refusal to negotiate, fires through-

out Moscow, and the prospect of a long winter deep in Russian territory. On October 19, Napoleon began the long, painful retreat from Russia, which, by the time his armies crossed the border at the Berezina River, had decimated his army.

Borovik, Genrikh (1929–) and Artyom (1960–2000)
journalists

Two well-connected journalists, father and son, from the postwar Soviet era, the Boroviks gave an international polish to Soviet journalism. Genrikh Aviezerovich Borovik was born in 1929. He first made his reputation in the late 1950s with his reports about the Cuban revolution for the weekly *Ogonek,* featuring interviews with Fidel Castro and Ernest Hemingway. From 1966 to 1972, he worked in New York City for the Soviet news agency, Novosti Press. At his luxurious apartment in Moscow, he hosted Arthur Miller, Norman Mailer, John Updike, and Hemingway's widow, Mary. His government connections, his ability to interview reclusive personalities like the Soviet spy Kim Philby and the CIA defector Edward Lee Howard, and his chairmanship of the Soviet Peace Committee, a KGB-controlled organization, led many to assume he also had intelligence connections. In addition to his foreign correspondence, he wrote several books of journalistic value about his travels in Cuba, Argentina, and the United States. An English-language version of the book, *The Philby Files: The Secret Life of Master Spy Kim Philby,* which he coauthored with Philip Knightley, was published in 1994.

His son, Artyom Genrikhovich Borovik, was born in 1960 and followed in his journalistic footsteps. Born in Moscow, he was educated at the elite Moscow English School, and then at the Dalton School in New York City, during his father's tenure there for Novosti Press. In 1981, he graduated from the prestigious Moscow Institute of International Relations (MGIMO), the training school for Soviet diplomats. After a tour of duty in the Soviet embassy in Peru, he turned to journalism and worked on *Ogonek,* by the 1980s a liberal voice, supportive of Mikhail GOR-BACHEV's glasnost (openness) campaign. The editor in chief, Vitali Korotich, sent Borovik to cover the AFGHANISTAN War. Borovik's accounts of the war were distinguished by their honesty and sensitivity in portraying the horrors of war for young Soviet soldiers. A product of the cultural elite of the late Soviet era, like his father, he moved easily between the worlds of Soviet and international journalism. A translation of his writings on the Afghan war, *The Hidden War: A Russian Journalist's Account of the Soviet War in Afghanistan,* was first published in English to some acclaim in 1992. Artyom Borovik was killed in an airplane crash on March 9, 2000, with eight others on a charter flight going from Moscow to Kiev.

Botvinnik, Mikhail Moiseevich (1911–1995)
chess player

One of the greatest Russian and world chess players of all time, Botvinnik held the title of world champion for all but two years from 1948 to 1965. Botvinnik was born in St. Petersburg to a dental technician and a dentist who separated when he was nine. He started playing chess at the age of 12. Two years later, in 1925, the first intimation of future greatness came when he defeated the then world champion, José Raul Capablanca, in a simultaneous exhibition. Although he won the title of chess master in 1927, he did not devote himself full time to chess until he completed his engineering studies at the Leningrad Polytechnic Institute in 1933. By then he had won two Soviet chess championships, in 1931 and 1933. His first major international victory came in 1935 at the Moscow International, where he tied for first with Salo Flohr, For the rest of the 1930s, Botvinnik continued to consolidate his position as one of the rising young stars in international chess. After winning the 1941 USSR chess champi-

onship, he spent most of World War II using his engineering skills at a high-tension laboratory in the Urals, for which he later received an Order of the Badge of Honor. By the end of the war Botvinnik had emerged as the almost unchallengeable dominant Soviet chess player, winning back-to-back USSR championships in 1944 and 1945. Negotiations were in progress for a highly anticipated match with Alexander ALEKHINE, the eccentric Russian émigré and then world champion, when Alekhine died in Portugal in 1946. The world title remained vacant until 1948, when the 34-year-old Botvinnik won a special tournament organized by the International Chess Federation. For the next 25 years, Botvinnik held the title from 1948 to 1956, 1958 to 1960, and 1961 to 1963, losing only to Vasily Smyslov in 1957 and Mikhail TAL in 1960, before reclaiming his title. Known for his orderly, pragmatic, even cold approach to chess, Botvinnik became, more than any other Soviet player of his era, the exemplar of the superiority of the Soviet chess "system" and, hence, in the ideological context of the cold war, of the superiority of the Soviet system itself. By 1963, when he lost the world title to Tigran PETROSIAN, Botvinnik was no longer able to keep up a young cadre of, mostly Soviet, contenders. Although he won the Hastings Tournament in 1966, he announced his retirement in 1970 and returned to his other intellectual passions: electrotechnical theory and computer chess programs.

Breshko-Breshkovskaia, Ekaterina Konstantinovna (1844–1934)
revolutionary

Affectionately known as the "Grandmother" of the Russian Revolution, Breshko-Breshkovskaia participated through all the major stages of the revolutionary movement between 1861 and 1917. Like other revolutionaries of her generation, Breshko-Breshkovskaia was born into a noble serf-owning family and was disillusioned by the terms under which serfs were emancipated in 1861. Under the influence of populist

Ekaterina Breshko-Breshkovskaia *(Hulton/Archive)*

exile in 1896, she played a key role in the revival of POPULISM under the banners of the newly formed Party of Socialist Revolutionaries (PSR). She toured the United States in 1904 on a fundraising mission. Back in Russia, she was arrested in Simbirsk province in 1907 as part of the repression that followed the 1905 Revolution. This time she was sentenced to perpetual exile in Siberia. She returned to Petrograd, a triumphant survivor of exile, and promptly threw her support behind Aleksandr KERENSKY, who was emerging as one of the democratic socialist leaders of the Provisional Government. After the Bolshevik victory in October, she supported the "democratic counterrevolution" that sought a middle course between the BOLSHEVIKS and the monarchist army officers behind the White movement. She left Russia for exile in Czechoslovakia, where she founded Russian-language schools, before retiring to a farm near Prague. There she died at the age of 90. Her memoirs were published in an English translation with the title *Hidden Springs of the Russian Revolution: Personal Memoirs of Katerina Brezhkovskaia* (1931).

Brest-Litovsk, Treaty of (1918)

Known in some quarters as the "indecent peace," the Treaty of Brest-Litovsk was the controversial agreement that marked a separate peace between Soviet Russia and Germany during World War I. By this treaty, Russia gave up huge territories in the west, including the Baltic provinces and Ukraine, and was obliged to demobilize the army. The value of the treaty to Germany, which had hoped to transfer a large number of troops to the western front, was to a large extent nullified by the drawn-out negotiations, though the occupation of Ukraine was a great economic gain for the Germans. Discussions about a peace with Germany caused the first serious crisis within the ranks of the recently victorious BOLSHEVIKS. The promise of peace had been one of the main Bolshevik slogans when they seized power, and LENIN rushed to conclude an agreement that would allow the Bolsheviks

ideas, she carried out educational work among the peasantry, but when this was labeled subversive in 1871, she abandoned her husband and family and joined her sister Olga in founding a socialist commune in Kiev. Organized around craft workshops, the commune became a center of debates between followers of LAVROV and BAKUNIN. Although convinced of the necessity of terror, she joined the populist "To the People" crusade in 1874, but was arrested after three months. One of the defendants in the "Trial of the 193" (January 1878), Breshko-Breshkovskaia became the first woman to be sentenced to hard labor in Siberia. She became internationally famous after the American journalist George F. Kennan, traveling in Siberia in 1885, wrote an account of her captivity. Allowed to return from the "breathing space" to consolidate their government, before the expected backlash from opposition forces taking shape in the south. Opposition to the treaty within the party came from two sources—Leon TROTSKY and Nikolai BUKHARIN. Bukharin and the Left Communists opposed any peaceful relations with bourgeois imperialist governments and supported a revolutionary war to the end. Trotsky's position, supported by the majority of the Bolshevik Central Committee, was defined by the slogan "neither peace nor war," in expectation of a German proletarian revolution. When Trotsky, acting as commissar for foreign affairs, first told the German negotiators at Brest that the Soviet government would cease to fight but would not conclude a peace, the Germans continued their advance on Petrograd. Shaken by the German advance and by Lenin's threat to resign unless a treaty was signed, the Central Committee reversed its decision and supported Lenin by a small majority. Soviet Russia's separate peace with Germany gave further encouragement to the Allied military intervention in northern Russia that hoped to install a government that would reopen hostilities with Germany. With Germany's defeat in November 1918, the Soviet government unilaterally abrogated the treaty. While the Ukraine was brought back into the newly formed Soviet Union, the former Baltic provinces—reconstituted as the nations of Estonia and Latvia—as well as Lithuania, remained independent until 1940.

Brezhnev, Leonid Ilich (1906–1982)
ruler

Leader of the Soviet Union from 1964 to 1982, Brezhnev presided over a long period of relative stability and international power that, however, led to the country's demise a decade after his death, in great part as a result of the stagnation and corruption that were also hallmarks of his rule.

Brezhnev was born in the Ukrainian town of Kamenskoe, renamed Dneprodzerzhinsk in 1936, to a working-class family. He left school at age 15 and briefly worked in amateur theater troupes before eventually becoming a land surveyor. In 1931 he joined the COMMUNIST PARTY and returned home to the Ukraine to enroll in the Kamenskoe Metallurgical Institute. In the late 1930s, like other hard-working young Party activists of his generation, Brezhnev began to advance his political career in the late 1930s at a time when brutal purges had depleted the party ranks. In 1939 he became first secretary of the Dnepropetrovk's regional party committee. Brezhnev spent World War II as a minor political officer in the Ukraine and the Caucasus, eventually attaining the rank of major general. He played a part in the important battle around Novorossiisk, although later writings would greatly embellish his role. After the war he returned to party work in Dnepropetrovsk and, in 1949, was elected to the Central Committee of the Ukrainian Communist Party. Increasingly important appointments followed during the 1950s, especially as KHRUSHCHEV—whom he had befriended in the late 1930s—gained the upper hand in the post-Stalin political struggles. After a stint in Kazakhstan, where he took part in the Virgin Lands Campaign, Brezhnev returned to Moscow in 1956, becoming a full member of the Presidium (Politburo) after the defeat of the ANTI-PARTY GROUP that tried to oust Khrushchev in 1957. In 1960 he was named titular head of state of the Soviet Union, a prominent position though with little real power.

Although not a leader of the conspiracy that overthrew Khrushchev in October 1964, Brezhnev benefited from its outcome—perhaps because of his relatively unthreatening political persona—and became first secretary of the Communist Party of the Soviet Union. Advocating a policy of "stability of cadres" that appealed to party members who had survived STALIN's terror and Khrushchev's bureaucratic reorganizations, Brezhnev gradually consolidated his power over the next decade, even as his health began to fail. For the next 18 years, a conservative party bureaucracy diluted or defeated reformist attempts and arbitrary Stalinist terror gave way to selective persecution of political, religious, and nationalist activists, who were often harassed at work or imprisoned in "psychoprisons," while economic growth fueled by the postwar recovery slowed down and corruption spread through the system. With Brezhnev in office, the Soviet Union appeared at the peak of its international power, even though excessive military spending ultimately contributed to the domestic crisis of the 1980s. The August 1968 WARSAW PACT invasion of Czechoslovakia was later justified by the Brezhnev Doctrine, which defended the Soviet Union's right to intervene in Soviet-bloc countries where it felt socialism was threatened. Brezhnev's pursuit of détente with the United States and its allies led to concrete achievements in disarmament and the 1975 Helsinki Agreement. The cold war competition was transferred to places such as Angola and Ethiopia, leading to the disastrous 1979 Soviet invasion of AFGHANISTAN, which embroiled the Soviet Union in an unwinnable war and whose far-reaching consequences are still being felt today.

The final years of Brezhnev's rule were marked by his declining health and an inability to perform his basic duties, the subject of numerous unofficial jokes from Soviet citizens increasingly cynical about their rulers and communism itself. He died of heart failure in November 1982, three days after reviewing the traditional October Revolution parade in the cold of a Moscow winter.

Brighton Beach

A neighborhood in southeast Brooklyn, New York, bounded by the Atlantic Ocean to the south and nestled between Manhattan Beach and Coney Island, which in the last three decades Brighton Beach has become the home to a new wave of mostly Jewish émigrés from the Soviet Union. The neighborhood dates to the late 1860s and was named after its more famous English counterpart. Some prominent early landmarks were the Hotel Brighton, the Brighton Beach Racetrack, and the Brighton Beach Baths built in 1907. As the demand for housing increased in the 1920s, more than 30 six-story apartment buildings were built in the neighborhood, and the area gradually came to have a large number of Jewish residents, mostly of East European origin. By the 1970s the wood-frame houses and bungalows of earlier years had considerably deteriorated, even though the 1920s Art Deco apartment buildings were still in good condition. The availability of housing and commercial stock and the East European Jewish character of the neighborhood made it an attractive place to resettle the large numbers of Soviet Jewish émigrés who arrived in the 1970s and 1980s. The maritime character of the neighborhood, with its expansive boardwalk and beach front, and the fact that almost three-quarters of the recent immigrants came from ODESSA and the Black Sea region contributed to it being sometimes known as "Little Odessa." The dissolution of the Soviet Union in 1991 and the lifting of previous restrictions on emigration brought another wave of immigrants to the neighborhood, even as immigrants from other nations started to settle in the outskirts of the neighborhood. By the early 21st century, Brighton Beach was no longer the final destination for emigrants from the former Soviet Union, but with its Russian-language signs for restaurants, nightclubs, bookstores, bathhouses, and fruit stands dominating the neighborhood landscape, it still remained their symbolic gateway into New York and the United States.

Brodsky, Joseph (1940–1996)

poet

One of the most accomplished Russian-born poets of the postwar period, Joseph Brodsky lived through political persecution, followed by exile in the United States, before winning the 1987 Nobel Prize in literature. Born to a Jewish family in Leningrad, Brodsky lived through the harrowing nine-hundred-day siege of his hometown by the invading Germans. He dropped out of school at age 15 to become a factory worker, educating himself through his love of reading. Already a prominent poet in his late teens, he befriended Anna AKHMATOVA and became recognized as one of the leaders of a revitalized group of Leningrad poets. He supported himself by working at a variety of odd jobs, which earned him an arrest in 1964 on a charge of "parasitism," Soviet legal jargon for someone who lacked officially approved gainful employment. Although Brodsky was a recognized poet, he was not a member of the official Soviet Writers' Union. Sentenced to five years of hard labor in the Far North, he was released after 18 months following protests from Soviet and Western writers. In 1972 he was stripped of his Soviet citizenship and eventually settled in New York City, where he began a second career as a prominent poet, publishing in both English and Russian. For the next two decades, he taught literature at several universities, publishing frequently and receiving important awards for his work. In 1977 he was granted U.S. citizenship, and in 1981 he was awarded one of the coveted MacArthur Foundation "genius" awards. In 1987, he became the second-youngest recipient of the Nobel Prize for literature. In 1991–92 he held the position of poet laureate of the United States. Among his more prominent poetry volumes are *Selected Poems* (1973), *A Part of Speech* (1980), *History of the Twentieth-Century* (1986), and *To Urania* (1988). An autobiographical collection of essays, *Less Than One* (1986), received a National Book Critics Circle Award, while another, *On Grief and Reason,* was published in 1995. Despite his international prominence and Nobel Prize, Brodsky's work began to be published in his homeland only in the late 1980s, during GORBACHEV's period of glasnost (openness) and then more fully in the 1990s after the Soviet Union dissolved.

Bronze Horseman (Myodnyi Vsadnik)

A bronze equestrian statue of PETER I the Great that assumed great symbolism as a result of a poem by Alexander PUSHKIN, the *Bronze Horse-man* has become one of the iconic symbols of the city of St. Petersburg. The statue was commissioned by CATHERINE II the Great, who wanted to make an explicit connection between her reign and Peter's. After consultations with her philosophe correspondents, Diderot and Voltaire, she chose the French sculptor Etienne Falconet to build the statue. In 1782 a towering sculpture was unveiled showing Peter in control of an unpredictable mount representing Russia, while his free hand points forward. On the granite base of the sculpture are two inscriptions, one in Russian and one in Latin, that state simply "To Peter I from Catherine II." While impressive, the sculpture gained much in symbolism from the poem "The Bronze Horseman," written by Pushkin in 1833. In the poem, the protagonist loses his fiancée and his sanity in the great flood that ravaged St. Petersburg in 1824. In his mind he is chased through the empty streets of the city by the imposing sculpture of Peter the Great. To Pushkin, the sculpture symbolized the oppressive autocratic state as well as the destructive potential of St. Petersburg, a city that appears as unnatural and bureaucratic in many works of 19th-century Russian literature. The statue sits on the former Senate Square, which in another twist of symbolism was the site of the abortive DECEMBRIST uprising of 1825 and was renamed Decembrists' Square one century later.

Budennyi, Semyon Mikhailovich (1889–1973)

field marshal

Budennyi was a legendary Soviet military hero of the civil war, known for his cavalry skills and his distinctive handlebar mustache. He was born in the southern province of Rostov, joined the czarist army in 1903, and saw action during the RUSSO-JAPANESE WAR of 1904–5. During World War I he served with distinction as a noncommissioned cavalry officer and was decorated four times. He joined the BOLSHEVIKS in 1918 and during the civil war made a brilliant career, becoming the commander of the First Cavalry

Army with Kliment Voroshilov as his political commissar. The long march from the north Caucasus to Poland in 1920 earned him great fame. After the civil war, he became inspector of the Red Army Cavalry (1924–37), an appointment that gradually diminished in importance as mechanized warfare became more widespread. In 1935 he was promoted to the rank of marshal, one of four in the Red Army at the time. A strong supporter of STALIN, he sat on the special military court that sentenced Marshal Mikhail TUKHACHEVSKY and other leading Red Army commanders to death as part of the 1937 purge that decimated the Soviet Union's officer corps. After the German invasion of June 1941, he was appointed commander of the southwestern front with responsibility for the Ukraine and Bessarabia. His command was short-lived and disastrous, as he proved "bewildered" by the new mechanized warfare, and he was dismissed only a few months later, in September 1941. His close relationship to Stalin protected him from the more serious reprisals common at the time, and he was reassigned to administrative tasks. He never returned to active command but remained commander in chief of various Caucasian fronts until January 1943, when he was appointed commander of the Red Army Cavalry. He was a member of the Central Committee of the Communist Party (1939–52), as well as a member of the Presidium of the Supreme Soviet, the latter a purely decorative position. He continued to concern himself with horses and horse breeding. His memoirs were published in Russia in 1959, and as he grew older he became a symbol of a heroic age of Soviet life that had passed.

Bukhara

An ancient center of civilization in Central Asia founded in the first century A.D., on an oasis on the Zeravshan River, 270 miles to the southwest of Tashkent. After its capture by the Arabs in 709, Bukhara became an important center of medieval Islamic learning, subsequently ruled by Persians, Turks, and Uzbeks. The modern history of Bukhara begins with its inclusion into the Uzbek state founded by Khan Sheybani after the conquest of the Timurid domains in Transoxania in 1500–1507. In 1555, Abdullah Khan transferred the seat of government from SAMARKAND to Bukhara, which became the capital of the Bukhara Khanate that survived until the 20th century. After a succession of internal feuds had weakened its power, Bukhara was conquered in 1740 by Nadir Shah of Persia. Although Bukhara regained its independence in 1754, it did not recover its supremacy over areas like KHOREZM, Merv, Badakhshan, Tashkent, and the Fergana valley. The rulers of Bukhara, known by the title of emir, ruled over a predominantly Uzbek population with an admixture of Sarts and Tadzhiks. Within the framework of the Shariat and customary law, they had almost unlimited power, which they exercised with the support of Uzbek tribal chieftains and the Muslim clergy. In the mid–19th century, Bukhara became an object of desire in the long-standing struggle between Russian and British imperial interests. In 1866, the Russian army inflicted a disastrous defeat on the Bukharan army, leading to an 1868 treaty that surrendered some of Bukhara's best lands, including Samarkand, to Russia and established a Russian protectorate over the Bukhara khanate. A Russian political agent resided at Kagan, eight miles from Bukhara, and slavery was abolished, but otherwise Bukhara remained aloof from the transformation of the Turkestan area, especially around Tashkent, into a cotton-growing colony of Russia. In 1920, a coalition of Russians and local Communists, aided by the Red Army, deposed the last emir and established the Bukhara People's Soviet Republic on the territory of the now dissolved Bukhara khanate. Fierce resistance, led by BASMACHI guerrillas, ensued, but after a ruthless campaign of pacification that led to the destruction of over half of the region's arable land and livestock, and of hundreds of villages, the Communists established control in 1924. The Bukhara khanate was incorporated into the Soviet Union, and in the 1930s it became part of the Uzbek Soviet

Socialist Republic, which after 1991 became the Republic of Uzbekistan. A rich architectural heritage that includes the ninth-century tomb of Ismail Samanid and the *medressehs* of Ulugbek (15th century) and Mir-Arab (16th century) have made Bukhara a popular tourist destination in the region.

Bukharin, Nikolai Ivanovich
(1888–1938)
revolutionary and Soviet leader

A Russian Communist leader and skilled theoretician, Bukharin was a leading critic of Stalinist policies after the late 1920s and an advocate of a more gradualist approach to the transformation of the Soviet Union into a communist society. Born in Moscow to a family of school teachers, Bukharin's first taste of revolutionary politics came as a student during the 1905 Revolution. In 1906, while an economics student at the University of Moscow, he joined the Bolshevik faction of the Russian Social Democratic Labor Party and rose quickly within the ranks of the party. After several arrests he escaped to Germany in 1911, where he settled until the outbreak of World War I. During the war he moved to Switzerland, then Sweden, and eventually came to New York City in 1916, where he briefly worked with Leon TROTSKY in editing a radical Russian-language newspaper. With the fall of the monarchy in February 1917, Bukharin returned to Moscow, where he continued to occupy important posts in the Bolshevik Party and was elected to the party's Central Committee. After the October Revolution he was named editor of *Pravda,* the party newspaper, a position he held until 1929. Always independent-minded, he supported LENIN's overall civil war policy, later known as War Communism, but opposed him on the question of signing a separate peace with Germany in March 1918. Although in his well-known books *The ABC of Communism* (coauthored with the economist Evgenii Preobrazhensky) and *The Economics of the Transition Period,* Bukharin had forcefully called

Nikolai Bukharin *(Hulton/Archive)*

for an economy based on state control, militarized labor, and compulsory requisition of food, he became a strong advocate of the New Economic Policy developed by the party after 1921. As one of the preeminent leaders of the COMMUNIST PARTY, Bukharin became involved in the bitter power struggle that followed Lenin's death in 1924, initially supporting STALIN against Trotsky, KAMENEV, and ZINOVIEV. Closely identified with the more gradualist New Economic Policy, Bukharin became known as a leader of the Rightist wing of the party and an opponent of the Leftist policy of super industrialization at the expense of the peasantry. By the time Stalin had developed his policy of collectivization and rapid industrialization based on coercion and terror, Bukharin had been defeated within the party. He was removed from the party's Politburo and the editorship of *Pravda,* but allowed to remain a member of the Central Committee. In 1934 he was named editor of the newspaper *Izvestiia,* and in 1936 he chaired the commission that produced the draft of the 1936 Constitution, later known as the "Stalin Constitution." In February 1937, however, with the Great Purge in full swing, Bukharin was arrested on charges of counterrevolutionary activities. He served as the main defendant in the 1938 Moscow show trial, was found guilty, and was shot soon after. In the 1980s his defense of the mixed economy of the New Economic Policy was attractive to Communist reformers, including Mikhail GORBACHEV. In 1988, his verdict was reversed and he was fully rehabilitated by the Soviet Supreme Court.

Bukovsky, Vladimir Konstantinovich (1942–   )
writer

A leading member of the dissident movement of the 1960s and 1970s, Bukovskii was allowed to leave the Soviet Union in 1976, as part of an unusual exchange with the Chilean Communist Party leader, Luis Corvalan, imprisoned by the Pinochet government. The son of a COMMUNIST PARTY official, Bukovsky studied biology at Moscow State University, where he became involved with the Soviet dissident movement. He was first arrested in 1963 for illegally photocopying the book *The New Class* by the Yugoslav dissident Communist Milovan Djilas, and placed in a Leningrad psychiatric hospital. Freed in 1965, he was arrested again later that year for organizing a demonstration in support of the writers Andrei SINYAVSKY and Yuli Daniel, who at the time were being tried on charges of promoting anti-Soviet views in their works. He was sentenced to another term in a psychiatric hospital. Freed in 1966, he was rearrested in January 1967 and sentenced to a three-year term in labor camps for further political activities. In January 1971, he collected materials on the Soviet Union's abuse of psychiatric hospitals for political purposes, which were presented to the World Congress of Psychiatrists in Mexico City and led to the congress's condemnation of Soviet psychiatry. He was arrested once more and in 1972 was

sentenced to seven years in prison, to be followed by five years of exile. In December 1976, as part of the exchange for Corvalan, he left the Soviet Union and settled in England. He wrote his autobiography, *To Build a Castle: My Life as a Dissenter* (1978), and continued to work for the human rights movement. In 1983, he was appointed president of the human rights organization Resistance International.

Bulgakov, Mikhail Afanasievich (1891–1940)
writer

Virtually forgotten at the time of his death, with the posthumous publication of his most important works Bulgakov is now considered a major force in 20th-century Russian letters. Bulgakov was born in Kiev on May 15, 1891. His father was a professor of divinity at the Kiev Theological Academy. Bulgakov studied medicine and briefly practiced as a country doctor (1916–18), before traveling to the Caucasus in 1919 to write newspaper stories and plays. Arriving in Moscow in 1921, he first worked as a journalist before turning to literature and drama. His literary breakthrough came with the novel *The White Guard* (1926), which was soon adapted for the stage by the Moscow Art Theater (MkhAT) as *The Days of the Turbines*. Although its portrayal of White officers was considered by some to be overly sympathetic, the play was a big success, and Bulgakov began a long association with the Moscow Art Theater as dramatist, director, and author that was richly productive and controversial. A short satirical novel, *Heart of a Dog,* was also published at this time. In 1929, Bulgakov was dismissed from the MkhAT staff and his plays were banned, but after a personal appeal to STALIN the decision was reversed. *The Days of the Turbines* was restaged and once again proved a hit with theater audiences. Success and official acceptance proved fleeting as his next play, *Molière* (written 1930, published 1962), was in rehearsals for four years and when it finally opened in 1936, the censors shut it down after only seven days. During rehearsals he wrote a brilliant biography of Molière, *The Life of Monsieur de Molière*, published in 1966. Bulgakov's reputation as a major author, however, rests on the novel *Master and Margarita*, written between 1928 and 1940, but published in Moscow only in 1966. The novel exists in eight versions, and the final drafts were dictated to his wife on the eve of his death, as Bulgakov was now blind. Using irony and fantasy, Bulgakov reenacts the passion of Christ in an author's manuscript at a time when the Devil intrudes into modern Moscow. A daring novel that can be read on many levels, it caused a sensation when finally published. In the 1980s it also gave rise to a particularly devoted following by fans who, in the face of the authorities' refusal to erect a monument to Bulgakov, made their own loving tribute by adorning the stairwell of the apartment where he lived from 1921 to 1934 with graffiti from the novel.

Bulgakov, Sergei Nikolaevich (1871–1944)

theologian and philosopher

Bulgakov was, with Nikolai BERDIAEV and Semyon Frank, one of the leading representatives of the group of intellectuals gathered around the *Vekhi* movement who traveled from Marxism to a religious orientation in the aftermath of the 1905 Revolution, denouncing radicalism and political activism. Bulgakov was born in Orel province to the south of Moscow, and his father was an Orthodox priest. Bulgakov graduated from Moscow State University in 1894 and embraced the Marxist ideas popular among the youth of his day, becoming a prominent spokesman for the Legal Marxists. In 1901, he was appointed professor of political economy at the Kiev Polytechnic University and later at the Moscow Institute of Commerce. Following a Christian socialist orientation, he was elected in 1906 to the short-lived Second DUMA for the Constitutional Democratic (Kadet) Party. In 1918 he was ordained an Orthodox priest. During the Russian civil war he lived in the Crimea, teaching

at Simferopol University until he was dismissed in 1921 for his religious convictions. Bulgakov was part of the prominent group of intellectuals who were expelled from the Soviet Union in 1922–23. After a short stay in Prague, where he taught at the Russian faculty of law, he moved to Paris. From 1925 to 1944, Bulgakov served as dean of the St. Sergius Theological Institute in Paris, shaping it into one of the leading centers of Orthodox thought. Influenced by Vladimir SOLOVIEV, he devoted much of his work to the controversial idea of "sophiology," where Sophia is the feminine ideal essence of the world that exists in the mind of God. Bulgakov also worked actively to develop a worldwide ecumenical government, acting as an intermediary between traditionally hostile Protestant and Catholic groups in western Europe.

Bulganin, Nikolai Aleksandrovich (1895–1975)

Soviet official

A COMMUNIST PARTY official who benefited from an early alliance with KHRUSHCHEV after STALIN's death in 1953, Bulganin was prime minister of the Soviet Union from 1955 to 1958. Bulganin was born into a white-collar family in the Volga River port of NIZHNII-NOVGOROD, where he attended school. After joining the Bolshevik Party in 1917, he worked for the Cheka (secret police) during the civil war. During the 1920s he built a career in the Soviet economic sector, before becoming chairman of the Moscow Soviet in 1931, a position he held until 1937. During these years he developed a good working relationship with Nikita Khrushchev, then secretary of the Moscow Communist Party, and helped oversee the building of grand projects such as the Moscow Metro and the overall transformation of the city into a showcase of socialist architecture. Already a member of the Central Committee of the Communist Party in 1934, Bulganin was appointed chairman of the Council of People's Commissars (Sovnarkom) of the Russian Republic (RSFSR) of the Soviet Union in

1937. The following year, he became deputy chairman of the Sovnarkom for the entire Soviet Union, a post he held until 1941. Bulganin spent the first part of World War II as a traveling political commissar, before being promoted to deputy commissar of the Defense Ministry and member of the State Defense Committee. He continued his rise in the army and party bureaucracies after the war, obtaining the rank of marshal in 1947 and a seat on the party's Politburo in 1948. In the power struggle that followed Stalin's death in 1953, Bulganin sided with Khrushchev and benefited from his eventual victory, becoming defense minister in 1953 and prime minister (premier) in 1955. In 1957, however, he threw his lot in with the unsuccessful "ANTI-PARTY GROUP," led by MOLOTOV, MALENKOV, KAGANOVICH, and Voroshilov, which sought to remove Khrushchev from power. Unlike his co-conspirators, Bulganin was not punished by Khrushchev until 1958, at which time he lost his seat on the Politburo and his military rank of marshal, in addition to being fired as prime minister. For the next few years he worked at minor economic posts, first in the State Bank and then in the southern province of Stavropol as chairman of the local Council of the National Economy. He retired in 1960 and lived near Moscow in political obscurity until his death.

Bund

Political party. Derived from the Yiddish term for *union,* the Bund, or Jewish Bund, formed in Vilna in 1897 and was formally known as the General Jewish Workers Bund in Russia and Poland (after 1901, Lithuania was added to the title). By the time of its establishment, its activists, drawn mostly from the Russified Jewish intelligentsia who had benefited from the GREAT REFORMS of the 1860s, had a decade's worth of organizational and agitational experience. Its general aims were an end to anti-Jewish discrimination and a reorganized federal Russian Empire within the framework of socialism. By 1900 it was the most powerful socialist body in the

empire and had played an important part in the foundation of the Russian Social Democratic Labor Party (RSDLP) in 1898. Despite their common allegiance to Marxist principles, conflicts soon arose between the two parties, especially with Vladimir LENIN. They clashed over the Bund's emphasis on Jewish interests and over the nature of the party, with the Bund rejecting Leninist organizational principles in favor of a broad-based mass party modeled on the German Social Democratic Party. As a result of these broader disagreements and the Bund's demands to be recognized as the sole representatives of Jewish workers and its demands for internal autonomy within the RSDLP, the Bund seceded from the Russian Social Democratic Labor Party in 1903. The Bund rejoined the party in 1906 and thereafter generally sided with the Mensheviks. Like other Russian socialist parties, the Bund's fortunes declined in the period between 1907 and 1914 as a result of repression, emigration of many of its members, and a reduced commitment after the heady days of the 1905 Revolution. World War I particularly affected the Bund, since its traditional areas of recruitment were now the sites of the heaviest fighting with Germany. Bund leaders supported the platform of the Zimmerwald Conference of 1915, calling for peace without annexations or indemnities and for an emphasis on proletarian internationalism rather than patriotic nationalist demands. It supported the Provisional Government in 1917 but decided not to join it, following the general policies of the Petrograd Soviet. The majority of the party opposed the Bolshevik revolution, but the civil war further splintered the Bund organizationally and ideologically. The creation of an independent Poland in November 1918 broke up the unity of the prerevolutionary Bund, and with the formation of a Polish Bund, a substantial part of the party was now drawn into Polish interwar politics. In 1920, the Bund in Soviet territories split with a majority, led by M. Rafes, choosing to join the Communist Party and a minority, led by Rafail Abramovich, continuing as a separate Social Democratic group until its subsequent suppression. The Polish Bund continued to operate until World War II, and remnants of the organization existed in the United States as late as the 1960s.

Bunin, Ivan Alekseevich (1870–1953)
writer

The recipient of the Nobel Prize in literature in 1933, Bunin represents the last link to the "classical" tradition of nineteenth-century realist literature of TOLSTOY and TURGENEV. He was born in Voronezh into a provincial gentry family, and his most representative work draws deeply from this rural background. Working as a journalist, he first received literary recognition for his poetry, and was awarded the Pushkin Prize in 1901. Although generally apolitical, he initially joined Maksim GORKY's group of revolutionary and proletarian writers. The early, somewhat detached lyrical prose of works like *Antonovskie iabloki* (*Antonov Apples*) (1900) gave way to a more somber, even gloomy set of works about the Russian countryside. Typical of this vein are *Derevnia* (*The Village*) (1910), a portrayal of the poverty-stricken life of the Russian peasant, and *Sukhodol* (*Dry Valley*) (1912), where he portrays the life of a disintegrating manor house from the viewpoint of one of its female servants. A well-traveled man, he wrote his best-known work, *Gospodin iz San Franzisko* (*The Gentleman from San Francisco*) in 1916. It is a biting satire on Western bourgeois life, especially the power of money. He emigrated in 1920, setting in the south of France. His major postrevolutionary works treat ageless themes such as love (*Mitya's Love,* 1925) and the past (*The Life of Arseniev,* 1930) in the context of the Russia he left behind. Although Bunin never returned to Russia, he never left it behind, arranging for the transfer of his papers to Moscow shortly before his death. After his death, his works were published in the Soviet Union in large editions and he received posthumous recognition as a great Russian writer.

burlaki

Barge haulers. From the 16th to 19th centuries, *burlaki* hauled vessels along Russia's rivers with the help of towing ropes. To generations of 19th-century intellectuals, the use of men as draught animals was one of the most powerful symbols of capitalist exploitation. They were especially prevalent along the northern routes connecting Moscow and ARCHANGEL on the White Sea, the Volga route from Moscow to ASTRAKHAN, and the Dnieper River route in the Ukraine. *Burlaki* were hired at the beginning of the navigation in river towns like Nizhnii-Novgorod, Saratov, Rybinsk, and Kiev. Until the abolition of SERFDOM in 1861, most were serfs, hailing from land-hungry provinces along the Volga River, who had been temporarily released from their labor duties by their landlords. Occasionally they were joined by town dwellers and déclassé elements. Wages were not enough to cover expenses for the whole trip, and barge haulers were forced to borrow from the following years' wages. Although the terms of labor were fixed in written agreements, employers often arbitrarily reduced the previously agreed wage upon payment. Most *burlaki* were hired during winter, a time when prices fell and barge haulers needed advance payments. Usually they were hired in artels, groups of four to six, sometimes 10 to 40 men, which then merged to form larger artels of up to 150 men, bound by mutual guarantees. Haulers were paid only at the end of the season, so often they came home already in debt. Technical progress and the growth of steamship navigation in the 19th century brought an end to the need for bargemen. By midcentury there were about 150,000 bargemen, almost half a million fewer than at the beginning of the century, and their numbers continued to decline rapidly. By the beginning of the 20th century, *burlaki* had mostly disappeared, their memory celebrated in cultural icons, such as REPIN's painting *Volga Boatmen,* stories by GORKY and the journalist GILIAROVSKY, and *Song of the Volga Boatmen,* later a staple of Russian folk music.

C

calendar

For many centuries Russians used a calendar that began the year on September 1 and counted time from 5509 B.C.E., the year that Orthodox theologians considered marked the beginning of the world. In 1700 PETER I decreed the adoption of the Western system of year numbering, with the New Year beginning on January 1, 1700. However, the Western calendar Russians adopted was not the Gregorian calendar, introduced by Pope Gregory XIII in 1582, but the Julian calendar, first introduced by Julius Caesar in 45 B.C.E., and since abandoned in the West. It seems that the main reason Russia adopted the Julian and not the improved Gregorian calendar was deep-seated animosity toward the papacy. Russia's use of the Julian calendar caused great confusion in comparing Russian and Western dates. During the 17th century, the Russian calendar lagged 10 days behind the Gregorian calendar. In each successive century, the Russian calendar fell yet another day behind, so that Russian dates lagged 11 days behind the Gregorian system in the 18th century, 12 days in the 19th century, and 13 days in the 20th century. On January 26, 1918, the Soviet government announced that Russia would adopt the Gregorian calendar on February 1, 1918, which then became February 14 in the Gregorian style. In dating the events of the Russian past, historians often indicate dates in the Gregorian style as "New Style" (N.S.) and in the Julian as "Old Style" (O.S.). A revolutionary calendar, reminiscent of the French revolutionary calendar, that replaced weeks with periods of five numbered days and reckoned years from 1917 was devised in 1929 but never used.

Catherine I (1684–1727)

empress

The second wife of PETER I the Great and empress of Russia from 1725 to 1727, Catherine was born Marfa Skovronskaia, the daughter of a Lithuanian peasant. A few details are known about her youth: she worked as a servant, married a Swedish soldier, and eventually became part of the household of Prince Alexander MENSHIKOV, Peter's close collaborator. In 1703 she joined the Orthodox Church and was rechristened Ekaterina (Catherine) Alekseevna. She met Peter in Menshikov's household and the two became lovers, with Catherine often accompanying Peter in his military campaigns. The two were officially married in 1712, although some historians refer to a private marriage in 1707. Peter and Catherine had several children, but only two daughters, Anna and ELIZABETH, survived beyond an early age. In 1722, Peter changed the succession law to allow the ruler to name his or her successor, but he never named a successor. In 1724, however, Catherine was crowned empress consort but not named heir to the throne. The following year, however, after Peter's death, she was named empress with the support of the new power brokers such as Menshikov and the Imperial Guard's regiments created by Peter. Her reign, dominated by Menshikov, was brief and relatively uneventful, except for the creation of the Supreme Privy Council in February 1726. The council, composed of Menshikov and five other prominent nobles, was designed to deal with "matters of exceptional importance," in effect creating a group of associates to the monarch.

For the next four years it played a dominant role in Russian court politics until 1730, when the new empress ANNA IVANOVNA abolished it. Before her death in May 1727, Catherine appointed the future PETER II, grandson of PETER I from his first marriage, as heir to the throne, with the Supreme Secret Council, now expanded to include her daughters, as regents.

Catherine II (1729–1796)

empress

Known to later generations as Catherine the Great, Catherine was a German princess who ascended the Russian throne in 1762 as the result of a conspiracy against her husband, PETER III. She was born Sophia Augusta Frederica, the daughter of Prince Christian of Anhalt-Zerbst, a small principality near Prussia. She was engaged to her future husband, Peter, duke of Holstein-Gottorp, a grandson of PETER I the Great, at the age of 15. She converted to Russian Orthodoxy and adopted the name Catherine in 1744, a year before her marriage to Peter. Ignored by her husband, Catherine adapted to her new country, learning its language and customs and gradually developing a core of influential supporters. When Peter became emperor in 1762, he quickly alienated various sectors of Russian society, notably the Imperial Guard, which led a successful palace revolution against him in midsummer 1762. Peter was killed a few days later by Grigorii Orlov, Catherine's lover at the time, and Catherine was named empress, while her eight-year-old son, Paul, was named heir to the throne. Catherine denied complicity in her husband's death, but suspicions as to her role have lingered through the centuries. What appeared to be a brief regency until Paul attained majority evolved into a long and celebrated 34-year reign that cemented Russia's emergence as a major European power.

In foreign policy, Catherine continued her predecessors' policy of territorial expansion. Two successful wars with Turkey brought most of the northern shore of the Black Sea and the Cri-

mean Peninsula into Russian hands by 1784. She ended any vestiges of administrative autonomy in the Russian-controlled Ukraine. Russia took the lead in the three POLISH PARTITIONS (1772, 1793, and 1795), annexing over half of the former Kingdom of Poland. Her reign also witnessed the establishment of the first Russian colony in ALASKA in 1784.

Her domestic record was more mixed. Attracted by the ideals of the Enlightenment, she corresponded with leading French philosophes such as Voltaire and Diderot and tried to rule as an "enlightened despot." She started an ambitious program of reforms, convening a legislative commission, and preparing comprehensive plans for educational, legal, and administrative reform, but most were left unfinished. Aware of her dependence on the nobility for her power, she continued the policies of rulers after Peter the Great granted them greater privileges as in the Charter to the Nobility of 1785. The condition of the serfs also continued to deteriorate during her reign, leading some historians to describe it as the "zenith of SERFDOM." On the other hand, her patronage of literature and the arts was more successful, as her reign witnessed important cultural milestones such as the publication of satirical journals, the establishment of private printing presses, and the overall Westernization of Russian culture.

The PUGACHEV REBELLION of 1773–74 and the French Revolution brought out the more repressive aspects of her reign. The former was led by a Cossack who, in the tradition of previous rebels, claimed to be her deceased husband, the "true" Peter III and managed to gain substantial support among COSSACKS, serfs, and other disenfranchised groups along the Volga River basin, before he was defeated with great difficulty by the Russian army. The aftermath of the French Revolution stripped any remaining pretense of enlightened rule, as important intellectuals such as Aleksandr RADISHCHEV and Nikolai NOVIKOV were arrested for their work and, in the case of Radishchev, banished to Siberia. Catherine died on November 6, 1796, and was succeeded by her son, PAUL I, whom she had tried to skip over in favor of her grandson, the future ALEXANDER I.

Central Asian Revolt of 1916

Although the largest internal insurrection in the Russian Empire between the revolutions of 1905 and 1917, the Central Asian revolt of 1916, lost in the carnage of World War I, remained virtually unknown to contemporaries in Europe. Building on long-standing animosities between local Muslims and Russian colonial authorities, the revolt was triggered by the wartime imperial decree of June 15, 1916, which called for the draft of Muslim youths to perform labor duties behind the front lines. It spread quickly from the towns and villages of Central Asia to include the nomadic populations that covered the vast region between Kirghizia and Kazakhstan.

The various political units of Central Asia (present-day Kazakhstan, Kyrgyzstan, Tajikistan, Turkmenistan, and Uzbekistan) had been annexed into the Russian Empire between 1865 and 1885. Until the early 20th century, the region had for the most part received little attention from Russian bureaucrats and traders. By 1911, however, its vast expanses had become the site for large-scale cotton cultivation and the resettlement of landless Russian peasants, who now made up about 40 percent of the region's population. As *inorodtsy* (non-Russians), the local Muslim population was accorded virtually second-class status. It was, however, exempt from military service. Although the June 1916 decree sought to draft Muslim youths only for noncombat duties, it offended the sensibilities of a population that resented colonial Russian rule and felt besieged by the onslaught of Russian settlers. The rebellion caught local Russians by surprise and thousands of Russian settlers were killed in the summer, before the governor-general of Turkestan's troops was able to join the colonists and restore order in late 1916. Precise numbers are unavailable, but the estimates of those killed in the army's reprisals have reached 500,000.

The coming of the FEBRUARY REVOLUTION of 1917 in Petrograd gave new life to the demands of Central Asian Muslims. Activists based in Tashkent began to advance demands for broad autonomy within the framework of a future federalized state. This led to further tension with local Russian colonists, and by September 1917, the region had fallen into a civil war between Russians and Muslims that continued until 1920. The OCTOBER REVOLUTION and civil war of 1917–21 took the issue of autonomy and nationalism in a different direction, leading to the formation of the Soviet Union in 1922.

Chaadaev, Petr Yakovlevich (1793–1856)
writer

After university studies, Chaadaev served as an army officer in the prestigious Semenovsky regiment in the Napoleon Wars (1812–15). Friendly with many of the future DECEMBRISTS and sympathetic to their ideas, he was admitted to their secret society in December 1821, but by that point Chaadaev had resigned his commission and began a long sojourn in Europe. In 1826 he returned to Russia, settled in Moscow, and began work on his *Lettres philosophiques,* which he wrote in French. When published in the journal *Teleskop* in 1836, the impact of the first letter was described by contemporaries as a "shot in the dark" night of the repressive regime of NICHOLAS I. Chaadaev built on his unmitigated support of Western European values and his wholehearted condemnation of Russian culture to argue that Russia's future salvation could lie only in a reunion with the Roman Catholic Church. The government's reaction was swift. The journal's publisher was exiled to Siberia, the censor who had approved publication was dismissed, and Chaadaev was officially declared insane. In response, Chaadaev wrote his *Apology of a Madman,* a partial recantation of his views. His complete rejection of any value in Russian culture was one of the ideas that precipitated the division between SLAVOPHILES AND WESTERNIZERS among

Russian intellectuals. The complete French text of the *Lettres philosophiques* was not published until 1966.

Chagall, Marc (1887–1985)
artist

Chagall was born Mark Zakharovich Segal to a Jewish family near Vitebsk in czarist Belorussia. After three years of art studies in St. Petersburg, in 1910 he moved to Paris, where he lived in an artists' commune. In Paris he was greatly influenced by cubism, a dominant influence in his later work. Returning to Russia in 1914, he supported the OCTOBER REVOLUTION, and in 1918 he became director of the Vitebsk Popular Arts Institute. He worked with the State Jewish The-

ater in Moscow (1920–21) and was then made people's commissar for the fine arts in Vitebsk but soon fell out with Soviet authorities. He emigrated in 1922 first to Berlin and, in 1923, to Paris. With the exception of a brief interlude in the United States (1941–48), Chagall remained in Paris for the rest of his long life. Chagall's style—a distinctive mixture of folk art, primitivism, and cubism rich in reds, blues, and greens, with Russian and Jewish religious and provincial themes from his childhood as its subject—took shape early in his career. His art is populated with rabbis, musicians, acrobats, peddlers, and animals from his Belorussian years (e.g., *Return from the Synagogue,* 1925; *The Blue Violinist,* 1947). Although Chagall criticized organized religion, God is everywhere present in his work, often in the love of two human beings floating in space, daringly defying the rules of gravity as in paintings such as, *Over the City,* 1917; *Double Portrait with Wineglass,* 1917; and *The Bridal Pair before the Eiffel Tower,* 1938. Biblical scenes appear in his work from the mid-1920s onward. In later years his work achieved a more monumental scale, as he turned to widely acclaimed murals and stained-glass windows (Paris Opera, 1964; Metropolitan Opera, 1966; and the Jerusalem stained-glass cycle of *The Twelve Tribes,* 1961). Although Chagall never returned to Russia after 1922, his widow arranged for a successful exhibition of his work in Moscow in 1987.

Marc Chagall *(Hulton/Archive)*

Chaikovsky, Nikolai Vasilievich (1850–1926)
revolutionary

A product of the nobility, Chaikovsky played an influential role at several stages of the revolutionary movement. While a student at St. Petersburg University, he participated in student disturbances of 1868–69. In 1869 he also formed with Mark Natanson the first revolutionary populist organization in Russia, known as the Chaikovsky Circle. Until 1874, when it was closed by the authorities, the circle was the center of revolutionary POPULISM. Among its members were many future influential revolutionaries such as the anarchist Petr KROPOTKIN; Andrei Zheliabov, who would later direct the assassination of ALEXANDER II; and Pavel Akselrod, one of the first Russian Marxists. Chaikovsky emigrated in the fall of 1874 and by 1880 had settled in London, where he helped organize the Russian Free Press Fund. Attracted to religious ideas, he tried to establish a religious commune in the United States, eventually returning to London. In 1904 he joined the Socialist Revolutionary (SR) Party and returned to Russia the following year. By 1910, he had broken with the SRs, joined the more moderate Popular Socialist Party, and became involved in the burgeoning cooperative movement. During World War I he was one of the organizers of the Union of Towns and became active in defense work. During 1917 he sided with old revolutionary stalwarts like PLEKHANOV and Kropotkin in opposing the rising Bolshevik tide, albeit more actively. After the OCTOBER REVOLUTION he formed the Union for the Regeneration of Russia, an anti-Bolshevik organization that sought to bring together liberals and moderate socialists. After the Allied landing in the northern port of ARCHANGEL in August 1918, Chaikovsky headed the short-lived anti-Bolshevik government in the region. He emigrated in January 1919 and later participated as a member of the unofficial Russian delegation at the Paris Peace Conference. He remained abroad and died in London.

Chaikovsky, Peter Ilich   See TCHAIKOVSKY, PETER ILICH.

Chaliapin, Feodor Ivanovich (1873–1938)
singer

In a long and celebrated international career, Chaliapin established himself as one of the most famous bass singers of all time. Born to a poor family in KAZAN, east of Moscow, Chaliapin first learned his craft in small provincial companies where he took on both bass and baritone roles. He made his opera debut in Moscow in 1896 and joined the Bolshoi Opera in 1899. Here he developed his first signature role, playing the title role in MUSSORGSKY's *Boris Godunov*. Chaliapin defined the role for future generations through a sensitive portrayal that presented GODUNOV as noble and dignified, but tortured by guilt. His reputation growing, Chaliapin sang at La Scala in Milan (1901), traveled to the United States in 1908, and worked with DIAGHILEV in Paris (1908–9). Everywhere he performed, his singing and acting talents met with great acclaim. He emigrated from Soviet Russia in 1921 and worked in the United States (1922–25) before settling in Paris. After he moved to Paris, his health began to decline. In emigration, Chaliapin widened his repertory beyond the Russian operas that had initially brought him fame. Not only did he tackle expected roles such as King Philip II in Verdi's *Don Carlos*, he created the role of Don Quixote in Massenet's *Don Quichote*, and he surprised audiences with a gift for comedy as Don Basilio in Rossini's *Barber of Seville*. Chaliapin brought dramatic insight and force, as well as vocal skill, to the operatic stage. His autobiography was first published in Leningrad in 1926, and the following year in English as *Pages from My Life*. After his death in Paris, Soviet authorities approached his family many times requesting permission to move his remains from France to the Soviet Union. This was always rejected until finally, in 1984, permission was granted and he was reburied at Novodeviche Cemetery, Moscow, with great ceremony.

Chapaev, Vasili Ivanovich (1887–1919)
partisan leader

A former laborer, Chapaev was hailed as a hero of the Red Army during the Russian civil war, when he commanded a division in the Urals. His Twenty-fifth Rifle Division took active part in the capture of the town of Ufa in April 1919, an important stage in the struggle against Aleksandr

KOLCHAK's White troops. Chapaev's place in Soviet history as a legendary commander, however, owes more to the literary efforts of his political commissar, Dmitrii Andreevich Furmanov (1891–1926), than to the relative importance of his own military exploits. In his immensely popular novel *Chapaev* (1923), Furmanov glorified the commander he had worked with to create the image of a down-to-earth, cunning and wise, self-made revolutionary commander—a folk hero for the new Soviet era. The civil war provided ample adventure material for the Soviet public, and the civil war partisans, riding horseback into battle, replaced the prerevolutionary Cossack as the folk symbol of independence and daring. Chapaev became the prototype of tough, rude, loyal, and witty civil war commanders who treated their troops as equals but were ultimately wiser and more cunning than they. A man of the people, this folk hero was also contemptuous of brass and bureaucrats. The legend of Chapaev really took off with the wildly successful film adaptation *Chapaev* (1934), for many decades one of the genuinely popular films among Soviet audiences. An entire "cultural industry" developed around the figure of Chapaev that included songs and children's games. But the widespread existence of unofficial jokes and song parodies also revealed that the Soviet public must have also felt that Chapaev's glorification was excessive.

Chayanov, Aleksandr Vasilievich (1888–1939)

economist, writer

An influential agrarian economist of the 1920s who also contributed to art and archaeology and wrote science fiction, Chayanov became a victim of the purges of the 1930s. Born in Moscow, he graduated from the Moscow Institute of Agriculture in 1910 and was appointed to its faculty in 1918. By then he had already established himself as an important agrarian economist with the publication of his *Essays on the Theory of the Peasant Economy* (1912–13). In 1920 he was appointed director of the Research Institute for Agricultural Economics in Moscow, also known as the Chay-

anov Institute. Chayanov's work on the optimal size of peasant farms was much discussed during the 1920s and would later be rediscovered in the West during the 1960s. In 1927 he was accused without foundation of belonging to an anti-Soviet "working-peasant party" but was later released. Feeling the pressure of an increasingly intolerant and politicized scholarly climate, Chayanov reformulated his earlier views and now advocated the creation of massive factory farms. Nevertheless, he was arrested in 1930 and sentenced to death in 1937. He was executed in 1939. During the 1980s his earlier views on the peasant economy, still socialist in content, were reevaluated, as Mikhail GORBACHEV and like-minded reformists sought to find alternative paths of socialist development. Chayanov was formally rehabilitated in 1988.

Chechnya

An autonomous republic of the Russian Federation of about 5,800 square miles (15,000 square kilometers) located in the northern Caucausus, Chechnya has been the site of a brutal war for independence since 1992. Descendants of a mountain-dwelling people organized in clans, most of the 1.2 million Chechens are Muslim. From the 16th to the 18th century, the entire Caucasus region became the object of a three-cornered struggle among Ottoman Turkey, Safavid Persia, and Czarist Russia. In the mid-18th century Sheikh Mansur, a Chechen, led a resistance movement against foreign invaders, but he was captured by Russian forces in 1791. During the 19th century, Russia began its campaign to annex the lands of the northern Caucasus but met with fierce resistance in the areas of modern-day Chechnya and Dagestan. Especially noteworthy was the resistance movement led by Imam SHAMIL, known as the Lion of Dagestan, from the 1830s until his capture in 1859. At the time of the collapse of the Russian Empire and the Russian Revolution of 1917, the Chechens again rebelled against Russian rule, but by 1920 they had been brought under Soviet rule. During the 1930s, like other peoples of the Soviet Union, the Chechens were forced to join collective farms and suffered religious persecution. A territorial reorganization led to the formation of the Chechen-Ingush Autonomous Republic in 1936.

World War II brought massive changes to the Chechen lands. In February 1944 the Chechen and Ingush were deported en masse to inhospitable lands in Central Asia as punishment for their alleged collaboration with Nazi German occupation forces. The Soviet government abolished the Chechen-Ingush Autonomous Republic, and the Chechen and Ingush lived in internal exile until January 1957, when the republic was restored. The bitter experience of exile shaped generations of future Chechen leaders. In late 1991, at a time when the Soviet Union was beginning to unravel, Dzhokhar Dudaev, a Soviet army general of Chechen background, expelled the Communist government in Grozny, the Chechen capital. Elected president in October, Dudaev declared Chechnya an independent republic in November 1991. The Russian Federation that succeeded the USSR after December 1991 refused to recognize Chechnya's independence. In December 1994, Russian President Boris YELTSIN authorized an invasion of Chechnya by Russian troops. After bloody fighting that saw the almost complete destruction of Grozny, the Russians entered the capital in February 1995. The Chechens turned to guerrilla warfare, but after Dudaev was killed in a rocket attack in April 1996, both sides were willing to work toward a negotiated agreement signed in August 1996, in which they agreed to postpone a decision on Chechnya's status until 2001. After a wave of spectacular terrorist attacks by Chechen dissidents during 1999, Russian forces again moved into Chechnya in September 1999, beginning a second war that has shown no sign of abating.

Chekhov, Anton Pavlovich
(1860–1904)
writer and playwright
A writer known for his subtle, well-crafted plays and short stories, Chekhov stands with DOSTO-EVSKY, TURGENEV, and TOLSTOY as one of the great

Anton Chekhov *(Hulton/Archive)*

figures of Russian and world literature in the second half of the 19th century. The grandson of a serf and the son of a grocer, Anton Chekhov was born in Taganrog, a port on the Sea of Azov, an inlet of the Black Sea. He lived in Taganrog until 1879, when he left for Moscow to rejoin his family and begin medical studies at Moscow University. Always in financial straits, he supported himself and his family by tutoring and writing humorous sketches for publication. Of greater historical than literary value, these sketches helped Chekhov refine his skills as a short story writer. After graduation in 1884, he increasingly turned to writing, although he never completely abandoned medicine, which he practiced until 1892. His sketches attracted the attention of a prominent St. Petersburg publisher who encouraged him to devote himself to writing as a career. In 1888, he won the prestigious Pushkin Prize for literature awarded by the

ACADEMY OF SCIENCES. In 1890, he traveled to the distant island of Sakhalin on the Pacific Ocean, then the site of a penal colony. His heartfelt writings about his experiences were well received, contributing to his growing fame and more concretely to the introduction of some prison reforms. Later Chekhov's association with the theater came to dominate his life and work. His earlier one-act plays gave way to the major four-act dramas still in the international repertoire: *The Seagull* (1896), *Uncle Vanya* (1897), *Three Sisters* (1901), and *The Cherry Orchard* (1904). When first staged his full-length plays were poorly received, but a successful restaging of *The Seagull* by the newly established Moscow Art Theater under the direction of Konstantin STANISLAVSKY marked the beginning of a successful collaboration that benefited both Chekhov and the new theater. In 1900 he was elected to the Academy of Sciences but resigned two years later in protest over the academy's refusal to recognize the election of Maksim GORKY. In 1901, after a long bachelorhood, he married the actress Olga Knipper. Sick with tuberculosis during most of his adult life, Chekhov spent much time in the Crimea and in foreign health resorts. He never completely healed and while resting at a resort in Badenweiler, Germany, he died on July 15, 1904, and was buried in Moscow at the Novodeviche Cemetery. Though Chekhov was relatively unknown outside of Russia at the time of his death, the translation of his works into English made his work an essential part of the universal canon of modern drama.

Chernenko, Konstantin Ustinovich
(1911–1985)
Soviet leader

Chernenko's short-lived rule (1984–85) was seen as the last obstacle to the emergence of a younger generation of Soviet leaders after the long BREZHNEV era. Yet his career also demonstrates the importance of patronage in the late Soviet era. He was born to a peasant family in the region of Krasnoyarsk in Siberia. He joined

the COMMUNIST PARTY in 1930 and served soon after in the Cheka border guard detachments, before moving on to several party posts in Siberia. In the 1950s he was transferred to the recently annexed Moldavian S.S.R., where he met the then-party leader, Leonid Brezhnev. Chernenko became his loyal assistant and his career benefited immensely from Brezhnev's ascending star. Following Brezhnev's transfer to Moscow and emergence as KHRUSHCHEV's successor, Chernenko became a candidate member of the party Central Committee in 1966, a full member in 1971, and one of its secretaries in 1976. Two years later he joined the Politburo, a reward for years of devoted service to Brezhnev. Widely seen as Brezhnev's likely successor and the candidate of the status quo Brezhnevites, he was outmaneuvered by Yuri ANDROPOV, who became general secretary in November 1982. After Andropov's death in 1984, however, Chernenko's candidacy was successful, although questions about his health made it clear this was a stopgap measure, while younger politicians sorted out the succession behind the scenes. Not as reactionary or as incompetent as his opponents portrayed him, Chernenko saw the need for reforms and agreed to the transfer of substantial unofficial power to Mikhail GORBACHEV. He died in March 1985 of complications from emphysema after a long illness, and was succeeded by Gorbachev.

Cherniaev, Mikhail Grigorievich
(1828–1898)
general

A general of conservative and pan-Slav views whose penchant for independent action brought him into frequent clashes with the government of ALEXANDER II, Cherniaev played a leading role in the campaigns that led to the Russian conquest of Central Asia in the 1860s. Cherniaev first made his name in 1858, when he led an army detachment in support of rebels against the Khan of Khiva. In 1864, while completing a mission to build a defensive line between the Siberian and

Orenburg steppes, he seized the towns of Ali-Atka, Chimkent, and Tashkent from the Khan of Kokand. In 1865 he was appointed military governor of Turkestan, but he was dismissed the following year for exceeding his authority. As editor with Rostislav Fadeev of the reactionary journal *Russian World* (1875–78), he opposed the Czar's military reforms and advocated Pan-Slav imperialist views. His support of Slavs in their liberation struggles from Turkish rule led him to accept the command of the Serbian army in 1876. When the RUSSO-TURKISH WAR broke out the following year, he was refused permission to rejoin the Russian army. His fortunes improved again after 1881 with the new and more conservative czar, ALEXANDER III. In 1882 he was promoted to lieutenant general and appointed governor-general of Turkestan. In 1884 he became a member of the War Council.

Chernobyl

Home to the Chernobyl Power Plant near Kiev in Ukraine, Chernobyl was the site of the most severe nuclear accident to date, the consequences of which are still being felt in the region. On April 26, 1986, plant operators drastically reduced the power in reactor Number 4, one of the plant's four graphite reactors, by almost one-half as part of a controlled experiment to evaluate the response to a sudden loss of electrical power. The reactor overheated causing a meltdown of the core, and two explosions blew off the top of the reactor, releasing roughly seven tons of radioactive fuel out of the building. For more than 10 days, clouds of radioactive material were released into the atmosphere, blowing northward over Belarus and toward Scandinavia. About 70 percent of the radiation fell on neighboring Belarus. The disaster came early in the tenure of Mikhail GORBACHEV as Soviet ruler, and the Soviet government's initial response was one of secrecy. But after other nations called for a fuller disclosure, the government admitted to the magnitude of the accident. The Chernobyl accident is seen as one of the events that contributed to the development of Gorbachev's policy of glasnost (openness). The exact toll of the accident remains unclear, but scientists estimate that the people of the Chernobyl area were exposed to 100 times the radioactivity of the bomb dropped on Hiroshima in 1945. More than 600,000 people involved in the cleanup are known to have died or have fallen sick since 1986. In Belarus, which suffered the brunt of the exposure, babies were still being born without arms or eyes 10 years after the disaster. Other estimates note that over 15 million people were victimized by the accident. In 1991, reactor Number 2 was shut down, but five years later, despite the obvious symbolism of Chernobyl, the Ukrainian government announced plans to reopen the Number 2 reactor.

Chernyshevsky, Nikolai Gavrilovich (1828–1889)
writer

Best known to posterity for his political novel, *What Is to Be Done?*, Chernyshevsky was a journalist and a prominent intellectual leader in the 1850s and 1860s, known for his radical views. Chernyshevsky, the son of a priest, was born in the Volga River town of Saratov. After initial studies at the Saratov Seminary, he rejected his father's career to pursue studies in philology at St. Petersburg University. There his thinking began to take shape under the influence of the leading critic of the 1840s, Vissarion BELINSKY, who impressed on his followers the importance of social engagement in literature and criticism. After a brief attempt at teaching in Saratov, Chernyshevsky returned to St. Petersburg and joined the editorial staff of the progressive journal *The Contemporary* (*Sovremennik*) in 1853. Writing during the reformist decade that followed the death of NICHOLAS I and Russia's defeat in the CRIMEAN WAR, Chernyshevsky gained a reputation for well-crafted, increasingly blunt critiques of liberalism, advocating instead greater concern for Russia's peasantry, at a time when the Russian government was planning the abolition of SERFDOM. As Russia's political climate turned more conservative in the early 1860s, Chernyshevsky became increasingly popular among students. A letter from the émigré revolutionary leader Aleksandr HERZEN, intercepted by the authorities, led to his arrest in 1862. He was imprisoned in St. Petersburg's Peter and Paul Fortress, where he wrote *What Is to Be Done?*, a novel whose title succinctly captured the concerns and growing impatience of Russia's radicalized youth with the state of their society. The novel presented a world of well-intentioned, rational-thinking "new people," devoted to the transformation of Russian society, and introduced the character of Rakhmetev, a professional revolutionary who sought to live by this strict code. It became required reading for generations of future intellectuals and revolutionaries, including Vladimir LENIN, who wrote an important political tract of the same name in 1902. In 1864, Chernyshevsky was sentenced to seven years of labor and exiled for life to northern Siberia. The harshness of Siberian exile harmed his health, and in 1883, he was allowed to return to Saratov. Like Herzen, a pivotal though ambiguous figure in the development of Russian social thought, Chernyshevsky contributed to the intellectual development of both Populists and Marxists, rivals in the struggle for leadership of Russia's revolutionary movement. Both groups of revolutionaries were strongly influenced by his utilitarian aesthetics and philosophical materialism and his belief in historical determinism, tempered to account for Russia's comparatively slow development.

Chicherin, Boris Nikolaevich
(1828–1904)
historian and philosopher

One of the outstanding Russian liberal intellectuals of the 19th century, Chicherin was also a jurist who took part in politics. He was born on his family's estate in Tambov province but made his career in Moscow. By 1858, through several important historical studies, Chicherin had established himself as a leading historian. In his work, Chicherin became known as the advocate of the "statist" school of Russian historiography, arguing for the essentially progressive role of the Russian state. He tempered his defense of the state with the liberal beliefs in individual freedoms, property rights, and toleration of religious and ethnic minorities. Throughout his political life, he advocated substantial reforms, beginning with the abolition of serfdom, but always in the context of nonviolent, legal change. In 1861 he was appointed professor of law at Moscow University, but he resigned seven years later in protest against the government's interference in a tenure case. In 1881 Chicherin reentered politics when he was elected mayor of Moscow, but he was forced to resign in 1883 when his public views on popular government clashed with the autocratic preferences of ALEXANDER III. He returned to scholarship, publishing works such as *The Foundations of Logic and Metaphysics* (1894), *On Popular Representation* (1899), and *The Philosophy of Law* (1900). In the latter years of his life, he took part in the politics of the Tambov provincial ZEMSTVO. He died at the family estate on February 16, 1904. His four-volume memoirs were published posthumously from 1929 to 1934.

Chicherin, Georgii Vasilievich
(1872–1936)
revolutionary and diplomat

A Bolshevik of noble background, Chicherin served as Soviet foreign minister in the first decade after the October Revolution. Chicherin, a relative of the renowned liberal philosopher and historian Boris Nikolaevich CHICHERIN, was born on his family's estate in Tambov province. He graduated from St. Petersburg University in 1897 and joined the Foreign Ministry. In 1904 after years of involvement in the revolutionary movement, Chicherin resigned his government post, renounced all claims to family estates, and emigrated to Berlin. There he joined the Menshevik faction of the Russian Social Democratic Labor Party. Chicherin spent the next decade working with the labor movement in Great Britain, France, and Germany. World War I found him in London, where he engaged in relief work while speaking out against the war. The British government confined him to Brixton Prison as an enemy agent soon after the Bolshevik revolution of October 1917. In January 1918 he was freed in exchange for the British ambassador to Russia, Sir George Buchanan, who had been jailed by the BOLSHEVIKS. Chicherin returned to Russia for the first time in 14 years and joined the Bolshevik Party. He returned to diplomatic work for the Bolshevik government and participated in the final stages of the Treaty of BREST-LITOVSK, signed in March 1918. In May 1918 he was appointed commissar for foreign affairs, a position he held until 1930. As foreign minister, Chicherin's greatest achievement was to end the post-revolutionary isolation of the Soviet Union with regard to other European nations. Most impressively, he conducted the secret negotiations with Germany that led to the Treaty of Rapallo of April 1922 that reestablished commercial and diplomatic relations between the two nations. Never a member of the Bolshevik inner circles, Chicherin did not shape Soviet foreign policy, but he executed the policies with skill until his rapidly deteriorating health prevented him from doing so. He resigned in 1930 and lived the final years of his life in Moscow.

Chigorin (Tchigorin), Mikhail Ivanovich (1850–1908)

chess master

Widely considered to be the founder of the Russian school of chess, Chigorin is also recognized as one of the great pioneers in the theoretical study of chess openings. He was born in the town of Gatchina, home to one of the royal palaces near St. Petersburg, and grew up in an orphanage. A relative latecomer to the world of chess, Chigorin entered his first tournament at the age of 20, but by 1879 he had established himself as the leading Russian player, after winning the St. Petersburg championship. During the 1880s,

Chigorin became an internationally recognized chess player. In 1886–87 he defeated Wilhelm Steinitz, recently crowned as the first world chess champion, in a postal match held in London and St. Petersburg. This victory earned him the right to play Steinitz for the world championship in a match that was held in Havana in 1889. Chigorin was soundly defeated by Steinitz by a score of 10 to 6, with one draw. Other victories followed for Chigorin, including a cochampionship in New York a few months after his loss to Steinitz. Chigorin's questioning of the theoretical soundness of some of Steinitz's opening led to two games played by telegraph between the two masters, both of which Chigorin won. Steinitz accepted another challenge for the world title, and the rematch was held again in Havana in 1892. This time Chigorin played Steinitz more closely, but a colossal blunder in the 24th game allowed Steinitz to retain his title. Chigorin never challenged again for the world title, but he remained one of the leading players of his time, winning tournaments in Budapest (1896), Moscow (1899 and 1901), Kiev (1903), Vienna (1903), and St. Petersburg (1905). His influence on the development of 20th-century Russian chess was undisputable, as he was not only instrumental in organizing the first All-Russian tournament, but also in organizing the first correspondence chess tournaments, as well as the first interscholastic tournaments. Chigorin died in the Polish town of Lublin on January 25, 1908, at the age of 58, an early death hastened by alcoholism. Just a few months earlier, as if sensing his impending death, he burned his chess board.

Chinese Eastern Railway

A railroad built by Russia between 1896–1903 that connected the Pacific Ocean port of Vladivostok to the TRANS-SIBERIAN RAILROAD by cutting through Chinese territory in MANCHURIA. Arrangements for the construction of the Chinese Eastern Railway were made by Russia and China in a secret agreement of 1896 that followed the Sino-Japanese War of 1894–95. The rail line broke off from the Trans-Siberian Railroad at Chita, east of Lake Baikal and headed in a southeasterly direction into Manchuria through the city of Harbin before reentering Russian territory and ending at Vladivostok. It provided a quicker route to Vladivostok than the original route of the Trans-Siberian Railroad route. In 1898, Russia pressured China to allow the construction of another spur, the South Manchurian Railway, connecting Harbin with Port Arthur on the Yellow Sea, which Russia had recently leased from China. The product of Russian imperial designs at a time of Chinese political weakness, the Chinese Eastern Railway continued to be a bone of contention between the two nations after the OCTOBER REVOLUTION. Even after the Soviet Union renounced Russia's previous territorial claims over China in 1924, it held on to the Chinese Eastern Railway. The Chinese nationalist government briefly seized the line in 1927, but returned it in 1929. In 1935 the Soviet Union agreed to sell the railway to Manchukuo, the puppet government installed by Japan in Manchuria. As part of the Sino-Soviet Treaty of 1945 signed with the Chinese Nationalist government, the Soviet Union obtained a 30-year partnership agreement to manage the railway. Eight years later with the Chinese Communists in power, the Soviet Union yielded its share of the partnership to the Chinese government.

Chkalov, Valerii Pavlovich (1904–1938)
pilot

A record-breaking pilot in the 1930s, Chkalov was born in Nizhnii-Novgorod province, east of Moscow, to a working-class family. At the age of 15 he volunteered for the Red Army and worked as an engine fitter in the Nizhnii-Novgorod aviation park. From 1921 to 1924 he studied at various aviation schools in the Moscow region, qualifying as a fighter pilot. From 1924, he served in the Krasnoznamennoi (Red Flag) Fighter Squadron, where he gained distinction as a skillful pilot. As of 1930, he tested more than 70 types of airplanes and developed and introduced new aerial maneuvers such as the ascending corkscrew and the delayed *bochka* (barrel roll). Chkalov became one of "STALIN's falcons," celebrity pilots in an era when the regime promoted aviation as a heroic emblem of a new world forged by science and technology. He achieved several long-distance world records for his time: In November 1936 he and his crew completed the first direct flight from Moscow to Kamchatka, a distance of 9,734 kilometers, in 56 hours and 20 minutes. Eight months later, in July 1937, Chkalov flew with the same crew from Moscow across the North Pole to the outskirts of Portland, Oregon, a distance of 8,504 kilometers, in 63 hours and 16 minutes. On December 15, 1938, he died in an air crash while testing a new fighter plane. In his lifetime Chkalov was made deputy of the Supreme Soviet and awarded the Order of Lenin and the Order of the Red Flag. When he died, his hometown of Orenburg was renamed Chkalov in his honor, although in 1957 it reverted to its former name. He was buried at the Kremlin wall on RED SQUARE.

Chukovskaya, Lidia Korneevna (1907–1996)
writer

A poet, novelist, and literary critic who spoke out in defense of dissidents persecuted by the Soviet government, Chukovskaya was born in St. Petersburg, the daughter of the prominent writer Kornei Ivanovich CHUKOVSKY (1882–1969). She grew up in the literary atmosphere of her family's house in St. Petersburg and the country dacha in Kuokkala (Repino). Chukovskaya studied in some of the city's most prestigious schools, such as the Tagantsev Gimnasium and the Tenishev School. Her complaints against the arbitrary actions of the city's Communist Youth League (KOMSOMOL) led to an 11-month-long term of exile to the city of Saratov in 1926. Her father's intervention secured her release and return to Leningrad (as St. Petersburg was renamed in 1924). In 1928 she graduated from Leningrad

State University and obtained a position in the children's division of the Leningrad branch of the state publishing house, Gosizdat, working under the direction of Samuil Marshak, a close friend of her father. Under the pseudonym of Aleksei Uglov, she published a number of well-regarded children's stories, such as *Leningrad-Odessa* (1928), *The Story of Taras Shevchenko* (1930), and *On the Volga* (1931). Chukovskaya suffered personally from the terror of the 1930s: her husband was arrested in 1937 while she was under surveillance from the secret police. Of her many publications, the novel *Sofia Petrovna,* an account of the impact of the repression of the 1930s on simple, apolitical citizens, written in 1939–40 but first published in Paris in 1965, is considered her masterpiece. In the 1960s she emerged as a particularly courageous opponent of the Soviet government's persecution of literary and political dissidents. Her defense of the writers Andrei SINYAVSKY and Yuli Daniel during their 1966 trial and her repeated interventions on behalf of Andrei SAKHAROV and Aleksandr SOLZHENITSYN ultimately led to her expulsion from the Union of Soviet Writers in 1974. In 1978 she published a collection of her poetry under the title *On this Side of Death.* From 1976 to 1980 she published in book form under the title *Notes about Anna Akhmatova* the text of her notes of conversations she conducted with Anna AKHMATOVA in the years from 1938 to 1941 and from 1952 to 1962, an invaluable historical document of the poet whom the Soviet government had much maligned.

Chukovsky, Kornei Ivanovich (1882–1969)
writer

A writer, critic, historian, and translator, Chukovsky was perhaps best known to generations of readers as the author of popular children's stories. Chukovsky was born Nikolai Vasilievich Korneichukov in St. Petersburg, but grew up in ODESSA with his mother, a Ukrainian peasant. His writing career began while still in Odessa. He worked one year in London as a correspondent (1903–4), and by 1914 he had become a successful journalist. His knowledge of English helped him develop a second career as a translator, translating numerous authors including Walt Whitman. With the poet Nikolai GUMILEV, he published a work on the art of translation in 1919. As a literary critic, Chukovsky was particularly interested in the work of the radical poet Nikolai NEKRASOV (1821–77), producing an edition of his complete works that was published in 1927. But it was in the area of children's literature that Chukovsky made an indelible imprint in the Russian and Soviet world. Beginning with *The Crocodile,* published in 1917, he wrote numerous books that captivated children and adults with their humor, wordplay, metaphors, puns, and made-up words. Many of these stories later provided the material for radio, television, and film scripts. His own complete works were published in six volumes in Moscow (1965–69). Oxford University awarded him an honorary doctorate in literature in 1962. Chukovsky died in Moscow on October 28, 1969. His daughter Lidia Chukovskaya became a noted writer and literary critic in her own right.

Communist Party

The Communist Party was formally founded in 1919 when the former BOLSHEVIK Party was renamed the All-Russian Communist Party. Until 1991 it exercised a monopoly of power within the Soviet Union, while exercising a hegemonic influence over most other Communist parties elsewhere. Until his death in 1924, Vladimir LENIN dominated the party, although he carried no formal title. At the time of the Bolshevik revolution, the party had only about 200,000 members, most of who had joined during the revolutionary year of 1917. The civil war of 1918–21, during which the party changed its name from Bolshevik to Communist, tested its ability to organize a new government and rule a vast country in the process of disintegration. With ruthless determination and, some would

Joseph Stalin addressing the 19th Congress of the Communist Party of the Soviet Union at the Kremlin in Moscow, 1952 *(Library of Congress)*

argue, at the cost of silencing more democratic voices within the party, the Communists outlasted their rivals and emerged victorious by 1921. In 1921, other political parties were banned and Soviet Russia (known as the Soviet Union since 1923) became a one-party dictatorship. After Lenin's death, a period of stormy intraparty debates over the Soviet Union's future path developed among his closest advisers, with Joseph STALIN eventually emerging as his successor by 1929. Stalin's victory reinforced the already strong authoritarian tendencies within the party, which had been renamed All-Union Communist Party (Bolshevik) in 1925 to account for the multiethnic nature of the Soviet Union. In the late 1920s and early 1930s, the party presided over a period of dramatic social trans-

formations in the areas of industrialization and the collectivization of agriculture. By 1933, the party had about 3 million members, mostly based in urban centers, although collectivization expanded the rural base of the party. Yet, another social trauma still lay ahead for the party and the Soviet Union. The assassination of Sergei Kirov in 1934, the party leader of Leningrad, triggered a period of mass terror that greatly affected the Communist Party. The show trials and execution of former leaders and rivals of Stalin such as Nikolai BUKHARIN, Grigorii ZINOVIEV, and Lev KAMENEV on grounds of treason were only the tip of a nationwide campaign, now known as the Great Terror, or Great Purge. With the purges drawing to a close in 1938, party membership declined to 1.9 million. Party membership rebounded in response to the German invasion of the Soviet Union in 1941, and the Communist Party contributed to the eventual Soviet victory through its organization of the home front in support of the military effort. In the final years of Stalin's long rule, the party remained under the strict control of Stalin and his inner circle, without a party congress called between 1939 and 1952.

Nikita KHRUSHCHEV's Secret Speech at the Twentieth Party Congress of 1956 launched a campaign of de-Stalinization that peaked six years later at the Twenty-Second Party Congress of 1962, when Stalin's body was removed from its place of honor alongside Lenin in the LENIN MAUSOLEUM and buried in RED SQUARE along with other prominent Communist Party functionaries. Khrushchev's frequent administrative reorganizations and personnel turnover contributed to his own overthrow in October 1964. The collective leadership of Leonid BREZHNEV and Aleksei KOSYGIN that replaced him pledged themselves to a policy of "stability of cadres" that promised to end the terror of the Stalin years and the impulsiveness of the Khrushchev era. By the 1970s Brezhnev had emerged as the dominant figure in the leadership, the preferred choice of an aging group of party bureaucrats concerned with maintaining their hold on power. The constitution of 1977 legalized the monopoly of power that the Communist Party had enjoyed since 1921.

By 1985, after a three-year period of transition that witnessed the deaths of three elderly Soviet leaders (Brezhnev, Yuri ANDROPOV, and Konstantin CHERNENKO), Mikhail GORBACHEV was named first secretary of the Communist Party and was charged with the task of reforming the party and the Soviet Union. As Gorbachev advanced his reform program, the party found itself divided, with some members calling for greater reforms and others resisting what seemed to be the end of their personal privileges. A big issue of the late Gorbachev years was the removal of the party's monopoly and "leading role" in the Soviet political system. In February 1990, the Communist Party, prodded by Gorbachev and other reformists, called for the end of its constitutional guarantee of power. In March 1990 the Congress of Peoples' Deputies repealed Article Six of the Soviet Constitution, which had guaranteed the party's political monopoly. In August 1991 hard-line party leaders in alliance with like-thinking members of the military and security services launched the failed AUGUST COUP hoping to halt the transformation of the Soviet Union. In the backlash against the plotters, Russian President Boris YELTSIN outlawed the party and confiscated its property on the eve of the dissolution of the Soviet Union itself in December 1991.

In post–Soviet Russia, the party reemerged from illegality as the Communist Party of the Russian Federation (CPRF) under the leadership of Gennadi Ziuganov. No longer the leading political force in Russia, it tried to slow the overall transformation of the country into a non-Communist society. Nevertheless, aided by the hardships suffered by ordinary Russians throughout the post-Soviet period, the Communists remained a formidable political force that won the largest bloc of seats in the 1995 parliamentary elections, while Ziuganov ran close to Yeltsin in the 1996 presidential elections, before losing in the second round. In the 1999 parliamentary elections, the party gained a plurality of the votes but was outnumbered by a pro-government alliance. Soon after his election in 2000, President Vladimir PUTIN surprised observers by forming a parliamentary alliance with the Communists, but in April 2002 the alliance collapsed and the CPRF lost its leadership positions in the parliament.

Congress of Berlin   See BERLIN, CONGRESS OF.

Copper Revolt (1662)
The Copper Revolt of 1662 was one of the briefest, but most intriguing disturbances in the reign of ALEKSEI MIKHAILOVICH (1645–76), a reign that witnessed frequent expressions of domestic

discontent. By the late 1650s the beginning of a long war with Poland over Ukraine (1654–67), cholera epidemics (1654–57), bad harvests (1656–58), and major military reverses (1659–61) had resulted in increasing distress for Muscovy while imposing a heavy financial drain on its resources. The roots of the Copper Revolt lay in the financially strapped government's decision to increasingly substitute copper coinage of lesser value for silver coins, while maintaining their previous parity. As the copper coins depreciated, an inflationary spiral rapidly set in, accompanied by food shortages. The spark that led to the one-day revolt was the government's insistence on being paid in silver, while paying its obligations in copper. This smoldering discontent suddenly broke into the open on July 25, 1662, when a crowd of about 5,000 assembled in RED SQUARE to hear soldiers and traders attack rich speculators and profiteers. Later, the crowd marched to Kolomenskoe, the czar's summer residence, where Aleksei Mikhailovich addressed the crowd in a conciliatory manner. Another crowd of about 5,000 in Moscow was not as easily placated, with some engaging in looting of merchant depots, and by the afternoon almost 10,000 people were milling about Moscow. The Czar's troops arrested about 2,000 at Kolomenskoe, while in Moscow over 200 of the supposed ringleaders were arrested. The next morning 18 were summarily executed, and the demonstration ended soon after. Although the revolt was suppressed with ease by the government, it undoubtedly contributed to the decision to withdraw the debased copper coinage from circulation in 1663 and to replace it with a more stable silver system. But the roots of deeper discontent remained, ready to be stirred by a much more serious rebellion, soon to be led by Stenka RAZIN.

Cossacks (Russian: *kazaki*; Ukrainian: *kozaky*)

Drawing their name from the word of Turkic origin that means "free warrior," the Cossacks developed as an important military community, which for many centuries asserted its autonomy with regard to the states of Russia and Poland-Lithuania. Originally situated in the territories of modern Ukraine and southern European Russia, Cossack communities later developed in southern Siberia and the Far East. The irregular frontier troops of the Crimean Khanate and the principality of Ryazan during the 15th century were known as Cossacks, and in the following century large and vigorous Cossack communities arose along the banks of the middle and lower Dnieper and of the Don and its tributaries. Their ranks were increased by people, mostly peasants, fleeing Polish-Lithuanian religious oppression and Muscovite heavy taxation and political tyranny. More important, they were fleeing the growth of SERFDOM in both states. Some Don Cossacks established themselves, also during the 16th century on the Rivers Ural and Terek, and there formed autonomous communities. Life in the Cossack territories had some resemblance to that in the American Wild West. Apart from military raids, the occupations of the Cossacks were hunting, fishing, and from the 17th century, agriculture. Principles of direct democracy governed their internal organization, with elected atamans (hetmans). Relations between the Russian government and the Cossacks were for a long time unstable, ranging from direct service, as in the conquest of Siberia, to uneasy alliance vis-à-vis TURKEY, and to several open rebellions. The Cossacks were gradually brought under central authority in the 18th and 19th centuries, retaining local self-government, and they became a prosperous, exclusive, hereditary estate of the realm with a growing internal differentiation between Cossacks and non-Cossack peasants. The government created new Cossack communities (ASTRAKHAN, Orenburg, Siberia, Transbaikalia, Kuban, Amur, Semirechye, Ussuri); some non-Russian peoples (Kalmyks, Bashkirs) were also made Cossacks. All Cossacks were obliged to serve in Cossack military units, which distinguished themselves in many wars, and by the late 19th and early 20th centuries they had completed the evolution from rebels to feared elite

Soviet Cossack guards attack in the Crimea, ca. 1940 *(Library of Congress)*

cavalry units of the Russian army, who were often used for police purposes.

Cossack communities responded to the FEBRU-ARY REVOLUTION by forming small autonomous republics with elected *atamans,* and in the spirit of the times, by establishing the All-Russian Cossack Union. Most Cossacks were hostile to the Bolshevik seizure of power, taking an active part in the civil war on the White side, and in the Kuban region, for example, continuing guerrilla warfare until 1924. Soviet rule impacted heavily on Cossack life. After 1920, richer Cossacks were deprived of their wealth, traditional forms of local administration were abolished, Cossack soldiers were relieved of their special military and police duties, and Cossack cavalry units were abolished. Cossacks were forced to engage in collective farming, and resistance to collectivization was fierce, especially in the Kuban region during 1932–33. As a result, many were deported from their lands and resettled in Kazakhstan or Siberia, even though in 1936 they were officially "forgiven" and some cavalry units were given the appellation of Cossack. During World War II, Cossack units fought in both the Soviet and German armies; those of the latter who had taken part in the Italian campaign were compulsorily repatriated by the British, and many were banished to the labor camps of the GULAG. Nevertheless, despite the turmoil of the early Soviet era, some Cossack customs and traditions survived, most notably the distinctive Caucasian-derived dress and the fine horsemanship, especially in the areas of the Don and Kuban Rivers. Cossack organizations experienced a sudden revival in the final years of the Soviet Union, with the formation of Cossack associations in the Russian south, the north Caucasus, and the Ural Mountains. In 1990, various Cossack associations came together in a national union, and by 1992 Cossack associations had appeared not only in traditional Cossack lands, but in various northern cities, such as St. Petersburg and Moscow.

Costakis, George (1912–1990)
(Georgii Dionisovich Costakis)
art collector

A famous art collector, Costakis almost single-handedly preserved the legacy of the Russian avant-garde from neglect and destruction through his savvy and dedication. He was born in Moscow, the son of a wealthy Greek tobacco merchant who lost his tobacco plantations in Uzbekistan at the time of the Russian Revolution. Early on, he developed a passion for collecting, beginning with rare stamps, icons, porcelain, and silver. He first worked at the Greek embassy in Moscow before moving on to the Canadian embassy, where his modest salary was paid in foreign currency, which enabled him to enlarge his collection. In the post-STALIN years he met Vladimir Tatlin, Aleksandr RODCHENKO, and other surviving leaders of the remarkable avant-garde movement that had flourished between 1910 and 1925. Over time he found and contacted over 100 members of the avant-garde, and by the mid-1960s he had amassed a collection of almost 2,000 avant-garde works. During the KHRUSHCHEV years he counted on the support of powerful politicians like the minister of culture, Ekaterina FURTSEVA, but after 1964 he came into more frequent conflict with a government that now realized the true value of his collection. Considered a speculator by the KGB, he was forced to leave the Soviet Union in 1978 and leave behind a large part of his collection as a form of payment for his exit visa. Costakis settled in Athens and lent his surviving collection for exhibits in the United States, England, and Western Europe that further opened the eyes of the West to the achievements and depth of the Russian avant-garde.

Crimean War (1853–1856)

A war fought by Russia against an alliance of Great Britain, France, the Ottoman Empire, and Piedmont-Sardinia. The roots of the war lay in several long-term mid–19th-century conflicts: the weakness of the Ottoman Empire, Russia's policy of championing the interests of the Ottoman Empire's Slavic subjects, and the overall conflict between Russian and British interests in Asia. The issue that triggered the war, however, was a dispute over which Christian power was to control the holy places in Ottoman-ruled Palestine. By 1853 Napoleon III, emperor of the French, had maneuvered the Sultan to grant the French certain privileges to Catholics in the Holy Land. Czar NICHOLAS I, who had long seen Russia as the protector of Christians in the region, now demanded a Russian protectorate over all Orthodox subjects of the Ottoman Empire. Great Britain and France, already nervous about the extension of Russian influence over the Ottoman Empire, sided with Turkey. Confident of British and French support, Turkey declared war on Russia in October 1853. The destruction of the Turkish flotilla at Sinop by Russian naval forces led by Admiral Pavel NAKHIMOV threatened to tilt the balance of this RUSSO-TURKISH WAR in favor of the Russians, and Great Britain and France declared war on Russia in March 1854.

The war, the first major European conflict for Russia since its victory in the Napoleonic Wars, proved to be disastrous for Russia. Although Russian soldiers fought heroically, their commanders generally proved incompetent. The centerpiece of the war was the yearlong siege of the fortress city of SEVASTOPOL on the Crimean Peninsula, which began in September 1854. After one year of steady bombardment the Allies overran Russian defenses and captured the city. The prospect of further military defeats, the death of Nicholas I in 1855, and the threat of active Austrian intervention against Russia convinced the new czar, ALEXANDER II, to sue for peace. The ensuing Treaty of Paris, signed in March 1856, laid down harsh terms for Russia. Russia was prohibited from rebuilding both its Black Sea fleet and the fortress of Sevastopol. It surrendered all claim to a protectorate over Orthodox subjects of the Ottoman Empire, as well as the territory of southern Bessarabia and its protectorate over Wallachia and Moldavia, the core principalities of the future Kingdom of Romania. Russia's defeat in the Crimean War is generally credited with providing the necessary motivation for the GREAT REFORMS implemented by Alexander II, especially the abolition of SERFDOM, which was seen as the symbol and cause of Russia's competitive backwardness in relation to Great Britain and France. It is also credited with turning Russia's future imperial ambitions eastward toward Central Asia and the Far East. In 1871, during the Franco-Prussian War, Russia unilaterally abrogated the clause that prohibited it from building its Black Sea Fleet.

Cyrillic alphabet

An alphabet originally developed in the ninth century that has survived with important modifications to serve as the present alphabet of most Eastern and Southern Slavic peoples. Legend has it that two Greek missionaries from Constantinople, St. Cyril (after whom it is named) and St. Methodius, "Apostles to the Slavs," invented the alphabet to assist in their efforts to Christianize the Moravians. Recent scholarship suggests that St. Cyril may have devised the older Glagolitic alphabet, but that the Cyrillic alphabet was perhaps devised by one of his followers. The alphabet, originally consisting of 43 letters, was based on Greek and Latin letters in the ninth-century uncial script, with additional letters invented to represent Slavic sounds not found in Greek. Its usage eventually spread to the regions inhabited by the Russians, Ukrainians, Belorussians, Bulgarians, and Serbs, all of whom added or dropped letters to suit their own languages, so that modern Cyrillic alphabets in these countries range from 30 letters in Serbia and Bulgaria to 33 in Russia and Ukraine.

Over the centuries important changes have been made in the Cyrillic alphabet used in Russia. In the early 18th century, PETER I the Great introduced the civil Russian alphabet, a considerable simplification of the old Cyrillic alphabet. Church books continue to use the old alphabet, but after 1710 all other books had to use the civil alphabet. At this time, Peter also introduced Arabic numerals to replace the Slavonic ones then in use. Further changes were made by the Bolshevik government in 1918 to simplify orthography. Under Joseph STALIN, Central Asian and Siberian ethnic minorities adopted, mostly under pressure, the Russian-based Cyrillic alphabet for their written languages, with additional letters for sounds not found in Russian. The impetus behind this move was mostly political—another way to facilitate the integration of these nations into the Russian-dominated Soviet world. In areas, like Central Asia or Buriatiia, where a previous script had been in use, it also meant a break with their classical traditions. After 1991, some of these peoples and nations began to turn away from Cyrillic, as a symbol of Russian colonialism, and adapted Latin script for their languages.

Czech Legion

A corps of almost 40,000 Czech soldiers of the Austro-Hungarian army held in Russian prisoner-of-war camps, which by the accident of history came to play a crucial role in the early stages of the Russian civil war that followed the Bolshevik Revolution of October 1917. The Czech Legion in Russia was the most prominent of three such legions formed to fight the Central Powers and advance Czech interests with the goal of establishing an independent Czech state after World War I. Formed in late 1917, after negotiations between the Czech nationalist leader Jan Masaryk and the Bolshevik government, the Czech Legion in Russia was nominally under French command and posted to the eastern front, virtually dormant since the OCTOBER REVOLUTION. Their hopes of fighting the Central Powers diminished considerably after Soviet Russia pulled out of the war in March 1918, after signing the Treaty of BREST-LITOVSK. Still eager to fight and help establish Czech independence, the legion's leaders arranged with the BOLSHEVIKS to travel eastward along the TRANS-SIBERIAN RAILROAD to Vladivostok, where they would then be transported by ship back to France.

Trouble began in mid-May 1918 soon after the Czech soldiers had embarked in stages for Siberia. At Chelyabinsk, a minor clash with westbound Hungarian prisoners of war resulted in the Czech capture of the town. When local soviet leaders, acting on Bolshevik orders, tried to disarm the Czechs, more serious fighting broke out, this time between the Czechs and local Bolshevik troops. Better armed and organized, the Czechs gradually came to control most of Siberia along the Trans-Siberian Railroad. They now actively sided with Admiral KOLCHAK's White government based in the town of Omsk.

The Czech presence in Russia, accidental as it was, was also part of a broader foreign intervention in Russian affairs during the civil war. From 1918 to 1920, soldiers from 14 countries, primarily Great Britain, France, the United States, and Japan, landed on Russian territory, with the Japanese staying in the Russian Far East until 1922. The Czech Legion completed its evacuation in the spring of 1920, by which time the Bolsheviks were on their way to winning the civil war.

D

Dal, Vladimir Ivanovich (1801–1872)
writer

Dal was an important lexicographer and ethnologist born in Lugansk (Voroshilovgrad in Soviet times) on November 10 (22), 1801. The son of a physician, he enrolled in Dorpat University and graduated from that institution in medical studies. He then worked as a physician and as a civil servant, all the while collecting the flora and fauna of the Orenburg region near the southern edge of the Urals and satisfying his interest in Russian language and literature. He became a close friend of PUSHKIN and was among those present at the death of the poet. In 1838, Dal was elected corresponding member of the St. Petersburg Academy of Sciences for his work in the natural sciences. From his early youth, Dal also collected material on Russian folklore. In 1832 he published a collection of Russian stories and fables, using the pseudonym Kazak Luganskii (Cossack of Lugansk). He also wrote a number of original tales that won broad popular appeal and reflected influence by the naturalist school. In 1862, Dal published his *Poslovitsy russkogo naroda (Proverbs of the Russian People: A Collection of Proverbs, Sayings, Expressions, Sobriquets, Tongue Twisters, Nonsense, Riddles, Folk Wisdom and the Like)*, which listed over 30,000 proverbs and examples of humorous sayings. But his major work was without doubt the *Tolkovyi slovar zhivogo velikorusskogo yazyka* (Explanatory dictionary of the living great Russian language), published in four volumes between 1863 and 1866 after almost half a century of labors. This dictionary lists over 200,000 words and remains the greatest achievement of Russian lexicography. It has gone through numerous editions. For this, Dal was awarded the Lomonosov Prize of the ACADEMY OF SCIENCES and in 1863 was given the title of honored academician. He died in Moscow on September 22 (October 4), 1872. His complete works were first published in a 10-volume edition in St. Petersburg in 1897–98 and again in Moscow in 1956.

Danilevsky, Nikolai Yakovlevich (1822–1885)
writer

A biologist by training, Danilevsky became known as one of the most militant advocates of PAN-SLAVISM, an aggressive nationalist ideology that developed in Russia in the 1870s. Danilevsky was born in the province of Orel (Oryol) about 200 miles southwest of Moscow. As a young student Danilevsky participated in one of the provincial intellectual circles that grew from the Petrashevsky Circle in St. Petersburg. Danilevsky is best known for his book *Russia and Europe,* issued serially in 1868 and published as a book in 1870. In this work, Danilevsky laid out a philosophy that viewed history as the unfolding of distinct civilizations that often came into conflict. He maintained that the conflict of his time was an irreconcilable one between the Western (or Romano-Germanic) world and the Slavic world, of which Russia was the main component. Danilevsky argued that the Slavic world should counteract the West by focusing on its own natural traditions, primarily political absolutism, that differentiated the Slavic from the Western world. Danilevsky's ability to use his

Ekaterina Romanovna Dashkova, ca. 1790
(Hulton/Archive)

training in biology to present his nationalist views as scientific gave them an air of authority that added to their influence among followers of pan-Slavism. He also influenced later philosophers of history, such as Oswald Spengler.

Dashkova, Princess Ekaterina Romanovna (1743–1810)
(née Vorontsova)
writer

An immensely talented woman who excelled as a writer, art connoisseur, teacher, philologist, editor, naturalist, and musician, Dashkova was a noted and controversial intellectual during the reign of CATHERINE II. Born into the prominent aristocratic Vorontsov family, she was educated in the home of her uncle, Mikhail Vorontsov,

chancellor to Empress ELIZABETH. From 1758 she became close to the future empress Catherine II. She actively participated in the palace revolt that brought Catherine to the throne in 1762, although Dashkova's desire to be rewarded more prominently caused an initial rift between the two. Dashkova's first intellectual enterprise was the journal *Nevinnoe uprazhnenie,* which she established in 1763. From 1769 to 1783, she traveled in Europe, where she met leading intellectuals of the day such as Voltaire, Diderot, and Adam Smith. Back in St. Petersburg, from 1783 to 1794 she served as director of the ACADEMY OF SCIENCES and president of the Russian Academy, remarkable appointments for an 18th-century woman. During these years she founded two important publications, *Sobesednik liubitelei russkogo slova* (Companion for Lovers of the Russian Language) (1783–84) and *Novye ezhemesiachnye sochineniia* (1786–96), to which she attracted leading literary figures of her day, such as G. R. Derzhavin, D. I. FONVIZIN, Ia. B. Kniazhnin, V. V. Kapnist, and others. She took part in launching the *Dictionary of the Russian Academy,* as well as the periodical *Russian Theater* (1786–94). In 1794, the publication of Kniazhnin's tragedy *Vadim Novgorodskii* (1793) led to a final rift with Catherine II and Dashkova's removal from her posts. Dashkova played an invaluable role in promoting cultural enlightenment and education in Catherinian Russia. Her memoirs, first published in Russian in 1804–6 and later translated into English as *Memoirs of Princess Dashkova,* were very popular among readers and, while not always reliable in their exposition of historical events, they contain interesting information about the reign of Catherine II and about life in 18th-century Russia.

Davydov, Denis Vasilievich (1784–1839)
soldier and writer

The scion of an aristocratic family, Davydov embarked on a military career in 1801. As an adjutant to BAGRATION from 1806 to 1812, Davydov fought against the French, Swedes, and Turks, distinguishing himself with his bravery in conflict. During Napoleon's invasion of 1812, Davydov became known as the leading advocate and organizer of partisan warfare against the French. His nonconformist ideas and his hatred of ARAKCHEEV, the dominant military figure in the second half of the reign of ALEXANDER I, kept him on the sidelines of power. But despite his liberal ideas and his friendly relations with many prominent members of the future Decembrist movement, he never joined their secret societies. Davydov served in the army until 1832, when he retired with the rank of lieutenant general. As an author, Davydov wrote poetry and historical essays. He was a founder of the Arzamas literary circle, and the themes of his poetry reflect his moderate, freethinking outlook. In his historical writings Davydov forcefully argued for the importance of partisan warfare in turning "the soldiers' war" into a "people's war," while challenging the received wisdom of the day that it was the harsh winter climate that was most responsible for the French defeat after Napoleon's invasion of Russia. Works such as "Test Theory of the Partisan Movement" (1821), "A Meeting with General Suvorov" (1835), "Was It the Frost That Destroyed the French Army?" (1835), and "Diary of Partisan Warfare" (published posthumously in 1860) remain important sources for the study of the Russian army in the early 19th century. Readers of Tolstoy's *War and Peace* will recognize Davydov as the model for the character Denisov.

Decembrists

The name given to the participants in the uprising of December 14, 1825 (O. S.), in St. Petersburg that sought to prevent the accession of NICHOLAS I to the throne. The roots of the Decembrist movement go back to the spread of Western liberal ideas among junior aristocratic officers who served during the Napoleonic Wars. Dissatisfied by the lack of substantial reform during the reign of ALEXANDER I, officers formed

secret societies such as the Union of Salvation (1816–17) and the Union of Welfare (1818–20) to discuss concrete reforms such as the abolition of serfdom and the introduction of a constitution. By 1823 three new secret societies with more overt revolutionary goals had been formed: the Northern Society, the Southern Society, and the Society of United Slavs. The Northern Society, centered in St. Petersburg, was led by two Guards officers, Nikita Muraviev and Prince Sergei Trubetskoi, as well as a romantic poet, Kondratii Ryleev. Muraviev wrote a plan based on the U.S. Constitution that envisioned a federative constitutional monarchy with a bicameral legislature and an emperor whose powers would be similar to those of the American president. The Southern Society was based in the headquarters of the southern or Second Army in Podolia and was headed by Colonel Pavel Pestel. Of less aristocratic background than the leaders of the Northern Society, Pestel wrote a political manifesto, *Russkaia pravda* (Russian justice), in which he outlined a political vision that owed more to the radical traditions of the French Revolution than the liberal traditions of the American Revolution. Pestel called for the establishment of a centralized egalitarian republic in which every citizen had the right to receive a land allotment. Scholars have seen Pestel as the founder of an authoritarian Russian Jacobin revolutionary tradition that runs through Petr TKACHEV all the way to Vladimir LENIN. The Society of United Slavs was also formed by officers of the Southern Army but, in distinction to Pestel, emphasized the formation of a democratic federation of all Slavic peoples.

The three societies had not yet coalesced into a single movement and talk of concrete action remained in the future when the death of Alexander I in November 1825 and questions about who his successor would be provided members of the Northern Society with what seemed to be a favorable opportunity to lead a rebellion. Although Alexander had previously arranged for his brother Nicholas rather than his brother Constantine to succeed him, this arrangement was not widely publicized. The Northern Society seized on the confusion and the belief that Constantine was a more likely liberal reformer to launch an armed rebellion on Senate Square in St. Petersburg that was supported by 3,000 soldiers and sailors. Hastily planned and poorly coordinated, the St. Petersburg revolt and a related one in the Ukraine were both easily suppressed. In the criminal case that ensued, 36 conspirators, most of them members of aristocratic and well-to-do families, were sentenced to death. After further review, the new czar Nicholas I approved the executions of only five (including Pestel and Ryleev), while 88 conspirators were sentenced to hard labor in Siberia and 14 were sentenced to settlement in Siberia. Throughout his long reign Nicholas refused to commute the sentences of the exiled Decembrists. Only in 1856, after his death, did his son, ALEXANDER II, issue a full amnesty to the surviving Decembrists in Siberia. Considered to have been the first of a long line of Russian revolutionaries, the Decembrists were regarded as revolutionary martyrs by later generations. After the OCTOBER REVOLUTION, the site of their rebellion, centrally located in St. Petersburg (Leningrad, in Soviet Times) was renamed Decembrists' Square.

Demidov family

A Russian business dynasty whose fortune was first made in the field of metallurgy in the 18th century, the Demidov family grew in influence and prestige over the next century. The founder of the dynasty was Nikita Demidovich Antufyev (1656–1725), a serf and blacksmith from the Tula region. By the end of PETER I the Great's reign, Antufyev, who in 1702 had adopted the surname Demidov and is generally known as Nikita Demidov, had turned the iron foundry in Tula into one of the great centers of weapons production in imperial Russia. He also established foundries in the Ural Mountains region. As a reward for his efforts, Peter granted him noble status in 1720 as well as large estates. Nikita Demidov's son Akinfy Nikitich Demidov (1678–1745) expanded the

family fortune through landholding and by building factories in the region of the Urals. By the late 18th century the Demidovs controlled about 40 percent of Russia's output of cast iron. During CATHERINE II the Great's reign the family founded a school of commerce that was initially attached to the Moscow orphanage. By the early 19th century, the Demidovs became important benefactors of the arts and sciences, with contributions that ranged from the promotion of scientific education in Moscow to the establishment of an annual prize in literature.

Denikin, Anton Ivanovich (1872–1947)
general

The most important of the White commanders during the Russian civil war, Denikin was a rarity in the imperial army, an officer of humble background who had risen to divisional commander on the eve of World War I. Denikin joined the army in 1887, graduated from the General Staff Academy as an infantry officer, and fought in the RUSSO-JAPANESE WAR. He fought with bravery and distinction during World War I with the Southern Army. This and the democratic opportunities provided by the Russian army to men of nonnoble background after the FEBRUARY REVOLUTION ensured his rapid promotion in 1917. By August 1917 he had become commander in chief of the Southwest Army Group. Imprisoned by KERENSKY's Provisional Government after his support of General KORNILOV's march on Petrograd, Denikin escaped in October 1917. He joined the Volunteer Army being formed in southeastern Russia by Generals KORNILOV and ALEKSEEV, in opposition to the Bolshevik government. By October 1918, after the deaths of Kornilov and Alekseev, Denikin was in sole charge of the Volunteer Army. His troops' victories in the north Caucasus and COSSACK defeats in the Don region allowed Denikin to emerge as the commander in chief of the Armed Forces of South Russia (AFSR), with authority over the Volunteer Army and Cossack forces. In the summer of 1919, his troops mounted an offensive on Moscow that came within 200 miles of the capital before being turned back. Denikin's fortunes declined quickly afterward. The weakness of other White commanders did not permit a coordinated White offensive that would have challenged the BOLSHEVIKS simultaneously on various fronts. His own lack of political imagination, his insistence on a "Russia united and indivisible," and his insensitivity to the aspirations of national minorities in a highly multiethnic area prevented the development of a strong political base in the areas the Whites controlled. By November 1919, Denikin was on the defensive. The remnants of his forces fled to the Crimea and Denikin resigned in favor of Baron Petr WRANGEL and fled to Istanbul. He was offered refuge in England but chose to go to Belgium, later France, and finally the United States, where he died.

Dezhnev, Semyon Ivanovich
(1605–ca. 1673)
explorer

Dezhnev was a COSSACK explorer who, in 1648, became the first Westerner to sail through what is now the Bering Strait, separating Asia from North America. Nevertheless, because no records were kept of his journey, it was not until 1728, when Vitus BERING made the trip, that the existence of this body of water became widely known.

Dezhnev was born in Velikii Ustiug in northern European Russia, home to many Siberian explorers. He worked briefly as a sailor before moving to Siberia in the 1630s and working as a tribute collector for the czar's government. In 1638 he moved to Yakutsk on the Lena River, then the main Russian post in eastern Siberia. For the next decade he participated in several fur-trading and exploratory expeditions to the east and north to the Arctic Ocean. In 1648, after an initial setback, he took part in an expedition led by Feodor Popov, a Cossack, whose goal was to travel from the mouth of the Kolyma River on the Arctic Ocean around the eastern tip of Siberia and reach the Anadyr River, which empties into the Pacific Ocean. Seven ships left Kolyma in

June; by August only three remained to round the easternmost tip of Asia. The expedition, with Dezhnev as commander after Popov was wounded, shipwrecked off the coast of northeastern Siberia. After 10 weeks of overland march they reached the mouth of the Anadyr River. Only 26 of the more than 100 men who had left Kolyma survived the journey. After a difficult winter at the mouth of the Anadyr, Dezhnev and 13 survivors sailed upstream and founded Anadyrsk, the center for future Russian advances in the region. Dezhnev spent the next ten years exploring the area around the Gulf of Anadyr, rich in walrus rookeries. In 1662 he was relieved of his command and, after two years in Yakutsk, traveled back to Moscow to present the czar with furs and silver and other treasures and to account for his travels. Czar ALEKSEI MIKHAILOVICH rewarded Dezhnev with the title of ataman, a Cossack leader, and wealth. He returned to Yakutsk in 1665 with his nephew and commanded the Olenek River area, before returning to Moscow in 1671 with a large fur shipment. There he died in either 1672 or 1673.

Geographers of his era had long debated whether Asia and America were joined or whether there was a water passage between the two. In his 1648 journey, Dezhnev and his crew had unknowingly provided the answer, but his report attracted little attention at the time and was filed in a Siberian archive, to be rediscovered only in 1736, in time for Vitus Bering's famous expedition. The easternmost part of the Asian mainland, separated from ALASKA by the Bering Strait, now bears the name of Cape Dezhnev, in his memory.

Diaghilev, Sergei Pavlovich (1872–1929)
artistic impresario

The man most responsible for introducing the richness of early-20th-century Russian art to Western European audiences, Diaghilev was born in NOVGOROD, the son of a landowner. He grew up in the town of Perm and graduated with a law degree from St. Petersburg University in

1896. He then enrolled in the St. Petersburg Conservatory, where he studied with RIMSKY-KORSAKOV. Diaghilev was the driving force behind the influential journal MIR ISKUSSTVA (*World of Art*) (1898–1904). In 1899 he was appointed special assistant to Prince Volkonsky, the new director of the Imperial Theaters, his main task being the editing of the theater yearbook. Diaghilev spent the next decade organizing various artistic exhibitions and projects such as "Old Russian Portraits" (St. Petersburg, 1905), "Russian Art" (Paris, 1906), and a Russian Seasons series in Paris (1907–9) which drew attention to the talents of Rimsky-Korsakov, RACHMANINOFF, Glazunov, and CHALIAPIN. Having found his métier in bringing together musicians, painters, and dancers, Diaghilev began the artistic enterprise with which he is most closely associated, the Ballets Russes (1909–29). His brilliant vision of ballet productions as unifying vehicles for dance, choreography, sets, and composition introduced a vibrant Russian artistic scene and reawakened interest in ballet throughout the world. At different times over the next two decades, dancers such as Vatslav NIJINSKY (with whom he had a romance that scandalized the czar's court), Anna PAVLOVA, and Tamara KARSAVINA, choreographers such as Fokine, artists such as Benois, Matisse, Picasso, and Bakst, and composers like Debussy, Ravel, STRAVINSKY, PROKOFIEV, and Rachmaninoff all worked with the Ballet Russes. Although the revolution broke his links with Russia, Paris served as the center of this unique enterprise until the late 1920s, when Diaghilev's failing creative powers, financial difficulties, and stormy personal life contributed to a decline in the company's fortunes. In his last years he turned to the collection of Russian antiquarian books. He died in Venice.

Dmitrii Donskoi (1350–1389)
grand prince

The son of Ivan II, grand prince of Moscow, Dmitrii Donskoi is one of the heroes of Russian history, primarily for his victory over Mongol forces at the Battle of KULIKOVO, on the Don River (hence his name Donskoi) in 1380. This was the first major victory by Russian forces over the Mongol armies since their invasion of Russia in 1240. Although the Mongols were only temporarily defeated and, in fact, raided Moscow two years later and continued to receive tribute for another century, their mantle of invincibility was gone. Dmitrii also consolidated the supremacy of Moscow over rival principalities at a time of internal dissension both in the ranks of the Russian principalities and among the Mongols who ruled them. Among other achievements, Dmitrii's reign also witnessed the first introduction of firearms into the Muscovite armies and of new stone walls to replace the old wooden walls of the Moscow Kremlin.

Dmitrii inherited the throne of Moscow at the age of nine and during his minority received considerable help from the wise counsel of Metropolitan Aleksei, leader of the Russian Church. His father had been a weak ruler, and at the time of his death several relatives of Dmitrii claimed the principality of Moscow. An early challenger to the Muscovite throne was Prince Dmitrii of Suzdal, a distant relative who claimed seniority over him. After Moscow's population rallied behind young Dmitrii, Dmitrii of Suzdal agreed to recognize his position. A more serious challenge came from Prince Michael of TVER, who benefited from the Mongol policy of divide and rule, and obtained the title of grand prince that the Mongol rulers used to ascribe seniority among the Russian princes. Michael of Tver also allied himself with Olgerd of Lithuania, who himself tried to capture Moscow in 1368 and 1372. After repelling the Lithuanian offensive, Dmitrii signed a truce with Olgerd and turned on Michael, who recognized him as grand prince.

By 1378, following a Muscovite victory over Mongol troops near the Vozha River, Dmitrii had built up enough strength to concern the Mongols. Their new ruler, Mamai, set out to destroy the Muscovite threat, established an alliance with Grand Prince Jagiello of Lithuania, and agreed on a joint invasion of the principality of Moscow.

With an army of 200,000 Mamai planned to join up with Jagiello's armies in the upper Don River area. But before the two armies could join forces, Dmitrii crossed the Don at the head of 150,000 soldiers and engaged Mamai at the field of Kulikovo, in September 1380. After brutal fighting, the Mongols were routed. Jagiello's armies, two days removed from Kulikovo, chose not to fight Dmitrii's forces. The Battle of Kulikovo gave Dmitrii a concrete victory that allowed Moscow to assert leadership over other Russian principalities by presenting itself as the champion of Russian national interests over the Mongols.

Doctors' Plot (1953)

A "conspiracy" reported in Soviet newspapers in January 1953 whereby a group of nine Moscow doctors were allegedly plotting to kill prominent party, government, and army officials. It was alleged that these doctors, seven of whom were Jewish, had already been responsible for the sudden death in 1948 of Andrei ZHDANOV, the head of the Leningrad party organization and leader of the virulent anti-semitic campaign against "cosmopolitan" influences in Soviet culture in the early post–World War II years. The doctors were arrested and forced to confess (on orders from STALIN), then sentenced to death, although no public trial was held. Two doctors were executed before Stalin's death in March 1953 interrupted what many believe was the first stage in a new campaign of mass terror along the lines of the Great Purge. In April 1953, the COMMUNIST PARTY newspaper, *Pravda*, which had published the original charges, announced that the Doctors' Plot had been a hoax, and the surviving doctors were released from prison. For many decades the true motives behind the accusations eluded explanation. Although it was agreed that they were another symbol of the ANTI-SEMITISM of the postwar period, their role in the byzantine intrigues of Stalin's inner circle were less clear.

domovoi (pl. *domovye*)

A central figure in Russian folklore, the *domovoi* is a household spirit who represents the spirit of a family's founding ancestor and is said to live in a stove, the traditional focal point of Russian homes, especially in peasant communities. Because of the spirit's connection to a family's ancestors, belief in the *domovoi* has survived well into the modern era. The *domovoi*, whose name derived from the Russian word for house (*dom*), looked after a household's welfare and was known by a number of mostly affectionate terms, such as "grandfather," "fellow," or "the master." Legends differ on their exact origins but agree that the *domovye* developed from malicious spirits that fell from the heavens into places inhabited by humans, often down their chimneys and into their stoves. Although his main duty is to protect the household, the *domovoi* is known as a mischief maker who enjoys playing tricks on the inhabitants of the household, sometimes by knocking on walls or throwing plates around and sometimes by assuming animal shapes such as dogs, cats, or snakes. In rural areas especially, in addition to the housebound *domovoi*, there is a *dvorovoi* who lives in the *dvor* (courtyard). In some cases, the *domovoi* had a wife, the *domovikha*, who lived in the cellar or henhouse. She helped good wives with their chores and annoyed the lazy ones by tickling their children in the middle of the night. The *domovoi* was traditionally represented by an elongated carved wooden statue that sometimes depicted an old man with a fur-covered face and sometimes was made to resemble the likeness of the head of the household.

Dorzhiev, Agvan (1853–1938)
scholar and diplomat

A Buriat Buddhist leader who fell victim to STALIN's purges. Dorzhiev was born in Verkholensk in Irkutsk province. After studying theology in Tibet, he became the spiritual leader of Buriat Buddhists in Russia, founded monasteries in Irkutsk province, and heavily engaged in the work of introducing secular education to the Kalmyks and Buriats. He composed an alphabet for the Buriats, compiled collections of Buriat folklore, and wrote historical studies. In 1913 he was largely responsible for building a Buddhist temple in St. Petersburg. During his frequent visits to Tibet, Dorzhiev became a friend of the Thirteenth Dalai Lama and represented his interests to the Russian government. When the BOLSHEVIKS came to power, Dorzhiev reformed the lifestyle and curriculum of the Buddhist monasteries in the Russian Empire. The Soviet government recognized him as the diplomatic representative of the Dalai Lama and for a time relied on his services to maintain friendly relations with the Buddhist leader. After the formation of the Mongolian People's Republic, Dorzhiev and the Buddhist clergy in the Soviet Union were subjected to repression. In 1936 Dorzhiev was banished from the Buriat-Mongol ASSR and lived in Lakhta in the Leningrad region. In 1937, he was arrested and was banished to Ulan-Ude, where he was imprisoned. Dorzhiev died in prison the following year.

Feodor Mikhailovich Dostoevsky, ca. 1880
(Hulton/Archive)

Dostoevsky, Feodor Mikhailovich (1822–1881)

writer

A prolific Russian novelist, Dostoevsky has come to occupy a prominent place in the canons of world literature. Born in Moscow, Dostoevsky attended the Military Engineering College in St. Petersburg from 1837 to 1841 and was subsequently commissioned into the army. While in college his father, a wealthy landowning doctor, died with rumors that he was murdered in 1839 by the serfs of his country estate. In 1844 Dostoevsky resigned his commission to devote himself to literature. His first major work, *Poor Folk,* was published in 1846 and received high praise, especially from radical circles. In 1849, he was arrested for his links to the Petrashevsky Circle, an intellectual group sympathetic to early socialist ideals. He was sentenced to death together with 14 other members of the circle. Facing the firing squad, he learned that his sentence had been commuted at the last moment; instead, he served four years of hard labor in Siberia, followed by two years of internal exile. In 1859 he was amnestied and returned to St. Petersburg. A changed man who abandoned his earlier radical views and in somewhat poor health, Dostoevsky now devoted himself fully to writing. His Siberian experience provided the material for *Memoirs from the House of the Dead* (1861–62). More successful and in line with his later work was *Notes from the Underground* (1864). His first wife, whom he had married in Siberia, died in 1863, and in 1865 he traveled with a female companion to Germany. The decade that followed his return to St. Petersburg saw the publication of his great novels, *Crime and Punishment* (1866), *The Idiot* (1868), *The Possessed* or *The Devils* (1871), followed by his crowning literary achievement, *The Brothers Karamazov* (1880). These were all written at a time of great personal turmoil, increasingly poor health, and poverty. Through other literary vehicles, such as the magazine *Time and Epoch* (1861–65), the weekly *The Citizen* (1873–74), and his *The Diary of a Writer,* which was published in separate volumes between 1876 and 1881, Dostoevsky publicized a unique blend of nationalist, Russian messianic, democratic, and Christian views that also show an appreciation for European civilization. By the time of his death in February 1881, he was recognized as one of the Russian literary giants of the day. He was buried in the Alexander Nevsky monastery in St. Petersburg. In the decades that ensued, his literary reputation grew worldwide, in great part because of the efforts of his second wife, Anna Grigorievna. In the 20th century his work came to be seen as anticipating that of Nietzsche and Freud, albeit with unique Russian spiritual themes that later found an echo in the work of Aleksandr SOLZHENITSYN.

Dovzhenko, Aleksandr Petrovich (1894–1956)
film director

One of the leading representatives of the Soviet avant-garde in cinema, Dovzhenko was born to a COSSACK family. After early stints as a schoolmaster, a painter, and a diplomat in Berlin, he entered the world of the cinema. Two of his early films deserve the label classic of both Soviet and world cinema, *Arsenal* (1929) and *Earth* (1930). They used a variety of cutting-edge techniques of the day but are infused with Dovzhenko's distinctive lyricism, full of poetic imagery and surrealistic symbols. In the changing context of Soviet politics of the time, official critics denounced them as "counterrevolutionary" and, in the case of *Earth,* as "too realistic" in its portrayal of a peasantry on the verge of collectivization. He partially redeemed himself with *Shchors* (1939), the story of a Ukrainian Red Army hero of the civil war, presented in a way that conformed to official accounts. During World War II, he shot *Battle of Ukraine* (1943), distinguished by its use

of over 20 cameramen distributed along the battlefront. He turned to color for *Michurin* (1949), a botanist who had been elevated to cult status by Soviet officialdom. At the time of his death he was working on *Poem of the Sea,* which was distributed posthumously in 1958.

Dukhobor

A term that translates as "spirit wrestlers," Dukhobor is the colloquial name of a religious sect whose members were active in 18- and 19th-century Russia before emigrating to Canada after 1898. The Dukhobors were disciples of one of the many nonconformist religious movements that developed in resistance to the Orthodox Church reforms introduced by Patriarch NIKON in 1652 that resulted in the church schism of 1666–67. While some of these nonconformist groups were OLD BELIEVERS who defended the traditional ways of Russian Orthodoxy, a minority adopted more extreme forms of worship, with mystical and often orgiastic overtones. Among these were the Dukhobors, who in addition to rejecting the authority of the state and the church also distinguished themselves by rejecting the authority of the Bible. Pacifist by conviction, they also rejected military service. A small minority practiced collective nudism. The Dukhobors centered their religious activities around a *Book of Life,* a collection of hymns and proverbs, which were read and sung at gatherings that featured simple peasant food. Like other religious sectarians, especially those who did not recognize the authority of the state or refused to perform military service, the Dukhobors were persecuted by the czarist government. Already in 1840–41, a group that had previously settled near the Sea of Azov had been deported to the Caucasus. In 1898, with the assistance of British Quakers and the vocal support of Leo TOLSTOY, about 7,500 Dukhobors emigrated to Canada, first settling in the province of Saskatchewan, which welcomed them with land and exemption from military service. In 1907 most of the Dukhobors moved on to British Columbia when the Saskatchewan government insisted on individual, rather than communal, land ownership. By the 1990s only about 5,000 Dukhobors remained in Canada.

Duma

A term derived from the Russian root for "thought" or "thinking" that is generally associated with deliberative political bodies throughout Russian history, and more specifically with the parliament that existed from 1906 to 1917 and was revived after the dissolution of the Soviet Union in 1991. In addition to the State Duma created in 1905, Russian history witnessed a "boyar duma" and municipal or town dumas. In 1700 PETER I the Great abolished the rank of boyar and the boyar duma as well. The State Duma of the late imperial period was the product of concessions made by the government of NICHOLAS II to popular demands for a more representative government during the course of the 1905 Revolution. For the remainder of the imperial period the State Duma served as the lower chamber of the legislature, while the Council of State, established in the early 19th century, served as the upper chamber.

Four dumas were convened between 1906 and 1917. Historians have long debated the extent to which these served as a parliamentary institution that could have paved the way for the transformation of Russia into a Western-style constitutional monarchy. The franchise was limited to male taxpayers and property owners grouped into four electoral classes (landowners, townspeople, industrial workers, and peasants) that, with the exception of the five largest cities, elected delegates who, in turn, chose the members of the Duma. Moreover, the powers of the duma were limited. Finally, the czar had the power to veto the assembly's acts and to dissolve it. And yet this was the first instance of representative government, albeit limited, in Russian history.

In theory, the Duma's consent was required for all legislation, but this rule was often disregarded in practice. All taxpayers and property owners were enfranchised; elections were indirect (save in the five largest cities) through electoral colleges based on social status. Though Duma members could question ministers, the latter were not responsible to the Duma. Legislation could be introduced by the Duma, and laws had to be passed by it and the State Council and signed by the emperor.

Nicholas II used his power to dissolve the Duma on three occasions: in July 1906, June 1907, and in February 1917, on the eve of his abdication. The First Duma lasted only 73 days, from May to July 1906, when the czar dissolved it for excessive criticism of government policy. The Second Duma (March-June 1907) had, like the First, a radical, antigovernment majority that the czar found unmanageable. In June 1907, Prime Minister Petr STOLYPIN crafted a new electoral law that gave greater representation to the upper classes, and the elections to the Third Duma returned a conservative majority that ensured that this was the only duma to serve its full five-year term. The composition of the Fourth Duma (1912–17) was even more conservative than the third, but in the course of World War I, the Duma clashed frequently with the government over the conduct of the war, leading the czar to dissolve it on the eve of what proved to be the February Revolution.

Following the czar's abdication, the Duma set up a provisional committee that in turn set up a Provisional Government that was to rule Russia until a popularly elected Constituent Assembly convened to decide future political arrangements. This Provisional Government ruled until October 1917, when it was overthrown by the BOLSHEVIKS acting in the name of the soviets, a rival institution representing workers, soldiers and peasants that had spread throughout Russia in the last half of 1917. Previously planned elections to the Constituent Assembly were held, and in January 1918 it met for one day but was closed by the Bolshevik government. The institution of the Duma disappeared from Russian history until the final days of the Soviet period, when the parliament of the Russian Federation was reestablished and given the name Duma.

Durova, Nadezhda Andreevna
(1783–1866)

soldier and writer

Durova was the first woman in the Russian Empire to hold the rank of officer in the armed forces, and the only woman until 1917 to hold the St. George Cross. Born in Kiev, Durova grew up in a military household; her father was a captain of hussars. She married in 1801, gave birth to a son in 1803, but in 1806 ran away from home and joined a COSSACK regiment disguised as a man. In 1807, she fought at the Battle of Friedland against Napoleon's armies, where it emerged that she was a woman. ALEXANDER I interviewed her, promoted her to officer rank, and gave her a commission in the Mariupol Hussars. In 1811, she was transferred to the Lithuanian Uhlan Regiment. Durova fought at BORODINO, where she suffered shell shock, and marched westward with Alexander's armies, serving as an orderly to General KUTUZOV. Passed for promotion in 1815, she submitted her retirement but withdrew it when Napoleon escaped from Elba. In 1816, she retired from the army with the rank of staff captain. In retirement and until the end of her life, she insisted on being addressed as "Aleksandr Andreevich Aleksandrov," her masculine alias. With Aleksandr PUSHKIN's encouragement, her memoirs were first excerpted in the journal *Sovremennik* (*The Contemporary*) in 1836. Received to great acclaim, from 1837 to 1840, Durova added to her memoirs with less success than in the first installment. In 1840, she abandoned her brief attempt at a literary career and returned to a long quiet life on her estate of Elabuga on the foothills of the Urals. When she died in 1866, she was buried with full military honors.

Dzerzhinsky, Feliks Edmundovich
(1877–1926)

revolutionary and Soviet official

Dzerzhinsky is best known for his work as the first director of the Cheka, the political police established by the BOLSHEVIKS during the Russian civil war and the forerunner of the OGPU and the KGB. Born into a Polish gentry family, he joined the Lithuanian Social Democratic Party in 1895 and soon became a full-time revolutionary. He met LENIN in Stockholm in 1906 and was elected to the Bolshevik Central Committee. Repeatedly arrested, imprisoned, and exiled, Dzerzhinsky spent a total of 11 years in jail before the FEBRUARY REVOLUTION liberated him from a Moscow prison. During the OCTOBER REVOLUTION, Dzerzhinsky directed the defense of the Smolny Institute—the headquarters of the Bolshevik Party—and the capture of the central post and telegraph offices. When the Extraordinary Commission for Combating Counter-revolution and Sabotage (Cheka) was established in 1917, Dzerzhinsky was appointed as its first director with a mandate to defend the revolution from its opponents. In July 1918, the insurgent Left Socialist Revolutionaries briefly held him prisoner but inexplicably released him, a mistake they quickly came to regret when he launched the Red Terror after Fanny Kaplan's attempted assassination of Lenin in August 1918. He became people's commissar for internal affairs in March 1919 and hence would integrate the functions of the militia and the political police. The growing power of the Cheka and its parallels with the czarist police that had persecuted them as revolutionaries troubled many Bolshevik leaders, but Dzerzhinsky maintained Lenin's unconditional support during the civil war. In the post–civil war period Dzerzhinsky continued as head of the political police through the several incarnations and permutations that revealed the difficulties the COMMUNIST PARTY faced in shaping and controlling the fearful weapon it had created. Because of his organizational talents and tireless dedication to work, Dzerzhinsky was assigned numerous other tasks in the early years of the revolution: chair of the committee for universal labor conscription, chair of the commission for improving the lot of children, people's commissar of transport (1921), and chair of the Supreme Council of the National Economy (1924). Although he sided with STALIN at important junctures, such as the 1922–23 Georgian affair, he was never Stalin's man. His death in July 1926 opened the way for a more pliable, pro-Stalin head of the political police. During the rest of the Soviet era, the regime promoted Dzerzhinsky as "Iron Felix," the symbol of incorruptible, ruthless Soviet power. His statue stood in front of KGB headquarters until after the failed AUGUST COUP OF 1991, when it was removed to a sculpture park near the Moscow River.

E

Ehrenburg, Ilya Grigorievich
(1891–1967)
writer and journalist

A prolific Russian writer of Jewish background, Ehrenburg began his career as a poet before turning to fiction and journalism, where he found great acclaim. Born in Kiev, the son of an engineer, he became involved in revolutionary activities at age 16. Arrested in 1908, he escaped to France and lived in Paris from 1909 to 1917. His love-hate relationship with Western culture found an early outlet in *Julio Jurenito* (1921), a novel that satirizes contemporary civilization. Ehrenburg returned permanently to the Soviet Union in 1924, and after experimenting with various literary trends, embraced socialist realism (at least in theory) by 1932. In subsequent work, Ehrenburg showed an ability for writing about topical themes on the minds of Soviet readers. In *The Second Day* (1933), he evoked the conflicting emotions generated by rapid industrialization. He revealed himself as an outstanding war correspondent, first during the Spanish Civil War and then during World War II. His two-volume collection, *War* (1941–42), struck a chord among readers for its moving portrait of a nation resisting the German onslaught. *Storm* (1948), a forceful attack on the West, reflects the international tensions of the first years of the cold war. In the years after STALIN's death in 1953, Ehrenburg emerged as a leading spokesman for cultural liberalization, and he is most frequently noted for his work *The Thaw* (1954), which, with its imagery of spring after a long frozen winter, aptly captured the mood of expectation in intellectual circles that followed STALIN's death. The final work of his long career was a multivolume autobiography, *People, Years Life* (1960–61), where between sketches of people in his life, he tackled the difficult issues of personal survival during the Stalin years. Like many intellectuals and artists of his generation, he was able to walk the fine line between criticism of the regime and approval from it, with only occasional mishaps. In 1963, with a new cultural freeze on the horizon, conservative cultural commentators harshly criticized his memoirs. He died in Moscow on August 31, 1967.

Eisenstein, Sergei Mikhailovich
(1898–1948)
film director

The most famous film director, producer, and theorist of the Soviet cinema, Eisenstein was a brilliant innovator who embraced political and historical topics in his work, and as a result encountered government opposition in the 1930s and 1940s, leaving many projects unfinished. Born in Riga, the son of an architect, Eisenstein first trained as a civil engineer (1916–18). A Red Army volunteer in 1918, he worked in a theatrical propaganda group during the civil war. In 1921 he became a director for the Proletkult (proletarian culture movement) theater, where he worked with the great Vsevolod MEYERHOLD. In 1925 his first film, *Strike!*, was released, followed by *Battleship Potemkin*, which received its premiere at Moscow's Bolshoi Theater. *Battleship Potemkin*, based on events around the sailors' mutiny during the 1905 Revolution, is still considered one of the classics of Soviet and world cinema, and its "Odessa steps" scene is one of the most cited and identifiable. With *October* (dis-

Sergei Eisenstein, ca. 1940 *(Hulton/Archive)*

worked on what became his most popular film, *Aleksandr Nevskii,* completed in 1938. Although shelved for a while in 1939 in deference to the Soviet Union's nonagression pact with Germany, when released again in 1941, the film played an important role in stirring up Russian nationalism against a new Teutonic invader. His next project was the monumental *Ivan the Terrible,* released in two parts. The first was released in January 1945 to an enthusiastic reception, including STALIN's, for which Eisenstein and his associates received a Stalin Prize. The second part, focusing on the troubling conclusion of Ivan's reign, inevitably suggested similarities between Ivan and Stalin. The film was withdrawn in 1946 and not screened until 1958 in a different political climate. An earlier film, *Bezhin Meadow,* had also encountered problems with Soviet cultural watchdogs and was abandoned in 1937. Eisenstein's health suffered, in great part owing to the stress of completing *Ivan the Terrible* under Stalin's frequent interference, and he died of a heart attack in 1948. He is buried in Novodevichi Cemetery in Moscow.

tributed in the West as *Ten Days That Shook the World*) (1927), shot to commemorate the 10th anniversary of the Bolshevik revolution, Eisenstein continued the combination of highly artistic, politically engaged films that also worked as Bolshevik propaganda. *The General Line,* his film about the collectivization of agriculture, commissioned by Goskino in 1926, ran into political problems when completed three years later, on the eve of the collectivization campaign. With heavy editing it was released as *The Old and the New* in 1930. Seeking a change and an opportunity to explore the new possibilities opened by sound film, Eisenstein traveled to the United States with his close assistants Grigorii ALEKSANDROV and Eduard Tisse. Although he was treated with great respect befitting his status in the world of cinema, the visit produced no concrete results. A subsequent trip to Mexico led to the unfinished work *Que Viva Mexico!* After his return to Moscow in 1932, Eisenstein taught at the All-Union State Institute of Cinema (VGIK) and

Elena Pavlovna (1806–1873)
grand duchess

The wife of Grand Duke Mikhail Pavlovich, brother to Czars ALEXANDER I and NICHOLAS I, Elena Pavlovna became the hostess of one of the most influential salons in St. Petersburg in the 1850s and 1860s. A German princess by birth, Elena Pavlovna arrived in Russia in September 1823, three months before her marriage. The marriage was not a happy one; Mikhail Pavlovich's rigid, militaristic interests did not coincide with hers, and all of the couple's children but one died before reaching adulthood. Elena Pavlovna became a patron of the arts and scholarship, and steeped herself in the study of Russian culture and internal affairs, learning from books and from the many important visitors to her salon. The death of her abusive husband in 1849 allowed her to fully dedicate herself to her salon, which became a center of wide-ranging cultural and political discussion in the final years of the reign of Nicholas I. The accession of her nephew, ALEXANDER II, to the throne and Russia's defeat in the CRIMEAN WAR opened an era where reform was discussed openly in government and public circles. Because she was the senior member of the imperial family, Elena Pavlovna's influence grew through her connections with a new coterie of reformists bureaucrats. Poor health forced her to leave Russia in 1856 for treatment at European spas, but she continued her involvement in reformist politics. She convened the Wildbad Conference (1857), where she responded to the call of influential politicians that a testing ground for emancipation of the serfs was needed by offering her Karlovka estate with more than 15,000 serfs. After she returned to St. Petersburg in 1858, reform discussions were far less tentative, and Elena Pavlovna's salon became the vehicle for broadening the contact between St. Petersburg bureaucrats and members of the intelligentsia. It also provided the means for informal unofficial contact between the emperor and reformist officials in the bureaucracy. As the drafting of the emancipation decrees increasingly became its raison d'etre, Elena Pavlovna's salon declined after the publication of the EMANCIPATION ACT in March 1861. Her own interests changed and she became an active supporter of the arts and charity, founding the Russian Musical Society in St. Petersburg and its Conservatory. Just before her death, she helped establish the Eleninskii Clinical Institute to assist provincial doctors in bringing medical innovations to the peasantry.

Elizabeth (1709–1762)
(Elizaveta Petrovna)
empress

The youngest daughter of PETER I The Great and his second wife, Marfa Skavronskaia, who reigned as CATHERINE I after Peter's death. Elizabeth was born in Kolomenskoe, near Moscow. In the decades that followed her father's death, she was passed over for the throne several times. In 1726, at her mother's insistence she became a member of the Supreme Privy Council, which

played a dominant role in Russian politics until it was abolished by Empress ANNA in 1731. Elizabeth became empress in November 1741 as a result of a palace revolution carried out by the Imperial Guards that removed the infant emperor IVAN VI and the regent, his mother Anna Leopoldovna. The change in government has been portrayed, with some exaggeration, as the end of the era of the "German party," first installed by Empress Anna. Charming and easygoing, Elizabeth was more interested in enjoying the privileges of power, leaving the running of the state to a series of favorites, some of whom, like Count Ivan Shuvalov, were extremely able, while others, like Count Peter Shuvalov, were corrupt. She was rumored to have secretly married a Ukrainian Cossack, Aleksei Razumovsky, to whom she remained romantically attached throughout her life. Childless, early in her reign she named her nephew Peter, son of the duke of Holstein and her sister Anna, as her successor.

On the surface Elizabeth tried to restore the spirit of her father's reign, bringing back the Senate, but in practice the main trends of her reign were more in line with those that had come after Peter's death. Elizabeth continued the Westernizing cultural policies of her predecessors, but because of her own French sympathies, her reign witnessed the emergence of French culture over German culture as the culture of the court. Other important achievements of her reign include the abolition of the death penalty and the founding of Moscow University in 1755 and of the Academy of Arts in 1757. Important St. Petersburg architectural landmarks, such as the Winter Palace, designed by Bartolomeo RASTRELLI, were built during her reign, too. Her frivolous, lavish lifestyle, including a collection of 15,000 dresses, made a dent in the finances of the empire. More substantially, perhaps, her reign saw the nobility gain important privileges at the expense of their serfs, whose living conditions and legal status continued to deteriorate. In 1746, nonnobles were no longer allowed to purchase serfs, while in 1760 landowners received the right to banish their serfs to Siberia for a number of offenses.

Elizaveta Petrovna, ca. 1750 *(Hulton/Archive)*

During her reign, Russia scored important military and diplomatic victories, most notably over Sweden in 1743, which brought an end to centuries of intermittent conflict and added a large part of Finland ("Old Finland") to the empire's borders. Her government continued the alliance with Austria, established in 1726, but also established good relations with France, Austria's traditional rival. In 1756, Russia joined Austria and France against Prussia and Great Britain in the Seven Years' War. By 1762, Prussia was on the verge of total defeat, when Elizabeth died and her German-born successor, PETER III, reversed course and gave up the costly gains Russia had won on the battlefield. She died in St. Petersburg on January 5, 1762.

Emancipation Act (1861)

The legal document that abolished SERFDOM in Russia, the Emancipation Act was signed by ALEXANDER II on February 19, 1861 (O.S.) and announced publicly 12 days later. The Emancipation Act was the product of a long process begun by Alexander II soon after he assumed the throne in 1855, and the final result shows an attempt to find a compromise between the goal of emancipating Russian serfs and preserving as much as possible the interests of the serf-owning gentry. The basic provisions of emancipation first had been outlined in a document known as the Nazimov Rescript (1857), in which Alexander II rejected the request of Lithuanian nobles to free their serfs without land, calling instead for emancipation with land and for the organization of peasants into communes. In its final form the Emancipation Act covered more than 50 million peasants, of whom 20 million were owned by private landowners. The act gave land to serfs employed in farming but not to household serfs. With the exception of Ukraine, land was given not to individual peasants but to peasant communities organized around the institution of the peasant commune (*mir*). The land was not given freely; peasants were assessed with "redemption payments" to be paid in installments over the next 49 years. Individual peasants were given the option known as the "pauper's allotment," in which they would receive only one-quarter of their allotted land but would not be required to pay for the land. The Emancipation Act was the centerpiece of a broader attempt to modernize Russian society known as the GREAT REFORMS. Although the Emancipation Act implemented a major transformation of Russian society with relatively little violence, disappointment with its provisions among radical intellectuals and large sections of the peasantry fueled the rise of a revolutionary movement that shaped Russian politics for the next half-century.

Ermolova, Maria Nikolaevna (1853–1928)
actress

Considered to be one of the leading representatives of a romantic style of acting, Ermolova was born in Moscow, the daughter of a *prompter* of the Malyi Theater. Prior to her completion of studies at the Moscow Theatrical School, Ermolova had already joined the Malyi Theater. Ermolova's frequent portrayal of romantic heroines such as Joan d'Arc and Mary Stuart endeared her to the segment of the intelligentsia and theatergoing public that symphatized with the revolutionary movement. After the OCTOBER REVOLUTION, Ermolova acted in numerous productions with more explicit revolutionary themes. In 1920, with Vladimir LENIN in attendance, she was honored for her work in a career that spanned 50 years. Later that year, Ermolova was named People's Artist of the Soviet Republic, the first artist to receive such a distinction. Ermolova retired from the stage in 1921. Her home of more than 30 years in the fashionable Boulevard Ring of central Moscow was later made into a museum.

Esenin, Sergei Aleksandrovich (1895–1925)

poet

One of Russia's most beloved popular poets, together with PUSHKIN and MAYAKOVSKY, Esenin's brief and turbulent life ended in a suicide that sparked a wave of sympathy suicides among his distraught public. Esenin was born to a peasant family in Ryazan province; rural and religious themes pervaded his poetry. He began writing poetry by the age of nine, and nine years later he had become a famous poet, published by the leading Petersburg magazines. He welcomed the OCTOBER REVOLUTION but did not join the BOLSHEVIK Party, preferring instead the elemental resistance to authority that he found in peasant rebels such as Emelian Pugachev and the peasant anarchist Nestor MAKHNO (who appears in his poems as Nomakh), both of whom he celebrated in his poems. A bundle of contradictions, Esenin celebrated the dignity of rural life but embraced urban decadence, living like a "peasant dandy." He drew deeply from religious themes but mixed them with irreverence for symbols of tradition such as churches and convents that bordered on hooliganism. Embracing outrageous exhibition-

ism, he led a life marked by legendary alcoholic binges. After a marriage in 1917 that lasted only one year, he married the American dancer Isadora Duncan in 1921, his senior by 18 years, even though neither spoke each other's language. Together they toured Europe and the United States, a celebrity couple with an affinity for scandal. Estranged from his Russian land, Esenin soon sank further into alcoholism and misery. He left Duncan in 1925, returned to Russia, and married for the third time in September 1925. Three months later, however, he hanged himself in the Hotel Angleterre in Leningrad (St. Petersburg), leaving a remarkable farewell poem, "Do svidania drug moi" (Goodbye, My Friend), written in his own blood. Never accepted by the Soviet literary establishment, he instead became a revolutionary romantic idol to the common Soviet citizen, who was charmed by his handsome appearance, his bohemian lifestyle and his irreverence toward authority. An edition of his collected works appeared soon after his death, and a smaller one came out in 1948 at the height of Stalinism. Some of his poems were turned into songs and became immensely popular. His grave in Vagankoe cemetery remains a popular site of artistic pilgrimage.

Evdokiia Feodorovna (1669–1731) (née Lopukhina)

empress

The daughter of a palace functionary, Feodor Abramovich Lopukhin, Evdokiia Feodorovna was the first wife of PETER I the Great, whom she married in February 1689. She was raised in the traditional world of Muscovite women and had little in common with the future czar, three years her junior. She bore Peter three sons, Alexis, Alexander, and Paul, but only Alexis (1690–1718) survived to adolescence. Their marriage was brief and unhappy, and the couple divorced in 1698, after which Peter forced Evdokiia to enter a nunnery. In the summer of 1718, her son and heir to the throne, Alexei, was sentenced to death on charges of treason but died in the Peter and Paul Fortress in St.

Petersburg on the eve of his execution. Evdokiia left the convent soon after her son's death but was soon captured on Peter's orders and confined to the Uspenskii Monastery. PETER II, her grandson, formally rehabilitated Evdokiia and she died on September 7, 1731 at the Novodevichi Convent in Moscow.

exile system

The official use of exile as a system of punishment first appeared in the Law Code of 1649, where it was included as a penalty in 11 instances. In the centuries that followed criminals, religious dissenters, disgraced officials as well as political prisoners were at one time or another exiled to Siberia. Until 1917, banishment in the form of hard labor, permanent settlement, or temporary residence became a central feature of the czarist penal system. Most, but not all, of the exiles were banished to Siberia, and it is with Siberia that the exile system is most closely associated. As with other contemporary exile systems, such as Britain's use of Australia as a penal colony, exile provided Russian authorities with the opportunity to free European Russia of "undesirable" elements while colonizing recently acquired territories. By 1662, exiles composed 10 percent of Siberia's Russian and other immigrant population. The use of Siberia as an exile destination slowed down somewhat during the early 18th century, as Peter the Great demanded large quantities of unfree labor for construction projects such as the city of St. Petersburg. In the late 18th century, it again increased as serf owners were granted the right to exile insubordinate serfs and their families. Reformist government official Mikhail SPERANSKY's Exile and Convoy Regulations of 1822 sought to alleviate the most extreme conditions by humanizing the exile system, but the reform efforts were neutralized by the growing number of exiles, mostly criminals, arriving to Siberia. From a yearly rate of 8,000 in the 1830s, by the turn of the 20th century there were about 300,000 exiles in Siberia.

A group portrait of convicts in Siberia, ca. 1880 *(Library of Congress)*

Their ability to escape with ease created a host of social issues that threatened the well-being of Siberia's free and indigenous population. After the EMANCIPATION ACT of 1861, peasant communes received the right to sentence their own peasants to administrative exile. Beginning with Polish nationalists in the 1790s and the DECEMBRISTS in 1826, political prisoners were late arrivals to the Siberian exile population. Although their historical visibility was high, thanks to the many memoirs they wrote, political prisoners composed at the most 1 percent of the total exile population. In 1900 the Exile Reform Law sought to reduce the number of exiles by curtailing the communes' right to banish peasants. On the other hand, growing political strife in the final decades of the ROMANOV DYNASTY led to greater numbers of political prisoners being sent to Siberia. Other discussions about reforming or ending the exile system did not bear fruit, despite growing awareness of the danger of a politically radicalized population. Only in April 1917, after the fall of the monarchy, did the successor Provisional Government abolish the system of punitive exile. Ironically, the BOLSHEVIKS, many of whom had suffered under the exile system, brought the system of exile and hard labor back into practice in the 1920s and 1930s, on a much greater and harsher scale than that of the czarist period.

F

Fabergé, Karl Gustavovich (1846–1920) (Karl Peter)

jeweler

Designer of the world-famous bejeweled Easter eggs made for the Russian imperial family from the 1880s to 1917. Fabergé was born in St. Petersburg into a family of French Huguenot origin that had settled in the Russian Empire. They entered the jewelry business in 1842 when Fabergé's father, Gustave Fabergé, opened a small shop in St. Petersburg. Karl Fabergé learned his craft at Dresden, Frankfurt-on-Main, Italy, and Paris, before taking over the family business in 1870. He developed a reputation for brilliant jewelry designs that used rock crystals and semiprecious marbles with diamonds and precious metals. Fabergé expanded the possibili-ties of jewelry by integrating the new trends of the Arts and Crafts and Art Nouveau movements into his designs and by making not just the jewel, but the boxes they came in, a work of art. His achievements were first recognized at the Pan-Russian Exhibition in Moscow (1882), where he won a gold medal and in 1885 when he became the court jeweler to the ROMANOV DYNASTY. Although he made numerous decorations and official gifts for the court, Fabergé's fame rests on the splendid Easter eggs that he made for the families of the last two czars, beginning in 1885. The first egg, which he made for Alexander's Danish wife, contained a jeweled hen from the Danish collection. Under ALEXANDER III he made one Easter egg every year for the czar's wife, and under NICHOLAS II, he made two,

Richly decorated and highly ornate Fabergé eggs, pictured as part of a Russian art exhibition *(Hulton/Archive)*

one for the czar's wife and one for his mother. Every egg had a different design based on a topical event, such as the coronation or the inauguration of the TRANS-SIBERIAN RAILROAD, which was kept secret until the greatly anticipated official presentation of the egg to the imperial family. Fabergé's reputation spread worldwide after the 1900 Paris World Exhibition, where his art was featured. Of the 54 eggs he designed for the imperial family, 47 survive; 10 are in the Kremlin, the rest scattered around the world, mostly in private collections. In February 2004 Russian industrialist Viktor Vekselberg acquired the Forbes collection of Fabergé, including nine imperial eggs. Vekselberg announced plans to return the eggs to Russia.

Fadeev, Aleksandr Aleksandrovich (1901–1956)

writer

One of the more talented representatives of literary socialist realism, Fadeev also prospered in the treacherous world of Soviet literary politics as a faithful advocate of the official party line in literature during the harshest years of Stalinist rule. He was born Aleksandr Bulyga in the town of Kimry, near Moscow. In 1918 he joined the BOLSHEVIK Party and took part in the civil war of 1918–20, which later served as the background for the events described in his first novel, *The Rout,* which tells of the adventures of a band of Red guerrilla fighters in the Siberian Far East. Published in 1927 at a time when the emerging school of socialist realism had still not been fully co-opted to serve the interests of the Soviet estate, the novel was quite frank in its depiction of civil war life and was well received by the Soviet public and literary establishment. From 1929 to 1940 he worked on a second, more ambitious novel, *The Last of the Udege,* about an indigenous Siberian people embarking on the Soviet-style panacea of socialist development, which he never completed. In the meantime, Fadeev had entered literary politics, first as head of the proletarian literature movement RAPP and later as a member of the Union of Soviet Writers,

which he headed from 1946 to 1954. This period coincided with the worst years of Andrei ZHDANOV's postwar campaign of anti-Western cultural orthodoxy. Although a loyal executor of the government's commands in the field of literature, Fadeev himself was not exempt from the government's watchful eye. In 1945 he published his best-known work, *The Young Guard,* about the World War II exploits of partisan fighters in the Donbas region behind German lines, for which he later received the Stalin Prize for literature. Nevertheless, the novel was subject to criticism that he failed to show the leading role of the COMMUNIST PARTY in the struggle against the Germans, and in 1951 he published a revised version that did precisely that. The course of events after STALIN's death in 1953 affected him deeply. Disillusioned by the "Secret Speech" of February 1956, where Premier Nikita KHRUSHCHEV denounced Stalin's crimes and personality cult, Fadeev committed suicide three months later.

False Dmitrii

impostors

The name given to three pretenders who claimed the Muscovite throne during the chaotic period known as the TIME OF TROUBLES (1598–1613). Each of the pretenders claimed to be the true Dmitrii of Uglich, the young son of IVAN IV whose mysterious death in 1591 was widely blamed on Boris GODUNOV, the de facto regent during the reign of his brother-in-law FEODOR I (1584–98) and czar from 1598 to 1605. The first False Dmitrii, most likely a monk named Grigorii Otrepev, surfaced in 1601 but soon fled to Poland-Lithuania. There he gathered support from important nobles, but no official recognition from the Polish government, and married Marina Mnizech, the daughter of a local aristocrat. In October 1604, he returned to Muscovy with the armed assistance of Polish and Lithuanian nobles. Despite repeated defeats, the False Dmitrii's troops persisted until April 1605, when Boris Godunov suddenly died. Godunov's young son, FEODOR II, was named czar, but after numerous intrigues he and his mother were murdered. False Dmitrii entered Moscow victorious in June 1605 with help from prominent local boyars and was proclaimed czar. False Dmitrii quickly alienated his Polish-Lithuanian patrons by failing to act on his promise to introduce Catholicism to Russia and his Muscovite supporters by his untraditional behavior and his Polish entourage. In 1606, he was overthrown and murdered by a group of boyars, led by Vasili Shuisky, who then assumed the Muscovite throne until 1610.

The second False Dmitrii, claiming to be the recently murdered czar although quite unlike him in appearance, emerged in August 1607 and attracted significant support in southern Russia, mostly from peasants. By the spring of 1608 he had established a base, complete with court and administration, at Tushino, on the outskirts of Moscow (hence his nickname, Thief of Tushino). His troops ravaged northern Russia, and his authority soon rivaled that of Czar Vasili Shuisky, who in 1610 forced the pretender to flee to Kaluga. While there the second False Dmitrii continued to press his claims until fatally wounded in October 1610 by one of his own followers. A third and last False Dmitrii emerged in 1611 and raided the plains before retiring to PSKOV (hence his nickname Thief of Pskov), where he was betrayed and executed. The Time of Troubles ended with the election of Michael Romanov as czar.

famines

Famines have been a recurrent event in Russian history, a result of drought and other conditions, and have contributed to social unrest in the countryside and unrest in urban centers. The severe famine of 1891–92, which affected the Volga region following the comparatively calm 1880s, aroused renewed social and political activ-

A group of children, deserted by their parents and most of them barefoot, in the Volga district, an area hit hard by famine, 1921 *(Library of Congress)*

ity on the part of the political opposition. It is also remembered for the relief work led by civic figures such as Leo TOLSTOY. The famine also contributed to the ideological debates between populists and Marxists, with the latter arguing that the further impoverishment of the peasantry was ultimately advantageous for the development of capitalism, which in turn would advance the cause of the proletarian revolution. Smaller famines and food shortages affected· Russian localities in the years after the 1905 Revolution. Likewise, during World War I and the Russian civil war, drastic food shortages caused by transportation problems affected Russian urban centers and contributed to the political unrest of those years. In 1921 outright famine again struck the Volga region, the tail end of a period of unrest and severe need. The famine was one of several causes that marked the end of draconian civil war food procurement policies and ushered in the New Economic Policy. Internal relief work as headed by Maksim GORKY and other non-Communist intellectuals, most of whom were thereupon expelled from Russia, while foreign relief work was chiefly undertaken by American and British missions, most notably by Herbert Hoover's American Relief Administration and the American Friends Service Committee. The next major famine, that of 1932–33, was purposely exacerbated by the authorities to break the resistance of peasants to the collectivization of agriculture. The harvests in those years were adequate (and indeed grain was exported), but the grain was removed from the countryside by armed detachments chiefly composed of internal security troops and members of the Communist Party youth organization, the KOMSOMOL. Many towns in the areas principally affected (Ukraine, north Caucasus, the Volga region, and Kazakhstan) also suffered. The last major famine, in 1946–47, was partly caused by drought, but partly, especially in the areas unaffected by drought (such as central Russia), by the peasants' resistance to the rigorous restoration of the collective farm system, which had been somewhat relaxed in the war years. One result of this famine was the delay,

compared with other countries, of the postwar upward trend in the birthrate. At the time, the Soviet government denied the existence of famine and refused all offers of help from abroad.

February Revolution (1917)

The first of two revolutions in 1917, the February Revolution resulted in the overthrow of the Russian monarchy and the ROMANOV dynasty that had ruled Russia since 1613. Dissatisfaction with the autocratic form of government in general and the government of Czar NICHOLAS II in particular had been building for decades. It had accelerated since the outbreak of World War I, as numerous military defeats and a pervasive sense of governmental incompetence and corruption further discredited the government of Nicholas II. Against a background of rising discontent with the war, inflation, shortages of food and fuel, and with Nicholas II still away from the capital at the front, demonstrations broke out in Petrograd, as the city of ST. PETERSBURG had been renamed in 1914, on March 8, 1917 (February 23 according to the Russian Julian calendar used in pre-revolutionary Russia). The demonstrations across the city were led initially by working-class women, who used the occasion of International Women's Day to voice their demands for bread and an end to the war, and brought together close to 100,000 protesters. By March 10 (February 25, O.S.) the demonstrations had spontaneously transformed into a general strike that closed down the city of Petrograd. The strike turned into an uprising when troops posted to the Petrograd joined the demonstrators. On March 11 (February 26), the government tried to restore its authority by ordering its loyal troops to shoot on the crowds, killing or wounding several hundred demonstrators. It also closed down the parliament (DUMA) and arrested some radical politicians. That evening the regiment from the garrison that had been ordered to shoot on the demonstrators agreed not to further use violence against the crowds. By the next day, March 12 (February 27), the bulk of the garrison had joined the mutiny against the government. That same day, Czar Nicholas dispatched eight regiments from the front to Petrograd to restore order, but their commanding officer, in consultation with the army's high command, did not enforce the order, thus marking the end of the czar's government. With the czar powerless and away from the capital, two different groups moved to fill the power vacuum that ensued. Later in the day of March 12, moderate members of the Duma, who had refused to acknowledge the czar's order to dissolve, formed a Provisional Government intended to rule Russia until a constituent assembly could be called to decide its future government. That same evening, the workers and socialist leaders formed the Soviet of Workers' Deputies to represent their interests. The Soviet had first been formed during the 1905 Revolution, before being shut down by the government in the final months of 1905. Now reconstituted, the Soviet was soon renamed the Petrograd Soviet of Workers' and Soldiers' Deputies to take into account the influential role of rank and file soldiers in the revolution. On March 13 (February 28), the czar's ministers were arrested. On March 15 (March 2), Nicholas II abdicated in favor of his brother, Michael, who in turn abdicated the following day in favor of the Provisional Government.

Fedorov, Nikolai Feodorovich
(1828–1903)
philosopher

A reclusive thinker who never published a book, Fedorov's ideas about solar energy, space travel, and labor armies were highly influential in the first decades of Soviet rule. Little is known about Fedorov's own life, except that he worked as a librarian for 25 years at Moscow's Rumiantsev Museum (later Lenin Library). Fedorov's highly idiosyncratic ideas combined a belief in the primacy of Russian Orthodoxy and czarism with great faith in the possibilities of interplanetary travel. In his vision the future world would be united by Orthodoxy, czarist rule, and a common language, which linguists would uncover from before the time of the Tower of Babel. Society would be organized along utopian lines in rural communes, situated around a cemetery with a model of the Moscow Kremlin at the center. Communal life would be built around a daily regime of mind control, open diaries, public confession, and the regulation of sexuality. Each commune would be assigned a specific task of humanity's broader mission: victory over death, resurrection of the dead, and the settlement of outer space. Rejecting both capitalism and socialism, Fedorov believed that the perfect classless society would be realized when humankind conquered nature, following which it would devote its energies to the resurrection of the dead. At one time or another scholars such as Konstantin TSIOLKOVSKY, an early pioneer of the Soviet space program; Vladimir VERNADSKY, a prominent earth scientist; and Leonid Krasin, an industrialist close to the BOLSHEVIKS were under the sway of Fedorov's ideas.

Fedorov, Svyatoslav Nikolaevich
(1927–   )
eye surgeon

A pioneer in the development of eye surgery, Fedorov became an international medical celebrity, and in the post-Soviet political environment has harbored presidential political ambitions. Fedorov was born in Ukraine to a military father who was sent to the camps in 1937. Fedorov was a member of the COMMUNIST PARTY until August 1991. He graduated as a doctor from the Medical Institute in Rostov-on-Don and became a physician. He was a professor and corresponding member of the USSR ACADEMY OF SCIENCES (Russian Academy of Sciences, from 1991) and the USSR Academy of Medical Sciences (Russian Academy of Medical Sciences, from 1991). After graduation he worked as an ophthalmologist in various hospitals, and in 1957 he became head of the clinical department of the branch of the Gelmgolts Scientific Research Institute of Eye Diseases, Cheboksari. In 1960 he was the first eye surgeon to place an artificial crystal in a patient's eye. The Soviet medical establishment condemned him for this and he had to stop practicing but later moved to the Arkhangelsk Medical Institute. He continued implanting artificial plastic and then silicon crystals and by 1965 he had performed 62 such operations. He was head of Moscow Institute (1967–74), director of the Moscow Scientific Research Laboratory for Experimental and Clinical Eye Surgery (1974–80), and director of the Moscow Scientific Research Institute of Eye Microsurgery (1980–86). In 1986 Fedorov met Nikolai Ryzhkov, then USSR prime minister, and made a great impression on him. With Ryzhkov's support, by a joint decree of the Central Committee of the Communist Party and the USSR Council of Ministers, the institute was transformed into an interbranch scientific research complex for eye microsurgery, with Fedorov as its director. In 1991 he was appointed a member of the Higher Consultation Coordination Council of the Russian Federation Supreme Soviet, and in 1992 he became vice president of the Russian Club (for those who had arrived in Russian society). He was elected to the USSR Congress of People's Deputies in March 1989 and became a member of the Supreme Soviet. In June 1990 he was elected president of the Russian Federation Union of Lessees and Entrepreneurs. At the time of the AUGUST COUP OF 1991 COUP, Fedorov supplied Boris YELTSIN and his supporters defending the home of the Russian Parliament, known as the Russian White House, with mobile medical equipment and food. He left the Communist Party in August 1991, and joined Democratic Russia. He has published over 400 scientific papers.

Feodor I (1557–1598)
(Feodor Ivanovich)
czar

The youngest son of IVAN IV by his first wife, Anastasia, Feodor became ruler after his father's death in 1584. Aware that his son was ill-equipped to rule, Ivan provided for a regency council in his will. Of the five regents, Boris GODUNOV, brother-in-law to the new czar, proved to be the most able and served as de facto ruler dur-

ing most of Feodor's reign. Feodor's reign was a time of foreign policy successes but increasing domestic tensions, inherited from his father's long reign and wars. Muscovy continued its good relations with Elizabethan England. War with Sweden (1590–95) brought Muscovy renewed control over much of the coast of the Gulf of Finland, as well as parts of Karelia. Russian penetration of western Siberia, begun in the last years of Ivan IV's reign, continued apace, with Muscovites soon establishing a permanent presence in the area. Another important achievement of Feodor's reign was the elevation of Metropolitan Job, head of the Russian Orthodox Church and an ally of Boris Godunov, to the rank of patriarch. The Russian patriarch now ranked fifth in seniority in the Orthodox world, behind the patriarchs of Constantinople, Alexandria, Antioch, and Jerusalem. In domestic affairs, labor shortages and declining tax revenues resulted from the flight of peasants escaping famine conditions and the burdens of heavy taxation. Unable to cultivate their estates, nobles were less able to provide the czar with military service. Godunov's attempts to limit the peasant's freedom to migrate, while reducing taxation, did not bear the desired fruits. Feodor's death on January 7, 1598, without a male heir or designated successor, marked the end of the Rurikid dynasty, which had provided Muscovy with rulers since Ivan the Great in 1462. For the next decade and a half, Muscovy fell into the TIME OF TROUBLES, a period of dynastic and social turmoil, aggravated by foreign invasion, out of which emerged Russia's next and last ruling dynasty, the Romanovs.

Feodor II See GODUNOV, BORIS and FALSE DMITRII.

Feodor III (1661–1682)
czar

Feodor, the son of Czar ALEKSEI MIKHAILOVICH by his first marriage and half brother to the future PETER I, reigned from 1676 to 1682. A well-educated and devout young man with literary aspirations, Feodor was in ill health for most of his short reign. His mother's family, the Miloslavskys, initially dominated court politics, although by the end of his reign the boyar Vasili GOLITSYN served as de facto ruler. Feodor continued his father's main policies, especially with regard to religion. Former Patriarch NIKON was allowed to return from exile, but he died en route in 1681; his rank of patriarch was posthumously restored. Persecution of the OLD BELIEVERS, who had broken off from the church in resistance to Nikon's reforms, continued unabated. AVVAKUM, their leading spokesman, was condemned to death and burned alive in 1682. An important change that prefaced Peter's later reforms was the abolition of the policy of precedence (*mestnichestvo*) in the army, under which the hierarchy of command was determined by ancestry rather than ability. Feodor's government also abolished the practice of cutting off the hands and feet of thieves, substituting for it the penalty of deportation to Siberia. In foreign affairs, the Treaty of Bachkisarai (1682) with Turkey recognized Muscovy's rule over the city of KIEV. Feodor's first wife, Agafia Grushevskaia, gave birth to a son in July 1681, but they both died within a few days. The grieving czar was convinced to remarry for dynastic reasons, but a few months after marrying Marfa Apraksina, his health took a turn for the worse and he died in April 1682, without designating an heir. His brother Ivan and his half brother Peter were designated as co-czars, with his sister SOPHIA Alekseevna as regent, an arrangement that lasted until 1689, when she was forced to retire to a convent, and until 1696, when IVAN V died, leaving Peter as sole ruler.

Feodosii Kosoi (16th century, dates unknown)

heretic

Feodosii Kosoi was the head of one of the heretical movements that found support among the peasantry and urban lower classes in the struggle against the feudal order and the official church in the mid–16th century. A slave, Feodosii Kosoi

fled Moscow in the 1540s to the remote Beloozero Monastery and became a monk. He later settled in the Novoozero region and in 1551 started preaching what he called the "New Teachings." In 1553 he was arrested in connection with another case and imprisoned in a Moscow monastery, but he escaped to Lithuania. His New Teaching was an important influence in the formation of a radical current among the Polish-Lithuanian anti-Trinitarians. In his teachings, Feodosii Kosoi repudiated the basic dogmas of the Orthodox Church, including the divine nature of Christ and the resurrection of the dead; denied saints, miracles, and the need to worship icons and the cross; and called for the abolition of monasticism. He not only rejected the feudal church and its hierarchy, dogmas, and rituals, but the whole system of feudal exploitation, spoke out against wars, and preached the equality of all people. His New Teaching gave voice to a developing peasant-heretical tradition in Russia that would more fully express itself in the following century during the Great Schism of the Orthodox Church which gave birth to the OLD BELIEVER sect as well as other sectarian groups in the following centuries.

Feofan Grek (14th–15th century, dates unknown)

artist

Also known as Theophanes the Greek, Feofan Grek was a painter of Greek origin who came to Russia from Constantinople in the late 14th century. Known primarily for frescoes that adorn churches, he was also an accomplished book illustrator. He successfully adjusted the style of the Byzantine Renaissance to the simpler, less sophisticated Russian traditions of the time. His frescoes are full of energy and dynamism, and the holy images, although painted in laconic brush strokes, possess deep psychological penetration. Over the centuries Feofan Grek's work, like that of Andrei RUBLEV, was forgotten until the 20th century, when his frescoes were rediscovered during renovation to the Church of the Transfiguration in Novgorod. Feofan Grek's work is also in evidence in the distinctive multi-tiered iconostasis of the Annunciation Cathedral of the Moscow Kremlin, where he worked with Prokhor Gorodetskii and Rublev. He is also believed to be the author of the small icon known as the *Don Virgin*, which DMITRII DONSKOI carried into battle against the Mongols in 1380, the first significant victory of Russian forces since the MONGOL CONQUEST of 1237–40. The icon is different in that it shows the Virgin Mary looking tenderly at her son rather than at the viewer. Believed to have miraculous powers, the icon was said to have saved Moscow in 1571 from a raid by Crimean Tatars. Feofan Grek is believed to have died some time between 1405 and 1419.

Fetisov, Vyacheslav Aleksandrovich (1958–)
hockey player

A celebrated hockey player in both the Soviet Union and the United States, Vyacheslav Fetisov's career from 1976 to 1998 reflected the impact of a changing international political climate on the world of amateur and professional sports. Born in Moscow, Fetisov joined the prestigious Soviet army team, known by its Russian-language initials CSKA, at the age of 18. For the next 13 years, Fetisov would shine as an outstanding defenseman, leading the Soviet army team to 13 championships while winning the annual award given to the best Soviet player on three occasions. His talents were also recognized beyond the Soviet borders; he was named European player of the year three times. Fetisov was also a centerpiece of the Soviet national teams that dominated international competitions during those years, winning seven gold medals at the World Championships and two Olympic gold medals. To his dismay, Fetisov was also on the receiving end of one of the most celebrated moments in American sports at the 1980 Winter Olympics in Lake Placid, New York, when a plucky amateur squad defeated a heavily favored, more talented Soviet team on the way to a surprising gold medal.

In 1989, after a long legal battle marked by KGB surveillance, Fetisov was awarded a visa and left the Soviet Union. He joined the New Jersey Devils of the National Hockey League (NHL) who owned his NHL rights after drafting him in 1983. Fetisov's entry into the NHL marked the beginning of an exodus of talented Soviet players, at first a curiosity, given the realities of cold war politics, but which continued steadily after the dissolution of the Soviet Union in 1991 to the extent that Russian players are now commonly a part of North American professional hockey. Already past his prime when he joined the NHL, Fetisov did not really make his mark in the league until 1995, when he was traded to the Detroit Red Wings and joined four other talented Russian players—Sergei Fedorov, Slava Kozlov, Vladimir Konstantinov, and Igor Larionov. Together they became known as the "Russian Five" and were an integral part of the Detroit teams that won two successive Stanley Cups in 1997 and 1998. But as before, his personal victories were not without emotional suffering. On the way home from a victory rally after winning the 1997 Stanley Cup, Fetisov was seriously hurt in the automobile accident that left his teammate Konstantinov and the team trainer with severe brain damage and paralyzed. After his retirement, Fetisov returned to Russia, where he coached the Russian team to a Bronze Medal at the 2002 Winter Olympics held in Salt Lake City. He then was appointed Sports Minister for the Russian Federation, a post he currently holds.

Figner, Vera Nikolaevna (1852–1941)
revolutionary

Born in KAZAN province into the family of a wealthy noble, Figner left Russia via an early marriage to pursue her goal of becoming a doctor. In 1872 she enrolled at Zurich University, where she also came into contact with the émigré colony of Russian revolutionaries and students. At first she resisted pressures to join the revolutionary movement and return to Russia to participate in the "To the People" crusade. In 1875, however, on the verge of graduation, she returned to Russia and worked as a medical aide in Samara and Saratov provinces. A reluctant convert to revolutionary terrorism, she became a member of the Central Committee of the PEOPLE'S WILL, the group that assassinated ALEXANDER II in 1881. She was arrested in 1883 and tried the following year. Her death sentence was commuted to life imprisonment, which she began to serve in solitary confinement at Schlusselburg Fortress. Twenty years later, she was sent into exile, then released after the 1905 Revolution. She joined the Socialist Revolutionary Party in 1908, but left soon after the disclosure of the AZEV affair. Revered as a heroine of the revolutionary movement, she traveled widely outside of Russia between 1906 and 1915, lecturing and raising funds for the revolutionary cause. After the OCTOBER REVOLUTION, she worked for the cause of non-Bolshevik revolutionaries, first as honorary president of the Political Red Cross, then for the Society of Political Exiles. She wrote her memoirs and spent her last years in a special home for old revolutionaries. She died on the eve of the German invasion in 1941, 10 days before her 89th birthday. She is buried in Moscow's Novodevichi Cemetery.

Filaret (1554?–1633)
(Feodor Nikitich Romanov)
patriarch and coruler

Filaret was a pivotal figure in the turbulent events of the TIME OF TROUBLES that ended with the election in 1613 of his son MICHAEL ROMANOV as czar. Born Feodor Nikitich Romanov, he was the nephew of Anastasia Romanova, the first wife of IVAN IV. During the reign of his cousin FEODOR I (r. 1584–98), he served in various capacities as a military and diplomatic adviser. After Feodor's death he was banished to a northern monastery by his rival Boris GODUNOV and forced to take monastic vows, at which time he adopted the name Filaret. Filaret reemerged as a power broker following Boris Godunov's sudden death in 1605 when the first FALSE DMITRII freed a number of Godunov's former rivals. Filaret was appointed metropolitan of Rostov. In 1610, during the latter stages of the Time of Troubles, he

was imprisoned by the Polish king Sigismund III, who held him hostage while trying to place his son Wladyslaw on the Russian throne. While in prison, Filaret's son Michael was elected czar of Russia by the ZEMSKII SOBOR of 1613, an event that formalized the end of the Time of Troubles and the beginning of a new Russian dynasty. Filaret was not freed by the Poles until 1619, after the signing of an armistice between Poland and Russia. Back in Moscow, he was appointed patriarch as well as given the title Great Sovereign. From 1619 until 1633, Russia essentially had two rulers with two courts, although the experienced and forceful Filaret was the true power behind the throne.

Filaret (1782–1867)
(Vasili Mikhailovich Drozdov)
theologian and ecclesiastical leader

A distinguished leader of the 19th-century Russian Orthodox Church, Filaret was known for his gift of oratory and biblical scholarship. He was born Vasili Drozdov and graduated from the Trinity Monastery near Moscow in 1803. In 1808 he took his monastic vows, at which time he adopted the name Filaret. That same year he began to teach philosophy at the St. Petersburg Theological Academy, eventually becoming its rector. In 1818 he was appointed to the Holy Synod, the governing body of the Russian Orthodox Church. From 1819 to 1821, when he was transferred to Moscow, Filaret was archbishop of Tver. In 1826 Filaret became metropolitan of Moscow, a post he held until his death. In 1823 he first published an influential *Catechism,* which after several revisions was adopted as a standard school textbook in 1839. Filaret was the driving force behind the translation of the Bible from Old Church Slavonic into modern Russian, a project that was heatedly opposed by traditionalist members of the clergy, but was finally completed in 1858. A modernizer in some respects, Filaret was less tolerant of Old Believers. In July 1856 he was instrumental in reversing the ruling that had allowed OLD BELIEVERS to conduct services in their Rogozhsk suburb of Moscow seven months earlier. A long-time opponent of serfdom, Filaret is considered the author of the EMANCIPATION ACT of 1861 that abolished serfdom.

Florensky, Pavel Aleksandrovich (1882–1943)
polymath and scholar

Described by contemporaries as a man of "superhuman" erudition, Florensky excelled in theology, philosophy, mathematics, and physics. The son of a railway engineer, Florensky was first educated in Tbilisi, Georgia. He graduated with a degree in mathematics from Moscow University, where he studied under the father of the poet Andrei BELY. Florensky then entered the Moscow Theological Academy, graduating in 1908. In 1911, he became an Orthodox priest and returned to the academy to teach philosophy. With his work *The Pillar and the Foundation of Truth* (1914), he established his reputation as an important and original religious thinker of his time. Banished by the czarist authorities to Central Asia, he returned to Petrograd after the October Revolution and studied advanced physics at the ACADEMY OF SCIENCES. Florensky was one of the main contributors to the *Soviet Technical Encyclopedia* (1927–36). Contemporaries wrote that he liked to scandalize the new Communist elite by appearing at Academy of Sciences scholarly conferences wearing his priest's cassock. Florenskywas arrested in 1928 and briefly exiled to Nizhnii-Novgorod (Gorky). Arrested again in 1933, he spent the rest of his life in different camps of the GULAG, including the notorious Solovki camp. Little is known about his life in the camps, but it is presumed he died in 1943.

Fonvizin, Denis Ivanovich (1744–1792)
playwright

A representative of the Russian Enlightenment, Fonvizin is considered to have been the first Russian playwright of any significance. After entering the civil service, he wrote his first major play, *Brigadir* (1769), a satire on Russian Fran-

cophiles, which brought him to the attention of the influential statesman Nikita Panin. Panin, who had helped CATHERINE II gain the throne in 1762 and at the time was head of the College of Foreign Affairs, made Fonvizin his secretary. Fonvizin now turned to writing plays with political themes, among them *On the Recovery of Grand Duke Paul Petrovich* (1771) and *In Praise of Marcus Aurelius*. His later works ran into trouble with the censors. His best-known play, *The Callow Youth* (1781–82), a satire on the nobility, was initially banned and was performed only after the intervention of Prince Grigorii POTEMKIN, then Catherine's favorite. The censors also banned a later play, *Honest Person's Friend* (or *The Traditionalist*). Fonvizin also produced *Universal Court Grammar*, a satirical account of his published exchange with Catherine II in the journal *A Companion for Lovers of the Russian Language*. After suffering a stroke in 1785 that left him partly paralyzed, he turned to religious mysticism in the last years of his life. The most successful of Fonvizin's plays combined the styles of 18th-century French comedy with native Russian comedy, an important synthesis in the development of a Europeanized Russian culture.

Frunze, Mikhail Vasilievich (1885–1925)
military commander

One of the leading Red Army commanders during the Russian civil war, Frunze was born in Pishpek, then a part of Russian Turkestan, modern-day Kyrgyzstan. Already imbued with revolutionary ideas, he traveled in 1904 to St. Petersburg to pursue his education; instead he joined the BOLSHEVIKS and was expelled from the city months later for his part in a demonstration. During the 1905 Revolution, he first took active part in the six-week-long textile strike in Ivanovo-Voznesensk, home to the first soviet (workers' council) in Russian history, then was at the barricades in Moscow during the unsuccessful December insurrection. Arrested, he was sentenced to 10 years of hard labor, followed by exile in 1914 to Irkutsk province, but he escaped to Chita in 1915. The revolutionary year 1917 first found Frunze at the head of the Bolshevik movement in Minsk, Belorussia. In October 1917, at the head of 2,000 workers and soldiers, he was instrumental in the Bolshevik victory in Moscow, after a weeklong battle. During the Russian civil war he fought with distinction, defeating KOLCHAK's forces in the Urals in 1919. As commander of the eastern front, he secured Bolshevik control of Turkestan, including the nominally independent Emirate of BUKHARA. In November 1920 he led the capture of Crimea, routing WRANGEL's troops and ending the White military presence in Russian territory. Frunze sided with STALIN in his struggles with TROTSKY, particularly on the issue of using ex-czarist officers whom Trotsky had recruited during the civil war. After Trotsky's resignation in 1925, Frunze was appointed people's commissar of war in January 1925, Frunze was the author of the "unitary military doctrine," which envisaged that the military should be trained for offensive action and dedicated to carrying out one of the goals of the COMMUNIST PARTY, world revolution. Frunze helped lay the foundations of the efficient Soviet machine by introducing conscription and standardizing military uniforms and formations. He died on October 31, 1925, after a prolonged illness. After his death, his hometown was renamed Frunze, by which name it was known until the end of Soviet rule in 1991. It has been renamed Bishkek, capital of Kyrgyzstan. The Military Academy in Moscow was renamed the Frunze Academy, a name it retains to this day.

Furtseva, Ekaterina Alekseevna (1910–1974)
Soviet official

One of the few women to rise to the top of Soviet politics, in 1957 Furtseva became the first woman to be chosen to the COMMUNIST PARTY Politburo, known as the Presidium from 1946–64. A protégé of Nikita KHRUSHCHEV, Furtseva's prominence was due more to her ability to follow the party line than to any special commitment to women's politics. She began her political career as first party secretary of one of the Moscow city districts (1942–50), before becoming second secretary of the entire Moscow city party apparatus. In 1954, with Khrushchev on the ascendance, she became the first secretary of the Moscow Communist Party, essentially the top party city official, a formidable achievement for a woman in the 1950s. She had also risen in the Communist Party apparatus during these years, becoming a candidate member of the Central Committee in 1952, and a full member of the Central Committee in 1956. That same year she was elected as a Central Committee secretary, an important stepping stone toward the pinnacle of party power, the Politburo, which she reached in 1957. By 1960, however, her fortunes had changed. She lost her Central Committee secretaryship and her Presidium seat the following year. Instead she was appointed minister of culture, a position she held through the fall of Khrushchev and into the BREZHNEV era. Her conformist, conservative cultural outlook dismayed the Soviet intelligentsia and was emblematic of the Brezhnev regime's attempt to restrain the limited freedoms the cultural intelligentsia had gained during parts of the Khrushchev era.

futurism

A literary and artistic trend, futurism flourished with particular strength and originality in Russia between 1910 and 1930. Its name and its principal idea, the abandonment of the past and the creation of a new art consonant with the machine age, initially drew from the ideas of Italian and French futurism. Most Russian Futurists, however, were far more uncompromising in their rejection of existing society and, with the onset of the Russian Revolution, were presented with a much greater social canvas to realize their ideas. There were several organized groups of Futurists, the most important, the cubo-futurists, being also the most radical in both the artistic and the political sense. Their leader and theorist was

Velimir KHLEBNIKOV, the most outstanding of all futurist artists. The poet Vladimir MAYAKOVSKY also belonged to this group. Futurists generally welcomed the Bolshevik revolution as consonant with their own social and political extremism. In the first years of the Bolshevik regime, when the cultural policy of the government was in the hands of unorthodox and open-minded BOLSHE-VIKS like Aleksandr Bogdanov and Anatolii Luna-charsky, futurists had a highly visible role. They established the influential group LEF (Left Front of Art) (among whose members were PASTER-NAK, Kirsanov, and N. Aseyev). During the 1920s most prominent futurists became disillusioned with Soviet rule; Khlebnikov died in 1922 and Mayakovsky committed suicide in 1930. LEF itself abandoned revolutionary Futurism in 1926 in favor of a more "socially constructive" program. In 1929 the group became REF (Revolutionary Front of Art), and the following year it joined RAPP (the All-Russian Association of Proletarian Writers). Despite their exaggerations, which sometimes went beyond the limits of comprehension, the Futurists had an important influence upon Russian poetry through their linguistic innovations.

G

Gagarin, Yuri Alekseevich (1934–1968)
cosmonaut

The first man to orbit the earth in a space capsule, Gagarin became the symbol of the spectacular successes of the Soviet space program in the late 1950s and early 1960s, beginning with the launching of SPUTNIK in 1957. He was born near Smolensk in western Russia, the son of a collective farmer, and joined the Soviet air force in 1955, eventually rising to the rank of major. He graduated as a fighter pilot from the Chkalov Military Aviation School in 1957, and in 1960 he was selected as a possible future cosmonaut. He competed with German TITOV for the distinction of being the pilot on the first manned flight, winning out, some said later, because his more engaging personality and peasant background reflected better on Soviet science for propaganda purposes. On April 12, 1961, he made his historic 108-minute flight aboard *Vostok-1*. A member of the COMMUNIST PARTY since 1960, Gagarin became a Soviet and international celebrity, a member of the USSR Supreme Soviet, and an ambassador for Soviet science and technology. In 1962 he published a book of memoirs, *Till We Reach the Stars*. He continued his previous work as a test pilot and helped train a new generation of Soviet cosmonauts. He died in an air crash in March 1968 while testing a fighter plane. After his death, numerous monuments were built and streets renamed in his honor across the Soviet Union, including Gagarin Square in Moscow with its gigantic monument to Gagarin. His ashes are buried in the Kremlin Wall.

Soviet cosmonaut Major Yuri Gagarin on his way to his spaceship *Vostok*, 1961 *(Hulton/Archive)*

Galich, Aleksandr Arkadievich (1918?–1977)
(born Ginzburg)
musician and writer

A popular singer of satirical ballads whose songs circulated clandestinely, Galich was born in Ekaterinoslav (Dnepropetrovsk). His family moved to Moscow, and he attended the Stanislavsky Studio. During World War II he toured the front with theatrical troupes. After the war, Galich turned to writing plays, film scripts, as well as songs, which brought him the greatest recognition. He became a popular singer of satirical ballads, accompanying himself on the guitar. Like Bulat OKUDZHAVA and Vladimir VYSOTSKY, Galich enjoyed an immense popularity that was in great part due to the growing availability of tape recorders, which made it possible for his songs to be recorded and duplicated. This was the era of *magnitizdat,* uncensored recordings of popular songs that circulated clandestinely, much like the better-known phenomenon of *samizdat* (self-publishing). Eventually, the recordings reached the wrong hands, because he was severely reprimanded in 1968 and expelled from the Union of Writers and the Union of Cinematographers in 1971, making it almost impossible for him to gain legal employment. He was forced to emigrate in 1974, settling first in Munich, then in Paris. He worked with Radio Liberty, broadcasting regularly to the Soviet Union. He died in Paris on December 15, 1977, when he accidentally electrocuted himself while "fumbling" with his stereo equipment. Under GORBACHEV's policy of glasnost (openness), he was rehabilitated and posthumously reinstated in the Union of Cinematographers in 1988.

Galiev, Sultan Mirsaid (1880–1940)

revolutionary

The most famous Muslim national Communist in the Soviet Union, Galiev attempted to graft on aspects of Islamic teaching to Marxism-Leninism, thereby giving it a distinctly non-European national face. Of Tatar ethnicity, he was born in present-day Bashkortostan and taught and published in Ufa. He took part in the Muslim Congresses of May and July 1917, and joined the Bolshevik Party after the OCTOBER REVOLUTION. In January 1918, he was appointed chair of the newly created Central Muslim Commissariat. As member of the inner collegium of the People's Commissariat of Nationalities, he worked closely with its commissar, STALIN. Drawing from LENIN's belief that imperialism was the highest stage of capitalism, Galiev argued to the Muslim world

that all oppressed colonial peoples should cooperate with the BOLSHEVIKS by forming national liberation movements, an idea that was later developed more extensively by Mao Zedong and Ho Chi Minh. While the Bolsheviks were engaged in consolidating and spreading Soviet power to the borderlands of the former Russian Empire, they supported Galiev's ideas, recognized an independent Muslim Communist Party, and allowed for a Muslim Military College under Galiev's direction. Some of Galiev's other ideas, notably the creation of an autonomous Islamic Soviet Socialist Republic, began to take a pan-Islamic coloration that diverged from the increasingly nationalist-statist agenda of the Bolshevik Party. By 1923, with the establishment of Soviet power in the Turkestan region, Galiev's views now posed a threat to Bolshevik rule and hegemony in the area. He was first arrested in May 1923, at Stalin's instigation, and accused of "national deviation." Released soon after owing to international pressure, he was rearrested in November 1923 on a charge of treason and sentenced to 10 years' hard labor. In 1928 he was sent to the notorious Solovki labor camp near the White Sea. Galiev was rearrested in early 1938, sentenced to death in December 1939, and executed in January 1940.

Gapon, Georgii Apollonovich (1870–1906)

priest and trade union leader

An Orthodox priest who became an influential trade union leader at the instigation of the St. Petersburg police, Father Gapon's career captures some of the contradictions of the attempts by some in the government to promote "police socialism." Seeking to undermine Marxist influence over the growing urban proletariat, police officials under the influence of Sergei ZUBATOV developed the strategy known as "police socialism." They encouraged the formation of trade unions that would press for what they considered to be fair workers' demands, but without the broader revolutionary agenda of the socialist movement. In 1903, Father Gapon founded the

Assembly of Russian Workers of St. Petersburg to advance workers' conditions within a framework the police could approve. Social Democratic infiltration of the group soon brought tensions with regard to goals and tactics, pushing the assembly toward more confrontational tactics, such as strikes, than Gapon would have preferred. In December 1904, the assembly became involved in a mass strike after some of its members were dismissed. Gapon then drew up a manifesto to the czar, expressed in a mixture of religious and secular language, appealing for more social justice. It proved immensely popular and soon collected over 150,000 signatures. On Sunday, January 9, 1905, Gapon headed a long procession of workers whose goal was to present the petition to Czar NICHOLAS II in the Winter Palace. The police overreacted, fired on the crowd, and killed more than a hundred people including women and children. Known as BLOODY SUNDAY, the incident destroyed what was left of the myth that the czar was the loving father of the people and sparked what became the 1905 Revolution. Although the incident shocked and radicalized Gapon, his police contacts eventually caught up with him, as the Socialist Revolutionaries assassinated him in 1906 as an "agent provocateur."

Gasprali (Gasprinsky), Ismail Bey (1851–1914)

reformer

An advocate of moderate secular and liberal reform among the Muslims of the Russian Empire, Ismail Bey Gasprali was a Crimean Tatar who became known as the "father of pan-Turkism." Gasprali, sometimes referred to as Gasprinsky, was born in Gaspra, a village in the Crimea, to an impoverished Tatar noble family. He entered the Moscow Cadet Corps and later lived in Paris and Istanbul, before returning to his native Crimea. From his life in these places, he absorbed a distinctive blend of Slavophile ideas, liberalism and reformist, which he sought to blend into an ideology of pan-Turkism. A champion of education as the best vehicle for pro-

gress, he founded his first school, or *medrese*, in the Crimea in 1882. Known as Jadidism (New Method), Gasprali's educational philosophy sought to renew Islamic schooling through a synthesis of Islamic culture and Western-style technical education. His school was a success and soon Gasprali was traveling through the Muslim regions of the Russian Empire as far as BUKHARA, promoting jadidist education. As a publicist, Gasprali was driven by the belief that linguistic unity was the prerequisite for political unity. In 1883 he founded the newspaper *Terdzhuman* (*Tercuman*, or Interpreter), one of whose goals was the promotion of a pan-Turkic language based on modern Ottoman Turkish that would be understood by all Turkic peoples from Istanbul to Turkestan. For the next three decades, the newspaper was in the forefront of Muslim intellectual life in the empire. Gasprali also published periodicals for women and children and a satirical journal entitled *Kha, kha, kha* (*Ha, Ha, Ha*). He was also active in the political awakening of Russian Muslims, participating in three Muslim congresses where he defended his message of pan-Turkism. A moderate with regard to Russian culture and the empire, he advocated cultural and political cooperation based on the healthy development of a Muslim national culture that would lead to mutual cultural understanding between Russian Muslims and non-Muslims. At a time of growing nationalist assertiveness, this message did not resonate well with the younger generation of Russian Muslims. By the time of his death, a network of jadidist schools had developed, extending from the Crimea and the Volga at one end to the eastern borders of Central Asia on the other. Gasprali's educational legacy is uncontested and essential in understanding the intellectual and political development of the Muslims of the Russian Empire.

Ge, Nikolai Nikolaevich (1831–1894)

artist

Of French origin, Ge joined the Academy of Arts in 1850. From 1857 to 1869, he studied in Italy, settling in Florence, where he concentrated mainly on landscapes and religious paintings. Back in Russia, he joined the Peredvizhniki (WANDERERS) movement in 1870 and continued to explore moral and religious themes. His famous *Peter I Interrogates the Tsarevich Aleksei* (1871) dates from this period. Ge abandoned a promising career as an art teacher and traveled to the Ukraine, where he spent 10 years studying Lev Tolstoy's religious writings. His religious paintings are particularly expressive and, with their emphasis on suffering, stand out from the comforting familiarity of other religious paintings of the era. Not long before his death, he completed a cycle of works on the Passion of Christ, beginning with *What Is Truth?* (1890), that portrays Pilate's interrogation of Christ, and continuing with *Crucifixion* (1891) and *Golgotha* (1892).

Giers, Nikolai Karlovich (1820–1895)
statesman and diplomat

Russian foreign minister during the reign of ALEXANDER III, Giers engineered the surprising transition from a Russian alliance with imperial Germany to one with republican France. Giers was born in the town of Radzivilov in the province of Volhynia in the western part of the Russian Empire. He entered the Russian foreign service in 1838, first working in the Asian department of the Foreign Ministry. After serving in numerous posts abroad, including ambassador to Iran (1863) and Sweden (1872), in 1875 Giers was appointed assistant foreign minister and director of the Asian department of the Foreign Ministry. With Foreign Minister Aleksandr GORCHAKOV increasingly unable to fulfill his duties and discredited after the CONGRESS OF BERLIN in 1878, Giers became de facto foreign minister during the last years of ALEXANDER II's reign, even as Gorchakov remained the titular minister until 1882. As foreign minister, Giers sought to maintain Russia's recent pro-German orientation through the Three Emperor's League that also included Germany and Austria-Hungary and committed the three empires to a policy of friendly neutrality should one of them be at war with a fourth power (except the Ottoman Empire). First established in 1873, the league had recovered from disagreements following the RUSSO-TURKISH WAR and was in place again from 1881 to 1887. In 1887, with Russia and Austria-Hungary at odds over the Balkans, the agreement was allowed to lapse, but Russia signed a secret Reinsurance Treaty with Germany that was to be renewed in 1890. By 1890, however, with Emperor Wilhelm II in full control over foreign policy, Germany discontinued the Reinsurance Treaty. Building from a series of French loans designed to spur Russian industrialization, Giers arranged for a diplomatic understanding between France and Russia, signed in 1891, by which the two countries would consult each other in case of war. In January 1894, after French insistence overcame the Russian preference for a rapprochement with Germany, the diplomatic understanding was upgraded to a formal military alliance. As foreign minister, Giers was known for a cautious but firm style that matched that of Alexander III and kept Russia out of war during his tenure. Giers died in office on January 26, 1895.

Giliarovsky, Vladimir Alekseevich (1853–1935)
journalist

Born to a middle-class family that had settled in the northern province of Vologda. Like many youths of his day, Giliarovsky was strongly influenced by the writings of the radical journalist Nikolai Chernyshevsky, particularly by the romantic character of Rakhmetov in *What Is to Be Done?* (1863). In 1871, seeking to emulate Rakhmetov, Giliarovsky set out for the Volga region, "to serve the people," beginning a 10-year period of wanderings during which he worked as a barge hauler, fireman, paint factory worker, breaker of wild horses, circus actor, and provincial theater actor. Giliarovsky participated in the RUSSO-TURKISH WAR OF 1877–78 as a volunteer and, in 1881, settled in Moscow, the city with which he became most closely identified. His first book of stories, *Trushchobnye liudi* (Tenement people) (1887), described with honesty and sympathy the world of Moscow's slum dwellers. By order of the czarist censorship, all copies of the book were burned before publication. Giliarovsky worked extensively for various newspapers as a journalist in prerevolutionary times, earning the nickname "king of Moscow reporters." After the revolution, Giliarovsky wrote several volumes of well-received memoirs that further cemented his reputation with the Soviet reading public. Among these are *Moi skitaniia* (My wanderings) (1928), in which he recounted his early wanderings across provincial Russia, and *Liudi teatra* (People of the theater) (published posthumously, 1940), in which he wrote of his many friends and acquaintances in the world of culture, including CHEKHOV and ERMOLOVA. His most popular work, however, was *Moskva i moskvichi* (Moscow and Muscovites), first published in 1923 and revised in 1935, which warmly captured for posterity his old Moscow world of artists, beggars, thieves, and ordinary people. Because few authors could write as knowingly about both the high society and the lower depths of prerevolutionary Moscow, this work came to occupy a place of honor among a reading public in the 1960s and 1970s that was beginning to trade revolutionary enthusiasm for a nostalgia about the past.

Ginsburg, Moisei Yakovlevich
(1892–1946)
architect
Ginsburg was born in the Belarussian capital of Minsk. His father was an architect, a family tradition that Ginsburg's own son and grandson would later continue. After graduating from the Academy of Arts in Milan in 1914, he returned to Russia, where he received an engineering degree from the Rizhskii Polytechnic Institute in Moscow in 1917. He spent the years of the civil war (1918–21) in private practice in the Crimea. Back in Moscow after the civil war, he worked actively in his profession throughout the 1920s as a teacher and editor. He taught at Vkhutemas

(State Higher Art and Technical Studios) and the Moscow Institute of Higher Technology, became a founding member of the Society of Contemporary Architects (OSA) in 1925, and edited the journal of the Moscow Architectural Society, *Arkhitektura*. Ginsburg became known as the leading theorist and practitioner of constructivist architecture. In his work *Style and the Epoch* (1924) and the journal of the Society of Contemporary Architects, *Sovremennaia arkhitektura* (Contemporary architecture), which he founded and edited (1926–30) with Aleksandr VESNIN, Ginsburg strongly upheld what he called the "mechanization of life"—the integration of scientific and technological discoveries into the process of rational, artistic creation. Like other architects of the revolutionary period, Ginsburg was concerned with the problems of mass housing in the context of the new socialist order. His most important contribution, "a landmark of constructivist architecture," was the six-story building block he built between 1927 and 1929 for the People's Commissariat of Finance (Narkomfin) in Moscow, an example of the *dom-kom-muna* (house commune) that would provide collective living quarters for its residents. As Ginsburg's influence in Moscow waned with the 1930s backlash against constructivism and other avant-garde styles, he returned to his theoretical writings about standardization and mass housing. His final works were in distant places like Alma-Ata in Kazakhstan (Administration Building of the Turkestan-Siberia Railroad, 1929–34) and Kislovodsk in the Caucasus (Ordzhonikidze Sanatorium, 1925–37).

Ginzburg, Evgeniia Semyonovna
(1904–1977)
memoirist
Ginzburg first became known outside the Soviet Union as the author of two poignant volumes of memoirs of her 18 years in the GULAG labor camps. She was born in Moscow and graduated in history from Kazan State University, in the Tatar Autonomous Republic of the Russian Fed-

eration. Her first husband, Pavel Aksenov, a leading member of the Tatar province COMMUNIST PARTY, was arrested in 1937 at the height of the Great Purge. Ginzburg was arrested soon after as the wife of an "enemy of the people" and began a long journey through various camps in the GULAG, especially in the remote area of Magadan on the Sea of Okhotsk. She was released and rehabilitated in 1955. Drawing entirely from memory, she began drafting her manuscript in 1959, while writing articles and educational materials to support herself. By 1962, she had completed over 400 typescript pages. The magazine *Yunost* (*Youth*) published a few excerpts, but with a growing freeze refused to publish the entire manuscript. Circulated through the *samizdat* network, Ginzburg's memoirs struck a deep chord among its readers. A first volume was published in English to great acclaim as *Journey into the Whirlwind* (1967), and a second followed in 1979 as *Within the Whirlwind.* They were finally published posthumously in the Soviet Union in 1988 in *Yunost,* the same journal that had refused them two decades earlier. Her son, Vasili AKSENOV, who had been separated from his parents at the age of four, joined her in Magadan in the early 1950s and went on to become a prominent Soviet novelist.

Gippius, Zinaida Nikolaevna (1869–1945)
writer

One of the leading representatives of Symbolist poetry and the Silver Age, Gippius was born in Tula province, the daughter of a government official, and grew up in Tbilisi, Georgia. She published her first poems at the age of 19 in the journal *Severnyi vestnik* (*Northern Herald*). A member of the Religious and Philosophical Society, she wrote metaphysical poems, as well as an important novel, *The Devil's Puppet* (1911). Her marriage, of over 50 years, to another Symbolist poet, Dmitrii Merezhkovskii, formed one of the more remarkable partnerships in Russian literature. A talented poet and literary critic, she was

admired and feared as the star of St. Petersburg literary life and intrigue in the last decade before the revolution. She welcomed the FEBRUARY REVOLUTION and was disheartened by the Bolshevik victory in October, which she condemned as a victory of the vulgarity she had always despised. She left Russia in 1919 with Merezhkovskii for Poland, then settled in France. In Paris, she continued her role as literary salon hostess (the Green Lamp) and wrote bitterly anti-Bolshevik pieces in the émigré press. She wrote a biography of Merezhskovskii after his death in 1941. Her prerevolutionary diaries, published much later in Paris, reveal perplexing sexual confusion. She considered herself the mentor of both Bely and BLOK. Her memoirs and correspondence reveal a sharp intellect and a sardonic malicious sense of humor. A collected edition of her poetry was first published in Munich in the 1970s.

Glinka, Mikhail Ivanovich (1804–1857)
composer

The first Russian composer to break from imitation of Western traditions, Glinka is generally considered the father of Russian music. A student of the Irish composer and pianist John Field, who moved to Russia in 1802, Glinka first made his name as a pianist and singer. He studied in St. Petersburg and Berlin. Well traveled in Russia and abroad, he enjoyed the friendship of GRIBOEDOV, PUSHKIN, Zhukovskii, and Mickiewicz, and the acquaintance of leading composers like Berlioz, Liszt, and Mendelssohn. His fame rests primarily on two operas, *Ivan Susanin, A Life for the Tsar* (1836), which is the first example of the introduction of Russian themes into his music, and *Ruslan and Liudmilla* (1842), based on a poem by Aleksandr Pushkin. He also wrote songs, chamber works, and music for piano, and two orchestral works that play on Spanish themes. Although he spent much time in western Europe, his pioneering use of nationalist themes, Oriental themes, and Russian folk songs most influenced later generations. Among them were the members of the Moguchaya

Kuchka (The Mighty Handful), a group of young composers (Balakirev, Cui, MUSSORGSKY, Borodin, and Rimsky-Korsakov) who went on to create a distinct national Russian school of music. Balakirev edited and published Glinka's works after his death.

Godunov, Boris Feodorovich (1552?–1605)
czar

Czar of Russia during the first part of the early-17th-century TIME OF TROUBLES, Godunov led a life that became the subject of a well-known tragedy by Aleksandr PUSHKIN, later made into an opera by Modest MUSSORGSKY. Born to a prominent boyar family of Tatar origin, Godunov was educated at the court of IVAN IV. His fortunes benefited from his marriage to the daughter of Maliuta Skuratov, the head of Ivan's *oprichnina,* which he also joined, and from his sister's marriage to Ivan's feeble son, the future FEODOR I. After Ivan IV's death in 1584, Godunov gradually outmaneuvered his main competitors for influence over the new czar, the Mstislavskii, Shuiskii, and Romanov families, and concentrated power in his hands as regent. As regent, Godunov was universally recognized as a skillful statesman who advanced Russia's territorial interests in the west toward the Baltic, in the southern steppes, and in promoting a more energetic attempt to colonize Siberia in the east. He was also instrumental in obtaining the agreement of the patriarch of Constantinople in 1598 for the establishment of a separate Russian PATRIARCHATE, thus enhancing the status of the Russian Church. Under Godunov's regency, the legal status of serfdom was further guaranteed by an edict of 1587 that bound serfs to the land. In 1591, the 10-year old prince Dmitrii of Uglich, Ivan's youngest son and possible heir to the throne, died under highly mysterious circumstances. Godunov was never able to dispel the suspicions that he was responsible for Dmitrii's death. Nevertheless, when Feodor died childless in 1598, the Assembly of the Land chose him as czar. As Godunov relied on the minor gentry in his ongoing attempt to consolidate the autocracy, he antagonized many of the prominent Muscovite boyar families who had suffered heavily under Ivan IV. Increasing peasant discontent and famine contributed to the period of social breakdown known as the Time of Troubles, which historians traditionally date from 1598 to 1613. As opposition to his rule grew, many boyars turned their support to an impostor who claimed to be the real Dmitrii of Uglich who had escaped Godunov's attempted assassination, hence the name FALSE DMITRII. With the support of Polish and Lithuanian nobles, False Dmitrii invaded Muscovy in 1604. Godunov was on the verge of defeating False Dmitrii when he died unexpectedly in April 1605, leaving his wife and young son, FEODOR II, to rule over a profoundly divided Muscovite state. Feodor reigned for only a few months but was killed with his mother, as False Dmitrii entered Moscow in June 1605 and was crowned czar. The events of Boris Godunov's life and, most notably, the lingering suspicions over his role in the death of Dmitrii of Uglich cast him—unfairly—for future generations in the tragic role of a Russian version of Shakespeare's Richard III.

Gogol, Nikolai Vasilievich (1809–1852)
writer

One of the masters of 19th-century Russian literature, Gogol eluded easy classification from his contemporaries and later generations of readers. Of Ukrainian origin, Gogol arrived in St. Petersburg in 1829, and after a short stint in the civil service, he became a private tutor. By 1831 he had become part of the elite literary world inhabited by PUSHKIN and the critic Vissarion BELINSKY. His early stories and sketches of Ukrainian life, *Evenings on a Farm near Dikanka, Arabesques,* and *Mirgorod,* were well received for their novelty and ability to capture rural life. Larger success and acclaim came with the play *The Government Inspector* (1836), a satire of provincial bureaucrats. He spent the next decade abroad, mostly in Rome,

Nikolai Gogol *(Library of Congress)*

where he wrote the work regarded as his masterpiece, *Dead Souls,* published in 1842. A satirical account of serf-owning provincial nobles, the novel also comments on the failings of the human condition. His short stories, particularly "The Overcoat" (1842) and "The Nose," introduced surreal elements that would influence later generations and bring him closer to 20th-century themes. Gogol also wrote successfully in the historical genre, as in *Taras Bulba,* a portrait of life among the Zaporozhe COSSACKS. Increasingly under the influence of a fiercely ascetic priest, Gogol became convinced of his divine mission to bring about the moral regeneration of Russia. After his return to Russia he clashed in a famous exchange of letters with his former friend Belinsky, who felt that Gogol's religious orientation betrayed the earlier value of his work. Gogol spent the last 10 years of his life working on the continuation to *Dead Souls* but, less than a week before his death, burned the manuscript. With an outstanding body of work that combines the realism of early works, elements of surrealism, social criticism, mysticism, and political conservatism, Gogol stands apart from his contemporaries, transcending the labels they sought to place on him.

Golden Horde

Drawn from the Tatar term *altun ordu* (golden army), the Golden Horde is the name traditionally given to the medieval Mongol-Tatar state formed by BATU KHAN, grandson of Chinggis (Genghis) Khan, following the MONGOL CONQUEST of Russia. More correctly known as the Khanate of Kipchak, the Golden Horde comprised most of southern Russia and western Siberia, with its capital at SARAI on the lower VOLGA RIVER. The majority of the northern Russian principalities conquered between 1237 and 1240 became vassals of the Mongol state and paid tribute to the ruling khans, by traveling once a year to Sarai. Under Khan Uzbek, Islam became the dominant religion of the Golden Horde in the 14th century. The Golden Horde's hold over Russia was first challenged by grand prince of Muscovy, DMITRII DONSKOI, who led Russian troops to their first victory over a Mongol force at the Battle of KULIKOVO in 1380. In 1395 a more serious challenge came from the south when Timur (Tamerlane) began his conquest of the Golden Horde. After Timur's death, the Golden Horde broke into four independent khanates: ASTRAKHAN, Crimea, KAZAN, and Sibir (Siberia). This fragmentation of the Golden Horde facilitated the rise of Muscovy as the dominant Russian principality and challenger to continued Mongol rule of Russia. In 1480 IVAN III, grand prince of Muscovy, formally ended the practice of paying tribute to the khans, a step traditionally seen as the end of Mongol rule in Russia. Nevertheless, with the exception of the khanate of Crimea, the four successor khanates of the Golden Horde continued to rule large parts of European Russia until their defeat in the mid-16th century. The khanate of Crimea, protected by the rising power of Ottoman Turkey, preserved its independence until 1783 during the reign of CATHERINE II the Great.

Golitsyn, Vasili Vasilievich (1643–1714)
statesman

A member of an ancient princely family with numerous branches and a long tradition of service to the czar, Prince Vasili Golitsyn was the main adviser to SOPHIA during her regency (1682–89). Golitsyn first rose to prominence in 1676 during the reign of ALEKSEI (1645–76), when he was awarded the rank of boyar and appointed to military command in Ukraine. During the reign of Aleksei's son FEODOR III (1676–82), Golitsyn played a leading role in the commission that recommended the abolition of *mestnichestvo,* a cumbersome system that allotted positions in the army, government, and diplomatic corps on the basis of hereditary precedence. With his lover Sophia as regent for her brother IVAN V and her half brother PETER I, Golitsyn reached the peak of his influence in Russian politics. Golitsyn was able to reform the Muscovite penal code but ran into solid opposition from the traditionalist members of the ruling elite when he sought to introduce far-reaching reforms, such as the abolition of serfdom, initiation of widespread education, the establishment of religious toleration, and the promotion of industry. Golitsyn had more lasting success in military and diplomatic affairs. In 1686 he negotiated an advantageous treaty of "eternal peace" with Poland, which recognized Russia's control of KIEV and the eastern bank of the Dnieper River. In 1689, Russia and China ratified the Treaty of NERCHINSK that established the Russo-Chinese border along the AMUR RIVER, opening the way for further Russian exploration and expansion toward the Pacific Ocean. Although he succeeded in rallying European support for a Holy League against the Ottoman Empire, the military campaigns that followed in 1687 and 1689 against the Crimean Tatars, allies of the Ottomans, resulted in disasters that contributed to the downfall of Golitsyn and Sophia's regency in 1689. With Sophia overthrown, Golitsyn was exiled to the northern town of Kholmogory, where he eventually died on May 2, 1714.

Goncharov, Ivan Aleksandrovich (1814–1891)
writer

Best known for his masterful psychological study of a slothful gentleman in the novel *Oblomov,* Goncharov worked for the government as editor of an official newspaper and, between 1856 and 1873, as censor. He first came to the attention of the Russian reading public with the novel *The Frigate Pallas* (1858), a gripping account of his trip to Japan in 1852–53 as secretary to Admiral Putiatin that fed Russians' growing interest in the ocean and sea adventures. *Oblomov* (1859) was actually the second, and by far most successful, volume of a trilogy, begun with *A Common Life* (1847) and completed with *The Precipice* (1869). The latter depicts a frequent theme in the literature of the era, an ordinary family confronted by the arrival of a nihilist. In *Oblomov,* Goncharov portrays an indolent, guilt-ridden landowner who spends most of his day in his bathrobe trying to get out of bed, and contrasts him with his foil, his efficient secretary Stolz, who not unintentionally has a Germanic name. The novel's eponymous hero became the symbol of the agreeable laziness that was held to be a typical Russian characteristic that to some critics was a "disease," known to this day as *oblomovshchina.*

Goncharova, Natalia Sergeevna (1881–1962)
artist

A prominent exponent of a fusion of Russian and European artistic styles, Goncharova came from a noble background that made her an exception in the artistic circles she frequented. She enrolled in the Moscow School of Painting, Sculpture and Architecture in 1898, hoping to study sculpture. Here she met her lifelong companion and collaborator, Mikhail Larionov. Goncharova's early work attempted to combine the Russian traditions of the icon and cheap popular print known as *lubok* with post impressionist ideas. In 1906, she sent her work to an exhibit organized by the promoters of the journal *MIR ISKUSSTVA*. Impressed by her and Larionov's work, DIAGHILEV invited them to contribute to an upcoming exhibition in Paris at the Salon d'Automne. The next years saw the production of some of her better-known works—*The Wreath* (1907), *Golden Fleece* (1908), *Jack of Diamonds* (1910–11), and *Union of Youth* (1910). She helped organize and took part in the Donkey's Tail Exhibition, held in Moscow (1912), which displayed her work along with that of Larionov, Vladimir TATLIN, Kazimir MALEVICH, and others. The exhibition featured works that revealed Russian folk art influences using bright colors. She also designed the sets for Diaghilev's production of *Le Coq d'or* (1914). In 1915, she left Moscow with Larionov and settled permanently in Paris in 1919.

Gorbachev, Mikhail Sergeevich
(1931–)
Soviet leader

The last leader of the Soviet Union, Gorbachev came to power in 1985 and tried unsuccessfully to preserve the country as a unified and Communist political entity. Gorbachev was born into a peasant family in the village of Privolnoe, located in the fertile southern agricultural province of Stavropol, at the edge of the northern Caucasus region. Both his grandfathers suffered from the repression—exile in one case, arrest and torture in the other—unleashed by STALIN's government on the peasantry in the 1930s, a fact that could have derailed his career had it been publicized in the 1950s or 1960s. The German occupation of the Stavropol region from August 1942 to January 1943 further disrupted

his youth. After the war, Gorbachev worked several summers at his village's machine-tractor station driving farm machinery, earning in 1949 with his fellow villagers an Order of the Red Banner of Labor for overfulfilling the harvest quota.

In 1950 Gorbachev was admitted to the Law Faculty of Moscow State University, the country's most prestigious university, a difficult achievement for a rural youth. He joined the KOMSOMOL, the COMMUNIST PARTY youth organization, later that year and by 1952 had become a full member of the Communist Party. In 1953, he married a fellow university student, Raisa Titorenko, and their daughter Irina was born four years later. After graduation in 1955, Gorbachev returned with this family to Stavropol, where he was appointed first secretary of the city's Komsomol. Under the patronage of Feodor Kulakov, his career advanced smoothly in Stavropol in the 1960s, especially after Kulakov was named secretary of the Agriculture Department of the Central Committee in Moscow. In 1970 Gorbachev was appointed first secretary of the Stavropol region, and the following year he was appointed full member of the Central Committee, becoming a member of the Soviet elite at the young age of 40. With the continued mentorship of Kulakov and two other influential party leaders with Stavropol connections, Yuri ANDROPOV and Mikhail SUSLOV, Gorbachev continued his rise through the party apparatus, taking over Kulakov's post in the Central Committee after his death in 1978; two years later he gained full membership in the Politburo. Despite several poor harvests, his reputation for energy and competence contrasted sharply and positively with other members of the aging BREZHNEV leadership, and in the final years of Brezhnev's rule, he was seen as the rising young star of Soviet politics. With an ill Andropov in power after Brezhnev's death in 1982, Gorbachev was given increasingly important responsibilities, leading observers to believe he was next in line to succeed Andropov. The election of Konstantin CHERNENKO as party general secretary in February 1984 was a temporary setback. But in March 1985, after Chernenko's death, Gorbachev was chosen general secretary.

His years in power were promising and tempetuous to the fore. In domestic affairs he presided over an overhaul of the Soviet leadership, bringing reformist allies such as Alexander YAKOVLEV, Nikolai Ryzhkov, and Eduard SHEVARDNADZE. Gorbachev began his term by signaling his commitment to a more open political culture in recalling the dissident physicist Andrei SAKHAROV from internal exile, and in more traditional Soviet fashion, by seeking to improve labor discipline through a widely unpopular campaign to reduce alcohol consumption. The more ambitious agenda of perestroika (economic restructuring) and glasnost (political openness) for which he is widely known met with mixed and unexpected results. Economic reforms consisting of moderate attempts to move toward a limited market economy met with resistance in the Communist Party and government establishment, leading to inflation, shortages, and declining production by 1990. Political change, on the other hand, quickly surpassed what Gorbachev had originally envisioned. In rapid succession, an astonished Soviet public saw the Communist Party lose its leading role in the economy, a deep reevaluation of hitherto taboo topics in Soviet history such as the dark aspects of Stalin's rule, relatively open elections for a new Congress of People's Deputies, the reemergence of a thriving, creative artistic and intellectual climate, and democratic elections in the 15 Soviet constituent republics, which brought democratic and nationalist movements into positions of power.

In foreign policy, Gorbachev overcame initial American suspicions and became a full partner in the peaceful dismantling of the cold war apparatus by reversing the Soviet occupation of AFGHANISTAN, refraining from interference in the Eastern European revolutions of 1989, withdrawing Soviet troops from Eastern Europe, agreeing to the reunification of Germany, and sharply reducing nuclear arsenals. For these achievements he received the 1990 Nobel Peace Prize.

With his economic reforms stalled, the emergence of nationalism within the 15 Soviet republics doomed his program to failure. From the NAGORNO-KARABAKH crisis of 1988 to nationalist struggles in Georgia and Lithuania in the spring of 1991, and the election of Boris YELTSIN as president of the Russian Republic, the future of the Soviet Union as a reformed federal entity was increasingly in question. The conservative putsch of August 19, 1991, designed to preempt the signing of a new union treaty, failed to dislodge Gorbachev from power but accelerated the decline of the Communist Party and the dissolution of the Soviet Union. Under house arrest in the Crimea during the AUGUST COUP, Gorbachev returned to power after a few days to a different country. With all but Russia and Kazakhstan declaring their independence by October 1991, Gorbachev was unable to stop the final dissolution of the Soviet Union, which took place on December 25, 1991.

Out of power, Gorbachev established the Gorbachev Foundation, a think tank, lectured outside of Russia, and wrote several volumes of memoirs. He ran for president as a social democrat in the 1996 election but received less than 1 percent of the votes cast in the first round. In September 1999, his wife died of cancer. A decade removed from power, Gorbachev remained more admired outside of Russia than inside.

Gorchakov, Aleksandr Mikhailovich (1798–1883)
statesman and diplomat

As foreign minister during the entire reign of ALEXANDER II, Gorchakov played a central role in restoring Russia's power and prestige after the humbling defeat suffered in the CRIMEAN WAR (1853–56). Born to a prominent Russian family he was a one-time classmate of Aleksandr PUSHKIN. At the precocious age of 22 Gorchakov was already participating in top-level Russian diplomatic delegations. A series of appointments to Russian embassies in western Europe, culminating with the post of ambassador to the Austrian court at the time of the Crimean War, seasoned him as a diplomat and brought him to the attention of the new czar Alexander II. Gorchakov was named foreign minister in 1856 in time to conduct the negotiations that led to the Treaty of

Paris that ended the Crimean War in that same year. Defeated in war and forbidden to place warships in the Black Sea, Russia, under Gorchakov's guidance, looked eastward and waited for the right moment to undo the most onerous clauses of the Treaty of Paris. That moment came in 1870 when Russia took advantage of European preoccupation with the Franco-Prussian War to unilaterally abrogate the provisions that banned Russian warships from the Black Sea. As foreign minister, Gorchakov also presided over Russian expansion into Central Asia, although the foreign ministry was often put on the spot by ambitious generals such as Mikhail CHERNIAEV who would present it with de facto conquests. Nevertheless, Gorchakov successfully defended Russian expansion to the outside world. In 1864, in the early stages of the Russian imperial thrust into Central Asia, Gorchakov issued a much-quoted circular that defended Russia's actions in terms of a civilizing mission analogous to that articulated by other European empires and the United States to justify their own territorial expansion. In the last decade of his life, Gorchakov's diplomatic touch began to lose its luster. In 1873 he agreed to join Germany and Austria-Hungary in the League of Three Emperors, an alliance that was undermined by personal rivalry with the German chancellor Otto von Bismarck. In 1877, the foreign ministry was unable to resist Russian pan-Slav public pressure to enter a war with Turkey. Following Russia's victory in the RUSSO-TURKISH WAR OF 1877–78, Gorchakov was unable to restrain his ambitious aide Nikolai Ignatiev from overplaying the Russian hand at the Treaty of SAN STEFANO (1878). The backlash in European capitals over that treaty's terms led to the Congress of Berlin of that year that took away many of Russia's diplomatic and territorial gains, and was seen by Gorchakov as his greatest diplomatic defeat. In declining health and taking the blame for the decisions of the Congress of Berlin, the octogenarian Gorchakov was minister only in name for the last four years of his life while his future successor, Nikolai GIERS, ran the Foreign Ministry.

Gorky, Maksim (1868–1936)
writer

Gorky, born Aleksei Maksimovich Peshkov, is often accorded the not entirely flattering title "father of Soviet literature." Although he came to advocate the ideas of socialist realism and made many compromises with the STALIN regime in his last years, his whole body of work is more rich and complex than the epithet might suggest. Born to a family of artisans, and orphaned from an early age, he was raised by his relatives in a strongly patriarchal household, and was given little formal education. As a young man, he tramped around Russia, taking many odd jobs, experiences that he later drew on for his richly realistic stories and that he would later recall compellingly in his three volumes of autobiography, *My Childhood* (1913), *My Apprenticeship* (1918), and *My Universities* (1923). A writer since 1892, he achieved his first major success in 1898 with short stories that chronicled his vagabond life, then with his play *The Lower Depths* (1902). He joined the Bolshevik Party in 1905, and his later writings were strong critiques of capitalist society from a Marxist viewpoint (*Mother*, 1907; *The Artamonov Business*, 1925; *Klim Sangin*, 1927–36). For many years, the royalties from his works were one of the main sources of income for the BOLSHEVIKS. During a lecture tour of the United States (1906), he scandalized American audiences by openly traveling and living with a woman who at the time was not his wife, the actress Maria Andreeva. From 1906 to 1913 he joined the émigré colony on Capri, where he displayed his independent, anti-Leninist streak by founding with Aleksandr Bogdanov the left-wing Vpered (Forward) faction and by joining Anatolii Lunacharsky in developing the quasi-religious ideology of "God-building," an attempt to supplement Marxism with a new religion for the working classes. After the 1917 February Revolution, he expressed his non-Bolshevik social democratic views in his newspaper, *Novaia zhizn (New Life)*, which opposed the Bolshevik seizure of power and published the reservations of ZINOVIEV and KAMENEV. After the revolution,

Maksim Gorky *(Library of Congress)*

he was critical of Bolshevik excesses but was instrumental in saving many intellectuals from terror and starvation. He lived in Italy during most of the 1920s, at first a critic of the Soviet regime, but later its defender. After returning to the Soviet Union, Gorky became head of the Writers' Union and helped advance the literary agenda of the COMMUNIST PARTY, through the doctrine of socialist realism. For someone who had been quite critical of LENIN, Gorky had few negative things to say about the Stalin regime, praising instead some of its more troubling features such as forced collectivization and the White Sea Canal, built with prisoner labor. A long-time sufferer of tuberculosis, he probably died of natural causes, but for a long time there were questions about the circumstances of his death. At the 1938 BUKHARIN show trial, government prosecutors alleged that the "anti-Soviet Bloc of Rightists and Trotskyites" was responsi-

ble, while others believed that Stalin may have been involved in his death. Between 1932 and 1990, his hometown of Nizhnii-Novgorod was known as Gorky in his honor.

Grand Embassy (1697–1698)

The name given to the unprecedented extended visit that Peter the Great made to western Europe in 1697–98. The first reigning Russian sovereign to travel abroad on a peaceful mission since the 11th century, Peter impressed his hosts with his curiosity, his appetites, and his informality. Having recently defeated the Ottoman Empire and captured the Black Sea port of Azov in July 1696 and become sole ruler after the death of his co-czar, IVAN V, Peter felt confident enough to embark on his long-desired tour of the West. Traveling under the alias Peter Mikhailov, he and his party visited Riga, Königsberg, and Berlin before arriving in Amsterdam in August 1697. In Amsterdam he worked in the shipyards of the Dutch East India Company and visited workshops and factories where he learned about clock making, dentistry, and anatomical dissection. The embassy left for London in January 1698 and stayed until May on the invitation of King William III. Here Peter added knowledge of the scriptures, love of drink, and general rowdiness to the reputation he had developed. Returning to Russia via Austria, he heard news of the *streltsy* (musketeers) revolt in Moscow in early 1698, which forced him to shorten his visit and return home. Although the embassy had specific goals, such as gaining the support of Western monarchs for further war against Turkey, it is best remembered for the broader symbolism of Russia's opening to the West and for its success in attracting Western technical specialists. Peter's vigorous program of Westernization clearly owed much to his experiences in the West. Equally important, he recruited a large number of military and technical experts who were to have a great impact on Russian life as teachers, officers, and administrators. In 1717, Peter undertook a second journey to western

Europe that took him to Copenhagen, Amsterdam, Paris, and Berlin. He again surprised his cultured European hosts by the informality of his manner, as when he met the seven-year-old French king Louis XV and picked him up and embraced him. The tour was far less successful than the first one, resulting only in the Treaty of Amsterdam, a minor personal agreement of friendship between the Russian czar and the French and Prussian kings that involved no military obligations. Having failed in his attempt to persuade the French from supporting Sweden, he returned to St. Petersburg in October 1717.

Great Reforms

A series of individual reforms issued by the government of ALEXANDER II, the Great Reforms sought to modernize Russia after the debacle of the CRIMEAN WAR. The centerpiece of the Great Reforms was the EMANCIPATION ACT of 1861, which abolished SERFDOM in Russia. The terms of Emancipation were somewhat complicated, as the government sought to balance a number of interests: concern for the status of the gentry, fear of the social upheaval that might accompany emancipation, and reluctance to give former serfs large quantities of land outright. Thus peasants only received half of the land that they had cultivated for their former masters. The land was to be bought through "redemption payments" that were spread over a period of 49 years. Peasants did not receive the land as individuals but rather as members of a peasant commune that was collectively responsible for fulfilling a village's obligations to the state. Other reforms followed. The abolition of serfdom made it necessary to address the issue of rural self-government, a role that had essentially been exercised by the landowners themselves. In January 1864 the government introduced a new institution, known as the ZEMSTVO, at the district and provincial levels. Representation in the *zemstvo* (pl. *zemstva*) was to be decided on the basis of indirect election that apportioned delegates according to landownership. The *zemstva* were to appoint boards that would organize the delivery of practical services such as schools, roads, medical care, and establish food reserves. The judicial reforms (1864) were in the long run perhaps the most successful of all, introducing modern justice to a system that was archaic, secretive, and extremely vulnerable to corruption. The judicial reforms made the judiciary an independent branch of government, reduced to two the number of legal procedures for conducting cases, and introduced trial by jury for criminal offenses and justices of the peace for minor cases. The municipal reform of 1870 reorganized urban government and introduced the *zemstvo* model to many towns. The military reforms of 1874 are generally considered the last of the Great Reforms. Military service to be determined by lot was extended to all Russians, not just the lower classes, and the onerous terms of pre-reform Russia reduced from 25 to six. Other changes that aimed at improving the quality of the professional corps also followed. The Great Reforms were controversial in their time, especially criticized by an impatient younger generation that felt the reforms did not go far enough. Nevertheless, they introduced important changes to Russian life and set the tone for Russia's development in the next half-century, even as subsequent rulers sought to roll back many of their provisions.

Griboedov, Aleksandr Sergeevich (1795–1829)
writer

A precocious genius who entered Moscow University at the age of 11, Griboedov left a literary legacy that consists mainly of one extraordinary play, *Woe from Wit*, considered to be Russia's first comedy of manners. By the age of 16 Griboedov had completed university studies in literature, law, natural science, and mathematics and studied four languages. His plans to earn a doctorate were interrupted by Napoleon's invasion, and Griboedov served in the army, 1812–16. An early interest in the theater found expression in several translations and adaptations of foreign plays, which Griboedov undertook. In 1818, he was forced to leave St. Petersburg in connection with a duel, and accepted a post in the Russian embassy in Persia. During these years he completed *Woe from Wit* (1816–23), but the censors did not allow its publication until 1833, four years after his death. In 1828 he was appointed ambassador to Persia. A promising literary and diplomatic career was cut short the following year when a crowd invaded the Russian embassy in Tehran and killed all its occupants, including Griboedov.

Grigorenko, Petr (Petro) Grigorievich (1907–1987)
general and activist

Like his fellow dissident Andrei SAKHAROV, Petr Grigorenko provides an example of a member of the Soviet elite who sacrificed his privileges and endured official harassment to advocate human rights causes. Grigorenko was born in the Ukraine into a poor peasant family. He joined the Komsomol in his youth and participated in grain requisitioning expeditions during the 1920s. He later joined the Red Army and served as a division commander during World War II. After the war he lectured for many years at the prestigious Frunze Military Academy in Moscow, and was promoted to major general in 1959. In 1961, a speech highly critical of Stalinism at a local party meeting resulted in his dismissal from the academy, his loss of rank, and expulsion from the party. He was sent to the Far East in 1963 and the following year imprisoned in a psychiatric hospital, the new tool that the KGB (secret police) was developing against dissenters. He became a forceful advocate for the cause of the Crimean Tatars, arguing for their right to return to their historic homeland in the Crimea after their mass deportation to Central Asia by STALIN in 1944, accused of pro-German sympathies. For this he was arrested again in 1967 and imprisoned in a psychiatric hospital. Grigorenko became one of the founders of the Helsinki monitoring group in Moscow. In 1977, he was

allowed to leave the Soviet Union with his wife to visit their son in the United States but was stripped of his citizenship soon afterward. He spent his final years in the United States, a human rights campaigner to the end.

Gromyko, Andrei Andreevich (1909–1989)
diplomat, head of state

For almost three decades as foreign minister of the USSR (1957–85), Gromyko was the forbidding face of Soviet diplomacy, privately dubbed by Westerners Mr. Nyet (Mr. No). He was born to a peasant family in the village of Starye Gromyki, located in present-day Belarus. He joined the COMMUNIST PARTY as a student in 1931. An agricultural economist by training, he began his studies at the Economics Institute in Minsk but graduated from the Minsk School of Agricultural Technology in 1936. He then joined the staff of the journal *Voprosy Ekonomiki* (*Problems of Economics*) with the Institute of Economics in Moscow. Like other talented, ambitious, well-educated young Soviets of his generation, Gromyko suddenly benefited from the Great Purge that decimated the ranks of higher-level party and state officials. In 1939 he was appointed to head the American department of the USSR People's Commissariat of Foreign Affairs (later known as the Ministry of Foreign Affairs). In 1943, with little previous background, he was appointed ambassador to the United States, a post he held until 1946. As such he led the Soviet delegation to the Dumbarton Oaks conference in Washington, D.C., held in 1944, which put in place the foundation for the United Nations. In 1945, he attended the Yalta and Potsdam Conferences. From 1946 to 1948, he headed the Soviet Union's mission to the United Nations in New York, returning to Moscow in 1949 to serve as first deputy foreign minister. The final year of STALIN's life brought a brief demotion when he was appointed ambassador to the United Kingdom in 1952, but after Stalin's death in 1953, he returned to his post of first deputy foreign minister. A candidate member of the Central Committee since 1952, he gained full membership in 1956. After the failure of the ANTI-PARTY GROUP to unseat Nikita KHRUSHCHEV in 1957, Gromyko replaced MOLOTOV as foreign minister.

For the next 28 years, he survived various changes in Soviet leadership, becoming a full member of the Politburo in 1973, from where he consolidated his control of Soviet foreign policy. Gromyko made the Soviet Union an indispensable actor in international affairs, without whom no major crisis could be resolved. He supported the 1968 WARSAW PACT invasion of Czechoslovakia and was one of the small group of insiders who made the fateful decision to invade AFGHANISTAN in 1979. At the same time he was active in the disarmament negotiations that led to the SALT and START treaties and that helped usher in an era of reduced tensions with the United States and Western Europe in the 1970s.

A somewhat reluctant convert to the cause of internal reform, Gromyko was one of the "kingmakers" who supported GORBACHEV's election as party secretary in March 1985. He was also one of the early victims of Gorbachev's reformist course when Eduard SHEVARDNADZE replaced him as foreign minister in June 1985. In deference to his status, however, Gromyko was appointed chairman of the Presidium of the Supreme Soviet, the ceremonial position of head of state in the Soviet system. In September 1988, Gorbachev appointed himself to that post, and in April 1989 Gromyko resigned from the Central Committee, along with other elderly party leaders. His memoirs, published in 1988, provide an important account of the internal world of Soviet diplomacy by someone who besides his grim public persona was a connoisseur of English literature.

Guchkov, Aleksandr Ivanovich
(1862–1936)
industrialist and politician

A scion of an OLD BELIEVER Moscow business family, Guchkov played an important role in the final decades before the Russian Revolution as founder and leader of the moderate conservative Octobrist Party after the 1905 Revolution. His support of STOLYPIN's dissolution of the second DUMA and the introduction of a far more restrictive franchise in June 1907 earned him the antagonism of liberal, democratic politicians in the following decade. As speaker of the Third Duma (1907–12), he also earned the wrath of the imperial family for his harsh attacks on RASPUTIN in 1912 and for circulating correspondence between Rasputin and the empress, which he had somehow obtained. During World War I he took an active part in the Progressive Bloc in the Duma, and as chair of the Duma committee on military and naval affairs pressed for greater parliamentary involvement in the conduct of the war. From 1915, as chair of the War Industries Committee, he assumed an even more vocal role in criticizing the government's war effort for its inefficiency. During the final days of the FEBRUARY REVOLUTION, he took great pride in traveling to Pskov with V. V. Shulgin to arrange for the abdication of the Czar Nicholas II. His parliamentary background made him an obvious choice for minister of war and navy in the first Provisional Government. But events were moving too quickly for a man of moderately conservative views, and when, in May 1917, the Petrograd garrison issued the famous ORDER NO.1 that, among other things, undermined officers' authority over soldiers, he resigned from the government. After the OCTOBER REVOLUTION he fled to Paris, where he occupied a prominent role in the Russian émigré community until his death almost 20 years later.

gulag

Drawn from the Russian acronym for the Chief Administration of Camps, a branch of the secret police created in the 1930s, the term *gulag* has become synonymous with the vast empire of concentration camps, labor camps, and transit prisons that developed in the Soviet Union during Joseph STALIN's long rule. The history of labor camps in the Soviet Union begins almost from the first year of the Bolshevik seizure of power in 1918. Labor camps were known to be in existence as early as mid-1918 and were legalized by decrees in September 1918 and April 1919. The widespread use of labor in prisons, however, was sanctioned only in the late 1920s under Stalin. The labor camps built and administered by the gulag served a dual function: as a place to put the masses of detainees (commonly known by the Russian term *zeks*) and to help curtail an immense shortage of labor that resulted from Stalin's industrialization policies. Gulag prisons were originally centered in Karelia, along the White Sea coast, and in Vorkuta and Pechora, in the Arctic regions of European Russia. By the late 1930s gulag labor camps were set up just about everywhere in the Soviet Union, including Moscow. The gulag's role in industrializing the Soviet Union became increasingly more important and by the end of the 1930s was responsible for much of the country's logging and extraction of copper, gold, and coal. Millions were sent to the gulag camps and about 900,000 died in them. The majority sent to the camps were so-called political prisoners—intellectuals, party and army officials who had been (usually falsely) accused of being "enemies of the people," spies, or saboteurs. The harsh and often deadly conditions in the gulag camps have been attested to by a number of survivors, perhaps the most noteworthy being Aleksandr SOLZHENITSYN, whose book *The Gulag Archipelago* (translated into English in 1974) was one of the first comprehensive accounts of the Soviet camps.

Gumilev, Nikolai Stepanovich
(1886–1921)
poet

One of the major Russian poets of the 20th century, Gumilev was born on April 3, 1886, in Kronstadt, the naval base outside St. Petersburg, the son of a naval doctor. He spent his youth alternating between Tsarskoe Selo and Tbilisi (Tiflis), where he first came under the influence of revolutionary Marxism. He published his first volume of poetry, *Put Konkvistadorov,* in 1905, then traveled to Paris, where he studied French literature at the Sorbonne (1907–8). He married the noted poet Anna AKHMATOVA, in 1910; their son, Lev Nikolaevich, was born in 1911. By 1914, Gumilev was a well-known literary personality in St. Petersburg, and with his wife and Osip MANDELSTAM, a leader of the influential Acmeist school of poetry that developed in opposition to the Symbolists. A lifelong interest in Africa, especially Ethiopia, led to several voyages, most notably in 1913 as part of an expedition organized by the Russian ACADEMY OF SCIENCES. When World War I broke out, Gumilev served in cavalry regiments and was twice awarded the St. George Cross. His *Notes of a Cavalryman* stems from this period. After the FEBRUARY REVOLUTION of 1917, he went on a military mission through Scandinavia and Britain to France, trying to get to the eastern front. He returned in April 1918 through London and Murmansk to Petrograd. His marriage to Akhmatova ended in 1918, and the following year he married Anna Engelhardt. An active lecturer, translator, and editor during the chaotic revolutionary years, he was elected chairman of the Petrograd Union of Poets over the more pro-Bolshevik Aleksandr BLOK. He was arrested in August 1921, charged with participating in an anti-Bolshevik monarchist conspiracy, and shot by the Cheka, together with 61 others. For the next six decades he became a nonperson in Soviet literature, excluded from all major anthologies, despite his obvious importance. The new political environment promoted by GORBACHEV after 1985 and the centenary of Gumilev's birth provided an opening for the reappearance of his work.

Gurdjieff, George Ivanovich
(1874?–1949)
(George Gurzhiev)
occultist

A highly charismatic and controversial figure, worshiped by some as a mystic teacher, derided by others as a charlatan, Gurdjieff played an important role in the reawakening of interest in mysticism and the occult in early-20th-century Russia and Europe. Gurdjieff was born in Alexandropol (Leninakan) in Armenia, to an Armenian mother and a Greek father who was a carpenter and traditional storyteller. In later years, Gurdjieff obscured the details of his life, but it seems that he left home at the age of 16 to pursue secret knowledge among the holy men of India, China, and Tibet. By 1905 he was back in the Caucasus practicing as a hypnotist and teacher of the occult. He moved to Moscow in 1911, where he developed a strong following through his lectures and personal presence, but his plans to establish a teaching institute were interrupted by war and revolution. Gurdjieff was one of the first to make use of the Western interest in Eastern esoteric thought and mysticism, developing an eclectic system that combined elements of Sufism with yoga exercises and dervish dancing. He was not well educated, and his influence grew only after the recruitment of Petr OUSPENSKY, a talented philosopher who tried to give clarity to his rather cryptic thoughts. During the Russian civil war he returned to the Caucasus before emigrating to Turkey, from where he followed Ouspensky to England. With Ouspensky's help in 1922 he founded a teaching center, the Institute for the Harmonious Development of Man, in Fontainebleau, France, where they both taught until their break in 1924. The school featured an intensive daily regime of "intentional suffering" that combined manual labor with question-and-answer sessions with the "Master." A serious car accident limited his teaching and compelled him to write down his thoughts and revelations. He died in the Paris suburb of Neuilly. His writings, published posthumously, include works that draw on Indian and Persian esoteric traditions and an account of his alleged early meetings with wisemen of the East, *Meetings with Remarkable Men,* which was turned into a relatively successful film in 1979.

H

Hague Peace Conferences (1899, 1907)

Two conferences called by NICHOLAS II to discuss universal peace and disarmament, which met in The Hague, capital of the Netherlands. The czar's original appeal for a conference to consider reducing excessive armaments was met with skepticism and ridicule by many, who considered it a propaganda ploy by a government that was hard-pressed to keep up with an arms race with Austria yet pursued aggressive policies in the Far East. Nevertheless, the idea of a peace conference struck a chord with European public opinion. The First Hague Peace Conference met from May to June 1899 and was attended by representatives of 20 European nations and Japan, China, Siam, Persia, Mexico, and the United States. While the conference failed to agree on disarmament or compulsory arbitration of disputes, it did agree to restrictions on the use of balloon warfare, gas, and expanding bullets, as well as the creation of a permanent court of arbitration. The Second Hague Peace Conference met from June to October 1907 and focused on issues of international law. A third convention was planned for 1915 but never met, because of World War I. Although the initial lofty goals were not achieved, the two conferences advanced the acceptance of arbitration in solving international disputes, served as the forerunners of a long series of international conferences on peace and disarmament, and influenced the form of the future League of Nations.

Hannibal, Avram Petrovich
(1697–1781)
engineer and general

The great-grandfather of Russia's greatest poet, Alexander PUSHKIN, Hannibal was an Ethiopian prince who by accident of fate was involuntarily brought to St. Petersburg at an early age. Hannibal was born in Lagona, Ethiopia, the son of a reigning prince. At the age of nine he was kidnapped and brought to Turkey. Accounts differ on the means by which he came to the court of PETER I the Great. Some note that he was bought by Russian agents, others that he was kidnapped by them, and others that he was presented, together with two other African boys, to the czar by the Ottoman sultan. Peter adopted the boy, nicknamed him Hannibal, and baptized him, hence his Russian name Avram Petrovich Gannibal (Hannibal). For the next 10 years Hannibal followed Peter faithfully in his many travels. Skilled in mathematics and engineering, he took part in the construction of the Kronstadt naval base. Peter took an interest in his studies and in 1716 sent him to France for further training. While abroad, he took part in the War of the Spanish Succession (1704–14), in which he was wounded. After six years, he returned to Russia. Hannibal's fortunes changed in 1725 with Peter's death. He fell out of favor and was banished to Siberia, where he worked on the construction of the Selechinsk fortress. In 1730, he was allowed to return to European Russia and his honors were restored. Later in life, he was promoted to general.

Helfand, Aleksandr Lazarevich
(1876–1924)
(Parvus)
revolutionary entrepreneur

Aptly named "the merchant of revolution" by his biographers, Helfand was a talented and flamboyant personality who, in the decade before the Russian Revolution of 1917, made a successful career in the demimonde where revolutionary politics and commerce intersected. He was born into a Jewish family near Minsk, but grew up in ODESSA. While at the University of Basel, he became a Marxist and later worked in Germany as a socialist journalist, writing under the pseudonym of Parvus. In Switzerland, he also first established the connections with Russian revolutionaries that would continue through the rest of his career. During the RUSSO-JAPANESE WAR (1904–5), he presciently argued that Russia's defeat in the war could lead to a revolution that could spread to other countries. A brief but important intellectual friendship with Leon TROTSKY developed during the 1905 Revolution when Helfand worked with Trotsky in the St. Petersburg Soviet. Helfand's influence on Trotsky is most visible in the idea of "permanent revolution," which Helfand argued could start with a mass strike such as the one that gripped Russia in October 1905. Arrested in April 1906, he was exiled to Siberia but soon fled and returned to Germany. A partnership with GORKY to collect the latter's European royalties as his literary agent ended bitterly, with Gorky accusing Helfand of embezzlement, allegations that permanently tarnished his reputation within the revolutionary movement. Helfand next surfaced in 1910 in Istanbul, where he made a fortune channeling resources from the German government to the Young Turk movement. In 1915 he moved to neutral Copenhagen, a center of wartime intrigue, where he developed a number of business projects linking Germany and Russia that most likely served as cover for his political interests. After the FEBRUARY REVOLUTION of 1917, he was involved in the negotiations with the German government that resulted in LENIN's return journey to Russia on the "sealed train." In the summer of 1917 the KERENSKY government forcefully tried to link Lenin to German funds, accusations that the BOLSHEVIKS were never able to shake off. Ironically the Bolshevik victory in October 1917 undermined Helfand's role as revolutionary

middleman. After the war, he returned to his Berlin villa where he lived until his death.

Hermitage

The popular name for the State Hermitage Museum, an art museum located in St. Petersburg that is the largest public museum in Russia and the home to what is considered to be one of the world's greatest collections of art. CATHERINE II the Great first founded the Hermitage Museum in 1764 to serve as the home of the royal court's art collection, built from western European works she purchased from private collectors. Her successors, notably ALEXANDER I and NICHOLAS I, substantially added to the collection. The collection was first housed in the Hermitage building, also known as the Small Hermitage, an annex to the Winter Palace built by the French architect Lamothe. As the collection grew, the museum expanded into the Old Hermitage, another private gallery near the Winter Palace, built in 1775–84. After a fire in the Winter Palace in 1837, the Hermitage buildings were rebuilt, and a New Hermitage (1839–50) was added to house the ever-growing royal collection. Nicholas I first opened the collection to the public in 1852. Following the OCTOBER REVOLUTION of 1917, the collection was nationalized and the museum became known as the State Hermitage Museum. With the Winter Palace no longer serving as the imperial residence, in Soviet times it became another of the magnificent buildings—totaling five—that housed the vast art collection. The buildings themselves, among the best examples of imperial architecture, are part of the attraction that the Hermitage exerts on its visitors.

The original collection was built from the renowned collections of private collectors such as Baron de Thiers, Count Heinrich Bruhl, and Sir Robert Walpole. In addition to paintings by the great masters, it included cameos and statues. With later purchases, the Hermitage's collection of western European art became one of the best in the world, especially strong in Italian, Spanish, Dutch, and Flemish paintings, with

The Hermitage Royal Museum, ca. 1900 *(Library of Congress)*

major works from Raphael, Rembrandt, Van Dyck, Velázquez, El Greco, Murillo, Caravaggio, and Rubens. The addition of the Schukin and Morozov collections brought major impressionist and postimpressionist paintings by artists such as Matisse, Van Gogh, Gauguin, Cézanne, and Picasso to the museum. Karl FABERGÉ's golden eggs are also part of the museum's collections. The museum also holds a special collection of jewelry, ancient gold artifacts, as well as Russian art. Dependent on Soviet-era cultural subsidies that paid for growing additions to the collections, many of which lay in package crates in the museum's basements for lack of room to display, the museum faced difficult financial choices in the post-Soviet period. Recent agreements, especially with the Guggenheim Museum of New York, to display parts of its collections in the various museum annexes that have sprouted in the last decade are helping the museum to regain its financial footing.

Herzen, Aleksandr Ivanovich (1812–1870)
revolutionary theorist

Long considered the "father of Russian socialism," Aleksandr Herzen was the illegitimate son of a wealthy nobleman who left him a large fortune that supported his writing and journalistic activities. Born in Moscow, Herzen was strongly influenced by the example of the DECEMBRISTS, swearing with his young friend the poet Nikolai Ogarev, to rid Russia of tyranny. He attended

Moscow University, where he joined radical student circles that confirmed his earlier political feelings. In 1835 and again in 1841, Herzen was sentenced to internal exile, first in Viatka and later in Novgorod, for his clandestine political discussions and writings. In 1847, inspired by European developments, he traveled to France for a visit, but never returned to Russia. Disenchanted by the outcome of the 1848 revolutions in western and central Europe and by European politics in general, he settled in London in 1852, where he lived for the next 11 years. His time in London was extremely productive and established him as the leading oppositionist voice in exile. He wrote his multivolume precocious memoirs, *My Past and Thoughts* (1842–45), one of the classics of 19th-century Russian memoir literature, and started the Russian Free Press. In 1857 he became the publisher of the influential émigré newspaper *Kolokol* (*The Bell*), which although initially censored was widely read by Russian official and intellectual circles, especially after the death of NICHOLAS I in 1855 gave way to a less oppressive Russian government under ALEXANDER II. Herzen's voice was especially influential during the period preceding the emancipation of

the serfs in 1861, when he helped shape the terms of the debate, particularly through his advocacy of the Russian peasant commune. During these years he began to develop his views on Russian socialism, a romantic-agrarian type of socialism based on the belief that the egalitarian communal instincts of the Russian peasant would pave the way to a future free society in conjunction with the leadership of progressive intellectuals. These ideas formed the core of the Populist movement that held sway over Russia's intelligentsia and students from the 1860s through the 1880s. By the early 1860s, however, Herzen's ideas and willingness to engage the czar in pragmatic reforms was coming under criticism from more impatient young radicals who viewed the older generation of intellectuals as talkers instead of doers. Herzen's influence also suffered from his support of the POLISH REBELLION OF 1863–64, which triggered a nationalist backlash throughout Russian society. In 1864, Herzen moved to Geneva with the goal of establishing links with a younger generation of Russian radical students in Swiss universities. Unsuccessful in this goal, he stopped publishing *Kolokol* in 1867 and died in Paris three years later.

I

Ilf and Petrov
writers

The most popular satirists of the early Soviet period, Ilf and Petrov met in Moscow in 1925 and for the next decade collaborated as partners on humorous sketches and stories. Ilf (1897–1937) was born Ilya Arnoldovich Faizelberg in ODESSA, the son of a bank clerk. After graduation from the Odessa Technical School, he took a number of jobs, including telephone operator, statistician, and accountant, while writing poetry and editing a humorous magazine. He moved to Moscow in 1923, where he worked as a reporter and contributed to several humor magazines. Petrov (1903–42), born Evgenii Petrovich Kataev, also hailed from Odessa and was the son of a schoolmaster. His older brother Valentin Kataev was the author of the socialist realist classic *Time Forward!* (1932). Petrov also moved to Moscow in 1923, where his experience as a reporter and a police criminal investigator initially inspired him to write detective stories. Their two novels about the wheeling and dealing of successful operators during the NEP years, published as *Dvenatsat stulev* (*The Twelve Chairs*) (1927) and *Zolotoi telenok* (*The Golden Calf*) (1931), became instant classics and have remained so ever since. A sojourn in the United States in the 1930s as correspondents for the newspaper *Pravda* resulted in the book *Odnoetazhnaia Amerika* (*Little Golden America*), a pointed but humorous description of a country both had admired. Ilf and Petrov also wrote many humorous gems such as "How Robinson Was Created" (1932), a spoof on editorial interference and censorship that still rang true half a century

later. Ilf died in Moscow of tuberculosis. After Ilf's death, Petrov continued to write for *Pravda* and for humor magazines. During World War II, he worked as a war correspondent, but he was killed when the Germans shot down the plane in which he was flying back to Moscow from Crimea.

Ilya Muromets
legendary character

A mythical warrior or BOGATYR in the traditional folk epics (*byliny*) composed between the 10th and 12th centuries, Ilya Muromets, or Ilya of Murom, was said to be part of the court of VLADIMIR I, the ruler who brought Christianity to KIEVAN RUS. Unlike most other legendary figures from Vladimir's entourage, Ilya Muromets was said to be of peasant origin. He was an invalid for the first 30 years of his life until a miraculous cure set him on the path to heroic deeds. Given a magic horse, Ilya traveled to Vladimir's court, where he became known for his strength, generosity, and devotion. Some scholars have noted that the legend about his long period of immobility links him to the Eastern Christian tradition of "pillar-like immobility," while the name Ilya represents the Slavic form of the name Elijah, the Old Testament prophet who ascended to heaven in a chariot of fire. Whereas other *bogatyri* seem to represent the nobility or clergy of early Kiev, Ilya is the symbol of the peasant masses, perhaps the reason for the enduring popularity of his legend. His zeal is tempered by an independent streak, while his uncommon strength is only used reluctantly as a last resort.

Iskander, Fazil Abdulovich (1929–   )
writer

An Abkhazian who writes in Russian, Iskander was born in the Black Sea port of Sukhumi. He graduated from the prestigious Gorky Literary Institute in Moscow in 1954. He first came to wider prominence in 1966 with the publication of *The Goatibex Constellation.* The novel, a satire on the crackpot Michurinist and Lysenkoist theories of genetics that had gained currency under KHRUSHCHEV, features bureaucrats who try to crossbreed an ordinary goat with an ibex, hoping to solve the Soviet Union's perennial food shortages. Iskander's distinctive blend of simple plots and a witty conversational style that cloaks strongly satirical stories came into sharper focus in subsequent works. In *The Thirteenth Labor of Hercules* (1978), he comments on the virtues of humor and the dangers of humorlessness through a parable about the last Roman emperors. Recognized as a subtle critic of the late-BREZHNEV Soviet system, with his next two books he crossed the line between acceptable and unacceptable criticism. *Sandro of Chegem* (1983) and *The Gospel According to Chegem* (1984) are now considered Iskander's major works, but although quickly translated into English, they were not published in full in the Soviet Union until the GORBACHEV era. Featuring Uncle Sandro as the main character, Iskander recreates the history of his Abkhazian village from the 1880s to the 1960s. Through the words of Sandro, an independent and irreverent narrator, Iskander comments gently but incisively on modernization, the Soviet experience, and, of course, STALIN.

Ivan I (1301–1340)
(Ivan Danilovich)
ruler

Known as Ivan Kalita (Moneybags) for his ability to increase his influence with the Mongol court through lavish payment of tribute, Ivan I was instrumental in making Moscow the preeminent Russian principality. Ivan succeeded his brother Yuri Danilovich as Prince of Moscow in 1325. Three years later after assisting in the GOLDEN HORDE's destruction of the Principality of Tver, he obtained the title of grand prince in recognition of his role as the foremost of all the Russian princes. Crafty and economical, Ivan consolidated his position by accumulating Russian territories and by pleasing the khan of the Golden Horde through the collection of tribute. The death of the head of the Russian Church, Metropolitan Petr, while on a visit to Moscow provided Ivan with an opportunity to increase Moscow's influence, when Petr was later canonized and his shrine became a place of worship. Ivan convinced his successor, Metropolitan Theognost, to transfer the seat of the Russian Orthodox Church from Vladimir to Moscow, thus adding spiritual leadership to the substantial financial and political power that the principality now enjoyed. Ivan was succeeded by his son, Simeon the Proud, who continued the work of enlarging Moscow's domains and influence.

Ivan II (1326–1359)
grand prince

Grand prince of Moscow from 1353–59, Ivan was the third son of IVAN I, also known as Ivan Kalita, who had greatly increased the status of the principality of Moscow in relation to other Russian states. Ivan succeeded his older brother Simeon the Proud, who had enlarged the territory of Moscow, but died from the plague at the early age of 36. Compared to his brother, Ivan was seen as a weak ruler and was known as Ivan the Meek. During his reign, Ivan relied significantly on the metropolitan of Moscow, ALEKSEI, a remarkable ecclesiastical and political leader who was later canonized by the Russian Orthodox Church. Ivan's reign witnessed an important long-term change in the region's balance of power involving the GOLDEN HORDE, Moscow, and Lithuania. Beginning in 1357 the Golden Horde, which had ruled over the Russian principalities for more than a century, began to fragment and was engulfed by civil war for the next two decades. To the west, however, the Lithuanian state under Olgerd was beginning to emerge as a major power. Ivan II was succeeded by his nine-year old son Dmitrii, who would later gain fame as DMITRI DONSKOI after leading the Muscovite armies in the pivotal Battle of KULIKOVO, the first Russian victory over the Mongols since the Mongol conquest.

Ivan III (1440–1505)
(Ivan Vasilevich)
ruler

Known as Ivan the Great for his leadership in refusing to pay further tribute to the Mongol khans of the GOLDEN HORDE, Ivan was the first Russian ruler to adopt the title "czar." The son of Vasilii II, Ivan assumed the title of grand prince upon Vasilii's death in 1462. Between 1470 and 1480, he greatly enlarged the Muscovite territory by annexing the Novogorod Republic, the principality of Tver, and several other principalities. In 1480 he formally broke with centuries of subjugation to Mongol rule when he ceased paying tribute to the khan. Although minor conflicts with the Mongol continued for at least another century, the date is generally used to mark the end of the Mongol era of Russian history. In 1493 he took the title of "sovereign of all Russia," claiming for Moscow the inheritance to the legacy of KIEVAN RUS and contesting the claims of Poland and Lithuania to the same territory. In 1497 his government introduced Muscovy's first legal code (Sudebnik), an important step in the centralization of judicial power of the state. Following the death of his first wife, Maria, in 1467, he married Zoe (Sofia) Paleologos, a niece of the last Byzantine emperor, in 1472. The dynastic link to the former Byzantine Empire allowed Ivan to transfer to himself much of the imperial prestige, including the emperor's emblem of the two-headed eagle, and to make the claim that Moscow was its direct successor, the Third Rome.

Ivan IV (1530–1584)
(Ivan Vasilievich)
czar

Better known in history as Ivan the Terrible, Ivan was the first Russian ruler to be known as "czar," Russian for the word *Caesar*. Ivan was three years old at the time of his father's death, and his youth was dominated by the threats and conspiracies of prominent boyar families jockeying for power. He was crowned czar at the age of 17. The early years of his reign, influenced by the good advice of the church and loyal boyars and of his first wife, Anastasia Romanova, were constructive and progressive. He called the first ZEMSKII SOBOR in 1549, and this body approved reforms in the law and in local administration. In 1551 a church council took place that regulated and improved the church's position in the state. In 1550 and 1556, reforms were made in the army and in the military service owed by the gentry. With improved forces, Ivan conquered the most important of Moscow's traditional enemies KAZAN, ASTRAKHAN, and the Livonian Order. He had by 1560 established the authority of the czar, greatly strengthened the state, and undertaken commercial relations with England.

The second half of his reign was characterized by his extreme behavior—uncontrollable rages, suspicion of the whole boyar class, and a harsh personal despotism. These were exacerbated by the death of his wife, Anastasia, in 1560 and his belief that she had been murdered. His withdrawal from the boyars and the church, and his insistence on personal control, found its most extreme form in the creation of the *oprichnina*—parts of the state that were separately governed by officials (*oprichniki*) who acted as his personal police and whose function was to kill those whom he considered his enemies. The internal disintegration of the state coincided with pressure from its enemies in the Crimea and in the northwest, where the LIVONIAN War was revived, with Poland and Sweden joining forces against Muscovy. In 1581 the czar killed his son Ivan in a fit of rage; the event appeared to have finally destroyed his mental balance. He died in 1584 and was succeeded by his son FEODOR I.

Ivan V (1666–1696)
(Ivan Alekseevich)
ruler

The son of Czar ALEKSEI MIKHAILOVICH and half brother of PETER I the Great, Ivan was co-czar of Russia from 1682 until 1696, but only in name, since his poor health precluded him from assuming the responsibilities of government. When his elder brother FEODOR III, who had ruled from 1676 to 1682 died without an heir, the complications of Aleksei's two marriages come to the fore. Factions surrounding the Miloslavsky family of Aleksei's first wife and the Naryshkin family of his second wife disputed the throne until a compromise was found. Ivan, as representative of the former, and Peter, as representative of the latter, were named corulers, but because of Ivan's ill health and Peter's young age, Aleksei's firstborn, SOPHIA, was installed as regent. This arrangement lasted until August 1689, when Sophia's bid to attain full power was defeated. Peter, until then formally the junior of the two corulers, was acknowledged as main ruler, even though he did not actually assume control of the government until 1696, allowing instead a series of advisers to rule in his name. Ivan remained a coruler until his death. Despite his illness and purely ceremonial role while coruler, Ivan affected the Russian monarchy long after his death. His daughter ANNA reigned as empress from 1730–40 and his grandson, the unfortunate infant IVAN VI, was briefly acknowledged as ruler from 1740 to 1741 but then overthrown by Peter's own daughter ELIZABETH.

Ivan VI (1740–1764)
(Ivan Antonovich)
emperor

An ill-fated infant who inherited the Russian throne in October 1740 at just under two months old, Ivan was overthrown almost a year later and spent the rest of his short life in solitary confinement until assassinated in Schlusselburg fortress. Ivan, a great grandson of Czar IVAN V (Peter the Great's half brother), became czar after the death of his great aunt, Empress ANNA. Anna's designated regent, Ernst Johann BIRON, was overthrown within a month and succeeded by Ivan's mother, Anna Leopoldovna. Anna Leopoldovna's increasingly unpopular regency was marked by struggles among German favorites such as Burkhard Munnich and Andrei OSTERMANN, and the interference of foreign ambassadors in court politics. As discontent with Anna Leopoldovna's regency grew in St. Petersburg, the Imperial Guards turned their support to ELIZABETH, Peter the Great's daughter from his second marriage. In November 1741, acting to forestall plans to transfer guards units out of the capital, Elizabeth seized power, arresting the "baby emperor," the regent, and her ministers. Elizabeth reneged on a promise to allow Anna Leopoldovna's family to return to Germany, banishing them instead to Kholmogori in the far north in 1744. Ivan was separated from his family and in 1756 was transferred to Schlusselburg fortress. On July 5, 1764, when a disgruntled army officer tried to release Ivan, his jailers stabbed him to death under long-standing orders from Elizabeth, confirmed by CATHERINE II, that he be killed if any attempt was made to rescue him. In 1780, long after his parents had died, Catherine allowed Ivan's surviving siblings to settle in Denmark, where they lived as her pensioners.

J

January Insurrection See POLISH REBELLION OF 1863–64.

John of Kronstadt, Father (1829–1908)
priest

Born Ivan Ilich Sergeev, John of Kronstadt became a major religious figure in late imperial Russia and the object of a popular cult. After his ordination, he went to Kronstadt, an island near St. Petersburg, where his sermons attracted large congregations from all classes of society. Father John began as an activist priest, ministering to the poor, building shelters, developing employment programs, and becoming a forceful advocate of the temperance movement. An opponent of radical reform, he opposed the Christian anarchist teachings of Lev TOLSTOY. Father John emphasized frequent communion at a time when the laity seldom received communion more than four or five times a year. He also developed a form of public confession, in part a practical response to the sheer number of people who came to see him for confession, where the faithful shouted their sins simultaneously. Kronstadt became a place of pilgrimage, a place where the faithful alternated with hawkers selling souvenirs, photographs, and trinkets. A profound believer in the power of prayer, he brought to his services an intense feeling of emotional immediacy, which also shines through in his spiritual autobiography, *My Life in Christ*. By 1894, his reputation was such that he was asked to minister to the dying ALEXANDER III, and in the process he attracted an international audience. In 1964 he was canonized by the Russian Church in exile and in 1990 by the Russian Orthodox Church in Moscow.

Joseph of Volotsk (1439-1515)
(Iosif Volokolamsky, Ivan Sanin)
abbot and theologian

Founder of the Volokolamsk Monastery, Joseph was a prominent religious figure of his time whose activities influenced monastic life in Russia as well and the overall development of church-state relations. Joseph (also known as Joseph of Volokolamsk) was born Ivan Sanin in the Russian town of Volokolamsk, about 60 miles northwest of Moscow, in 1439, although some sources cite 1440 as his year of birth. At the age of seven, he began to study with an elder of a nearby monastery, and at the age of 20 he left home and joined the Borovsky Monastery. By the time he was appointed abbot of the monastery in 1477, Joseph had come to believe in an ascetic monasticism centered on strict community life and social work among the local community. This went against the traditions of a luxurious monastery that was personally supported by IVAN III and which was seen as a training ground for the future religious elites.

In 1479, Joseph left Borovsky Monastery with a few devoted followers and returned to his home region of Volokolamsk, where he founded his own monastery in accordance with his ascetic beliefs. In the half-century after its founding, the Volokolamsk Monastery became known for its rigor, discipline, and practical work in the community. It received financial support from those who had benefited from the monks' labor, while its students later came to staff numerous positions in the Russian clergy and state.

Joseph was involved in two important religious controversies of his time. In the 1490s he took a leading role in the church's attack on a religious current that arose in NOVGOROD that questioned basic Christian dogmas such as the Trinity and the divinity of Christ as well as the existing structure of the Orthodox Church. Known by the inflammatory and misleading name of "Judaizers," these religious dissidents were eventually condemned in 1504 as heretics. Some of their leaders were executed and others were imprisoned. Joseph is also known for his role in the controversy between "possessors" and "non-possessors" that embroiled the church in the early 16th century. The "non-possessors," led by NIL SORSKY, argued that the church should not only divest itself of its landholdings and other forms of wealth but should also be independent of the state. Joseph of Volotsk and his followers (also known as Josephites) defended the more traditional position that the church should be rich and powerful and closely allied to the secular ruler. The Church Council of 1503 decided in favor of Joseph's position. At the time of his death, the legacy of Joseph and the Volokolamsk Monastery as defenders of religious orthodoxy was solidly established. Joseph was canonized in 1578.

July Days

A failed uprising against the Provisional Government in Petrograd (St. Petersburg), the July Days of 1917 marked an important turning point in the convoluted politics of Russia's revolutionary year. Although the BOLSHEVIKS did not organize the uprising, as the Provisional Government later charged, they did support it once it had started and suffered the brunt of the reprisals that followed.

The uprising began on July 16, 1917, when a regiment of machine gun troops took to the streets of Petrograd to protest against the unsuc-cessful military offensive that the Provisional Government had launched on July 1 in Galicia, but which had faltered after almost two weeks. Echoing the slogans used by the Bolsheviks since LENIN's return to Russia in April 1917, the demonstrators called for the Petrograd Soviet of Workers' and Soldiers' Deputies to seize power from the Provisional Government. The Petrograd Soviet, controlled by the moderate socialist Menshevik and Socialist Revolutionary Parties, refused to heed the demonstrators. The following day, Petrograd civilians and sailors from the Kronstadt naval base, a Bolshevik stronghold, joined the ranks of demonstrators, swelling their number to over 400,000. Random shooting throughout the city resulted in the deaths of close to 50 people. Pressured by the situation and their own rank-and-file, Lenin and the Bolshevik leadership agreed to assume the direction of the protests, with some reluctance since they considered the attempt to seize power to be premature. By the morning of July 18, the demonstrations lost their force as news spread of the arrival of troops to defend the government and the Provisional Government's attempt to portray Lenin as a German agent took root. Two days later, Alexander KERENSKY became prime minister and the cabinet of the Provisional Government gained more moderate socialists.

The immediate consequence of the July Days was a temporary weakening of the Bolshevik Party in the form of government reprisals that led to the arrest of prominent leaders, including Leon TROTSKY, and Lenin's quick escape to Finland, shorn of his trademark goatee to avoid detection. In the short-term, the Provisional Government gained support among liberal and conservative sectors worried about the rapid deterioration of the situation and the growing power of workers and soldiers. But by late August, with the failure of the KORNILOV putsch, the Provisional Government had squandered what little political capital it had left and Bolshevik popularity was again on the rise, opening the way for their successful insurrection on November 7, 1917.

K

Kaganovich, Lazar Moiseevich
(1893–1991)
Soviet official

An important member of Joseph STALIN's inner circle, Kaganovich developed a reputation for ruthlessness among an already ruthless group. He was born in Kiev to Jewish parents. A leather worker at the age of 14, Kaganovich joined the BOLSHEVIK Party in 1911 and spent the next years organizing underground workers' groups. During 1917 he worked in the town of Gomel in Belarus, organizing the Bolshevik seizure of power there at the time of the OCTOBER REVOLUTION. A talented organizer, he advanced rapidly in the ranks of the party, joining the All-Russian Executive Committee of the Russian Soviet Federated Socialist Republic (RSFSR) soon after the revolution. During the civil war he worked as a political commissar in the Red Army. An early ally of Stalin, he became a secretary of the Central Committee of the COMMUNIST PARTY in 1924, and the following year he was appointed first secretary of the Ukrainian Communist Party. In 1928, Stalin recalled Kaganovich to Moscow, where he again worked in the Party Secretariat. In 1930 he became a full member of the Politburo, as well as first secretary of the party in Moscow. From this position he directed the transformation of Moscow into a "showcase of socialism." Among his achievements at this time was the construction of the Moscow Metro, a subway system with elegant stations that were supposed to be underground palaces for the masses who used the system. He also oversaw the destruction of numerous older structures, especially churches such as the Cathedral of Christ the Savior. While in Moscow, he was instrumental in advancing Nikita KHRUSHCHEV's career, which he would probably later regret. In 1935 he became people's commissar for Transport, a post he held until 1944. During these years Kaganovich also served as a troubleshooter for Stalin, organizing the collectivization campaigns of 1929–32 and taking an active part in the purges of the 1930s. Trusted by Stalin, Kaganovich held numerous posts in the next decade. While working as transportation commissar, he was appointed to serve as commissar for the oil industry. During World War II, he was a member of the State Defense Committee and traveled to various fronts, especially the Caucasus, as a political commissar. From 1938 to 1953, he was deputy chairman of the Council of People's Commissars, known as the Council of Ministers after 1946.

In 1957 Kaganovich joined MALENKOV, MOLOTOV, and other old-guard Stalinists in the unsuccessful attempt to overthrow his former protégé Khrushchev, an episode that would later be known as the ANTI-PARTY GROUP. He was removed from all his posts and appointed a factory director in the Urals, a milder punishment than what Kaganovich had earlier accorded his rivals. He returned to Moscow in 1961 but lost his party membership in 1962. He applied for reinstatement in 1964, after Khrushchev had been overthrown, but was denied; his hard-line Stalinist past was too much even for a more conservative leadership. He lived as a pensioner in Moscow until his death in 1991 at the age of 98.

Kalashnikov rifle

A Soviet-designed assault rifle, first introduced into the Soviet army in 1949, the Kalashnikov rifle has become one of the most widely used rifles in the contemporary world, a symbol of the guerrilla and nationalist warfare of the late 20th and early 21st centuries. It is a reliable and adaptable rifle distinguished by a separate gas return tube, a box magazine that holds 30 rounds. Also known as the AK-47, the rifle was first designed in 1942 by Mikhail Timofeevich Kalashnikov (b. 1919), a soldier in the Soviet army. Kalashnikov was born to a peasant family in the Altai region of Siberia. After secondary school, he found employment as an apprentice at a railway depot and was working as a clerk for the Turkestan-Siberian (Turksib) railway administration when he was called up to the Red Army in 1938. While completing instruction in the army's tank mechanical school in the Kiev military region, Kalashnikov designed a tank running-time meter that first brought him to the attention of senior military leaders. In October 1941 he was severely wounded while fighting in the region of Briansk. While recovering from shell shock, Kalashnikov began to sketch out the design for a submachine gun, which he later built while on sick leave and sent to the Moscow Aviation Institute. A second version of the rifle was developed in June 1942 and tested by specialists at the Dzerzhinsky Ordnance Academy. Impressed by the abilities of a self-taught designer, the Red Army posted Kalashnikov with the research division of its Main Ordnance Directorate. By 1944 Kalashnikov had designed an experimental model of a self-loading carbine. After competitive testing, the army adopted the rifle in 1949. The rifle has been updated several times since, but its popularity remains undiminished, as evidenced by sales of more than 70 million units by the mid-1990s.

For his efforts, Kalashnikov received a Stalin Prize and was posted to Izhevsk, where he still lives, to work in small arms design for the army. He has been decorated many times by the Soviet government and, after 1991, the Russian government. In addition to the Stalin Prize, he was twice named Hero of Socialist Labor, awarded a LENIN PRIZE in 1964, and decorated with three Orders of Lenin and the Order of the Red Banner of Labor. In 1996, the Russian government awarded him the Order for Distinguished Services to the Motherland, and three years later, the 50th anniversary of the adoption of the Kalashnikov rifle by the Soviet army was celebrated with great fanfare.

Kamenev, Lev Borisovich (1883–1936)
revolutionary and Soviet leader

A prominent Old Bolshevik and associate of LENIN, Kamenev became one of the first major victims of the Great Purge of 1936–38. Kamenev was born in Moscow to Jewish parents. He briefly studied law at Moscow University, but after joining the Social Democratic Party in 1901, he worked for the next six years as a propagandist in Tbilisi, Georgia, and St. Petersburg and was frequently arrested. In 1909 he emigrated to western Europe, where, together with Grigorii ZINOVIEV, he became one of Lenin's closest lieutenants and helped direct the Bolshevik organization from abroad. In 1914 he returned to St. Petersburg to edit the party newspaper *Pravda* and to coordinate the work of the six Bolshevik members in the Fourth State DUMA. In October 1914 he and the Bolshevik Duma deputies were banished to Siberia for their opposition to Russian participation in World War I. A moderate within the party, during 1917 Kamenev was at odds with Lenin's policy of immediate seizure of power, advocating instead a socialist coalition government. His estrangement from Lenin's course did not last long, and soon he was back in the inner circles of Bolshevik power, most notably as chairman of the Moscow Soviet. In the early 1920s, Kamenev was one of the most powerful Bolsheviks, as one of five members of the party's Politburo, as an understudy of Lenin in the Council of People's Commissars, and as a member of the "triumvirate" (with Zinoviev and STALIN) that moved against TROTSKY in the first phase of the power struggles after Lenin's death. By 1926, however, Stalin had outmaneuvered him and Zinoviev, and Kamenev was shunted off to Italy as ambassador. In 1927 he joined forces with Zinoviev and Trotsky in a belated and unsuccessful attempt to oppose Stalin. Twice expelled from the party but both times readmitted, he was arrested with Zinoviev in 1935 on the trumped up charge of planning the assassination of Stalin's close associate Sergei Kirov in December 1934. They were both expelled from the party once more and sentenced to five years' imprisonment. The following year, Kamenev and Zinoviev became the main defendants at the first show trial, were sentenced to death, and were executed in 1936.

Kandinsky, Vasili Vasilievich (1866–1944)

artist

Known in the West as Wassily Kandinsky, Kandinsky trained in law and economics at Moscow University. At the age of 30 he left Russia to study art in Munich. In Munich and elsewhere in Germany, he was an active participant in the numerous art groups and movements that flourished in the decades before World War I, such as the Phalanx and the Berlin Secession. With Franz Marc he founded the Blaue Reiter group. Kandinsky was the first Russian painter to produce purely abstract works. Initially these were Expressionist abstractions, but he later was influenced by Kazimir MALEVICH's geometrical designs and by Paul Klee's work. In 1914 he returned to Russia, where he helped establish the arts after the Russian Revolution of 1917, but he left in 1921 after disagreements over the trends to subordinate art to industry and utilitarian needs. He joined the influential Bauhaus school of design and architecture in Weimar, Germany, where he taught with his friend Klee. In 1933, he left Germany for France, where he lived until his death. By the end of his life, Kandinsky had produced a remarkable variety of abstract works. He is also known for his theoretical writings, such as *Con-*

Klein Welton #IV, a color lithograph by Vasili Kandinsky, 1922 *(Library of Congress)*

cerning the Spiritual in Art (1912) and *Point and Line in Plane* (1926).

Kapitsa, Petr Leonidovich (1894–1984)

physicist

Cowinner of the 1978 Nobel Prize in physics with two Americans, Kapitsa was a prominent Russian physicist who survived several clashes with STALIN, including his refusal to work on the Soviet atomic weapons program. Kapitsa was born on the island of Kronstadt, near St. Petersburg; his father was a military engineer. He first studied physics at the Petrograd Polytechnic Institute under the guidance of Abram Ioffe, one of the leading physicists in Russia (later the Soviet Union), then at the Petrograd Physical and Technical Institute. After graduation in 1919, Kapitsa taught electrical engineering at the same institute. In 1921, he traveled to Cambridge,

England, during a thaw in British-Soviet relations to study with Ernest Rutherford, the director of magnetic research at the Cavendish Laboratory in Cambridge. After earning a Ph.D. in physics from Cambridge in 1923, Kapitsa became deputy director of the Cavendish laboratory. In 1929 he was elected a fellow of the Royal Society, the first foreigner in over 200 years to obtain that honor. Kapitsa stayed in England until 1934, when he returned to the Soviet Union for a holiday. Stalin prohibited him from returning to Cambridge, and after a brief stand-off, Kapitsa agreed to stay in the Soviet Union. His Cambridge laboratory was transported back to Moscow, where it served as the basis for the newly founded Institute for Physical Problems, which Kapitsa headed from 1936 to 1946. In 1939, Kapitsa was chosen a member of the Soviet ACADEMY OF SCIENCES; in 1941 and again in 1943, he received the Stalin prize for physics.

Kapitsa's refusal to work on the Soviet atomic weapons program led to house arrest from 1946 to 1953. He was allowed to continue his work, and after Stalin's death in 1953 he was restored to his position as director of the Institute for Physical Problems. While in England in the 1920s, Kapitsa had built upon Rutherford's research on producing magnetic fields, before turning to the effect that magnetic fields have on metals. He became intrigued by the impact of very low temperatures on the magnetic properties of metals. He published his first findings on the superfluidity of helium II. Kapitsa found that at extremely low temperatures helium becomes a better conductor than copper. Kapitsa also designed improved plants for the liquefaction of hydrogen and helium. The Nobel Prize he received in 1978 was based on this lifetime work on low-temperature physics.

Karamzin, Nikolai Mikhailovich
(1766–1826)
writer

The author of influential works of history and poetry, Karamzin was an important figure in Russia's cultural development. Karamzin first gained attention with the publication of his *Letters of a Russian Traveler, 1789–90,* published in 1792. An important milestone in the development of Russian literature, the *Letters* discussed Karamzin's travels in western Europe, where he had been well received in literary circles. The *Letters* introduced Russian readers to a more cosmopolitan world and to a more polished literary language that avoided Old Church Slavonic influences in favor of colloquial Russian. Modeled on Sterne's *Sentimental Journey,* they also contributed to the development of sentimental literature in Russia. Another important work of Karamzin's was the fictional story "Poor Liza," which is generally seen as an early contribution to the Russian literature of social protest that flourished in the 19th century. Through two major works, Karamzin also contributed to the development of Russian historiography. In the *Memoir of Ancient Russia* (1811), he criticized Russia's 18th-century rulers while arguing for a strong monarchic state. Well received by the public and by Emperor ALEXANDER I, Karamzin was appointed court historian on the basis of this work. In 1818 he began a multivolume *History of the Russian State,* a massive endeavor that was very popular with the Russian reading public. At the time of his death, after 11 volumes, Karamzin had reached only the early 17th century. In retrospect, Karamzin's work, especially the *History of the Russian State,* stands the test of time less for its scholarly achievements than for its influence on Russian literature.

Karpov, Anatolii Yevgenievich
(1951–   )
chess player

The world chess champion from 1975 to 1985, Karpov has been a Soviet master since the age of 15, the youngest Soviet player to have achieved such an honor. Born in Zlatoust, a town in the Urals, Karpov learned to play chess at the age of six. At 13, he began to receive lessons from the great player and former world champion Mikhail BOTVINNIK. Two years later he became a Soviet master. Karpov's first international victory came in 1969 when he won the World Junior Championship. The following year after several victories in major chess tournaments, he obtained the title of international grandmaster. Karpov became the subject of world attention in 1974 when he won the right to challenge the then-world champion Bobby Fischer for the title. When Fischer refused to play Karpov, the International Chess Federation (FIDE) deposed him and named Karpov the new world champion. At the peak of his game, Karpov proceeded to win seven major tournaments in the next two years, then to successfully defend his world title twice against Viktor Korchnoi in 1978 and 1981. The matches with Korchnoi were fiercely contested and framed in a cold war context, as Korchnoi was a Soviet defector, while Karpov, a COMMUNIST PARTY member, had long been an emblem of the Soviet chess establishment. A similar context framed Karpov's title defense in 1984–85, when he faced Garry KASPAROV, a Soviet Jewish player at a time when the Soviet Union was embarking on the reformist era of the GORBACHEV years. While the staid Karpov again symbolized to many the old regime, the brash and younger Kasparov represented to many the new Soviet Union that was beginning to emerge after the long BREZHNEV rule. The match was surrounded by controversy, when Karpov was saved from near defeat by the intervention of the FIDE president, who arranged for a new championship match later in 1985. In November 1985, Karpov lost his title to Kasparov. Two attempts to regain the crown from Kasparov in 1987 and 1990 were unsuccessful. In 1993, Karpov failed to qualify as the official challenger to Kasparov. He did continue to win important tournaments, with his most impressive victory coming in 1994 at an international tournament in Spain, which he won without losing a single game.

Karsavina, Tamara Platonovna (1885–1978)
ballerina

One of the leading ballerinas of her time, Karsavina was a founding member of Diaghilev's Ballets Russes. After studying at the Imperial Ballet School, she made her debut in 1902 and became prima ballerina for the Mariinskii Theater in St. Petersburg. In 1909 she joined DIAGHILEV for the first season of the Ballets Russes. Her most famous roles over the succeeding years included *Le Spectre de la Rose,* which she danced with NIJINSKY, *The Fire Bird,* and *Giselle.* After the Russian Revolution, she settled in London in 1918, where she helped found the Royal Academy of Dancing. In the following decades Karsavina performed to great acclaim all over the world, charming audiences with her supreme artistry, her diversity, her sensitivity, and her beauty. In 1930 she published an early autobiography, *Theatre Street.* Later works such as *Ballet Technique* (1956) and *Classical Ballet: The Flow of Movement* (1962) focused on dancing theory and technique. Her older brother Lev Platonovich Karsavin (1882–1952) was a historian and philosopher who in *Vostok, zapad i russkaia idea* (*East, West and the Russian Idea*) (1922) articulated the basic position of the "Eurasian" school that emphasized the anti-European nature of Russian culture. He was expelled from Russia in 1922, settling in Germany then Lithuania, which was annexed by the Soviet Union in 1940. Arrested in 1948, he died in a labor camp.

Kasparov, Garry Kimovich (1963–   )
chess master

One of the most dazzling and controversial players in contemporary chess, Kasparov became the youngest world chess champion in history in 1985 at the age of 22. Kasparov was born in Baku, in the then Soviet republic of Azerbaijan. He first caught the attention of the chess world in 1975, when at the age of 12 he won the Azerbaijan championship, followed by the world junior championship four years later. In 1982, at the age of 19, he became a candidate for the world championship, and two years later he first won the right to challenge the reigning world champion, Anatoli KARPOV, for the title. For nearly the next decade Kasparov and Karpov's battles for chess supremacy took place in the context of rapid change in Soviet life, and the two players were made to represent two sides of these changes. Kasparov's youth and his brash playing style contrasted with the cautious style of Karpov to produce a celebrated contest in which Karpov was portrayed to represent the Soviet chess establishment under challenge by a new generation of players like Kasparov. The 1984 match went on for 16 months without a decision until stopped by the president of the International Chess Federation (FIDE). The following year in a rematch, Kasparov defeated Karpov to become world champion. Another battle for the world championship in 1986 ended in a draw, with Kasparov retaining his title under international rules. In 1990 Kasparov defeated Karpov once again in the last of the major matches between the two Soviet champions. In the final years of the Soviet Union, Kasparov participated in politics and was elected to the Congress of People's Deputies on a reformist slate. The 1990s brought many changes to the world of international chess, with Kasparov always at the center. In 1993, Kasparov, still the world champion, and the British challenger Nigel Short challenged the dominance of FIDE by holding a championship match under the sponsorship of the Professional Chess Association. In turn, his old nemesis, Karpov, won the FIDE championship held to fill in the vacancy left by Kasparov. By the mid-1990s both Kasparov and Karpov were claiming the title of world champion. Most recently, Kasparov was in the public eye in connection with his competition against Deep Blue, a chess computer created by International Business Machines (IBM). In 1996, Kasparov went from a loss in the first game—the first time a computer had defeated a world championship under chess match conditions—to win the entire match by a score of four to two. In 1997, however, Kasparov was defeated in a six-game series by an upgraded version of Deep Blue that could process 200 million chess positions per second. By 2000, the breach with FIDE had been healed, but Kasparov lost the world championship to a new challenger, his former pupil, Vladimir Kramnik. In early 2003, Kasparov announced plans to play another computer, known as Deep Junior.

Katyn Forest Massacre (1940–)

Katyn Forest, about 12 miles west of Smolensk, was the site of a mass slaughter of Polish officers by Soviet NKVD (secret police) troops, estimated to have taken place in the spring of 1940. Knowledge of the massacre first became public in April 1943, when Nazi German radio announced the discovery of eight mass graves in the area with the bodies of over 4,000 officers, bound and shot in the back. The bodies were believed to be part of a contingent of 15,000 Polish officers and soldiers captured and deported to Soviet prison camps in late 1939, when Soviet troops marched into eastern Poland as part of the NAZI-SOVIET PACT. The other 11,000 bodies have never been accounted for. Although the Soviets denied the charge and blamed the Germans for the massacre, all signs pointed to NKVD responsibility. When the Polish government-in-exile called for an International Red Cross investigation, the USSR broke diplomatic relations. Public discussion of the massacre in Poland and the Soviet Union was suppressed during the cold war, but the issue simmered just under the surface, contributing to the distrust and resentment Poles felt toward the Soviet Union as a client Communist state. Finally, in 1987, in the spirit of glasnost promoted by Mikhail GORBACHEV, a joint Soviet-Polish commission was established to investigate the massacre. In 1990, the Soviet government admitted that NKVD units were responsible for the crime. A joint Polish-Russian collection of documents, with a foreword by Alexander YAKOVLEV, was published in 1997.

Kazakov, Aleksei (1891–1919)
fighter pilot
Widely considered Russia's most successful fighter pilot during World War I, Kazakov was born in the province of Kherson. He began his career in the cavalry but in 1915 joined the

newly formed Russian air force. At a time when aerial warfare was in its infancy, the record confirm that Kazakov shot down 17 planes; he may have been responsible for bringing down more airplanes in remote rural areas. Kazakov's most widely known fighting tactic was to ram the enemy aircraft in midair, a risky but effective method. After the OCTOBER REVOLUTION of 1917, Kazakov joined the White forces that sought to overthrow the Bolshevik government. On August 1, 1919, he was killed in an air crash. The timing of his death, soon after the Allies had ceased supporting the Whites in July 1919, and his great expertise at landing airplanes have led many to believe that he purposely crashed his plane out of depression over the fate of the White cause.

Kazan

A city on the Volga River, located about 500 miles east of Moscow, Kazan is the political and cultural center of Russia's Tatar Muslim population. Kazan was founded in the late 14th century and in 1445 became the capital of the Khanate of Kazan, one of the states that formed as the GOLDEN HORDE began to fragment. In 1552, after a long campaign it was captured by the troops of IVAN IV the Terrible. The famous cathedral of St. Basil's in Moscow was built to commemorate its capture, an important turning point in Russian history. The city declined during the following centuries and suffered great damage in 1774 during the PUGACHEV REBELLION. In 1781, CATHERINE II designated it a provincial capital, and the city recovered to become an important regional transportation and manufacturing center. Kazan became an important intellectual and cultural center in the 19th century following the foundation in 1804 of Kazan University, which counted Lev TOLSTOY and Vladimir LENIN among its famous students. In Soviet times, Kazan became the capital of the Tatar Autonomous Soviet Socialist Republic, which after 1991 became known as Tatarstan, an autonomous republic within the Russian Federation. By the mid-1990s its population had reached 1.4 million.

Kerensky, Aleksandr Feodorovich (1881–1970)
politician

The central figure behind the Provisional Government that succeeded NICHOLAS II in February 1917, Kerensky was born in Simbirsk (now Ulyanovsk), the son of a headmaster who once taught the man who later overthrew him, Vladimir LENIN. A lawyer by trade, Kerensky joined the Socialist Revolutionary Party in 1905 and was briefly imprisoned and exiled. Returning from exile in 1906, he began a successful career as a defense lawyer in political cases. In 1912 he was part of the delegation that traveled to Siberia to investigate the LENA GOLDFIELDS MASSACRE, which left 170 miners dead. That same year he was elected to the Fourth DUMA for the Trudovik (Labor) faction of the Socialist Revolutionaries. By the time of the FEBRUARY REVOLUTION, Kerensky had developed parliamentary connections and a not insignificant mass following from his highly visible activities as a radical lawyer. Already a deputy chairman of the Petrograd Soviet, Kerensky entered the Provisional Government as minister of justice. Over the next six months, he accumulated power in the Provisional Government, becoming minister of war and navy in May 1917, prime minister in July after the defeat of a pro-Bolshevik insurrection, and supreme commander in chief in September after the murky KORNILOV affair. By then, Kerensky's policy of strongly supporting the war, despite its great unpopularity, and postponing basic reforms until the convening of a democratically elected Constituent Assembly had destroyed what little support the government had left. On October 25, Kerensky fled Petrograd in disguise, as the BOLSHEVIKS and their allies took over the city, proclaiming a Soviet government. After the OCTOBER REVOLUTION, he remained active in anti-Soviet politics. In hiding after October 1917, he did not leave Russia until

May 1918. In London and Paris he unsuccessfully lobbied for Allied support for a democratic Russian government. From Paris he edited the newspaper *Dni* (*Days*), a critic of both communism and Nazism. In 1940, on the eve of the German occupation, he moved to the United States and settled in Stanford, California. He edited a three-volume collection of documents on the Provisional Government and rewrote his memoirs, published as *The Kerensky Memoirs: Russia and History's Turning Point* (1965). He died of cancer in New York City in 1970.

Khlebnikov, Velimir Vladimirovich (1885–1922)
poet

One of the leading and most inventive representatives of Russian FUTURISM, Khlebnikov was born near the Caspian Sea port of ASTRAKHAN. His father was a scientist, and he studied at Kazan University in 1903, and later at St. Petersburg University (1908–11). His first poems were published in 1908, and he soon became known for his brilliant verbal experiments that influenced many of his contemporaries from GUMILEV to MAYAKOVSKY. A central figure in the Futurist movement, Khlebnikov took part in many of its "happenings" across Russia. Unlike many of his Futurist colleagues, Khlebnikov shunned the spotlight, preferring instead to work on utopian projects for global and cosmic reform. He adopted a style that was half-serious, half-naive, and enjoyed calling himself "president of the globe." Apart from his love for grammatical experiments, Khlebnikov introduced influential primitive, archaic, and exotic elements in his poetry, evident in works like *Lesnaia Deva, Shaman I Venera, Truba Gul-Mully* (all from 1921) and *Zangezi* (1922). He identified with revolution in a general, not political, sense. In his own life he became a homeless vagrant, showing complete disregard not only for any career possibilities but also for any type of settlement that would restrict his life. Information about his final years is sketchy, but it appears he died of hunger and neglect in a village near Novgorod. Unlike his fellow Futurist Mayakovsky, Khlebnikov wrote works that were too esoteric to establish a wide popular following during his lifetime. Beginning with a five-volume edition of his collected works, published in Leningrad in 1928–33, his posthumous reputation soared, and he is nowadays considered the greatest Russian Futurist poet.

Khmelnitsky, Bogdan Mikhailovich (1595?–1657)
Cossack leader

A Cossack leader in Ukraine whose rebellion against Poland led to the controversial agreement of Pereiaslavl that brought the Ukraine under Russian rule. Khmelnitsky was the son of a minor nobleman in Chigirin district in the Ukraine. He received a fine education at a Jesuit college in Lvov, where he learned several languages. As a soldier in the Polish army, he fought the Turks in 1620 and the Russians in the 1630s. In 1645 he traveled to France as a Polish emissary to discuss the possible use of Cossack troops in the French campaigns against Spain. In 1647, Khmelnitsky became unhappy with his service with the Poles and was briefly arrested for planning an uprising against the king of Poland. In 1648, he started the rebellion in the Ukraine for which he is known, leading the Zaporozhian COSSACKS, who recognized him as their chief (hetman). After initial successes against the Poles, most of the Ukraine joined his rebellion. An armistice with the Polish government followed, during which he began negotiations with the Russians about the possible annexation of the Ukraine. After another round of battles with the Poles, Czar ALEKSEI MIKHAILOVICH called an assembly of the land (ZEMSKII SOBOR), which agreed to declare war on Poland and strive for the annexation of Ukraine. In January 1654, Khmelnitskii and his Cossack followers pledged loyalty to the czar at Pereiaslavl. Two months later the czar announced his intention to grant Ukraine broad privileges of autonomy. In the years that followed, Khmelnitsky tried to convince skeptical COSSACKS of the benefits of the arrangement with Moscow. Disagreements over the true meaning of the Pereiaslavl agreement provided the foundation for the long-standing autonomous feelings of Ukrainians and for the development of a Ukrainian nationalist movement in the 19th century.

Khorezm

One of the main oases and oldest centers of civilization in Central Asia, situated along the delta of the Amu Darya River, Khorezm belonged to Russia (later the Soviet Union) from 1873 to 1991. The first mention of Khorezm appears in Persian chronicles of the sixth century B.C. Before the Arab conquest of 712, Khorezm had developed as an Iranian-speaking polity whose people adhered to Zoroastrianism and whose art integrated Hellenistic and Buddhist influences with local features. The emirs of northern Khorezm unified the area in 995, and the Khorezm oasis, with its capital at Urgench, became a major seat of Arabic learning, the home of Al-Birunni and Avicenna. Under Muhammad II (1200–1220) and other rulers known as Great Khorezmshahs, Khorezm was the center of an empire that included Central Asia and Iran. However, in 1220 it was conquered and laid waste by Genghis Khan and included in the GOLDEN HORDE. Aware of its strategic and commercial importance, the Mongols promoted the prosperity of the oasis, especially Urgench, until conquered by Timur in 1388. By this time the population of Khorezm had already been Turkicized. A century of struggle between the Timurids and the Golden Horde for Khorezm was followed by Uzbek conquest in 1505. Soon Khorezm became an independent Uzbek state, known in Russia and western Europe as the Khiva Khanate. Internal feuds, raids by Turkmen, Kazakh, and Kalmyk tribesmen, and wars with neighboring BUKHARA weakened the state, and in 1740 it was conquered by Nadir Shah of Persia. Persian rule lasted only a few years, but it was not until the beginning of the 19th century that Khorezm again rose to power and prosperity. Its khans subjugated most of the Turkmen tribes, but their attempts to extend their rule to the Kazakhs, who were Russian subjects, and their attacks on Russian merchants led to hostilities with Russia. A first Russian expedition against Khorezm (1839–40) was unsuccessful, but in 1873 the khan was compelled to cede the right bank of the Amu Darya and recognize Russian suzerainty. Russia took over Khorezm's foreign relations, but aside from the release of about 15,000 slaves, it did not interfere much with Khorezm's internal life. Thus, Khorezm did not participate in the rapid economic transformation that Russian Turkestan underwent as a Russian colony. In 1920 the Red Army seized the oasis, deposed the khan, and declared the establishment of the Khorezm People's Soviet Republic. With the national delimitation of Central Asia in 1924, the oasis was divided into three parts, the Khorezm oblast and the Kara-Kalpak Autonomous Republic in Uzbekistan and the Tashauz oblast of Turkmenistan. Long isolated by the desert, the construction of a railway link from Khorezm to Chardzou on the Amu Darya River in the 1950s greatly improved the economic prospects of a region that now depends mostly on irrigated agriculture, sheep raising, horse breeding, and cotton processing. The dissolution of the Soviet Union in 1991 did not end the political division of the Khorezm oasis; now it is part of the republics of Uzbekistan and Turkmenia.

Khrushchev, Nikita Sergeevich (1894–1971)
Soviet ruler

The eventual successor to Joseph STALIN, Nikita Khrushchev left his mark on Soviet politics as an inconsistent and impulsive reformer, while the West remembers him as a slightly buffoonish leader who banged a table with his shoe at the United Nations.

Khrushchev was born on April 17, 1894, to a peasant family in Kursk province, southern Russia. In 1909, the family moved to Yuzovka, in

Nikita Khrushchev (right) and Fidel Castro *(Library of Congress)*

the sprawling Donbas mining region of the Ukraine, where Khrushchev took various jobs as apprentice mechanic, machine repairman, and metal fitter. In 1918 he joined the Bolshevik (later Communist) Party and during the civil war served as political commissar in Budenny's famous First Cavalry Army. After a stint as deputy director of a mine, Khrushchev entered the Ukrainian Communist Party apparatus; by 1929, with the help of Lazar KAGANOVICH, he was transferred to Moscow. Two years later, he was appointed first secretary of the Bauman district in Moscow. Working with Kaganovich on the construction of the Moscow Metro, Khrushchev continued his rise through the Moscow party bureaucracy, becoming first secretary of the

Moscow city party organization in 1934. Four years later he was named first secretary of the Ukrainian Communist Party, a position that involved him deeply in the implementation of the bloody purges throughout the Ukraine. A member of the party's Central Committee since 1934, he was appointed a full member of the Politburo in 1939 at the young age of 45. Khrushchev spent World War II mostly as a political commissar visiting various fronts, including Stalingrad, where his eldest son died in battle. He retained his party posts in the Ukraine and, after some minor setbacks in 1947, returned to Moscow to serve directly under Stalin as a Central Committee secretary for agriculture.

Stalin's death in March 1953 propelled Khrushchev to the highest echelons of Soviet power and a fierce succession struggle. By December 1953, Lavrenty BERIA, Stalin's feared political police chief, had been executed and Georgii MALENKOV had been prevented from concentrating too much power in his hands. With Malenkov as prime minister, Khrushchev became first secretary of the COMMUNIST PARTY. By 1955 he had outmaneuvered Malenkov, who resigned as prime minister but retained his seat on the Party Presidium (Politburo). Khrushchev's defining moment came after the 20th Party Congress in February 1956, when he read his famous "Secret Speech," in which he condemned Stalin's personality cult and the purges of the 1930s—the first public criticism of Stalin since the 1920s. The Secret Speech marked the beginning of a period of inconsistent de-Stalinization, especially evident in the field of culture. In June 1957, Khrushchev defeated one last attempt by old-guard Stalinists, later known as the ANTI-PARTY GROUP, to remove him from power. As Soviet ruler, Khrushchev faced numerous foreign policy challenges such as dissension within the Soviet bloc, most notably the failed Hungarian Revolution of 1956, growing policy differences with Communist China, and tensions with the West, symbolized by the building of the Berlin Wall and the 1962 Cuban Missile Crisis, which brought the world to the brink of nuclear conflict.

By October 1964, resentment over his impulsive bureaucratic reorganizations and policies that appeared erratic reached a head among his Politburo colleagues. While on vacation near the Black Sea, he was removed from office and replaced by Leonid BREZHNEV as party general secretary. Khrushchev retired to a dacha near Moscow, where he composed his memoirs, first published posthumously in the West. He died in September 1971 in Moscow and was buried, not in the Kremlin Wall with other Communist leaders, but in the city's Novodeviche Cemetery. Although unsuccessful in his own reforms, he influenced a whole generation of young party activists, including Mikhail GORBACHEV, who later enjoyed positions of power in the late 1980s.

Kibalchich, Nikolai Ivanovich (1853–1881)

revolutionary and inventor

One of the five terrorists from the revolutionary organization PEOPLE'S WILL hanged for their role in the assassination of Czar ALEXANDER II on March 1, 1881. Kibalchich was also one of the pioneers of Russian rocket science. He was born on October 10, 1853, in Chernigov province; his father was a priest. Fascinated with trains, he entered the St. Petersburg Transportation Institute in 1871 but transferred two years later to the Medico-Surgery Academy. Active in revolutionary politics, he was imprisoned in 1875–78 for engaging in revolutionary propaganda. After his release, he joined the populist organization Land and Liberty. When Land and Liberty split in 1879, he sided with the People's Will faction, which advocated revolutionary terrorism, and became a member of its Executive Committee. By this point his interest in trains had given way to a fascination with explosives. As the People's Will "main technician," he directed the preparation of the bombs that were used to assassinate the czar. He was arrested on March 17, 1881, and sentenced to death. Together with Andrei Zheliabov, Sofia Perovskaya, and two others, he was hanged on April 3, 1881. While in prison awaiting his death, Kibalchich worked out an original project for the development of a flying machine based on rocket principles. For the next three decades, Kibalchich's plan lay buried in the czarist police archives until discovered by N. A. Rynin and published in the journal *Byloe* in 1918. Kibalchich's design played an influential role in spurring interest in space travel in the 1920s and 1930s.

Kiev

The present-day capital of Ukraine, Kiev (Kyiv in Ukrainian) is considered to be the cradle of eastern Slavic culture and civilization. Built mostly on hills that overlook the Dnieper River, which flows south into the Black Sea, Kiev was first founded in the fifth century, but it was only in the ninth century that it appears more prominently in historical accounts. The city's favorable location along the routes that linked Scandinavia and Constantinople brought it relative prosperity and the attention of Varangian (Viking) adventurers who had already taken NOVGOROD in 862. In 882 they took Kiev and made it the capital of the state known as KIEVAN RUS. With the conversion to Orthodox Christianity of VLADIMIR I and his court in 988, Kiev also became one of the leading religious centers of medieval Europe, with enduring architectural symbols such as the Cathedral of St. Sophia and the Perchersky (Cave) Monastery, both founded in the 11th century. War with nomad peoples along the southern frontier was a frequent feature of early Kievan history. In 1240, the city was captured, sacked, and destroyed by the Mongol armies of BATU KHAN. Mongol rule continued until 1362, when the city became a part of Lithuania. In the next three centuries Kiev changed hands frequently: invaded by the Crimean Tatars in 1482; annexed by the Poles in 1569; and finally given to Russia in 1686 as part of the "eternal peace" signed between Poland and Russia. For the next 300 years, with a few brief interruptions, Kiev would belong to the Russian Empire and its successor, the Soviet Union. During the 18th century the city was fortified, the Cathedral of St. Sophia was restored after centuries of neglect, and the baroque style Church of St. Andrew was built. In the 19th century Kiev emerged as an important commercial, industrial, educational, and cultural center, with a large multiethnic population that included Ukrainians, Jews, Poles, and Russians. During the 1905 Revolution, the city was the site of political disturbances and a POGROM against its Jewish population. The period of the Russian Revolution and civil war (1917–21) ranks among the most chaotic of Kiev's long history. At different times Ukrainian nationalists, Germans and Poles controlled the city, before the Soviets emerged triumphant in 1920. In 1934, Kiev became the capital of the Ukrainian Soviet Socialist Republic, replacing its recent rival, the industrial city of Kharkov. The German Army occupied Kiev from 1941–43 causing great damage to the city and its people. Close to 200,000 of its inhabitants were killed, of which the mass execution of Jews at BABI YAR ravine is the best known and most infamous example. Widespread reconstruction after World War II restored Kiev to its position as the third-largest city of the Soviet Union. After the collapse of the Soviet Union, Kiev, now known by its Ukrainian name, Kyiv, and with a population of almost 2.7 million, became the capital of the new independent Ukraine.

Kievan Rus

An East Slav state that flourished between the ninth and 13th centuries around the city of KIEV, Kievan Rus is considered the cradle of Russian culture and civilization. In the ninth century, Kiev emerged as an important center of trade on the Dnieper River linking Scandinavia with Byzantium. Over the next two centuries Kievan Rus produced a number of outstanding rulers. These include Princess Olga (ca. 890–969), who converted to Christianity; VLADIMIR the Great (ca. 956–1015), who introduced Christianity to Russia; Yaroslav the Wise (1019–54), who introduced the first Russian legal code; and Vladimir Monomakh (1053–1125), who briefly checked

the process of fragmentation that set in after the death of Yaroslav. The continuation of these feuds after the death of Vladimir Monomakh contributed to the disintegration of Kievan Rus and the rise of regionalism in areas like Galicia, Volhynia, Novgorod, and Vladimir. Kiev's decline also corresponded to broader shifts in the patterns of international trade and political relationships. The negative impact of the Crusades on the Byzantine Empire was felt in Kiev, which was situated on the great trade routes from Scandinavia to Byzantium, and from western Europe to Central Asia. The rise of princely rule in Vladimir, an oligarchic republic in Novgorod, and a landed nobility in Galicia all contributed to the weakening of the prestige of the grand princes of Kiev. By the time of the MONGOL CONQUEST (1237–40), Kiev had entered a period of decline and fragmentation. Nevertheless, the memory of the Kievan era provided a strong unifying symbol for Russian princes under the long period of Mongol rule. The princes of Moscow in particular attempted to claim for themselves the mantle of the Kievan legacy, as part of the process of "gathering of the lands" that had belong to Kievan Rus. Competing claims to the Kievan legacy have been one of the many points that long divided Russians and Ukrainians.

Klimov, Elem Germanovich
(1933–2003)

film director

As newly elected secretary of the Filmmakers' Union in 1986, Klimov helped lead the charge that gave artistic and intellectual momentum to the first years of GORBACHEV's perestroika (restructuring). Klimov began his professional life as an aviation engineer but later migrated to film, graduating from the prestigious All-Union State Institute of Cinematography (VGIK). As a student he gained a reputation for provocative, satirical short films. His first full-length feature, *Welcome, or No Trespassing* (1964), was a satirical look at the socialization of children in a Young Pioneer camp. In *Adventures of a Dentist* (1967), he continued his mordant criticism of Soviet bureaucracy. His next film, *Agonia* (*Agony*), was finished in 1975 but not released until 1985 as one of the opening salvos of the era of cultural glasnost (openness). In it, he treated the politically sensitive topics of RASPUTIN, NICHOLAS II and ALEXANDRA, and the last years before the revolution in a highly unorthodox (for Soviet times) but artistically compelling way. The film was a major hit and brought Klimov international recognition. His other major film from this period was *Come and See* (1985), a brutally realistic account of life in Nazi-occupied Belarus. His wife, Larissa Shepitko, was also an accomplished filmmaker who died with some of her crew in an automobile accident while filming *Farewell to Matyora,* based on Valentin Rasputin's story from 1976. Klimov completed the film and supplemented it with a short sequel, *Larissa,* a loving tribute to her memory. Klimov's broader contributions to Soviet film and Soviet cultural life came after May 1986, when the historic Congress of the Filmmakers Union unanimously elected him general secretary of the Filmmakers Union. In Soviet terms this practically made him the head of the Soviet film industry. With decision-making power wrested away from bureaucrats and given to filmmakers themselves, Klimov released all the films that had been shelved for the previous 30 years (literally hundreds, including all his own films), thus inaugurating a period when film was once again the most vital Soviet art.

Kliuchevsky, Vasili Osipovich (1814–1911)
historian

One of the most influential Russian historians, Kliuchevsky is considered to have set the tone for 19th-century Russian historiography. He was born in the provincial town of Penza, the son of a village priest. Educated in a seminary, Kliuchevsky possessed intellectual talents that opened doors that would have been closed to most people of his social background, and he was able to enroll in Moscow University, Russia's most prestigious university. There he studied

under the great historian Sergei Soloviev, whom he would eventually succeed as professor and lecturer. In 1871 he published his thesis on the historiographical value of the Ancient Russians' Saints Lives. While still a student Kliuchevsky taught in different Moscow educational venues, and when Soloviev died suddenly of cancer in 1879 at a relatively young age, Kliuchevsky was the surprise choice to replace him at Moscow University. Slow to publish, Kliuchevsky first made his reputation as a brilliant lecturer, and his lectures drew large numbers of students as well as public figures. Kliuchevsky was conservative by nature and had little interest in the world beyond Moscow. The underlying theme of his work was the development of Russians into a nation, a theme best expounded in his well-known *The Course of Russian History,* a five-volume opus based on Kliuchevsky's lectures at various institutions. He saw Russia as a European nation, and drawing from popular historians such as Jules Michelet, Kliuchevsky emphasized the role of the Russian people in the making of its history. In addition to *The Course of Russian History,* he published a work on the Boyar Council that defended the advisory role of this parliamentary body within the context of Russian autocracy.

In later years, his reputation drew him somewhat reluctantly and briefly into the world of politics. He participated in the ZEMSTVO constitutional movement in the years before the 1905 Revolution. In 1905 he was called to help draft the proposal for a consultative DUMA, or parliament, known as the August Manifesto, but withdrew when the reform was unsuccessful. In the half-decade before his death, a conflict with the rector of Moscow University led to his gradual retirement from all positions of importance. Kliuchevsky's influence endured long after his death through the work of the generation of historians whom he trained. In the years before World War II, the most prominent Russian historians of the era from the liberal Pavel MILIUKOV to the Marxist Mikhail Pokrovsky had all studied under Kliuchevsky.

Kobiakova, Aleksandra (1823–1892)
writer

Kobiakova was a popular writer from the 1860s whose work provides one of the few glimpses into the lives of women in the traditional patriarchal merchant family. Little is known about her early life in Kostroma, an old merchant town on the Volga River, before she moved to St. Petersburg in the late 1850s. The success of her first novel, *The Last Execution* (1858), a historical tale about 18th-century merchant life, opened the doors of the capital's literary world, including those of the progressive journal *Russkoe slovo* (*The Russian Word*). During the 1860s, *Russkoe slovo* continued to publish her work, including her second novel, *The Podovshin Family* (1860), about a woman's unhappy marriage to the son of an abusive merchant. The journal also solicited her autobiography, one of the few extant primary sources authored by a woman from a merchant background. Writing within the framework of the radical intelligentsia of the times, Kobiakova confirmed the received notions of the journal and its readers about the oppressive, tradition-bound world of merchant families they had read about in Aleksandr OSTROVSKY's popular plays. *A Woman in Everyday Merchant Life,* published in 1863 and considered her best work, further explores the themes of merchant life, this time from the point of view of a woman's psychological disintegration during her marriage to an abusive merchant. Kobiakova's later work, treating provincial life, received far less attention from the St. Petersburg reading public than her earlier work. Little is known about her later years.

Kolchak, Aleksandr Vasilievich (1873–1920)
admiral

Kolchak was one of the leading anti-Bolshevik White commanders during the Russian civil war. Born in St. Petersburg into a family of naval officers, he entered the Naval Academy and graduated in 1894. During a distinguished naval career he served in the RUSSO-JAPANESE WAR, then in World War I, where he became commander of the Black Sea Fleet in July 1916. Previously he had also participated in two polar expeditions (1900–1903 and 1908–11) as a hydrologist. Faced with the rapid disintegration of the army and navy after the FEBRUARY REVOLUTION, he resigned his commission in June 1917 and traveled to the United States. Looking for a way to join the anti-Bolshevik struggle after the OCTOBER REVOLUTION, he linked up with the British, who were concluding that a military dictatorship might be the best way to defeat the BOLSHEVIKS. In October 1918, with British help, Kolchak reached Omsk, home to the Directorate, a moderate socialist anti-Bolshevik government, where he was appointed minister of war and navy. A few weeks later, right-wing officers overthrew the Directorate and named Kolchak "supreme ruler of Russia." Kolchak's regime never lived up to its grandiose title. Its major military offensive in the spring of 1919 fell short of reaching its objective, the Volga River. Bolshevik forces, led by Mikhail FRUNZE, soon forced Kolchak to retreat behind the Urals. Politically, Kolchak was never to rally any support beyond the narrow coterie of White officers and liberal politicians. Instead, chaos, corruption, and repression became the hallmark of his regime, despite his own reputation for honesty. Kolchak's regime unraveled quickly after November 1919. Fleeing eastward from Omsk, he was captured and turned over to revolutionaries in Irkutsk, who in turn handed him to the Bolshevik troops that captured Irkutsk in January 1920. Fearing a White counteroffensive, the Irkutsk Bolsheviks executed him on February 7, 1920.

Kollontai, Aleksandra Mikhailovna (1872–1952)
revolutionary and Soviet official

One of the few women who occupied a prominent position in the early Bolshevik hierarchy, Kollontai (born Domontovich) was also an accomplished writer and theorist. She was born in St. Petersburg, the daughter of an imperial army general. In 1893, she married a distant relative, Vladimir Kollontai, and together they had a son. Her life changed dramatically in 1896 when after a visit to a textile factory, she left her husband and joined the Social Democratic revolutionary movement. A Menshevik until 1915, Kollontai spent the decade from 1908 to 1917 in exile, attending various socialist congresses, traveling through western Europe and the United States, and advancing the message that the liberation of women was possible only through Marxism. During World War I she was arrested and expelled from a number of countries because of her antiwar propaganda activities. During these years she joined the BOLSHEVIK cause and met her future close friend and collaborator, Aleksandr Shliapnikov. Back in Russia after the February Revolution, she was an excellent orator who spoke extensively at meetings of soldiers and sailors. At the Sixth Party Congress, she was elected to the Central Committee, and after the OCTOBER REVOLUTION, she was appointed commissar of social welfare in the first Soviet government. In 1919, she joined Inessa ARMAND in establishing the Party's Section for Women's Work (ZHENOTDEL), becoming its director after Armand's death in 1920. Always independent-minded, she joined the various internal party oppositions that flourished during the civil war: the Left Opposition in 1918 against the BREST-LITOVSK treaty and, with Shliapnikov, the Workers' Opposition in 1920–21, resisting what she saw as growing Bolshevik authoritarianism. Her influence within the party diminished after 1921; she was appointed Soviet representative to Norway in 1923 and ambassador to Mexico in 1926, the first Russian woman to be given such rank. From 1927 to 1930 she served again as ambassador to Norway and from 1930 to 1945, ambassador to Sweden. She thus escaped the ravages of the Great Purge at home. In the 1960s and 1970s, Kollontai's work and writings, especially her views on free love, much criticized at the time, received renewed attention from Western scholars as an early exemplar of Soviet feminism.

Kolyma labor camps

One of the main and most infamous components of the system of enforced labor, better known as the GULAG, that developed under Joseph STALIN's rule in the Soviet Union. The Kolyma labor camps were built around the substantial gold deposits found in the upper region of the Kolyma River in northeastern Siberia, which rises in the Kolyma Mountains and flows northeast into the Arctic Ocean. In 1931, three years after the first gold mines in the Kolyma region were established, the Soviet government founded the Dalstroi (General Industry and Highway Construction), centered in the town of Magadan on the Sea of Okhotsk, to promote mining in the region and develop its industrial infrastructure. The following year, in October 1932, the Dalstroi region was designated an autonomous territory. The first shipment of 10 prisoners had already arrived in February 1932; by the winter of 1932–33, the prison population had swollen to 11,000 of which it is estimated that only 25 percent survived the winter. Over the next two decades the prison population grew inexorably, surpassing 100,000 in the winter of 1939 and reaching 190,000 in 1941, before declining to 84,000 in 1944. The territorial scope of Dalstroi grew accordingly, reaching 700,000 sq km in 1936 and 2.3 million sq km in 1941. Working and living conditions were notoriously brutal, leading to high mortality rates that were offset by the large numbers of new arrivals. Prisoners of war, from Poland at the beginning of World War II and Japan at the end, were also sent to Kolyma. The final years of the Stalin era saw a renewed increase in the number of prisoners from a headcount of 108,000 in 1949 to almost 200,000 in January 1952. In March 1953, following Stalin's death, jurisdiction over Dalstroi was transferred to the Ministry of Metallurgy, while the labor camps themselves remained a part of the gulag, now a part of the Ministry of Justice. Over the next year the harsh labor regime relaxed slightly, and beginning in 1954 large numbers of camp inmates were released, as the camps were gradually closed down. According to some estimates, over 1 million prisoners died in the Kolyma labor camps from 1932 to 1954, and to successive generations of Soviet and Russian citizens, the name

Kolyma, like Magadan, immediately evoked horrible memories, which some authors such as Varlaam Shalamov, whose collected stories were later published in English as *Kolyma Tales,* first ventured to chronicle in the 1960s.

Komsomol

The acronym formed from the Russian words for "Communist League of Youth," the Komsomol was the branch of the COMMUNIST PARTY that enrolled members between the ages of 14 and 28. The Komsomol was first organized in 1918 during the Russian civil war to channel revolutionary youth activism in support of the revolution. In 1922 its organization was established, and two other supporting youth institutions were created, the Little Octobrists, for children less than nine, and the Young Pioneers, for children from nine to 14 years of age. Komsomol members were to serve as role models of Socialist behavior while engaging in socially useful tasks. Gradually and for the rest of its existence, the Komsomol increasingly became the gateway to full membership in the Communist Party. In the late 1920s and early 1930s, as Soviet society embarked on a far-reaching transformation, the Komsomol played a crucial role in advancing the Stalinist leadership's agenda of industrialization and collectivization through its members' revolutionary enthusiasm and ideological zealousness. Komsomol members were particularly active in enforcing the government's antireligious campaign. As membership in the Komsomol was opened in the 1930s, its numbers reached 9 million, almost three times the size of the adult Communist Party. In the postwar period, the Komsomol continued to serve as the institutional mechanism for conveying ideologically approved Communist and collectivist values to the Soviet youth. Komsomol members were at the forefront of ideologically driven economic campaigns, such as the Virgin Lands Project launched in 1954. At its peak in the 1970s and 1980s, membership in the Komsomol reached 40 million. By 1991, with the Communist system in disarray and unable to recruit any new members, the Komsomol disbanded.

Kondratiev, Nikolai Dmitrievich (1892–1938)
economist

An influential economist with an international reputation, Kondratiev was one of the first economists to be arrested by Stalin's police in the 1930s. Outside the Soviet Union, Kondratiev is still known for his ideas about economic long cycles, sometimes known as Kondratiev cycles. Kondratiev postulated the existence of long cycles of economic expansion and contraction with an average of duration of about 50 years, a theory that was well received outside the Soviet Union but dismissed as "wrong and reactionary" by the Soviet establishment. In the Soviet Union, Kondratiev was active in the economic policy debates of the 1920s as founder and first director of the Moscow Conjuncture Institute (1920–28), professor at the Timiriazev Agricultural Academy, lecturer at the Communist Academy, and a consultant for the Finance and Agriculture Commissariats and the State Planning agency (Gosplan). Although he was one of the authors of the first five-year plan for Russian agriculture (1923–24), Kondratiev opposed the general COMMUNIST PARTY line adopted in the late 1920s with its emphasis on rapid industrialization to be paid by a collectivized peasantry. His defense of private agriculture and proposals to redistribute wealth to the peasantry eventually got him into political trouble. In 1930 Kondratiev was charged with "right deviationism" and membership in a nonexistent Working Peasants Party. He was arrested and, after a public trial, sentenced to eight years in a labor camp, where he eventually perished. Kondratiev was rehabilitated during the late 1980s, and his work was published for the first time in half a century. The long-suppressed details of his death were also made public. Kondratiev was shot in 1938 on the very day he was due to be released from his eight-year sentence.

Konev, Ivan Stepanovich (1897–1973)
army commander

Konev distinguished himself in the final offensive campaigns that led to Soviet victory in World

War II. Born to a peasant family, Konev was conscripted into the Russian imperial army and served as a noncommissioned officer during World War I. In 1918 he joined the Red Army and the COMMUNIST PARTY (CPSU). During the civil war he served mostly as a political commissar, although he was part of the troops that put down the uprising at the Kronstadt naval base in March 1921. He then transferred to the regular officer corps in 1924, graduated from the Frunze Military Academy in 1926, and was given progressively higher commands until appointed commander of the North Caucasus Military District in January 1941. When Nazi Germany invaded the USSR in June 1941, Konev was appointed commander of the Nineteenth Army and Western Army Group that fought in the Battle of Moscow in 1941. As commander of the Second Ukrainian and then First Ukrainian fronts he took part in the battles that liberated Kharkov (1943) and Kirovograd (1944), before moving into Romania in April 1944. In January 1945, Konev's armies invaded Germany from the south, while Georgii ZHUKOV entered from the center and Konstantin Rokossovsky from the north. For his wartime service he was promoted to marshal of the Soviet Union. As a senior Soviet officer, Konev was appointed to a number of important assignments after the war: Soviet representative on the Allied Control Commission in Vienna, chief of the Soviet ground forces (1945–55), deputy minister of war (1946–50), first deputy minister of defense (1955–60), commander in chief of the WARSAW PACT forces, and commander in chief of Soviet occupation forces in East Germany, 1961–62. He presided over the special court that sentenced secret police chief Lavrenty BERIA to death in December 1953. He was a member of the Central Committee of the CPSU, 1952–73. He was twice named a Hero of the Soviet Union.

Kopelev, Lev Zinovievich (1912–)
writer and dissident
A dedicated Communist in his youth, Kopelev became a prominent and influential dissident in the post–World War II period. Born in Kiev, as a teenager and young Communist Kopelev took an active part in the collectivization of agriculture campaign. He then graduated from the prestigious Moscow Foreign Languages Institute and became a Soviet specialist in German-language propaganda. His protests against the barbaric behavior of Soviet army troops in conquered Germany led to his arrest in 1945. He was sentenced to 10 years, which he spent in a *sharaga* (scientific research institutes that employed imprisoned scientists from the GULAG). There he met Aleksandr SOLZHENITSYN, who later modeled Rubin, one of his characters from his novel *The First Circle,* on Kopelev. Released in 1954, Kopelev later played a not unimportant role in the behind-the-scenes activity that led to the publication of Solzhenitsyn's seminal *One Day in the Life of Ivan Denisovich* (1962). Using his former COMMUNIST PARTY connections, Kopelev personally delivered the sensitive manuscript to Aleksandr TVARDOVSKY, editor of the journal *Novyi Mir,* in which the book was first published. A prolific writer, Kopelev published his own work and translations of German writers until 1966, when he became active in the human rights movement and was expelled from the Communist Party. In 1977, he was expelled from the Union of Writers, fired from all his jobs, and was not allowed to publish anymore. He and his wife, Raisa Orlova, emigrated to West Germany in November 1980 and were stripped of their Soviet citizenship the following year.

Korbut, Olga Valentinovna (1955–)
athlete
The unexpected star of the gymnastics competition at the 1972 Munich Olympic games, Korbut was born in Grodno, Lithuania. She trained with the Grodno Armed Forces team and first gained fame in the Soviet sports world when she became USSR champion in 1970, an achievement that she repeated in 1974, 1975, and 1976. At the 1972 Olympics she confounded Western stereotypes about Soviet athletes with her mixture of personality and showmanship, and led the Soviet team, while winning individual gold

and silver medals. For these achievements the Soviet sports community made her an Honored Master of Sports in 1972. Korbut also performed well at the 1976 Montreal Olympic Games, but she was overshadowed by an equally magnetic gymnast, the Romanian Nadia Comaneci. Nevertheless, she still led the Soviet team and won an individual silver medal. With her Olympic career behind her, she completed studies at the Grodno Pedagogical Institute in 1977, and the following year she joined the Minsk Armed Forces team. With Comaneci, Korbut was one of the gymnasts whose achievements and charisma raised the popularity of female gymnastic to new levels.

Kornilov, Lavr Georgievich (1870–1918)
general

For a brief moment in the late summer of 1917, General Kornilov represented the last hope of the conservative forces in Russia who sought to forestall the rapid disintegration of the Provisional Government. Kornilov was born near Karaganda in Russian Kazakhstan, the son of an officer in the Siberian Cossack Army. He graduated from the Mikhailovskoe Artillery School in 1892 and from the Academy of the General Staff in 1898, and was posted to Central Asia. He fought during the RUSSO-JAPANESE WAR of 1904–5, then served as military attaché in China (1907–11). A brigade and later division commander during World War I, he was wounded and taken prisoner by the Austrians in 1915 but escaped the following year. As commander of the Petrograd district after the FEBRUARY REVOLUTION of 1917, he was ordered by Alexander KERENSKY to put the imperial family under guard at Tsarskoe Selo. Kornilov was later appointed commander of the South-Western front in summer 1917. The events that followed have remained unclear after many decades. In late August, Kornilov marched on Petrograd at the head of his "Wild Division." Kornilov later maintained that he had done so on Kerensky's request; Kerensky insisted that this was an attempted coup d'état by Kornilov, representing the last-ditch attempt by conservative and monarchical Russia to reverse the course of the revolution. Regardless of the real motivation, the march failed when Kornilov's detachments disintegrated under the influence of working-class and revolutionary propaganda. The pendulum of Petrograd revolutionary politics now swung back in favor of the workers and their key allies, the BOLSHEVIKS, who could rightly claim they had put down an attempt to defeat their revolution. Kornilov was dismissed and imprisoned for high treason. After the OCTOBER REVOLUTION, he managed to escape and join fellow officers like General ALEKSEEV who were organizing the Volunteer Army in Novocherkassk in southern Russia to fight the BOLSHEVIKS. After Alekseev's death in 1918, Kornilov was appointed commander in chief and led the White retreat into the Kuban region. He was killed in April 1918 while his troops were attacking Ekaterinodar (now Krasnodar).

Korolenko, Vladimir Galaktionovich (1853–1921)
writer

A writer of Ukrainian-Polish background who advocated humanitarian causes and became known as an energetic opponent of any form of injustice, Korolenko was born in Zhitomir. His father was a Ukrainian judge and his mother a member of the Polish nobility. After completing secondary education at Rovno, he studied at the Petersburg Technical Institute (1871) and the Petrovskaia Agricultural Academy in Moscow (1874). A member of the POPULIST movement, Korolenko was in frequent trouble with the czarist authorities during the 1870s and 1880s. He was expelled from school, arrested, and exiled several times between 1879 and 1881 to places like the Russian North, the Urals, and remote Yakutia (Sakha) in Siberia. In 1885, he was exiled again to Nizhnii-Novgorod on the Volga. A journey to the United States to the 1893 World Exhibition gave him material for the description of the first mass emigration from Russia to America at the end of the 19th century. His populist tendencies and moral integrity made him known and influential among the intelligentsia. Korolenko was active in important causes of his day, defending Udmurt peasants accused of ritual murder (1895–96), resigning in protest (with the playwright Anton CHEKHOV) from the Russian Academy after the czar annulled its election of Maksim GORKY, investigating the 1903 Kishinev pogrom, and speaking out in favor of Mendel BEILIS, a Jewish bricklayer accused of ritual murder in 1911. Korolenko's political sympathies were with the Populists, and he served as editor of their influential periodical, *Russkoe Bogatstvo* (*The Russian Wealth*), from 1908 to 1914, although not continuously. After 1902, he mostly lived in the Ukrainian town of Poltava. After the OCTOBER REVOLUTION and during the civil war, he protested vigorously against acts of injustice and terror committed by all participants. Korolenko completely rejected Communist claims of speaking in the name of the whole people, and he was sharply rebuked by LENIN. He died of hunger and deprivation in Poltava during the 1921 famine. A prolific writer, Korolenko is best known for his short stories and his three-volume *Istoriia moego sovremennika* (*History of My Contemporary*), which chronicles his own life in the years between 1905 and 1921. Although a 10-volume edition of his collected works was published after STALIN's death, his brutally honest diary of the civil war in the Ukraine was not published during Soviet times.

Korolev, Sergei Pavlovich (1907–1966)
space rocket designer

The leading designer of the Soviet space program of the 1950s and 1960s. Korolev's contributions were kept secret until after his death in 1966. He was born in Zhitomir, the Ukraine, on January 12, 1907, and graduated from the Odessa Professional School in 1924. Attracted to aviation, he began constructing gliders and worked in Odessa glider clubs. After further studies he graduated in 1929 from the Bauman Higher Technical School in Moscow with a degree in aeromechanics. In 1930 he became a senior design engineer at the Central Air Dynamics Institute. At this time he became acquainted with the pioneer scientist Konstantin Tsiolkovsky and absorbed his interest in rocket and space technology. In 1931, together with F. Tsander, Korolev organized the Group for the Study of Cosmic Travel (GIRD), and in 1933 he transferred to the newly created Institute for Jet Research. During these years Korolev became a leading figure in the development of the Soviet ballistic missile program, but in June 1938, the NKVD (secret police) arrested him for allegedly selling information to a German company. Sentenced to 10 years' hard labor, he was dispatched to Kolyma, but from 1940 he worked in a special prison laboratory on military uses of rocket planes. He was thus one of a remarkable band of scientists who did pioneering work while in prison. Korolev was released in July 1944 and appointed to the team that evaluated German rocket technology after the war. Rehabilitated after STALIN's death in 1953, Korolev joined the COMMUNIST PARTY in 1953 and was elected a corresponding member of the USSR ACADEMY OF SCIENCES. Later in 1958, he became a full academician and was awarded the LENIN PRIZE. During the 1950s his penchant for theoretical research, construction work, and teaching made him a major designer and builder of the space rocket vehicles that placed the Soviet space program at the forefront of space technology. Beginning with the first artificial earth satellite in 1957, Korolev was actively involved in the design of many Soviet rockets, including *Vostok*, *Voskhod*, *Elektron*, *Molniya-I*, and *Kosmos*. He also directed the launches of interplanetary probes to Venus (1961–65) and Mars (1962). His first marriage did not survive the camps and he later married one of his assistants. Korolev died of cancer on January 14, 1966, and is buried in the Kremlin Wall. He was long known in the Soviet press only as "The Designer," and the full story of his arrest was not printed until 1987.

Kosmodemianskaia, Zoia Anatolievna (1923–1941)
partisan fighter

Kosmodemianskaia was born in rural Tambov oblast (province) on September 13, 1923. Her father was an office worker, and she joined the KOMSOMOL in 1938. In October 1941 during World War II, while a tenth-grade student in Moscow, she volunteered for service in a partisan detachment. With a group of other Komsomol members she was sent behind German lines but was captured in late November near the village of Petrishchevo in Moscow oblast trying to set fire to a German supply depot. Tortured by the Germans, she resisted courageously, gave no information, and allegedly made a heroic, defiant speech before her execution by hanging on November 29, 1941. Hard-pressed for victories, the government immediately began constructing a cult that portrayed her as a Soviet Joan of Arc, despite her very short military career and the relative unimportance of her mission. She was proclaimed a Hero of the Soviet Union posthumously on February 6, 1942. A monument to her memory was erected on the Minsk Highway near the village where she was captured and executed. After the war she was reburied in Moscow's Novodeviche Cemetery.

Kosygin, Aleksei Nikolaevich
(1904–1980)
Soviet official

An important figure in the leadership that came to power following the ouster of Nikita KHRUSH-CHEV in 1964, Kosygin served as prime minister from 1964 until his death in 1980. He was born in St. Petersburg to a working-class family. At the age of 15 he joined the Red Army and fought in the civil war. In 1924 he finished the secondary schooling he had interrupted and spent the next five years working with consumer cooperatives in Siberia. While in Siberia, he was promoted rapidly, especially after joining the COMMUNIST PARTY in 1927. In 1935 he graduated from the Leningrad Textile Institute and began working as a textile engineer. His work drew the attention of the new city party leader, Andrei ZHDANOV, at a time when the ranks of the party and government were being depleted by the Great Purge. A talented administrator, Kosygin rose rapidly

through the government, from USSR commissar for the textile industry in 1939 to minister of light industry in 1953 and deputy chairman of the Council of Ministers. He also rose within the party, becoming a full member of the Politburo in 1948. Sheer luck saved him from being caught up in the LENINGRAD AFFAIR, the deadly purge orchestrated by Georgii MALENKOV in 1949–50 against the protégés of Zhdanov, who had died in 1948. After some career setbacks, Kosygin again benefited from the decline of Malenkov's post-Stalin influence in 1955. In 1957, he became a candidate member of the Presidium (Politburo) and the following year was appointed as director of Gosplan, the state planning agency. By 1960 he was once again a full member of the Presidium, albeit with far more administrative authority, since he was also named first deputy prime minister. Blocked by Khrushchev from becoming prime minister, Kosygin joined the anti-Khrushchev conspiracy of October 1964, although in a secondary role. While BREZHNEV assumed the post of party general secretary, Kosygin became prime minister, and in this capacity tried to launch the "Kosygin reforms" in 1965, a package of reforms designed to make enterprises more self-sufficient, yet responsible for their performance. Threatened by changes that could minimize its leading role in economic affairs, the party bureaucracy successfully diluted their impact. The Soviet-led WARSAW PACT invasion of Czechoslovakia in August 1968 and the subsequent chill in Soviet political life put an end to the type of reformism proposed by Kosygin. Loyal to Brezhnev, he continued to serve as prime minister until October 1980, two months before his death.

Kovalevskaia, Sofiia Vasilievna
(1850–1891)
mathematician

The first Russian woman to hold the rank of professor at an institution of higher learning, Kovalevskaia was born Sofia Korvina-Krukovskaia in Moscow to a well-educated noble family. Her father was an artillery general in the imperial army. Her precocious interest in mathematics was reportedly sparked by her father's school notes on differential and integral equations that were used as temporary wallpaper in the children's rooms of the family estate. Nevertheless, at age 17 she was studying with a mathematics professor from the St. Petersburg Naval Academy. A marriage of convenience in 1868—common to Russian women of her time seeking emancipation—to Vladimir Kovalevsky, a paleontologist, brought her to Germany. Unable to attend university lectures, she took private courses at Heidelberg and Berlin, where she studied with Weierstrass for four years. In 1874, remarkable research papers on partial differential equations, integrals, and Saturn's rings earned her a doctorate in absentia from the University of Gottingen. Unable to find a teaching position in Europe, Kovalevskaia returned to Russia, where her husband was expecting a lectureship at Moscow University. The position never materialized and Kovalevsky committed suicide in 1883 after his name came up in connection with shady business deals. In 1884 Kovalevskaia's mentor, Weierstrass, helped arrange a mathematics lectureship at the University of Stockholm; in 1889, she was promoted to the rank of professor. While at Stockholm, she carried out important research and wrote *On the Rotation of a Solid Body About a Fixed Point* (1888), which earned her the prestigious Prix Bordin from the French Academy of Sciences. She also served as editor of the journal *Acta Mathematica*. Further research on this subject won her a prize from the Swedish Academy of Sciences, and in 1889 she was elected a corresponding member of the Russian ACADEMY OF SCIENCES. At the height of her career, Kovalevskaia died in Stockholm on February 10, 1891, from influenza complicated by pneumonia. Kovalevskaia was also an accomplished writer. In *Recollections of Childhood* she describes the early life of a woman of the intelligentsia. A fictionalized version appeared as *The Sisters Rajevsky*. Other novels such as *Vera Vorontsov, The University Lecturer,* and a drama, *The Struggle for Happiness,* were highly regarded.

Kozlov, Petr Kuzmich (1863–1935)
explorer

The leader of the 1907–9 expedition that discovered the remains of the ancient city of Khara-Khoto in the Gobi Desert, Kozlov was born in Smolensk province, the son of a herdsman. After graduating from military school he took part in the Central Asian expeditions of PRZHEVALSKY, Pevtsov, and Roborovskii. From 1899 to 1901, he directed his first Mongolian-Tibetan expedition, which made important contributions to the knowledge of the ethnography, climate, vegetation, and geology of eastern Tibet. The results of this expedition were published in eight volumes, *Mongolia and Kam (Mongolia i Kam)* (1905–8). His most important discovery would come with the expedition he led to Mongolia and Szechuan, China, in 1907–9. Amid the sands of the Gobi Desert his team uncovered the ancient city of Khara-Khoto, along with materials that revealed much about the culture of the Tanguts, including over 2,000 volumes of books written in Tangut, Chinese, and other languages. The published results of this expedition did not appear until 1923, when Kozlov published *Mongolia and Amdo and the Dead City of Khara-Khoto (Mongoliia i Amdo i mertvyi gorod Khara-Khoto)*. He undertook his last major expedition to Mongolia and Tibet between 1923 and 1926. This time in the mountains of Khentei, his team uncovered the burial mound of Noin-Ula, belonging to the Hunnic aristocracy and dating back to the Christian era.

Kronstadt Rebellion (1921)

An uprising of sailors in March 1921 at the Kronstadt naval base that shook the foundations of the Soviet state and convinced LENIN and the COMMUNIST PARTY of the need to move toward a more moderate economic policy, later known as the New Economic Policy (NEP). Located on the island of Kotlin in the Gulf of Finland, about 14 miles west of Petrograd (St. Petersburg), which commanded the approach to the city, the naval base grew around the town of Krontstadt, founded in 1703 by PETER I the Great, and the fortress built in 1710. The sailors of Kronstadt had a long tradition of political activism, having mutinied in 1825 and 1882 and during the revolutions of 1905 and 1917. From the time of the 1917 Revolution they had provided some of the most ardent support to the BOLSHEVIKS. By 1921, however, after three long years of economic hardship and growing political repression, the feeling that the Bolsheviks had lost touch with the original goals of the Russian Revolution had become widespread among the sailors. The 1921 uprising was a clear sign of the distance that had developed between the regime and its early supporters.

The revolt began in February 1921 in solidarity with striking workers in Petrograd, whose demands were met by violence from the Soviet government. On February 28, sailors meeting on board the battleship *Petropavlovsk* approved a resolution that called for secret-ballot elections open to all socialist parties, not just the Communist, for the soviets, which were the centerpiece of the revolutionary democracy they had supported in 1917. They also called for the abolition of the Cheka, the political police, whose existence, they believed, was no longer necessary now that the civil war had ended. Other demands included the abolition of TROTSKY'S labor armies and an end to forceful grain requisitioning from the peasantry. When the Communist Party responded by calling the sailors counterrevolutionaries and demanding their surrender, the sailors set up a Provisional Revolutionary Committee. The initial Red Army offensives against the sailors across the frozen Gulf of Finland were successfully repelled by the Kronstadt garrison, but eventually the sailors were defeated on March 18.

In defeat, the revolt had two important consequences. Shocked by the rebellion among its once most loyal supporters, the Communist Party moved to liberalize the economy after the privations of the civil war. At the same time, it tightened the lid on political expression by outlawing the remaining non-Communist parties.

Kropotkin, Petr Alekseevich (1842–1921)
scientist and revolutionary

Like Mikhail BAKUNIN, Russia's other prominent 19th-century anarchist, Kropotkin was born into a prominent aristocratic family. Unlike Bakunin, he was more of a theorist than a man of action, and he also became a respected international scholar who made important contributions in the field of geography. Born in Moscow and educated at an elite military school in St. Petersburg, Kropotkin served in the army in the Far East, where he made pioneering explorations. He resigned his commission in 1867 and joined the revolutionary movement, journeying from POPULISM to socialism to anarchism. Kropotkin was a leading member of the Chaikovsky Circle, agitating among workers in St. Petersburg and advocating anarchist insurrection and social revolution. While in Switzerland in 1872, he joined the First International, siding with Bakunin against Marx. Back in Russia, he was arrested in 1874 but escaped in 1876, and spent the next 40 years in western Europe. In exile, he became one of the best-known propagandists in the international anarchist movement, advocating a theory of anarchist communism based on mutual aid. Kropotkin opposed all state power and advocated the abolition of states and private property, as well as the transformation of humankind into a federation of mutual-aid communities. He spoke at lectures and discussions, wrote articles in the anarchist and liberal press, and produced pamphlets and books. He was expelled from Switzerland in 1881 and imprisoned in France, 1883–86, before settling in London, his home for the next three decades. As a geographer, Kropotkin contributed to knowledge about Manchuria and eastern Siberia, and proved that the main structural lines of Asia run from southwest to northeast. Kropotkin welcomed the FEBRUARY REVOLUTION of 1917 and returned to Russia the same year. His support for the war effort and the Provisional Government left him with little influence after the Bolshevik revolution of October 1917. The BOLSHEVIKS made tactical use of

Prince Petr Kropotkin *(Library of Congress)*

the anarchists before the OCTOBER REVOLUTION but came down hard on them afterward. Kropotkin served as the conscience of the anarchist movement and protested against the Allied intervention and the growing excesses of the new regime. His funeral was the last great anarchist demonstration, and his home in Moscow became a shrine and a museum until 1938. Kropotkin was and remains the most widely read anarchist writer, and his version of anarchist theory was the most influential contribution to the anarchist movement in Russia as elsewhere, though his direct participation was only slight.

Krupskaya, Nadezhda Konstantinovna (1869–1939)
revolutionary

LENIN's longtime companion, spouse, and comrade, Krupskaya was born in St. Petersburg. Her father, an impoverished military officer, harbored secret radical sympathies, and Krupskaya grew up with a desire to promote the well-being of Russia's downtrodden masses. Before becoming a Marxist, she was strongly influenced by Tolstoyan ideals. She met her future partner, Vladimir Lenin, in 1894 through the Social Democratic underground circles of the capital. Both were arrested in 1895–96, and she was allowed to accompany him into exile by claiming to be his fiancée. They formally married in July 1898 but never had children; the revolutionary cause was their full-time occupation. She then followed Lenin a year later, moving with him from place to place in 1901–16. During these years, Krupskaya made an invaluable and overlooked contribution as Lenin's main secretarial assistant to the growth of the BOLSHEVIK faction. She also kept her lifelong interest in education and the movement for the emancipation of women, helping ensure that the party did not ignore these issues. Krupskaya returned with Lenin from Switzerland aboard the "sealed train" in April 1917. In the period leading up to the OCTOBER REVOLUTION, she saw little of him as their political paths and views briefly diverged. Unconvinced of the need for an early Bolshevik revolution, she instead worked on reforming education. She visited him twice while he was hiding in Finland, after the failure of the JULY DAYS. After the October Revolution, they were reunited. Krupskaya was appointed deputy people's commissar of enlightenment under Anatolii LUNACHARSKY, where she continued her work on education. STALIN's rudeness toward her was the spark that made Lenin plan his dismissal from influential posts, but Lenin's illness intervened and it was never done. After Lenin's death in 1924, her status as Lenin's widow protected Krupskaya from Stalin's animosity and growing vindictiveness. Opposed to Lenin's deification by his successors, she tried without success to influence the management of the Lenin cult. She died on February 27, 1939.

Kruzenshtern, Ivan Feodorovich (1770–1846)
admiral and explorer

A sailor and explorer, Kruzenshtern is best known for directing the first Russian naval expedition that traveled around the world from 1803 to 1806. He graduated from the Imperial Naval College in St. Petersburg in 1788, and in 1793 he began a six-year tour of duty with the British fleet. From 1803 to 1806 he commanded the first Russian naval expedition to circumnavigate the globe. Kruzenshtern commanded the ship *Nadezhda* (Hope), while Captain Iu. F. Lisianskii commanded the *Neva*. Among the other participants in the expedition was the 16-year-old Otto von Kotzebue, later to visit Easter Island and the South Pacific on his own expeditions (1815–18), and Fabian von Bellinghausen, who became the first to circumnavigate Antarctica (1819–21). Apart from detailed geographic and statistical descriptions of Kamchatka, Russia's American possessions, the Pacific Ocean islands, and the coastal regions of southeastern China, the expedition members conducted important ethnological and oceanographic investigations. Their descriptions from the voyage contain data about the socioeconomic structure, religions, customs, and traditions of the various peoples of Kamchatka, Sakhalin Island, and Oceania. Kruzenshtern's account of his expedition, *Voyage around the World in 1803, 1804, 1805 and 1806,* was first published between 1809 and 1813. In subsequent years, he devoted himself to education and the introduction of new pedagogical techniques, as director of the Naval College from 1827 to 1842. An honorary member of the ACADEMY OF SCIENCES since 1806, Kruzenshtern was one of the founding members of the Russian Geographical Society and member of many foreign scientific societies.

Krylov, Ivan Andreevich (1769–1844)
writer

Known as the "Russian La Fontaine" and beloved by generations of Russian children, Krylov was a journalist, critic, and playwright who found his niche in writing fables. Krylov was born into a middle-class Moscow family that had fallen into hard times; his father was an army officer who died while he was still a child. To help his mother,

Krylov began working when he was 10 years old as a merchant's clerk. A lonely boy, he wrote prolifically and, by his teens, had tried his hand at opera, comedy, and drama. Although he had no formal education, he managed to learn several languages. After a stint in Tver, Krylov moved to St. Petersburg, where he was befriended by the leading journalists of the day, Nikolai NOVIKOV and Aleksandr RADISHCHEV. With their assistance he edited a satirical journal in 1789–90 with the initial encouragement of the empress, CATHERINE II. When Catherine abandoned her liberal sympathies and imprisoned Novikov and exiled Radishchev, Krylov was fortunate to receive only a minor scolding from the censors. For the next decade, Krylov withdrew into obscurity, reemerging in 1805 as a translator of La Fontaine's fables. Inspired by this work, he began to compose his own fables, the first volume of which, *Basni,* was published in 1809 to great acclaim. Czar ALEXANDER I was impressed by the effort and offered him a sinecure at the St. Petersburg library, where he remained until 1840. Krylov used his free time well, writing eight more volumes of original verse fables, with the last one appearing in 1843, one year before his death. All in all, he wrote more than 200 fables.

As a fabulist, Krylov enjoyed great success in his lifetime both in Russia, where school children memorized his tales, and in Europe and England, where his fame spread thanks to the efforts of translators. The secret of his success seems to have derived from his affable personality, which his fables reflect, and his ability to write stories that poke fun at private and public vices in a gentle, rather than bitter manner. In the deceptively nonthreatening genre of the fable and using the colloquial language of peasants that he had first heard while working near Volga River barges in Tver, he was able to express his critical views in a way that appealed to a wide audience. His fables did not lose their appeal after the Russian Revolution, and the centenary of his death was celebrated with great fanfare in 1944. A monument to Krylov was erected at one end of Moscow's famous Patriarch's Pond.

kulak

An epithet, derived from the Russian word for "fist," that assumed an important role in the Russian and political vocabulary of the first three decades of the 20th century. The initial application of the term, in prerevolutionary 1917, referred to those peasants who chose to break away from the village commune under the provisions of the land reform inaugurated by Prime Minister Peter STOLYPIN in 1906. Known as the "wager on the strong," Stolypin sought to create a class of landowning peasants that would be less vulnerable to revolutionary propaganda by virtue of having a stake in land ownership. In many villages, kulaks became prominent figures, owning their homes and livestock and often hiring other peasants to work their fields. There was also an element of resentment against kulaks that would reemerge in postrevolutionary political discourse. Response to the reforms was not overwhelming—by 1916 only 10 percent of peasants had taken advantage of the opportunity—but a full assessment of the appeal of this program is not possible because of the role of World War I and the Russian revolutions of 1917, followed by a different landholding structure inaugurated by the Soviet government.

After the 1917 Revolutions the term *kulak* found its way into Communist propaganda to refer to the comparatively prosperous peasants whom the Soviet government disenfranchised and subjected to heavier taxation. Under the New Economic Policy, wealthier peasants briefly received preferential treatment. In the difficult decades after the revolution, however, notions of wealth among the peasants were purely relative; in some cases commentators made the wry observation that a kulak had two cows where a regular peasant had only one. The onset of collectivization in 1929 added another dimension to the term, which was now used quite broadly by the government and its propaganda machinery to designate any peasant who opposed collectivization. As the struggle over collectivization intensified, the government announced a policy of "dekulakization," or "liquidating the kulaks as a class." In human terms, this meant the disappearance of more than 5 million peasant households; their members were either killed or deported to labor camps or to remote areas as "special settlers." The losses to Soviet agriculture caused by the collectivization campaign and dekulakization were immense, and their impact was felt for decades to come.

Kuleshov, Lev Vladimirovich
(1899–1970)
film director

One of the great pioneers of early Soviet cinema, Kuleshov was born in Tambov, and started in the film industry as a stage designer in 1916. As the first documentary filmmaker during the Russian civil war, he developed many of the techniques of editing and special effects that would help Soviet propaganda films attain an overall high artistic quality in the 1920s. His first film, *Na krasnom fronte* (On the Red Front), was one of the first agit-films screened around the country on the agitational trains developed by the BOLSHEVIKS. In 1919 he founded the State Film School, where he taught until 1930. Some of the more prominent names of Soviet cinema in the 1920s, including Vsevolod PUDOVKIN, Boris Barnet, S. Komarov, and his future wife, Aleksandra Khokhlova, were graduates of his influential workshop. His better-known films include the classic *The Extraordinary Adventures of Mr. West in the Land of the Bolsheviks* (1924) and an adaptation of Jack London's *By the Law* (1926). In the 1930s, Kuleshov was attacked for "formalist" tendencies in his work, particularly his strongly held belief that actors should submerge their identities and become complete instruments of the director. He partially redeemed himself with his 1940 production, *The Siberians,* which portrayed STALIN in a way that pleased the authorities. From 1944 on, he taught again at the State Film Institute (VGIK), but his creative spark no longer burned as brightly from the pressures of political harassment and World War II.

Kulikovo, Battle of (1380)

A battle ending in a Russian victory over Mongol forces that has traditionally been celebrated as a turning point in the Russians' attempt to free themselves from Mongol rule but whose importance was more symbolic than real. The showdown at Kulikovo followed a series of clashes between MOSCOW and the GOLDEN HORDE during the 1370s, including a minor Muscovite victory near the Vozha River in 1378. The battle of Kulikovo itself was fought on September 8, 1380, in an area known as Kulikovo Field (Kulikovo Pole), where the Nepriadva River flows into the Don. The Russian armies, led by Grand Prince Dmitrii of Moscow, son of IVAN II, chose to fight on a hilly terrain intersected by streams that minimized the Mongol cavalry's ability to simply surround the Russians. Later, highly embellished accounts of the battle estimated as many as hundreds of thousands on each side, but a more realistic estimate places the numbers of each army at less than 10,000 soldiers. By the end of the day, the Mongol armies led by Khan Mamai had been routed. Their Lithuanian allies reached the battle site two days later and chose not to fight. For his leadership in battle, Dmitrii was henceforth known as DMITRII DONSKOI, in remembrance of the site by the Don River where his armies had first defeated the Mongols. The Russian victory at Kulikovo was the first major defeat of the Mongols since they had conquered the lands of KIEVAN RUS in 1240–42. It strengthened the claims of the rulers of Moscow to an ascendancy over the other Russian principalities. But it marked only the beginning of the end of Mongol rule over Russia. In 1382, only two years after the battle, Mongol armies led by Khan Tokhtamysh entered Moscow and sacked and burned the city. It was only in 1480 that a later Muscovite prince, IVAN III, was able to successfully shake off Mongol rule after the battle of the UGRA RIVER.

Kurchatov, Igor Vasilievich (1903–1960)
physicist

Considered the father of Soviet nuclear power, Kurchatov was born near Chelyabinsk in the Urals. He was educated at Tauride University in Simferopol, the Crimea, graduating in physics. After graduation he taught in Baku before moving to Leningrad (St. Petersburg), where he taught at Leningrad University and the Leningrad Physico-Technical Institute. Kurchatov's research in the 1930s on nuclear chain reactions under neutron bombardment and artificial radioactivity and his theory of nuclear isomerism established him as a major authority on nuclear energy. In 1943 he was elected to the USSR ACADEMY OF SCIENCES and to its Presidium, and provided with a laboratory in Moscow, which subsequently became the Kurchatov Institute of Atomic Energy. He was also appointed director of the Soviet attempt to build an atomic bomb. During these years Kurchatov skillfully handled administration and research while having the unenviable job of working directly under secret police chief Lavrenty BERIA. Kurchatov joined the COMMUNIST PARTY in 1948. He supervised the first Soviet atomic test in 1949 and the first hydrogen bomb test in 1953. After STALIN's death in 1953, he tried to promote collaboration with Western scientists and protected geneticists (the discipline had been banned as a bourgeois pseudoscience in 1948), informing KHRUSHCHEV that Trofim LYSENKO was a charlatan. However, Khrushchev was deaf to reason where Lysenko was concerned. Kurchatovium, the 104th element of the periodic table, is named after him.

Kursk, Battle of (July–August 1943)

Kursk, in southwestern Russia, was the site of the largest tank battle in World War II, involving about 6,000 tanks and 4,000 airplanes on both sides. The stage for a major confrontation was set when German forces, already defeated at Stalingrad, decided to prevent Soviet forces from reinforcing by attacking the salient near the city of Kursk. German plans called for the concentration of the German Ninth Army and the Fourth Panzer Army to form two pincers that would encircle Soviet forces. For this operation all available German armor was to be concentrated. Together the Germans had 35 divisions with close to 1,800 tactical airplanes and 3,000 tanks, including the German Mark VI Tiger, considered the world's most powerful tank. The German attack was repeatedly postponed owing to equipment delays and top-level disagreements, so that by the time it actually began on July 4, the Germans had lost the crucial element of surprise. A Soviet counterattack on July 11 neutralized the initial German attack on the northern side. A second German attack on July 10, on the southern side of the salient, was more successful and led to the tank battle at the village of Prokhorovka. Close to 1,500 tanks were engaged while a furious air battle raged overhead. As both sides brought up reinforcements, the battle escalated until the Germans, concerned about the impact of the Allied landing in Sicily, suspended their maneuvers and began a withdrawal on July 17. Soviet forces then opened their offensive while Soviet partisans attacked the German rear. When the battle ended in mid-August 1943, the estimated losses on the German side were 70,000 troops killed and captured and 2,950 tanks and 1,400 aircraft destroyed—irreplaceable losses so soon after the disaster at STALINGRAD. Soviet losses were also heavy, but the men and weapons could be quickly replaced. The Kursk battle marked the end of German offensives on the eastern front and was followed immediately by the first Soviet summer offensive of the war.

Kutuzov, Mikhail Ilarionovich (1745–1813)
field marshal

Kutuzov began his military career as a lecturer in mathematics at the Artillery School in 1759, at the age of only 14. First posted in Poland in 1764–65, he fought in the Turkish wars of 1768–74 and 1787–91. After a mission to Constantinople (1792–94), Kutuzov was appointed director of the Cadet Corps in 1794. Several government appointments followed in the next decade: in Finland (1795–99), as governor of Lithuania (1799–1801), and governor of St. Petersburg (1801–02), after which he retired.

Kutuzov was brought back to face Napoleon and the invading French army at the Battle of Austerlitz (1805), but he was forced to defer to ALEXANDER I's leadership. Another round of government appointments followed: governor of Kiev (1806–7), of Moldavia (1808), of Lithuania (1809–11). Kutuzov was again in Moldavia as commander of the Russian army in the RUSSO-TURKISH WAR OF 1811, and he negotiated the Peace of Bucharest. Kutuzov succeeded BARCLAY DE TOLLY a few weeks before the Battle of BORODINO, and despite temporarily surrendering Moscow to the French in September 1812, subsequently he drove Napoleon's armies out of Russia by December 1812. He was widely popular among his people but disliked by Alexander I. An officer who was highly rated by SUVOROV, Kutuzov was able to play his bulky form and folksy manner to advantage against his opponents, who tended to underestimate him. His legend as the wise old man who had defeated Napoleon was greatly enhanced by the sympathetic portrait of him written by Tolstoy in *War and Peace* (1868–69).

Kuznetsov, Anatolii Vasilievich (1929–1979)
writer

One of the brightest lights among a stellar group of young Soviet writers in the early 1960s, Kuznetsov was born in Kiev and lived through the German occupation of the Ukraine during World War II. At the age of 15, he received a national prize for a short story submitted to *Pionerskaia Pravda* in 1946. He worked as a construction worker on some of the grand hydroelectric stations of the 1950s—Kakhovka (1952) and Irkutsk (1956). His convincing description of young workers in the novel *Prodolzhenie legendy* (1956) won him national and international acclaim. He was accepted into the elite Gorky Literary Institute in Moscow, graduating in 1960. His career changed substantially with the events surrounding his sensational work, *Babi Yar,* a novel that told about the Nazi German mass murder of Jews in the BABI YAR ravines of

Kiev. (YEVTUSHENKO's famous poem of the same name drew from Kuznetsov's original account.) Heavily censored by the authorities, Kuznetsov began to consider emigration. At the height of his popularity among Soviet youth, he sought political asylum in 1969, while on a trip to London to research LENIN's life in Britain. An uncensored translation of *Babi Yar* was published in the West to great acclaim soon after, but Kuznetsov was unable to otherwise replicate his previous literary success. Instead he worked for Radio Liberty and gained a wide Soviet audience through broadcasts that appealed to listeners through their style, wit, and honesty. He died in London of heart failure, a month after the birth of his daughter.

L

Landau, Lev Davidovich (1908–1968)

physicist

Landau was a prominent Soviet theoretical physicist who received the 1962 Nobel Prize in physics, primarily for his work in the field of cryogenics, or low-temperature physics. Born and raised in a Jewish family in Baku, Azerbaijan, Landau attended universities in Baku and Leningrad, graduating from Leningrad State University in 1927. After pursuing postgraduate studies in Denmark, Switzerland, and the United Kingdom, he moved to Kharkov, in Soviet Ukraine, in 1932 to work for the Physico-technical Institute. In 1937 he was appointed to teach theoretical physics at the S.I. Vavilov Institute of Physical Problems in Moscow. The following year he was arrested and held until 1939. Following his release he worked with the noted physicist Petr KAPITSA and was admitted to the USSR ACADEMY OF SCIENCES. Landau worked in several fields and published over 100 papers and numerous books, including a nine-volume *Course of Theoretical Physics,* cowritten with Y. M. Lifshitz and published in 1943. Among his contributions to Soviet physics are works in atomic and nuclear physics, stellar energy, as well as contributions to the development of Soviet space technology. His work on the behavior of liquid helium, developing mathematical theories that explain the superfluidity of liquid helium at temperatures near absolute zero, as well as the possibility of predicting the sound wave diffusion of liquid helium at two speeds account for his lasting reputation. For this he was cited for the Nobel Prize.

In January 1962, he was injured seriously in an automobile accident, suffering seemingly irreversible brain damage and loss of memory. He was treated by the celebrated Soviet psychologist Alexander LURIA, who during World War II had developed novel treatments to restore the psychological functions of patients with severe head injuries. With Luria's guidance, Landau made a significant recovery.

Lavrov, Petr Lavrovich (1823–1900)

revolutionary theorist

Lavrov was a respected intellectual with interests in mathematics, ethics, and history who made important contributions to the development of POPULISM as a revolutionary ideology. An army officer of gentry origin, Lavrov espoused reformist sentiments that brought him into contact with St. Petersburg radical circles in 1855. He contributed to liberal journals on sociology, philosophy, and anthropology and edited the *Encyclopedic Dictionary* (1864–66). He was arrested for revolutionary activities in 1866 and banished to Vologda province, in the north. While in Vologda he wrote his most important contribution to Russian radical social thought, *Historical Letters* (1868–69). Lavrov emigrated from Russia in 1870, becoming an important member of the revolutionary émigré community. He joined the First International and edited the journal *Vpered!* (*Forward!*) from 1873 to 1876, in which he continued to advocate a relatively moderate political line. Widely respected for his gentility and humanity, Lavrov often vacillated in his ideas. For example, at the time of the PEOPLE'S WILL's assassination of ALEXANDER II, he was temporarily swayed by the ideas of revolutionary terrorism. A similar vacillation characterized his philosophical views. He began as an advocate of "subjectivist sociology," arguing that progress came about from the deliberate action of "critically thinking individuals," intellectuals who were morally obligated to promote progress until all social institutions were based on truth and justice. Later, in part under Marxist influence, he came to allot a greater role to the supposed objective laws of social development; however, he never became a full-fledged historical determinist, and his rationalistic secular progressivism rested on a suppressed ethical impulse. His idea that the Russian intelligentsia and the educated classes owed a moral debt to Russia's oppressed classes and his reworking of the Petrine idea of service to argue that the intelligentsia's duty was service to the people were crucial influences in the development of populist thought of the 1870s.

Lena Goldfields massacre (1912)

A massacre of miners in April 1912 that achieved great notoriety in the Russian press and contributed to the revitalization of worker activism on the eve of World War I, after the wave of repressions that had followed the 1905 Revolution. The Lena Goldfields, a complex of highly profitable gold mines located almost 2,000 miles to the northeast of Irkutsk in Siberia, belonged to the Lena Gold-Producing Association, a joint stock society dominated by English interests. Count Sergei WITTE, the former prime minister, and prominent members of the royal family were among its shareholders. Although dividends were high for its investors, worker conditions were deplorable. Working days of 16 hours were not uncommon and few provisions were made for the safety of workers. The mines were run as a typical company town; workers were paid low wages, often in kind with shoddy goods from the company shops. A spontaneous strike that began on February 29, 1912, over the sale of rotten horseflesh at the company store developed into a full-fledged strike involving over 6,000 miners. Organized into strike committees, the miners demanded eight-hour workdays, pay raises, and the abolition of fines paid to the employers. After

an initial threat of fines and then partial concessions failed to quell the strike, the administration decided to suppress it with violence. On April 5, as a crowd of about 2,500 gathered to protest the arrest of strike committee members, a detachment of soldiers and security guards was ordered to open fire on the workers. When the shooting was over, about 250 workers were killed and more than 270 wounded. News of the massacre and the ensuing outrage helped promote worker solidarity and pressured the government to send an investigative commission to the mines. An independent commission of lawyers sympathetic to the workers, including Aleksandr KERENSKY, also traveled to the mines on a fact-finding mission. The strike continued until August 12, when the final party of workingmen decided to leave the mines. In all, about 9,000 men left the Lena mines. Outrage over the massacre led to sympathy strikes across Russia that involved over 700,000 workers.

Lenin, Vladimir Ilich (1870–1924)
revolutionary and Soviet leader

An important Marxist theorist, Lenin led his Russian Communist (Bolshevik) Party to power in October 1917 and was the first leader of the new Soviet state until his death in January 1924. He was born Vladimir Ilich Ulianov on April 24, 1870, in the VOLGA RIVER town of Simbirsk, later renamed Ulianovsk in his honor, the third of six children. His father was a school inspector whose position gave him noble status, while his mother was the daughter of an army doctor. The execution in 1887 of Lenin's older brother, Aleksandr, after an unsuccessful attempt on the life of Czar ALEXANDER III changed the family's fortunes and set Lenin on the path of becoming a revolutionary. After completing his law studies with distinction in 1892 as an external student, he moved to St. Petersburg, where he briefly practiced law but soon became involved in revolutionary circles, gaining notoriety as a fierce debater and defender of revolutionary Marxism. After a brief trip to Switzerland in 1895, he returned to St. Petersburg and joined his future antagonist Yuli MARTOV in founding the Union of Struggle for the Emancipation of the Working Class, a Marxist group that sought to organize the capital's industrial workers. One of its early members was Nadezhda KRUPSKAYA, later to become his wife and lifelong partner. In 1897, Lenin was arrested and sentenced to three years of Siberian exile, and Krupskaya joined him a year later. Freed from most distractions, he wrote copiously and quickly produced his first major study, *The Development of Capitalism in Russia* (1899), an attempt to study contemporary Russian society from a Marxist perspective.

Released from exile, he settled in western Europe and joined Georgi PLEKHANOV and Martov in editing the revolutionary socialist newspaper *Iskra* (*The Spark*). In his influential pamphlet *What Is to Be Done?* (1902), Lenin developed his own views about the organization of an underground revolutionary party, arguing for a small, disciplined party of full-time professional revolutionaries. This brought him into conflict with Plekhanov and Martov, and eventually led to a split in the Russian Social Democratic Party in 1903, between supporters of Lenin, known as BOLSHEVIKS (majority), and Martov, known as Mensheviks (minority). After a brief return to Russia on the occasion of the 1905 Revolution, Lenin left again in 1907, moving frequently, before settling in Switzerland in August 1914. For the next few years, he spoke and wrote actively against World War I and its support from many moderate socialists. Another important work, *Imperialism: The Highest Stage of Capitalism* (1916), argued that the war was a conflict between rival imperialist powers and that only the overthrow of capitalism could end it. He attended the two Zimmerwald Conferences organized by antiwar socialists, but by 1916 his hopes for revolution in Russia were dwindling. He even wrote privately that he feared he would not see revolution in his lifetime.

After the abdication of NICHOLAS II in March 1917, Lenin returned to Russia thanks to the mischievous efforts of the German government,

Vladimir Ilich Lenin, ca. 1920 *(Library of Congress)*

which provided a "sealed train" for the passage of Lenin and his retinue through German soil in the hopes that Lenin would create trouble for the new Russian government. Back in Petrograd (St. Petersburg), Lenin argued for an uncompromising Bolshevik policy calling for the overthrow of the Provisional Government, the transfer of power to the Petrograd Soviet, and an end to the war. Through the summer of 1917 the Bolshevik Party's fortunes rose, despite the temporary setback of the failed insurrection of the JULY DAYS that forced Lenin to flee to Finland. From hiding, he insisted to his reluctant comrades on the need to overthrow the Provisional Government, eventually overcoming their resistance after his secret return to Petrograd in mid-

October. He finally convinced his party to support an immediate insurrection to coincide with the forthcoming Second Congress of Soviets. Lenin's analysis proved correct, as the Provisional Government fell without much resistance on October 25 (November 7), 1917.

As chairman of the Council of People's Commissars, Lenin quickly nationalized land, demobilized the army, and arranged for peace with the Central Powers. From December 1917 to November 1920, the Bolshevik government fought a bloody civil war that brought great hardship and threatened to fragment Russia permanently. Surrounded by White forces and their foreign allies, isolated from other socialists who felt the revolution was premature, and mired in a deep economic crisis of industrial production and severe food shortages, the dictatorial underpinnings of Lenin's Bolshevism rose to the surface: internal opposition within the party was restricted, other socialists like the Mensheviks and Socialist Revolutionaries (SRs) were persecuted, and a new ruthless secret police—the Cheka—was established to root out enemies of the revolution. In 1919, the Bolshevik Party was renamed COMMUNIST PARTY and the Third International was established to coordinate and guide the efforts of other loyal communist parties. Anti-Bolshevik peasant revolts, riots, strikes, and demonstrations were common during the civil war, culminating in the March 1921 rebellion at the Kronstadt naval base, an erstwhile hotbed of pro-Bolshevik radicalism. Under great pressure from Lenin, that same month the Communist Party approved a degree of free trade and small manufacture while retaining control of the "commanding heights" of the economy, a less radical program known as the New Economic Policy, which remained in place until the late 1920s.

Between May 1922 and March 1923, Lenin suffered three strokes that partially paralyzed him and took away his power of speech. His final writings reflect his disillusionment with the bureaucratization of the party (*Better Fewer, but Better*) and the shortcomings of its main leaders (*Last Testament*), especially STALIN's rude personal style. He

died on January 21, 1924. His warnings to others calling for Stalin's removal went unheeded. His remains were embalmed and placed in RED SQUARE in a specially designed LENIN MAUSOLEUM that became a place of state-sponsored pilgrimage during the remainder of the Soviet period and still stands a decade after the dissolution of the Soviet Union.

Leningrad, siege of (1941–1944)

One of the examples of heroic Soviet resistance to the German invaders during World War II, the siege of Leningrad lasted from August 1941 to January 1944. In August 1941 German forces surrounded the city and cut the Leningrad-Moscow railway. When an initial attempt to capture the city failed, the Germans released their Panzer divisions to fight elsewhere, and settled down for a siege of the city. Hitler wanted to level the city and hand territory over to the Finns, who, being recent victims of Soviet aggression in the WINTER WAR of 1939–40, were fighting on the side of the Germans. Finnish troops advanced on Leningrad from the north but halted at their pre-1939 border, altering the initial German plans to use the Finns to surround the city. German artillery and aircraft pounded the city and Leningrad's 3 million people faced a long winter of likely starvation. The only supply route open to the city was across Lake Ladoga. Soviet naval units brought in food and fuel and took out refugees. When the lake froze, the Soviets sent supplies in by truck. About 500,000 people managed to leave the city, but the starving in the city continued. Incredibly, so did war production. The factories, despite bombardment and a malnourished work force, turned out tanks, ammunition, and other war matériel. Soviet forces vainly tried to break the siege, but not until January 1943 were they able to make a breach wide enough and deep enough to relieve the city. By then, amid reports of cannibalism and desperate thefts of food, hundreds of thousands had died. The complete lifting of the siege came in January 1944, when Soviet

Leningrad inhabitants, including women, using shovels and picks construct antitank ditches during the siege of Leningrad, 1942. *(Library of Congress)*

forces, fighting along a broad front, drove the Germans more than 50 miles from the devastated city. For the first time in 900 days, the survivors of Leningrad could walk the rubble-filled streets without the fear of a German air raid. STALIN declared Leningrad a Hero City; one of thirteen Soviet cities to receive such a designation in recognition of their suffering and heroism during World War II. Dmitrii SHOSTAKOVICH, one of the Soviet Union's greatest composers and an air raid warden, wrote his Seventh Symphony during the siege. He was evacuated to perform it in Moscow. The US premiere of what became the Leningrad Symphony raised money for relief. The saga of Leningrad's ordeal and heroism was well publicized in the United States and did much to strengthen support for the wartime alliance.

Leningrad affair (1949–1950)

A major purge that resulted in the execution of about 200 members of Leningrad Communist Party members and academics in the late 1940s, whose details remained unknown until revelations in the glasnost era of Mikhail GORBACHEV. The events surrounding the purge started in February 1949 with the dismissal of P. S. Popkov, first secretary of the Leningrad City Committee. In the course of 1949 almost all the leading figures in the central bureaucracy with links to the Leningrad region disappeared from public sight. The most prominent were N. A. Voznesensky, president of the Gosplan and member of the Politburo, M. I. Rodionov, chairman of the Council of Ministers of the RSFSR; A. A. Kuznetsov, secretary of the Central Committee and member of the Orgburo, the Organizational Bureau of the Central Committee. Little was said at the time about their fate, although most of the arrested were ritually accused of Titoist sympathies, the Communist deviation of the moment. News began to leak out in the mid-1950s when KHRUSHCHEV accused MALENKOV and BERIA of directing the purge. The true motive seems to have been Malenkov's desire to rid the organization of followers of his rival A. A. ZHDANOV, who had died in 1948, allegedly of natural causes. Although the death penalty had been abolished at the time of the arrests, it was reintroduced in time for the execution, apparently in September 1950, of Voznesensky, Kuznetsov, Popkov, Rodionov, and close to 200 others connected in some capacity to the Leningrad political establishment. One rising star with Leningrad roots who managed to avoid arrest was Aleksei KOSYGIN, future prime minister of the Soviet Union in the 1960s, even though he lost his Politburo seat.

Lenin Mausoleum

A monument, first built on Moscow's RED SQUARE in 1924, to house the sarcophagus containing the embalmed body of Vladimir LENIN. By the time of Lenin's burial on January 27, 1924, a temporary wooden mausoleum had been built according to a design developed by the architect Aleksei SHCHUSEV. This structure was rebuilt and enlarged in May 1924, at which time Lenin's embalmed body was brought into the building. The mausoleum was remodeled again in 1929–30, following another design by Shchusev. Its size was increased considerably from 1,300 to about 5,800 square meters, attaining the look it has to this

day with marble, granite, and porphyry. Lenin's body was removed from the mausoleum during World War II and evacuated beyond the Ural Mountains until April 1945, when it was returned to Red Square. Through the remainder of the Soviet era, the mausoleum served as the architectural focus of Red Square, the site for the ceremonial changing of the guard of honor, and a place of touristic pilgrimage for close to 2 million yearly visitors who stood in long lines waiting to catch a quick glimpse of the deceased leader. The roof of the mausoleum served as the reviewing stand from which the Soviet elite viewed important demonstrations such as the May Day parade. From 1953 to 1961, the mausoleum was renamed the Lenin-Stalin Mausoleum while STALIN's body was interred there. In October 1961, Stalin's remains were moved to the Kremlin wall next to those of other prominent Soviet figures. Since the fall of the Soviet Union, the issue of a proper burial for Lenin has resurfaced with some frequency, but all proposals have run into determined opposition from Communists who consider it the final line in the sand in the dismantling of the Soviet legacy.

Lenin Prizes

A set of prizes, first established in June 1925, designed to honor achievements in the areas of science and letters. Initially the prizes were awarded solely in the fields of science and the social sciences. Among the initial honorees was D. B. Riazanov in 1927 for his work on revolutionary history and his contributions to the first edited volumes of the works of Karl Marx and Friedrich Engels, and N. Ia. Marr in 1928 for his work in linguistics. Between 1935 and 1956, Stalin Prizes took the place of Lenin Prizes. A Central Committee resolution from September 1956 reinstituted the Lenin Prizes for science and technology and introduced a new category in literature and the arts. In 1960, a third category in journalism and publishing was added to the other two. The prizes were awarded yearly on the date of LENIN's birthday (April 22) and provided the recipients with a gold medal with Lenin's image and a cash payment initially set at 7,500 rubles. International Lenin prizes for foreigners who, in the eyes of the party and Soviet government, promoted peace and international understanding were first awarded in 1949 (known as Stalin Prizes from 1949 to 1956). Their recipients received the Lenin medal and a cash award of 10,000 rubles.

Lermontov, Mikhail Iurevich (1814–1841)
writer

Perhaps the truest romantic of all Russian poets in his character and work, Lermontov was born in Moscow to a family that originally came from Scotland (Learmont). He entered Moscow University in 1830 but was expelled two years later. He then attended the School of Cavalry Cadets in St. Petersburg and in 1834 received a commission as a cornet in the Life Guard Hussars (Hussars of the Guard). His literary career began controversially enough with the poem "Death of a Poet," protesting against the death of the poet Aleksandr PUSHKIN in a duel (1837), and the cover-up that followed. The poem stirred St. Petersburg society and earned Lermontov a court-martial and a posting to the Caucasus, at the time a turbulent frontier region. Confrontational by nature, Lermontov was killed, like his hero Pushkin, in a duel. Lermontov's place in Russian literary history rests on two major works, the novel *A Hero of Our Time* (1840) and the poem "Demon." In *A Hero of Our Time,* the first major prose novel of Russian literature, he further develops the themes of the "superfluous man" begun by Pushkin. Lermontov not only created one of the great romantic heroes of 19th-century Russian literature, he also contributed greatly to the creation of a romanticized image of the Caucasus, an exotic borderland peopled by bandits and free men. In "Demon" he created a brilliant supernatural portrait of demoniac love, which influenced generations of Russian artists, including Mikhail VRUBEL, who painted a whole cycle of works based on the poem.

Leskov, Nikolai Semyonovich (1831–1895)
writer

Considered by many to be the ablest of Russian storytellers, Leskov was born in the town of Gorokhovo on February 16, 1831. In his work, Leskov incorporated experiences from extensive travel across Russia from the time of his childhood through his professional life to produce colorful, satirical accounts of Russian provincial life that reached a broad public because they were written in the voice of the lower middle classes. His best-known novel, *Cathedral Folk* (1872), presents a panoramic view of the provincial clergy, drawn from his childhood travels with his grandmother to various monasteries, while *Enchanted Wanderer* (1873) uses material from a visit to the monasteries of Lake Ladoga. In early novels such as *Nowhere to Go* (1864) and *At Daggers Drawn* (1870–71), Leskov invited the wrath of the radical intelligentsia for his attacks on them, but following a trip to western Europe in 1875, he became more sympathetic to the intelligentsia and critical of the Orthodox Church. In later years he became a Tolstoyan in his political views. Leskov's popularity in his lifetime rested more on picaresque tales such as "The Tale of Cross-Eyed Lefty from Tula and the Steel Flea" (1881). But contemporary audiences are probably more familiar with "Lady Macbeth of Mtsensk District" (1866), a bleaker work that ends with a double suicide by drowning, which Dmitrii SHOSTAKOVICH adapted for an opera in 1934 amidst great criticism from Soviet cultural watchdogs. Other works by Leskov include *The Sealed Angel* (1873), *On the Edge of the World* (1875), *Trivialities of Clerical Life* (1878), and *Night Birds* (1891). He died on March 5, 1895 in St. Petersburg.

Likhachev, Dmitrii Sergeevich (1906–2000)
scholar

An eminent scholar with an international reputation, Likhachev was instrumental in fostering the general cultural revival that characterized the GORBACHEV era in the late 1980s. Likhachev was born to a prominent intelligentsia family in St. Petersburg and graduated from Leningrad University in 1928. Soon after graduation he was arrested and exiled to the Solovki concentration camp, which the BOLSHEVIKS had established on the grounds of the ancient SOLOVETSKII MONASTERY. He spent three years in the camp before being released in August 1932. In good graces with the Soviet government, Likhachev began working at the Institute of Russian Literature (Pushkinskii Dom) from 1938. In 1946, he was appointed to the faculty of Leningrad University, and in 1954 he returned to the Pushkinskii Dom as head of section and specialist in ancient Russian literature. In 1970, he was elected to the ACADEMY OF SCIENCES and began to speak out in favor of the protection of ancient monuments. His refusal to condemn his fellow academician Andrei SAKHAROV brought him a beating from government thugs and general political trouble. Unable to publish as a historian, he retreated from public life. In 1985, he became Mikhail Gorbachev's adviser on cultural and historical matters and joined the editorial board of the journal *Nashe nasledie* (*Our Heritage*). In 1987 Gorbachev's wife Raisa, a longtime admirer, appointed Likhachev director of the Soviet Cultural Fund, and she became his deputy. Likhachev worked in favor of historical preservation and called for the return of artifacts and archives taken out of Russia after the 1917 Revolution. International recognition soon followed in the form of honorary doctorates from Oxford and Cambridge and other foreign universities. Likhachev was elected to the Congress of People's Deputies in 1989.

Liubimov, Yuri Petrovich (1917–)
theater director

One of the leading theater directors of the late Soviet period, Liubimov gained recognition beyond the borders of Russia in the post-Soviet period. He was born in the Volga River town of Yaroslavl, to the northeast of Moscow. Liubimov studied in Moscow and graduated in 1939 from the Shchukin School of Theatre at the prestigious Vakhtangov Theatre. He served in the Red Army during World War II and was discharged in 1946. In 1946 he joined the Vakhtangov Theatre company as an actor, where he stayed until 1964. A COMMUNIST PARTY member since 1952, Liubimov was appointed director of the Taganka Drama and Comedy Theater in Moscow in 1964 at the dawn of the BREZHNEV era. In the next few decades, under his direction the Taganka Theater gradually became known for imaginative, often experimental productions that tested the limits of Brezhnev-era Soviet orthodoxy. The Taganka also became known as the artistic home of the ill-fated actor and bard Vladimir VYSOTSKY, whose early death in 1980 drew a spontaneous outpouring of emotion from Moscow residents. Early on, Liubimov found an unlikely defender in Yuri ANDROPOV, head of the KGB (secret police) and future general secretary of the Communist Party, whose daughter had married an actor in the Taganka troupe. Andropov protected Liubimov from some but not all of the frequent harassment of cultural officials who disapproved of the Taganka's unorthodox productions. In the early 1980s, with several of his productions canceled by the Ministry of Culture—most notably a production of *Boris Godunov*—Liubimov grew increasingly frustrated with Soviet censorship. In 1983, while traveling in Great Britain he issued a series of public declarations to which the Soviet government responded by revoking his citizenship, in effect condemning him to exile. While in exile, Liubimov was in great demand as a director throughout Europe. His productions won several prizes in Austria, Great Britain, Italy, and the United States. He returned to Moscow in 1988 to a different political climate and was able to stage the previously suppressed *Boris Godunov*. He also staged a spectacle in memory of his friend Vladimir Vysotsky. In 1989 both his citizenship and his directorship of the Taganka Theater were restored. Throughout the 1990s Liubimov and the Taganka Theater maintained their leading position in the world of Russian theater, staging various important productions, including one of Boris PASTERNAK's *Doctor Zhivago.*

Livonian War (1558–1583)

A long, protracted, and ultimately unsuccessful war that resulted from IVAN IV's attempt to gain access to the major seaports along the eastern Baltic Sea, the Livonian War brought Russia into conflict with Poland, Lithuania, and Sweden. The war began in 1558 with the Russian invasion of Livonia, a Baltic territory then ruled by the Livonian Order of the Teutonic Knights. Livonia itself was part of a greater Livonian territory that also included Estonia, Courland, and the island of Oesel. The Muscovite armies won several victories in the first years of the war, seizing more than 20 Livonian towns and fortresses, including Dorpat (Iuriev). In response, the Livonian Order dissolved itself in 1561 and transferred the greater Livonian territories of Estonia to Sweden, Courland to Poland, and Oesel to Denmark, while Livonia itself came under the protection of Lithuania. The order's decision had the effect of expanding the number of Russia's opponents to include Poland, Lithuania, and Sweden. Nevertheless, the first phase of the war ended with the Russian capture of Polotsk from Lithuania in 1563 as well as in seizure of large stretches of Lithuanian territory. Emboldened by its victories, Russia rejected a Lithuanian peace proposal in 1566. During the late 1560s, however, as Ivan's attention shifted to domestic problems, most notably the campaign of terror conducted by the *oprichnina* as well as trouble along the southern frontier with the Crimean Tatars and their Ottoman allies, Russia's position deteriorated. In 1569 Lithuania and Poland became one state as a result of the Union of Lublin. In 1576 they named Stefan Báthory, a veteran Transylvanian commander, as their monarch, and three years later Báthory's troops recaptured Polotsk. With PSKOV under siege, in 1582 Ivan agreed to a peace treaty, by which Russia renounced all its claims to Livonia and returned all the Lithuanian terri-

tories occupied by its armies. One year later, Russia came to terms with Sweden and agreed to give up its claims to Estonia and surrender Russian towns in the Gulf of Finland. As a result of the Livonian War, Russia lost what little access it had to the Baltic Sea, which it would recover only in the early 18th century after the Great Northern War.

Lomonosov, Mikhail Vasilievich (1711–1765)

scholar

Russia's leading intellectual of the 18th century, Lomonosov was in the words of the poet Aleksandr PUSHKIN a "one-man university." Known in his lifetime for his literary and philological contributions, in posterity he has been justly recognized as a scientific pioneer in fields like electricity, heat and energy conservation, metallurgy, astronomy, and even early work in atomic theory. The son of a fisherman and trader, Lomonosov was born in the ARCHANGEL region near the White Sea. A precocious learner, he enrolled in the SLAVIC-GREEK-LATIN Academy in Moscow in 1731. After five years of studies in extreme poverty, his ability was recognized and he traveled to St. Petersburg for further study. Almost immediately he was chosen to pursue advanced studies in chemistry, metallurgy, and mathematics at the Universities of Marburg and Friedburg in Germany. Lomonosov's early work in revising the rules of Russian grammar and literature established him as the founder of modern Russian literature. He was an important pioneer of Russian historical studies, although they lack the scholarly rigor that came with 19th-century works. Nevertheless, his critique of the Norman theory of Russia's origins remains an important contribution to the subject. Lomonosov's stellar scientific career, beginning with his return from Europe in 1741, coincides with the reign of Empress ELIZABETH I. He was appointed adjunct professor of physics in 1742 and full professor of chemistry in 1745 by the Russian ACADEMY OF SCIENCES, becoming the first Russian to gain equal status with the foreign scholars who dominated the academy in its first century. Through public lectures inaugurated in 1746, he contributed to the diffusion of scientific knowledge among Russian audiences. Thanks to Elizabeth's support, he established the first Russian glass and mosaic manufacturing industry, producing among others mosaics that celebrated Russian historical themes like Peter the Great or the Battle of Poltava. In his final years he devoted more time to administrative tasks at the academy. He also laid the groundwork for the foundation of Moscow University, established in 1755 and named after him since 1940. In the 1760s Lomonosov's influence began to decline, the result of age, illness, and a changing political climate around the time of Elizabeth's death in 1761. He died in St. Petersburg in April 1765, and is buried in the city's Aleksandr Nevsky Monastery.

Lunacharsky, Anatolii Vasilievich (1875–1933)
revolutionary and writer

A Bolshevik since 1904, as commissar of enlightenment Lunacharsky played an important role in the areas of culture and mass education in the first decade after the OCTOBER REVOLUTION of 1917. Lunacharsky was born in Poltava, the Ukraine, and pursued college studies in Kiev, where he first joined a Marxist revolutionary group. In 1892, he was forced to flee Russia, settling down first in Zurich, where he met Rosa Luxemburg, and, in 1894, in Paris. In 1896, Lunacharsky returned to Russia and resumed his political activities in the social democratic movement. Frequently arrested, during one of his terms of internal exile he met Alexander Bogdanov, a talented Marxist philosopher who would later clash with Vladimir LENIN. In 1904, while traveling in Paris, Lunacharsky met Lenin, eventually choosing to side with him and other BOLSHEVIKS in the factional struggle against the Mensheviks. During the 1905 Revolution, Lunacharsky was back in St. Petersburg as editor of *Novaia zhizn* (*New Life*), the first legal social democratic newspaper. Arrested again in the reprisals that followed the 1905 Revolution,

Lunacharsky escaped and fled to western Europe, where he lived in various locations until the FEBRUARY REVOLUTION permitted him to return to Russia. Intellectually restless and open to new ideas, Lunacharsky was influenced by the spiritual current within Russian Marxism that Lenin denounced as a deviation in his work *Materialism and Empirio-criticism*. His work *Religion and Socialism* (1908), in which he argued that socialism was the new religion of humankind, was well received in European intellectual circles. Lunacharsky broke with Lenin, although he would later return to the Bolshevik fold a few months before the October Revolution. In April 1917, Lunacharsky accompanied Lenin in the famous "sealed train" that brought many Bolsheviks back to Russia from Switzerland through Germany. Imprisoned by the KERENSKY government during the anti-Bolshevik backlash that followed the JULY DAYS, he was freed by the October Revolution, after which he was appointed commissar of enlightenment in the Bolshevik government. Despite limited resources in a nation torn by war and hunger, Lunacharsky advanced an ambitious agenda, reorganizing the Soviet educational system by introducing progressive education that also allowed students—many of them of working-class background—to gain vocational skills. The attempt to rush the formation of new working-class elites through hastily organized Workers' Faculties was less successful. One area where Lunacharsky's efforts are generally given high marks was the mass campaign to eliminate adult illiteracy. By 1929, amid a major social upheaval, Lunacharsky had little influence with STALIN and his inner circle. He was replaced as commissar of enlightenment and appointed to diplomatic posts. At the time of his death in 1933 he had been appointed Soviet ambassador to the newly installed Spanish republic.

Luria, Aleksandr Romanovich (1902–1977)
psychologist

One of the pioneers of modern neuropsychology, Luria was born in the city of KAZAN, to the east of

Moscow. He graduated in 1921 with a degree in social sciences from the University of Kazan and with a degree in medicine from the First Moscow Medical Institute in 1937. Luria's first important contributions were in the areas of child psychology. From 1924 to 1934, he collaborated with the eminent psychologist Lev Vygotsky in investigating the thought, speech, and play of children, and in devising educational and therapeutic methods for helping disturbed children. In 1932, his first major work, *The Nature of Human Conflicts,* was published in English. After Vygotsky's death in 1934, Luria turned to neuropsychology, concentrating initially on the impairment of speech through brain lesions; his important research in this area was published in *Travmaticheskaya afaziia* (Traumatic aphasia) (1947). During World War II, he developed novel methods of restoring the psychological functions of patients suffering from head injuries. His work was widely acclaimed in 1962 when he applied those methods in the astonishingly successful rehabilitation of the celebrated Soviet physicist Lev LANDAU, who had sustained severe and seemingly irreversible brain damage in a car crash. Luria's most original and influential research centered on the psychological effects of localized brain tumors; the findings are presented in his monumental *Higher Cortical Functions of Man* (1962). Luria's influence extended beyond the borders of the Soviet Union, and most of his major works have been translated into English. His most widely read book in English is perhaps *The Mind of the Mnemonist* (1968), a case study of a man with virtually unlimited powers of memory. He died in Moscow on August 14, 1977.

Lvov, Georgii Yevgenevich (1861–1925)
statesman

A reformer from a princely aristocratic family, Lvov was the first head of the Provisional Government following the abdication of Czar NICHOLAS II in March 1917. Lvov was born in the province of Tula, about 100 miles south of Moscow. He graduated from Moscow University with a law degree and entered the civil service.

In 1893 he resigned his post and returned to Popovka, the family estate in Tula, where he joined the local ZEMSTVO, one of the district and provincial assemblies that had been established during the GREAT REFORMS, and became one of its leaders. Lvov gained some recognition for his organizing relief work for wounded soldiers during the RUSSO-JAPANESE WAR (1904–05). In 1905 he joined the Kadet (Constitutional Democratic) Party and the following year was elected to the short-lived first DUMA that had been established during the 1905 Revolution. Lvov was again in the public eye during World War I as chairman of the All-Russian Union of Zemstvos and the Union of Zemstvos and Towns, both of which were voluntary associations that tried to assist the war effort by organizing supplies for the army and relief for the wounded. Chosen to head the Provisional Government as prime minister and minister of the interior following the abdication of Czar Nicholas, Lvov was overshadowed by more forceful personalities such as Pavel MILIUKOV and Aleksandr KERENSKY. On July 7 [July 20], following the anti-government demonstrations of the JULY DAYS, Lvov resigned his posts, allowing Kerensky to become prime minister. Soon after the OCTOBER REVOLUTION he was arrested on charges of counterrevolutionary activity by the Cheka in Ekaterinburg and released after three months. Fleeing eastward through Siberia, he traveled to the United States in November 1918 to plead for American intervention in the Russian civil war. In exile in Paris, Lvov played an active role in the Russian émigré community, particularly in supporting refugees and victims of the 1921 famine. Shortly before his death in Paris in March 1925, Lvov reconciled himself with the Soviet government.

Lysenko, Trofim Denisovich (1898–1976)
agronomist

The spokesman for highly unconventional theories of biological inheritance, Lysenko became the vehicle for a vicious ideological campaign against biology and genetics in the final decade of STALIN's rule (1943–53). After early research into plant physiology and development, some of which bore legitimate intellectual fruit, Lysenko became a spokesman for highly unconventional theories of inheritance based upon the work of a Russian horticulturist, I. V. Michurin. His fierce attacks upon Mendelian genetics were officially endorsed by the COMMUNIST PARTY of the USSR in 1948. There followed a period in which the whole of Soviet biology, but especially genetics, was ravaged by ideological conflict. Serious scientists were pilloried, laboratories closed or transformed into heavens of "Michurinist" biology, and the

teaching and practice of biology perverted. It seems clear that Lysenko himself connived at these abuses and used his position as president of the Lenin Academy of Agricultural Sciences to do so. Although he was discredited after the death of Stalin, he found a new patron in Nikita KHRUSH-CHEV, before being finally demoted from positions of influence after 1964. The consensus of several generations condemns Lysenko for the irreparable harm done to entire fields of Soviet science and the human cost—including imprisonment and death—suffered by those who, like Nikolai VAVILOV, spoke out against his ideas or were otherwise considered his opponents.

M

Machajski, Jan Waclaw (1866–1926)
revolutionary theorist

Machajski was born into a lower-middle-class Polish family in Russian-occupied Poland. As a youth he was influenced by the ideas of Polish nationalism and revolutionary socialism. In 1892 he became a Social Democratic agitator. He was arrested soon after and banished to Siberia. He escaped to western Europe in 1903. While in Siberia (1898), he wrote a series of highly influential essays that were published in Geneva in 1905 in a book entitled *Umstvennyi rabochii* (The Intellectual worker). In these essays, Machajski argued that the development of capitalism had brought forth a new class of intellectual workers—the intelligentsia—and that socialism was the class ideology of this intelligentsia rather than of the working class. He further argued that the victory of socialism (as well as anarchism), either through revolutionary or parliamentary means, would lead to the creation of a system in which capital owners would be replaced by administrators, who would continue to exploit the working classes through their educational advantages and expertise. As an alternative, Machajski proposed a "Workers' Conspiracy," a secret group of revolutionaries organized along Bakuninist lines. Through agitation, direct action, and a general strike, this Workers' Conspiracy would ultimately help bring about a truly proletarian revolution and a classless society. Many socialists and anarchists were attracted to what became known as Machaevism. Machajski returned to Russia during the 1905 Revolution and found several organizations of followers. In 1907 he produced a single issue of a paper, *Rabochii zagovor* (*Worker's Conspiracy*). He was again arrested in 1911 and fled to western Europe. He returned to Russia in 1917, and while he accepted the Bolshevik Revolution, he called for a more far-reaching worker revolution. In 1918 he published a short-lived newspaper, *Rabochaya revolyutsiya* (Worker revolution). He worked as a technical journalist during his final years.

Makarenko, Anton Semyonovich (1888–1939)
educator

Makarenko was a schoolmaster whose work in the 1920s with homeless children and juvenile delinquents brought him great, some would claim excessive, acclaim in the Soviet Union. The son of a railway painter, Makarenko attended teacher education courses in Kremenchug, Ukraine (1905), taught in provincial schools, and graduated from the Poltava Teachers Institute in 1917. During the civil war he was appointed director of a colony for juvenile delinquents in Poltava, then in 1920 of the "Maksim Gorky" colony near Kharkov. During the 1920s his reputation grew for his work with homeless orphan children (*besprizorniki*), a legacy of the upheaval of revolution and civil war. Makarenko tried to base his relations with his charges on a humane approach, stressing the necessity of trust and mutual respect, and also of collective work. Gradually, strict discipline, conformity, and collectivist slogans became more distinctive in Makarenko's work. Initially, with many Soviet educators influenced by the "progressive" ideas of John Dewey and other American educators, Makarenko came in for criticism. But with the turn toward a more radical political orientation in the late 1920s, Makarenko's work received acclaim from the government, which identified his approach to education as a key to the development of a new Soviet man. Makarenko became the director of a new commune for homeless orphans in Kharkov and an educational celebrity of sorts, traveling widely and lecturing on educational problems. During the Stalinist period up to the late 1980s, Makarenko was treated as a major figure in the history of education. In later years, a more sober evaluation followed, praising his achievements in educating wayward children but acknowledging the limits of his approach.

Makhno, Nestor Ivanovich (1889–1935)
anarchist revolutionary

Born Nestor Mikhnenko to a peasant family near Hulyai-Pole in the southeastern Ukraine, Makhno was attracted to anarchism from an early age. Imprisoned at the age of 19 for the murder of a policeman, in 1910 he was sentenced to death. Because of his youth, the sentence was commuted to 10 years imprisonment to be served in Moscow's Butyrki prison. There he studied the writings of anarchism, met and befriended Peter Arshinov, with whom he worked closely for the next decade. Here he also contracted the tuberculosis that would ultimately kill him. Released after the FEBRUARY REVOLUTION of 1917, he returned to the Ukraine, where he engaged in revolutionary agitation. During the civil war, Makhno organized the Revolutionary Insurgent Army of Ukraine, a formidable peasant guerrilla force that fought both Reds and Whites. Makhno's army fought Austrians and Germans, Ukrainian nationalists and Russian Whites and played a crucial role in the successive defeats of Hetman Pavlo Skoropadsky, Semyon Petliura (1918), DENIKIN (1919), and WRANGEL (1920). His army used guerrilla tactics, taking advantage of the mobility of his cavalry. His raids involved great violence and, although he condemned ANTI-SEMITISM, POGROMS and great brutality. At the peak of his power, he controlled a large portion of the southeastern Ukraine from his base around Hulyai-Pole, where he tried to establish an anarchist peasant polity. Given the strategic significance of the Ukraine and the BOLSHEVIKS' increasing determination to control it, this proved unworkable. Makhno was temporarily allied with the Red Army in 1919 and 1920, and his movement operated legally in Soviet territory, but discord soon developed between his band and the Red Army. His alliance with the Bolsheviks was only tactical, a case of choosing the lesser of two evils, papering over profound ideological differences. With Ukraine in their hands, the Bolsheviks turned on Makhno in late 1920 and destroyed his army and regime. He fled Soviet Russia in August 1921, eventually settling in Paris after stays in Romanian and Polish detention camps. In exile, he dabbled in émigré anarchist politics, worked as a shoemaker, wrote three volumes of memoirs covering the first year of the revolution, and died in poverty and isolation. Idealized by some like the poet ESENIN as a true revolutionary leader in the tradition of other peasant rebels, Makhno was vilified by the Bolsheviks as a bandit. In the post-Soviet era, Ukrainian historians have begun to reevaluate Makhno's legacy in the light of Ukrainian resistance to Soviet rule.

Malenkov, Georgii Maksimilianovich (1902–1988)
Soviet official

Presumed to be STALIN's likely successor on the eve of the dictator's death in 1953, Malenkov was outmaneuvered by Nikita KHRUSHCHEV within a few years. Born in Orenburg to a middle-class family, during World War II he served as a Communist political officer on the eastern and Turkestan fronts. The patronage of Lazar KAGANOVICH, a member of Stalin's inner circle who recognized his organizational skills, helped Malenkov advance in the party apparatus. As director of the Communist Party's Central Committee's department for party personnel in the mid-1930s, he took an active part in implement-

Georgii Malenkov (left) and Joseph Stalin watching May Day parade in Moscow, 1949 *(Library of Congress)*

ing the Great Purge with regard to the COMMU-NIST PARTY. A Central Committee member in 1939 and Politburo member in 1946, in the first few years after World War II, Malenkov locked horns with Andrei ZHDANOV, the dominant figure in Stalin's inner circle. Zhdanov's unexpected death in 1948 freed Malenkov to move against his supporters in a purge of the Leningrad party apparatus in 1949–50, known as the LENINGRAD AFFAIR, whose full extent was not revealed until the late 1980s. At the time of the Nineteenth Party Congress of October 1952, the first in 13 years, Malenkov delivered the closing report, to many a sign that Stalin was considering him his successor. After Stalin's death in March 1953, Malenkov became prime minister and party general secretary, but was forced to give up one

post under pressure from colleagues reluctant to concentrate too much power in the hands of one individual. Malenkov gave up his party post, thus allowing the new party secretary—Khrushchev—to consolidate the party as his power base. By late 1953 Malenkov and Khrushchev had removed police chief Lavrenty BERIA as a threat, but then quickly found themselves at odds for power. In 1955 Malenkov was forced to resign as prime minister, and in 1957 he lost his remaining influence as a result of the defeat of the ANTI-PARTY GROUP that sought to remove Khrushchev. In a sign that Soviet political life had changed somewhat since Stalin's death, Malenkov's punishment was not death or a term in a labor camp, but an appointment as manager of a hydroelectric plant in Kazakhstan. He later returned to Moscow, where he lived quietly for several decades until his death.

Malevich, Kazimir Serafimovich (1878–1935)
artist

Malevich, a painter of Polish origin, was one of the forerunners of 20th century abstract painting. He studied in Kiev and at the Moscow Art School. Starting as a follower of the impressionists, Malevich progressed through phases of Cézanne and Van Gogh influences, expressionism, fauvism, and cubism to the creation of his own style, which he called Suprematism, in which only geometrical elements were used in construction. His first Suprematist paintings were exhibited in 1915 in Petrograd; they were formal arrangements of geometrical elements, notably a black square on a white ground. In 1918 he showed his famous "white on white" series. Malevich attempted to re-create the two-dimensional spirituality of icons through the medium of abstract painting. After the 1917 Revolution and the Bolshevik seizure of power, when many painters proclaimed utilitarian social functions of art as the only true ones, Malevich continued to insist on the primarily spiritual values of abstract paintings. From 1919 to 1921, he taught art in Moscow and Leningrad. During the 1920s he traveled to Weimar, Germany, where he met Wassily KANDINSKY and published his own *The Non-Objective World*. Unlike Kandinsky, CHAGALL, and many other Russian artists, he remained in Russia after the revolution, and in the last years of his life was forced by the obligatory doctrine of socialist realism to cease his original creative work, and painted only a few intimate portraits in a stiff "realist" manner. Malevich died in poverty in 1935.

Manchuria

A historic region of northeastern China that became the object of Russian expansionist interests from the late 17th century to the early 20th century. The plains of Manchuria were home to the nomadic Manchu peoples who invaded China in 1644 and established the Qing dynasty, which remained in power until 1911. Russian exploration in the vicinity of the AMUR RIVER led to the first conflicts between Russians and Chinese and the first attempt to fix a boundary between the two nations through the Treaty of NERCHINSK (1689). By the terms of the treaty, in effect until 1858, the Amur River valley and Manchuria itself remained firmly under Chinese control. By the mid-19th century, however, Russia was able to exploit China's political weakness and annex large amounts of land neighboring Manchuria. In 1858, the Treaty of Aigun gave the left bank of the Amur River to Russia, while the Treaty of Peking (1860) established the two countries' frontier along the Amur and Ussuri Rivers, with Russia gaining all land between the two rivers and the Sea of Japan. As a result of the two treaties, China surrendered more than 400,000 square miles of land north and east of historic Manchuria and lost its access to the Sea of Japan.

During the last decade of the 19th century, Russia began to assert its power in the region, seeking to absorb Manchuria into its economic sphere of influence, even while the region remained nominally Chinese. Competing interests over a thinly populated but potentially rich land brought Russia and Japan into greater conflict between 1895 and 1905. After the First Sino-Japanese War (1894–95), Japan briefly gained control of the Liaodong Peninsula but was prevented from making any permanent gains in the region by the concerted diplomatic efforts of Russia, Germany, France, and Great Britain. In 1898, concerned over the Japanese expansion in the region, Russia in turn arranged for a 25-year lease of the southern part of the peninsula, including the towns of Dalian and Port Arthur. In 1900, Russia moved to occupy the rest of Manchuria, which it held until the RUSSO-JAPANESE WAR of 1904–05. The Russian-controlled CHINESE EASTERN RAILWAY, a spur of the TRANS-SIBERIAN RAILROAD that cut through the heart of Manchuria and linked Chita in eastern Siberia with Vladivostok on the Pacific Ocean, was completed in 1903. In 1904 the Russians completed a railroad linking the city of Harbin in central Manchuria with Port Arthur. War broke out between Japan and Russia in February 1904 and was fought mostly across parts of Manchuria. As a result of the Treaty of Portsmouth of August 1905, which ended the war, both sides agreed to restore Manchuria to China.

In 1931 Japan invaded Manchuria and established a puppet state known as Manchukuo. Soviet forces briefly occupied Manchuria in 1945–46, after Japan's defeat in World War II, but at the conclusion of the Chinese civil war in 1949 the area was once again firmly under Chinese control.

Mandelstam, Nadezhda Yakovlevna (1899–1990)
writer

The widow of the poet Osip Mandelstam, Mandelstam was born Nadezhda Yakovlevna Khazina in the Volga River town of Saratov. She grew up in Kiev, where she studied art under Aleksandra Ekster. In 1919, she met her future husband, and they married soon after. She shared her husband's increasing political problems and his early exile experiences until his arrest in May 1934. As the wife of an "enemy of the people," she was prohibited from living in Moscow, moving instead to Tashkent, Ulianovsk, and other cities, where she tried to make a living teaching English. During these long decades, she tirelessly kept her husband's literary heritage alive, by memorizing his poems being the person most responsible for saving one of the greatest 20th-century Russian poets from oblivion. In 1958, she was allowed to return to Moscow. Mandelstam achieved international recognition with the publication of two outstanding and poignant volumes of memoirs that are generally considered among the best testimonies of the STALIN era. The memoirs were published in Russian in New York and Paris and translated into English

as *Hope Against Hope* (1970) and *Hope Abandoned* (1972).

Mandelstam, Osip Emilovich (1891–1938)
poet

One of the best and most famous Russian poets of the 20th century, Mandelstam was born into a Jewish merchant's family in Warsaw and grew up in St. Petersburg. He enrolled in St. Petersburg University, where he studied French literature. He published his first poems in the magazine *Apollon* at the age of 19. With Anna AKHMATOVA and Nikolai GUMILEV, he founded the Acmeist movement in 1912, which sought to bring a clearer, more direct style to a Russian literary world dominated by symbolism. During the Russian Revolution of 1917 and the ensuing civil war, he emerged as a voice stressing human values and the absolute importance of human dignity. The political culture of Communist Russia was alien to him and he published two novels as well as poetry during the 1920s. Later he acquired an individual poetic voice of exceptional clarity. Although shy by nature, he was amazingly bold in openly criticizing STALIN in a poem, written in November 1933, where he referred to him as a Kremlin mountaineer, with leering cockroach whiskers, who enjoyed killing peasants with his half-human gang. His arrest, only a matter of time, came in May 1934. Mandelstam spent his last four years between prison, exile, and labor camps. He died in December 1938 in transit to the Arctic Circle concentration camps in the Magadan region, but his burial place remains unknown.

Martov, Yuli Osipovich (1873–1923)
revolutionary

One of the prominent early leaders of the Russian Social Democratic Labor Party (RSDLP), Martov was Vladimir LENIN's main antagonist before the party split into two factions, Menshevik and Bolshevik. He was born Yuli (Iulii)

Osipovich Tsederbaum in Istanbul, Turkey, into a middle-class Russian Jewish family. At the age of four, he moved with his family to ODESSA, where he grew up and became active in revolutionary youth politics, initially as a member of the BUND, the Jewish socialist party. He was first arrested for revolutionary activism in St. Petersburg in early 1892, but by December of that year he had been released and formed the St. Petersburg Group for the Emancipation of Labor. An accomplished theorist in his own right, Martov developed the idea of agitation among the workers in his pamphlet "On Agitation" (1896), which was to play a central role in the subsequent development of Russian Marxism. In November 1896 he joined Lenin and other St. Petersburg Marxists in forming the Union of Struggle for the Emancipation of the Working Class, a forerunner of the RSDLP. Within a month the group's leaders, including Lenin and Martov, had been arrested. Martov spent three years in Siberian exile. Upon his release in 1899, he joined Lenin and the founder of Russian Marxism, Georgii PLEKHANOV, in western Europe. Together they brought new life to the recently founded RSDLP, especially through the publication of the party newspaper *Iskra* (*The Spark*). Differences with Lenin soon surfaced while Plekhanov sided with Martov. At the Second Party Congress, held in Stockholm in 1903, the party split into two factions over Lenin's concept of a highly centralized party composed of professional revolutionaries. After a vote taken at the congress, supporters of the majority view were called BOLSHEVIKS and led by Lenin, while supporters of the minority view were called Mensheviks and led by Martov. In western Europe until 1917, Martov and other Menshevik leaders developed a two-stage theory of Marxist revolution designed to account for Russia's belated capitalist development. In the first stage, a bourgeois or capitalist revolution, the socialists would help overthrow the monarchy and then become part of the opposition. They would then press for reforms and educate the working classes for a second, socialist, revolution that would take place—as per Marx—when the conditions of economic and political development came to

fruition. By the time Martov returned to Russia in May 1917, the Menshevik Party was in control of the Petrograd Soviet of Workers' and Soldiers' Deputies, cooperating with the moderate Provisional Government. Martov disagreed with his own party's growing moderation and its inability to end Russia's participation in World War I, but he also was critical of what he saw as Lenin's irresponsible calls for "all power to the Soviets." Still a Menshevik, he formed his own Internationalist faction but was reduced to the sidelines as the Bolsheviks seized power in October 1917. Following the OCTOBER REVOLUTION, he developed a position that, although critical of the Bolshevik regime, considered the revolution itself "historically necessary" and sought to position the Mensheviks as a loyal opposition within a soviet democracy. This was perhaps theoretically sound but politically untenable, as the country teetered on the brink of disintegration and the Bolsheviks hung on to power more desperately, and political parties moved toward more extremist positions. Isolated and defeated, he emigrated again in 1920, settling in Berlin, where he edited the important Menshevik newspaper *Sotsialisticheskii vestnik* (Socialist messenger) from 1920 until his death in 1923.

Mayakovsky, Vladimir Vladimirovich (1893–1930)
poet

A leading Futurist poet and active supporter of the October Revolution, Mayakovsky provided many of the most vivid words and images of early Soviet literature and propaganda. He was born in Georgia and educated in Kutaisi and, after 1906, in Moscow. Mayakovsky joined the BOLSHEVIK Party in 1908, and after a stay in solitary confinement at Moscow's Butyrki prison, he began writing poetry. A leading representative of Russian FUTURISM, he enjoyed scandalizing society with his poems. His early poems were published in the Futurist collection *A Slap in the Face of Public Taste* (1912). Other publications of the prerevolutionary period include *Vladimir Mayakovskii* (1913), *A Cloud in Trousers* (1915), and *The*

Spinal Flute (1916). During World War I, his anti-war poetry gained him many admirers. Maya-kovsky was in his element during the early years of the Soviet regime, supplying brilliant captions to cartoons and posters, contributing to Soviet commercial advertising in the 1920s, and writing politically engaged poems that celebrated the October Revolution. He was the leader of the Left Front in Art (LEF) and his poems "150,000,000" (1920) and "Vladimir Ilich Lenin" (1924) glorified the deeds of the BOLSHEVIKS. His plays, *Mystery-Bouffe* (1918), *Bed Bug* (1929), and *The Bath House* (1930), drew on traditional dramatic themes, with a new presentation. He traveled widely but gradually lost faith in the revolution and the party; together with misfortune in love, this drove him to suicide. He shot himself in Moscow and a new myth began to surround him as the greatest poet of the revolution, a myth that was greatly supported by the government, which sought to present him as an exemplar of socialist realism. In the STALIN era he was lionized as a leading poet of proletarian culture, and his name was given to prominent streets, squares, and theaters.

Mazepa, Ivan Stepanovich (1639?–1709)

Cossack leader

A leader of the Ukrainian COSSACKS, Mazepa found himself entangled in the politics of the Great Northern War (1700–25) between Sweden and an emerging Russia, led by czar PETER I. Mazepa had been elected hetman, or leader, of the Ukrainian Cossacks in 1687. During his tenure as hetman, Mazepa built churches and promoted the spread of education. He also sought to promote the interests of the more privileged Cossacks at the expense of rank-and-file Cossacks and the peasants living in Cossack lands. Nevertheless, it was his desire to reassert Cossack independence, compromised since the extension of Muscovite rule over Ukraine in 1654, which led to Mazepa's undoing. Having already conducted unsuccessful secret negotiations with the Polish king Stanislaw Leszczyński in 1705 in the hope of gaining an ally against

Peter. Mazepa turned to a stronger rival of Peter's, the Swedish king Charles XII. As King Charles continued to press his advantage over Russia in the early stages of the Great Northern War, he found an ally in Mazepa. In 1708, King Charles chose to move his armies into Ukraine, where he hoped to join forces with Mazepa's Cossacks before continuing his attack against Peter's armies. However, Mazepa was only able to deliver about between 2,000 and 3,000 Cossack troops to a Swedish army of about 25,000 soldiers. Mazepa fought with Charles XII at the Battle of POLTAVA of July 1709, which ended in a decisive Russian victory. Defeated, Mazepa joined Charles XII in seeking safety in Ottoman territory to the south, where he died soon after.

Medvedev, Roi and Zhores Aleksandrovich (1925–)

scholars

Twin brothers, Roi and Zhores Medvedev, played an important role in the intellectual history of the BREZHNEV and GORBACHEV eras. The two brothers were born in 1925 in Tbilisi, Georgia; their father was a Red Army commissar who perished in the GULAG labor camps. Roi, a historian, studied philosophy at Leningrad University and later worked as a researcher for the USSR ACADEMY OF SCIENCES. Zhores graduated from the Moscow Agricultural Academy and became known as a biologist and gerontologist. By the late 1960s they were both raising important and taboo questions within their fields in works circulated through the unofficial *samizdat* network. Zhores's work criticized the LYSENKO regime in Soviet science under STALIN; he also wrote a remarkable study of Soviet mail censorship. He was arrested in 1970 and sent to a psychiatric hospital in Kaluga, but after strong protests from the international scientific community organized by his brother, he was released after two weeks. Zhores emigrated in 1973, settling in London, but still kept in close touch with his brother and Soviet affairs, writing an early biographical study of Yuri ANDROPOV. In the meantime Roi had been expelled from the COMMUNIST PARTY in 1969 after writing a pioneering study of the Great Purge of the 1930s that was published in English as *Let History Judge*. Although harassed by the KGB (secret police), his excellent connections in the party allowed him to develop a remarkably prolific and successful career as a dissident historian whose books were regularly published in the West. Among his many publications from this period are *On Socialist Democracy* (1975), *Khrushchev* (1982), and *All Stalin's Men* (1984). He also maintained links with the Soviet *samizdat* community, editing a *samizdat* magazine, *Politicheskii dnevnik* (*Political Diary*) and an almanac, *Dvadsatyi vek* (*Twentieth century*). He also cowrote a number of books with Zhores, including *A Question of Balance* (1971) and *Khrushchev: The Years in Power* (1975). With the liberalization of politics under Mikhail Gorbachev, Roi Medvedev, a staunch Leninist, emerged as a strong defender of Gorbachev's policies. He was elected to the 1989 Congress of People's Deputies, where he spoke out forcefully on human rights, ethnic issues, and East-West relations.

Melnikov, Konstantin Stepanovich (1890–1974)

architect

A visionary architect who came into prominence during the experimental 1920s but, unwilling to adapt to the changing ideological directives that affected his field, spent the last four decades of his life in relative obscurity. Melnikov began his creative career as an artist, studying painting in Moscow (1905–11) before switching to architecture, and enrolling in the Moscow School for Painting, Sculpture and Architecture, between 1912 and 1917. After the 1917 Revolutions, Melnikov found employment with the Moscow city soviet, while teaching at the influential Vkhutemas (Higher State Art and Technical Studios) from 1921 to 1923. His first work was the design of the façade and factory structures of the AMO automobile works in Moscow. In a decade that sought to find innovative approaches to everyday problems such as mass housing and

workers' leisure, Melnikov contributed seven worker clubs and four garages to the city's landscape. He also designed the sarcophagus used to display LENIN's body after his death in 1924. His innovative designs for the Soviet pavilion at the 1925 International Exhibition of Decorative Arts in Paris brought him international acclaim. But the most talked about of his buildings was the house he built for himself on a plot of land he received from the government as a reward for the successful Paris show. Long fascinated by cylinders, circles, and curves, Melnikov designed a house composed of two intersecting cylinders, forming the footprint of the numeral eight, with hexagonal windows. Melnikov participated in the polemical discussions that were a central part of architectural professional discourse, but he was too much of an individualist to formally join one of the existing associations with ideological platforms. Thus, he never joined the Constructivists led by Moisei GINSBERG and Aleksandr VESNIN, and his association with the Association of New Architects (ASNOVA) was brief. With the spread of government-controlled socialist realism to all fields of creative activity in the 1930s, Melnikov was labeled a "formalist" and denied most major commissions by the architectural establishment. The exception was the interior to the Central Department Store in Saratov, which he designed in 1949. He devoted his last years to the painting that had been the source of his first creative work.

Mendeleyev, Dmitrii Ivanovich (1834–1907)

scientist

One of Russia's most prominent scientists, Mendeleyev's best-known contribution to world science was the periodic table of elements, which he first devised in 1869. He was born in the Siberian town of Tobolsk, the son of the headmaster of the local secondary school, and educated at the St. Petersburg Pedagogical Institute. After postgraduate work in Germany at Heidelberg University, Mendeleyev returned to Russia and taught at St. Petersburg University from 1857 until 1890, when he resigned after a disagreement with the minister of education. Besides his periodic table, Mendeleyev engaged in important research on gases and liquids, crystallography, meteorology, and organic chemistry. A man of many talents, Mendeleyev had interests that extended beyond scientific scholarship. From 1893 until his death, he directed the Chamber of Measures and Weights. A successful industrialist and a recognized spokesman for Russia's emerging managerial class, he participated in various enterprises that developed Russia's rich mineral resources around the turn of the century, such as coal from the Donets, Kuznetsk, and Karaganda basins, oil from Baku, and metals from the Urals. Influenced by the German economist Friedrich List, he devoted much time to the study of tariffs as a prerequisite for economic development, and he served on a government commission on customs tariffs. Among his many publications, two that stand out are *Foundations of Chemistry* (1869–71), a summation of the achievements of classical chemistry that was translated into English in 1892, and *Essays in Historical Chemistry*, published posthumously in 1911. His daughter married the poet Aleksandr BLOK.

Menshikov, Aleksandr Danilovich (1673–1729)
official

A close, but controversial, collaborator of PETER I the Great, Menshikov rose from humble origins as a stable boy to the dominant figure in the government of Peter's first successor, his second wife CATHERINE I. After serving in Peter's "toy regiments," Menshikov became his adjutant and accompanied Peter on the original GRAND EMBASSY in 1697–98. From 1702 to 1708, he served in various administrative capacities as governor of Schlusselburg and then governor-general of Ingria, Karelia, and Estonia. Named prince of Izhora by Peter, he became governor of St. Petersburg in 1708. An able commander, in

1708 his troops destroyed the capital of the Cossack leader, Ivan Mazepa, who had sided with the Swedish king, Charles XII, during the Great Northern War. Menshikov's fondness for money got him in trouble in 1714–15 when he was formally accused of corruption. This did not significantly alter his standing with Peter, and in 1720 he was named head of the War College. He was in trouble again, in 1723–24, on the charge of concealing over 30,000 runaway serfs on his estates. After Peter's death he threw his support to Catherine I, the former Marfa Skavronskaia, whom he had introduced to Peter. As a member of the Supreme Privy Council, he dominated court politics during her reign (1725–27). Scheming to remain in power, he maneuvered to have his daughter Anna Menshikova engaged to the young Peter Alekseevich, Peter the Great's grandson, who stood to inherit the throne. Menshikov's plans backfired when his rivals, the Dolgorukii family, persuaded, without too much effort, the future PETER II to renege on his engagement and banish Menshikov to Siberia, where he died a few years later.

Merjani, Shihabeddin (1818–1899)
scholar

A Tatar reformist intellectual, Merjani sought to spark an Islamic cultural revival through the advancement of scientific knowledge. Although his main concern was religious reform, Merjani was a historian and teacher who had studied at the *medresses* of BUKHARA and investigated the manuscripts and rare materials at the SAMARKAND library. An essay on the history of the Uighurs, published in 1865, gained him membership in the St. Petersburg Academy of Sciences, where he subsequently presented papers on the history of the Volga Tatars. Travels to the Middle East in 1886–87 rekindled his interest in Islamic reformist ideals. Shortly after his return to KAZAN in 1887, he was appointed language teacher at the Russo-Tatar Teachers' School. His contact with the Russian teachers at this school, as well as with the professors at Kazan University, allowed him to compare the reform prospects in two different societies, Islamic and Russian, and contributed to his critical assessment of Tatar needs. Merjani wrote over 20 works, all but one of them in Arabic, the exception being his history of the Volga Tatars, the first such attempt in the modern Tatar language. His thinking was grounded in his conviction that Islamic cultural revival depended both on a return to original Islam and on a turn away from the conservative scholastic philosophy that had led Muslim science and education to stagnate. Influenced by the Russian and Tatar cultures that coexisted in Kazan, Merjani also advocated learning Russian, for Russian science then offered the Tatars the shortest bridge to reach the world of modern science.

Meyerhold, Vsevolod Emilevich (1874–1940)

actor and director

An innovative director, Meyerhold was one of the giants of Russian experimental theater. Born into a German-Jewish family near Penza, he converted to Orthodoxy and was given the name Vsevolod. After studies with the renowned theater producer Vladimir NEMIROVICH-DANCHENKO and the director Konstantin STANISLAVSKY, he worked for the Moscow Art Theater (1898–1902). In 1902 he founded the New Drama Company and served as its producer. In 1905 he returned to Stanislavskii's studio, but the following year he moved to St. Petersburg, where he remained until 1917, as chief producer of the Komissarzhevskaia Theater and the Aleksandrinskii Theater. An early interest in cinema resulted in two films made in 1915 and since lost, *The Strong Man* and *Dorian Grey,* that influenced contemporary filmmakers. After the revolution he joined the Bolshevik Party in 1918 and was briefly placed in charge of all Moscow theaters by the commissar of enlightenment, Anatolii LUNACHARSKY. Meyerhold established his own theater in 1920 and, with occasional interruptions, worked there until it was closed down in 1938.

Among those complaining about the tenor of his productions was LENIN's wife, KRUPSKAYA, who labeled his theater a "madhouse." He collaborated with the poet MAYAKOVSKY in various daring and modernistic productions but felt increasingly alienated from the theater, especially after Mayakovsky's suicide in 1930 and with the growing conservatism and conformism of Soviet cultural life. Meyerhold found it increasingly hard to work during the 1930s as the cultural authorities repeatedly criticized his work as "formalist." Information about his final years has remained scanty. He was arrested in 1939 and sent to labor camps. For many years it was believed he died in 1942, but scholars have recently established that he was shot on February 2, 1940.

Michael Romanov (1596–1645) (Mikhail Feodorovich)

czar

Elected czar in February 1613, Michael inaugurated the ROMANOV DYNASTY, which was to rule Russia until 1917. Only 16 at the time of his coronation five months later, Michael came to power at the end of the TIME OF TROUBLES, a period of dynastic instability, foreign invasion, famine, and social upheaval. Considered a weak ruler by most historians, in his long reign Michael nevertheless reintroduced a measure of stability into Russian life after the dislocations of the Time of Troubles.

Michael's elevation to the throne of Russia came as the result of a meeting of the ZEMSKII SOBOR (Assembly of the Land). His name had been first proposed in 1610, after Czar VASILI IV had been deposed, but he lost to the Polish prince Wladyslaw, son of King Sigismund, who was offered the Russian throne pending an agreement that included his conversion to Russian Orthodoxy. In 1613, after a three-year interregnum that witnessed the Polish occupation of Moscow and the formation of a Russian national army of liberation, Michael was one of six or seven candidates whose names were proposed to

Michael Romanov, ca. 1640 *(Hulton/Archive)*

the assembly. With little information about the deliberations of the assembly, historians have speculated that Michael's chances benefited from belonging to the Romanovs, a well-connected family that had built up a certain amount of goodwill in the decades since the reign of IVAN IV. Michael was the son of Feodor Romanov, whom Boris GODUNOV had forced to take religious orders and exiled to the north, and who had since made a career in the church as Metropolitan FILARET. His grandfather, Nikita Romanov, and his great aunt, Anastasia Romanova, the first wife of Ivan IV the Terrible, were fondly remembered as people who tried to curb the murderous instincts of Ivan the Terrible.

The most urgent tasks facing Michael and his advisers were reestablishing internal order and fending off the Polish and Swedish armies that still controlled parts of Russia. In 1617, Russia signed the Treaty of Stolbovo with Sweden, according to which the Swedes returned Nov-

gorod while keeping a strip of territory on the Gulf of Finland, blocking Russian access to the sea. Peace with Poland proved more elusive. In 1618 at Deulino, both sides agreed to a 14-year truce that allowed Poland to keep Smolensk in exchange for the return of notable Russian prisoners held since 1610, including the czar's father, Metropolitan Filaret. In 1634, after two years of hostilities, a more lasting peace was signed, according to which Poland kept territories in western Russia but renounced Wladyslaw's claims to the Muscovite throne.

During the first decade of his reign, the Assembly of the Land stayed in Moscow, assisting the young czar. After 1619, Metropolitan Filaret, now patriarch of the Russian Church, more experienced and forceful than Michael, was given the title of great sovereign and served as coruler until his death in 1633 at the age of 80. The Assembly of the Land met 16 times during Michael's reign, at first almost continuously, and after 1632, meeting to consider special taxes or vexing problems of foreign policy. At the time of Michael's death in 1645, the country had recovered but was burdened by an almost desperate financial situation. After his death, a specially convened Assembly of the Land confirmed Michael's designation of his only son, ALEKSEI MIKHAILOVICH, as his successor.

Mighty Handful

composers

The Mighty Handful (Moguchaia kuchka), also sometimes known as "the Five," was the name given to the group formed by Mily Balakirev, Aleksandr Borodin, Cesar Cui, Modest MUSSORGSKY, and Nikolai RIMSKY-KORSAKOV. Following in the footsteps of Mikhail GLINKA, they drew on Russian national themes and sought to free Russian classical music from German academic traditions. In this they were opposed by the RUBINSTEIN brothers, Anton and Nikolai, who sought to identify Russian music with Western music. A major difference between the two camps was that the Rubinsteins had solid academic music training, while the Mighty Handful was composed mostly of amateurs brought together by their love of music. Of the five, Rimsky-Korsakov was the only one who by virtue of persistence acquired mastery of his art. Rimsky-Korsakov's compositions in particular and tireless revisions of his associates' music (much of which they left incomplete) created a Russian national tradition that made a valuable contribution to musical history. The Mighty Handful's interest in a national style was part of a broader social exploration of neglected folk and patriotic themes that swept through 19th-century Russian intellectual circles in response to the Westernization of the 18th and early 19th centuries.

Mikhailovsky, Nikolai Konstantinovich (1842–1904)
revolutionary theorist

Mikhailovsky was the leading populist philosopher and sociologist in the intellectual debates that divided the revolutionary movement over the role of capitalism in the development of Russian society. Although Mikhailovsky flirted with radical agitation while a student in St. Petersburg in the early 1860s, he eventually decided to concentrate on serious journalism and writing. During his long career as a public intellectual, he was associated with two important journals: *Otechestvennye zapiski* (*Notes from the Fatherland*) from 1869 to 1884, and *Russkoe bogatstvo* (*Russian Wealth*) from 1892 until his death. Like many in the Russian intelligentsia, he was briefly seduced by the attraction of terrorism in the last years of ALEXANDER II's reign. In 1881 he interceded in vain with the new czar, ALEXANDER III, to spare the arrested leaders of the PEOPLE'S WILL Party from their death sentences (they had assassinated Alexander II). Mikhailovsky is known in Russian social thought for his theory of progress, developed primarily in 1869–70, according to which humankind could escape the fragmentation of human nature induced by capitalism and instead create a better society based on cooperation and solidarity, in which the individual's

interests would nevertheless be safeguarded and harmonized with those of the collective. Like Aleksandr HERZEN, he believed that the homegrown institutions of the peasant commune and the workers' artel could provide the seeds for this collectively harmonious society. Mikhailovsky's ideas are emblematic of a populist worldview that accepted important components of Marxism, such as its theory of historical stages, but tried passionately to write a different scenario that would end with the victory of a collectivist, peasant-based socialism. Prominent Marxists of the 1890s, such as Petr Struve, and especially Vladimir LENIN, for whom morality was class-specific and not absolute, harshly criticized what they saw as Mikhailovsky's "ethical" socialism as well as his insistence on a special path for Russia that could bypass capitalism. As the 19th century came to an end with a rapidly industrializing Russia and a thriving Social Democratic (Marxist) movement, Mikhailovsky and POPULISM seemed to have lost the debate, but with the formation of the Socialist Revolutionary Party and the rise of Viktor Chernov as an important theorist, populism underwent one last revival.

Mikhalkov, Nikita Sergeevich (1945–   )
film director and actor

An internationally recognized film director and actor who has become a public figure in the cultural world of post-Soviet Russia, Mikhalkov was born in Moscow into a prominent Russian artistic family of painters and writers. His father, a children's literature author, also wrote the lyrics to the old Soviet national anthem. His mother was a poet, while his brother, working under the name Andrei Konchalovsky, has gained an international reputation as a film director. Well connected from birth in Russian cultural circles, Mikhalkov studied in the acting schools of the distinguished Stanislavsky and Vakhgantov Theaters. Among his early acting credits was a role in his brother's film *A Nest of Gentry* (1969), based on the novel by Ivan TUR-

GENEV. Mikhalkov also studied directing at VGIK, the state film school in Moscow, under the supervision of the prominent filmmaker and teacher Mikhail Romm. By the time of his first directed feature, *At Home Among Strangers* (1974), Mikhalkov had already established himself as a leading Soviet actor, with over 20 film appearances. As a director he first gained international recognition with his second feature, *A Slave of Love* (1976), in which the crew of a silent film attempts to complete a movie at the time of the 1917 Russian Revolution. His next film, *An Unfinished Piece for Piano Player* (1977), won the first prize at the San Sebastian Film Festival, while his adaptation of Ivan GONCHAROV's classic novel *Oblomov* (1980) confirmed his status as a major presence in the Soviet and international world of film. Further acclaim came in 1987 with *Dark Eyes*, another literary adaptation, this time of several of Anton CHEKHOV's short stories. The film's leading actor, Marcello Mastroianni, won the Best Actor award at that year's Cannes Film Festival as well as an Academy Award nomination. In 1992, *Close to Eden*, or *Urga*, a portrait of Mongols in the remote borderlands between Russia and China, earned Mikhalkov an Academy Award nomination for Best Foreign Language Film. His next film, the highly praised *Burnt by the Sun* (1994), tackled the complex issues of the 1930s through the portrait of a family led by a retired military hero, played by Mikhalkov himself, and won the Academy Award for Best Foreign Language Film. Most recently, Mikhalkov acted and directed in *The Barber of Siberia*, a historical drama set at the turn of the 20th century involving an American woman and a Russian military cadet banished to Siberia.

Miklukho-Maklai, Nikolai Nikolaevich (1846–1888)
ethnographer

An ethnographer who became internationally recognized for his first-hand research in New Guinea, Australia, and Southeast Asia, Miklukho-Maklai was born into a railway engineer's family in Novgorod province. His father died in

1857, and his mother had to raise five children alone. While still a student, Miklukho-Maklai read the revolutionary political literature of the day, especially the works of Aleksandr HERZEN and Nikolai CHERNYSHEVSKY. Arrested at age 15, he spent three days in jail for his role in a student demonstration. In 1863 he entered St. Petersburg University but was expelled the following year for political activism and deprived of the right to study at any other Russian university. He moved to Germany and graduated in 1868 from the University of Jena, where, under the influence of Charles Darwin's ideas, he became interested in the impact of environment on the mutability of organic forms and decided to study marine fauna. After graduation, Miklukho-Maklai traveled briefly along the coast of the Red Sea, gathering zoological data while observing the living conditions of the local inhabitants before returning to St. Petersburg in the summer of 1869 and joining the staff of the Zoological Museum of the Russian ACADEMY OF SCIENCES. With a growing interest in the zoology of the Pacific Ocean, in September 1869 he submitted a proposal to the Russian Geographical Society for a long-term expedition to the Pacific region. The proposal was accepted.

Following the advice of other scholars, Miklukho-Maklai revised his proposal to study the almost unknown island of New Guinea, for which he set sail in November 1870 and arrived in September 1871. Except for a brief interlude in 1882 when he visited Russia, for the next 16 years Miklukho-Maclay criss-crossed the region between New Guinea, Dutch Indonesia, Australia and the Malay Peninsula, engaging in ethnological research at a time when Great Britain and Germany were asserting their interests in the area and Australian colonists were laying claim to eastern New Guinea. Miklukho-Maklai emerged as a forceful defendant of the interests of the region's indigenous population, especially in New Guinea. In 1884 he married Joan Robertson, the widowed daughter of a former prime minister of the Australian colony of New South Wales. Three years later, gravely ill from years of wandering and disease, Miklukho-Maklai returned with his family to St. Petersburg in 1887. Less than a year later he died in a hospital on April 14, 1888, at the age of 41. Although well known in the latter years of his life, Miklukho-Maklai and his work were forgotten soon after, despite the efforts of his friends and colleagues. In 1923 the Soviet government began to recover his scholarly legacy by publishing the diaries of his travels in New Guinea. Other more complete scholarly editions followed in the 1950s, while the Institute of Ethnography of the USSR Academy of Sciences was renamed in his honor.

Mikoyan, Anastas Ivanovich
(1895–1978)
Soviet official

Mikoyan was an astute Bolshevik politician who managed to survive the turbulence of high Soviet politics and remain close to the levels of power under STALIN, KHRUSHCHEV, and BREZHNEV. An Armenian by ethnicity, Mikoyan received a theological education but joined the BOLSHEVIKS in 1915. In the early stages of the Russian Revolution, he served as a Bolshevik organizer in the Caucasus. When anti-Bolshevik forces captured Baku in 1918, through sheer luck Mikoyan escaped the fate that awaited the famous 26 Baku commissars, who were rounded up, transported across the Caspian Sea, and shot in the desert. Close to Stalin from the early moments of the civil war, Mikoyan rose rapidly inside the COMMUNIST PARTY hierarchy in the 1920s and 1930s, joining the Central Committee in 1923 and the Politburo in 1935. As a government official, he specialized in trade and distribution; between 1926 and 1949, he served in succession as people's commissar for trade, supplies, food, and, finally, foreign trade. After Stalin's death in 1953, he astutely threw his lot with Khrushchev, eventually becoming deputy prime minister from 1955 to 1964. Khrushchev sent Mikoyan to Cuba, where he fell in love with Castro's revolution, saying that it reminded him of his youth. In

October 1964, Mikoyan played an important, and by all accounts sincere, role in easing the power transition from Khrushchev to Brezhnev, once the Politburo turned against his former ally. Mikoyan remained in ceremonial roles for a few more years before retiring. When his old ally Khrushchev died in 1971, Mikoyan managed to send a wreath to the funeral. In 1988 his son, Sergo Mikoyan, was the first of the children of the old elite to acknowledge openly the responsibility of their parents for the terrible Russian past since the revolution.

Miliukov, Pavel Nikolaevich
(1859–1943)
historian and politician

The leading liberal politician between the 1905 and 1917 Revolutions, Miliukov served as foreign minister in the first Provisional Government after the abdication of NICHOLAS II. Miliukov lectured at Moscow University from 1886 to 1894, but was dismissed for his sympathies with the student movement. When the 1905 Revolution broke out, Miliukov was lecturing in Chicago, but he quickly returned to Russia and played a crucial role in that turbulent year. Uncompromising in his rejection of the Czarist regime, Miliukov emerged as the dominant figure in the newly formed Party of Constitutional Democrats (Kadets), Russia's preeminent liberal party until the October Revolution. In 1905, his politics were slightly to the left of those of his liberal colleagues, rejecting the czar's October Manifesto and pressing for a Constituent Assembly in conjunction with more extreme revolutionaries. Eventually, he came to terms with the post-1905 semiconstitutional settlement. He served as a Kadet deputy in the Third and Fourth DUMAS (1907–12, 1912–17). During World War I, he was one of the loudest critics of the government's war effort, joining the Progressive Bloc that demanded a role in managing the wartime economy. He became notorious in November 1916 in a thunderous speech in which he catalogued the government's failings and then queried whether this was "stupidity or treason," nimbly raising the issue on many people's minds that the czar's German-born wife's allegiances were not entirely with Russia. After the FEBRUARY REVOLUTION, Miliukov's erudition and intellectual brilliance did not help him in the chaos of Russia's revolutionary politics in 1917, when he quickly proved unable to adapt to a rapidly changing situation. He was appointed minister of foreign affairs in the first Provisional Government but was its first political casualty when his note to the Allies reasserting Russia's postwar territorial aspirations was leaked to the public, and he was forced to resign by socialist public opinion, which interpreted it as a continuation of czarist imperialist foreign policies. He watched the disintegration of the Provisional Government from the sidelines and after the October Revolution helped form the Volunteer Army under General ALEKSEEV. After the defeat of the anti-Bolshevik resistance in 1920, Miliukov moved to France, where he was active in émigré politics and wrote numerous works, including a *History of the Russian Revolution*, in which he had played an important role.

Miliutin, Dmitrii Alekseevich (1816–1912)

official

Together with his brother Nikolai Alekseevich Miliutin (1818–72), Dmitrii Miliutin was one the leading officials whom historians have called "enlightened bureaucrats" deeply involved in the planning and execution of Czar ALEXANDER II's Great Reforms. Born in Moscow into the family of an insolvent factory owner, Miliutin graduated from the Moscow University pensionate with a silver medal in 1832. After a junior officer commission, he entered the Military Academy in 1836, and upon graduation was posted to the Guards general headquarters with the rank of staff captain. After active service in the Caucasus, in 1840 he embarked on an extended tour of western Europe, from which he developed an intense interest in political economy, law, and administration to add to his interests in history and geography. From 1845 to 1856 he taught at the academy and continued to publish while also devising operational plans for the impending Russian campaign against Turkey. His scholarly interests and commitment to military education found expression in his role as one of the founders of the historical journal *Voennyi zhurnal* (Military Journal) and, in 1858, of *Voennyi sbornik* (Military Review). After further service as chief of staff to the Caucasian armies, he became deputy war minister in 1860 and the following year, minister of war. Although not a democrat, he did pursue his goal of military reform with conviction and energy. His nationalist feelings came to the surface, as with other contemporaries, in his strong defense of Russia's brutal suppression of the POLISH REBELLION OF 1863–64. As a military reformer, Miliutin advocated the creation of a national army that transcended class divisions, and his reforms of the czarist army, while not entirely successful in achieving this goal, did introduce new standards of professionalism and modernity. He was promoted to field marshal and named a count in 1878, but his influence waned dramatically after the assassination of Alexander II. The new czar, ALEXANDER III, hardly a reformer, had little use for Miliutin, who resigned as minister in May 1881. For his services he was rewarded with a seat on the State Council, the highest but ultimately powerless consultative political body in the empire prior to the 1905 Revolution.

Minin and Pozharsky

patriotic leaders

Two 17th-century Russian patriots whose monument stands on Moscow's RED SQUARE in tribute to their contributions during the last stage of the TIME OF TROUBLES (1598–1613). Kuzma Minin (?–1616) was a butcher from the Volga River town of Nizhnii Novgorod, while Prince Dmitrii Mikhailovich Pozharsky (1578–1642) had gained some military experience in previous years. Although the Time of Troubles dated to 1598 and the end of the Rurikid dynastic line, the event that set the stage for the intervention of Minin and Pozharsky was the deposition of Czar VASILI IV in 1610 after a five-year period that had witnessed three czars and the emergence of two impostors claiming to be Prince Dmitrii of Uglich, dead since 1591. With the throne vacant, Polish and Lithuanian armies entered Moscow and imposed their candidate, Prince Wladyslaw, son of the Polish king. A nationalist backlash soon took place centered around the town of Nizhnii Novgorod, where in September 1611 Kuzma Minin, an elder in the town council, proposed the formation of a fund to raise an army to dislodge the foreign invaders. After calling for volunteers, he proposed Prince Dmitri Pozharsky as the army's leader. Pozharsky, a nobleman from Vladimir in central Russia, had distinguished himself in an earlier campaign in 1608. The response to Minin's appeal was impressive, and an army led by Pozharsky set off for Moscow, gaining recruits along the way. On the outskirts of Moscow it joined another army led by Prince Trubetskoi, and in August and September 1612, Pozharsky's army attacked the Polish-Lithuanian troops. By November 1612, the Polish troops inside the Kremlin surrendered. The endgame of the Time of Troubles took place in 1613, when an assembly of the land (ZEMSKII SOBOR) met composed of representatives from across Russia and chose MICHAEL ROMANOV as the new czar, thus marking the beginning of the ROMANOV DYNASTY, which would rule Russia until 1917. Pozharsky was allegedly offered the crown first, but he refused it. For his efforts Minin was made a noble. In 1818, an imposing monument to the two leaders was erected in the center of Red Square. Later it was moved to the edge of the square, closer to St. Basil's Cathedral, where it now stands.

Mir Iskusstva (World of Art)

An influential artistic movement at the turn of the 20th century that rejected the then dominant utilitarian view that art should serve a socially useful function, advocating instead art for art's sake. In this, they were reacting with particular vehemence to the ideas of the Peredvizhniki (WANDERERS), who had dominated artistic discourse in Russia from the 1870s through the 1890s. The movement took its name from the journal founded in 1898 by Sergei DIAGHILEV and the painter Aleksandr Benois, which acquainted readers with the latest trends in western European art while reevaluating the traditions of Russian art, especially ancient art. Although the journal ceased publication in 1904, its tenets continued to influence Russian art for the next decades. The movement also organized several exhibitions to which leading Russian artists such as Mikhail VRUBEL, Isaak Levitan, and Valentin Serov sent their work. The most prominent members of Mir Iskusstva left Russia after the 1917 Revolutions, among them Benois, Leon Bakst, Nikolai ROERIKH, and Mikhail Larionov. In emigration a few of them collaborated with Diaghilev, by then a longtime resident of Paris, in his Ballets Russes.

Molotov, Vyacheslav Mikhailovich (1890–1986)

revolutionary and Soviet official

A revolutionary who became one of STALIN's most loyal associates, Molotov was the stubborn face of Soviet diplomacy until his influence waned in the mid-1950s as Nikita KHRUSHCHEV consolidated power. Molotov was born Vyacheslav Scriabin, into a middle-class family related to that of the composer Aleksandr SCRIABIN. In 1906 he joined the Bolshevik Party and helped found the newspaper *Pravda,* which he also edited. In 1909 he was banished to the northern province of Vologda for his revolutionary activity, where he remained until 1911. At the time of the FEBRUARY REVOLUTION of 1917, Molotov was a member of the Russian bureau of the Bolshevik Party's Central Committee. Unlike his future mentor Stalin, Molotov argued for opposition to the Provisional Government, the line that LENIN would advocate after his return to Russia in April 1917. In October 1917, as a member of the party's

Military-Revolutionary Committee, Molotov was involved in the organizational aspects of the insurrection in Petrograd that brought the BOL-SHEVIKS to power. He spent most of the civil war engaged in party organizational work, and in 1920 he was appointed head of the COMMUNIST PARTY in Ukraine, a position he held until 1925. During these years Molotov began his rise through the party ranks, with the help of Stalin. A member of the Central Committee since 1921, he entered the Politburo in 1925. In the following decades he held numerous posts of growing importance, but he is perhaps best known for his efforts as commissar for foreign affairs, to which he was appointed in May 1939, succeeding Maxim Litvinov. Molotov's appointment signaled an important change in Soviet foreign policy which culminated with the signing of the pact with Nazi Germany that bears his name, the Molotov-Ribbentrop Pact, in August 1939. Otherwise known as the NAZI-SOVIET PACT, this nonaggression agreement between two ideological enemies shocked the world and set the stage for World War II after Germany felt free to attack Poland when the USSR indicated it would not object. Molotov was at Stalin's side during all the wartime conferences with the United States and Great Britain. Even after his wife, who was Jewish, was sent to a labor camp, Molotov remained Stalin's loyal aide, a bizarre sign of the mixed devotion and fear that Stalin inspired in his inner circle. In 1949 Molotov was replaced as foreign minister by Andrei VYSHINSKY, but he regained his position in March 1953 after Stalin's death. Molotov supported Khrushchev against BERIA in the early maneuverings that followed Stalin's death, but his influence declined as Khrushchev pursued a more reformist path. In 1957, after he was replaced by Andrei GROMYKO as foreign minister, Molotov joined other old-guard Stalinists such as KAGANOVICH and MALENKOV in the anti-Khrushchev opposition known as the ANTI-PARTY GROUP. In defeat, unlike the others he refused to acknowledge any mistakes but was nevertheless demoted to serve as Soviet ambassador to the People's Republic of Mongolia. He later also

Vyacheslav Molotov *(Library of Congress)*

served as Soviet representative to the International Atomic Energy Agency in Vienna. In 1964, during one of Khrushchev's periodic de-Stalinization campaigns, he was expelled from the Communist Party. Twenty years later, with the conservative Konstantin CHERNENKO briefly in power, Molotov was readmitted to the party. He died in obscurity in the village of Peredelkino outside Moscow.

Mongol conquest

Mongol armies first appeared on the eastern banks of the Volga River in 1236, after conquering China, Central Asia, Iran, and Transcaucasia over the previous three decades. Their leader was BATU KHAN, grandson of Genghis (Chinggis) Khan. Batu Khan, who already ruled the steppes to the north of the Aral Sea and Lake Balkhash, began to penetrate farther west, and within four years he had conquered the Volga Bulgarians and the politically fragmented Russian principalities with the exception of Novgorod, capturing the great city of Kiev in December 1240. Batu established the GOLDEN HORDE, with its capital at SARAI on the eastern banks of the Volga, near ASTRAKHAN, and from there the Mongols ruled the Russian principalities through a system of tribute. After about a century, the Mongol grip on its vassal states began to weaken. During the 14th century, the western and southern Russian principalities fell under the sway of the newly established Grand Duchy of Lithuania. Within the territory still held by the Golden Horde, the small principality of Moscow absorbed many of its neighbors until it felt strong enough to challenge the Horde. In 1380 the Muscovite Prince DMITRII DONSKOI led a coalition of Russian princes to defeat the Tatars at the Battle of Kulikovo. The defeat was mostly a harbinger of future changes, because it was not for another hundred years that Moscow was able to fully shake off its tributary burdens. In 1480, IVAN III formally proclaimed that Moscow would not pay tribute, a claim that was enabled by the Battle of the Ugra River. Although the Mongols continued to raid Russian territories throughout the late 16th century, their power declined as a result of internal divisions. During the 15th century, the Golden Horde disintegrated into a number of khanates (Astrakhan, Crimea, KAZAN, and Siberia). With the exception of the Crimea, they fell to the growing power of Muscovy during the 16th and early 17th centuries.

Moscow (Moskva)

An urban settlement on the confluence of the Moscow and Neglinnaia Rivers that emerged from relative obscurity in the 14th century to lead the process of unification of the subjugated Russian principalities in their struggle against Mongol rule. The first recorded mention of the town dates back to 1147, when records show that it belonged to Prince Yuri Dolgoruki of Vladimir-Suzdal, one of the principalities that formed part of KIEVAN RUS. A minor town at the time of the MONGOL CONQUEST in 1240, Moscow survived through luck, geographical location, and the cunning of its ruling princes, and in 1340, its prince IVAN I (Kalita) was awarded the title of grand prince by the Mongol khan. In 1380, during the reign of DMITRII DONSKOI, Muscovite forces defeated the Mongols at the Battle of Kulikovo field, the first Russian victory over the Mongols in more than a century. Up through the reign of IVAN III the Great, the principality of Moscow—also known as Muscovy—continued to increase its power by annexing or conquering neighboring territories. In 1480, Ivan the Great formally renounced the payment of tribute to the Mongols at SARAI, an event usually considered to mark the end of Mongol rule in Russia, although military confrontations between the two sides continued until the late 16th century. Together with its emergence as a military power, Moscow benefited from its importance as a center of spiritual power. In 1320, the metropolitan of the Russian Orthodox Church moved to Moscow. By 1589 the importance of Russia in the Orthodox world was recognized with the establishment of a PATRIARCHATE in Moscow. After briefly experiencing foreign rule during the TIME OF TROUBLES (1598–1613), Moscow flourished during the 17th century, developing a unique culture that was different from the West yet open to Western influences. The reign of PETER I the Great (1689–1725) marked an important turning point in the fortunes of the city. Seeking to align Russia closer to Western culture, Peter established a new capital on the banks of the Neva River, near the Baltic Sea, which he named St. Petersburg. In 1712, St. Petersburg formally became the capital of Russia. For the next 200 years, with the exception of the brief reign of PETER II, Peter the Great's grandson, who attempted to restore Moscow as capital, Moscow was relegated to second-city status, although new rulers were still officially crowned in the Kremlin. Overshadowed by St. Petersburg, a few events stand out in the city's

Rooftop view of Moscow, overlooking the Uspensky Cathedral and the Moscow River, ca. 1918 *(Library of Congress)*

history between 1712 and 1918. In 1771, the city suffered from a plague epidemic that led to widespread riots. In 1812, still an important urban center, Moscow was invaded by Napoleon Bonaparte's armies after their victory at the Battle of BORODINO. As the French prepared to enter Moscow, thinking that its capture would lead Czar ALEXANDER I to sue for peace, a series of fires broke out, quickly negating its value to the French occupiers. A month later, Napoleon left the city and began his disastrous retreat in the middle of the Russian winter. Architectural change came to Moscow, first as part of the reconstruction that followed the French occupation and later in the 19th century through the efforts of an emerging wealthy business class that sought to leave its mark on the city.

Moscow regained its status as the seat of Russia's government in March 1918, when the newly installed Bolshevik regime transferred its offices from Petrograd (St. Petersburg), while German forces advanced on Petrograd. Moscow's new status was made permanent after the establishment of the Union of Soviet Socialist Republics in December 1922, with Moscow as the Soviet capital. Joseph STALIN's long rule left its mark on Moscow, as part of his effort to transform the city into a showcase of socialism. A subway system known as the Metro was begun in the 1930s with near-palatial stations. At the same time, the industrializing policies of the Soviet regime brought an unprecedented wave of rural migrants to the city, drastically increasing its population from 1.6 million in 1912 to 4 million in 1937. Soon after the beginning of hostilities with Germany in June 1941, German forces advanced on Moscow. By October 1941 they had reached the city's outskirts, threatening to capture the Soviet capital and military headquarters. A Soviet counterattack in December 1941 forced the Germans to retreat, and gradually the Soviet war effort gained strength (see MOSCOW, BATTLE OF). In the postwar period, the city continued to grow in population, reaching 5 million in 1959 and 7 million in 1970. During the era of Mikhail GORBACHEV, Moscow was, together with Leningrad (St. Petersburg), a stronghold of reformist ideas and politics. In August 1991, when Communist hard-liners attempted to overthrow Gorbachev, the spirited resistance of many Muscovites helped prevent the coup from succeeding. At the time of the dissolution of the Soviet Union, the city's population had reached 9 million. In the 1990s, Moscow continued to be at the center of Russia's turbulent politics while becoming the showcase for the new Western-style economy that emerged after the fall of communism.

Moscow, Battle of (1941)

A winter battle fought between October and December 1941 on the outskirts of MOSCOW that marked the first land defeat for the Germans since their invasion of the Soviet Union in June 1941. The attack on Moscow was one of three major offensives launched by the Germans in the summer of 1941, the other two being attacks on the key Soviet cities of Leningrad and Kiev. By July 1941, the 60 divisions led by Field Marshal Feodor von Bock had captured Smolensk, a major transportation link and gateway to Moscow, a few hundred miles to the west. While the German Army Group Center expected to take Moscow by mid-September, Hitler hesitated as to the priority of his objectives, ordering instead to halt the advance on Moscow and dispatch Bock's tank

commander General Heinz Guderian to assist the fighting around Kiev, which fell in September 1941. The attack on Moscow, code-named Operation Typhoon, resumed in late September, by which time most observers agree the Germans had precious little time as the long winter season approached. In the first 10 days of the offensive, the Germans advanced to within 60 miles of Moscow, taking Kalinin (Tver) to the north and Tula to the west. By mid-October, however, rain and mud had begun to slow down the German advance, and by November a harsh early winter had set in. The Germans, expecting an early conquest of Moscow, had not issued winter clothing or supplies to their troops, but Hitler refused to allow the troops to retreat, thus adding to the number of casualties. Nevertheless, the Germans pressed on and by early December they were within 25 miles of the city center.

Up to this point an orderly evacuation of key government officials and diplomatic personnel to the Volga River town of Samara had been taking place. The approaching advance of the Germans triggered a temporary panic and looting among some Moscow residents not authorized to leave. In response STALIN publicly announced his intention to remain in the city, while ordering the police and the NKVD (secret police) to shoot looters and those fleeing Moscow. The arrival of over 100,000 fresh troops from Siberia and the Far East allowed the Red Army to mount a counteroffensive that pushed the Germans to about 60 miles from Moscow. Finally, as German losses from the cold and the fighting escalated, Hitler ordered the offensive abandoned. The German advance on the Central Front was halted and the country's capital had not fallen. The Soviets had resisted successfully but at a great cost, with over 600,000 troops killed or captured. The Germans held on to most of the territories they had gained in this offensive until 1942, but together with their inability to seize Leningrad, the air of inevitable victory that had marked the first six months of the German invasion had begun to dissipate as a result of the Battle of Moscow.

Mussorgsky, Modest Petrovich
(1839–1881)
composer

One of the most original and influential of Russia's 19th-century nationalist composers, known for his operas and song cycles, Mussorgsky was born in Karevo and trained at a military academy in St. Petersburg. Although he was destined for a career as a guards officer, his life was changed by an encounter with the Russian nationalist composer Aleksandr Dargomyzhsky in 1857. Through him, Mussorgsky joined a circle of young nationalist composers, later known as the MIGHTY HANDFUL, (Moguchaia kuchka) or Mighty Five. The following year, he resigned his military commission, intending to devote himself to music. Like three other members of the Five, Mussorgsky had no real training in music, except for some basic instruction he received from Mily Balakirev, the fifth member of the group. That he was self-taught makes his considerable musical achievements all the more remarkable. Unable to make a living only as a composer, Mussorgsky entered the civil service in 1863. His first work to gain public attention was the symphonic poem *Night on Bald Mountain,* first performed in 1867. The following year he completed the opera *Boris God-unov,* considered to be his masterpiece. However, it was not performed in public until 1874. Other works followed, notably the piano suite *Pictures at an Exhibition,* which he wrote in 1874 for his recently deceased friend, the architect Victor Hartmann. In his lifetime Mussorgsky's work, full of bold nationalist themes, relying on folk music and dramatic choirs, was rarely performed as originally written. Other performers rearranged it, sweetening or diluting its original impact for the audiences of the day. At his untimely death at the age of 42, Mussorgsky left several important works unfinished, among them the operas *Khovanshchina* and *The Fair at Sorochinsk.* He was fortunate that his friends and long-time colleagues from the Five, RIMSKY-KORSAKOV and Cesar Cui, respectively, took it upon themselves to complete the two operas. Mussorgsky's reputation continued to grow with the reorchestration of *Boris Godunov* by Rimsky-Korsakov in 1896 and orchestration of *Pictures at an Exhibition* by the French composer Maurice Ravel in 1922. For many years only these reorchestrations were known by the wider listening public. And only in the latter half of the 20th century did performers stage Mussorgsky's work in full and as he had originally intended.

N

Nabokov, Vladimir Vladimirovich (1899–1977)
writer

The product of a prominent noble family, Nabo-kov was born in St. Petersburg on April 23, 1899. His father, V. D. Nabokov, was a well-known lib-eral politician who took part in the Provisional Government of 1917. After the OCTOBER REVOLU-TION of that year, the Nabokov family fled Russia for Berlin, where the elder Nabokov was assassi-nated in 1922, the victim of a bullet intended for his colleague, Pavel MILIUKOV. His son Vladimir graduated from Cambridge University, and after marrying his lifelong partner, Vera Slonim, in 1925 settled again in Berlin to work as a writer. Under the pseudonym of V. Sirin, he wrote a series of works in Russian that focused on the themes of loss and exile, of which *Dar* (*The Gift*, 1937) is perhaps the most representative. Fleeing the Nazis, the Nabokov family moved to France in 1937, before settling in the United States in 1940. Nabokov embarked on a new career as an academic, teaching at Wellesley College and Cor-nell University, and more remarkably as an English-language author, beginning with *The Real Life of Sebastian Knight* (1941). An American citi-zen since 1945, Nabokov combined the charac-teristic themes of the émigré writer, such as loss and longing, with a more modern literary fasci-nation with illusion, parody, distortion, multiple worlds, and language itself. The publication of *Lolita* (1958) thrust Nabokov onto the center stage of public notoriety that included an obscen-ity trial as many readers fixated on the love affair between a middle-aged émigré and a teenaged girl and ignored other themes of the book. The Nabokovs moved to Montreux in 1959, his final

Vladimir Nabokov *(Library of Congress)*

stopping place, where he continued to publish, notably *Pale Fire* (1962), his autobiography, *Speak Memory* (1966), and the family chronicle *Ada* (1969). He died in Montreux at the age of 78, his reputation firmly established as a Russian and American writer and with his devotion to record-ing precise details above generalities, a major influence on contemporary literature.

Nagorno-Karabakh

A region in the southern Caucasus, formally a part of the republic of Azerbaijan, but with an Armenian majority, that in 1988 erupted as the first flashpoint of the ethnic conflict that would mark the final years of the Soviet Union. An independent khanate in the 18th century, Nagorno-Karabakh became part of the Russian Empire in 1828. By the time of the Russian Revolution of 1917, the region's population was about 75 percent Armenian. In 1923, at the creation of the Union of Soviet Socialist Republics, Nagorno-Karabakh was given the status of an Autonomous Region and placed under Azerbaijani control. Further territorial changes in 1930 isolated Nagorno-Karabakh from Armenia, leaving it entirely within the borders of Azerbaijan.

In February 1988, inspired by Mikhail GORBACHEV's reformist rhetoric, Armenians in the Karabakh region began a series of demonstrations requesting to be united with the Armenian S.S.R. When the Soviet government offered to hold high-level discussions about the region's status, thousands of demonstrators in the Armenian capital of Yerevan marched in solidarity with the Karabakh Armenians. As the Soviet government hesitated, the demonstrations in Yerevan grew in frequency while the number of demonstrators reached the hundreds of thousands. The Azerbaijanis responded in kind to a perceived threat to the integrity of their republic, but on February 28–29, 1988, at Sumgait, an industrial town north of Baku, events took an ugly turn, leading to attacks on the town's Armenian population and the deaths of more than 30 people. As the crisis became more intractable, the possibility of a compromise disappeared and the Soviet government placed Nagorno-Karabakh under direct presidential rule from July 1988 to November 1989. But this also failed to solve the crisis. The discontent of both Armenians and Azerbaijanis with the Nagorno-Karabakh situation gave voice to both Armenian and Azerbaijani nationalist demands in the final two years of the Soviet Union.

With the dissolution of the Soviet Union in December 1991, the region declared its independence and sought to join the now independent republic of Armenia. War broke out between Armenia and Azerbaijan, and by 1994 the Nagorno-Karabakh Armenians had seized control of most of the region's territory to the west, linking up with Armenia. By the time a cease-fire agreement was negotiated later that year, about 15,000 people had been killed in the conflict and over 1 million had been displaced from their homes.

Nakhimov, Pavel Stepanovich (1802–1855)
admiral

The commander of the Russian Black Sea Fleet during the CRIMEAN WAR, Nakhimov distinguished himself for his heroism during the unsuccessful defense of SEVASTOPOL, during which he was killed. Prior to his service in the Crimean War, Nakhimov had circumnavigated the world in 1822–24. As commander of the Black Sea Fleet, however, he gained notoriety in the West as the officer behind the destruction of a Turkish flotilla at Sinop in 1853, soon after the Ottoman Empire had declared war on Russia in October 1853. Nakhimov's destruction of the Turkish flotilla, which was anchored at the time of the attack, was denounced by the British in particular as a massacre and an atrocity. It contributed to turning a Russo-Turkish conflict into a broader one that brought Great Britain, France, and Sardinia to declare war on Russia. Together with admirals V. A. KORNILOV and V. I. Istomin and General E. I. Totleben, a talented military engineer, Nakhimov led the resistance of 18,000 Russians, mostly sailors, to the siege of the naval base of Sevastopol begun in September 1854, the centerpiece of the allied campaign in the Crimea. Of the four, only Totleben survived, although he was seriously wounded. Nakhimov took over the command after Kornilov and Istomin had perished, but he too was killed in July 1855. The siege continued until September 1855, when after one year of bombardment, the allied troops finally broke through the city's defenses.

In 1944, as part of its campaign to rehabilitate czarist military officers such as SUVOROV and

KUTUZOV, the Soviet government created a naval decoration, the Nakhimov Order, while naming naval schools after Nakhimov.

Nazi-Soviet Pact

The name usually given to the 10-year Non-Aggression Pact signed between the Soviet Union and Nazi Germany on August 23–24, 1939. Sometimes known as the Molotov-Ribbentrop pact, after the Soviet and German diplomats who signed it, the pact dramatically changed the geostrategic balance in Europe by removing the threat to Germany of having to fight a two-front war, as in World War I. The published component of the pact merely stated that neither side would join in an attack on the other for a period of 10 years. The pact had a secret protocol, however, that promised the Soviet Union the eastern third of Poland and spheres of influence over Latvia, Estonia, and Finland. Under the original terms of the pact, Lithuania was to fall under Germany's sphere of influence. The secret protocol also stated that the Germans would not contest a Soviet claim to Bessarabia, a Romanian province that had been part of Russia until 1918.

News of the pact shocked the outside world, especially communist party members in western Europe who had spent most of the 1930s fighting fascist movements in places such as Austria, Spain, and France. Many of them left their parties at this time. Freed from concern over Soviet intentions, Adolf Hitler launched the German invasion of Poland on September 1, 1939, starting what became World War II. Soviet troops marched into eastern Poland two weeks later and annexed Estonia, Latvia, and Lithuania in 1940. The Soviet Union admitted to the existence of the secret protocol only in 1989.

Nechaev, Sergei Gennadievich
(1847–1882)
revolutionary

Nechaev was a fanatic and controversial revolutionary who, through his belief that revolutionaries should suppress any moral considerations, raised some difficult issues for the Russian revolutionary movement. The son of a waiter, Nechaev was born in the town of Ivanovo, north of Moscow. Like others of his generation, as a student Nechaev took part in disturbances in St. Petersburg and was compelled to emigrate to Switzerland in 1869. In Geneva he met and impressed the seasoned anarchist revolutionary Mikhail BAKUNIN, 33 years his senior. Claiming to be the head of a powerful clandestine organization, Nechaev enlisted Bakunin in writing several propaganda brochures and in collaborating on a pamphlet entitled "The Catechism of the Revolutionary." Authorship of this pamphlet was debated for some time, but it seems that most of the credit should go to Nechaev. In it, Nechaev begins with the then widespread idea that true revolutionaries should be exclusively concerned with their one passion, revolution. He further argued that revolutionaries should suppress all moral inhibitions and be prepared to kill, manipulate, and compromise opponents and those who stood in the way—ideas that created a storm in what was still a highly idealistic revolutionary movement. Nechaev also argued for strict organizational rules, dictatorial centralization and secrecy in developing a revolutionary organization. These organizational ideas placed him in the tradition of the Decembrist Pavel Pestel, and would later resurface in the writings of Petr TKACHEV and Vladimir LENIN. Nechaev returned to Moscow in August 1869 and promptly founded a revolutionary organization called People's Retribution. When one member protested some of Nechaev's techniques, he was murdered by Nechaev and four of his colleagues. The case received much publicity and shocked the Russian radical intelligentsia. Nechaev was forced to flee again, but this time he was ostracized by the revolutionary émigrés, including Bakunin. In 1872 he was extradited from Switzerland as a common criminal, and sentenced to 20 years' hard labor. Instead, he was held in solitary confinement in St. Petersburg's PETER AND PAUL FORTRESS, where he died, possibly a suicide.

Neizvestny, Ernst Iosifovich (1925–)

artist and sculptor

An influential figure among unorthodox Soviet artists, Neizvestny will be most readily remembered for the testy but ultimately respectful relationship he developed with Nikita KHRUSHCHEV. Born in Sverdlovsk (Ekaterinburg), he studied at the Surikov State Institute for the Arts. He served in the Red Army during World War II (1942–45) and was severely wounded. After the war he worked as a sculptor at the studios of the USSR Agricultural Exhibition in Moscow. Over the years he developed a monumental cubist style, which was neither that of "official" socialist realism, nor a reflection of the fashionably abstract work then being produced in the West, and thus he was criticized by proponents of both traditions. Neizvestny became known to the world following his public confrontation with General Secretary Khrushchev when the latter launched a violent verbal attack against modern art while visiting the Manezh exhibit in Moscow in November 1962. Yet Khrushchev eventually changed his evaluation of Neizvestny's art, because at the time of Khrushchev's death, he was commissioned to sculpt the memorial to Khrushchev in Novodeviche Cemetery in Moscow. An active supporter of human rights and dissident causes, Neizvestny was expelled several times from the Artists' Union between the 1950s and 1970s. He emigrated in 1976, first to Switzerland then the United States, where he has lived since. In 1991, the Soviet citizenship that had been revoked when he emigrated was restored.

Nekrasov, Nikolai Alekseevich (1821–1877)

poet and publisher

A poet recognized for his passionate denunciations of SERFDOM and the misery of the lower classes, Nekrasov enjoyed great popularity among the intelligentsia of the mid-19th century. He was the owner and editor of the influential journals *Sovremennik* (The contemporary) and *Otechestvennye zapiski* (Notes of the fatherland).

Nekrasov was born into the noble family of a retired officer and serf-owner and spent his childhood on the family estate in Yaroslav province. In 1832 Nekrasov entered the Yaroslavl Gymnasium but did not complete his studies. In 1838 his father sent Nekrasov to St. Petersburg to enroll in the training academy for noble officers, but he instead joined the Faculty of History and Philology at St. Petersburg University. In punishment, his father ceased to provide Nekrasov with financial support, forcing him into a student life of hunger and deprivation far removed from the privileged circumstances of his childhood. His early attempts at literature were unsuccessful, but Nekrasov eventually found success as a poet, with the encouragement of the influential critic Vissarion BELINSKY, whom he met in 1845. By 1847 Nekrasov had become the editor and publisher of *Sovremennik,* the literary journal that published Belinsky, Aleksandr HERZEN, Lev TOLSTOY, Feudor DOSTOEVSKY, Ivan TURGENEV, and other leading authors of the Russian world of letters. Under Nekrasov's direction, *Sovremennik* also became the leading voice of Russia's emerging revolutionary movement. In 1866 the auhorities closed the journal, but two years later Nekrasov was publishing a new journal, *Otechestvennye zapiski,* which he edited until his death. Although Nekrasov's influence through his editorial work and publishing was immense, he is best remembered by Russians through poems such as "The Railway," "Peasant Children," "Russian Women," and "Who Lives Well in Russia?," the latter a historical epic written from 1864 to 1876. Several of his poems were also put to music by leading composers of his day, such as Peter TCHAIKOVSKY and Modest MUSSORGSKY.

Nemirovich-Danchenko, Vladimir Ivanovich (1859–1943)

theater director and producer

Born in Georgia, Nemirovich-Danchenko was one of two brothers who played an active part in the culture of the late imperial and early Soviet periods of Russian history. While his older brother Vasili (1848–1936) was a prolific and popular author of historical narratives, Vladimir Nemirovich-Danchenko became one of the central figures in the development of 20th-century Russian and Soviet drama. Born in Georgia, Nemirovich-Danchenko studied at Moscow University from 1876 to 1879, developing a reputation as an amateur actor and critic. Under the influence of his friend Anton CHEKHOV, he began to write novels and plays, but his signal contribution to Russian drama would come from a different source. In 1898 he joined forces with Konstantin STANISLAVSKY to found the Moscow Arts Theater (MkhAT), which quickly became an important force in Russia's cultural life. Blending Stanislavsky's directorial genius and Nemirovich-Danchenko's abilities as a producer, the Moscow Arts Theater contributed immensely to the development of Russian drama through its productions of Chekhov's works and its promotion of an influential new style of acting, as developed by Stanislavsky. During the early Soviet period Nemirovich-Danchenko and Stanislavsky further consolidated the identity of the Moscow Arts Theater as a venue for producing Russian classical works. Nemirovich-Danchenko also organized an operatic school within the Moscow Arts Theater, which sought to train opera artists as singers and actors. The school was later renamed the Nemirovich-Danchenko Musical Drama Theater, and in 1939 it grew further by incorporating the Ballet Collective of the Moscow Art Ballet. During the final decade of his life, Nemirovich-Danchenko's work became more conservative, in line with the harshly conformist Stalinist cultural politics of those years.

Nerchinsk, Treaty of (1689)

The first diplomatic agreement between Russia and China, the Treaty of Nerchinsk was a political and commercial pact that also established the boundaries between the two empires. The treaty was a result of growing incidents of armed confrontation in the AMUR RIVER region between Russian settlers and COSSACKS on one side and troops of the Manchu Qing dynasty that had ruled China since 1644. Negotiations were conducted in the town of Nerchinsk, which the Russians had established in 1654, and the treaty was signed on August 27, 1689. According to the treaty, China recognized Russian possession of the region east of Lake Baikal, up to the Argun River, with the Stanovoi Mountains serving as the boundary north of the Amur River. In turn, Russia recognized Chinese control of the Amur River valley. Russian commercial caravans also received the long-sought right to enter the Chinese capital, Peking (Beijing). With some minor revisions in 1727, the Nerchinsk agreement remained the basis of Sino-Russian relations until 1858. In that year, with a greatly weakened Chinese Empire, the Treaty of Aigun gave the left bank of the Amur River to Russia, while the Treaty of Peking (1860), established the new Sino-Russian boundary along the Amur and Ussuri Rivers, giving Russia about 400,000 square miles of Chinese land.

Nicholas I (1796–1855)
(Nikolai Pavlovich)
czar

Known as the "Iron czar," Nicholas was the third son of Emperor PAUL I, who became emperor in 1825 when his older brother, Emperor ALEXANDER I, died childless in Taganrog. Nicholas was born in Tsarskoe Selo, the imperial suburb outside St. Petersburg. Not expected to become ruler, Nicholas received a purely military education instead, to which scholars attribute the passion for order and discipline that became evident once he became czar. In 1817 he married Alexandra of Hohenzollern, a Prussian princess. Together they had seven children—four sons and three daughters. Nicholas's reign began with the suppression of the DECEMBRIST revolt, which had been initiated by reform-minded officers who sought to take advantage of the public confusion surrounding the succession to the throne after Alexander's death by declaring their allegiance to his brother Constantine, the presumed heir.

Unbeknownst to the public, Constantine had no desire to be czar and had secretly abdicated his rights in 1820. His own personality and training and the impact of a revolt led by younger members of prominent Russian aristocratic families shaped the strongly autocratic character of Nicholas's reign. To most Russians and foreign observers, the reign of Nicholas was a time of order, militarism, and a growing bureaucracy, best summarized by his education minister's formula of "Orthodoxy, autocracy and nationality." In domestic affairs his concern for order resulted in repressive policies but did not close him completely to the empire's need for reform. Thus, he was the originator of the political police known as the Third Section, and he set the tone for tighter discipline in the army, greater censorship in universities and intellectual life, and restrictions on foreign travel. But he also charged Mikhail SPERANSKY, the reformist bureaucrat, with codifying Russia's laws, the first code since 1649. He sought to alleviate the condition of the serfs, specifically that of Crown peasants, through minor changes that did not challenge the institution of SERFDOM itself. His foreign policy was also informed by a concern for order across Europe, and under Nicholas Russia played the role of the "gendarme of Europe," intervening to suppress revolutions in Poland (1830–31) and Hungary (1848), and raising the fear of Russian expansionism in European capitals. Nicholas also waged successful wars against Persia (1826–28) and Ottoman Turkey (1828–29), but a renewed conflict with the latter in 1853 drew Russia into the quagmire of the CRIMEAN WAR (1853–56), where Russia was defeated by a coalition led by Great Britain, France, and Turkey.

Nicholas II (1868–1918)
(Nikolai Aleksandrovich)
emperor

The last ruler of the ROMANOV DYNASTY and the last emperor (czar) of Russia, Nicholas II was executed by the Bolshevik revolutionaries who took power in October 1917. Nicholas was the eldest son of Czar ALEXANDER III and as such received the education befitting an heir to the throne. The assassination of his grandfather, ALEXANDER II, by revolutionaries and the conservative education he received from his principal tutor, Konstantin Pobedonostsev, made the young Nicholas a strong believer in divinely ordained autocratic rule. In 1890 he began a world tour that took him to Egypt, India, China, and Japan, where he escaped an assassination attempt by a local policeman. He returned to St. Petersburg in 1891 through Siberia, following the route of the projected TRANS-SIBERIAN RAILROAD, whose construction he inaugurated. In 1894, against the wishes of his parents, Nicholas married Princess Alice of Hesse-Darmstadt, who adopted the Russian name ALEXANDRA FEODOROVNA and over the next decade bore him four daughters and one son. Alexander III's unexpected death in October 1894 brought the 26-year-old Nicholas to the throne without more than passing acquaintance with governance. His uncompromising adherence to the principle of autocracy in a speech to the Tver gentry alienated an important segment of Russia's progressive nobility. His coronation ceremony in MOSCOW in May 1896 was marred by a mass stampede, with over 1,200 casualties, and by the widespread perception that Nicholas did not care about the deaths since he proceeded with the festivities.

Nicholas's first decade in power was marked by a renewal of clandestine and revolutionary political activities, including the formation of Russia's first political parties and a recession that led to strikes in industrial areas and overall political discontent. In foreign affairs, Russia's eastward expansion marked by the construction of the Trans-Siberian Railroad, completed in 1903, led to the occupation of Port Arthur in 1896 and Manchuria in 1900 and eventually war with Japan in 1904. Losing a war that most Russian and foreign observers expected to win and a deteriorating economic situation contributed to the revolution that broke out across Russia in 1905, sparked by the January massacre of unarmed workers in St. Petersburg, known as

BLOODY SUNDAY. Nicholas was able to slow down revolutionary activities only with the issuance of the October Manifesto, granting civil rights to Russians and providing for a legislative assembly (DUMA) with limited powers. The decade from 1905 to 1914 saw the development of a semi-constitutional regime in Russia, much to the dismay of Nicholas and his wife, who remained steadfast in their belief in autocratic rule. Also during this time, the sinister monk Grigorii RASPUTIN gained influence with Alexandra because of his supposed ability to control the hemophilia of the heir to the throne, Alexis.

The outbreak of World War I in July 1914 tested Russia's military power and the limits of its constitutional experiment. Early Russian defeats by the German army compelled Nicholas to join the command at the front, leaving Alexandra, now dependent on Rasputin, to clash with representatives of the Duma who wanted greater participation in the conduct of the war effort. Continued military defeats, food shortages, and a widespread revulsion against corruption at the imperial court led to spontaneous protests in Petrograd in February 1917. Ten days later Nicholas was forced to abdicate, and when his brother Michael refused the throne, the fate of the Romanov dynasty was sealed. With the Provisional Government in power, Nicholas and his family were first kept at the palace of Tsarskoe Selo, but in August 1917 they were moved to Tobolsk, in Siberia. After the OCTOBER REVOLUTION, the BOLSHEVIKS moved the family to Ekaterinburg in the Urals. With civil war raging across Russia and the future of the Bolshevik government in doubt, LENIN approved the execution of Nicholas, his wife, and children, which was carried out in July 1918.

Nijinsky, Vaslav Fomich (1890–1950)
dancer and choreographer

One of the greatest names in the history of ballet, lauded at his peak as the "God of Dance," Nijinsky was born in Kiev to a family of Polish descent. He enrolled at the St. Petersburg Impe-

rial Ballet School in 1900, displaying an exceptional virtuosity that gained him leading roles early in his career at the Imperial Theater. In 1908, he met Sergei DIAGHILEV, who immediately recruited him for his Ballets Russes, which toured Europe to great acclaim in 1909 with Nijinsky as the star dancer. Nijinsky astounded western audiences with his technical accomplishment, his apparent ability to hover in the air, and his interpretive abilities. In 1911, Nijinsky was dismissed from the Imperial Theaters, ostensibly because his costumes were too revealing, but more likely because the imperial family did not approve of his love affair with Diaghilev. He left Russia, never to return, and now performed exclusively for Diaghilev, developing his skills as a choreographer in works like *L' Après-midi d'un faune, Jeux,* and *Le Sacre du printemps,* the latter causing a furor among audiences for its extreme barbarity and originality. His sudden marriage to a Ballets Russes dancer and his behavior during the 1913 tour of South America marked the beginning of his final estrangement from Diaghilev, and after refusing to dance on one occasion, he was dismissed from the company. He danced for four more years, but in 1917, only 10 years after his debut, ravaged by mental disease, he was confined to an asylum, where he spent the last three decades of his life. He died in London. His sister Bronislava Nijinska (1891–1972), an extraordinary dancer and teacher who appeared with her brother in the first season of the Ballets Russes, has the distinction of being the first female choreographer.

Nikitenko, Aleksandr Vasilievich (1804–1877)
censor and writer

A talented man of letters known to later generations for the invaluable diary he kept for half a century, Nikitenko was born a serf into a family owned by count Sheremetev. By virtue of his talents he rose to become secretary of a district branch of the Bible Society, which developed in Russia in the 1820s with the goal of spreading the Holy Scriptures, particularly the Gospels. Persuaded by influential intercessors such as the poet Vasilii Zhukovskii, who later became a tutor to the future ALEXANDER II, Sheremetev agreed to give Nikitenko his freedom in 1824. In 1828, he graduated from St. Petersburg University and six years later began a long career on the faculty of literature that lasted until 1864. In 1855 he was elected academician. Nikitenko began writing in 1826, while still a student, publishing works of criticism and the history of Russian literature that, while eclectic in their conception, met with mixed reviews. In 1833, Nikitenko began working for the government's censorship office, where he gained a reputation as a lenient censor whose main concern was to produce quality literature within the guidelines of Russia's censorship laws in the conservative reign of NICHOLAS I. Radical authors like Aleksandr HERZEN sought him out, knowing that Nikitenko approached his task from the vantage point of a writer. He wrote various essays on censorship and, under Alexander II's more liberal regime, served as a member of the Main Censorship Directorate from 1860 to 1865. Nikitenko's main literary contribution are the diaries he kept from 1826 until his death, in which readers gain a unique insight into the world of a cultured man of peasant background and moderate views. The diaries were first published in 1889–92, and a scholarly edition appeared in three volumes in 1955–56. An abridged English edition was published as *Diary of a Censor*.

Nikitin, Afanasii (unknown–1472)

merchant

A 15th-century merchant from Tver, Nikitin journeyed to India, and left for posterity one of the first extended descriptions of the region and its people available in any European literature. Nikitin left his hometown of Tver in 1466 on business, sailing down the Volga River to the Caspian Sea to Derbent and Baku. After crossing the Caspian he arrived in Persia, where he spent almost one year. In 1469, he left Persia, sailed

around the Arabian Sea, and arrived in India. While in India, he kept a record of the lives of its peoples, their occupations, social structure, government, and religions. On his return trip he sailed again on the Arabian Sea, the eastern coast of Africa, crossed the Arabian Sea once more, traveled from Hormuz through Tebriz and Trebizond, across the Black Sea, and landed in Cafu (Feodosiia) in 1471. A literate and sophisticated man, Nikitin left a clear account of his journeys in his book *Khozhdenie za tri moria* (Journey over three seas), which portrays with great equanimity for the era the various religious faiths and customs of the regions he visited. Scholars have seen Nikitin as an example of broader humanist, cosmopolitan currents that, although not a coherent movement as in western Europe, found individual representatives in 15th-century Muscovy.

Nikon (1605–1681)

ecclesiastical leader

Patriarch of MOSCOW and all Russia from 1652 to 1658, Nikon initiated liturgical reforms that led to a major schism within the Russian Orthodox Church in the 1660s. Of Mordvinian background, Nikon was born to a peasant family near the Volga River town of Nizhnii Novgorod. In 1626 he became a priest and married, settling down at Makariev Zheltovodsky Monastery. In 1636, he briefly traveled to Moscow, before being assigned to the Anzerskii Monastery, on the Solovetskii Islands of the White Sea. Back in Moscow in 1646, after living in other distant monasteries, Nikon was installed as abbot of Novospasskii Monastery. He befriended the young czar Aleksei and was named patriarch in 1652. As patriarch, Nikon created a court reminiscent of his predecessor FILARET, the father of Czar MICHAEL ROMANOV, who had ruled with his son as great sovereign from 1619 to 1633. Following in Filaret's spirit, Nikon also advanced ideas that placed the church on a level superior to the state. His PATRIARCHATE witnessed the construction of several monasteries, most notably the Resurrection monastery outside Moscow, better known as New Jerusalem, begun in 1656 as a replica of the Church of the Holy Sepulchre in the Holy Land. Nikon is perhaps best known for the controversial reforms he initiated in 1654 with the aim of updating the liturgy of the Russian Church. His proposed reforms included the standardization of church ritual and correction of church books. While accepted by the church leadership, the reforms met with enormous opposition from sections of the clergy and laity, which led to a formal break within the Orthodox Church once they were accepted by the Church Council of 1666–67. In the meantime, Nikon's claims regarding the church's supremacy over the state led to conflicts with Czar Aleksei, and Nikon was deposed as patriarch in 1658. The Church Council of 1666–67 also met to consider Nikon's case, condemning him and exiling him to Ferapontov Monastery, where he lived until 1676. In 1676, Nikon was transferred to Kirillov Monastery. Five years later, while on his way to the Resurrection Monastery in New Jerusalem, Nikon died in Yaroslavl.

Nil Sorsky, Saint (ca. 1433–1508)
monk

A widely respected monk of his time, Nil Sorsky's writings in defense of the supremacy of the contemplative spiritual life influenced Russian monasticism for centuries. Born Nikolai Maikov, Nil Sorsky adopted his name from the Sora River in northeast Russia, besides which he founded his own monastery after returning from pilgrimages to Constantinople and Mount Athos. Sorsky's belief that monks should renounce property and live up to their vows of poverty drew him into the controversy between "possessors" and "non-possessors" that divided the Russian Orthodox Church at the turn of the 16th century. The controversy was ostensibly about the issue of church property, but related to it was the broader question of the proper relationship between the church and secular rulers. The possessors, led by JOSEPH OF VOLOTSK, argued that the church should be rich and powerful and closely allied to the secular ruler, who in turn acted as the church's natural protector. The "non-possessors," of which Sorsky became the chief spokesman, defended the view that the church should not only divest itself of its wealth, particularly its monastic landholdings, but it should also be independent of the state. The Church Council of 1503 decided in favor of the "possessors." Although later church councils declared some of his followers to be heretics, the church canonized Nil Sorsky. His feast day is celebrated on May 7.

Nizhnii Novgorod

The third-largest city in the Russian Federation, with a population of about 1.8 million, Nizhnii Novgorod is Russia's largest river port and a major industrial center and transportation hub. The city was first founded in 1221 as a frontier fortress on a strategic site where the Oka River meets the Volga River in European Russia, about 250 miles east of Moscow. Like other ancient Russian cities, Nizhnii Novgorod developed around a *kremlin,* or citadel, and suffered from Tatar raids in the 13th and 14th centuries. By 1350, however, it had become the capital of the principality of Suzdal-Nizhnii Novgorod and briefly contested the increasingly powerful principality of Moscow, until annexed by the latter in 1392. Due to its proximity to Tatar centers of power, Nizhnii Novgorod served as a base for IVAN IV's successful attack against KAZAN in 1552. During the TIME OF TROUBLES, Nizhnii Novgorod served as one of the centers of the national movement that liberated Moscow from Polish rule in 1611. In 1817 the nearby annual Makarev Fair, which had been founded in 1525, was moved to Nizhnii Novgorod. Until its closure by the Soviet government in 1930, the annual fair, and the city's transportation links to European Russia and Asia, made Nizhnii Novgorod one of Russia's leading commercial centers. Already a center of industrial activity in czarist times, with flourmills and the Sormovo metal works established in 1849, the city benefited from the transfer of several factories to the area during WORLD

WAR I. With the introduction of five-year plans in 1928, Nizhnii Novgorod grew to become one of the Soviet Union's leading industrial centers, and the site of a huge automobile plant (built 1930–32), one of the early showpieces of Stalinist industrial development. In the following decades, the city also attracted an engineering plant, aircraft industries, and railroad and textile industries. In 1932 the city's name was changed to Gorky in honor of the writer Maksim GORKY, who was born in the city. Closed to foreigners because of its industries, the city became well known outside the Soviet Union when the dissident writer Andrei SAKHAROV was banished there (1980–86) for his criticisms of the Soviet government. In 1991, the name reverted to Nizhnii Novgorod. During the 1990s under the leadership of the governor of Nizhnii Novgorod, Boris Nemtsov, the city was relatively successful in making the transition to a post-Soviet, mostly capitalist economy.

Novgorod

One of Russia's most ancient cities, Novgorod challenged MOSCOW for supremacy until the late 15th century and continued to play an important commercial role in northwestern Russia until the foundation of ST. PETERSBURG in 1703, after which it declined in importance. Situated on the Volkhov River near Lake Ilmen, south of St. Petersburg, Novgorod was founded sometime in the fifth or sixth century. In 862, the semilegendary Rurik—considered to be the founder of the Russian monarchy—became prince of Novgorod. By the ninth century Novgorod had become secondary to KIEV, which was emerging as the leading city of the early Russian world, in great part due to its closer proximity to Constantinople. Nevertheless, in 1136 Novgorod achieved formal independence from Kiev. The city successfully resisted Tatar attacks in the late 13th century. Unlike other Russian cities, which were subjugated by the 13th-century Tatar-Mongol invasions, Novgorod successfully resisted conquest and by the 14th century had grown into an important outpost of the Hanseatic League of Baltic Sea towns. It also developed a distinctive form of oligarchic government that reflected its commercial orientation and was centered on the institution of the Veche, in contrast to the autocratic model of government that developed in Novgorod's later rival, the principality of Moscow. Internal divisions in Novgorod and superior Muscovite military strength led to a decisive victory by Moscow in 1471, after which Novgorod was forced to pledge allegiance to IVAN III. In 1478, when the Novgorod leaders sought Lithuanian help and refused to recognize Ivan, Muscovite troops besieged the city, after which Novgorod surrendered without fighting. Harsh reprisals, executions, and deportations of prominent boyar families followed, and by 1489 all traces of Novgorod's previous independence had vanished. Almost one century later, in 1570, the city again suffered the wrath of a Muscovite ruler, this time at the hands of the *oprichnina,* the special institution created by IVAN IV "the Terrible" to spread terror throughout Russian society. In 1610, during the final and most chaotic stage of the TIME OF TROUBLES, Novgorod was captured by Sweden, which held it until the signing of the Treaty of Stolbovo (1617). In relative decline over many centuries, Novgorod suffered severe damage under the WORLD WAR II German occupation from 1941 to 1944 but underwent substantial reconstruction in the postwar decades. Today, although it is a small commercial center of close to 300,000 inhabitants, it preserves a rich architectural legacy dating as far as back to the 11th century.

November Insurrection See POLISH REBELLION 1830–31.

Novikov, Nikolai Ivanovich (1744–1818)
journalist and publisher

The most influential publicist of the late 18th century, Novikov was also one of Russia's most prominent Freemasons. The arc of Novikov's public career coincided with the reign of CATHERINE II, with whom he had a contentious relationship that alternated between collaboration and conflict. Novikov was first educated at home, then at Moscow University. In 1767, he first appeared as a writer for the Legislative Commission. His first publishing venture, the satirical journal *Truten (Drone)* (1769), was closed after one year by order of Catherine, after engaging in a running dialogue or dispute with Catherine's journal *Vsiakaia vsiachina (This and That)*. The authorities also closed three other journals, *Pustomel (Chatterbox)*, *Zhivopisets (Painter)*, and *Koshelok (Bag)*. He became a Freemason in 1775. In 1779 Novikov moved from St. Petersburg back to MOSCOW to manage the publishing arm of Moscow University. In 1783, he established his own enterprise, which over the next decade issued over 1,000 books of translations and originals, including *The Library of Old Russian Authors,* in 30 volumes. Novikov was arrested in 1792, charged with being a Freemason, and sentenced to 15 years in prison to be served at Schlusselburg Fortress to the east of St. Petersburg. Over 20,000 copies of his book were burned. Czar PAUL I commuted his sentence in 1796, after Catherine's death. Novikov settled on his estate but remained inactive for the rest of his life. Novikov was one of the main figures of the Russian Enlightenment, an ardent promoter of human rights, education, justice, and tolerance, and a critic of serfdom, which to him was the main source of Russia's ills.

Novocherkassk massacre of 1962

A massacre of striking workers in the industrial city of Novocherkassk in Rostov province in southwestern Russia that took place on June 1, 1962. The strike resulted from the Soviet government's announcement of substantial increases in the price of meat and butter. In protest, workers acompanied by their families took to the streets of Novocherkassk and marched towards the local headquarters of the Communist Party. The marchers adopted the prerevolutionary symbols of labor protest, such as singing the *Internationale* while they displayed their loyalty to the regime by carrying portraits of Vladimir LENIN. The government, perhaps unaware of the irony, responded much like the czarist government during the BLOODY SUNDAY massacre of 1905, shooting at the demonstrators. At the end of the day, 24 people had been killed and 69 wounded. The dead were buried in secret places throughout Rostov province; seven alleged leaders of the demonstration were executed; and many others were sent to labor camps of the GULAG. The Soviet government successfully covered up the news of the massacre, but over the next two decades details began to filter out through the underground *samizdat* press or foreign radio stations such as Radio Liberty. In the first volume of *The Gulag Archipelago,* Aleksandr SOLZHENITSYN makes reference to the events in Novocherkassk. It was only in the late 1980s when one of the imprisoned strike leaders was released that the first open discussion of the Novocherkassk massacre took place among the Soviet public. In 1992, relatives of those killed during the massacre were finally informed of where the bodies had been buried.

Nureyev, Rudolf Hametovich
(1938–1993)
dancer

World famous ballet dancer and choreographer, he was born into a Tatar family in Ufa, now Bashkortostan, in the Russian Federation. After training in Ufa, he moved to Leningrad in 1955, graduating three years later, a promising talent. As a soloist with the Kirov Ballet of Leningrad (1958–61), he became an overnight sensation, rapidly considered among the best young virtuoso dancers of the ballet world. While in Paris in 1961, he sought political asylum. The following year in London, Nureyev began an historic partnership with the renowned British ballerina Margot Fonteyn, and became a favorite of Western critics and audiences. Combining technical accomplishment and subtle, emotional performances, Nureyev left a deep mark on Western male dancing. Although his interpretations of traditional classics (Siegfried in *Swan Lake* and Albrecht in *Giselle*) were constant favorites, he also worked in neoclassical and modern idioms, representing every major 20th-century choreographer. Despite his versatility, it is as a supreme exponent of the classical school in ballet that he made his international reputation, both with his own performances and through the many imaginative productions that he mounted with Western companies–including *La Bayadère, Raymonda, Swan Lake, The Sleeping Beauty, Don Quixote* (of which he also directed a film), *The Nutcracker,* and *Romeo and Juliet.* In 1982, he became an Austrian citizen, and served as director of the Paris Opera Ballet from 1982 to 1989. Nureyev returned for the first time to the Soviet Union in November 1987, and danced again at the Kirov, the scene of his first triumphs, in November 1989.

O

Ob River

A river that rises in southwestern Siberia on the northern side of the Altai Mountains and flows into the Arctic Ocean, the Ob is joined by the Irtysh River in western Siberia to form a river system of about 3,400 miles, the largest in Asia and the fourth-largest in the world. In its early stages the Ob drains more populated regions of Siberia, flowing in a northern direction past the cities of Barnaul, Novosibirsk, and Tomsk. Past Tomsk it flows in a generally northwestern direction through western Siberia before joining with the Irtysh at Khanty-Mansiisk, after which it turns sharply to the north for the last 500 miles of its course before emptying into the Gulf of Ob, an arm of the Arctic Ocean, near the town of Salekh. In its total course the Ob drains a vast area of more than 1 million square miles and, although navigation is closed in the winter months, it serves as the region's main route for the transportation of lumber and grain. The lower reaches of the Ob formed the easternmost part of the vast trade network developed by Novgorod merchants and peasants across northern Russia in the centuries before 1450. In turn, the upper basin of the Ob was part of the Khanate of Siberia, one of the successor states to the Mongols' GOLDEN HORDE, until 1582, when the Khanate was conquered by the Muscovite state. In the early 17th century, the Ob river basin was the staging point for the further Russian exploration and conquest of Siberia. During the STALIN years, the vast unpopulated area spreading between the right bank of the Ob and the Arctic Ocean was the site of hundreds of camps of complete isolation for political prisoners.

October Revolution (1917)

The second of two revolutions in 1917, the October Revolution (also known as the BOLSHEVIK Revolution) led to the establishment of a Bolshevik-led Soviet government that in 1923 became known as the Union of Soviet Socialist Republics, or Soviet Union, which ruled Russia and the lands of the former Russian Empire until 1991. The seeds of the October Revolution were planted in the inability of the Provisional Government, formed during the FEBRUARY REVOLUTION, to effectively establish its authority in the city of Petrograd (ST. PETERSBURG) and across Russia during the spring and summer of 1917. Its authority was already limited by the system of "dual power" that had been created as a result of the FEBRUARY REVOLUTION, by which the Provisional Government shared de facto power with the Petrograd Soviet of Workers' and Soldiers' Deputies, the leading members of a nationwide network of soviets that sprang out in the early months after the fall of the monarchy. Unable to stop rampant inflation and improve the supply of food to the cities, the Provisional Government also lost much of its meager political capital because of its continuing commitment to fighting World War I, a policy with which the leader of the Provisional Government, Aleksandr KERENSKY was closely identified. During the summer of 1917, the government beat back a premature Bolshevik-supported rising in Petrograd, known as the JULY DAYS, which temporarily weakened the leftist forces allied to the Bolsheviks and forced Vladimir LENIN to seek refuge in Finland. By August 1917, however, the Provisional Government was now being threatened from the right, as conservative and middle-class Russians pinned their hopes on a military solution, personified by General Lars KORNILOV, which would stop what they saw as the disintegration of Russia. As Kornilov marched on Petrograd, the city's workers, often Bolshevik supporters, played a crucial role in defeating the threat of a military coup. Although the Provisional Government remained in place, the real winners of the Kornilov incident were the Bolsheviks, who emerged as the consistent opponents of the war that was seen as the root of most of Russia's problems.

On September 26 (September 13) the Bolsheviks gained a majority in the Petrograd Soviet, a crucial development in their growing political strength. One week later they also had a majority in the Moscow Soviet. With support for the Bolsheviks rising throughout the country, especially in urban centers, Lenin called for an uprising from his hideout in Finland. Sensing the reluctance of the Petrograd Bolsheviks to move against the Provisional Government, Lenin returned to Petrograd under disguise on November 5 (October 23). After meeting with the executive committee of the Bolshevik Party Lenin gained their support for an uprising, although there were still some misgivings. With elections to the Constituent Assembly that would decide Russia's future system of government scheduled for later in November 1917, it was crucial that the Bolsheviks act quickly while the fortunes of the Provisional Government were at their lowest ebb. They also wanted to present the Second All-Russian Congress of Soviets scheduled to meet in early November with a de facto situation. On November 7 (October 25), they occupied strategic points throughout Petrograd. With assistance from Bolshevik sympathizers in the Petrograd garrison, the Kronstadt naval base and the working-class Red Guards, the Bolsheviks succeeded in capturing the Winter Palace and members of the Provisional Government who had not managed to escape. On the morning of November 8 (October 26), the residents of Petrograd awoke to a new Soviet government. One week later, after extensive fighting in the city, the Bolsheviks triumphed in Moscow, and throughout the winter and spring months that followed Soviet power was proclaimed in other Russian cities.

Odessa

A port on the Black Sea with a rich multicultural history, Odessa belonged to Russia from 1791 to 1991, when it became part of an independent Ukraine. Although Odessa itself was founded in 1794 as a Russian naval fortress, it is believed the area was the site of a Greek trading colony in ancient times. Crimean Tatars also traded in the area in the 14th century, and control of the area passed from Lithuanian to Tatar to Turkish hands. In the course of the Russo-Turkish war of 1787–92, Russian troops stormed the Turkish settlement in 1789 and annexed it for Russia in 1792. In 1805 it became the residence of the viceroy of the province of New Russia. Odessa's importance in the 19th century was tied to the spectacular growth of the Russian grain trade, for which the city served as the main port. In 1854, the French and British allies bombarded Odessa in the course of the CRIMEAN WAR. The first all-Russian census of 1897 recorded a population of about 400,000. It was during the 19th century that Odessa developed its multicultural character, with significant Bulgarian and Jewish colonies in addition to its Ukrainian and Russian populations. The anti-Semitic POGROMS that occurred with greater frequency in Russia after 1881 also took their toll on the city's Jewish population, contributing to large numbers of emigrants from Odessa. During the 1905 Revolution, Odessa was the site of internal disturbances triggered by a workers' strike supported by the mutinying sailors of the battleship *Potemkin*. These events would be later celebrated in Sergei EISENSTEIN's classic 1926 film of the same name. During World War I, Odessa was briefly captured by the Austrians then changed hands several times during the civil war that followed the Bolshevik revolution of 1917. In 1919, as part of the Allied Intervention during the Russian Civil War, Odessa was briefly occupied by the French and then, as the fortunes of the anti-Bolshevik White movement declined, it served as one of the embarkation points for Russians seeking to escape the country during 1920. In Soviet times, the city developed a colorful reputation as the center of a criminal underworld, celebrated in the works of such writers as Isaac BABEL. During World War II Odessa was occupied by German and Romanian troops from 1941 to 1944 and suffered great damage. With the renewal of Jewish emigration from the USSR in the 1970s, many of the area's Jewish residents resettled in the BRIGHTON BEACH area of New York City, which became colloquially known as Little Odessa. In 1991, with the dissolution of the Soviet Union, Odessa became a part of newly independent Ukraine, at which time its population was estimated at about 1 million.

Okudzhava, Bulat Shalvovich
(1924–1997)
poet and balladeer

One of the first Soviet-era performers to develop a wide following through the spread of clandestine tape recorders, throughout his career Okudzhava skillfully negotiated the high wire between official tolerance and mass popularity. Okudzhava was born in Moscow to a Georgian father and an Armenian mother. Both parents were Communist Party officials; his father was shot during the Great Purge and his mother spent 19 years in the GULAG. Okudzhava volunteered for service at the front in 1941 and served in the Red Army through the end of World War II in 1945. After the war he enrolled in Tbilisi University in Georgia, and graduated in 1950. Back in Moscow, he found employment as a schoolteacher and in publishing houses. He published his first volume of poetry in 1953, and in 1955 he joined the COMMUNIST PARTY after the rehabilitation of his parents. Okudzhava was part of a very influential generation of Soviet artists, writers, and performers that included Vasily AKSENOV, Yevgeni YEVTUSHENKO, Andrei Voznesensky, Bella AKHMADULINA, and others who tried to create a hybrid of high culture and popular culture, dis-

tinguished by its high artistic standards. His deceptively simple, often nostalgic ballads that sang with equal feeling of ants, paper soldiers, and the lost world of Moscow's Arbat district were not considered antiestablishment and were thus mostly tolerated by the government. Nevertheless, the songs circulated clandestinely, through the system known as *magnitizdat,* during the BREZHNEV era. In the GORBACHEV years, Okudzhava attained official recognition, and his songs became part of the collective soundtrack of the late 1950s and 1960s, often featured in films and documentaries that celebrate that era.

Old Believers

Also known as Old Ritualists, a more precise translation of the Russian term *staroobriadtsy,* Old Believers was the appellation given to the Russian Orthodox faithful who broke with the church in the 17th century and to their descendants. The introduction of a series of liturgical reforms by Patriarch NIKON in 1653 set in motion the events that led to the church schism of 1666. Nikon's opponents objected to his attempts to introduce changes such as making the sign of the cross with three fingers, a new spelling of Jesus, and a return to Greek liturgical texts, all of which they saw as a betrayal of a true Muscovite culture. They found an articulate defender in the archpriest AVVAKUM, who was first exiled and eventually executed for his opposition to the reforms. Initial opposition to Nikon also took violent forms, as in the case of the SOLOVETSKY MONASTERY, where monks and their allies carried out a war of resistance that lasted from 1668 to 1676. Persecution of Old Believers began soon after the schism, increased during the reign of FEODOR III (1676–82), was made official policy in 1684 during the regency of SOPHIA, and continued periodically into the 19th century. During the 18th century the Old Believers split into "priestist" (*popovtsy*) and "priestless" (*bezpopovtsy*) factions. The former organized their own ecclesiastical hierarchy and in some cases, while keeping their own rites, reconciled with the Orthodox

Church. The latter embraced a more radical rejection of the Orthodox Church, questioning not only the priesthood but also all sacraments except baptism and confession. Large Old Believer communities developed in the northern reaches of the VOLGA RIVER and in the relatively remote regions of the Altai Mountains and Lake Baikal in Siberia. An important Old Believer community also took shape in Moscow, where several Old Believer families established business dynasties in the course of the 19th century that played a central role in the development of a Russian entrepreneurial class and in the politics of pre-revolutionary Russia. Prominent industrialists such as Pavel RIABUSHINSKY and Aleksandr GUCHKOV hailed from Old Believer families and emerged as spokesmen for this business elite in the first decade of the 20th century.

Oleg (unknown–913)
ruler

Considered to be the founder and first historical ruler of KIEVAN RUS, much of our knowledge about Oleg is shrouded in mystery and is drawn from the 12th-century *Primary Chronicle*. According to the chronicle, Oleg became the ruler of the city of NOVGOROD in 879, succeeding his kinsman, the legendary Rurik. In 882 he led an expedition against the city of KIEV, captured it, and made it his capital and the center of a state and civilization that would flourish for the next three centuries until the Mongol conquest. Most of Oleg's reign as grand prince of Kiev was spent on military campaigns against neighboring peoples along the waterways of the Volkhov and Dniepr Rivers. The Derevlians, in particular, seem to have resisted Kievan expansion. On the whole, Oleg followed the traditional pattern of maintaining a conquered people's allegiance through system of tribute.

In 907, Oleg led a campaign against Constantinople. Although Byzantine sources say little about this campaign, Russian chronicles retell it extensively, adding colorful details, such as how Oleg nailed his shield on the gates of Constantinople, that cannot be confirmed elsewhere. Nevertheless, four years later, in 911, Oleg signed an advantageous commercial treaty with the Byzantine state, the first between the established empire and the upstart Kievan state. Upon Oleg's death, Prince Igor, alleged to be Rurik's son, succeeded Oleg as grand prince of Kiev, ruling from 913 to 945.

Olga (ca. 890–969)
ruler

The first Russian saint and first female ruler of Kiev, Olga was the wife of Grand Duke Igor of Kiev, who ruled from 913 until 945. Following Igor's death in battle with the Derevlians, who threatened Kiev, Olga was called to serve as regent for her young son, Sviatoslav. As with the early rulers of Kiev, most of the information about her reign is drawn from the 12th-century *Primary Chronicle*, which praised her as "the wisest of women." Accounts of her background agree that she came from the northern town of PSKOV, but they dispute whether she was of Slavic or Scandinavian forebears, part of a larger debate about the origins of the early rulers of Kiev. The main events of her reign were the continuing battles with eastern steppe tribes and her own conversion to Christianity. She avenged Igor's death by defeating the Derevlians and imposing heavy tribute duties on them. Olga is also credited for regulating the collection of tribute by establishing depots throughout the country. The *Primary Chronicle* tells of her conversion in 954 or 955 and a subsequent trip to Constantinople, where she was well received by the Byzantine emperor Constantine Porphyrogenitus. There are various accounts, not always reliable, about her trip to Constantinople. Some claim that she artfully dodged a marriage proposal from the emperor. Her conversion to Christianity remained a relatively isolated episode, until the reign of her grandson VLADIMIR I (sometimes known as Vladimir the Great), who was baptized and adopted Christianity as the official religion of the Kievan state in 988.

Order no. 1 (1917)

A product of the early days of the FEBRUARY REVOLUTION, Order no. 1 played a crucial role in hastening the disintegration of the Russian army in the first months after the abdication of Czar NICHOLAS II. The order was issued by the Petrograd Soviet of Workers' and Soldiers' deputies on March 1 (14), 1917, on the eve of the announcement of the czar's abdication. The order called for the formation of elected committees of soldiers who would administer military affairs. It also struck a blow in the name of the dignity of the common soldier by prohibiting rudeness toward soldiers on the part of officers, while abolishing the use of honorific titles for officers. It did not, however, abolish military discipline; it only stipulated that when off duty, soldiers were entitled to the full rights of individual citizens. Finally, Order no. 1 established that the primary loyalty of rank-and-file soldiers was to the Petrograd Soviet, not the Provisional Government. Although in its original form, the order was intended to apply only to the Petrograd garrison, other units and garrisons quickly adopted similar versions. Its effect was to convulse the hierarchical patterns of the army by stripping officers of most of their power over rank-and-file soldiers.

Ordzhonikidze, Grigorii Konstantinovich (1886–1937)

revolutionary and Soviet official

Ordzhonikidze was a Georgian Bolshevik at the center of the Soviet industrialization campaign of the 1930s who committed suicide in 1937 after a falling out with STALIN. Ordzhonikidze, often known by his nickname Sergo, was born in Kutaisi province in Georgia. He joined the Social Democratic Party in 1903 and sided with the BOLSHEVIKS in their disputes with the Mensheviks. After the 1905 Revolution, he moved to Germany for two years. Back in Russia in 1907, he worked in Baku before being arrested and exiled to Siberia. He escaped and reached Paris in 1910, where he met LENIN; two years later,

became a member of the Bolshevik Central Committee. During the Russian civil war, he served as a political commissar in the Caucasus, later becoming party leader in Transcaucasia in 1921–26. An early supporter of his fellow Georgian, Joseph Stalin, Ordzhonikidze rose to positions of great influence in the late 1920s and early 1930s: chair of the Central Control Commission and Rabkrin (responsible for discipline among party and state officials) (1926), chair of the Supreme Council of the National Economy (VSNKh) (1930), and commissar for heavy industry (1932). In the latter two positions, he played a central role in implementing the party's decisions with regard to rapid industrialization. In 1926 he had been elected a candidate member of the Politburo and in 1930 a full member, revealing that he was a member of Stalin's inner group. Although details remained sketchy for decades, it seems that Ordzhonikidze, whose brother had been tortured and shot, argued with Stalin over the purges. He died suddenly in 1937, officially of a heart attack, but it was widely believed that he committed suicide. At the Twentieth Party Congress in 1956, KHRUSHCHEV alleged that he had been forced to commit suicide by Stalin.

Orlova, Liubov Petrovna (1902–1975)

actress

Perhaps the most famous comedy actress of the Soviet era, Orlova was born to a distinguished Russian noble family, distantly related to the Tolstoys. Attracted to music and choreography, she studied at the Moscow Musical Conservatory and the Moscow Ballet School, and acted in the prestigious Nemirovich-Danchenko Musical Theater, before appearing in her first film, *Petersburg Night* (1926). Together with her husband, the film director Grigorii ALEKSANDROV, and the composer Isaak Dunayevsky, Orlova took part in some of the most popular and entertaining comedies of the 1930s (*The Happy-Go-Lucky Fellows*, 1934; *Volga-Volga*, 1938; and *The Bright Way*, 1940). In *Circus* (1936), she captivated audiences with a convincing American-accented Russian, playing the role of an American actress. The film also featured "The Song of the Motherland," one of the most popular Soviet songs of all time, which went on to become the signature song of Radio Moscow through the Soviet years. Although her particular strength was musical comedy, she played many other roles as well. In *Spring* (1947), she played two twins in the typical case of altered identities, and in *Meeting on the Elbe* (1949), she played an American spy. Orlova continued to work in the theater well into her late years. After her death, her husband made one final tribute to her and her work, the documentary *Liubov Orlova*, shortly before his own death.

Ostermann, Count Andrei Ivanovich (1686–1747)
official

An important adviser to PETER I the Great, Count Ostermann was the dominant voice in Russian foreign policy from the time of Peter's death in 1725 until 1741, when he was removed by ELIZABETH. The son of a Protestant pastor, Ostermann was born Heinrich Johann Friedrich Ostermann in Westphalia, and entered the service of Peter the Great in 1704, allegedly after killing a fellow student at the University of Jena. In 1708, he was appointed interpreter at the foreign office and promoted to secretary in 1710. A loyal servant of Peter and his adopted country, Ostermann rose rapidly through the ranks of the Russian government. Historians consider his own diplomatic skills to have been greatly responsible for the advantageous terms that Russia obtained from Sweden at the Treaty of Nystadt which ended the Great Northern War (1700–1721). For these and other services, Peter awarded him the rank of baron and appointed him vice president of the foreign office. It was after Peter's death, however, that Ostermann reached the peak of his power. He was one of the original six members of the Supreme Privy Council, which served as the real rulers of Russia until 1730. Ostermann's own field of expertise remained foreign policy, where

he served as vice chancellor of the College of Foreign Affairs. By supporting the autocratic prerogatives of the new empress, ANNA IVANOVNA, he survived the crisis of 1730 caused by the failed attempts by members of the Supreme Privy Council that she accept limitations on her powers. The foundation of Ostermann's policies was an alliance with Austria, signed in 1726. This allowed Russia to counter French attempts to limit Russia's growing role in European affairs by supporting its neighbors, Poland, Sweden, and the Ottoman Empire. An initial consequence of this antagonism with France was Russia's intervention in the War of the Polish Succession (1733–35), which ended with the defeat of the French-sponsored candidate, Stanyslaw Leszczynski, and the installation of the Russian-approved Augustus III as king of Poland. His policies toward the Ottoman Empire were less successful, as the RUSSO-TURKISH WAR OF 1736–39 brought costly victories on the battlefield, but few tangible results at the negotiating table. Dissatisfaction with the outcome of the war gave those who advocated a French and Prussian orientation in the court ammunition with which to attack Ostermann. With the death of Anna in 1740 and the short-lived reign of the infant IVAN VI, Ostermann was caught in a web of intrigue, much of it directed by the French through their ambassador in St. Petersburg. When Ivan VI was overthrown in November 1741 and replaced by Peter's daughter, Elizabeth, Ostermann was arrested and sentenced to death. While on the scaffold, his sentence was commuted to exile in Siberia, where he lived the final six years of his life.

Ostrovsky, Aleksandr Nikolaevich (1823–1886)
playwright

A prolific writer who dominated Russian dramaturgy in the second half of the 19th century, Ostrovsky is generally considered the true founder of Russian drama, completing, in the words of the writer Ivan GONCHAROV, the foundation begun by Denis FONVIZIN, Aleksandr GRI-

Aleksandr Ostrovsky *(Library of Congress)*

of the wealthy merchant class or officials who objected to their satire. Although Ostrovsky is most closely associated with plays about the merchant class, he also embraced other themes. In *The Forest* (1871) and *The Wolves and the Sheep* (1875), he portrayed the changing mores of his times, focusing on noble landowners affected by the abolition of SERFDOM, as well as adventurers seeking to profit from these changes. Ostrovsky's historical plays borrowed from 16th- and 17th-century themes. His fairy tales also found resonance with the public and to this day occupy an important role in the repertoires of many theaters. Because of the anticapitalist themes that could be inferred from his plays about the merchant classes, Ostrovsky's plays were frequently staged throughout the Soviet era. They provided a continuity with the prerevolutionary period that is especially evident in the extent to which many of the titles of Ostrovsky's plays have become popular proverbs in everyday spoken Russian.

Ouspensky, Petr Demianovich
(1878–1947)
philosopher

Ouspensky is best known for his interests in mysticism and theosophy and for his association with GURDJIEFF. Ouspensky was born into a prominent intellectual and artistic family in Moscow. His father was a mathematician and mathematics played an important role in Ouspensky's work. His first book, published in 1909, was a volume of mathematical philosophy entitled *The Fourth Dimension.* Ouspensky followed his many interests in Nietzsche, biology, mathematics, and dreams through his own course of reading. His encounter with theosophy began in 1907, and from that moment on he plunged into research that would prove the existence of a universe beyond the material world through linking mathematical theory with esotericism. In 1908 his studies took him to the Middle East and then, between 1909 and 1911, into mystical experiments devoted to exploring the possibility

BOEDOV, and Nikolai GOGOL. Working within the parameters of Gogol's critical realism, Ostrovsky wrote plays that touched upon the problems of contemporary society, particularly the merchant class of the city of MOSCOW, whom he often portrayed in negative tones. Born and educated in Moscow, Ostrovsky found employment in the court system, where he personally encountered the world of the petty merchant class of Moscow. In plays such as *Family Affair* (1850), *Poverty Is No Crime* (1854), and *The Storm* (1860), he satirized this world, portraying it as oppressively patriarchal and backward and rife with bribery and lawlessness. Written at the end of the repressive reign of NICHOLAS I and before the onset of the more liberal climate of the Great Reforms of ALEXANDER II, many of these plays were banned by the censors, often at the request of an objective magic apart from the experience of subjective mysticism. His major work, *Tertium Organum,* appeared in 1912. Here, Ouspensky argued that habitual patterns of thought, especially those created by materialistic science, had impaired thought itself, and that the essential requirement was for the individual to evolve psychologically into a new state of higher consciousness. Ouspensky lectured widely on the subject and eventually met Gurdjieff, with whom he would be associated during the next decade. From 1915 to 1924, he served as the "Master's" apostle, propounding his ideas and methods, lending a veneer of intellectual legitimacy to a man many considered a charlatan. In 1921 Ouspensky settled in England, where he developed a large and devoted following, especially after his break with Gurdjieff and the appearance of *Tertium Organum* in English translation. He spent the World War II years in the United States but returned to Surrey in England, where he died on October 2, 1947.

P

Pale of Settlement

A term that refers to the territory where Russian Jews were legally allowed to reside, the Pale of Settlement was established in 1791 by the government of CATHERINE II the Great and abolished in 1917. As a result of the late 18th-century POLISH PARTITIONS, large numbers of Jews found themselves under Russian rule for the first time. The Pale included 25 provinces in the western part of the Russian Empire, a region that coincides with the present-day boundaries of the republics of Latvia, Lithuania, Belarus, Ukraine, and parts of Poland. From 1804 to 1835, the Pale of Settlement also included the provinces of Astrakhan and the Caucasus region. During the reformist period of the 1860s under ALEXANDER II, the government relaxed restrictions on Jewish residence. Nevertheless, by 1880, only about 5 percent of the Russian Empire's 5 million Jews were living in varying degrees of legality outside the Pale. As part of ALEXANDER III's overall repressive response to the assassination of his father, Alexander II, previous restrictions on Jewish residence were reinforced and new ones were added, beginning in 1882. From 1882 until 1905, the Temporary Rules of 1882 prohibited Jews from residing outside of towns and large villages. Inside the Pale and across the empire, a large number of Jews responded to the government's discriminatory practices and the increasing number of POGROMS by emigrating. Between 1881 and 1914, more than 2 million Russian Jews left the empire. The development of intellectual and political movements such as the Haskalah, Zionism, and the socialist BUND inside the Pale was another response to Russian repression and the overall poverty of the Jewish masses. The borders of the Pale were extended eastward during World War I to accommodate several hundred thousand Jews who, along with ethnic Germans and Poles suspected of disloyalty to the empire, had been resettled away from the regions bordering Germany and Austria-Hungary. The Provisional Government abolished the Pale of Settlement in 1917.

pan-Slavism

A 19th-century intellectual current based on the idea that the Slavic nations of eastern Europe had common cultural traditions that should result in international political solidarity among them. Articulated as early as the 17th century, pan-Slavism first began to take shape in the 1830s under the influence of the ideas of the German philosopher Johann von Herder, as a movement to promote Slavic culture at a time when most Slavic peoples, with the exception of Russians, were under foreign rule. An important milestone in the transformation of pan-Slavism into a movement with more explicit political goals was the First pan-Slav Congress held in Prague during the revolutionary year of 1848. Presided over by Frantisek Palacky, the congress brought together Slavs from Bohemia, Poland, Croatia, Serbia, Dalmatia, and Silesia, all under Austrian rule, and had a strong anti-Russian bent.

To the extent that Russia was both an oppressor of Slavic nations such as the Poles and Ukrainians and a potential liberator of Slavs under Austrian or Ottoman rule, its position within the pan-Slav movement was always controversial. To non-Russian Slavs, pan-Slavism could lead to a federation of relatively equal Slavic nations or it could provide the cover for Russian imperialism in eastern Europe and the Balkans. Also within Russia, pan-Slavist ideals underwent a transformation in the aftermath of the disastrous CRIMEAN WAR (1854–56) from an ill-defined romantic Slavophilism to a more militant and nationalistic Russian pan-Slavism. Influential in shaping this transformation were Rostislav Fadeev (1824–83) and Nikolai DANILEVSKY (1822–85). Fadeev was an army general who wrote an influential pamphlet, *Russia and the Eastern Question,* which was issued in serialized form in the late 1860s and 1870s, while Danilevsky wrote *Russia and Europe* (1871), a treatise that featured Russian civilization as distinct from that of Europe. Fadeev argued that Russia should lead the liberation of Slavic lands ruled by Austria and the Ottoman Empire and form a Russian-dominated Slavic federation. Danilevsky also saw a fundamental conflict between Russia and western Europe and also envisioned the long-term emergence of a Slavic federation dominated by Russia. The ideas of Fadeev and Danilevsky were influential in shaping popular opinion in the 1870s and pressuring a reluctant Czar ALEXANDER II and his foreign minister, Aleksandr GORCHAKOV, in provoking the RUSSO-TURKISH WAR OF 1877–78. Pan-Slavism declined somewhat in the following decades but resurfaced in the years leading up to World War I, as Serbia challenged Austria in the Balkans, with the expectation of Russian support as a protector of Slavs. Unable to prevent the Austrian annexation of Bosnia in 1908, Russia felt more duty-bound to support Serbia when the crisis caused by the assassination of Archduke Franz Ferdinand in June 1914 resulted in the outbreak of World War I. Although the Bolshevik government renounced pan-Slavism in the aftermath of the Russian Revolution in favor of the new goals of international communism and world revolution, after World War II pan-Slavist themes were rearticulated in the context of Soviet domination of eastern Europe.

Pashukanis, Evgenii Bronislavovich (1891–1937)
Soviet legal theorist

A Bolshevik of Lithuanian origin, Pashukanis became the most prominent legal theorist of the early Soviet period. He began his legal studies at St. Petersburg, but owing to his involvement in revolutionary politics, he was forced to complete them in Munich. He joined the BOLSHEVIK Party in 1918, first working as a people's judge and later as a legal adviser to the Commissariat of Foreign Affairs. In his most influential book, *General Theory of Law and Marxism* (1924), Pashukanis tried to construct a Marxist theory of law by reducing legal phenomena to social relationships based on a market economy. Hence all law, in his view, is private and bourgeois; as such it is incompatible with socialism and destined to "wither away" in socialist society. This position led Pashukanis to conclude that since crime and litigation were the result of class conflict, it followed that the ending of private property presaged the end of crime. Pashukanis and his followers developed the theory of commodity exchange, which would lead to the withering away of law. This was because it was believed that all law emanated from capitalism; hence under socialism there would be no socialist law. This theory gained ascendancy in the 1920s and Pashukanis himself became vice president of the Communist Academy and director of its Institute of Soviet Construction and Law. In the less experimental 1930s, Pashukanis's ideas ran up against the new realities of Stalinist society. In 1931 Pashukanis recanted his views, accepting that even in socialist societies, law served the interests of the state. Nevertheless, Pashukanis continued to teach and worked in the preparation of the 1936 ("Stalin") Constitution. In 1936 he was appointed deputy commissar of justice. The Stalin Constitution of 1936 was a deathblow to Pashukanis's theories as socialism now required criminal laws to protect state assets. The notion that law would disappear along with classes and the state as the Soviet Union approached socialism was no longer tolerated and in January 1937,

Pashukanis was arrested, tried, and executed. Vilified for two decades as an "enemy of the people," Pashukanis was rehabilitated in 1957.

Pasternak, Boris Leonidovich
(1890–1960)
writer

One of the great Russian writers of the 20th century, Pasternak became a symbol of the cultural struggles in the first decade after STALIN's death, when he was pressured to renounce the Nobel Prize in Literature he received in 1958. Pasternak was born in MOSCOW to a cultured and well-connected Jewish family. His father was a well-known painter and friend of Lev TOLSTOY; his mother was an accomplished pianist. A student at the universities of Moscow and Marburg in Germany, he began to study music but instead received a diploma in philosophy. Beginning with his first volume of poetry, *The Twin in the Clouds,* published in 1914, Pasternak established himself as a major Russian poet, whose work was in touch with new modernist currents but grounded in a philosophical approach to history. Other volumes such as *Above the Barriers* (1917), *My Sister Life* (1922), and *Themes and Variations* (1923) consolidated his reputation in the early postrevolutionary period. In *The High Malady, 1905* and *Lieutenant Shmidt,* published between 1924 and 1931, he tried to tackle larger historical themes, but with less success. After two volumes of poetry in 1931 and 1932, Pasternak's published output diminished, as Soviet literary politics enforced the officially approved doctrine of socialist realism, an area where Pasternak was found wanting. Criticized for his formalism and concern with individual matters, only two other volumes of original poetry were published after 1932. To make a living, he turned to translation, and his translations of Shakespeare and Goethe, as well as of other English, German, French, Armenian, and Georgian writers are considered to be of the highest standards.

Despite the greatness of his poetry, Pasternak's reputation outside of Russia rests primarily

Boris Pasternak, 1958 *(Library of Congress)*

on *Doctor Zhivago,* his only novel (written between 1946 and 1956) and the source of the controversy that surrounded the 1958 Nobel Prize. In the spirit of the cultural thaw that followed Stalin's death in 1953, Pasternak had submitted his novel, a work that raised important philosophical and humanistic questions about the Russian Revolution, to the prestigious literary journal *Novyi mir,* expecting its publication. The censors, however, refused to publish it. But Pasternak had previously given a copy of the manuscript to an Italian publisher, expecting that it would be published abroad only after publication in the Soviet Union. The Italian publisher went ahead and published the Italian translation in 1957, and English- and Russian-language versions followed in 1958. Extremely well received in the West, *Doctor Zhivago* (which was made into an acclaimed film) was the basis on which Pasternak was awarded the 1958 Nobel Prize. Soviet literary officials immediately began a major campaign denouncing Pasternak, pressuring him to renounce the prize and expelling him from the Soviet Writers' Union. Under such pressure, he refused the prize, but the stress of the scandal ultimately affected his health and hastened his death, which came on May 30, 1960, in the artists' colony of Peredelkino, near Moscow. His later work, including *Doctor Zhivago,* was not published in the USSR until 1987, at which time Pasternak was also publicly rehabilitated.

Patriarchate

The office of the head of the Russian Orthodox Church, the Patriarchate was first established in 1589 during the reign of FEODOR I. Until then the Russian Church had been in theory at least subordinate to the patriarch of Constantinople. The establishment of a Russian patriarch was the product of negotiations between Boris GODUNOV, the de facto ruler during Feodor's reign, and Jeremiah the patriarch of Constantinople. The first Russian patriarch was Metropolitan Job, a friend of Boris Godunov. Two outstanding 17th-century patriarchs were FILARET, the father of Czar MICHAEL ROMANOV, and NIKON, the force behind the controversial reforms that split the Russian Church in the 1660s. Filaret ruled as great sovereign with his son, while Nikon regarded his office as equal to or perhaps higher than the czar's in importance.

Perhaps the implicit challenge to the czar's authority as well as PETER I's own view of the church as an obstacle to reform inspired his actions toward the church. When Patriarch Hadrian died in 1700, Peter kept his seat vacant until 1721, when the Spiritual Reglament of the Church, authored by Feofan Prokopovich, created a new system of rule for the church. Under the Spiritual Reglament, the office of the patri-

arch was abolished and replaced by a Holy Synod, consisting of 10 clerics, later expanded to 12. For the next two centuries, the work of the Holy Synod was supervised by the ober-procurator of the Holy Synod, a lay official appointed by the czar. This situation continued until 1918, when a church council elected Patriarch Tikhon to continue the Patriarchate. Upon Tikhon's death in 1925, however, the Soviet government prevented the election of a new patriarch, a sign of a more uncompromising attitude toward the church that would intensify in the 1930s.

World War II and the need to rally the Soviet population around more traditional symbols changed the government's policy toward the church. In 1943, Metropolitan Sergei was elected as the first patriarch in almost two decades. Sergei died in 1945 and was succeeded by Alexis, who in turn was succeeded by Pimen in 1971. The current patriarch, Alexis II, assumed his post in 1990 after Pimen's death, the first patriarch since the 1917 Revolution to be freely chosen by the church without government interference. During the 1990s the patriarch led the church in its attempt to reassume its former position as one of the pillars of Russian national identity, a goal that often led the church in appearing to be intolerant of other faiths, Christian and non-Christian alike, which it felt were making inroads in Russia at the expense of Russian Orthodoxy.

Paul I (1754–1801)
(Pavel Petrovich)
emperor

The son of CATHERINE II, Paul reigned briefly from 1796 until 1801, when he was overthrown and assassinated during a palace revolt. Soon after his birth, he was taken from Catherine by Empress ELIZABETH and raised away from his parents. His own son, Alexander, would later be raised by Catherine in a similar pattern. Although he was long reputed to have been the son of one of Catherine's lovers, Paul grew up believing that he was the son of Czar PETER III, who had been overthrown and assassinated in 1762. His shock at his mother's complicity in Peter's removal and his belief that she had ordered his assassination were powerful forces in shaping his antagonistic relationship with Catherine. These negative feelings were later augmented by Catherine's long reign and her apparent attempts to bypass Paul as her heir, in favor of Paul's eldest son, Alexander. Paul married twice. His first wife died in 1776 during childbirth. Later that year he married Sophia Dorotea of Württemberg, a German princess who adopted the Russian name Maria Feodorovna. The couple had four sons, two of whom reigned as emperors, and six daughters. In 1783 Paul retired to Gatchina Palace near St. Petersburg, where he gave free reign to his love of military parades and discipline, creating a court of marked contrast to that of Catherine's. As ruler, Paul was frequently driven by the desire to reverse many of his mother's policies, with often unpredictable results. Early measures such as the creation of Russia's first two ministries and prohibitions on serf labor on Sundays as well as the breaking up of serf families hinted at a reformist streak, but the latter were also driven by his hatred of the nobility. Of longer-lasting impact for the stability of the monarchy and the country was his 1797 decree imposing the system of male primogeniture. His foreign policy was dominated by the wars surrounding France but was inconsistent toward revolutionary and Napoleonic France. Driven by antirevolutionary sentiment, in 1798 he joined the second coalition against France, but with Napoleon in power after 1799, Paul began a more pro-French policy. Ironically, he was a victim of the last of the palace revolutions he had sought to abolish, when in March 1801 he was assassinated in a conspiracy led by Guards officers, who placed the future ALEXANDER I on the throne.

Questions about his sanity have accompanied evaluations of Paul's reign since his own time, with historians generally presenting his reign as a temporary aberration between the relatively enlightened reigns of Catherine the Great and Alexander I (at least his first decade). More recent research has emphasized a more enduring legacy of Paul's short reign for subsequent rulers: a militaristic style, increasing censorship, a government of ministries, and a paternalism tinged with early features of a 19th-century police state.

Pavlov, Ivan Petrovich (1849–1936)
physiologist

One of Russia's best-known scientists and the winner of the 1904 Nobel Prize in physiology, Pavlov was a pioneer in the study of the heart, the nervous system, the digestive tract, as well as reflex behavior. Pavlov was born in the provincial capital of Ryazan, to the southeast of Moscow, the son of a village priest. First educated at a theological academy, he pursued medical

Ivan Petrovich Pavlov *(Library of Congress)*

studies at the University of St. Petersburg and the Military Medical Academy, also in St. Petersburg. He distinguished himself as a student and was asked by Sergei Botkin, one of Russia's most prominent physicians, to establish what amounted to one of Europe's first laboratories for experimental work with animals, where he established a tradition of working with unanesthetized dogs. His early research focused on blood pressure, then moved on to the study of the digestive tract. He developed what is known as "Pavlov's pouch," which advanced the possibilities for experiment and observation. From 1884 to 1886, he pursued postgraduate studies in Breslau (now Wroclaw, Poland) and Leipzig, Germany. In 1891 he became director of the physiological department of the Institute of Experimental Medicine. Six years later he became a professor at his old academy, the Military Medical Academy.

Despite numerous achievements, Pavlov's fame rests mostly on his work on conditioned reflexes, begun in 1897. Using dogs, he measured the degree to which they formed an association between arbitrary stimuli such as a metronome beat and the delivery of food. Over the next four decades he continued these studies, eventually applying their lessons to the study of human psychology. Pavlov's work had a crucial influence on the development of behavioral psychology in the 20th century.

In 1904 he became the first Russian, and first physiologist, to receive a Nobel Prize, awarded to him mostly for his work on digestive glands. In 1915 he received the Copley Medal from the Royal Society. His own homeland recognized his achievements with an election to the ACADEMY OF SCIENCES in 1907, a position he held until his death in 1936. Although opposed to the Bolshevik revolution and communism, he maintained his status as an academician and the Soviet government allowed him to continue his research. It built him a special laboratory in 1935 in Leningrad (St. Petersburg). A prolific writer, his most influential work was translated and published in English as *Conditioned Reflexes* (1927).

Pavlova, Anna Pavlovna (1881–1931)
dancer and teacher

A beloved dancer who did much for popularizing classical ballet throughout the world, Pavlova was born in St. Petersburg. There she studied at the Imperial Theater School and made her debut at the prestigious Mariinskii Theater in 1899, becoming a prima ballerina in 1906. Originally a member of the Imperial Russian Ballet in St. Petersburg, she made guest appearances abroad that gave her a taste for independence. After several international tours, she joined Sergei DIAGHILEV's Ballets Russes in 1909, featuring in *Les Sylphides*. Seeking independence and control of her career, she left Diaghilev's company in 1911. After one last trip to Russia in 1914, she settled in London, where she formed a small ballet company, which was never permitted to be more than a background to her own highly individual performing genius. With this company she ceaselessly toured around the

Anna Pavlova *(Library of Congress)*

world, and in over 5,000 performances she brought her art to new places in the Near East, Australasia, the Pacific, South America, North America, and the Far East. The choreography and music that formed most of her repertory was often banal, but the content of her program was unimportant in light of her interpretations, which gave life to the most uninspired material. She did not restrict her performances to the large cities and permanent theaters, believing, with almost religious fervor, that it was her mission to dance whenever and wherever people would come to see her. Pavlova died in The Hague, the Netherlands. She inspired a whole generation to take up dance, including Frederick Ashton, Robert Helpmann, and Alicia Markova, and even today to the general public her name is synonymous with dancing.

People's Will (Narodnaya Volya)

Populist revolutionary organization formed in 1879 after the split of the "Land and Liberty" (Zemlia i Volya) organization. While the other faction to emerge from the split, "Black Repartition," rejected terrorism, People's Will broke from mainstream POPULISM in its rejection of a gradualist approach that emphasized education of the peasantry. It also adhered to the "Jacobin" idea of a seizure of power by a dedicated minority, while advocating violence and the use of terror against government officials. Among those who joined People's Will were about 70 army officers. People's Will also established cells among workers in St. Petersburg, MOSCOW, Kharkov, and Rostov-on-Don. In 1879, the Executive Committee of the group ordered the assassination of ALEXANDER II, which it finally succeeded in doing on March 1, 1881, after several unsuccessful attempts. The nationwide sympathy uprising that they had expected to follow news of the czar's death did not materialize. Instead, the czar's son, ALEXANDER III, launched a ruthless campaign against terrorists and revolutionaries in general that practically destroyed People's Will. Among those apprehended were five members of its Executive Committee, including Sofia Perovskaya, Andrei Zheliabov, and Nikolai KIBALCHICH, who were executed by hanging on April 3, 1881. What was left of the organization managed to remain organized in small groups in Russia or in emigration. In 1887 the St. Petersburg group, led by Alexander Ulianov (LENIN's older brother), attempted the assassination of Alexander III, for which Ulianov and others were executed. Some of the younger People's Will members carried their tradition into Russian social democracy, later becoming BOLSHEVIKS, but the majority remained populists and combined with other groups to form in 1902 the Party of Socialist Revolutionaries, which through its Fighting Organization continued the People's Will tradition of terror.

Peredvizhniki See WANDERERS.

Peter and Paul Fortress

The first structure built on the future site of St. Petersburg, the Peter and Paul Fortress was intended to defend the city from naval attack but was never used for that purpose. Construction of the fortress began in May 1703 and was not completed until 1740. By then the fortress was delineated by massive stone walls 12 feet thick and 40 feet high. Three hundred cannons were mounted on the bastions of the fortress. In addition to the buildings connected with its military role, the fortress contained the Mint, where Russia's currency was coined since 1724, and the Cathedral of St. Peter and St. Paul, with its elegant slender golden spire, one of the city's landmarks. Built between 1712 and 1733 by the Italian architect Domenico Trezzini, the cathedral became the final resting place of all czars beginning with Peter the Great. Only PETER II, who died in Moscow, and NICHOLAS II, who was executed in the Urals town of Ekaterinburg by the BOLSHEVIKS, were not buried in the cathedral at the time of their death. The fortress was also known to generations of revolutionaries as a jail for political prisoners. The five DECEMBRISTS sentenced to death in 1826 for their role in the conspiracy were executed on the grounds of the fortress. The members of the PEOPLE'S WILL who assassinated ALEXANDER II, radical writers such as Nikolai CHERNYSHEVSKY, Maksim GORKY, and revolutionaries such as Peter KROPOTKIN and Leon TROTSKY were all imprisoned in the fortress's Trubetskoi Bastion. Today, a museum celebrates this revolutionary legacy. During the OCTOBER REVOLUTION of 1917, the fortress's personnel sided with the Bolsheviks, and the attack on the Winter Palace was planned from its grounds. In 1941–44, during the siege of Leningrad, the local authorities successfully camouflaged the cathedral's spire, and damage to the fortress was limited. Every day at noon a cannon is fired from the fortress.

Peter I (1672–1725)
(Petr Alekseevich, Peter the Great)
emperor

A greatly influential ruler whose military victories and Westernizing policies decisively brought Russia into the concert of European nations and civilization and established the foundations of the modern Russian state, Peter is more commonly known to subsequent generations as Peter the Great. The youngest son of Czar ALEKSEI by his second marriage, to Natalia Naryshkina, Peter was not given the education reserved for an heir to the throne, instead, he learned freely from his frequent visits to the foreigners' quarter in MOSCOW. When his half brother and successor to Aleksei, FEODOR III, died in 1682 without issue, his half sister SOPHIA prevented Peter from becoming successor as the patriarch and leading boyars wanted, and instead engineered for Peter and his half brother, the sickly IVAN V, to serve as corulers with Sophia as regent. While Sophia's favorite, Prince Vasili GOLITSYN, ruled in her name, Peter retired to the village of Preobrazhenskoe near Moscow with members of the Naryshkin family. Successive defeats at the hands of Crimean Tatars in 1687 and 1689 and other problems led to the overthrow of Sophia

in 1689 and the emergence of Peter as the de facto ruler. With the death of Ivan V in 1696, Peter became sole ruler of Russia. His first major initiative was to undertake his famous GRAND EMBASSY (1697–98), an extensive journey across Brandenburg, the Netherlands, Britain, and Austria, a sign of his interest in European culture and his desire to recruit European technical and military expertise.

Russia's participation in what became the Great Northern War (1700–1721) allied with Poland against Sweden was the military centerpiece of Peter's reign and the motive for many of the reforms that came to characterize his reign. The war began badly for Russia as Charles XII of Sweden defeated Peter's navy at the Battle of Narva on the Baltic Sea in 1700. Peter reorganized his armies and the government, and nine years later at the Battle of POLTAVA in Ukraine, he defeated the Swedes, a turning point for the war. The war dragged on until 1721, when the Peace of Nystadt awarded Russia a long-sought coastline on the Baltic.

During this long war, Peter brought many changes to Russian government and society, even though not all of them achieved long-term results. Some were substantial changes needed for military victory. He also brought Western experts to provide the technical expertise necessary to explore mines and build a naval fleet. Through state companies Peter sought to promote commercial activity in Russia. He created a system of obligatory service for the gentry, who were now required to provide civil or military service. In 1722 this service system was given a hierarchical structure through the TABLE OF RANKS, which allowed individuals to advance from one position to another, theoretically on the basis of merit, and at a certain stage they received noble status. Other changes were more symbolic but equally important. On the banks of the Neva River near the Gulf of Finland, he built a new capital, St. Petersburg (named after the apostle) that would serve as Russia's "window on the west," a strikingly beautiful, Western-looking city designed in contrast to Moscow, representative of the old Russia. Beginning with the attempt to force men to shave their beards, Peter also sought to change the way Muscovite men and women looked and acted, pressing them to wear Western-style dress and encouraging women to participate in public life. He brought Russia's old calendar closer in line with the Western CALENDAR (although until 1918 the calendars would not be the same) and modernized the CYRILLIC ALPHABET that Russia used. In 1721 Peter adopted the Western-sounding title of emperor. Other reforms sought to weaken the power of the Orthodox Church by abolishing the PATRIARCHATE and creating a Holy Synod, controlled by Peter to supervise the Russian Church.

Not all of Peter's reforms can be evaluated in positive terms. His attempts to create a society based on gentry service harshened the terms of SERFDOM for the bulk of the Russian population. His embrace of Western styles for the nobility resulted in a cultural and social gap between elites and the Russian masses that would contribute to the turbulent character of Russian politics in the 19th and 20th centuries. His attempt to change the succession process by allowing the emperor to choose his or her own successor inaugurated a period of palace revolutions that continued throughout the 18th century, where the Imperial Guards often intervened to choose rulers. Having been complicit in the death of his own son Alexis in 1718, Peter was succeeded by his second wife, who ruled as CATHERINE I (1725–27), although real power was held by the Supreme Privy Council, a group of prominent statesmen who had worked closely with Peter throughout his reign.

Peter II (1715–1730)
(Petr Alekseevich)
emperor

The son of PETER I the Great's ill-fated son, Aleksei Petrovich, Peter ascended to the throne in May 1727 at the age of 11, and reigned for fewer than three years before dying of smallpox. He succeeded Peter's second wife, who had reigned briefly as CATHERINE I. One of Peter's first acts was to free his grandmother, EVDOKIIA Lopukhina,

Peter the Great's first wife, from the Schlusselburg Fortress, earl of St. Petersburg prison, where Catherine I had sent her in a petty act of revenge. Behind the scenes a battle among aristocratic factions raged over whom the young Peter would choose as his future bride. While Catherine was still alive, Prince MENSHIKOV had persuaded her to choose his daughter, Maria Menshikova, as Peter's wife, which she did soon before her death. The Dolgorukii faction, fearful of Menshikov's growing power, convinced Peter without much difficulty to break the engagement and exile Menshikov and his family to Siberia, where he died in 1729. Although Peter made a few cosmetic changes such as restoring Moscow as the capital of Russia and moving the court there, real power still lay in the hands of the Supreme Privy Council, which Peter the Great had set up before his death. In November 1729, the engagement of Peter to Catherine Dolgorukaia, the daughter of Aleksei Dolgorukii, was announced and the wedding set for January 18, 1730. On the morning of his wedding Peter died of smallpox, leaving once again the Supreme Privy Council to decide the tangled issue of the succession to the throne.

Peter III (1728–1762)
emperor

Born Karl Peter Ulrich of Holstein-Gottorp, the future Peter III was the son of Anna Petrovna Romanova, the daughter of PETER I the Great and Duke Karl-Friedrich of Holstein-Gottorp. Raised in Kiel, Germany, Peter was often mentioned as a possible future king of Sweden, but in 1742 his aunt Empress ELIZABETH of Russia proclaimed him as her heir. A marriage was arranged to Sophia Augusta Fredericka of Anhalt-Zerbts, from another princely family. His future wife arrived in Russia in 1744 and converted to Orthodox Christianity, adopting the name Catherine. The marriage was not a happy one. On Elizabeth's death in December 1761, Peter succeeded to the throne, but his reign lasted only eight months. Although generally portrayed as a weak and ineffectual ruler, some of his initial policies met with approval. By his manifesto of February 18, 1762, he freed the nobility from the compulsory state service instituted by his grandfather Peter the Great. He also abolished the Secret Chancellery and Elizabeth's advisory cabinet to simplify the structure of government. His proposal to secularize church lands was in line with discussions during Elizabeth's reign, and was finally implemented by his wife, ruling as CATHERINE II. Peter's foreign policy, ruled by his own strong pro-Prussian feelings, proved more problematic. At a crucial juncture in the Seven Years' War, he signed a peace treaty with Prussia in April 1762, returning all the provinces Russia had conquered, and saving Frederick the Great from certain defeat. He then negotiated an alliance with Prussia, signed in June 1762. While controversial, this pro-Prussian tilt was not entirely unpopular among Russian policymakers, but his plans for war against Denmark to reconquer Schleswig, essentially using Russian money and troops to pursue the interests of the Duchy of Holstein-Gottorp, alienated the all-powerful Imperial Guards. On June 28, 1762, Peter was overthrown in a palace revolt organized by the Orlov brothers and other Guards officers, working in alliance with Catherine. Placed under house arrest at his Ropsha country estate, he was murdered on July 6, 1762. The evidence suggests that Catherine had not been informed of the plotters' intention to dispose of her husband. In the tradition of Russian monarchical impostors, the circumstances of his death allowed future rebels like Emelian Pugachev to claim they were actually Peter III, who had escaped from prison.

Petrosian, Tigran Vartanovich
(1929–1984)
chess player

A chess player of Armenian descent, Tigran Petrosian reigned as world champion from 1963 to 1969. Petrosian was born in Tbilisi, Georgia, and his parents taught him chess when he was eight years old. Both parents died in 1945, when Petrosian was 16, after which he briefly took his father's old job as a caretaker in a war veteran's

home. In his spare time, he played chess, and his local reputation grew after winning a couple of tournaments. The year after his parents' death he had only recently moved to Yerevan, Armenia, when he placed first in the Armenian championship at age 17. In 1948, Petrosian repeated as Armenian champion. The following year he moved to Moscow, where he continued to astound the world of chess with his skills. In 1951 he won the Moscow city chess championship and placed second in the Soviet national championship. By 1952 he was an international grandmaster, and after strong finishes in international tournaments in Sweden and Switzerland, he was considered among the best young players in the world. Through the 1950s and 1960s Petrosian continued to be in the elite of the Soviet chess world, winning numerous Moscow city championships and Soviet national championships. Not until 1962, however, did he win the right to challenge his countryman and world champion Mikhail BOTVINNIK for the world title, after winning the candidates' tournament in Curaçao. After two months of play Petrosian emerged as the world champion, a title he held until 1969, when he was defeated by another Soviet player, Boris SPASSKY. During the first three years of his tenure as world champion, he was chief editor of the monthly chess magazine *Shakhmatnaya Moskva* (Moscow chess). He was known in the chess world as "Iron Tigran" for his tenacious, if uninspiring, play and his ability to outlast opponents. In 1968 he received a master's degree in logic from Yerevan University, writing a dissertation entitled "Chess Logic." Petrosian continued to play in Soviet and international tournaments after losing the world title to Spassky, winning many of them or finishing in the top positions. He died of cancer in Moscow in August 1984.

Pirogov, Nikolai Ivanovich (1810–1881)
physician

One of the pioneers of contemporary surgery and anatomical research, and the first to use plaster casts, Pirogov was born in Moscow into a military family. His father's sudden death in 1824 disrupted a cultured, comfortable early life. After graduation from the Medical Faculty of Moscow University at age 18, with a specialization in surgery, Pirogov began teaching at Dorpat (now Tartu) University. Two years of observation in Germany (1833–35) convinced him of the need to raise surgery to the level of a science through special study of anatomy and physiology. As head of the surgical clinic of the St. Petersburg Medico-Surgical Academy (1841–56), Pirogov lectured in anatomical pathology, pioneering the use of frozen cadavers for research, which he developed in over 12,000 dissections. During these years his accomplishments were many, first using chloroform in Russia, developing the theory and use of anesthesia (which he first tested on himself), originating the intravenous administration of anesthetic ether, and introducing mass use of anesthesia for military surgery during the siege of SEVASTOPOL during the CRIMEAN WAR. Frustrated by conditions at the Medico-Surgical Academy, he retired from teaching and hospital work in 1856. After three stormy years as curator of the Odessa and Kiev educational districts, he retired to his estate in southern Ukraine in 1861, which he rarely left in the following 20 years. In 1862, while traveling in Europe as a mentor for young Russian scientists in training, he performed successful leg surgery on Giuseppe Garibaldi, who had been severely wounded at the Battle of Aspromonte, near Calabria in southern Italy. In 1870, he served as a representative of the Russian Red Cross during the Franco-Prussian War (1870–71), and in 1878 he served as a surgeon during the RUSSO-TURKISH WAR. Pirogov was the author of a classic four-volume work on surgical anatomy, *Anatomia topographica* (1851–59), and the standard reference work on field surgery, *Foundations of General Military Field Surgery,* first published in German in 1864, which was based on his experiences during the siege of Sevastopol. Pirogov was also a renowned educator and liberal publicist who spoke out against restrictions on edu-

cating women and the poor. After his death, the Pirogov Society was founded in his honor in 1883. Until its final suppression in 1922, it was the main Russian medical society, and through its renowned "Pirogov congresses," a public forum for liberal views in late imperial Russia.

Platonov, Andrei (1899–1951)
(Klimentov, Andrei Platonovich)
writer

A novelist, journalist, and poet who attained cult status decades after his death, Platonov was born Andrei Platonovich Klimentov in the town of Voronezh in the Black Earth region of southern Russia. After graduating from the Voronezh Polytechnic Institute, he began to work as a journalist. In 1927 he moved to Moscow. Two years later he published the first of two important short story collections, *Makar the Doubtful,* which was followed by the novels on which his reputation as a major writer rests: *Chevengur* (1929) and *The Foundation Pit* (1930). Platonov warned about the dangers that industrialization posed to human values and about the overall direction of the revolution, especially what he saw as its bureaucratization. In the overheated ideological climate leading up to the enshrinement of socialist realism as official Soviet literary dogma at the 1934 congress of the Union of Soviet Writers, Platonov came under attack from literary officials and critics. He published very little after 1934. In a second collection of short stories, *The River Potudan* (1937), he attempted to work within the literary formulas of socialist realism while preserving the worldview of his earlier work. During World War II he returned to the journalism of his early years and worked as a war correspondent. In 1947 the government denounced his work as slanderous, and Platonov was essentially silenced and his work suppressed until his death. The Russian reading public first rediscovered Platonov in the 1960s, when his works began to appear through the *samizdat* (self-publishing) literary underground. In the late 1980s they were officially reissued.

Platonov, Sergei Feodorovich
(1860–1933)
historian

One of the leading Russian historians of the early 20th century, Platonov contributed to the development of Russian historiography by advocating careful and thorough archival research and analysis. Platonov was born in the town of Chernigov in southwestern Russia near the Ukrainian border. His father was a typographical technician in the government's employ who had been transferred from his native Moscow. In 1869 the family moved to St. Petersburg, and, with the goal of pursuing a university education, Platonov was enrolled in one of the city's gymnasiums. Although profoundly interested in history since his childhood, Platonov entered the literature faculty at St. Petersburg University, from which he graduated in 1882. After graduation he taught modern Russian history at the Alexander Lyceum in St. Petersburg while pursuing graduate work toward a master's thesis. Attracted to the period of the TIME OF TROUBLES he wrote a thesis analyzing tales and legends about the Time of Troubles as a historical source, which he defended in 1889. That same year, he was invited to teach at St. Petersburg University but encouraged to complete a doctoral dissertation in order to be a full-fledged member of the faculty. For this purpose he wrote the work for which he is perhaps best known, *Essays on the Time of Troubles in the Muscovite State in the XVI–XVIIth Centuries* (1890). Platonov spent most of his teaching career at St. Petersburg University and was elected to the Russian ACADEMY OF SCIENCES in early 1917. During this time he wrote two other works, *Lectures on Russian History* (1899) and *History of Russia* (1909), which became standard textbooks until the early 1920s. The *Lectures,* in particular, published in numerous editions, joined Vasili KLIUCHEVSKY's *Course of Russian History* as one of the two pillars

of Russian historiography of the late imperial period. After the OCTOBER REVOLUTION Platonov was allowed to maintain his post at the university, renamed Leningrad State University after 1924. During the 1920s he wrote other influential books: *Boris Godunov* (1921); *Time of Troubles* (1923), a more popular accessible synthesis of his earlier work; *Moscow and the West in the XVI–XVIIth centuries* (1925); and *Peter the Great: Personality and Activity* (1926), his last published work. By the late 1920s, at a time of increasing ideological debate, Platonov's apolitical or non-Marxist teachings were the source of suspicion among his more ideologically intolerant colleagues. In 1930 he was arrested on fabricated charges of participating in a monarchist plot against the Soviet state. After a trial, he was convicted and exiled to the Volga River town of Samara (known as Kuybishev during Soviet times), where he died in January 1933.

Plekhanov, Georgii Valentinovich
(1857–1918)
revolutionary

The "father of Russian Marxism," Plekhanov began his revolutionary career as a populist. When the revolutionary organization Land and Liberty, of which he had been a member in the 1870s, split into two factions in 1879 over the issue of terrorism, Plekhanov became a leader of its nonterrorist faction, Black Repartition. The other faction, People's Will, went on to plot and carry out the execution of the czar, ALEXANDER II, in March 1881. Plekhanov emigrated to Switzerland in 1880, and there he came into contact with the ideas of Marxism that would shape his further development as a revolutionary. In 1883 he was the main force behind the foundation of Ozvobozhdenie Truda (Emancipation of Labor), the first self-proclaimed Russian Marxist revolutionary organization. He represented Russia in the Socialist International and became one of its leaders. For the next decades Plekhanov worked to spread the message of Marxism throughout Russia while polemicizing with the populists, a task that was made easier by the foundation of the Russian Social Democratic Labor Party in 1898. On the major issues that divided the young party in the next decade, Plekhanov alternated from early support of LENIN's Bolshevik wing to support of the Mensheviks. Personal issues connected with his desire to maintain his senior position in the movement seem to have been as important as his commitment to orthodox Marxism. In 1910, he split with the Mensheviks and set up his own subfaction, briefly collaborating with Lenin. During World War I, Plekhanov advocated an Allied victory as the best policy for advancing the socialist cause, a view that set him at odds with Lenin. After 37 years of émigré politics, Plekhanov returned to Russia after the FEBRUARY REVOLUTION of 1917 and set up a bitterly anti-Bolshevik social democratic organization, called Unity. He died after the Bolshevik revolution.

Plevitskaya, Nadezhda Vasilievna
(1884–1940)
singer and spy

Born Nadezhda Vinnikova, Plevitskaya was a renowned Russian singer who embarked on a second career as a Soviet intelligence agent while living in France. Plevitskaya was born in the village of Vinnikovo, Kursk province, the 12th child in a peasant family. By 1906 she had already become a famous mezzo-soprano who entertained members of the imperial family and government ministers. Her first husband was the ballet soloist Edmund Plevitskii, and her second husband a young officer, Iurii Levitskii, whom she soon left. In 1921 she married Nikolai Skoblin, a major-general in the imperial army 11 years her junior, and immigrated with him to Paris. In Paris, Plevitskaya became the darling of the Russian émigré community, attracting large crowds at Russian restaurants and numerous admirers. One of her songs, *"Zamelo tebia snegom Rossii,"* became close to an unofficial anthem for émigré White Russians. She also toured Europe with equal success. Details of her other life are

sketchy, but at some point in the 1930s she was recruited by the OGPU-NKVD (secret police), who at the time were very interested in penetrating Russian émigré circles. She used her influence on Skoblin, and they eventually took part in the NKVD-organized kidnapping and assassination of the former White General Evgeni Miller in Paris, 1937. It is likely that she was also involved in the kidnapping of General Kutepov that had also taken place in Paris seven years earlier, although this was never proven. Skoblin disappeared and was probably executed by the NKVD, but Plevitskaya was arrested by the French police. After a long, sensational trial she was sentenced to 15 years in prison for her part in Miller's murder. She died soon after while serving her sentence in Rennes prison. The Soviet press often reported on her singing career, without mentioning her intelligence activities.

Plisetskaya, Maya Mikhailovna
(1925–)
ballerina

The leading ballerina of the Bolshoi Ballet during the 1950s and 1960s, Plisetskaya is most identified with the dual role of Odette/Odile in Tchaikovsky's *Swan Lake*. Born into a Moscow family of dancers—she was the niece of the dancers Asaf and Sulamith Messerer—Plisetskaya studied with Agrippina Vaganova, a teacher of other prominent Soviet dancers. Plisetskaya joined the Bolshoi Company after graduation from the Bolshoi Ballet School in 1943. With the Bolshoi she was given lead roles and developed a style that combined technical virtuosity with unique acting portrayals that made the fullest expressive use of her body, especially her arms. In addition to *Swan Lake*, Plisetskaya danced in classical ballets such as *The Fountain of Bachkisaray, Don Quijote, Giselle,* and *Sleeping Beauty.* She also performed in modern Soviet ballets such as *The Stone Flower* (1954). Plisetskaya toured with the Bolshoi Ballet, performing in numerous countries including the United States, India, and China. In 1964 she was awarded a Lenin Prize for her artistic work. In later years, Plisetskaya turned to choreography, as in a 1972 performance of *Anna Karenina*.

Pobedonostsev, Konstantin Petrovich (1827–1907)
statesman

A conservative political philosopher and advocate of unfettered autocracy, Pobedonostsev wielded great influence in the late 19th century as tutor to the last two czars of the Romanov dynasty, ALEXANDER III and NICHOLAS II. Pobedonostsev was born in Moscow, the son of a priest who taught at Moscow University. In 1846 he graduated from the Oldenburg School of Law in St. Petersburg and entered the civil service, first working in the Moscow office of the Senate. His publications on the history of Russian civil law led to a lectureship on civil law at Moscow University, where he developed a reputation as an articulate and organized lecturer. In 1861 Czar ALEXANDER II invited him to serve as tutor to his son, Alexander Alexandrovich, the heir to the throne, during the imperial family's visits to Moscow. Four years later, the appointment became a permanent one, and Pobedonostsev left Moscow University for St. Petersburg. Pobedonostsev arrived at the capital toward the end of the reformist decade of Alexander II's reign. Pobedonostsev's views took on distinctly conservative, if not reactionary, tones, and he came to oppose all of Alexander's reforms, otherwise known as the GREAT REFORMS, at a time when the czar himself was having second thoughts about the political course he had charted up to the 1860s. Pobedonostsev continued to rise through the imperial hierarchy, with appointments to the Senate in 1868, to the Council of State in 1872, and, most important, as procurator of the Holy Synod of the Russian Orthodox Church in 1880. He held the latter position—essentially the chief administrator of the church—until 1905, when pressured to resign in the course of the 1905 Revolution. From this position and through his close rela-

tionship with the last two czars, Pobedonostsev greatly influenced the development of the repressive, nationalistic, authoritarian political agenda of the Russian government, especially during the 1880s. Even though his direct political influence declined in later years, his rigid personality and inflexible political views made him a symbol or lightning rod of a regime that in the years preceding the 1905 Revolution was seen as out of touch with the people of Russia.

pogrom

A term that denotes a mob attack on ethnic or religious minorities, often encouraged or tolerated by the authorities. In Russian history pogroms are most commonly associated with the mob violence and massacres of Jews and attacks on their property that were common in the late 19th and early 20th centuries. Although the city of ODESSA witnessed a pogrom in 1871, there were few other such incidents before 1881, when a wave of pogroms followed the assassination of czar ALEXANDER II. From April through December 1881, at least 12 localities, mostly in the Pale of Settlement, including KIEV and Odessa, witnessed anti-Jewish pogroms. In 1883, there were at least four other major pogroms including places outside the Pale such as NIZHNII NOVGOROD. These attacks on Jewish communities and property triggered a wave of Jewish emigration, largely to the United States. All together, between 1881 and 1914 almost 2 million Jews left the Russian Empire. The next major violent episode was a three-day pogrom in the Moldavian city of Kishinev in April 1903, which resulted in the death of 45 Jews and the looting of 700 houses and 600 businesses. Anti-Semitic violence increased again during the 1905 Revolution and subsequent years, with over 300 separate pogroms that left about 1,000 casualties and thousands more wounded. Beginning in April 1905, pogroms spread from Zhitomir to Kiev, Białystok, Simferopol, and Yaroslavl, before peaking in an orgy of violence in Odessa from October 18 to 21, which left about 500 Jews dead. The publication of the anti-Jewish fabrication known as *The Protocols of the Elders of Zion* in January 1906 sparked a new wave of violence with pogroms in Gomel, Yalta, Vologda, Simbirsk, and again Białystok. The port of Odessa was an epicenter of anti-Semitic violence during these years; in addition to the pogroms already mentioned, it witnessed one in July 1906, one in May 1907, and one in June 1907. The outbreak of World War I triggered more anti-Jewish violence in the areas near the front. The 1917 Russian Revolution and the civil war that followed triggered yet another round of anti-Semitic violence, again concentrated in Ukraine. Although the Soviet government prohibited anti-Semitic violence, it was unable to prevent it among its own troops, let alone among the Whites and the various nationalist and bandit groups that emerged. It is estimated that by the end of the civil war in late 1920, close to 2,000 pogroms left a total of 100,000 dead Jews and 500,000 homeless. These numbers would unfortunately pale when compared with the horrendous human cost of the Nazi German occupation of parts of the USSR during World War II, as a result of the Germans' extermination of Jews and other minorities.

Polish partitions

Three 18th-century territorial divisions of the Kingdom of Poland by its neighbors, Russia, Prussia, and Austria, that took place during the reign of CATHERINE II. By the early 1770s, Poland's internal divisions and a weak, decentralized political system had led to a political paralysis that fed the territorial ambitions of its three neighbors. In the First Partition (August 1772), Poland lost territories with a total of about 4.5 million people, which amounted to one-third of its territory and close to one-third of its population. Russia pushed its border westward up to the Western Dvina River and the Dnieper River, an area with about 1.3 million people. Austria took an equally large, but more densely populated, territory that included Galicia, western Podolia, and the city of Lvov (Lem-

berg or Lwow), while Prussia took a smaller area in northwestern Poland that enabled it to link its East Prussian territories with those to the west of Poland. In the next two decades, Poland tried to institute a number of reforms to prevent further action by its neighbors, including instituting a hereditary constitutional monarchy, but it proved to be in vain. Russia took the lead in promoting the Second Partition, which came in January 1793. Russia obtained a vast territory with about 3 million inhabitants that included most of Lithuania and most of western Ukraine. Prussia took the area known as Great Poland, as well as the towns of Danzig (Gdansk) and Thorn, while Austria did not participate in the Second Partition. A great Polish uprising led by Tadeusz Kościuszko in March 1794 failed to stem the tide toward the completed dismemberment of Poland, which came with the Third Partition of October 1795. Austria took the city of Kraków and land to the north up to the Bug and Vistula Rivers, while Prussia pushed its border eastward to the Niemen River, adding the city of Warsaw to its domains. Russia again seized the largest amount of territory, adding the rest of Lithuania and Ukraine up to the Niemen and Bug Rivers, an area with an estimated 1.2 million inhabitants. After the Third Partition, Poland ceased to exist as an independent state until 1918.

Polish Rebellion of 1830–31

Also known as the November Insurrection, the Polish rebellion of 1830–31 was the first of two 19th-century attempts by Polish patriots in Russian-occupied Poland to undo the legacy of the 18th-century Polish partitions. By 1830, the disappointments and animosities of almost four decades of Russian rule had boiled over. Inspired by the recent French Revolution of 1830 which had overthrown Louis-Philippe, Polish soldiers formed a secret society, the National Association against Russia, to overthrow their Russian overlords. Confident of French aid, Polish members of the Warsaw Training School who feared their replacement by Russians openly rebelled on

November 29, 1830, attacking Russian cavalry companies and assaulting the Russian grand duke's residence in Warsaw. Polish army regiments, citizens, and prisoners, joined the insurrection. Grand Duke Konstantin Pavlovich, brother of Czar NICHOLAS I, fled the city. The rebels set up General Jozef Chlopicki (1771–1854) as Polish ruler with dictatorial powers. The Poles, who had been formally ruled in a separate Kingdom of Poland with the Russian czar as their king, increased the stakes of their revolt by announcing the end of the Russian succession to its throne on January 25, 1831. While Russian troops rested in the winter and prepared for an upcoming campaign, the Polish side began to suffer from internal dissension. On May 26, 1831, Russian forces won the battle of Ostroleka, moved westward, and seized Warsaw on September 8, 1831. The rebellion collapsed with its leaders fleeing Poland. Russia, which had quelled sympathetic uprisings in the Ukraine and elsewhere, now fully incorporated its part of Poland as a Russian territory. It also launched an aggressive policy of Russification with the goal of destroying all vestiges of Polish nationhood. Temporarily defeated, the Poles in Russia would rise again in 1863 in another ill-fated rebellion.

Polish Rebellion of 1863–64

Three decades after the November Insurrection, Russian-occupied Poland rose again for its independence in 1863. Known as the January Insurrection, it was also unsuccessful. Although Czar ALEXANDER II tried to implement a reformist program with concessions to the Poles in education, religion, and administration, the fundamental issue of Polish autonomy remained unaddressed. The authoritarian manner of the czar's viceroy in Warsaw provoked both the moderate gentry and the more radical youth to agitate for independence in 1861. The czar's appointment of his brother Konstantin Nikolaevich, a leading liberal member in St. Petersburg court politics, as viceroy of Warsaw in 1862 and his promise to grant local voting rights did not mollify the Poles.

Instead there was an attempt on Konstantin's life. The Russian administration in Warsaw responded by trying to draft the young rebels, mostly students, into the Russian army. Many fled into the forests, where they formed a revolutionary assembly. Open rebellion erupted on January 22, 1863, spreading rapidly through the country and into neighboring Lithuania. Bands of poorly equipped and inexperienced youths conducted guerrilla warfare against Russian soldiers for almost two years. British, French, and Austrian attempts at mediation failed and together with the rebellion itself contributed to a nationalist and conservative backlash in St. Petersburg, where Alexander's reformist impulse had begun to slow down. The Polish rebels set up a clandestine government in Warsaw and Lithuania but they were suppressed by May 1864, never having received the military aid promised by Napoleon III of France. The Russians killed or exiled the participants and confiscated their property. Poland lost all vestiges of self-government and was reorganized as a Russian province; the Russian language became obligatory in Polish schools.

Poltava, Battle of (1709)

A turning point in the Great Northern War fought between Sweden and Russia from 1700–21, the Battle of Poltava also marked the emergence of Russia as a major European power. In 1708, after years of desultory fighting and meddling in Polish politics, which followed the important Swedish victory at the Battle of Narva in November 1700, the Swedish king, Charles XII, invaded Russia in the hope of bringing the war to an end. Charles's somewhat unorthodox strategy involved a detour through Ukrainian lands, where he hoped to form an alliance with the Cossack leader Ivan MAZEPA, before turning to attack Moscow. Mazepa, however, was only able to deliver about 2,000 Cossack troops, far less than expected. In October 1708, at Lesnaya, the Russians were able to intercept and defeat 15,000 Swedish soldiers traveling to reinforce

Charles's army in Ukraine. After a long, hungry winter, Charles XII prepared for a final offensive against the Russian army, despite shortages of troops and weapons. In May 1709 a Swedish force of about 20,000 laid siege to the small fortress of Poltava in Ukraine. By late June, the Russians had brought 80,000 troops, led by czar PETER I and his main military adviser, Prince Aleksandr MENSHIKOV, to lift the siege. On July 8, 1709, the two sides engaged in battle. The Swedish plan of attacking the main Russian defensive position by charging past the initial lines was never fully implemented, in great part because Charles himself was recovering from previous injuries. A Russian force of 40,000 soldiers counterattacked and defeated the Swedes. Charles XII and his Cossack ally, Mazepa, were able to flee with about 1,500 troops and sought asylum in Turkish territory to the south. Although the Battle of Poltava was in hindsight an immensely important victory for the Russian army, like Charles at Narva, Peter was not able to press his advantage to quickly conclude the war. Working in the Ottoman court and with French diplomatic assistance, Charles XII was able to convince Turkey to declare war on Russia in 1710, and the Great Northern War itself would continue until 1721.

Popov, Oleg Konstantinovich
(1930–1999)
circus artist

Known as the "Sunshine Clown," Oleg Popov was the longtime top clown with the Moscow State Circus and one of the world's most famous clowns. He was born in Vyrubovo, near Moscow. He joined the circus at the age of 14 as a juggler and slackwire artist. From 1945 to 1950, he studied at the State Circus School (School of Circus Art) in Moscow and specialized in tightrope walking, but he also studied juggling, acrobatics, and animal training. He made his debut at Tbilisi, Georgia, in 1949. At 20, he became a clown specializing in the art of mime. After working as an assistant to the performer Karandash (Pencil), he substituted for an injured clown at Saratov and decided to make clowning his career. Popov was an extremely popular artist and huge box-office success throughout the Soviet Union. He performed abroad with equal success. In 1956 he became the first Soviet clown to perform outside the Soviet Union when he appeared with the Moscow State Circus in Brussels, Paris, and London. Five years later he toured Cuba, Canada, the United States, and Italy. His familiarity with different circus disciplines enabled him to parody other acts on the bill and his frequent appearances in the ring ensured a sympathetic reception for the talented company. However, the character of the mischievous boy whom he created and his own happy-go-lucky personality dominated his performances. He worked in films and musicals, sometimes with his wife, Alexandrina Ilynitchna. He was made Artist of Merit in 1957, and awarded the Clown d'Or at the Monte Carlo International Circus Festival in 1981. He created the Popov school of clowns and also taught young performers. He wrote his memoirs in Russian, *Moi Geroi* (*My Hero,* 1961) and an autobiography that appeared in French as *Ma Vie de Clown* (*My Life as a Clown*) in 1968. In 1993 he was elected to the International Clown Hall of Fame.

Popova, Liubov Sergeevna
(1889–1924)
artist

An influential member of the Russian artistic avant-garde. Popova's career was cut short at age 35 when she died of scarlet fever two days after the death of her infant son, whom she was nursing. After an early career painting traditional landscapes, Popova traveled to Paris in 1912 and spent a year studying art. She returned to France and Italy for a brief stay in 1914. These trips were highly important in changing her style toward FUTURISM and constructivism. In 1914 and 1915 she took part in important Russian exhibitions such as the *Bubnovyi valet, Tramvai V,* and *0.10.* In addition to the canvas, she began to design textiles and rugs and in 1917 worked with Vladimir Tatlin in designing the Café Pittoresque in Moscow. After the Russian Revolution she abandoned painting and turned to more utilitarian concerns, continuing her textile designs, now for the First State Textile Printing Factory in Moscow, and designing theater sets and costumes. Two of her best-known sets were for Vsevolod MEYERHOLD's *The Magnanimous Cuckold* (1922) and *Earth on End* (1923). Stark and functional, the sets were designed so that actors could use them at any time and for any performance. With Aleksandr RODCHENKO she was one of the leading forces of constructivism. Before her untimely death, she was working on avant-garde dress designs that emphasized lightness, efficiency and hygiene.

populism

Known in Russian as *narodnichestvo,* populism is an ideological and intellectual movement that dominated radical thought from the 1860s to the 1880s. Although populism's tenets are often fluid, at the core of its ideology is a firm belief in the uniqueness of Russia in comparison with the West and in the viability of agrarian or peasant socialism as a path for future development. Its forerunners were Alexander HERZEN and Nikolai CHERNYSHEVSKY, who articulated the basic position that, drawing from its inherently socialist peasant communes, Russia could attain socialism by means of a peasant revolution, thus avoiding the capitalist stage that Marxists were arguing was an inevitable part of historical development. Its core support came from the young people who attended universities in the 1860s at a heady time when the GREAT REFORMS initiated by ALEXANDER II opened up a world of possibilities to intellectuals. Revolutionary populism was especially strong in the 1870s, although much of its emotional capital was spent in the naive and spectacularly unsuccessful campaign of going "to the people" (1874), when more than a thousand students descended upon the countryside only to find how wide the gap was between themselves and the peasantry they had idolized. Most of

these populists were influenced by BAKUNIN's view that the peasants were inherently revolutionary and were ready to rise against their landlords and the state, needing only a spark. Others, notably the Chaikovsky Circle, followed LAVROV in believing that it was first necessary to educate and train peasant leaders. In 1876 a predominantly Bakuninist underground organization, Land and Freedom, was founded, but it had little success and in 1879 split into two factions: PEOPLE'S WILL (Narodnaya Volya) and Black Repartition (Chernyi Peredel). People's Will accepted the "Jacobin" ideas of a seizure of power by a revolutionary minority, recently advocated by Petr TKACHEV, and advocated the use of terror to achieve revolutionary goals. Black Repartition, named after the millenarian peasant goal of universal redistribution of land, rejected terrorism and remained committed to the idea of building a revolutionary movement through education and propaganda. Members of People's Will assassinated Alexander II in 1881, while leaders of Black Repartition, like Georgii PLEKHANOV, emigrated. The assassination of the czar, the heavy repression that followed, and the dispersal of many of the original populists theorists and activists marked the end of what is sometimes known as the classical stage of revolutionary populism.

Potemkin, Grigorii Aleksandrovich (1739–1791)
statesman

An able statesman who was romantically involved with CATHERINE II the Great, Potemkin remained her most trusted adviser until his death. He was born in Smolensk province and educated at the recently established Moscow University. Potemkin first came to the attention of Catherine as one of the participants in the 1762 palace revolt that overthrew her husband, PETER III, and placed her on the throne. For his efforts he was rewarded in 1763 with an appointment as assistant procurator of the Holy Synod. He distinguished himself during the Russo-Turkish War of 1768–74, after which he marshal and president of the War Department. In this capacity he introduced important reforms of the Russian army and also built the Russian Black Sea Fleet. He organized Catherine's victorious tour of New Russia and the Crimea in 1787, from which time comes the expression "Potemkin village," commonly associated with him. In anticipation of her visit, Potemkin ordered the erection of fake villages to make the newly conquered area appear more populated than it really was. During the second Russo-Turkish war of Catherine's reign (1787–1792), Potemkin acted as commander in chief of the Russian forces. Potemkin died in October 1791 while traveling to begin peace negotiations with Ottoman diplomats.

Potemkin Mutiny (1905)

A naval mutiny that took place during the 1905 Revolution aboard one of the ships of the Black Sea Fleet, the *Potemkin* Mutiny was later immortalized as the subject of Sergei EISENSTEIN's groundbreaking film, *Battleship Potemkin* (1925). Six months into the revolutionary events of 1905 and at the tail end of the unsuccessful RUSSO-JAPANESE WAR, radical sailors in the Black Sea Fleet were planning a mutiny that would strike across the entire fleet. The plan was to capture the fleet's battleships with the hope of sparking a major nationwide insurrection. On June 14, 1905, the crew of the *Potemkin,* named after Catherine the Great's favorite, Prince Grigorii POTEMKIN, protested living conditions aboard the ship, especially the quality of the meat served to them. When the officer staff overreacted and killed their spokesman, the sailors mutinied, seized the ship, and sailed toward the port of ODESSA, hoping to link up with workers who had been on strike for several weeks. On June 16, sailors went ashore and contributed to the revolutionary ferment in the city by placing their dead comrade's body at the foot of the city's distinctive marble staircase. When thousands of sympathizers gathered in support of the sailors, the czarist authorities moved to end the disturbances, again overreacting by shooting into the

Prince Grigorii Aleksandrovich Potemkin *(Library of Congress)*

was rewarded with positions of power and, for several years, the affections of the empress. In 1774 he was appointed viceroy of New Russia, the steppe area north of the Black Sea and the Sea of Azov, recently conquered from the Ottoman Empire. He also became a count and governor-general of Ukraine. The romance with the empress lasted until 1776, but unlike her other favorites, Potemkin continued to wield power in various capacities. In 1783, he played a crucial role in convincing the khan of the Crimea to abdicate in Catherine's favor, thus opening the way for the Russian annexation of the Crimea, an object of Russian desire since the 16th century. For these efforts he was made a prince and the following year promoted to field crowd, a scene that forms the climax of Eisenstein's film. It is estimated that more than 2,000 people were killed at the Odessa steps. The crew left Odessa on June 17, but once it became clear that other ships were not joining in the mutiny, they sailed toward the Romanian Black Sea port of Constança and surrendered to the Romanian authorities in exchange for safe refuge.

Prokofiev, Sergei Sergeevich
(1891–1953)

pianist and composer

A brilliant pianist and prolific composer, Prokofiev was born in Sontzovka, Ukraine. At the age of 14 he entered the St. Petersburg Conservatory, where he remained until 1915, studying under various gifted instructors, including RIMSKY-KORSAKOV and Glazunov. In his early work, Prokofiev mastered a great variety of styles as shown in the romanticism of the First Piano Concerto (1912), the classicism of his First Symphony (1918), and the barbaric dynamism of his Scythian Suite (1916) and the colorful opera *The Love for Three Oranges* (1921). Nevertheless his work wasn't always well received in prerevolutionary Russia. While his First Piano Concerto won him the Rubinstein Prize, the Second (1913) was met with derision, and his former teacher Glazunov walked out of a 1915 performance. In 1918 he left Russia to undertake a world tour, during which he appeared as conductor and performer of his own works. The tour resulted in a 15-year absence from Russia, during which time he settled in Paris, working under the general direction of Igor STRAVINSKY. Works from this period include the Second, Third, and Fourth Symphonies (1925, 1929, 1930). Back in the USSR in 1933, he gravitated toward more melodic works, although Soviet critics would occasionally criticize his work for excessive modernism. Among his more important works from this period are the ballets *Romeo and Juliet* (1938) and *Cinderella* (1945), the opera *War and Peace* (1942), based on TOLSTOY's work, music for plays such as *Boris Godunov* (1936) and *Hamlet* (1938), and the film score for EISENSTEIN's

Ivan the Terrible (1942–45). Amazingly prolific, by the time of his death he had written over 100 compositions that included operas, ballets, symphonies, separate concertos for piano, violin, and cello, songs, music for plays, and film scores. News of his death on March 5, 1953, was lost among the outpouring of emotion that accompanied Joseph STALIN's death that same day.

Przhevalsky, Nikolai Mikhailovich
(1839–1888)

explorer and geographer

Known for the discovery of the wild horse named after him, Przhevalskii was born near Smolensk to a poor gentry family of Polish background. After graduation from the Smolensk gymnasium, he joined the Ryazan infantry regiment and later graduated with honors from the Academy of the General Staff in St. Petersburg in 1861. He remained an officer of the Russian army throughout his later career as an explorer and scholar, reaching the rank of major general. Przhevalsky's reputation is based on five great expeditions, inspired and organized by his mentor Petr SEMENOV TIAN-SHANSKY: one to the recently annexed Ussuri area in the Russian Far East (1867–69) and four to Mongolia, Sinkiang (Xinjiang), and Tibet (1870–85). In one expedition alone (1871–73)—the basis of his book *Mongolia and the Land of the Tunguts* (1875–76)—Przhevalsky covered 11,000 kilometers. Przhevalsky was elected an honorary member of the ACADEMY OF SCIENCES in 1878. In addition to his book on Mongolia, he published *The Third Journey in Central Asia* (1883), *The Fourth Journey in Central Asia* (1888), and *Passages and Metereological Diaries*. In 1888, as he was preparing for his fifth journey to Central Asia, he moved across SAMARKAND and into Sinkiang, and caught cold while hunting and died on October 26, in the town of Karakol, later named Przhevalskii after his death. Przhevalsky's contributions to scholarship in the fields of orography, climatology, botany, and zoology are substantial. In over nine years in Central Asia, he covered more than 30,000 kilometers and charted a vast area from the Pamirs in the west to the Great Khangan (Hangyan Norvu) range in the east, and from the Altai in the north to central Tibet in the south, a region that was unknown in the West. From his travels he brought back an enormous botanical and zoological collection. His name is associated with the exploration of the Kunlun Mountains, the peaks of northern Tibet, the basins of the Lob-Nor and Kuku-Nor, and the sources of China's Yellow River. Przhevalsky discovered a whole series of animal life such as the Tibetan bear, the wild camel, and, most notably, a wild horse, which later was named the Przhevalsky horse.

Pskov

An ancient city in northwestern Russia, located about 150 miles to the southwest of St. Petersburg, Pskov figured prominently in the medieval period of Russian history until its annexation by Moscow in 1510. Pskov was founded in 903 along the shores of the Velikava River, not far from the southeastern edge of the historic Lake Peipus, or Chud, where in 1242 ALEXANDER NEVSKY defeated the Teutonic Knights who had captured the town during the previous year. Until 1348 Pskov remained a dependency of the city of NOVGOROD. As an independent principality, Pskov's development mirrored that of Novgorod in some respects, but its smaller size and a lesser degree of social differentiation accounted for important differences. Thus, the powers of the prince of Pskov were more greatly restricted than in Novgorod, and the institution of the *veche* played a far greater role than in Pskov's former "big brother." Unlike Novgorod, Pskov did not pose a threat to Moscow, and in fact requested Muscovite assistance against outside attacks. Annexation by Moscow in 1510 was followed by deportations and greater taxes, and Pskov slipped into relative obscurity. In 1648, however, the town was caught up in the urban rebellions that spread from Moscow to other cities across Russia, such as Novgorod, in protest against excessive taxation and the corruption associated with advisers to Czar ALEKSEI. During World War

II, Pskov was occupied by Germans from 1941 to 1944 and suffered extensive damage in the process. Currently, a city of less than 300,000 inhabitants, Pskov has managed to preserve important architectural structures, such as a 13th-century *kremlin* (citadel) and several 14th and 15th century churches.

Pudovkin, Vsevolod Ilarionovich (1893–1953)
film director

One of the great directors of Soviet silent cinema, Pudovkin was born in the town of Penza, in central Russia, on February 28, 1893. He began studying science at Moscow University, but shortly before graduation he was drafted to serve in World War I, where he was wounded and taken as a prisoner of war to Germany. On his return to Moscow, he became caught up in the artistic upheaval that accompanied the Russian Revolution, and in 1922 he joined the experimental film workshop run by the great Soviet theorist and filmmaker Lev KULESHOV. Pudovkin's early films showed an ability to work in various styles. *Shakhmatnaya goryachka* (Chess fever, 1925) was "light and inventive, while *Mekhanika golovnogo mozga* (The mechanics of the brain, 1926) was used as an instructional film for Ivan PAVLOV's experiments in physiology, and *Mat* (Mother, 1926) was a classic drama adapted from Maksim GORKY's novel about the 1905 Revolution. Pudovkin established his name in the field of Soviet cinema with two widely acclaimed films, *Konets Sankt-Peterburga* (The end of St. Petersburg, 1927) and *Potomok Chingis-Khan* (Storm over Asia, 1928). The former was intended as a complement to EISENSTEIN's *October,* while the latter treats the topic of revolution in Mongolia. With the advent of sound film, Pudovkin's career entered into a relative decline, accompanied by poor health. In the final years of his life, he produced two well-received historical films: *Admiral Nakhimov* (1946) and *Vozvrashchenie Vassilia Bortnikova* (The return of Vassili Bortnikov), the latter issued shortly before his death in Riga in June 1953. Overshadowed by the two other giants of the Soviet silent cinema—Eisenstein and DOVZHENKO—Pudovkin remained a respected film teacher, and texts like *Film Technique and Film Acting* (1954) still remained influential decades after his death.

Pugacheva, Alla Borisovna (1949–　)
singer

Born in Moscow, Pugacheva has been a superstar in the world of Soviet music for almost three decades, having sold more than 200 million records. She first trained in classical music at the Ippolitov-Ivanov School of Music in Moscow before enrolling in the Lunacharsky State Institute of Theatrical Arts, also in Moscow. She began her career as a singer at the age of 16 and spent the next decade traveling across the Soviet Union, performing with various bands, such as New Electron, Muscovites, and Happy Fellows. A hint of her future success came with a third-place prize at the All-Union Soviet Pop Festival in 1974. The following year, Pugacheva received a lucky break when the official Soviet representative to the Golden Orpheus Song Festival in Bulgaria was replaced at the last moment amid rumors of bad behavior. Chosen to take his place, Pugacheva won the Grand Prize, performing the song "Arlekino." She quickly capitalized on her success with broadcasts on Soviet television and recordings through the state recording house, Melodiya, and in 1978 again won an international competition, this time at the International Song Festival in Sopot, Poland. By the late 1970s Pugacheva had developed a distinctive style that combined Western pop songs delivered with great drama that harked back to the traditions of Russian variety music known as *estrada*. Her fame grew throughout the 1980s with numerous performances in European song festivals, and she continued to gather more awards, Soviet and international. Pugacheva also developed a career in television and cinema. In 1988 she toured the United States for the first time, performing in Seattle's "Bumbershoot" festival. One year later she performed at the Country Music Festival in Nashville, Tennessee. In 1991 she was named a National Artist of the USSR, the highest designation in the cultural world of the former Soviet Union. At home, Pugacheva was known for the lavish lifestyle of a celebrity, complete with a turbulent personal life that included four marriages. Although Pugacheva was not able to build on her fame beyond the Russian-language world, her iconic status in Russian society remains undiminished, even as she moves away from music and into ancillary fields such as fashion design.

Pugachev Rebellion (1773–1774)

Peasant uprising. The Pugachev rebellion was the last of four major peasant revolts that shook the Russian state in the 17th and 18th centuries. In September 1773, Emelian Ivanovich Pugachev (1726–75), a Don Cossack who had served in the Seven Years' War, raised the banner of rebellion along the eastern banks of the Volga River. Claiming to be the true emperor PETER III, who had actually been murdered during the palace revolt that placed his wife, CATHERINE II, on the throne in 1762, Pugachev issued a "manifesto" emancipating the serfs. Pugachev's imperial claims, fervent OLD BELIEVER preachings, the promise to abolish SERFDOM, and the discontent of ethnic minorities recently incorporated into the Russian Empire helped him recruit a motley "army" of COSSACKS, peasants, as well as nomadic Kazakhs and Bashkirs. The rebels were able to make their initial advance up the Volga River in great part because the bulk of the Russian army was occupied in a war with Turkey. Imperial armies sent by Catherine were at first unable to defeat the rebels, who sacked KAZAN and seized Saratov and marked a trail of destruction, looting and burning the nobles' estates in the region. Finally, while peasants and others throughout Russia awaited the coming of Pugachev as a savior, his ill-equipped, untrained men were overwhelmed by Catherine's forces, led most notably by Count Aleksandr SUVOROV (1729–1800), and were thoroughly defeated at Tsaritsyn (now Volgograd) in September 1774. Betrayed by his own troops, Pugachev was handed over to the imperial authorities, who took him to Moscow and paraded him around the city streets in an iron cage. After a trial in late December 1774, Pugachev was executed by quartering in January 1775. It is estimated that the rebels were responsible for about 3,500 deaths, of which almost half were nobles, the rest government officials, soldiers, and about 200 members of the clergy. On the rebel side the number of deaths reached about 20,000, not including those suffered by the Bashkirs and those killed by government troops in savage reprisals after the rebellion had died out. The Pugachev rebellion planted the fear of similar future peasant uprisings in the minds of officials and nobles. Some responded by seeking to entrench the institution of serfdom, others by beginning the long process toward the abolition of serfdom, capped by the EMANCIPATION ACT of 1861.

Pushkin, Aleksander Sergeevich (1799–1837)

poet

Regarded by Russians as their great national genius, Pushkin is also one of the great figures of world literature. Born into an old noble family, on his maternal side Pushkin descended from AVRAM PETROVICH HANNIBAL, the Ethiopian general brought to Russia during PETER I the Great's reign. True to his background, Pushkin received a first-class education and after graduation held various posts at the foreign office (1817–24). As a young man he was raised on the liberal ideals of the Enlightenment and the French Revolution, which often landed him in trouble. For political poems that he wrote while a member of the secret Union of Salvation. He was twice banished from St. Petersburg, in 1820 to New Russia in the south and in 1824 to a family estate. Although friendly to many of the DECEMBRISTS and politically sympathetic to their ideas, he did not join their movement or the insurrection they attempted in 1825. He published his first poem at the age of 15, and his early work shows the classical and romantic literary influences of the era. Long poems like *Ruslan and Liudmila* (1819), *Cau-*

Aleksander Sergeevich Pushkin *(Library of Congress)*

casian Prisoner* (1821), *Fountain of Bachkisarai* (1822), and *Gypsies* (1824) reveal the strong influence of Byron on his early work. Pushkin succeeded at many other forms such as historical and philosophical poems, like *Poltava* (1828), and *The Bronze Horseman* (1833); historical dramas like *Boris Godunov* (1825); short and long stories like *Belkin's Tales* (1830), *The Queen of Spades* (1834), and *The Captain's Daughter* (1836), as well as fairy tales in verse. His masterpiece is undoubtedly the novel "in verse," *Evgenii Onegin* (*Eugene Onegin*), written between 1823 and 1831, which has often been described as an encyclopedia of contemporary Russian life. Although he was on good personal terms with NICHOLAS I, who often served as his censor, Pushkin did not relate well to the intrigue-ridden court life of St. Petersburg. In 1837 he became entangled in one such intrigue over his wife's good name, and was fatally wounded in a duel.

Putin, Vladimir Vladimirovich (1952–)
president of Russia

The president of the Russian Federation since 2000, Vladimir Putin was born in St. Petersburg, then known as Leningrad, on October 7, 1952. His father was a factory foreman. Two brothers were born before him, but they both died young, one shortly after birth and the other of diphtheria during World War II. As an infant, Putin was baptized in the Russian Orthodox Church, despite the atheist policy of the Soviet government. As a youth, Putin was a devoted participant in sports, especially wrestling and judo, and the Russian form of self-defense known as sambo. After winning the St. Petersburg sambo championships several times, he attained the title of master of sports in sambo, and later reached the same title in judo.

Putin studied law at Leningrad State University, graduating in 1975. He then joined the KGB's (secret police) foreign intelligence unit, stationed in Leningrad and East Germany. While stationed in Dresden, his wife, Liudmila, also a Leningrad State University graduate and a schoolteacher, gave birth to their daughters. In 1990, Putin returned to Leningrad and retired from the KGB with the rank of colonel. After a short stint as an aide to the vice president of Leningrad State University, he entered city politics as an aide to Anatolii Sobchak, the liberal mayor of Leningrad, renamed St. Petersburg in 1991. From 1991 to 1994 he served as the chairman of the committee for foreign relations of the St. Petersburg Mayor's Office. In March 1994 he was appointed deputy mayor, a post he held until Sobchak's defeat in the 1996 mayoral elections. During these years Putin had studied for a candidate degree in economic sciences, which he received in 1996.

While Putin was out of work in St. Petersburg, Anatolii Chubais, an influential insider, recommended him for a job in Moscow with President Boris YELTSIN's administration. From 1996 to 1998, Putin served as deputy chief administrator of the Kremlin, with responsibility for the central government's relations with Russia's diverse

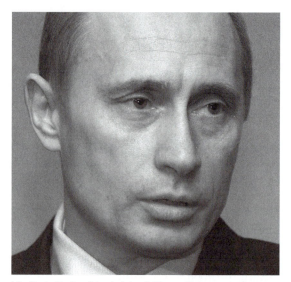

Vladimir Putin *(North Atlantic Treaty Organization)*

regions. In July 1998, he was appointed director of the Federal Security Bureau (FSB), one of the newly reorganized security services that replaced the old KGB. In March 1999, while remaining director of the FSB, he added another important portfolio, secretary of the Presidential Security Council, the advisory body coordinating the activities of the armed forces, security agencies, and the police.

Putin's appointment in August 1999 as prime minister, the fourth in less than a year, surprised most observers. Another surprise came on December 31, 1999, when Yeltsin resigned ahead of time and named Putin acting president. In March 2000 Putin was elected to a four-year term the initial results of which defied easy description. By early 2004 political life had become less chaotic, albeit less democratic; Yeltsin-era oligarchs had been co-opted; the war in CHECHNYA continued unabated; terrorism had become evermore present, especially in Moscow; and Russian coffers benefited from the country's emergence as a major oil producer. In presidential elections of March 2004, Putin gained easy reelection, garnering more than 70 percent of the vote.

R

Rachmaninoff, Sergei Vasilievich (1873–1943)
composer and pianist

The heir of TCHAIKOVSKY as the main exponent of Russia's classical tradition, Rachmaninoff was a piano virtuoso who is also considered Russia's last great romantic composer. Born to a military family in the Novgorod region, Rachmaninoff was trained in music by his mother from the age of four. He studied at the St. Petersburg Conservatory (1882–85) and then at the Moscow Conservatory, graduating in 1892 with a gold medal. After graduation he began his concert career, while working first as a teacher at the Mariinskii School, then as music inspector at the Ekaterinskii and Elizavetinskii Institutes. In 1897–98, he spent a year as conductor of Savva Mamontov's Moscow Private Orchestra. By this time he had already written his First Piano Concerto (1892) and a one-act opera, *Aleko,* and a stellar future lay ahead of him. The criticism of his First Symphony (1897) caused him to withdraw from writing, but with the help of hypnosis he composed his Second Piano Concerto (1901), an instant and enduring success. He achieved additional successes as a composer with his Second Symphony (1908), Third Piano Concerto (1909), and the choral works *The Bells* (1913) and *Vespers* (1915). The other areas of his career also flourished. An appointment as conductor with the Bolshoi Theater in Moscow (1904–6) was followed by a period in which he alternated between winters in Dresden and summers in Russia (1906–9). Rachmaninoff made his first visit to the United States in 1909, and after a guest appearance in Sweden in 1917, he decided to emigrate in response to the OCTOBER REVOLUTION of that year. He first lived in Paris and Switzerland before moving to the United States in 1935. Somewhat out of place in a modernistic age, Rachmaninoff managed to compose important pieces in the last decade of his life, including Rhapsody on a theme of *Paganini* (1934), his Third Symphony (1936), and Symphonic Dances (1940). On stage until the last few weeks of his life, at the time of his death Rachmaninoff was considered by many to be the greatest pianist in the world.

Radishchev, Aleksandr Nikolaevich (1749–1802)
writer

Radishchev is generally regarded as the founder of the revolutionary tradition in Russia. He was born to a prosperous landowning family whose serfs would later repay their generally humane treatment by hiding them in the forest for protection at the time of the PUGACHEV REBELLION (1773–74). Radishchev was educated at the Corps des Pages in St. Petersburg, graduating with distinction and earning a trip with other students to study law at the University of Leipzig, Germany. Radischchev later wrote of his student days in *The Life of Fedor Ushakov* (1789), dedicated to his good friend Ushakov, who had died an untimely death. Back in St. Petersburg in 1773, he entered government service but quit in 1775 in protest against the excessively cruel treatment given to Pugachev's defeated followers. With Count Aleksandr Vorontsov's assistance, he returned to government service in

1776. In his best-known work, *Journey from St. Petersburg to Moscow* (1790), he forcefully portrayed the inhumanity of SERFDOM and called for a revolution. As a result, he was charged with high treason and sentenced to death, but this was commuted to 10 years' banishment in Siberia and loss of noble status. He continued to write while in exile, and after CATHERINE II's death in 1796, PAUL I allowed him to return to his estates under police supervision. In 1801 ALEXANDER I gave him a full amnesty and made him a member of the commission for the codification of laws. But despairing of his efforts on behalf of the serfs, Radishchev committed suicide on September 11, 1802. Some have interpreted his suicide as an act of political defiance, pointing to a note found among his papers that read, "Posterity will avenge me." His *Journey* and his tragic life made a strong impression upon Russian progressive thought in the 19th century.

Raikin, Arkadi Isaakovich (1911–1987)
entertainer

A beloved and enormously popular entertainer and comedian, Raikin was born in Riga and grew up in provincial Russia before moving to Leningrad. Abandoning his original intention to study chemistry for the theater, Raikin graduated from the Leningrad Theatrical School in 1935. He worked as a dramatic actor for a few years in the Leningrad Theater for the Working Youth (TRAM) and the Lenin Komsomol Theater before turning to *estrada,* the distinctive Russian variety genre that combined verbal satire and comedy routines with music and dance. In 1939 Raikin won the All-Union Estrada Competition in Moscow, launching a career that would dominate Soviet *estrada* until his death. In the early post–World War II period, Raikin, like other Jewish performers, suffered from the extreme ANTI-SEMITISM of the late STALIN years. Prudently, he modified his act to include more satire of life in the capitalist West, as in skits like "Around the World in Eighty Days" (1951). In the KHRUSHCHEV years Raikin emerged as a mature comic whose packed performances in his Leningrad theater appealed to broad audiences ranging from celebrities to officials to common citizens. His repertoire tackled the permissible themes of shortages, poor service, shoddy products, bureaucratism, careerism, and alcohol abuse in a gentle, inclusive way that also relied on faces, gestures, and odd voices to entertain audiences. Many of his skits became part of the cultural canon of Soviet life in the 1960s and 1970s. Raikin's nationwide popularity was made possible by the spread of Soviet television in the 1960s and by the ease with which his brand of variety show adapted to the new medium. He moved to Moscow in 1981 and was named Hero of Socialist Labor. In his final years he turned to long, moralistic monologues that appealed less to his audiences. After his death, his son Konstantin followed in his footsteps.

Rasputin, Grigorii Efimovich (1872?–1916)
religious figure

A monk whose reputed healing powers brought him into the court of NICHOLAS II and ALEXANDRA, Rasputin became a symbol of corruption and decline in the final years of the ROMANOV DYNASTY. Rasputin was born Grigorii Efimovich Novykh in the Siberian town of Tobolsk. Details of his early years remain hazy, as he was wont to embellish them once he left Siberia. He is known, however, to have been influenced by the Khlysty (Flagellants), a religious sect. Rasputin arrived in St. Petersburg in 1903 with the reputation of being a *starets* (holy man) with healing powers and gained entrée into the upper reaches of imperial society. In 1905 he gained the loyalty of the empress Alexandra when he staunched the bleeding of the royal couple's heir, Aleksei, who suffered from hemophilia. A pious woman, Alexandra regarded Rasputin as a divine missionary and welcomed him into her circle, while Nicholas was less enthralled by Rasputin but respected his wife's gratefulness. Possessed of a large sexual appetite and advocating a philoso-

Grigorii Efimovich Rasputin *(Hulton/Archive)*

phy of repentance through sin, Rasputin became a controversial celebrity in the salons of high society. Eventually, his greed and desire for financial and political influence, coupled with the dissolute life he led, made him many enemies. In 1912 church authorities denounced him as an impostor and ordered him to return to Siberia. In 1914, however, he returned to St. Petersburg, and the following year, with Nicholas II residing in Mogilev with the command of the Russian armies during World War I, Rasputin's influence over Alexandra was now almost unchallenged. Isolated in the capital, Alexandra turned to Rasputin for political advice. Ministers rose and fell in rapid succession, depending on their ability to please Rasputin and Alexandra. Coupled with the Russian setbacks on the field of battle, the result was a whispering campaign that erro-

neously posited the existence of a German faction at the court, headed by the empress, who was of German origin, and aided by Rasputin. False as the rumors were, the damage to the image of the royal family was real. Identifying Rasputin as the source of the monarchy's and Russia's crisis, two distant relatives of the czar and the right-wing DUMA deputy Vladimir Purishkevich conspired to assassinate him in December 1916. After a bungled plot that only added to his legend, as he survived poison in his food and gunshots to his body, Rasputin finally died after being dropped into a hole in the frozen Neva River.

Rastrelli, Bartolomeo (1700?–1771)
(Varfolomeo Varfolomeovich)
architect

Born Bartolomeo Francesco Rastrelli in Paris, the son of the Italian architect and sculptor Bartolomeo Carlo Rastrelli (1675–1744), Rastrelli became the leading exponent of high baroque architecture in 18th-century Russia. He studied architecture in western Europe but was also influenced by 17th-century Muscovite architecture. His style was basically baroque but with rococo elements; his plans are completely cubic and rectilinear, with a complete absence of curves, and he is notable for his lavish use of decoration (grouped columns, moldings), color, and gilding. His magnificent interior enfilades were much copied. As court architect to Empress ELIZABETH, his principal works were the palaces of Peterhof (Petrodvorets) and Tsarskoe Selo (now Pushkin), the Summer Palace, and the Smolny Convent in St. Petersburg, in which he achieved a remarkable and exuberant fusion of rococo and native elements. Outside of St. Petersburg he built the St. Andrew's Cathedral in Kiev (1747–48). While all these are jewels of Russian architecture, the Winter Palace in St. Petersburg (1754–62) marked the culmination of Rastrelli's long and distinguished career and remains his masterpiece. Located on the banks of the Neva River, Rastrelli's Winter Palace set the tone for subsequent construction in the center of the city. With Elizabeth's death in 1761 and the dawning of the classical style, Rastrelli lost his preeminent position in St. Petersburg. He found employment in Kurland, at the court of Count BIRON, once the favorite of Empress Anna. Rastrelli died in 1771, but the exact date and place of his interment are unknown.

Razin, Stenka (ca. 1630–1671)

The leader of a 17th-century rebellion that was long celebrated in Russian song and folklore, Razin was born Stepan Timofeevich Razin into a prosperous Cossack family of the Don River area. In 1667 Razin gathered a band of loyal COSSACKS and landless peasants and during the next three years gained notoriety as a daring adventurer who raided the lands of the lower Volga and the Caspian Sea as far as Persia. By 1670 he returned to his stronghold on the upper Don River but soon planned a new set of campaigns, directed this time against Russian fortresses along the Volga River. After seizing ASTRAKHAN and Tsaritsyn (present-day Volgograd), Razin moved up the Volga River in a campaign that combined elements of a popular rebellion and anarchic looting. Razin's troops, which grew from an initial 7,000 to about 200,000 by the time they reached the river port of Simbirsk, directed their anger at the nobility and upper classes of the region, looting and burning their estates. They incited peasants and the lower classes to rebel against their masters and the bureaucracy but were careful not to rebel against the czar. In addition to the freebooting Cossacks who formed the core of his troops, Razin attracted the support of peasants, whose enserfment had recently been legalized in 1649, and some of the non-Russian ethnic minorities of the region. As the rebellion gained support beyond the Volga River valley and spread westward into the Donets and Don river valleys and engulfed parts of central European Russia around Penza and Tambov, Czar ALEKSEI sent a seasoned military commander, Prince Yuri Bariatinsky, to con-

front Razin's army at Simbirsk in October 1670. Though smaller in number, Bariatinsky's force included professionally trained regiments that easily defeated Razin's undisciplined and poorly equipped army. Razin managed to escape to his native region but was later betrayed by other Cossacks and, in April 1671 brought to Moscow, where he was tortured and publicly executed on June 16, 1671. The rebels continued fighting without Razin until December 1671, when their last stronghold, the town of Astrakhan, was captured by the czar's troops. Fearing reprisals and seeking to escape serfdom, the Razin rebellion triggered the exodus of many peasants to Siberia in search of land and freedom.

Red Square

One of the most easily recognizable Russian architectural landmarks, Red Square has long served as the symbolic center of the city of MOSCOW and, more broadly, of Russia and the Soviet Union. A vast, roughly rectangular open space of about 73,000 square meters, to the west Red Square is bordered by the walls of the Kremlin with the 19th-century GUM department store to the east, the 16th-century ST. BASIL'S CATHEDRAL at the south end, and the State Historical Museum at the north end. First known simply as "market square" and then "Trinity Square," the square itself dates back to the late 15th century, when the completion of the Kremlin walls created an open space on the eastern side of the Kremlin. It continued to take shape with the construction of the strikingly original St. Basil's Cathedral (1555–61), also known as the Cathedral of the Assumption, to commemorate the Muscovite capture of the city of KAZAN. The square's function was primarily commercial, and trading stalls occupied a large part of the square until 1679, when they were cleared out. It was not until the 1660s that the square became known as Red Square from the Russian term *krasnaya*, which means both "red" and "beautiful" (it has nothing to do with the later communist period of the USSR). In 1534 a

Celebration of the first of May in Red Square, Moscow, 1960 *(Library of Congress)*

rostrum was built, from which the czar and other officials could address Muscovites. Known as Lobnoe Mesto (Place of the Skulls), after 1685 it became the site of public executions. The Place of the Skulls was rebuilt several times, as late as 1786. In the 18th century, with the trading stalls removed, the square became the center of Moscow's cultural life, with the appearance of book stalls, the first public library, and the first building of Moscow University in the surrounding environs. In 1818 a statue to MININ AND POZHARSKY, who led the struggle against the Poles who had occupied the city during the TIME OF TROUBLES was erected in front of the Upper Trading Rows, near the center of the square. In 1930, the statue was moved closer to St. Basil's. The last quarter of the 19th century saw the construction of two important components of Red Square's current architectural ensemble. The dark-red State Historical Museum was built between 1874 and 1883 from a design by the architect O. V. Shervud. Along the other long side of the square, the Upper Trading Rows and Middle Trading Rows were completed in 1892–93, in a style that tried to match that of the Kremlin walls and towers. In Soviet times, the trading rows were nationalized and became known as the State Universal Store (GUM). The final addition to the ensemble of Red Square came with the construction of the LENIN MAUSOLEUM along the Kremlin side of the square. Following LENIN's death in 1924, a temporary wooden mausoleum was erected to house his embalmed body. A permanent structure was completed in 1930, at which time the observation platforms and fir trees were also added.

Throughout the Soviet period, prominent leaders were buried in the Kremlin walls near the mausoleum.

Because of its central, symbolic, and strategic location, Red Square has witnessed important events of Russian history, including several 17th-century riots, as well as fighting between supporters and opponents of Soviet power at the time of the OCTOBER REVOLUTION of 1917. Throughout the Civil War, Lenin repeatedly addressed workers and soldiers from a tribune erected on Red Square. In 1918, holding the May Day and October Revolution parades was started in the square, a tradition that continued throughout the period of Communist rule. As the Soviet Union became a military superpower, the parades increasingly became the site for the display of Soviet weapons, aircraft, and artillery. In the years since the dissolution of the Soviet Union in 1991, Red Square has retained its central importance in Russian life, and several architectural landmarks from czarist times have been restored. Lenin's body is still on display at the mausoleum, even though the honor guard has been removed. In 1990, Red Square was added to UNESCO's list of World Heritage Sites.

Repin, Ilya Efimovich (1844–1930)
artist

An artist who distinguished himself as a painter of historical themes, Repin was born on August 5, 1844, in Chuguev, in the Ukrainian region of Kharkov. His father was a military settler and Repin pursued studies at the Chuguev Military School of Topography. As a youth he worked with icon painters and studied with the painter I. Bunakov. In St. Petersburg after 1863, he first studied at the School of Graphic Art of the Society for the Encouragement of Art, then at the Academy of Arts (1864–71). A student of Ivan Kramskoi, one of the leaders of the artistic revolt against the academy that led to the formation of the Peredvizhniki (WANDERERS) movement, Repin joined the Wanderers in 1871. From 1873 to 1876, he studied in Italy and Paris. Back in

Russia, after four years in his native Chuguev (1878–82), he returned to St. Petersburg and from 1893 taught at the academy. The most accomplished of 19th-century realists, Repin was also the most prolific and versatile of Russian artists. He painted with equal facility portraits, historical and religious compositions, genre scenes, and landscapes. His works are done with an obvious gusto and a fine sense of color; his brilliant portraits of MUSSORGSKY and MENDELEYEV deserve special mention. A master of historical drama, he painted some of the best-known works of the genre: *The Volga Boatmen* (1873), *Easter Procession in Kursk Province* (1880–83), *Ivan the Terrible and his Son Ivan* (1885), and *The Zaporozhe Cossacks Write to the Turkish Sultan* (1891). Repin lived his last years in the Finnish village of Kuokkal, working chiefly on religious paintings. He died on September 29, 1930. Most of his paintings are held in the Russian Museum in St. Petersburg and at the Tretiakov Gallery in Moscow. In 1940, the Ilya Repin Museum was set up in Chuguev, and in 1958 a monument was erected in Moscow in his honor.

Riabushinsky, Pavel Pavlovich (1871–1924)
entrepreneur and politician

The leader of the third generation of a remarkable Moscow business dynasty of OLD BELIEVER stock, Riabushinsky also took part in the incipient democratic politics of the late imperial period after the Revolution of 1905. The eldest of nine sons (and sibling to 13 sisters), Riabushinsky inherited the leading role in the family business after his father's death in 1894. The Riabushinsky family empire had been built around textiles, one of several similar dynasties in the Central Industrial Region around MOSCOW. Under Riabushinsky's leadership, however, the family business expanded into a number of other areas such as banking (the Riabushinsky Bank, which in 1912 became the Bank of Moscow), publishing (the newspaper *Utro Rossii*), and automobiles (the AMO plant). He and his siblings also were active as cultural patrons, most notably in architecture, where they commissioned Feodor SHEKHTEL to build several mansions (1900–1902) and the Yaroslavl Railway Station (1902), the Riabushinsky Bank (1903), and the Moscow Merchants' Society (1909). As family leader, Riabushinsky also became involved in politics, emerging as a liberal, nationalist voice in Russian business circles. In 1913 he was elected chairman of the Society of Cotton Industrialists, and in 1915 he advanced the idea of the War Industries Committees and became a member of the Central War Industries Committee and chairman of the Moscow committee. He was a leader of the Progressive Bloc, which unsuccessfully sought to build a coalition of "progressive" forces in opposition to the czar. He spent most of 1916 convalescing in the Crimea and returned to Moscow around the time of the February Revolution to lead the All-Russian Union of Commerce and Industry. A cautious supporter of the Provisional Government in its early months, by August he was despairing of rule by a "gang of charlatans." After the OCTOBER REVOLUTION he emigrated to Paris, where he continued his work in émigré politics on behalf of the Union of Commerce and Industry until his death in 1924.

Rimsky-Korsakov, Nikolai Andreevich (1844–1908)

composer

A prolific composer, Rimsky-Korsakov also made a mark on Russian classical music as an unrivaled teacher and a promoter of Russian national themes. Originally a naval officer, Rimsky-Korsakov began his teaching career at the St. Petersburg Conservatory in 1871 as a professor of composition and instrumentation. Until 1884, he also served as Inspector of Naval Bands. From 1886 to 1900, he was conductor of the influential Free Music School Concerts inaugurated by a patron of Russian music, Mitrofan Beliaev. Among Rimsky-Korsakov's long list of distinguished students are Glazunov, PROKOFIEV, and STRAVINSKY. He composed extensively, writing 14

operas, numerous choral works and orchestral works, chamber music, vocal works, piano works, and 49 harmonized folk songs, first collected in 1875–76. His best-known operas include *The Snow Maiden* (1880–81), *Sadko* (1894–96), *Tsar Saltan* (1898–1900), and *The Golden Cockerel* (1906–7). He is now chiefly remembered for his orchestral work, *Sheherazade* (1888). He also revised and completed MUSSORGSKY's *Boris Godunov* and *Khovanshchina,* and Borodin's *Prince Igor.* In his last years he ran into trouble with the authorities. In 1905, he was dismissed from the conservatory for his vocal support of his students, taking part in the political protests of that revolutionary year. Shortly before his death, the censors banned his final opera, *The Golden Cockerel.* Although considered a superb craftsman and orchestrator of elegant and exuberant works, he has been criticized for the repetitions and clichés that inevitably found their way into such a large body of work. His operas were often based on national themes laced with folk music, and the ecclesiastical and oriental music he studied. As the most accomplished member of the Moguchaia kuchka (MIGHTY HANDFUL) group of nationalist composers, Rimsky-Korsakov helped define a distinctly Russian national school of music.

Rodchenko, Aleksandr Mikhailovich (1891–1956)

artist

One of the leaders of the constructivist movement in Russian art in the first decade after the Russian Revolution of 1917, Rodchenko was a versatile artist who worked in a wide range of media, including painting, sculpture, and photography. Rodchenko was born in St. Petersburg but moved with his family to KAZAN in 1907. He attended the Kazan Art School from 1911 to 1914, after which he moved to MOSCOW, where he studied at the Stroganov Artistic and Industrial Institute until 1916. Under the influence of Vladimir Tatlin, he embraced abstract art, and at the 1916 Futurist exhibit in Moscow organized by Tatlin, Rodchenko exhibited 10 of his paintings.

Like other similarly inclined artists, Rodchenko was particularly active in the first years after the OCTOBER REVOLUTION of 1917. In 1918, he served as the founder and first director of the Museum of Artistic Culture, as well as the Soviet government's Committee of Applied Arts. During the Russian civil war, he taught at the seminal artistic workshops known as Vhutemas. In the 1920s Rodchenko became known for his collages and photomontages and found steady work at Soviet publishing houses as a graphic artist, designing posters and book covers, including several for his friend the poet Vladimir MAYAKOVSKY. He designed the sets for Mayakovsky's 1929 play, *The Bedbug*. Rodchenko also worked in film, first collaborating with Dziga VERTOV in his newsreel series Kino-Pravda, and then between 1927 and 1930 as "constructor-artist" for films such as Boris Barnet's *Moscow in October* and *The Woman Journalist*.

Rodchenko traveled abroad only once during his lifetime, to the 1925 Paris Arts Deco Exhibition, where his design of a model "workers' club" was awarded four silver medals. Tainted by accusations of "formalism" from the Soviet cultural establishment, his work became more conventional after 1930. In the 1930s he returned to painting, both figurative and abstract, but was not allowed to exhibit, even as his photography was shown. Rodchenko was able to avoid the repression and terror that fell on some of the other leading figures of the postrevolutionary artistic world and died in Moscow on March 12, 1956.

Roerikh, Nikolai Konstantinovich
(1874–1947)
(Nicholas Roerich)
artist and designer

Born in St. Petersburg, Roerikh (sometimes spelled Roerich) was a prolific and original painter, who painted close to 7,000 pictures, and a man of extremely wide interests. He graduated from St. Petersburg University and the Academy of Fine Arts but began his professional life as an archaeologist. He first gained notoriety through his stage designs, based on Old Russian themes, for Sergei DIAGHILEV's productions of the Polovtsian Dances, a scene from *Prince Igor* (1909), and *The Rite of Spring* (1913), both of which were staged in Paris. He also designed sets for the Moscow Art Theater and Zimin's Private Opera that were distinguished by his meticulous attention to historical detail. From 1902, Roerikh took an active part in the MIR ISKUSSTVA movement, and in 1910 he was elected its chairman. Roerikh and his family traveled widely, moving back and forth from Russia with relative ease. From 1916, he lived in Finland and other Scandinavian countries. During 1920–23 he toured the United States with his pictures and enjoyed great success there, and developed a substantial following among those attracted to the mystical themes of his art. In 1923, Roerikh and his family went on an anthropological expedition to Central Asia, Mongolia, and Tibet. From 1928, he lived in the Himalayas at Kullu, near Simla, where he established the Urusvati Himalayan Research Institute, devoted to the botanical, ethnolinguistic, and anthropological study of the area. Convinced that culture and peace were prerequisites for each other, he spent much time promoting an international convention that would protect cultural treasures during times of war. Influenced by the example of the Red Cross banner, Roerikh suggested that a Banner of Peace, which he designed, be flown over cultural treasures. His efforts bore fruit in April 1935 when the then 21 members of the Pan-American Union signed the Roerich Pact at the White House, a treaty that still remains in force. Roerikh died at Kullu. A Roerich Museum exists in New York City.

Romanov dynasty

The Romanov dynasty ruled Russia from 1613 until the Russian Revolution of 1917 that abolished the Russian monarchy. The death without issue in 1598 of Czar FEODOR I, son of IVAN IV the Terrible, marked the end of the line of the Rurikids, who claimed to trace their ancestry back to Rurik, the legendary founder of the Russian state dynasty. From 1598 to 1613, Russia underwent a period of dynastic instability, social upheaval, and foreign invasion known as the TIME OF TROUBLES. To restore order to the country, a *ZEMSKII SOBOR* (assembly of the land) convened in January 1613 to elect a new monarch. After some deliberations, foreign candidates were removed from consideration, and the 16-year old MICHAEL ROMANOV emerged as the candidate with the most support. The Romanov family was a respected but not dominant aristocratic family that descended from a Moscow aristocrat whose daughter Anastasia Romanova had married Ivan IV. Anastasia's brother Nikita was a prominent official in Ivan's court, and his son became Metropolitan Filaret, a powerful member of the Russian Orthodox Church. Filaret's son was Michael.

Throughout the 17th century the principle of male primogeniture determined the order of succession. Thus, Michael (r. 1613–45) was succeeded by his son ALEKSEI (r. 1645–76), who in turn was succeeded by his son, FEODOR III (r. 1676–82). Feodor's death without children complicated the issue of succession because Aleksei had married twice and in-laws from both families, the Miloslavskys and the Naryshkins, advanced their own candidates. A compromise was reached by which two younger sons of Aleksei—IVAN V, a Miloslavsky, and PETER I, a Naryshkin—reigned as co-czars with their sister SOPHIA as regent. In 1689, Sophia was overthrown as regent and in 1696, after Ivan's early death, Peter assumed the throne as sole czar.

Peter I, later known as Peter the Great, reigned as czar from 1682 to 1725. In 1722 he introduced the principle of the reigning ruler choosing the successor to the throne, a principle that remained in place until the reign of PAUL I. From Peter's time onward, the Romanov rulers assumed the title of emperor or empress. The successions that followed from 1725 to 1801 were not smooth as the Imperial Guards frequently staged palace revolts to install new monarchs. Beginning with the reign of Peter's

second wife, CATHERINE I (r. 1725–27), the throne passed to PETER II (r. 1727–30), a grandson of Peter the Great; to Anna (r. 1730–40); to IVAN VI (r. 1740–41), an ill-fated infant; to ELIZABETH (r. 1741–62), the daughter of Peter the Great from his second marriage. Elizabeth, in turn, chose her nephew, the German-born PETER III (r. 1762), to succeed her, but after nine months he was overthrown and assassinated, and succeeded by his German wife, who reigned as CATHERINE II (1762–96). She alone of the 18th-century monarchs was succeeded by a son, the future Paul I. The death of Peter II in 1730 marked the end of the male line of the Romanovs. From Peter III onward, with the exception of Catherine II, the rulers of Russia belonged to the German family of Holstein-Gottorp (related to the Romanovs through Peter the Great's daughter), even though they retained the Romanov name.

Paul I (r. 1796–1801) brought relative order to the process of succession by restoring the principle of male primogeniture, even though he himself was overthrown and killed in a palace revolt. His son ALEXANDER I (r. 1801–25) assumed the throne, but when he died childless his younger brother, NICHOLAS I (r. 1825–55) was crowned emperor. Nicholas I was in turn succeeded by his son ALEXANDER II (r. 1855–81). After Alexander's assassination by terrorists, his son ALEXANDER III (r. 1881–94) assumed the throne. The last Romanov ruler was Alexander's son, NICHOLAS II (r. 1894–1917).

Rostropovich, Mstislav Leopoldovich (1927–)
cellist and conductor

One of the greatest cellists of his generation, Rostropovich is also known for having the courage of his convictions. Born in Baku in Azerbaijan, he first studied under his father, and made his musical debut in 1942. He graduated from the Moscow Conservatory in 1946 and began teaching there the following year winning first prize at the International Cellists' Competi-

Mstislav Rostropovich (left) with Bolshoi Theater opera star Galina Vishnevskaia, 1965 *(Library of Congress)*

tion in Prague in 1950 launched his career as a solo performer. He was awarded the LENIN PRIZE in 1963, later gaining a reputation as a conductor and a pianist. Rostropovich's troubles with the Soviet authorities began in the early 1970s when he gave refuge to the dissident writer Aleksandr SOLZHENITSYN. While traveling abroad in 1974, he and his wife, Galina Vishnevskaia, decided not to return to the Soviet Union, and in 1975 Rostropovich accepted an appointment as conductor of the National Symphony Orchestra in Washington, D.C., becoming its music director in 1977. They were both stripped of their Soviet citizenship in 1978. Rostropovich raised the National Symphony Orchestra to new heights, becoming in the process a leading musical celebrity. He received an honorary knighthood from Queen Elizabeth of Great Britain in 1987. Rostropovich and Vishnevskaia returned to great acclaim to the Soviet Union in January 1990, and their citizenship was restored. At the time of the AUGUST COUP of 1991 against GORBACHEV's government, Rostropovich coura-geously joined Boris YELTSIN and his supporters in the besieged Russian White House, home of the leadership of the Russian Republic and center of the resistance against the plotters.

Rubinstein, Anton Grigorievich (1829–1894)

pianist and composer

A virtuoso performer, Rubinstein is considered one of the greatest pianists of the 19th century. He was born in the town of Vykhvatinets in Podolsk province. By the time he was six, the Rubinstein family had moved to Moscow, where his younger brother Nikolai, also a talented musician, was born. A precocious talent, Rubinstein first made his debut in Moscow at the age of nine and then spent the next three years traveling through Europe with his teacher, Aleksandr Villoing. In 1844 he moved to Berlin, where he and his brother studied music theory for two years under Dehn. He spent another two years in Vienna studying composition before returning to Russia in 1848 and settling in St. Petersburg. There he wrote his first operas, including *Dmitrii Donskoi, Fomka the Fool,* and *The Siberian Hunters,* which were performed in 1852–53. After another foreign sojourn from 1854 to 1858, Rubinstein founded the Russian Music Society in St. Petersburg in 1859, and three years later the St. Petersburg, or Imperial, Conservatory, which he first directed until 1867. From 1871 to 1872 he directed the concerts of the Vienna Philharmonic, after which he engaged in a highly successful tour of the United States until 1873. During the 1870s he wrote a number of other operas, including a biblical opera *The Tower of Babel* (1870), *The Demon* (1875), and *The Maccabees* (1875), and *The Merchant Kalashnikov* (1880). He served a second term as director of the St. Petersburg Conservatory from 1887 to 1891. His autobiography was published in 1889. Rubinstein died in November 1894 in the town of Peterhof (Petrodvorets), outside of St. Petersburg. A prolific composer with more than 20 operas, six symphonies, and five piano concertos to his credit, Rubinstein is remembered more for his brilliant technique than for his own compositions. His brother Nikolai Grigorievich Rubinstein (1835–81) also had a successful career, and is remembered as the founder of the Moscow Conservatory (1864), which he directed until his death.

Rublev, Andrei (ca. 1360–1430)
icon painter

Rublev, the founder of the "Moscow School" of medieval painting, is the most important Russian medieval painter. Details about his early life remain sketchy. Born sometime between 1360 and 1370, he became a monk in middle age, first possibly at the Trinity–St. Sergius Monastery and later with more certainty at the Andronikov Monastery in MOSCOW, where he is buried. First mention of Rublev appears in 1405 as one of the painters of the Cathedral of the Annunciation in the Moscow Kremlin, working with his teacher Prokhor Gorodetskii and the famous Byzantine painter FEOFAN GREK (Theophanes the "Greek"). This church is the first example of the multitiered high iconostasis—the screen separating the sanctuary from the congregation—that would become traditional for Russian churches. In 1408, with Daniil Chernyi (the "Black"), he was commissioned to redecorate the great Dormition Cathedral in Vladimir. The result of their work is perhaps the finest surviving medieval Russian fresco, a depiction of the Last Judgment. Scholars agree that his greatest masterpiece is the icon, the *Old Testament Trinity,* originally painted for the Trinity–St. Sergius Monastery. Drawing from the biblical story of Abraham and Sarah offering food to three angels in the guise of travelers, Rublev's icon captured the Orthodox idea that they represented the Trinity in a harmonious and peaceful composition. An important part of the cultural flowering that accompanied Moscow's emergence as a leader among Russian cities in the late 14th century, Rublev's work builds on the simple traditions of Novgorod art and the elegance of Byzantine art, which he probably learned from Feofan Grek. To this he adds his own distinctive trait: a masterful use of light, both divine and natural. Later generations, however, did not hold Rublev in as high regard as today. Many of his frescos and icons were touched up and painted over. Only in the 20th century did careful cleaning and restoration reveal the original excellence of his work. His most important icons, including one found in a monastery shed in 1918 as well as the *Old Testament Trinity,* are now at Moscow's Tretiakov Gallery. Among the many artists inspired by his work was the filmmaker Andrei TARKOVSKY, whose *Andrei Rublev,* remains a classic of Soviet-era film.

Russian American Company

A colonial trading company that was first chartered by PAUL I in 1799, the Russian American Company was given a monopoly on trading privileges in the area known as Russian America until 1867, when Russia sold ALASKA to the United States. In addition to its commercial concerns, during the six decades of its existence the Company provided Russia's North American possessions with a civil administration. While Russian interest in Alaska had developed since the first exploratory voyages of Vitus BERING in 1732, the Russian presence was mostly limited to private traders who engaged in seasonal hunting of fur-bearing animals on the Aleutian Islands. The Russian American Company eventually grew from the efforts of Grigorii Shelikhov, a merchant who in 1784 had begun the first permanent Russian outpost on Kodiak Island, although he did not live to see its formal establishment. Seeking to gain control of the North Pacific fur trade, Shelikhov petitioned CATHERINE II the Great for a monopoly, but he died before the government took any action. In December 1799, Catherine's successor, Paul I, granted the charter creating the Russian American Company, with trading privileges over a vast area that included Alaska, the Aleutian Islands, and the territory of the North American Pacific coast down to latitude 55° north. According to the charter the government was to receive one-third of the profits. Under Aleksandr BARANOV, governor of Russian America from 1800 to 1818,

Russian activity in the area grew considerably. A permanent settlement was established on Sitka Island, and the town of New Archangel, founded in 1804, served as the capital of Russian America. Baranov organized the fur trade to maximize profits, and a second charter was granted in 1821, extending the company's monopoly to latitude 51° north. But the long-term outlook for the company and Russia's presence in America in general was not positive. By 1840 the fur trade was yielding fewer profits, and the Russian government took over the company, appointing the famous explorer Ferdinand von WRANGEL governor (1840–49). Nevertheless, despite his efforts, the distances involved in supplying the colony from Russia, the difficulty in attracting settlers to Russian America, the harsh climate, and the growing interest of the British and Americans in the area all pointed to decreasing Russian involvement in North America. Two decades later, when the U.S. government agreed to purchase Alaska from Russia, the company was dissolved.

Russo-Finnish War See "WINTER WAR."

Russo-Japanese War (1904–1905)

A war fought in 1904–5 that resulted from the long-term clash of interests in East Asia between two expansionist powers, the Russo-Japanese War marked the emergence of Japan as an East Asian power and, having triggered the 1905 Revolution in Russia, also exposed Russia's domestic vulnerability and military weakness. Attracted by the possible political gains from a "short, victorious little war," Czar NICHOLAS II ignored the advice of more seasoned officials such as his foreign minister and the former minister of finance, Count Sergei WITTE, and instead followed policies that provoked a conflict. The war itself was triggered by Russia's refusal to honor a 1902 agreement with Japan and withdraw from MANCHURIA, as well as from its insistence in obtaining commercial concessions in Korea. On February 6, 1904, Japan attacked the Russian naval fleet

based at Port Arthur. The following month the Japanese landed near Inchon and by late April faced the Russian defenses at the Yalu River. Overmatching the Russians by four to one, the Japanese crossed the river on May 1, cut off the Russian forces at Port Arthur from the main army in Manchuria, and began a nine-month siege of Port Arthur. The Russians received reinforcements via the just completed TRANS-SIBERIAN RAILROAD and launched two new offensives in October 1904 and January 1905, both of which proved indecisive. On January 2, 1905, after a 10-day intensive assault, the Japanese captured Port Arthur. Russian and Japanese again confronted each other at Mukden (Shenyang) between February 19 and March 10, 1905. Although outnumbered by the Russians, the Japanese forced a Russian surrender, even as both sides suffered heavy casualties (90,000 Russians and 50,000 Japanese). The defeat at Mukden effectively ended the land phase of the war.

The naval stage of the war proceeded almost in slow motion, as the Russian Baltic Fleet of 45 ships sailed from St. Petersburg in October 1904, but reached the war theater only in early May 1905. Intercepted by the Japanese at the Straits of Tsushima between Korea and Japan, over half the fleet was sunk or captured, and the Russians suffered about 4,000 casualties while over 7,000 sailors were captured, including three admirals. The Battle of TSUSHIMA essentially marked the end of the war, just as the Japanese were reaching the financial limits of their ability to conduct it. U.S. President Theodore Roosevelt offered to mediate, and both sides conducted negotiations at Portsmouth, New Hampshire. On September 5, 1905, the Treaty of Portsmouth was signed. According to its terms, Russia surrendered its leases at Liaoyang and Port Arthur, evacuated Manchuria, and gave the southern half of Sakhalin Island to Japan (which the Soviet Union would recover after World War II). Korea was recognized as being in the Japanese sphere of influence. Three years later, Japan annexed Korea. President Roosevelt received the Nobel Peace Prize for his efforts, while Nicholas II was now left with the purely domestic phase of the

1905 Revolution, which he defused with the October Manifesto.

Russo-Persian Wars

Between 1722 and 1911, the Russian and Persian Empires fought four major wars, which contributed to the southward expansion of Russian territory into the Caucasus and the acquisition of territories along the northwest shores of the Caspian Sea. In 1722–23 PETER I the Great launched a war with Persia, weakened by its own Afghan rebellions, to preempt possible Turkish expansion in the Caspian Sea region. The Russians seized the cities of Derbent, Baku, and Resht, while the Turks, threatened by Russian penetration of the area, seized the Georgian capital of Tbilisi, then a part of Persia. Protesting the Treaty of St. Petersburg (September 1723), which gave Russia control of the Caspian coastline between Derbent and Resht, the Turks forced a follow-up Treaty of Constantinople (1724). At the further expense of Persia, Turkey received parts of western Persia, including Tabriz and Kermanshah, and the Russians received territories in northern Persia and recognition of their previous conquests. A second Russo-Persian war ensued in 1804–1813, following the Russian annexation of Georgia and the Karabakh region, nominally under the suzerainty of the Persian shah. After a decade of inconclusive fighting, the Russians defeated a superior Persian force at the Battle of Aslanduz in 1812. The Treaty of Gulistan, which followed in 1813, confirmed Russian possession of the territories it had annexed earlier. War occurred again between 1825 and 1828, when Persia rejected Russia's overzealous interpretation of the Treaty of Gulistan and attempted to retake Georgia in 1825. After the Battle of Ganja on September 26, 1826, Russian troops took Yerevan and Tabriz in 1827 and marched into the Persian capital of Tehran in 1828. The Treaty of Turkomanchi set the Aras River as the Russian-Persian border, granted Russia the sole right to station warships in the Caspian Sea, imposed an indemnity to be paid by Persia, and gave territorial and commercial rights to Russia. Anti-Rus-sian feeling was still running high in Tehran the following year when a crowd stormed the Russian embassy and killed its occupants, including the ambassador, the noted playwright Aleksandr GRIBOEDOV. The final confrontation took place, under much more uneven circumstances, in 1911, when Russia sent troops to protect its interests in the sphere of influence it had carved out in northern Persia as a result of the Anglo-Russian agreement of 1907. Russian forces took Tabriz in the north and marched onto Tehran, forcing the regency government of Ahmed Shah (1898–1930) to shut down the assembly and accept their demands.

Russo-Swedish Wars

Between 1590 and 1808, Russia and Sweden fought seven major wars, mostly over the issue of access to and control of the eastern shores of the Baltic Sea. From 1590 to 1595, under Czar FEODOR I, Russia attempted to take northern Estonia from Sweden. After initial advances helped the Russians besiege Narva in early 1590, the two sides drew up a one-year armistice that gave the Russians control of several towns in the region. When the armistice ended, fighting resumed and by 1595 Sweden had regained control of the Baltic coast of Estonia and conquered most of Livonia (parts of present-day Estonia and Latvia). During the TIME OF TROUBLES (1598–1613), Sweden had actively intervened in the internal dynastic struggles of Russia and occupied the city of NOVGOROD. In 1613, with the new ROMANOV DYNASTY in place, the Muscovite armies sought to recapture Novgorod. Led by King Gustavus II, the Swedish armies stopped the Muscovite attack on Novgorod, but when they moved against MOSCOW itself, they were stopped at the town of Pskov, which successfully resisted a six-month siege in 1614. At the Treaty of Stolbovo of January 1617, Moscow regained Novgorod from Sweden and relinquished its territories on the Gulf of Finland and all claims to Estonia and Livonia. In 1656, in the course of the first Northern War, Czar ALEKSEI made peace with Poland and attacked Livonia and Estonia, concentrating his offensive on the town of Riga, which was besieged in the summer of 1656. The Swedes successfully resisted, driving the Russians back. After another unsuccessful Russian offensive in 1658, both sides concluded a truce.

The relative balance of power in the eastern Baltic changed during the Great Northern War (1700–1721), which marked the emergence of Russia as a great European power. After a Swedish victory at the Battle of Narva (1700), Peter the Great rebuilt and modernized his forces and won a decisive victory over his antagonist, King Charles XII, at POLTAVA in 1609. An intermittent war continued for another decade until the Treaty of Nystadt (1721) recognized Russia's victories. Twenty years later, encouraged by the French, King Frederick I launched an ill-advised attack on Russia to recover the territories lost at Nystadt. The Russians won at the Battle of Wilmanstrand in Finland in September 1741. Soon after Empress ELIZABETH, recently installed on the Russian throne, sought peace with Sweden. Unable to find a common ground, the Russians again invaded Finland, winning a major victory at Helsingfors (Helsinki) in August 1742. One year later at the Treaty of Abo of August 1743, Russia retained the Finnish territories it had captured, and the childless King Frederick I agreed to the election of Elizabeth's candidate, the future Aldolphus Frederick, as his successor to the Swedish throne.

Russia and Sweden went to war again in June 1788 when King Gustavus III invaded Russian Finland without the approval of his Diet (parliament), hoping to take advantage of Russia's own war with the Ottoman Empire. After major defeats at Fredrickshamm (Hamina) and in several naval battles and faced with resistance from his own officers, who considered the war illegal, Gustavus III led Swedish troops toward St. Petersburg in the winter of 1790. At the naval Battle of Svenskund (July 1790), a third of Russia's fleet was captured or destroyed. One month later, after Denmark had joined Russia and attacked the city of Göteborg, the Swedes agreed to the Treaty of Wereloe with Russia, which restored the prewar balance of power. The final confrontation between the two nations took place in 1808–9 in the course of the Napoleonic Wars in the aftermath of the Treaty of TILSIT (1807), which brought French and Russian hostilities to a temporary halt. When King Gustavus IV refused the French and Russian demand that Sweden end its alliance with Britain, Czar ALEXANDER I launched an invasion of Swedish Finland in February 1808. Rapid Russian victories in Swedish Finland and an unstable situation inside Sweden that led to the overthrow of Gustavus IV allowed Russian troops to enter northern Sweden. After the new Swedish king, Charles XIII, sued for peace, both sides signed the Treaty of Fredrikshamm (September 1809), by which Sweden relinquished its part of Finland and the Aland Islands to Russia. Finland became a grand duchy under Russian control until its independence one century later during the 1917 Russian Revolution.

Russo-Turkish War of 1877–78

One of 10 wars fought between Russia and the Ottoman Empire since the late 17th century, the Russo-Turkish War of 1877–78 was the last major conflict between the two empires prior to World War I. It differed from prior RUSSO-TURK-ISH WARS in the degree to which parts of Russian public opinion affected the Russian government's policy and to which outside European powers intervened in shaping the peace settlement between the two combatants. The most immediate cause of the Russo-Turkish War of 1877–78 was the 1875 uprising against Ottoman rule in the Balkans, that was suppressed by Turkey. News of heightened Ottoman repression against Christian subjects in the Balkans reached Russia, where it was used by the powerful PAN-SLAV lobby that had emerged during the 1870s to pressure ALEXANDER II to declare war on Turkey. Although Alexander II and his foreign minister, Aleksandr GORCHAKOV, were less enthusiastic about war than the Russian pan-Slavs proponents, Russia did eventually declare war on Turkey in April 1877 and was soon joined by Romania. Like other Russo-Turkish wars the

1877–78 war was fought in two main theaters: the Balkans and the Caucasus. In the Caucasus, the Russians gained several victories, capturing the fortress of Kars and threatening to take the eastern stronghold of Erzerum. The war effort in the Balkans was far bloodier for both sides. On July 19, 1877, the Russian army won a crucial victory at Shipka Pass in the Balkans. After a five-month siege, the Russians captured the city of Plevna, and led by General Mikhail SKOBELEV, the army began to advance toward Istanbul (Constantinople), reaching the city's outskirts in January 1878, at which point the Ottoman Empire called for peace negotiations.

Perhaps more than the war itself, the peace was highly controversial. The initial Treaty of SAN STEFANO concluded by Russia and Turkey in March 1878 aroused the opposition of other European nations, most notably Great Britain and Austria-Hungary, who feared that Russia had decisively tilted the balance of power in the Balkans in its favor. Under great diplomatic pressure, Russia agreed to participate in the Congress of BERLIN, which met in June–July 1878 and substantially revised the terms of the Treaty of San Stefano. The major change from San Stefano to Berlin involved the boundaries of the new state of Bulgaria and the extent to which it would be influenced by Russia. The war led to the creation of fully independent states in Serbia, Bulgaria, and Romania but did not remove the issues that contributed to the overall instability of the Balkans, as revealed by the Balkan Wars of 1912–13 and the outbreak of World War I in 1914.

Russo-Turkish Wars

Between 1678 and 1878, Russia and Turkey (Ottoman Empire) fought 10 major wars over control of the Ukrainian steppes, control of the northern shores of the Black Sea, and—as Ottoman power declined in the 19th century—the fate of Turkey's European possessions in the Balkans. An earlier conflict took place in 1568–69 when the Ottoman Empire tried to extend its reach to the Caspian Sea from the Black Sea by means of a canal designed to link the Don River with the VOLGA RIVER. With a third of the canal completed, the Turks laid siege to ASTRAKHAN but abandoned the project when they failed to seize the city. In 1678 the two empires first went to war following a Turkish invasion of Ukraine. By the Treaty of Radzin of 1681, the Ottoman Empire surrendered to Russia all claims to Ukrainian territories east of the Dnieper River. In 1695–96 PETER I attacked the Turkish fortress of Azov, on the Sea of Azov, an arm of the Black Sea. The initial failure of the campaign compelled Peter to order the construction of Russia's first navy, which helped him conquer Azov in 1696, although at the cost of more than 30,000 soldiers. It was in the context of this war that Peter organized his GRAND EMBASSY to western Europe, with the goal of gaining allies in his war against the Ottomans while learning about Western technological advances. The war ended with a truce in 1700, which allowed Russia to retain Azov in exchange for dismantling its Black Sea fleet.

The third war took place in 1710–11, as part of the Great Northern War fought between Russia and Sweden, as a result of the Ottoman sultan's refusal to hand over the Swedish king Charles XII, who had sought asylum at the Ottoman court after the disaster at the Battle of POLTAVA. After invading Moldavia with 60,000 soldiers in 1711, Peter did not receive expected aid from his secret allies among the Moldavians and Wallachians and was forced to negotiate peace terms. At the Treaty of Pruth (1711), Russia surrendered Azov and agreed to grant free passage to Charles XII. Turkey and Russia fought again briefly in 1722–23 in the context of a broader war between Russia and Persia. The fifth and final war of this first stage took place in 1736–39 and found Russia in alliance with Austria over control of the Turkish-controlled parts of Ukraine, while the Austrians pursued their goals in the Balkans. Control of various Ukrainian cities changed from side to side, while the Russian army invaded Moldavia. The Turks were successful against Austria and at the Treaty of Belgrade (1739); they gained Belgrade, northern Serbia, and parts of Bosnia and Wallachia from the Austrians. One month later, in October 1739, Russia and Turkey signed the Treaty of Nissa, by which Russia retained Azov and gained part of the Black Sea between the Donets and Bug Rivers. In exchange, the Russians agreed not to have a fleet on the Black Sea and to destroy their fortifications at Azov.

A second phase in the wars between Russia and Ottoman Empire, in which Russia increasingly had the upper hand, began with the war of 1768–74. The Russians advanced into Moldavia and Wallachia (present-day Romania), Georgia, and Crimea and destroyed the Ottoman fleet at the Battle of Cecme in the Aegean Sea in July 1770. After negotiations in 1773 failed to produce a peace settlement, the Russian army, commanded by Aleksandr SUVOROV, defeated most of the Ottoman army at Shumla in June 1774. The Treaty of Kuchuk-Kainardji of July 1774 confirmed the independence of Crimea, placed Moldavia and Wallachia under Turkish suzerainty, and awarded a large part of the northern shoreline of the Black Sea to Russia. The treaty also gave Russia the right to intervene in Ottoman affairs in order to protect the interests of Orthodox Christians living under Turkish rule. War resumed in 1787–92 following Russia's annexation of Crimea in 1783 and the Ottoman Empire's attempt to incite Russia's Muslim Tatar population to revolt against Russian rule. The Treaty of Jassy of 1792 awarded all lands east of the Dniester River to Russia.

The eighth war between Russia and Turkey occurred in 1806–12 in the context of the Napoleonic Wars, as the French encouraged Sultan Selim III to declare war on Russia. Most of the fighting ceased after an armistice of August 1807 that followed a Russian naval victory at the Battle of Lemnos in June 1807. The war itself did not end until both sides signed the Treaty of Bucharest of 1812, which reaffirmed Ottoman control of Moldavia and Wallachia and awarded the province of Bessarabia to Russia. In 1828, the two empires again went to war when Russia supported the Greek nationalists fighting for independence from the Ottoman Empire. The Russians captured Varna in the Balkans after a

three-month siege and Kars in the Caucasus. Under General Hans Diebitsch-Zabalkansky, the Russian army won several more victories in the Balkans before marching half-depleted into the town of Adrianople (Edirne). Here, the Treaty of ADRIANOPLE was signed in September 1829, giving Russia control of the mouth of the Danube River and access to the Straits of Constantinople, while recognizing the independence of Greece.

The final three conflicts between Russia and Turkey were part of larger international conflicts (the CRIMEAN WAR and World War I) or drew in other nations in determining peace terms between the two empires (the RUSSO-TURKISH WAR OF 1877–78). The Crimean War of 1853–56, fought primarily on the Crimean Peninsula, began as other Russo-Turkish conflicts had in the past but soon found an international coalition of Great Britain, France, Sardinia, and, to a lesser extent, Austria on the side of the Ottoman Empire against Russia. Under the Treaty of Paris (1856) Russia lost its control of the mouth of the Danube and was deprived of the right to maintain a navy on the Black Sea, a clause that it later revoked unilaterally in 1870. In 1877 Russia declared war on Turkey in great part to protect the interests of Christian Serbs under Ottoman rule. It was joined by Romania, a state formed from the union of the former Ottoman principalities of Moldavia and Wallachia. By January 1878, Russian forces had captured the European Ottoman strongholds of Plevna, Plovdiv, and Adrianople and threatened to advance on Istanbul (Constantinople). The Ottomans initially acceded to the Treaty of SAN STEFANO, signed in March 1878 but judged by other European nations to be excessively tilted in favor of Russia. The treaty was subsequently revised at the Congress of BERLIN in June–July 1878. The final confrontation between Russia and the Ottoman Empire took place during World War I, which ultimately resulted in the collapse of the two empires. While Russia had aligned itself with the Triple Entente, the Ottoman Empire joined the Central Powers in the fall of 1914. Most of the fighting between the Russian and Ottoman Empires took place in the Caucasus and eastern Anatolia.

S

St. Basil's Cathedral

A striking church with unique multicolored domes that stands at the south end of RED SQUARE in Moscow, St. Basil's has become a popular symbol of Russia. The church was commissioned in 1552 by IVAN IV "the Terrible" to celebrate the conquest of Kazan. Construction began in 1555 and was completed in 1679. The church was originally known as the Cathedral of the Intercession of the Virgin but eventually was named after BASIL THE BLESSED, the 16th-century holy man who died in 1552 and was later canonized by the Russian Orthodox Church. Little is known about the original architects, traditionally identified as Posnik and Barma. Legend has it that they were blinded by Ivan so that the church could not be replicated, but there is little evidence to support this. In the late 16th century the church was used to store the czar's Great Treasury. Fires in 1626, 1668, and 1737 damaged the church and, during the brief French occupation of Moscow in 1812, soldiers plundered the church. A complete restoration was conducted from 1839 to 1845 to replicate its early 17th-century appearance. During the Soviet era, the church became a museum.

St. George's Day

There are two important St. George's Days in the Russian Orthodox Church calendar, the second of which is closely connected to the development of SERFDOM in early modern Russia. The first St. George's Day falls on April 23 and commemorates the death of St. George the "Dragon Slayer," in A.D. 303. A holiday that rivaled Easter in some parts of the Orthodox world, on this St. George's Day, peasants marked the end of the long winter by driving out their cattle into the spring pastures and celebrated the oncoming spring by slaughtering a lamb and other festivities. The second St. George's Day commemorates the building of a church dedicated to St. George in Kiev in 1051–54. It falls on November 26 around the time of the pre-Christian celebrations of the end of the agricultural year, after the crops had been harvested and threshed. How the custom began is still unclear, but during the mid-15th century, the Muscovite government began to restrict peasant movement, except for a brief period around the second St. George's Day. At first the measure applied only to indebted peasants, allowing them to move only after they had paid their debts. The 1497 law code (*sudebnik*), passed in the reign of IVAN III, permitted peasants to move only in a two-week period around St. George's Day. The 1550 law code further restricted the right to move. In 1592, the peasants' right to move was universally canceled, thus marking the virtual enserfment of the peasantry, now bound to the land that was written into law in 1649. Although the abolition of their right to move was supposedly "temporary," peasants were not allowed to move freely again until 1906, for even the EMANCIPATION ACT of 1861 had limited their freedom to move through the institution of the commune.

St. Petersburg

Founded in 1703 by PETER I the Great to serve as Russia's "window on Europe," St. Petersburg served as the capital of Russia from 1712 until 1918, when the BOLSHEVIKS chose Moscow as the capital of Soviet Russia. The inhospitable region on which St. Petersburg was founded was controlled by Sweden in the late 16th century. In the early stages of the Great Northern War, the Russian armies captured the delta of the Neva River, which Peter chose as the site of his future capital. The first construction took place on Zavachy Island, the site of the PETER AND PAUL FORTRESS, which was designed to defend the city from naval attack. Human losses to hunger and the cold were enormous in the first years of the city's construction, but in the remainder of the 18th century and first half of the 19th century, St. Petersburg gained the architectural gems that have earned its reputation as one of the most beautiful cities in the world. In the late 19th century, St. Petersburg became an industrial city and by 1900 counted more than 100 metal plants. Along with the industries and factories came a large working class that was receptive to the radical message of socialist agitators and revolutionaries. The BLOODY SUNDAY massacre of unarmed workers at the gates of the Winter Palace in January 1905 triggered the nationwide 1905 Revolution that almost brought the downfall of the government of NICHOLAS II. Twelve years later, the city, known as Petrograd since the outbreak of World War I in an effort to remove the German associations of its original name, was the site of the demonstrations of February 1917 that did lead this time to the collapse of the Russian monarchy. During the rest of 1917, events in Petrograd drove the engine of revolutionary change, culminating in the OCTOBER REVOLUTION that brought the Bolsheviks to power.

The Soviet period was not kind to St. Petersburg. In March 1918 the Bolsheviks, feeling the pressure of advancing German forces, transferred the capital to Moscow. As hunger took root in urban Russia, the city's prewar population of 2.2 million dropped to about 600,000 in 1920. In 1924 the city's name was changed again, this time to Leningrad, in honor of Vladimir LENIN. Following the assassination of the city's Communist Party leader, Sergei Kirov, Joseph STALIN's government launched a campaign of mass arrests

that particularly affected Leningrad's residents. Leningrad was only emerging from the terror of the Great Purge of 1936–38 when it found itself under siege by the Germans, who had invaded the Soviet Union in June 1941. From September 1941 to January 1944, a period of 900 days, the city resisted heroically, refusing to surrender despite continued bombings, starvation, and disease (see LENINGRAD, SIEGE OF). Through a tenuous link across the frozen waters of Lake Ladoga, the city was occasionally supplied, but by the time the siege was lifted, more than 1 million residents had lost their lives and almost 10,000 buildings had been destroyed. The postwar period witnessed the gradual reconstruction of Leningrad, and the city's population recovered, growing from 2.3 million in 1945 to 5 million in 1989. In the final years of Soviet rule, Leningrad emerged along with Moscow as one of the strongholds of reformist sentiment. A few months before the fall of the Communist government on October 1, 1991, amid strong opinions on both sides, the residents of Leningrad voted in a city-wide referendum to rename their city St. Petersburg. In 2003, in great part due to the patronage of President Vladimir PUTIN, a native of the city, the major landmarks and buildings of St. Petersburg were renovated and beautified at great cost, as the city celebrated its tercentenary with great pomp.

Sakharov, Andrei Dmitrievich
(1921–1989)
physicist and political activist

Considered the father of the Soviet Union's hydrogen bomb, from the 1960s until his death Andrei Sakharov became the country's most famous human rights advocate, for which he was awarded the 1975 Nobel Peace Prize. Sakharov was born in Moscow, the son of a high school teacher. He graduated with a degree in physics from Moscow State University in 1942 but was evacuated to Central Asia along with his department, where he worked in a weapons plant until the end of World War II. Back in

Moscow, he studied theoretical physics at the Lebedev Institute of Physics of the ACADEMY OF SCIENCES, and received a doctorate in 1947, at the relatively young age of 26. In 1948, his mentor Igor Tamm recruited him for the ultrasecret project of developing Soviet thermonuclear weapons, which had been started at Joseph STALIN's insistence. Sakharov's mathematical contributions to the creation of the Soviet hydrogen bomb that was tested in August 1953 were central to the success of the program. Honors and privileges followed, most notably membership in the USSR Academy of Sciences at the age of 32.

Although relatively apolitical in the 1950s, Sakharov's growing doubts about the dangers of nuclear testing opened the way to a more profound questioning of the Soviet system, especially after the more conservative BREZHNEV regime was installed in 1964. His 1968 essay "Reflections on Progress, Peaceful Coexistence and Intellectual Freedom" remains a milestone in the development of the democratic dissident movement in the Soviet Union. It also marked the beginning of his troubles with the Soviet authorities as his secret clearance and many of his privileges were revoked after its publication in the underground *samizdat* press, although he was able to continue other work at the Lebedev Institute. In 1970 he was one of the cofounders of the Committee for Human Rights, becoming over the next decade one of the leading Soviet human rights advocates together with his second wife, Yelena Bonner. His tireless work and his prominent position in the Soviet scientific world gained him a worldwide audience, which ultimately led to his 1975 Nobel Peace Prize. The Soviet media vilified him for his work and he was not permitted to travel to Oslo to receive the prize on the grounds that he possessed military secrets from his earlier work. In January 1980, after publicly criticizing the month-old Soviet invasion of AFGHANISTAN, Sakharov was arrested and placed on internal exile in Gorky (Nizhnii Novgorod), a city that was closed to foreigners because of the presence of defense-building

industries. Although harassed by the KGB (secret police) and in poor health, Sakharov remained in contact with the outside world.

By the time Sakharov was released from internal exile in December 1986, Mikhail GORBACHEV's government was embarking on its attempted reforms and seeking out the moral authority of intellectuals such as Sakharov. Sakharov was sympathetic to Gorbachev's reforms but pressed for even greater liberalization of the political process. In March 1989 he was elected to the new Congress of People's Deputies, where he played an active role in the small but vocal liberal bloc that chipped away at the monolithic power of the COMMUNIST PARTY. Derided by many for his outspokenness, Sakharov died suddenly in December 1989 from a heart attack. His death triggered a wave of mourning among Russians who suddenly felt deprived of a clear moral leadership as they worked to redefine their political destiny.

Saltykov-Shchedrin, Mikhail Evgrafovich (1826–1889)
writer

A masterful writer of satire, Saltykov-Shchedrin was a prominent representative of the realistic traditions that dominated Russian literature in the mid–19th century. He began his career in government service in St. Petersburg, but as a result of his involvement in the Petrashevsky Circle, he was banished in 1848 to the province of Viatka. He returned to the capital in 1855 and worked in the Ministry of the Interior, where he participated in drafting plans for the emancipation of the serfs. In 1858, he was appointed deputy governor of Ryazan province and subsequently of Tver. In 1868, however, his satirical writings led to his dismissal from government service and he was forbidden to have any kind of state appointment. Saltykov then devoted himself fully to literature, which he had explored in an early work, *Provincial Sketches* (1856–57). He was coeditor of the leading radical journal, *The Contemporary,* and edited its successor, *Notes of the*

Fatherland. His work, primarily satire, consisted of novels, sketches, and stories that sought to expose the inequities of contemporary conditions and the pettiness of officialdom. His best-known work, *The Golovlev Family* (1872–76), skewers a clan of country gentry. During Soviet times, the main public library in Leningrad (St. Petersburg), affectionately known as the *publichka,* was formally known as the Saltykov-Shchedrin library.

Samarkand

An ancient city along the Silk Road to China, Samarkand was a part of Russia and the Soviet Union from 1868 until 1991; it is now part of Uzbekistan. Early references to Samarkand date back to 329 B.C., when it was mentioned as Maracanda, capital of Sogdiana, a kingdom conquered by Alexander the Great. In the eighth century, Samarkand was captured by Arabs. From the ninth to the 11th centuries, control of the city changed hands frequently, and it was ruled by a succession of Persian and Turkic rulers. In 1220, it was destroyed by Genghis Khan. In 1369, Timur rebuilt it as his capital. It soon became the most important cultural center in Central Asia and a rich trading city on the Silk Road, the point where a network of other important routes converged. In 1500, Uzbeks conquered the city; by 1550 they had moved their capital from Samarkand to BUKHARA, initiating a period of decline for the city that lasted until the 18th century. Samarkand was annexed by Russia in 1868. Economic revival was facilitated by the construction of a railway (1896) that restored its earlier status as a trade nexus. Under Russian and Soviet rule, both Bukhara and Samarkand were overshadowed by Tashkent, which became the capital of the Uzbek Soviet Socialist Republic in the 1930s. Samarkand contains gems of 14th- and 15th-century architecture including Registan Square, a complex of 15th-century colleges, 13 mausoleums from Timur's time, including his own from 1405, the Shah-Zindah mosque, and the mosque of Bibi-Kanum (1404).

San Stefano, Treaty of (1878)

Signed between Russia and the Ottoman Empire on March 3, 1878, the Treaty of San Stefano brought an end to the RUSSO-TURKISH WAR OF 1877–78. Representing the Russian side at San Stefano (the present-day Turkish village of Yeilkoy) were Nikolai P. Ignatev (1832–1906), who until 1877 had been the Russian ambassador in Constantinople, and Aleksandr I. Nelidov. The main provisions of the treaty recognized the independence of Romania, Serbia, and Montenegro, all former provinces of the Ottoman Empire that had managed to gain varying degrees of autonomy in previous decades but not formal independence. Bulgaria was to become autonomous under the suzerainty of the Ottoman sultan, with the Russian army remaining in the country for two years. The treaty was seen by the other European powers as excessively favorable to Russia and was superseded four months later by the Treaty of Berlin (see BERLIN, CONGRESS OF), which among other provisions reduced the size of the new Bulgarian state and forced Russia to return some of the Turkish territories it had received at San Stefano.

Sarai

The capital city built by the Mongol leader BATU KHAN in 1254, Sarai was the original administrative center of the GOLDEN HORDE. In old Russian historical sources it appears as Sarai-Batu, Old Sarai, and Great Sarai. It was built on the eastern banks of the Volga River. In 1260, it was supplanted as the capital by Sarai-Berke, also known as New Sarai, built by Berke Khan. The princes of Rus paid their tribute to the Mongol court at Sarai and were occasionally summoned to confirm their subservience to their Mongol overlords. The famous world traveler Ibn Battuta visited the city at its peak in 1333 and wrote glowingly of its beautiful bazaars and broad streets, teeming with Mongols, Kipchaks, Russians, Byzantines, and Cherkessians. After 1361, however, Sarai-Berke became a pawn in the internal struggles of the Golden Horde, frequently seized by pretenders to the throne of Khan. Tamerlane's armies reached the city in 1395 and destroyed it. The first substantial archaeological excavations were carried out in 1843–51 by A. V. Tereschchenko, followed by two major excavations in Soviet times (1922 and 1959–67). They confirmed Ibn Battuta's account, revealing a city with substantial palaces, mosques, and other prominent buildings. Today the village of Selitrennoe stands on the site of Old Sarai, while the village of Tsarev in the Volgograd Oblast stands on the site of New Sarai.

Scriabin, Aleksandr Nikolaevich (1872–1915)

composer

A relative of the revolutionary and Soviet official known as MOLOTOV, Scriabin was one of the few Russian composers who tried to incorporate the mystical themes that dominated Russian literature in the early 20th century. Scriabin was born in Moscow and entered the Moscow Conservatory in 1888. In 1897 he married Vera Isakovich, a fellow pianist. The following year he began teaching at the Moscow Conservatory, where he remained until 1903, after which he dedicated himself to composing and piano tours. Scriabin began his career as a composer-pianist, highly influenced by Chopin and Liszt, but in the early 1900s he developed an idiosyncratic, increasingly complex style that sought to incorporate his growing interest in mystical philosophy. His First Symphony was conceived to glorify art as religion. His 1907 orchestral piece *Poem of Ecstasy* was full of complex harmonies and unpredictable developments. For his orchestral tone poem, *Prometheus, The Poem of Fire* (1910) he tried to link tone and color by designing a color keyboard that would project on a screen the colors that he believed corresponded to musical tones. The keyboard was not built, so for the performance of *Prometheus* Scriabin had to resort to projecting color slides on a screen. Scriabin's later work became more eccentric as he abandoned traditional harmony in search of a uni-

versal mystical chord. With him as a messiah, he envisioned a "liturgical act" designed to reach a supreme final ecstasy through poetry, dance, colors, music, and even scents that would bring spiritual regeneration to Russia and put humanity on a higher spiritual plane. Scriabin succeeded in sketching only preparatory exercises for the final "Mystery" before his death in Moscow in April 1915. In addition to his mystical beliefs, he is known for ten piano sonatas composed between 1892 and 1913, three symphonies, a piano concerto, and 24 preludes for piano, many of which are still widely played.

Semenov, Grigorii Mikhailovich (1890–1946)

Cossack commander

One of three prominent Cossack warlords who carried the traditional title of ataman, Semenov ruled large stretches of the Transbaikal area during the Russian civil war. Semenov was born in Siberia, near the town of Chita in the area east of Lake Baikal. He graduated from the Orenburg Military School in 1911 and fought during World War I. In July 1917, he was appointed commissar of the Provisional Government in Siberia to form a unit that would be dispatched to the western front of World War I. Instead he formed a Special Manchurian Detachment that served as the base for his private army in the following years. From October to December 1917, he organized a revolt against the Bolshevik government. In August 1918 in alliance with the CZECH LEGION, Semenov set up a military government in Siberia known as the Provisional Siberian Government. Conflicts arose with Admiral KOLCHAK, appointed supreme ruler of Siberia in November 1918, who at first did not recognize Semenov's authority but later appointed him commander of Chita military district. Tensions and rivalries between the two continued and Semenov's insistence on protecting his autonomy by disrupting supplies intended for Kolchak in western Siberia caused significant harm to the overall White effort. With Japanese support, Semenov proclaimed himself ataman of the Transbaikal Cossack army in 1919. After Kolchak's defeat, Semenov took over power in Siberia and the Far East, but was defeated by the Red Army in 1920. He fled Russia in September 1921 and spent the next two decades in Korea, Japan, and northern China. In September 1945 he was abducted by Soviet spies in Manchuria, tried, and hanged.

Semenov, Nikolai Nikolaevich
(1896–1986)
physical chemist and physicist
A distinguished scientist who contributed to the field of chemical kinetics, Semenov was the first Soviet citizen to be awarded a Nobel Prize. Semenov was born in the Volga River town of Saratov and graduated from St. Petersburg University in 1917 with degrees in physics and mathematics. After a brief stay in the Siberian town of Tomsk, Semenov returned to St. Petersburg, soon to be known as Leningrad, in 1920. From 1920 until 1928 he worked at the Leningrad Physico-Technical Institute. In 1931, the same year in which Semenov was elected a full member of the USSR ACADEMY OF SCIENCES, the Physico-Technical Institute was converted into the Institute of Chemical Physics of the USSR Academy of Sciences. Semenov was appointed its first director, a position he held until his death in 1986. Semenov's worldwide reputation rests on his research in chemical kinetics, particularly in the field that studies chemical reactions. He postulated that in a special type of reaction known as a branched chemical reaction the highly reactive molecules known as free radicals could create explosions that not only perpetuated themselves but also occurred at ever faster intervals. For his research he was awarded the 1956 Nobel Prize in chemistry, in conjunction with the British chemist Cyril Norman Hinshelwood, whose work paralleled that of Semenov. The Soviet government in turn decorated Semenov with the Order of Lenin seven times and the Order of the Red Banner of Labor, while the British Royal Society made him one of its foreign members in 1958. Semenov's most influential works, *Chemical Kinetics and Chain Reactions* (1934) and *Some Problems of Chemical Kinetics and Reactivity* (1954), were translated into English only a few years after their publication in the Soviet Union.

Semenov Tian-Shansky, Petr Petrovich
(1827–1914)
geographer and statistician
A leading member in the Russian Geographical Society and its virtual director from 1873, Semenov Tian-Shanskii was one of the driving forces behind the numerous scientific expeditions to Central Asia carried out by prominent scholars like Przhevalsky, Potanin, KROPOTKIN, and Komarov. He was educated at the universities of St. Petersburg and Berlin, and first made his reputation through extensive travels in Turkestan. There he studied the Tien Shan mountain range (hence the "Tian-Shansky" usually appended to his name), collected valuable mineralogical, botanical, and anthropological material, and proved that its origins were not volcanic. As a leading Russian scholar of his day, Semenov Tian-Shansky played an active role in the commissions that prepared the emancipation of the serfs in 1861 and the military reforms of 1874. As director of the Central Statistical Committee (1864–75), he organized the first Russian statistical congress in 1870, which laid the foundations for the influential *ZEMSTVO* movement. As chairman of the committee's successor, the Statistical Council (1875–97), he supervised Russia's first modern census in 1897. He became an honorary member of the ACADEMY OF SCIENCES in 1873 and a member of the Council of State in 1897. Among his numerous publications, two that stand out are the *Geographical and Statistical Dictionary of the Russian Empire*, published in five volumes (1863–85), and *Russia, Full Geographical Description of Our Fatherland*, which he edited with V. I. Lamansky and published in 19 volumes (1899–1914). Less known among his many scholarly activities was his love for Flemish and Dutch art, which he col-

lected extensively and which was the subject of his *Essays in the History of Netherlands Painting,* published in two volumes (1885–90). Before his death he gave his collection to the HERMITAGE Museum in St. Petersburg.

serfdom

A system that deprived Russian peasants of their freedom, serfdom developed gradually over the centuries and continued to provide the foundation for Russian rural society until its abolition in 1861. While peasant financial dependence on a landlord dates back to the period of KIEVAN RUS, the development of serfdom proper coincides with the expansion of the Muscovite state. As peasant indebtedness grew, and as the Muscovite state granted more land to the service gentry on whom it relied for military and administrative duties, peasants were increasingly bound to their landlords in a network of labor and financial duties. Traditionally, peasants had been allowed to leave their estates, provided they paid their debts around ST. GEORGE'S DAY in late autumn. By the late 16th century, at a time of famine and social turmoil, this freedom of movement became increasingly restricted, as the government proclaimed "forbidden years," when peasants could not leave their estates. The increasing frequency of forbidden years and the extension of the period when fugitive serfs could be returned to their masters were important markers in the progression toward complete serfdom. The Ulozhenie (Law Code) of 1649 brought these developments to a peak and is considered the document that fully established serfdom in Muscovite Russia. The code eliminated any statute of limitations on fugitive serfs and provided harsh penalties for those harboring them. As serfdom became a permanent feature of Russian social life, certain regional characteristics developed. Serfdom did not make any inroads in Siberia, colonized by Russians since the early 17th century, where the absence of a service gentry and the sheer vastness of the land made it unnecessary and almost impossible to enforce. During the

18th century, conditions for serfs worsened while the gentry strengthened their position, especially after the death of PETER I in 1725. Through successive laws and decrees, serfs were deprived of the right to volunteer for military service, purchase property, and seek temporary employment without their owner's permission. The prohibition against transferring serfs without the land they worked was gradually blurred as the century wore on, and serf owners were given the right to exile their delinquent serfs to Siberia. Peasant discontent over serfdom had been a main cause of rural rebellions as early as the TIME OF TROUBLES and the Stenka RAZIN revolt of 1670–71. In the late 18th century it again served as one of the main causes behind the far more serious and extensive PUGACHEV REBELLION that shook the foundations of the Russian state in 1773–74. The Pugachev Rebellion convinced the more progressive members of Russia's ruling circles that serfdom needed to be reformed or even abolished in the future. In the early 19th century, during the reigns of ALEXANDER I and NICHOLAS I, various projects were discussed in government circles, and some minor changes were implemented, such as Alexander's emancipation of serfs in the Baltic provinces, albeit without land. Both monarchs, although personally opposed to serfdom, shied away from acting forcefully from fear of the instability that might accompany far-reaching reforms or the outright abolition of serfdom. Only with the disastrous defeat in the CRIMEAN WAR did the government of ALEXANDER II obtain the necessary momentum and political desire to propose the emancipation of the serfs. After several years of discussion, the czar issued the EMANCIPATION ACT of 1861, freeing the serfs with some land, although not as much as the peasants had hoped for.

Serge, Victor (1890–1947)
revolutionary and writer

Born Viktor Kibalchich to a family of Russian exiles living in Belgium, Serge was the son of an Imperial Guards officer implicated in a plot to assassinate ALEXANDER II. In his childhood he soaked up revolutionary ideals and stories while traveling with his parents between Britain, France, and Switzerland. At the age of 18 he moved to Paris, hoping to find work as a draftsman, but instead he joined up with local anarchists he had met through the Russian émigré community. Turning to translations of Russian literature for his livelihood, he began to publish short pieces in the French anarchist press. As editor of *L'Anarchie* in 1910, he received a five-year prison sentence for his complicity in the terrorist activities of the Bonnot Gang. Following his release in 1917, he made his way to Barcelona, where he mingled with Syndicalists and followed the news from Russia. Disenchanted with Spanish revolutionaries and eager to see the land of his parents, he volunteered for military service in Russia in August 1917. Fourteen months later, after a period of internment in a French camp, he arrived in revolutionary Petrograd. After contacting GORKY and ZINOVIEV, he joined the Bolshevik Party and soon became a member of the Executive Committee of the newly founded Communist International (Comintern), where he put his knowledge of foreign languages to use. From the start Serge's relationship with the Soviet government and COMMUNIST PARTY was troubled. He was uneasy about the Bolshevik exercise of power and the cruelty practiced in the name of the revolution. After 1926, he became aligned with the Left Opposition and was expelled from the party in 1928. Under the pressure of increasing persecution, Serge's wife lost her sanity and was interned in a Red Army asylum. In 1933 Serge and his son were exiled to Orenburg. After an intense international campaign he was released in 1936 and allowed to leave the country with his wife and son. Serge settled in France, but in 1941 fled again with his son to escape the Germans, leaving his wife behind in a psychiatric asylum, where she died a few years later. After the Dominican Republic and Cuba turned them away, he settled in Mexico, where he remained until his death. His many writings about revolutionary Russia and the early Soviet period—novels, memoirs, and histories—are an invaluable source for the period, faithful to his socialist and libertarian views. Among them are *Year One of the Revolution, Memoirs of a Revolutionary,* and *The Case of Comrade Tulayev,* a novel about the Great Purge.

Sergei, Patriarch of Moscow (1867–1944)

church leader

Born Ivan Nikolaevich Starogodsky in the town of Arzamas, Patriarch Sergei led the Russian Orthodox Church during the most difficult years of Soviet antireligious persecution. A highly regarded church scholar, Sergei graduated from the Petersburg Theological Academy in 1890, later serving as its inspector (1899–1901). From 1905 to 1917, he served as bishop of Finland and Vyborg. In 1917 he was appointed bishop, then metropolitan of Vladimir, near Moscow. In 1925 he served as the deputy locum tenens of Patriarch Tikhon, but upon Tikhon's death the following year he was arrested for his role in attempting a secret election of a new patriarch, and imprisoned for six months. In 1927 he published a controversial declaration of loyalty to the Soviet regime, which led to internal (Catacomb Church) and external (Church in exile) splits within the church. To some it was a practical compromise, necessary for survival, to others a surrender to the atheism of the Soviet regime. After being named metropolitan of Moscow and Kolomna in 1934, Sergei was recognized as patriarch locum tenens by the church in 1937. He remained the head of the church during the worst years of persecution in the late 1930s, when only a handful of bishops were not sent to prisons or camps. During World War II he stressed the church's patriotic role, rallying to the side of the Soviet government. In exchange the government allowed the restoration of the PATRIARCHATE in September 1943, after almost two decades, with Sergei as patriarch. One year later, he died in Moscow and was succeeded by Aleksi as patriarch.

Sergius of Radonezh, Saint (1314–1392)
monk and mystic

A great mystic and ascetic who is also considered the patron saint of Russia, St. Sergius played a leading role in the monastic revival that unfolded in the northeastern parts of Russia during the 1330s at a time when the country was still under Mongol rule. Sergius was born Varfolomei Kirillovich into a noble family in the town of Rostov to the east of Moscow in 1314, according to some sources, or in 1322, according to others. The family moved to the town of Radonezh around 1328, but following his parents' deaths in 1334, Varfolomei moved into the forest with his brother, Stefan, to begin a life of seclusion and prayer away from the temptations and noise of Moscow. Stefan soon left to join a monastery, but Varfolomei remained behind, and after taking monastic vows he adopted the name Sergei. As word of Sergei's labors spread, other monks joined him in the forest. This group formed the core of the legendary Trinity Monastery (Trinity/Troitse–St. Sergius Lavra), established in 1337. Preaching patience, tolerance, and repentance, Sergius attracted and welcomed many followers who came to seek his guidance. These included quarreling Russian princes to whom Sergius preached a message of cooperation and nonviolence. In time the Trinity Monastery became one of the great centers of Russian Orthodox spirituality, a center of Christian civilization, and a place of pilgrimage. The monastery also attracted settlers who colonized and developed the land around it, thus becoming a model for future Russian monasteries in remote lands.

Sergius is also associated with the Battle of KULIKOVO in 1380, where the armies led by Prince DMITRII DONSKOI won the first Russian victory over the Tatar-Mongol armies since the MONGOL CONQUEST of 1240. Legend has it that Dmitrii consulted with Sergius for advice on whether to engage the Mongols in battle or pursue negotiations. Torn between his belief in nonviolence as a devout Christian and his national feelings as a Russian under Mongol domination, Sergius finally advised Dmitrii to do battle, supported his armies with money and the presence of two monks, and also predicted a Russian victory. Known for his humility, Sergius rejected most honors offered to him, including an appointment as metropolitan of Moscow, at the time the highest position in the Russian Orthodox Church. Only after great insistence did he accept to be ordained as priest and named as abbot of the monastery he had founded. The Russian Orthodox Church now commemorates his life on October 8, the date of his death according to the new calendar. His relics are still maintained in the Trinity's monastery main cathedral.

Sevastopol (Sebastopol)

A town on the southwestern point of the Crimean Peninsula, in present-day Ukraine. Although not officially founded until 1783, when the Crimea became a part of the Russian Empire, the site of modern Sevastopol had seen important settlements going back to the late fifth century B.C.E. Over the centuries the Greek colony of Chersonesus gave way to Roman, Byzantine, Genoese, and Tatar settlements. With the establishment of Russian rule during the reign of CATHERINE II the Great, the site became a strongly fortified naval base and was named Sevastopol. Its strategic location on the Crimean Peninsula commanding access to the northern shores of the Black Sea have twice made Sevastopol the site of extended sieges that have given the city a heroic reputation. During the CRIMEAN WAR (1853–56), Sevastopol held out for 349 days from September 1854 to September 1855 to combined British and French forces assisted by Turks and Sardinians. Lev TOLSTOY, who took part in the defense of the city, celebrated the heroism of the common Russian soldier in his *Sebastopol Sketches* (1855). The second long siege of the city came in 1941–42, when Sevastopol endured a nine-month siege at the hands of German and Romanian troops who captured the city and held it until 1944. For its resistance, Sevastopol later received the official Soviet designation of "hero city." As a major naval base, Sevastopol was also the site of one of the several naval mutinies that took place during the 1905 Revolution.

With the collapse of the Soviet Union in 1991, the status of Sevastopol, by 1996 a city of about 370,000 inhabitants, became a subject of dispute between the successor states of Ukraine and Russia. In 1954, Nikita KHRUSHCHEV had arbitrarily assigned Sevastopol and the entire Crimean Peninsula to the Ukrainian S.S.R. In 1991, Sevastopol's status had the added complexity of being the headquarters of the Soviet Black Sea Fleet. Both Russia and Ukraine laid claim to the fleet. In mid-1995 the two countries reached an agreement dividing the fleet, but questions persisted over the status of Sevastopol, with some Russian politicians arguing that it should be a part of Russia. A second accord was reached in 1997. Eighty percent of the fleet was given to Russia while Russia dropped its claims to Sevastopol, agreeing instead to lease the port.

Shamil, Imam (1796?–1871)
resistance fighter

Known as the Lion of Dagestan, Shamil led the resistance of north Caucasian Muslims to Russian conquest and colonization for more than 25 years. He built an Islamic ministate, defied death and capture countless times, and fought one of the longest guerrilla campaigns in history. Born in 1796 or 1797, Shamil was a sickly boy until age six, but then he grew to be a tall, athletic man distinguished by his long, black beard. After the first two imams died in 1832 and 1834, Shamil was chosen third imam of Dagestan, a title that combined religious and political leadership. From 1834 to 1859, he led a successful guerrilla war against the Russians, inflicting humiliating defeats on czarist troops and preventing the establishment of firm Russian control in the Caucasus. During these years he created a virtual state in the lands he controlled that was characterized by a harsh legal and financial order in the name of fighting the Russians. At the peak of his power, he had a standing army of about 14,000 soldiers and could

count on a reserve army of almost 40,000 men. In the 1850s, Russian troops began making inroads into his strongholds through a policy of forest clearing and an "Advanced Chechen Line" of fortresses. After Russian troops captured his stronghold of Vedeno in spring 1859, Shamil retreated for one final stand but surrendered a few months later in August 1859 at Gunib in Dagestan. Captured, he was taken to St. Petersburg, where ALEXANDER II complimented him on his fight and gave him an estate in Kaluga, in central Russia. On a pilgrimage to Mecca, he died in Medina, where he is buried. At the time of his surrender Shamil was considered a great resistance fighter all over Europe, celebrated for his courage.

Shchusev, Aleksei Viktorovich (1873–1949)
architect

An established architect from the prerevolutionary period with an affinity for historical styles, Shchusev survived the political and cultural upheavals of the first revolutionary decades. Born in Kishinev (now Moldava), he studied at the St. Petersburg Academy of Arts and traveled on scholarship around Russia and abroad (1894–98). Among early works are churches based on the Novgorod and Pskov styles of medieval architecture; more ambitious was the Kazan Railway Station in Moscow (1913–26), done in 17th-century style. His prestige carried over into the revolutionary period. After LENIN'S death, he was chosen to design the LENIN MAUSOLEUM, first a provisional wooden structure (1924), then the permanent one (1929–30) that exists to this day on RED SQUARE. Although Shchusev displayed an uncanny ability to reorient his work to the prevailing styles of the day, the socialist realism of the 1930s with its emphasis on historical, neoclassical forms was better suited to his own preferences than the experimental, modern styles of the 1920s. In addition to large works in Moscow, such as the theater on Mayakovsky Square and the Hotel Moskva near

Red Square—a collaborative design—Shchusev built important projects in Georgia and Uzbekistan. With the Marx-Engels-Lenin Institute (1933–38) in Tbilisi, which combined classical and Georgian styles and won him the 1941 Stalin Prize, and the Opera (1933–40) and Alisher Navoi Theater (1933–47) in Tashkent, Shchusev attempted a "social regionalism" that drew from regional traditions. One of his last projects was the Komsomolskaia Metro station in Moscow (1945–52), whose richly ornate interior with chandeliers and mosaics synthesizes Stalinist and rococo styles. Shchusev received academic honors from both regimes: academician of the St. Petersburg Academy of Arts (1910), member of the USSR Academy of Architecture (1939), and full member of the USSR ACADEMY OF SCIENCES (1943).

Shekhtel, Feodor Osipovich
(1859–1926)

architect

One of the most important architects of the prerevolutionary era, Shekhtel was born in the provincial town of Saratov; his parents were Volga German immigrants. He arrived in Moscow in the mid-1870s and first worked as a book designer, illustrator, and theater decorator. Starting as an independent architect in the 1880s, he first made his mark with designs for villas (*osobniaki*) for wealthy business patrons, the first of these being the Morozov house (1893). Although his work ranged widely, including designs for office buildings, banks, sanatoriums, factories, and cinemas, Shekhtel's most productive phase came in association with the wealthy Riabushinsky family. They commissioned some of the works for which he is best known: the stunning Riabushinsky mansion (1900–1902), later inhabited by Maksim GORKY before his death, the Riabushinsky Bank (1903), and the printing house of the Riabushinsky-owned newspaper *Utro Rossii* (1907). The patronage of the Riabushinsky family was also important in securing other commissions, such as the Yaroslavl Railway Station (1902) and the building of the Moscow Merchants Society (1909). Shekhtel worked successfully in various styles, developing a distinctive blend of old Russian architecture and Art Nouveau. He was among the first in Moscow to explore the possibilities of iron, glass, and reinforced-concrete technology. Shekhtel also made important contributions to the professional development of Russian architecture. In 1896 he joined the faculty of the Stroganov Institute, teaching theory of composition. After the OCTOBER REVOLUTION of 1917, he taught at the prestigious and influential Vkhutemas (Higher State Artistic-Technical Studios) (1919–22). He was president of the Association of Moscow Architects (1908–22) and sat on several committees, the last one the program committee and jury of the competition for the Palace of Labor (1922–23).

Shevardnadze, Eduard Amvrosievich
(1928–   )

politician

A resilient and savvy Georgian politician, Shevardnadze has built three distinct and important careers in Soviet and Georgian politics. He was born in Mamati, Georgia, joined the COMMUNIST PARTY in 1948, and graduated from the Party School of the Georgian Central Committee in 1951 and the Kutaisi Pedagogical Institute in 1959. Shevardnadze began his first career, rising through the Georgian party apparatus in predictable fashion: first secretary of the Georgian KOMSOMOL (1957), first deputy minister of internal affairs (1964), minister of internal affairs (1965). Charged with combating crime and corruption, he built a formidable dossier against the Georgian first party secretary, V. P. Mzhvanadze, who ruled the republic as a private business. After seeing the information, Leonid BREZHNEV named Shevardnadze first party secretary of Georgia with the special task of cleaning up Mzhavanadze's affairs and purging his appointees. As a reward, Shevardnadze was elected to the Soviet Communist Party's Central Committee in 1976 and a candidate member of the party's Politburo in

1978. A long-standing professional acquaintance with Mikhail GORBACHEV paid off in March 1985, when he was made a full member of the Politburo. His second career began in July 1985, when he succeeded Andrei GROMYKO as Soviet foreign minister. Despite the absence of diplomatic training or experience and lack of foreign languages, Shevardnadze became a superb ambassador of Gorbachev's "new thinking" in foreign policy. Warning of the possibility of a right-wing coup, he resigned his post in December 1990 and left the party in June 1991. Loyal to Gorbachev during the AUGUST COUP of 1991, he was reappointed Foreign Minister in November 1991 as part of Gorbachev's desperate attempt to forestall the dissolution of the Soviet Union, which nevertheless came one month later. With post-Soviet Georgia in danger of collapse from civil war and chaotic rule, Shevardnadze began his third career in 1992 as President of independent Georgia. Relying on controversial Russian assistance his forces put down the threat of Abkhazian separatism and routed the Gamsakhurdia forces. Shevardnadze survived various assassination attempts on the way to a second presidential term in 1997. In December 2003, however, he resigned after a wave of public protests.

Shevchenko, Taras Grigorievich
(1814–1861)
(Hryhorovych)

poet

The most renowned Ukrainian poet, Shevchenko was also an artist and an ardent supporter of Ukrainian nationalism. Though he was born a serf, his master recognized his talents and sent him to St. Petersburg to study art. There he met a number of influential artists and writers such as the poet Vasili Zhukovsky, tutor to the future ALEXANDER II, and the artists Karl Briullov and Alexei Venetsianov. A member of the secret Pan-Slavic Society, the Brotherhood of Saints Cyril and Methodius, in 1847 he was arrested and banished to Orenburg for 10 years, during which time he was prohibited from painting or

writing. Released from exile, he returned to St. Petersburg, where his friends raised a fund to buy his freedom in 1858. Shevchenko, writing in a popular romantic style, was a seminal influence in the development of Ukrainian literature and the Ukrainian national movement. His main poems, many of which celebrate the Ukrainian peasantry, are found in the collection *Kobzar* (1840). Shevchenko died on February 26, 1861, only a week after the decree on the emancipation of the serfs was issued.

Shmidt, Otto Iulevich
(1891–1956)

scientist and polar explorer

A ubiquitous figure in the fields of administration, education, and polar exploration in the 1920s and 1930s, Shmidt was born in Mogilev province and graduated from Kiev University in 1913. He joined the Bolshevik Party soon after the OCTOBER REVOLUTION of 1917, playing important administrative roles in food supply and education during the Russian civil war. He also taught at the Moscow Forestry Institute (1920–23), the Second Moscow University (1923–26), and Moscow State University from 1926 until his death. As executive editor of the *Great Soviet Encyclopedia* from 1924 to 1941 and chief editor of the journal *Priroda* (Nature), he was active in the field of popular education. In 1930 he became director of the Arctic Institute in Leningrad (St. Petersburg), and from 1932 to 1938, headed the Main Administration of the Northern Sea Route (Glavsevmorput), the de facto ruler of the Soviet Union's northern Asian territories above the 62nd parallel. Between 1929 and 1937 Shmidt participated in four important polar expeditions. The first, on the icebreaker *Sedov* (1929), established a scientific station on Franz Josef Land. The second, on the *Sibiriakov* (1932), was the first to navigate the whole Northern Sea Route in one season. The third was the ill-fated *Cheliuskin* expedition (1933–34), which met with disaster when the ship was crushed on the ice. The difficult rescue of the stranded crew captivated Soviet audiences and the title of hero of the Soviet Union was awarded for the first time to the pilot rescuers. The final expedition in 1937 established the first floating station at the North Pole. For these achievements, Shmidt also received the Hero of the Soviet Union award in 1937. Shmidt was also a respected mathematician who published important work on the abstract theory of groups and algebra. Dismissed in the course of the Great Purge of the 1930s, he continued academic work as a professor of mathematics at Moscow State University. He died in Moscow on September 7, 1956.

Sholokhov, Mikhail Aleksandrovich (1905–1984)
writer

A prominent writer from the Soviet years who was awarded the Nobel Prize in literature in 1965, Sholokhov was born in a small Cossack village in Rostov oblast in the region of the Don River. He was later educated in Moscow, where he worked as a teacher, clerk, and journalist. After the OCTOBER REVOLUTION of 1917, he embarked on several food procurement expeditions to confiscate grain from peasants for the hungry cities of the north. Sholokhov first emerged as a writer during the mid-1920s with *Donskie rasskazy* (*Tales of the Don*, 1925). Although not a Cossack himself, Sholokhov drew deeply from Cossack themes in this and the works that followed. His four-volume masterpiece *Quiet Flows the Don* was published between 1928 and 1940. It is often considered a Soviet version of TOLSTOY's *War and Peace* for its rich historical canvas and its attempts to portray the complex impact of the revolution and civil war on the lives of COSSACKS and peasants. Far more nuanced than the many proletarian novels that sought to conform to the strictures of socialist realism, *Quiet Flows the Don* quickly became a classic of Soviet literature, bringing acclaim and official privileges to Sholokhov. His next novel, *Virgin Soil Upturned,* ran into some problems with the censors; the first volume was published in

1932, but the second did not appear until 1960. Sholokhov joined the COMMUNIST PARTY in 1932 and received numerous Soviet awards, including the LENIN and Stalin PRIZES. In the post-Stalin era after 1953, he first spoke out in favor of the literary thaw, criticizing Stalinist literary bureaucrats, but he gradually came to articulate more conservative views. He condemned Boris PASTERNAK for initially accepting the 1958 Nobel Prize in Literature (although Sholokhov would not renounce his own Nobel Prize seven years later), and called for harsher sentences against Andrei SINYAVSKY and Yuli Daniel after their landmark 1966 trial for "slander" and "defamation" of the Soviet state. Questions about the true authorship of the early parts of *Quiet Flows the Don,* although never fully substantiated, arose periodically during his life.

Shostakovich, Dmitrii Dmitrievich (1906–1975)
composer

A brilliant composer, Shostakovich repeatedly ran afoul of Soviet cultural authorities during the Stalin era but endured to produce a large body of work. Shostakovich first studied at the Leningrad Conservatory and after graduation was appointed to its faculty, where he taught from 1939 to 1948. In early works such as his First Symphony (1925) and his opera *The Nose* (1927), based on a story by GOGOL, he revealed an innovative, cosmopolitan, and witty talent. The next few years saw some important, well-received works, including his Second and Third Symphonies (1927, 1929), which glorified the young revolutionary society, and the ballet *The Golden Age* (1929–30). But his opera *Lady Macbeth of Mtsensk* (1930–32) drew the wrath of cultural commissars for its "formalism," at a time when socialist realism was hardening into official dogma. Over the following decade, Shostakovich managed to find the right balance between artistic creativity and official sanction, with works such as the Seventh ("Leningrad") symphony (1941) that met expectations while withholding his more controversial works. STALIN's death in March 1953 enabled him to return to large-scale symphonic expression in his Tenth Symphony (1953), but he continued to suffer official harassment, especially after the appearance of his Thirteenth Symphony, which included a text by the poet Yevgenii YEVTUSHENKO that touched on Russian ANTI-SEMITISM. By 1960 he was in good graces again with the Soviet establishment, becoming secretary of the RSFSR Union of Composers. A prolific composer who wrote operas, ballets, choral works, oratorios, symphonies, song cycles, as well as music for plays and films, Shostakovich had a highly individual, austere style. His later works, including the Fourteenth and Fifteenth symphonies (1970 and 1972), are bleakly obsessed with mortality.

Shukshin, Vasili Makarovich (1929–1974)
actor and writer

A multitalented actor, writer, and film director, Shukshin was much beloved by Soviet audiences of the 1960s and 1970s for his ability to project a complex, "everyday man." Shukshin was born into a Russian family in a remote Siberian village. At the age of 15 he left home, beginning a period in his life where he had many occupations including fitter, house painter, sailor, radio operator, KOMSOMOL official, and school principal. He arrived in Moscow in 1954. Without any previous studies or training in cinema, he passed the difficult entrance exams to the prestigious State Film School in Moscow, graduating in 1960 as a film director. He attended Mikhail Romm's seminal workshop with other young directors whose talents would blossom in the 1960s, including his good friend Andrei TARKOVSKY. His debut film, *There Was a Lad* (1964), introduced a fresh talent to Soviet audiences. His most popular and important film, *Snowballberry Red (Kalina Krasnaya)* (1974), for which he wrote the script, directed, and played the lead role, featured an imperfect hero, a former criminal trying to go straight by working on a collective farm. Shuk-

shin also excelled at writing, publishing short stories in the prestigious journal *Novyi mir*, as well as a novel about Stenka RAZIN, the 17th-century rebel and COSSACK leader. However, his plans to turn it into a film tentatively entitled *I Came to Give You Freedom* were squelched by the cinema bureaucracy. Always carrying his native Siberia in his work, Shukshin was one of the leading *derevenshchiki* (VILLAGE PROSE) writers who presented the virtues of rural life and morality and the conflicts and tensions that arose between rural and urban dwellers. Together with writers like Yuri TRIFONOV, Valentin Rasputin, and Feodor ABRAMOV, Shukshin reached a large Soviet audience and maintained high artistic standards during the BREZHNEV era. His unexpected death from a heart attack while on location was felt as a national tragedy. Soon after his death, a small hill decorated with red snowball berries, in memory of his most popular film, appeared at the Novodevichi Cemetery in Moscow, not far from the graves of CHEKHOV, GOGOL, and BULGAKOV. He received a posthumous LENIN PRIZE (1976).

Sikorsky, Igor Ivanovich (1889–1972)
aircraft designer

A talented aeronautical engineer, manufacturer, and inventor, Sikorsky is most often associated with the development of the helicopter as a viable means of air transport. Sikorsky was born in Kiev, capital of the Ukraine, where his father was a professor of psychology at St. Vladimir University. He graduated from the St. Petersburg Naval Academy and then pursued further studies in Paris and the Kiev Polytechnic Institute. In 1908, impressed by the news of Count Ferdinand von Zeppelin's dirigible, he turned to the study of aviation. In 1913, at the age of 24 he designed, built, and flew the first successful four-engine airplane, known as the *Grand*. During World War I, he designed four-engine bombers for the Russian army. Opposed to the Bolshevik Revolution of 1917, he left Russia in 1918 and settled in Paris but was not able to make a living

Igor I. Sikorsky *(Library of Congress)*

building aircraft. In 1919 he moved to the United States, where he remained for the rest of his life, taking American citizenship in 1928. In 1923, after several years of hardship, he joined other Russian refugees in forming the Sikorsky Aero-Engineering Company, of which the composer Sergei RACHMANINOFF was a large investor and vice president. The firm soon became a part of the United Aircraft and Transport Company, one of the early giants of American aviation. In the late 1920s Sikorsky invested a lot of his time and resources in the development of multi-engine "aerial yachts," or flying boats. In 1929 he sold 56 such aerial yachts to wealthy investors, but with the crash of the stock market in October 1929 Sikorsky was never paid for them. United continued to support Sikorsky's work on aerial yachts, which culminated in the construction of the S-42 Clipper Ship for Pan

American Airways, but the planes were never profitable, and they were no longer built after 1938.

Sikorsky's work on helicopters proved far more successful. During the 1920s and 1930s a number of designers in the United States and abroad had experimented with helicopter design. It was not until 1939, however, when Sikorsky tested his VS-300, that the helicopter became truly practical. By 1945, the final year of World War II, the U.S. army was using Sikorsky-designed helicopters. In the 1950s their use became more widespread, both for military and peaceful purposes. By that time, Sikorsky's company was one of the leading manufacturers of helicopters.

Simonov, Konstantin Mikhailovich (1915–1979)

poet and journalist

A widely published Soviet author whose wartime fiction and journalism gained him an important place in the world of Soviet letters. Simonov was born on November 28, 1915, in St. Petersburg. The son of a military instructor who sided with the BOLSHEVIKS during the civil war, Simonov traveled with his father's unit, growing up mostly in the provincial towns of Saratov and Ryazan. In 1930 he entered a factory school in Saratov, but his studies there were interrupted in 1931 when the family moved to Moscow, where he worked as a factory mechanic while pursuing part-time university studies. In 1934 he entered the prestigious Gorky Institute of Literature, from which he graduated in 1939. During these years he began to write poetry, and his verses first appeared in journals such as *Molodaya Gvardiia* (Young guard) and *Oktiabr* (October). In 1940 his first volume of poems, *Verses, 1939,* was published, based mostly on his yearlong experience as a military correspondent in Mongolia. During World War II, however, Simonov made his mark on Soviet literature. In 1941 he was called up for army duty and spent most of the war as a correspondent for the army newspaper

Krasnaya znamia (Red flag). As a war correspondent, he traveled to many fronts and was present during the final Soviet assault on Berlin in 1945. A party member since 1939, he was given an army rank and during the war was promoted to lieutenant colonel, followed by a promotion to full colonel after the war.

In addition to his reportage, Simonov published a number of plays and novels, of which the best known is perhaps *Days and Nights* (1944), set in the city of Stalingrad in late 1942 on the eve of the Soviet counteroffensive that turned the tide of the Battle of STALINGRAD and of the war itself. Simonov continued to mine war themes after the war in novels such as *Comrades in Arms* (1952) and *The Living and the Dead* (1959). While working within Soviet ideological strictures, Simonov wrote expressively about the impact of war on soldiers and families in a direct, conversational style that also managed to convey the emotions of his characters.

For his literary efforts, Simonov was rewarded with important positions in the party and Soviet literary world. He also traveled extensively as a Soviet literary ambassador. Simonov was a member of the Central Committee of the COMMUNIST PARTY from 1952 to 1956 and twice served as deputy to the Supreme Soviet of the USSR. He first served as editor of the influential literary journal *Novy mir* from 1946 to 1950 and again from 1954 to 1958. He first served as secretary of the Union of Soviet Writers from 1946 to 1950 and was appointed to a second term in 1967. Simonov balanced some relatively independent political stands without losing his respected position in the Soviet literary establishment. After being dismissed as editor of *Novy mir* in 1958 for approving the publication of the controversial novel by Vladimir Dudintsev, *Not by Bread Alone*, Simonov was sent to Tashkent as correspondent for the Central Asian Bureau of the Communist Party's newspaper, *Pravda*. Likewise, his refusal to sign a statement of support for the 1968 WARSAW PACT invasion of Czechoslovakia did not jeopardize his position as secretary of the Union of Soviet Writers, a post he continued to hold until

the year of his death. In addition, he received a 1974 LENIN PRIZE and was made a Hero of Socialist Labor in 1977.

Sinyavsky, Andrei Donatovich (1925–1998)
writer

Together with his codefendant, Yuli Daniel, Sinyavsky was involved in a landmark trial in the mid-1960s that marked the end of the post-Stalinist thaw in Soviet literature. Sinyavsky was born in Moscow and graduated from Moscow State University in 1952. By the time of his arrest in 1965, he had written an important study of poetry in the early revolutionary period and had established himself as a literary scholar and author. But after 1956 Sinyavsky, writing under the pseudonym of Abram Tertz, and his colleague Daniel (pseudonym Nikolai Arzhak) had been smuggling manuscripts of short stories, short novels, and essays that were highly critical of Soviet life. Among Sinyavsky's contributions from this time were *On Socialist Realism* (1960), a thorough critique of the official Soviet literary doctrine, and *The Trial Begins* (1960), a fictional exposé of Soviet justice. Although critical, the works were not explicitly anti-Soviet. Nevertheless, the KGB (secret police) sought to identify and prosecute the authors. Their identities were finally established and Sinyavsky and Daniel were arrested in September 1965 for disseminating anti-Soviet literature and were placed on trial. Despite a brave defense by both defendants, they were found guilty. In February 1966, Sinyavsky was sentenced to seven years hard labor (the maximum sentence), while Daniel received five. The trial—and the harshness of the sentences—shocked the Soviet intelligentsia, for it was the first time that writers had been tried in an open court, and it marked an important milestone in the development of the dissident movement. Sinyavsky was released in 1971 and emigrated to Paris two years later, where he published his prison journal *A Voice from the Chorus* (1973) and became a celebrated literary figure. His critical take on Russian classical works, published in *Walks with Pushkin* and *In Gogol's Shadow*, triggered considerable controversy. With his wife, Mariya Rozanova, he founded and edited the journal *Sintaksis* and held a professorship at the University of Paris, Sorbonne. He first returned to the Soviet Union in 1989 for Yuli Daniel's funeral, and even though he lived in France, he continued to comment on the intelligentsia in the post-Soviet years. Two of his later works were published in English, *Soviet Civilization: A Cultural History* (1990) and *The Russian Intelligentsia* (1997), based on lectures he gave at Columbia University.

Skobelev, Mikhail Dmitrievich
(1843–1882)

general

A popular general of imperialist, pan-Slav views, Skobelev was one of the architects of Russian expansion into Central Asia. He first drew notice during the conquest of Kokand in 1875–76 when he led a cruel, punitive campaign against anti-Russian rebels. Once Kokand had been annexed by Russia and renamed the Fergana territory, Skobelev served as military governor of the region (1877–78). Like CHERNIAEV, Skobelev exemplified the activist military leader who took advantage of the hesitations of St. Petersburg officials to present them with de facto conquests. In the Balkans during the RUSSO-TURKISH WAR OF 1877–78, Skobelev further built the image of the "White General," wildly popular among his soldiers, even though there was more style than substance to the image. Home from the Turkish war, he returned to Central Asia and in 1880–81 he participated in the Akhal-Tekin expedition to the steppes of Turkmenia, and led the capture of Gheok Teppe in January 1881. British diplomats interpreted this and successive campaigns as part of a Russian design on British India, but Skobelev, who had earlier detailed plans for an invasion of India, now argued against it, having experienced the hardships of these campaigns. In early 1882 he delivered two anti-German speeches in St. Petersburg and Paris that stirred nationalistic feelings and embarrassed a government that had recently renewed the Three Emperors' League with Germany and Austria. Skobelev voiced support for Bosnians in their rebellion against Austria and spoke of an inevitable war between Germans and Slavs, a prominent theme in pan-Slav writings of the time. In the context of his public comments, his sudden death a few months later in July 1882 in a drinking binge at a brothel gave rise to unfounded rumors that he had been assassinated.

Slavic-Greco-Latin Academy
(1687–1814)

Founded in 1687 during the regency of SOPHIA Alekseevna, the Slavic-Greco-Latin Academy was the first establishment of higher education in Russia proper, and as such played an important role in the spread of education in 17th-century Russia. The academy was founded on the initiative of Simeon Polotsky and his pupil Silvestr Medvedev on the model of the influential Kievan Academy, which they had attended. The academy grew from the Bogoiavslensky Academy, founded by Polotsky and Medvedev in 1682, and was initially devoted to the preparation of educated students for the ecclesiastical and civil apparatus of the Muscovite state. Its somewhat cumbersome name reflected a profound controversy over whether its intellectual orientation should be Greek or Latin. The first directors and instructors of the academy were two Greek scholars from Constantinople, the Likhud brothers, Joakini and Sofroni. In 1694 they were removed at the insistence of the Patriarch of Jerusalem (Dosifei) and replaced with Russian scholars. In the early 18th century, following a reorganization of the academy by S. Yavorsky, Greek gave way to Latin as the main language of instruction. The main subjects of instruction were those of traditional medieval scholastics: grammar, rhetoric, sciences, as well as Slavonic, Greek, and Latin languages. In its heyday the academy was the leading center of education in Moscow, attracting students from the urban aristocracy, clergy, and merchant families as well as Ukrainian, Belorussian, Greek, Macedonian, and Georgian students. One of the academy's most famous alumni was the scholar Mikhail LOMONOSOV. Ironically, the founding of Moscow University in 1755, in which Lomonosov played an important role, marked the beginning of the decline of the academy's fortunes. Over the next half century, it gradually concentrated on the teaching of theology. In 1814, the academy was reincorporated as the Moscow Theological Academy and placed under the jurisdiction of the Trinity–St. Sergius Monastery.

Slavophiles and Westernizers

Two groups of 19th-century intellectuals who articulated a fundamental dichotomy in Russian thought that centered on different understandings of the value of autocracy, religion, and Russia's relationship to the West. Both intellectual currents developed from the endless philosophical discussions of the seminal Stankevich Circle of the 1830s, organized in Moscow by Nikolai Vladimirovich Stankevich (1813–40). Future Slavophiles and Westernizers served their intellectual apprenticeship in the Stankevich Circle discussing German romanticism and the works of Friedrich Wilhelm Joseph von Schelling and Georg Wilhelm Friedrich Hegel. By the 1840s, two different orientations began to emerge in more distinct form. The Slavophiles developed their ideas in reaction to the Westernization and bureaucratization of Russian society, which they traced to the pernicious influence of the reforms of PETER I the Great. Believing that Russia was politically, culturally, and morally superior to the West, they idealized the peasant, communalism, Russian Orthodox Christianity, and Russia's autocratic system of government, which they argued had been altered for the worse by Peter and his successors. They opposed the rationalism, secularism, and emphasis on individualism that they associated with western Europe. Instead they favored the notion of *sobornost*, a harmonious collective, organic type of social organization that

they insisted was intrinsic to Slavic peasant communities and political traditions. Although looking backward to an idealized past, the Slavophiles also advocated substantial reforms, such as the abolition of SERFDOM and the granting of civil rights. Among the leading representatives of the Slavophile movement were Aleksei Khomiakov (1804–60), Ivan Kireevsky (1806–56), and the two AKSAKOV brothers, Konstantin Sergeevich (1817–60) and Ivan Sergeevich (1823–86).

The Westernizers were a less ideologically coherent group whose identity was defined primarily by their rejection of the Slavophile message. Their social backgrounds were more diverse than those of the Slavophiles, who hailed primarily from the Moscow landowning gentry. They admired Peter the Great and felt that Russia's backwardness was due to not having undergone the same intellectual path of the West, most notably the absence of a Renaissance. They felt that Russia needed to become more like the West, rather than less. They also attacked other parts of the Slavophile philosophy. The literary critic Vissarion BELINSKY (1811–48) argued against romanticizing the Russian peasant. Aleksandr HERZEN (1812–70) sought to adapt European socialism to Russian conditions. The historian Timofei Granovsky (1813–55) did much to introduce Western ideas to students at Moscow University through his lectures on European history. They all rejected the emphasis on religion placed by the Slavophiles, advocating instead a philosophy of secularism or, in the case of Mikhail BAKUNIN (1814–76), atheism. Even though the terms *Slavophile* and *Westernizer* refer to a specific period of Russian intellectual history, to the extent that they embodied contrasting intellectual attitudes to Russia's relationship with the West, they retain some validity in understanding subsequent intellectual and political trends in Russia.

Solovetsky Monastery

One of the foremost Russian Orthodox monasteries, the Solovetsky Monastery developed as an important cultural, economic, political, and military center in the prerevolutionary period. Situated on the shoreline of Solovetsky Island on the White Sea, it was founded during the 1420s–1430s by monks of the Saint Cyril of Beloozero (Kirillo-Belozersky) Monastery. During the 15th and 16th centuries, its land holdings, located along the shores of the White Sea and its tributary rivers, grew substantially. With more than 50 salt works in the 1660s and its important role in handicrafts and commerce, the monastery became the economic center of the White Sea region. With 350 monks and more than 600 servants by the mid–17th century, it was also a political power, especially because its archimandrite (abbot) reported directly to the czar and not to the ecclesiastical authorities. Solovetsky Monastery also acquired importance as a major frontier fortress with powerful walls, towers, and a strong garrison, which successfully withstood foreign invasions in 1571, 1582, 1611, and 1854. In addition to the Solovetsky Chronicle composed in the monastery, it held many manuscripts and served as the starting point for the introduction of Christianity to the north. From the 1650s to the 1670s, the monastery became one of the strongholds of the traditionalist faction that opposed the reforms of Patriarch NIKON. In 1668 this resistance to reform turned into one of the most violent episodes of the Great Schism, when the monastery rose in a rebellion that lasted until January 1676, when a force of 1,000 *streltsy* (a hereditary military caste) finally stormed the monastery through a breach in the walls. Many monks, including the major leaders, were killed in reprisals, and the monastery came to occupy a prominent place in the chronicles of OLD BELIEVER martyrdom. After 1765, with the monastery reporting directly to the Holy Synod, its autonomy was further dissolved. With the secularization of ecclesiastical lands in 18th-century Russia, the monastery's economic power was disrupted, even though it continued to control substantial wealth until the early 20th century. From czarist times, the remote monastery had been used as a place of banishment, but under the Soviets it became a full-fledged labor camp for intellectuals. Many of its inmates were drawn for the construction of the infamous White Sea Canal in the

1930s. With its five-dome Cathedral of the Transfiguration and powerful walls (six meters deep, 10 meters high), the Solovetskii complex remains one of the best examples of medieval Russian architecture. In 1992 it was selected as a UNESCO World Heritage site.

Soloviev, Vladimir Sergeevich (1853–1900)
philosopher

The second son of the historian Sergei M. Soloviev (1820–79), Vladimir Soloviev achieved distinction as a poet and an advocate of humanism and a forerunner of 20th-century ecumenical thought. At the age of nine, Soloviev experienced the first of three visions of a beautiful woman that would change his life and help shape his theological views. Having completed secondary studies at Moscow Gymnasium No. 1, Soloviev entered the science faculty of Moscow State University in 1869, but later transferred to the philosophy faculty. After graduation in 1873, Soloviev began attending classes in the seminary of St. Sergius Monastery near Moscow. His master's thesis, "The Crisis in Western Philosophy," was accepted in 1874 and helped him secure a position as lecturer in Moscow University. The following year, however, he took a leave of absence and traveled to England, where he experienced for the second time the vision of his childhood. Instructed by the vision, he traveled to Egypt, where he claims to have seen the vision for the third time in November 1875. Soloviev now accepted Christianity and over the years developed a theology centered on the woman in the vision, whom he identified as Sophia, or Divine Wisdom. He held that Sophia, a feminine divine entity, was the ideal essence of the world held in the mind of God. Back in Russia, in 1877 he accepted a post in the Ministry of Education and lectured in philosophy at the University of St. Petersburg. His ideas developed under the influence of respected church elders known as *startsy*, Slavophile intellectuals, and the writer Feodor DOSTOEVSKY. In his *Treatise on Godmanhood* (1878), he developed the idea of a synthesis of religious conviction, scientific knowledge, and mystical experience in a system he called "godmanhood." In 1880 he received a doctoral degree based on the successful defense of his dissertation "Critique of Abstract Principles." A highly promising academic career was cut short in April 1881, when the authorities prevented him from lecturing after Soloviev issued an appeal for them to spare the lives of those convicted of assassinating Czar ALEXANDER II. Soloviev now was free to actively pursue his goal of reconciling the various Christian churches, a theme that he most forcefully articulated in his book *Russia and the Universal Church* (1889). In it, Soloviev called for the union of Catholic and Orthodox churches in a universal theocracy under the joint leadership of the Roman pope and the Russian czar. He traveled to Paris to raise support for this, but his ideas found little resonance among French Catholics. Soloviev was more influential at home, where he developed a following among religious philosophers and the poets of the early-20th-century Symbolist movement. His last work was the controversial *Three Conversations on War, Progress, and the End of History* (1899), where he presented a more apocalyptic rendering of his idea of a universal theocracy. He died in August 1900, while visiting the estate of the prominent Trubetskoi family.

Solzhenitsyn, Aleksandr Isaevich
(1918–   )
writer

One of the giants of 20th-century Russian literature, Solzhenitsyn is perhaps best known for his searing re-creation of the world of the enforced labor camps of the Soviet Union, published as *The Gulag Archipelago,* for which he received the Nobel Prize in literature. Solzhenitsyn was born in the town of Kislovodsk on the northern side of the Caucasus to a family of Cossack background. He never knew his father, who died shortly before his birth, and was raised by his mother. Solzhenitsyn graduated from the state university at Rostov-on-Don with

a degree in mathematics, but he also pursued his budding interest in literature through correspondence courses from Moscow State University. He fought with distinction during World War II, rising to the rank of artillery captain, but in 1945 he was arrested for writing critically about Joseph STALIN in a letter to a friend. He spent the next eight years in the prisons and labor camps of the GULAG that would provide the source material for his most powerful novels. In 1953 he was released from the labor camps but sentenced to an additional three-year term in internal exile in Kazakhstan. Finally free in 1956, he settled in the central Russian town of Ryazan and worked as a mathematics teacher. He achieved instant recognition in the world of Soviet letters after the submission of his short novel *One Day in the Life of Ivan Denisovich,* a powerful description of a typical day in a Soviet labor camp, which drew from Solzhenitsyn's own experiences. Published in 1962, the book was approved for publication through the intervention of General Secretary Nikita KHRUSHCHEV, who was in the middle of a political campaign of de-Stalinization. The growing cultural conservatism that followed Khrushchev's overthrow in 1964 contributed to the increasingly hostile official reception that Solzhenitsyn's subsequent works, which were now published through the Soviet literary underground known as *samizdat,* received. In novels such as *The First Circle* (1968) and *The Cancer Ward,* (1968) he continued to probe the nature and personal consequences of the system of political repression created under Stalin, topics that were central to his early work. For this body of work, Solzhenitsyn was awarded the 1970 Nobel Prize in literature, but aware of his own government's growing displeasure with his work and fearing that he would not be allowed to return to the Soviet Union, he did not travel to Sweden to receive the prize. His conflict with the Soviet authorities came to a head in 1973 when he authorized the publication in Paris of a copy of the manuscript recently seized by the KGB in Moscow. Published as *The Gulag Archipelago,* the novel attempted what Solzhenitsyn described as a literary-historical investigation of the vast network of labor camps that had mushroomed during the Stalin years. For his efforts, Solzhenitsyn was arrested and deported from the Soviet Union in February 1974.

In exile, he settled in Vermont and completed the second and third volumes of *The Gulag Archipelago.* Lionized by the Western press for his opposition to the Soviet system, he gradually came to antagonize his hosts for his equally powerful critiques of Western consumerism and individualism, articulating a political vision that called for the renewal of Russia's authoritarian and Christian traditions. He revised his earlier novel *August 1914,* first published in 1971, and made it a part of an ambitious series entitled *The Red Wheel.* His previously banned works were finally published in the Soviet Union during the late 1980s. After his citizenship was restored in 1990, Solzhenitsyn returned to Russia in 1994 in grand fashion, traveling westward to Moscow along the TRANS-SIBERIAN RAILROAD.

Sophia (1657–1704)
(Sofiia Alekseevna)
regent

The sixth child of Czar ALEKSEI and his first wife, Maria Miloslavskaia, Sophia ruled as regent from 1682 to 1689. She received an unusually good education from Simeon of Polotsk. On the death of her brother Czar FEODOR III in 1682, Sophia assumed the leadership of the Miloslavsky family faction against the supporters of her father's second wife, the Naryshkin family. During the *streltsy* (a hereditary military caste) riots of May 1682, Sophia exercised a moderating influence and engineered a compromise that placed her brother IVAN V, a Miloslavsky, and her half brother PETER I, a Naryshkin, as corulers, with herself as regent. In her regency she was assisted by her lover, Prince Vasili GOLITSYN, who proved to be a mostly capable administrator. In domestic affairs, her reign witnessed the institution of formal persecution of OLD BELIEVERS (1684), the transfer of the office of the Metropolitan of Kiev under the jurisdiction of the Moscow Patriar-

chate (1686), and the opening of the SLAVIC-GRECO-LATIN ACADEMY in Moscow (1686). In foreign affairs, Russia concluded a treaty of peace and alliance promising "eternal peace" with Poland in 1686 that recognized Russian control of part of the Ukraine. Less successful was the Treaty of NERCHINSK, signed in 1689, by which Russia established diplomatic relations with China but gave up its claims to the Amur region. Sophia's growing political ambitions and Golitsyn's unsuccessful campaigns in 1687–89 against the Tatar Khanate of Crimea led to widespread criticism that broke out into the open in 1689. Tensions between Sophia and the Naryshkin family grew until August 1689, when an attempt to use the disgruntled *streltsy* regiments against Peter I and his family backfired. One month later, Sophia was arrested and forced to retire to the Novodevichii Convent on the outskirts of Moscow, which she herself had endowed. There, Sophia lived as a nun under the name of Sister Susanna until her death on July 14, 1704.

Soviet-Polish War (1919–1920)

A 20-month war that took place during the final stages of the Russian civil war, the Soviet-Polish War developed from the need to define and consolidate the borders of the new independent state of Poland and the Bolshevik desire to spread their revolution westward into Europe. The fighting began in February 1919 on what is now Belorussian soil, as both countries sought to take advantage of the withdrawal of German troops from Poland as part of the World War I armistice. While Soviet troops advanced westward into Polish-held territory up to the Bug River, Polish troops pushed eastward into Soviet-held territory up to the Berezina River. While the BOLSHEVIKS believed that victory over Poland would allow them to link up with a revolutionary Germany and guarantee the success of their own revolution, the Polish leader Józef Piłsudski (1867–1935) was hoping to restore the borders of historic Poland before the 18th-century partitions that had led to its disappearance as a European state. At the peak of the Polish advance into Soviet territory, Piłsudski's troops attacked Kiev, capital of the Ukraine, in late April 1920, and captured it on May 7, 1920. Soviet troops reorganized under the young general Mikhail TUKHACHEVSKY, recently successful in establishing Soviet control of most of Siberia, and drove the Polish troops out of the Ukraine by June 1920. On July 4, 1920, Tukhachevsky's armies crossed the border into Poland. Advancing rapidly, they reached the Vistula River, on the outskirts of Warsaw, by mid-August 1920.

The turning point of the war was the battle for Warsaw. After a 10-day battle, known at the time as the "Miracle on the Vistula," Piłsudski's troops stopped the Soviet advance. On August 31, 1920, the last great cavalry battle in European history took place to the south of Poland, involving over 20,000 cavalry troops. The Poles won and through September 1920 further pushed the Soviet armies eastward to the Neman River almost 200 miles to the east of Warsaw. Defeated, the Soviets agreed to an armistice, which was formalized on October 12, 1920. After months of negotiations both sides signed the Treaty of Riga on March 18, 1921. According to the treaty, Poland received parts of the Ukraine and Belorussia, which it would later lose in World War II. The conclusion of the Soviet-Polish War in October 1920 helped the Bolsheviks to consolidate their control of Russia by freeing their armies for the final rout of the remnants of the White armies still fighting Soviet power. In November 1920, Baron WRANGEL, the last White commander, led the evacuation of over 150,000 White troops from the Crimea, thus marking the end of the Russian civil war.

Spassky, Boris Vasilievich (1937–   )
chess player

A chess child prodigy who became known for his tremendous attacking ability and willingness to sacrifice pieces for overall advantage, Spassky reigned as world chess champion from 1969 to 1972, when he was defeated by Bobby Fischer in

a highly publicized contest. Spassky was born in Leningrad, but at the age of four his family moved to the Ural Mountain region seeking shelter from the German siege of LENINGRAD. Here, the young Boris first learned to play chess and after returning to Leningrad in 1945 began formal studies. In 1953, at the age of 16 he became an international master and two years later, after winning the world junior championship in Antwerp, Belgium, gained the title of international grand master. In 1960 he contributed a minor footnote to popular culture when his ending sequence in a match against David Bronstein was used in the opening sequence of the James Bond classic film, *From Russia with Love*. In the early 1960s under the coaching of the international grandmaster, Igor Bondarevsky, Spassky developed into a world-class player, able to challenge for the world championship. He twice challenged reigning world champion Tigran PETROSIAN for the world title, losing by a slim margin in 1966 before defeating him in 1969. Three years later, when the controversial American player Bobby Fischer won the right to challenge him for the title, Spassky became a pawn in a sometimes farcical battle that preceded the actual matches, which was as much about the tense Soviet-American cold war relationship as it was about chess. After protracted negotiations that extended to matters such as the size of chairs, shape of the table, and lighting of the rooms, the matches were held in Reykjavík, Iceland, in July and August 1972. After 21 matches that included seven consecutive draws, Fischer gained the agreed-upon seven victories (to Spassky's four) necessary to win the championship. Spassky's defeat marked the first time in over 50 years that the world title was not held by a Russian or Soviet player.

Spassky returned to the Soviet Union and won the 1973 Soviet championship but lost out to another rising star, Anatoli KARPOV, in his bid to challenge Fischer and regain his world title. Throughout the 1970s and 1980s, Spassky continued to challenge for the top positions in the international world of chess, but he never had another opportunity to play for the world championship. In 1992 Spassky agreed to play Fischer, a rematch of their confrontation 20 years earlier. This was to be Fischer's first appearance after disappearing from the chess world in 1975, when he refused to defend his crown against Karpov. The match was held in Yugoslavia, at the time of the Bosnian War, in contravention of U.N. sanctions. After 30 matches played in Montenegro and Belgrade, Spassky was again defeated by Fischer.

Speransky, Count Mikhail Mikhailovich (1772–1839)

official

A talented official who briefly rose to a position of great influence under ALEXANDER I, succumbed to court intrigues in 1812, and returned under NICHOLAS I to compile Russia's first code of laws in almost two centuries. The son of an Orthodox priest in Vladimir province, Speransky was first educated in the local seminary, then at the prestigious Alexander Nevsky Seminary in St. Petersburg, where he was soon appointed to the faculty. Choosing government service over an academic career, Speransky quickly rose through the ranks, attaining the status of hereditary noble by 1797. By 1807, Alexander I appointed him deputy minister of justice and instructed him to prepare a comprehensive plan to reform government institutions. Speransky's plan, presented in 1809, preserved the emperor's sovereign power but provided for three branches of government that included a State Council with eight ministries, a network of representative assemblies albeit without legislative powers, and the Senate serving as the judicial branch. Drawing on growing anti-French feeling, conservative opponents led by N. M. KARAMZIN succeeded in tarnishing Speransky and his reforms with the brush of French subversion. Dismissed by Alexander in March 1812, he was subsequently pardoned and made governor of Penza (1816). As governor-general of Siberia (1819–22), Speransky introduced reforms that, although well intended, increased rather than reduced the burden on Siberian native peoples. Back in St.

Petersburg, Speransky was appointed to the State Council and entrusted by the new czar, Nicholas I, in 1826 with the monumental task of codifying Russian laws. By 1833, his staff had collected and ordered chronologically all the decrees and acts issued since the previous *Ulozhenie* of 1649, and published them as *The Complete Collection of Laws of the Russian Empire*. Historians still debate whether Speransky's 1809 reforms were the prelude to constitutional monarchy in Russia, but they agree that the codification of laws is his greatest legacy.

Sputnik

The name given to the artificial satellites launched by the Soviet Union from 1957 to 1961, derived from the Russian word for "traveling companion," Sputnik captured the imagination of the world and started the Space Age. Between 1957 and 1961 the Soviet Union launched 10 artificial satellites that used dogs, laboratories, and dummy passengers to set the stage for the first manned space flight, Yuri GAGARIN's historic circling of the earth in April 1961 aboard the spacecraft *Vostok-1*. The groundwork for what became the Sputnik program, under the direction of its chief engineer, Sergei KOROLEV, had been laid with the construction of the BAIKONUR COSMODROME in Kazakhstan in 1955 and the launching of the first intercontinental ballistic missile in August 1957.

In September 1957, the Soviet Union announced its intention of launching its first artificial satellite. Although the announcement was dismissed in some circles as another instance of Soviet propaganda, *Sputnik-1* was launched on October 4, 1957, triggering a period of intense scientific competition with the United States. After more than 4,000 orbits around the earth, *Sputnik-1* reentered the earth's atmosphere on January 4, 1958. On November 3, 1957, *Sputnik-2* had already been launched, this time with a dog—Laika—on board. The dog survived for a week until oxygen supplies ran out, while the satellite disintegrated in April 1958. The third Sputnik was launched in May 1958, four months after the United States had launched its first satellite, *Explorer-1.* In orbit for almost 700 days, *Sputnik-3* carried the first space laboratory and used solar power for the first time as its source of energy. For the next two years, the Soviet space program concentrated on its lunar exploration program and developed the *Luna* vehicles. *Sputnik-4,* launched in May 1960 and equipped with a dummy passenger and ejector seat, resumed the Sputnik program but it veered off course, eventually disintegrating in October 1965. The fifth and sixth Sputniks, launched in August and December 1960, both carried dogs, but whereas the dogs in *Sputnik-5* returned safely to earth and landed on parachutes, those in *Sputnik-6* were killed when the satellite burned as it sought to change orbit. *Sputnik-7* and *Sputnik-8* were both launched in February 1961 with the mission of probing the planet Venus, but they encountered problems and were lost. The last two Sputniks were launched two weeks apart in March 1961 with dogs aboard and served as working models for the *Vostok* spacecraft to be used in Gagarin's April 1961 flight.

Stalin, Joseph Vissarionovich
(1879–1953)
(Iosif Vissarionovich Dzhugashvili)
leader of the Soviet Union

The successor to Vladimir LENIN as leader of the Soviet Union, Joseph Stalin ruled the USSR for almost 25 years, creating in the process one of the most repressive regimes of the 20th century. Stalin was born Joseph Vissarionovich Dzhugashvili in the Georgian village of Gori, the son of an abusive cobbler and a housecleaner. In 1894 he enrolled in the Orthodox Theological Seminary in Tbilisi, the Georgian capital, but was expelled four years later for revolutionary activities. A member of the Russian Social Democratic Labor Party since 1898, Stalin sided with the BOLSHEVIKS in 1903, even as most Georgian Marxists opted for the Mensheviks. Known as Koba, in his early revolutionary years, he worked in the Bolshevik underground, was arrested, and was exiled to

Siberia several times. In 1912 he was elected to the Bolshevik Central Committee and, perhaps because of his non-Russian background, sent on a mission to western Europe to meet exiled party leaders and gather materials for a study of Bolshevik policy toward ethnic nationalities in Russia. He was again arrested soon after his return to Russia in 1913 and sentenced to Siberian exile.

Stalin returned to Petrograd after the February Revolution of 1917 and edited with Lev KAMENEV the party newspaper *Pravda,* which at first adopted a relatively conciliatory policy toward the Provisional Government that was later denounced by Lenin. After the Bolshevik revolution of October, Stalin became commissar for nationalities and, later, commissar for state control. During the civil war he served as a troubleshooter traveling to various fronts. His enmity with Leon TROTSKY, then commissar of war, dates from their many clashes over matters of policy. In 1922, he was appointed secretary-general of the Central Committee of the Communist Party, a relatively unglamorous position that other Bolsheviks thought was well suited for a solid, hardworking party bureaucrat. Even before Lenin's death in 1924, however, Stalin began to use this position to build a power base, successfully avoiding an attempt to remove him because of his rudeness toward others. In the complex power struggle that followed Lenin's death, Stalin gradually emerged as the power broker outmaneuvering his better-known rivals such as Trotsky, Kamenev, Grigorii ZINOVIEV, and finally, by 1928, his one-time ally, Nikolai BUKHARIN. As the leader of an ambitious and devoted group of younger Bolsheviks, Stalin sought to bring into life his slogan of "socialism in one country," by embarking the Soviet Union on a crash program of industrialization, based on the forceful collectivization of the peasantry.

By 1934, after the completion of the First Five-Year Plan and a ruthless implementation of collectivization, Stalin and his group had dramatically transformed the Soviet Union. Soon after, however, following the assassination of one of his main lieutenants, Sergei Kirov, in December

1934, Stalin unleashed a campaign of terror that was initially directed against real and perceived enemies in the party and state bureaucracy, but eventually encompassed the army officer corps, officials at the republican and local levels, and countless civilians who were denounced on trumped-up charges. A vast network of labor camps in remote locations of the Soviet Union was created in the course of this terror campaign and integrated into the Soviet economy. The late 1930s were also marked by concern over Nazi Germany's expansionism and, after years of denouncing fascism and Nazism, in August 1939 the Soviet Union signed a nonaggression pact with Germany.

Nevertheless, Germany invaded the Soviet Union in June 1941, presenting the country and Stalin with its greatest challenge in decades. Although Stalin has been faulted for ignoring signs of the impending invasion, after a mysterious two-week disappearance in which German forces made bold inroads along the entire eastern front he rallied the country and led it to victory, albeit at a huge cost. By 1945, Stalin found himself at the peak of his power, the ruler of a devastated but undisputed superpower, especially after the Soviet Union developed atomic weapons in 1949. He reversed the few concessions he had made in the course of the war and the years between 1945 and his death in 1953 remain the least known of his long rule, shaped by increasing paranoia and secretiveness. It is widely believed that the alleged conspiracy known as the DOCTORS' PLOT, uncovered in January 1953, was the prelude to a larger mass purge, targeting Soviet Jews in particular, but cut short by Stalin's death from a cerebral hemorrhage in March 1953.

Stalingrad, Battle of (1942–1943)

One of the decisive battles of World War II, the Battle of Stalingrad marked the turning point in the war between Nazi Germany and the Soviet Union. The German advance into southern Russia and the Caucasus was halted and the Red Army began to roll back the German conquests, advancing into western Russia, the Ukraine, and eastern Europe and finally, Berlin. By summer 1942, with their attack on Moscow halted and their siege of LENINGRAD still in progress, the German armies sought to capture the oil fields of the Caucasus region and the Caspian Sea. While an army advanced down the Volga River on its way to the Caspian Sea and the major oil center of Baku, the German Sixth Army, led by General Friedrich von Paulus, advanced on the city of Stalingrad (known as Tsaritsyn until 1925 and as Volgograd since 1961). In addition to the symbolic power of carrying STALIN's name, Stalingrad was an industrial and communications center strategically located mostly on the west bank of the Volga River. On August 20, 1942, after a period of aerial bombardment, a large German force, aided by smaller Romanian and Italian contingents, began its attack on the city. For the next six months Soviet and German infantry fought a long, brutal, house-to-house battle.

The Red Army counteroffensive began on November 19, 1942, with the assistance of Siberian reinforcements and U.S. materiel provided through Lend-Lease. Led by General Georgii ZHUKOV, Soviet troops numbered almost 1 million soldiers. Breaking through Romanian

Three German soldiers walk through the ruins of Stalingrad, September 1942 *(Library of Congress)*

and Italian lines to the north, the Soviets encircled close to 300,000 German troops. Ordered by Hitler neither to surrender nor to attempt to break out to the rear, von Paulus waited for promised reinforcements and an airlift that never came. By January, the Sixth Army's situation was desperate; its soldiers were hungry and its ammunition was running low. On February 2, 1943, von Paulus, together with 24 generals and 90,000 soldiers, surrendered to the Soviets. The city of Stalingrad, almost completely destroyed in the fighting, was reconstructed after the war.

Stanislavsky, Konstantin Sergeevich (1863–1938)
actor and theater director
One of the most influential directors of the Russian theater, Stanislavsky (born Alekseev) was the son of a wealthy Moscow merchant. From 1877 to 1887, he directed an amateur group known as the "Alekseev circle." For the next decade he worked for the Society of Art and Literature until 1898, when he joined V. I. NEMIROVICH-DANCHENKO in founding the Moscow Art Theater (MkhAT), which would be at the center of Russian theater over the next century. With a team of outstanding actors and with plays by GORKY and CHEKHOV as the foundation of its repertoire, Stanislavsky was able to develop his famous Stanislavsky method of acting. A not entirely new idea that drew from the realistic traditions of the Russian theater, the Stanislavsky system appeared as something new and even revolutionary in comparison with the standards of the time. He developed a special technique called "reliving" that used the actors' emotional involvement to produce a realistic result. It was this tendency to identify the theater with life that prompted the most gifted of Stanislavsky's pupils, MEYERHOLD and Vakhtangov, to return to the idea of a "theatrical" or "representational" theater. Stanislavsky himself was not immune to the influence of symbolism that swept over Russian artistic life between the revolutions of 1905 and 1917. Under the experimentalism of the first decade of Soviet rule, Stanislavsky's theater

appeared old-fashioned and bourgeois. The emergence of socialist realism in the 1930s signaled a more favorable climate for Stanislavsky, but in the context of official dogmas, the life had been drained out of his system as was the case for most other art forms. Whereas Stanislavsky's genuine ideas have greatly influenced modern acting, both in Russia and abroad, the use made of his system during the last period of STALIN's rule severely harmed the Russian theater.

Starostin brothers
athletes
The Starostin brothers—Nikolai Petrovich (1898–1996), Aleksandr Petrovich (1903–81), Andrei Petrovich (1906–1987), and Petr Petrovich (1909–1993)—played a seminal role in the development of Soviet football (soccer) as players, coaches, and administrators. The Starostins made their career in Moscow, beginning in the 1920s in a Komsomol-sponsored team named Krasnaia Presnia, which after several transformations became known in 1935 as Spartak, to this day the most popular team in Moscow football. During the 1930s they were all football stars and led Spartak to several Soviet club championships. Nikolai played for the USSR national team in the 1920s and 1930s. In 1934 he was awarded the title of honorary master of sport. From 1955 to 1975, he managed his old team, Spartak. In 1967 he published *Zvezdy bolshogo futbola* (Stars of Great Football), a memoir about prominent Soviet football players, and a second volume in 1989, *Futbol skvoz gody* (Football through the Years). He served as Spartak team president well into his nineties. Aleksandr captained the Soviet national team in the 1930s, first wrote his memoirs, *The Captain's Story,* in 1935, and served as deputy chairman and chairman of the RSFSR football federation. Andrei also played for the Soviet national team in the 1930s, and was named master of sport in 1940. In 1959 he was appointed deputy chairman of the USSR football federation. He is the author of two books, *Bolshoi futbol* (Great Football) (1957) and *Povest o futbole*

(The Story of Football) (1973). Less is known about the youngest brother, Petr, who trained as an engineer. As mainstays of Spartak, the Starostin brothers personally suffered from the animosity of Lavrenty BERIA, the secret police chief and ardent follower of Dinamo Tbilisi, an opposing team. From 1939, hoping to weaken the dominant Spartak teams, he sought the arrest of the Starostin brothers on the charge that Spartak was running a "bourgeois" professional operation because its players were paid stipends. Repeatedly thwarted, he finally succeeded in 1942, and the Starostins were sent off to various labor camps, where they survived thanks to the protection of sympathetic guards who knew their identities. Only in 1955 were they allowed to return to Moscow, but the true nature of their long absence from Spartak was not publicly discussed until 1989.

Stolypin, Petr Arkadievich (1862–1911)
statesman

Together with Sergei WITTE, Stolypin stands out as one of the few able and innovative conservative czarist politicians in the final decades of the Russian Empire. Stolypin's family belonged to Russia's landed nobility. In 1885, he joined the Ministry of State Domains. As district marshal of the nobility in Kovno province (1889) and governor of Grodno province (1902) in Russia's multiethnic western borderlands, his duties brought him in contact with Great Russian, Polish, Lithuanian, and Jewish populations. Here he began to develop the ideas that would characterize his later career in politics: a belief that individual and not communal peasant land ownership was more productive and more conducive toward political stability in the countryside. In 1903 Stolypin was appointed governor of Saratov province, a region that later witnessed particularly severe peasant disturbances during the 1905 Revolution. As governor, his willingness to use extreme measures, such as hangings, in suppressing rural rebellions gave birth to the term "Stolypin neckties" and brought him to the

attention of the czar. In April 1906 he was appointed minister of the interior and, three months later, chairman of the Council of Ministers (prime minister). As prime minister, Stolypin continued the twin policies of repression and reform of land ownership that had characterized his earlier work. He did not hesitate to take unpopular measures, such as dissolving the first two popularly elected DUMAS in July 1906 and June 1907, followed by a suspension of the 1906 constitution and the construction of a new electoral system that was less representative but more stable. On the other hand, he tried to implement substantial land reform by encouraging peasants to leave the village communes and establish their own farms. Through the creation of the Peasant Land Bank, peasants could borrow money to buy land. Stolypin's government also encouraged the large migration of peasants from overpopulated European Russia to lands in Siberia and Central Asia. Stolypin was less successful at navigating the opposition of the court and bureaucracy to his broader plans to introduce reforms in other fields such as education, taxation, and local government. By the time of his untimely death, he was losing the support of the czar himself. On September 1, 1911, in the presence of the czar, he was assassinated by a Socialist Revolutionary double agent at the Kiev Opera House. Although scholars remain divided over the true impact and viability of his land reforms, post-Communist Russia has witnessed renewed interest in his work.

Stravinsky, Igor Feodorovich (1882–1971)
composer, pianist, and conductor

Stravinsky is widely considered to be the most influential composer of the 20th century. He was born in the town of Oranienbaum (now Lomonosov), near St. Petersburg. His father was a prominent opera bass, and Stravinsky grew up in a home exposed to the leading musical, theatrical, and literary figures of the day. Although trained in piano and musical theory from an early age, Stravinsky did not see a future in music until his early twenties. He graduated from St. Petersburg University in 1905 with a degree in law and philosophy. In 1907 he began to study with Nikolai RIMSKY-KORSAKOV, who recognized his brilliance and sought to shelter him from conventional academic training by offering individual lessons. Rimsky-Korsakov arranged for the performance of some of Stravinsky's early compositions in 1908. Later that year, Stravinsky began to work with Sergei DIAGHILEV, who commissioned him to arrange the 1909 summer season of his Ballets Russes in Paris. In 1910, again working for Diaghilev, Stravinsky, wrote a full-length ballet, *The Firebird,* which premiered in Paris and turned Stravinsky into an overnight sensation. The next few years witnessed an especially creative period of collaborations between Stravinsky and Diaghilev that revolutionized the world of ballet. Another acclaimed Stravinsky ballet, *Petrushka* (1911), featured Vaslav NIJINSKY in the title role. Stravinsky spent the next two years writing what turned out to be one of the most controversial and influential landmarks of modernist ballet and music, *The Rite of Spring.* First performed on May 29, 1913, it sparked an opening night riot among a sharply divided audience. World War I interfered with Stravinsky's successful work with the Ballets Russes. He spent most of the war in Switzerland with his wife and two children. Beginning with the pagan themes of *The Rite of Spring,* Stravinsky turned to more obvious Russian folk themes and text, which influenced his work over the next decade, as evidenced by *Renard* (1916) and *The Wedding* (1923). Cut off from Russia by the Russian Revolution, Stravinsky gradually abandoned the Russian themes and entered a neoclassical phase that would inform most of his work for the next three decades. The Stravinsky family left Switzerland in 1920 and settled in Paris, where they lived until 1939. Two important works from this period, the oratorio *Oedipus Rex* (1927) and the cantata *Symphony of the Psalms* (1930) reveal the influence of a religious conversion that Stravinsky had experienced in 1926. The deaths of his eldest daughter, wife, and mother and the onset

of World War II compelled Stravinsky to move to the United States. He remarried in early 1940 and first settled in Hollywood, California. After working on symphonies during the war years, Stravinsky produced his first full-length opera, *The Rake's Progress,* written between 1948 and 1951. Stravinsky's health declined after 1956, when he suffered a stroke, but he continued to work actively until 1966, when he completed his last major work, *Requiem Canticles.* Stravinsky died in New York City on April 6, 1971.

Suslov, Mikhail Andreevich (1902–1982)
Soviet official

Content to work away from the center stage of the ruling circles as the colorless guardian of ideological orthodoxy, Suslov was one of the most powerful men in the Soviet establishment from the mid-1960s until his death. Suslov was born to a Russian peasant family in the Saratov region of the lower Volga River valley. A teenager at the time of the 1917 Revolution, he joined the Communist Party's youth league (KOMSOMOL) during the civil war, becoming a full party member in 1921. The following year he was sent to Moscow, where he attended classes at the Institute for Red Professors as well as the Plekhanov Institute for Economics, from which he graduated in 1928. As a skilled propagandist he advanced within the party ranks and in the early 1930s played a role in removing alleged opponents of STALIN in the Urals and the Ukraine. Benefiting as others of his generation from the decimation of COMMUNIST PARTY ranks during the purges of the mid-1930s, in 1937 Suslov was appointed a party secretary of the Rostov region in southern Russia. Two years later he became first secretary of the Communist Party in the nearby Stavropol region, a position he held until 1944. From 1944 to 1946, he supervised the incorporation of Lithuania, occupied since 1940, into the Soviet Union. From 1947, when he became a secretary of the party's Central Committee until his death, Suslov worked in various capacities of increasing responsibility at the top levels of the Communist Party. From 1949 to 1950 he served as chief editor of the party newspaper, *Pravda*. In 1952 he held a seat in the expanded Presidium (Politburo), which he lost in 1953 but regained in 1955, after siding with KHRUSHCHEV in his struggle with Georgii MALENKOV. He again backed Khrushchev in the crucial showdown with the ANTI-PARTY group in 1957, but by 1964 he had grown tired, like others in the ruling inner circle, of Khrushchev's unpredictable maneuvers. He was one of the engineers of the conspiracy that overthrew Khrushchev in October 1964 and replaced him with a troika of Leonid BREZHNEV, Aleksei KOSYGIN, and Nikolai Podgorny, from which Brezhnev eventually emerged as the preeminent Soviet leader. From his post as supervisor of cultural and ideological affairs for the Communist party, Suslov was instrumental in blocking domestic reforms and enforcing ideological conformity within the Soviet bloc, as seen by the 1968 WARSAW PACT invasion of Czechoslovakia. While he was temporarily successful in delaying the rise of Yuri ANDROPOV, whom he considered a rival, Andropov first succeeded Suslov as ideological guardian and then Brezhnev as general secretary, after they both died in 1982. Ironically, Suslov's patronage of another emerging Communist leader with roots in the Stavropol region, Mikhail GORBACHEV, also opened the doors for more far-reaching reforms in the late 1980s.

Suvorov, Count Aleksandr Vasilievich (1730–1800)

military commander

To this day, Suvorov is celebrated and worshipped as Russia's greatest soldier, although his reputation has not traveled as well beyond Russian borders. A learned man, he related with ease and inspired the rank-and-file soldier, one source of his enduring popularity. Suvorov first distinguished himself in the Seven Years' War (1756–63), the RUSSO-TURKISH WARS of 1768–74 and 1787–92, as well as the 1768 and 1794 cam-

Count Aleksandr Suvorov, engraving *(Library of Congress)*

paigns in Poland. His best-known exploits came during the Italian and Swiss campaigns of 1799, which followed PAUL I's decision to join the anti-French coalition. Charged with neutralizing the French advance into Italy, Suvorov defeated the French in a series of brilliant attacks and conquered northern Italy. He was transferred to Switzerland, and a confusion in the allied command let to his troops being surrounded by the French. But through the celebrated, daring march through the St. Gotthard Pass, Suvorov escaped the French stranglehold. Suvorov also served as mentor for some of the officers who would lead Russia during the War of 1812, BAGRATION, DAVYDOV, and KUTUZOV. In 1797 Suvorov presented his views on warfare and training of troops in a treatise entitled *The Science of Conquest*. In it he recommends teaching subordinates by example, awareness of the environment, patience in military matters, and constant study. This treatise became a basic manual for all imperial commanders, and later for Soviet military commanders. At the moment of his greatest glory, having been promoted to the unprecedented rank of generalissimo, in January 1800 Suvorov found himself recalled to St. Petersburg in disgrace. Accused of a petty misdemeanor, he was banned from the imperial court and died a few months later. Although ALEXANDER I erected a statue in his memory, the cult of Suvorov that developed in the 19th century had certain anti-czarist connotations, given how Suvorov's career had ended. During World War II the Supreme Soviet established the Suvorov medal as the highest military decoration for gallantry in combat, and the cadet academy bears his name.

Sytin, Ivan Dmitrievich (1851–1934)
publisher

One of the major Russian publishers of the late imperial period, Sytin was born in Kostroma province, the son of a rural clerk who gave him little formal education. In a remarkable career, he became a multimillionaire while distributing popular education materials of generally high quality at minimum prices. After moving to MOSCOW in 1863, he worked in several bookshops before opening his first typography in 1876. From the beginning he was interested in publishing for a mass readership, starting with *lubki* (folk prints), before moving to cheap books for rural readers and the highly successful line of attractively illustrated calendars featuring practical information. By 1912 he was publishing 12 million of these yearly. In 1883, he founded I. D. Sytin and Company, a publisher that specialized in large print runs of cheap editions of Russian and foreign classics. The following year he started a successful partnership with Lev TOLTSOY and the Posrednik publishing house. Over the next years, they published over 250 titles with an emphasis on moral and spiritual literature, with Tolstoy penning 44 of them. By the 1890s, Sytin had become one of the most important Russian publishers. In the first decades of the 20th century he published various well-received encyclopedias, including the 14-volume *Popular Encyclopedia* (1911–12), a 10-volume *Children's Encyclopedia* (1913–14), and a *Military Encyclopedia* (1911–15) that had reached 18 volumes before the army ordered the suspension of its publication in the climate of military censorship that accompanied the outbreak of World War I. Sytin also published the popular magazine *Vokrug sveta* (*Around the World*) and the mass newspaper *Russkoe slovo* (*The Russian Word*), with a circulation of 1 million. His efforts to promote cultural literacy among the masses earned him the opposition of reactionary groups like the BLACK HUNDREDS, who were responsible for acts of vandalism against his enterprises. By 1914, Sytin had bookshops in over 60 Russian cities, and his two Moscow printing plants were responsible for 25 percent of Russia's book production. After the revolution the BOLSHEVIKS nationalized his presses, but he agreed to work as a consultant for the State Publishing House (Gosizdat) until his retirement in 1928. However, he refused LENIN's offer to become its director, citing his lack of formal education.

T

Table of Ranks

The commonly used name for a system that classified the Russian gentry in a hierarchy of seniority according to their service to the state, the Table of Ranks was first introduced by PETER I the Great in 1722, who drafted it in collaboration with his adviser Andrei OSTERMANN. With modifications over the next two centuries, it served as the organizing principle for the Russian army and bureaucracy until 1917. Formally known as the "Law about the State Service Order in the Russian Empire," the Table of Ranks organized military (army and navy), court, and civilian service in 14 parallel grades where each rank in one service had a corresponding rank in the other two. The first class was the highest rank and the 14th was the lowest. In theory, every official entering the three categories of state service began at the 14th rank and worked his way up the ladder through merit or length of service. Peter intended for the system to be open to advancement of gentry as well as nongentry officials. In the military ranks, officials in the 14 categories were given the status of hereditary nobility, while in the civilian and court ranks, only the top eight ranks assured hereditary nobility status, with the lower six awarding the right to personal nobility that could not be transferred to one's children. Although Peter's Table of Ranks resembled existing systems in European countries such as Prussia and Denmark, it was a significant departure for a society that had abolished a cumbersome system of social precedence (*mestnichestvo*) only 40 years before, especially with its emphasis on merit over social birth the basis for promotion. In an attempt to restrict entry into the nobility, in 1845 personal nobility was granted only when reaching the ninth level rather than the 14th.

Tal, Mikhail (1936–1992)
chess player

A daring, intuitive player who held the world chess championship from 1960 to 1961 with a style that went against the stereotype of the machinelike Soviet school of the 1950s and influenced a younger generation of Soviet chess players. Tal was born in Riga, the capital of Latvia, which during most of his lifetime was a part of the Soviet Union. At the age of eight he started playing chess with the Young Pioneers' chess club in Riga. Five years later he was taking private lessons with Alexander Koblencs, one of the leading Latvian players. Tal followed his first major victory, the 1953 Latvian championship, with back-to-back victories at the Soviet national championship in 1957 and 1958, during which time he also gained international grand master status. Tal's emergence energized the Soviet chess world, which for the previous decade or so had been dominated by Mikhail BOTVINNIK and his methodical, even scientific style of play, which had been elevated to the status of chess orthodoxy by the Soviet chess bureaucracy. In 1959, Tal won the international candidates' tournament held in Yugoslavia to choose the player who had the right to challenge Botvinnik for the world title. The match for the title began in 1960 with a quick victory by Tal in the first game. After 21 matches, Tal won the requisite six matches with only three defeats to unseat Botvinnik. At the age of 23, Tal became the youngest world champion ever, a record he held for 25 years until Garry KASPAROV won the title at the age of 22 in 1985. In poor health to defend his title, he lost the rematch to Botvinnik in 1961, the second time that Botvinnik had regained his title in the 25 years that he dominated world chess. Although Tal never regained his world title, he remained a strong international player, winning four more Soviet championships and playing competitively in four other candidates' tournaments for the world title between 1962 and 1985. In 1988 he surfaced again as world champion, this time of blitz, an ultrarapid variation of chess. Kidney failure was the reason behind his death in 1992.

Tarkovsky, Andrei Arsenevich (1932–1986)
film director

Tarkovsky became internationally famous for his film *Andrei Rublev,* which was completed in 1966 but could not be shown in the Soviet Union until 1971. He was born into a Russian family in Moscow; his father was the poet Arseny Tarkovsky, and he graduated from the State Film Institute (1961), where he studied under Mikhail Romm. His first film, *The Steam Roller and the Violin* (1961), was followed by *Ivan's Childhood* (1962), a film that pointed to a trend among young filmmakers in a direction away from the dogmas of socialist realism. Tarkovsky's breakthrough came with *Andrei Rublev,* which was awarded the International Critics' Prize, in 1969. Based on the life of the great medieval icon painter Andrei RUBLEV (ca. 1360–1430), the film deals with the relationship of a painter with the environment and the limits of artistic expression, a clear metaphor for the fate of Soviet artists in the BREZHNEV era. Tarkovsky made two more films, but the Soviet public and critics found him difficult to comprehend. He moved abroad and made films in Italy (*Nostalgia,* 1983) and Sweden (*The Sacrifice,* 1985, which won a prize at Cannes). Tarkovsky defected in 1984 and was deprived of his Soviet citizenship. He died of cancer in Paris. Under Mikhail GOR-

BACHEV's policy of glasnost (openness), he was recognized as a great director and all his previously banned films were shown.

Tchaikovsky, Petr Ilich (1840–1893)
composer

Perhaps Russia's most famous composer, Tchaikovsky first studied law at St. Petersburg School of Jurisprudence before entering the St. Petersburg Conservatory in 1862. After graduation, in 1865 he was appointed professor at the Moscow Conservatory. A disastrous marriage in 1877 (he was homosexual) compelled him to resign his professorship the following year. Again in St. Petersburg, he made his debut as conductor in 1887 with a program of his own compositions. In 1888 he undertook a successful international tour as a conductor, meeting other famous com-

Petr Ilich Tchaikovsky *(Library of Congress)*

posers, including Brahms, Grieg, Dvorak, Gounod, Massenet, and Paderewski. He visited the United States in 1891, then traveled to England to receive an honorary degree from Cambridge University. Versions of his death are contradictory. Some accounts note that he was forced to commit suicide, others that he died of cholera in St. Petersburg. An exponent of Russian romanticism who also introduced nationalist themes into Russian classical music, his works are among the best known in the Russian canon. Among these are the operas *Eugene Onegin* (1877–78) and *The Queen of Spades* (1890); the ballets *Swan Lake* (1875–76), *Sleeping Beauty* (1888–89), and *The Nutcracker* (1891–92); and the overtures *Romeo and Juliet* (1880) and *The Year 1812* (1880). In addition to these he left six symphonies, piano concertos, a violin concerto, chamber music, church music, and numerous arrangements.

Tereshkova, Valentina Vladimirovna (1937–)
cosmonaut

Tereshkova became a Soviet and world celebrity as the first woman to travel in space, when she circled the earth in June 1963 aboard *Vostok-VI*. Her father was a *kolkhoznik* (collective farm worker) in Yaroslavl oblast. She worked in factories in Yaroslavl and was a parachutist at the local aviation club until selected for training as a cosmonaut (Soviet astronaut) in 1962. In 1963 she married fellow cosmonaut Adrian Nikolaev, whom she later divorced. Their daughter, born in 1964, could claim to be the first child with two cosmonauts as parents. Tereshkova continued her studies, graduating from the Zhukovsky Aviation Academy in 1969. As a cosmonaut, she had entry into the Soviet Union's political establishment, joining the COMMUNIST PARTY in 1962 and becoming a candidate member of the Central Committee from 1971 to 1990. Well aware of her unique status, the Soviet government placed her in highly visible public relations positions. She was actively involved in the Soviet

Committee for Women, serving as chair from 1968 to 1987, but she failed to be reelected to the committee in 1987. She then became chair of the Soviet Society for Friendship and Cultural Relations with Foreign Countries. Tereshkova was elected to the landmark USSR Congress of People's Deputies in 1989. In 1992 she was appointed chair of the Presidium of the Russian Association for International Cooperation. She represented the Soviet Union abroad at many conferences and was known as a formidable, businesslike woman. A crater on the moon is named after her.

Tilsit, Treaty of (1807)

A treaty signed in July 1807 between Napoleonic France and Russia that inaugurated a five-year alliance between the two countries that was eventually broken by Napoleon's invasion of Russia in June 1812. The background to the Treaty of Tilsit was the War of the Third Coalition that began in 1805 when Russia joined Austria, Sweden, and Great Britain against France and Spain. After Napoleon's decisive victory at Austerlitz in December 1805, Austria was knocked out of the war, but the Russians continued, joined by Prussia in 1806. The French rout of the Prussians at Jena and Auerstadt, and a major victory over the Russians at Friedland on June 14, 1807, set the stage for peace negotiations at Tilsit, a town in East Prussia on the Niemen (Memel) River. The negotiations began on June 25, 1807, with a celebrated meeting between Napoleon and Emperor ALEXANDER I on a raft. By the time a treaty was signed on July 7, 1807, the two sides had agreed to an alliance. Two days later, a treaty was signed between France and Prussia. The terms of the Treaty of Tilsit were most onerous for the Prussians, who retained their independence only out of Napoleon's regard for the emperor of Russia. Prussia surrendered all territory west of the Elbe River, the Polish territories it had acquired in the last two partitions of Poland (see POLISH PARTITIONS), from which Napoleon created the Duchy of Warsaw, as well as the port of Danzig (Gdansk), which became a free city. The Prussian army was reduced in size, while the French continued to hold the Prussian forts and provinces they had seized until a war indemnity of 120 million francs was paid. Finally, Prussia agreed to close its ports to British vessels and join the Continental System that was blockading Britain.

Russia fared much better at Tilsit. Together with Prussia it recognized the sovereignty of Napoleon's three brothers as kings of Naples, Holland, and Westphalia. It agreed to withdraw its troops from the Danubian Principalities. In return France recognized in perpetuity Russia's Polish territories. France and Russia agreed to a treaty of alliance that essentially divided political control of Europe between them, an arrangement that lasted until 1812. A meeting in Erfurt in 1808 confirmed the alliance, and France recognized Russia's rights to Finland. Tensions and crises soon began to tear at the alliance. The French considered the Russians an unreliable ally that barely participated in Napoleon's 1809 war against Austria and that, after 1810, had essentially stopped participating in the anti-British blockade. The Russians were not only reluctant to enforce the blockade but also resented France's growing involvement in the Near East and were wary of Napoleon's rearrangement of the central European political map, especially the enlargement of the Duchy of Warsaw. By 1812, Napoleon had made the fateful decision that the invasion of Russia was the best course to further his goals.

Time of Troubles (1598–1613)
(Smutnoe vremia)

A period of dynastic and social instability in Russia between the end of the house of the Rurikids and the establishment of the ROMANOV DYNASTY, the Time of Troubles witnessed widespread social unrest and famine, invasions by Sweden and Poland, and five czars in MOSCOW in the span of 15 years. After the son of IVAN IV, Czar FEODOR I (r. 1584–98), died without children, his brother-

in-law and chief adviser, BORIS GODUNOV, engineered his own election as czar. Boris Godunov's reign (1598–1605) was marked by increasing harassment of nobles who opposed him, famine, and peasant upheavals. In 1604, an army of Poles, COSSACKS, and discontented Russians invaded Muscovy and put forth a pretender, known as FALSE DMITRII. False Dmitrii claimed to be Dmitrii of Uglich, Feodor's younger brother who had died in 1591 at the age of 10 under mysterious circumstances, for which many blamed Boris Godunov. When Boris Godunov, in poor health for many years, died in April 1605, his 16-year-old son Feodor succeeded him as czar. Ruling as FEODOR II, he was unable to gain the full allegiance of the boyar aristocracy who had once supported his father. In June 1605, as the armies of the False Dmitrii were advancing on Moscow, a group of boyars seized Feodor and murdered him and his mother on the orders of the pretender. The False Dmitrii ruled for only one year (1605–6) with the support of influential boyars, who had been ousted by Boris Godunov, and Polish troops. Soon, however, popular feeling turned against him and what was perceived as growing Polish Catholic influence at the court. In June 1606, the boyar Vasilii Shuiskii (r. 1606–10) led the overthrow of the False Dmitrii, whose death was followed by mob violence against his supporters on the streets of Moscow. Shuiskii seized the throne and ruled for the next four years but was violently opposed by Cossacks and some leading boyars. A second "False Dmitrii" appeared in 1608 and camped outside Moscow at Tushino, earning the nickname "the Thief of Tushino," and ruled over a large part of southern Muscovy. In 1610, Shuiskii was ousted by a group of boyars, the second false Dmitrii was killed, and the Russian throne was contested for the next three years. A third and fourth false Dmitrii claimed the throne, but the former was slain in 1611 and the latter was executed in 1613. The boyars offered the crown to the Polish king's son, Wladyslaw, and allowed Polish troops to march into Moscow, while lesser landowners offered it to the Swedish king's brother. With Polish troops sitting in the Kremlin and the possibility of a Polish king on the throne, Patriarch Hermogen helped transform the situation into a campaign of national resistance. After a First National Army fell apart, a Second National Army, led by the Nizhnii Novgorod merchant Kuzma Minin and Prince Dmitrii Pozharsky (see MININ and POZHARSKY), marched on Moscow and captured the Kremlin in 1612. A few months later, in January 1613, a meeting of the ZEMSKII SOBOR (Assembly of the Land) elected as czar the 16-year-old Michael ROMANOV (r. 1613–45), grand nephew of Ivan the Terrible's first wife, the first of the Romanov dynasty that would rule Russia for the next three centuries.

Titov, German Stepanovich (1935–2000)

cosmonaut

With his groundbreaking flight of August 4, 1961, Titov became the second Russian—after Yuri GAGARIN—to fly in space as well as the first one to sleep there. On August 4, 1961, Titov, a major at the time, stunned the world by riding his *Vostok-2* capsule for 17 orbits and an amazing 25 hours and 11 minutes. His impressive flight added more fuel to the space race of the 1960s and compelled the U.S. National Aeronautics and Space Administration (NASA) to stop a more cautious schedule of test flights and, more than six months later, send Lt. Col. John H. Glenn on a three-orbit flight around the earth. Titov's flight was also notable because he became the first human to sleep in a weightless atmosphere and the first to experience space sickness, the nausea that afflicts many astronauts. He later admitted that he almost decided to scrap the flight after a few orbits. Titov was born in Altai, in far south-central Russia, into a teacher's family. He graduated from military pilot's school in 1957 and was sent to a fighter pilot school in Leningrad (St. Petersburg). He was quickly drafted in 1959 into the top-secret space flight program. Titov competed with Gagarin for the pilot's seat on the first manned flight. Although

Titov saw himself as more urbane and better educated than Gagarin, the latter's more engaging personality and peasant background tilted the decision in his favor, especially in the eyes of Nikita KHRUSHCHEV, a key backer of the space program and himself a man of rural background. The August 1961 flight was Titov's first and last. He spent the rest of the decade in the Soviet air force, then returned to the space program as a senior official in the design department, where he helped draft a clone of the American space shuttle. He retired as a staff officer in the Defense Ministry. In 1995 Titov ran successfully for the Russian DUMA (parliament) on the Communist ticket. He wrote several books about space travel, including *The 17 Space Dawns* and *My Blue Planet.* He died on September 10, 2000, in Moscow.

Tkachev, Petr Nikitich (1844–1886)

revolutionary

A representative of the "Jacobin" tradition of conspiratorial revolutionary leadership often portrayed as a precursor of LENIN, Tkachev was born in Pskov province to an impoverished gentry family. He enrolled in St. Petersburg University in 1861, but was jailed soon after for his part in a student protest. He made his name in the 1860s as a revolutionary journalist, but was arrested again in 1869. In 1871, 16 months were added to his sentence for his association with the notorious revolutionary Sergei NECHAEV. Tkachev left Russia for Geneva in December 1873 for a short-lived collaboration with Petr LAVROV on his journal *Vpered!* (*Forward!*). Frustrated by Lavrov's moderate tactics, he founded his own journal, *Nabat* (*Tocsin*), in 1875. Over the following years, Tkachev developed an eclectic set of ideas that drew from the main revolutionary currents of the day. A populist at heart, he went against the mainstream populist belief in the revolutionary capabilities of the Russian peasantry, arguing instead that peasants alone could not carry out a successful revolution. He agreed with Mikhail BAKUNIN's call for an immediate uprising, but he believed in the need for an organized revolutionary elite. A temporary dictatorship would follow armed overthrow of the old order, but it would wither away once people had been educated in socialism. On other issues he remained a populist, believing that Russia needed to avoid going through the capitalist stage and that revolution could occur in Russia first, rather than in industrialized countries, as Marxists had argued. Sensing the imminent emergence of capitalism in Russia, Tkachev made insistent calls for immediate revolution by an organized revolutionary minority; this urgency, some believe, became despair and ultimately accounted for the insanity that claimed the last years of his life.

Tolstoy, Aleksei Nikolaevich (1882–1945)
writer

Born to the same aristocratic family as Lev Tolstoy and related to Ivan TURGENEV on his mother's side, Aleksei Tolstoy is now best remembered as the "comrade Count," because of his support for the Soviet government after the 1920s. He was born in Samara province and in the years before the 1917 Revolution achieved some success with works that satirized the disintegration of the Russian nobility. A supporter of the White cause, he emigrated after the OCTOBER REVOLUTION. While in emigration he completed an autobiographical novel, *Nikita's Childhood* (*Detstvo Nikity*) (1919–22), which foreshadows the success he would later have with historical works. Tolstoy returned to the Soviet Union in 1923, but was first regarded with some suspicion as a "fellow traveler." His published works from the 1920s, such as the futurist novel *Aelita* (1924) about an attempt to establish communism on Mars, while interesting and inventive, did not have the same resonance as his later realistic work, grounded in historical events. By the mid-1930s, however, he was widely praised as an exponent of socialist realism, next to Maksim GORKY and Mikhail SHOLOKHOV. Two works in particular account for his standing in the world of Soviet letters. The first, *The Road to Calvary* (*Khozhdenie po mukam*), a

trilogy written between 1919 and 1941, is a portrayal of the middle-class intelligentsia through the years of World War I and the 1917 Revolutions. The second, *Peter I* (*Petr Pervyi*), begun in 1929 and unfinished at the time of his death, is also a masterpiece of historical re-creation. It attracted the attention of STALIN, who seeing himself in Peter and the Soviet Union's historical moment in that of Petrine Russia, lavished great praise on the book.

Tolstoy, Lev Nikolaevich (1828–1910) (Leo Tolstoy)
writer

Widely considered one of the world's greatest novelists, Tolstoy imbued his writings with a strong moral content that greatly influenced his readers. A count by title, Tolstoy was born into a prominent aristocratic family and raised at the family estate in Yasnaya Polyana, to the south of Moscow. Both his parents died while he was a child, and he was raised by relatives. After a brief stay at Kazan University in 1844 and an attempt at independent study, Tolstoy gave up a formal education. For the next 15 years he drifted between managing the family estate, a life of pleasure in Moscow, and the army. In 1851, Tolstoy traveled to the Caucasus to visit his brother in the army and to enlist as a volunteer. While in the army, he began to write and published his first work, the semiautobiographical *Childhood* (1852), to substantial acclaim. Subsequent installments of his autobiography, *Boyhood* (1854) and *Youth* (1857), were equally well received. Tolstoy served with distinction in the CRIMEAN WAR (1853–56), which also provided the context for some outstanding war journalism, published as *Sebastopol Tales* (1855–56), which praised the heroism of the common soldier and condemned war—themes that would surface in later works. A short novel, *The Cossacks* (1862), also grew from his years in the Caucasus and the army. After the war, Tolstoy was seen as the rising star of Russian literature, but instead he retreated to Yasnaya Polyana in 1859, where he established a school for peasant children and managed the

Count Lev Nikolaevich Tolstoy *(Library of Congress)*

estate. In 1862 he married Sofia Bers, 16 years his junior, settling down to a period of rural domesticity that witnessed some of his greatest written work.

War and Peace, the massive novel about the War of 1812 and to many his greatest literary achievement, was published between 1865 and 1869. Originally intended to be a novel about the ill-fated Decembrist conspirators, the novel developed into a sprawling tableau depicting the lives of over 500 characters, both fictional and historical, with the eye for detail and psychological analysis that were becoming Tolstoy's trademark. The novel also included an extended exposition of a philosophy of history that questioned the impact of great men such as Napoleon on the making of history. His second masterpiece, *Anna Karenina* (1875–77), followed almost a decade later. Tolstoy moved away from the past

to portray the lives of contemporary Russians, focusing on three marriages of varying stability and happiness. He used the story of the leading character's passionate but adulterous affair to criticize the moral hypocrisy of his society.

By the late 1870s, Tolstoy had entered a period of personal turmoil, as he struggled with bouts of depression and embarked on a spiritual journey that led to an embrace of a radical Christianity based solely on universal love and resistance to the evil of violence, which he first chronicled in *A Confession* (1882). Increasingly didactic, Tolstoy wrote widely on topics ranging from capital punishment to vegetarianism, and while his writings brought him into conflict with official society and the Orthodox Church, he found a receptive audience in Russia and beyond. Renewed by his religious commitment, Tolstoy entered a third creative cycle that saw the publication of shorter pieces such as *The Death of Ivan Ilich* (1888); *The Kreutzer Sonata* (1889), which stirred Russian society with its frank discussion of sexual attraction and chastity; and *Resurrection* (1899). In his last published prose work, *Hadji Murad* (1904), Tolstoy returned to the historical fiction and the Caucasus of his younger days. As he tried to live according to the dictates of his increasingly strict beliefs, his relations with his wife deteriorated considerably. In November 1910, Tolstoy abandoned his home but soon contracted pneumonia and died at the village railway station of Astapovo. In his final years an ardent following developed around Tolstoy, much to his discomfort. Visitors traveled to Yasnaya Polyana to see him, while Tolstoyan communities devoted to a simple, nonviolent life sprang up around the world.

Ton, Konstantin Andreevich
(1794–1881)
architect

Born in St. Petersburg, Ton emerged in the mid–nineteenth century as the leading proponent of a "Russian style" in distinction to the classicism that had long prevailed in Russian architecture. His two brothers, Aleksandr Andreevich and

Andrei Andreevich, were also distinguished architects. Ton studied at the St. Petersburg Academy of Arts (1803–15), then moved to Italy (1819–28), where he gained recognition from the Rome and Florence academies. Returning to St. Petersburg in 1831, he was associated with the Academy of Arts for nearly 25 years, first as professor, then as rector. In his work, Ton sought to create a national style that would embody the official ideals of NICHOLAS I's reign: autocracy, Orthodoxy, and nationalism. Although he did not live to see its completion, Ton's greatest work was the Church of Christ the Savior in MOSCOW, built between 1832 and 1893. Intended as a memorial to the War of 1812, the church was a grand project that, when completed, stood over 100 meters in height, second only to the Kremlin in the Moscow skyline. Ton's other major work was the Great Kremlin Palace in Moscow (1838–49). Inside the Kremlin, Ton also constructed the Armory (1844–51), where collections of artworks, historical relics, weapons, and treasures are stored. He was not inflexible in his commitment to a Russian style. He modeled the two train stations he built for the first Russian railroad line (1844–51) on western European town halls, keeping the facades in the style of the Italian Renaissance. This composition and stylistic resolution can be attributed to Ton's understanding of the train stations as public buildings of citywide significance. His identification with the ideology of the autocracy made him a lightning rod for criticism by the late 19th century, when democratic journalism became widespread. In Soviet times, the majority of his churches were destroyed, including the Church of Christ the Savior, razed to make room for a proposed monumental Palace of Soviets that was never built. In the 1990s the church was rebuilt, at great cost and with great fanfare, as one symbol of Russia's break with its Communist past.

Trans-Siberian Railroad

A railway of 5,785 miles linking Moscow with Vladivostok on the Pacific Ocean, first built between 1891 and 1904. The Trans-Siberian railroad has since served as a symbol of the geographical expansiveness of Russia. The idea for the railroad surfaced after the foundation of Vladivostok in 1860. By 1880, Vladivostok had become a major port but lacked an adequate transportation link with European Russia. Planning for the railroad first began in the 1880s under the direction of Sergei WITTE and strong support from Czar ALEXANDER III. Advocates of the railroad believed it would facilitate the eastward movement of peasants from the overpopulated lands of European Russia to the mineral-rich and relatively fertile parts of Siberia. The eastward projection of Russian power and military might into Asia also figured in the arguments that led to the construction of the railroad. With Alexander III's approval, construction began in 1891 under the direction of the newly appointed minister of ways and communications and, later, minister of finance, Sergei Witte. The outbreak of the RUSSO-JAPANESE WAR in 1904 pressured the Russian government to rush the final stages of the railroad, which was first completed in 1905. The original route was a single-track railroad that went eastward from Chelyabinsk in the Urals through Omsk, Novosibirsk, Krasnoyarsk, Irkutsk, and Chita, east of Lake Baikal. From Chita, the railroad cut through Manchuria in China, before reentering Russian territory and reaching Vladivostok. The RUSSO-JAPANESE WAR highlighted the vulnerability of a railroad running through foreign territory. Thus a new line was built between 1908 and 1914 linking Chita with Vladivostok through Russian territory. Cutting through difficult, mountainous terrain, this stretch of the railroad cost almost twice as much per kilometer as that of any other section of the railroad. World War I also showed that there was too much traffic for a single-track railroad. By 1918, despite the turmoil of the Russian Revolution and civil war, most of the railroad had been double-tracked.

Between 1950 and 1970, the railroad was fully electrified. In 1974 another extension of the Trans-Siberian, known as the Baikal-Amur

Mainline (BAM), originally begun in 1938 but continued sporadically since, was given a prominent place in Soviet planning and propaganda, and construction began in earnest until its completion in 1991. The BAM departed from the Trans-Siberian Railroad west of Lake Baikal, circled its northern shore, and reached the Pacific Ocean to the northeast of Khabarovsk. Traversing stunning terrain, it is little used and poorly maintained. In the prerevolutionary era, the journey from one end of the Trans-Siberian to the other took nine days and the International Wagon Lits Company ran a "Trans-Siberian Express," with full amenities such as sleeping cars, library, chapel, and music room for its more affluent passengers. The journey now takes six days, and while passenger trains were best known in post-Soviet times, the Trans-Siberian Railroad has become an important route for container traffic between Europe and the Far East.

Tretiak, Vladislav Aleksandrovich (1952–   )

athlete

Russia's greatest hockey player and one of the most outstanding goaltenders in the history of hockey, Tretiak led Soviet Olympic teams to three gold medals between 1972 and 1984, during a decade that marked the emergence of Soviet hockey on the world stage. He was born in the Moscow suburb of Dmitrovo, and at the age of 10 began playing for the youth organization of the prestigious Central Red Army hockey team (TsKA). Five years later, he was training with the main squad and, in 1968–69, at the age of 17, became a team member. The following year he became the team's starting goaltender, beginning a distinguished career of 16 seasons, during which the Central Red Army team won 13 Soviet league championships. In 1972, the world hockey community witnessed Tretiak's world-class goaltending prowess at the Winter Olympics in Sapporo, Japan, where the Soviet Union won the gold medal in ice hockey. Later that year, the Soviet national team played a

Canadian All-Star team in a memorable series that surprised the heretofore dominant Canadians, who had expected to win with ease. With TsKA and the Soviet national team, Tretiak won numerous honors during his long playing career. From 1970 to 1984, he was chosen every year as goaltender to the Soviet League's First All-Star Team. Starting in 1981, he won the Golden Stick Award given to the best European player for three consecutive years. In addition to the three Olympic gold medals won at Sapporo in 1972, Innsbruck in 1976, and Sarajevo in 1984, Tretiak played in 10 world championships with the Soviet national team, which the team won four times. Curiously, Tretiak was not in goal during the one memorable loss suffered by the Soviet team in this period of international domination: the gold medal game of the 1980 Lake Placid Winter Olympics, won by the United States. Tretiak retired after the 1984 Winter Olympics, frustrated by the rigidity of the Soviet hockey establishment, which prohibited him from playing with the Montreal Canadiens of the National Hockey League (NHL), who had drafted him in 1983. In subsequent years he received offers to coach with the NHL but was not allowed to accept them. Nevertheless, in 1989 he became the first player from outside North America to be inducted into the Hockey Hall of Fame. Two years later, with the collapse of the Soviet Union, Tretiak was finally able to coach in the NHL, when he joined the Chicago Blackhawks. In 2003, he was elected to a seat in the DUMA.

Trifonov, Yuri Valentinovich (1925–1981)

writer

A prominent author from the late BREZHNEV era, Trifonov sketched sharp portraits of Soviet life in the great tradition of Russian realist writing. Trifonov was born in Moscow into the family of an Old BOLSHEVIK. His father, a founding member of the Cheka (czarist secret police), was a military specialist who foresaw an inevitable war with fascism and wrote a manuscript, "The Contours of the Coming War," that called for preparedness against a surprise attack. He was arrested in late 1937 as part of STALIN's purge of the Red Army and executed in 1938.

Trifonov graduated from the Gorky Literary Institute in Moscow in 1949. His first novel, *Students (Studenty)*, appeared in 1950 and was awarded a Stalin Prize in 1951. After Stalin's death in 1953, Trifonov spent most of the next decade trying to rehabilitate his father's name, an account of which he published as *The Campfire's Reflection* in 1965. He is best known for the realistic, contemporary cycle of novellas that appeared in the journal *Novyi mir,* where he chronicled the growing demoralization of the intelligentsia. Because Trifonov treated this topic from psychological rather than a political standpoint, his work was published without excessive interference from the censorship apparatus. His *House on the Embankment* (*Dom na Naberezhnoi*) (1976) was an instant success. Its title refers to the large gray apartment building across the Moscow River from the Kremlin, whose spacious apartments were reserved for members of the Soviet elite. Through fictionalized stories of some of its residents, Trifonov describes a world of cynical careerism, moral compromises, and heavy drinking that resonated with Soviet readers for its honesty and sensitivity. *The Old Man* (*Starik*) (1979) contrasts the pettiness and drabness of late Soviet life with the turbulence of the revolutionary years. His last novel, *Time and Place* (*Vremia i mesto*) (1981), deals in an openly critical manner with the then taboo topic of Stalin and his legacy. He died suddenly at the height of his creative powers on March 28, 1981, after complications from surgery.

Trotsky, Leon (1879–1940)
(Lev Davidovich)

revolutionary and Soviet official

A revolutionary, theorist, and prolific writer on a wide range of topics, next to Vladimir LENIN Trotsky played a central role in organizing the OCTOBER REVOLUTION of 1917 and consolidating Soviet

Leon Trotsky *(Library of Congress)*

power during the Russian civil war. Trotsky was born Lev Davidovich Bronstein to a relatively prosperous Jewish family in the Ukrainian village of Yanovka. At the top of his class in school in Nikolaev, the Ukraine, he joined the Social Democratic Party in 1896, a year before completing his secondary studies, then helped establish an illegal workers' organization, the South Russian Workers' Union. Arrested at the age of 19, he spent two and a half years in prison, and was then exiled to Siberia. In 1902, he escaped from Siberia and, adopting the name Trotsky, joined Lenin in London. Although Trotsky and Lenin worked closely together on the newspaper *Iskra* (*The Spark*), when the divisions within the Social Democratic movement hardened into two factions—BOLSHEVIKS and Mensheviks—at the London Congress in 1903, Trotsky sided with the Menshevik position. Trotsky returned to St. Petersburg during the 1905 Revolution and played an important role in the newly established St. Petersburg Soviet, a council that expressed workers' aspirations, eventually becoming its chairman. He was arrested in 1906 and banished to Siberia, but again he escaped, this time settling in Vienna. While in prison he worked out the theory of "permanent revolution," his signature contribution to Marxist theory. Trotsky argued that instead of a working-class revolution being preceded by a capitalist revolution, as traditional Marxists held, a revolution in Russia would trigger socialist revolutions elsewhere in Europe, which would in turn guarantee the success of the Russian revolution.

The outbreak of World War I in 1914 and his outspoken opposition to the war forced Trotsky to move often. He left Vienna for Zurich, and in November 1914 he moved to Paris, where he became one of the editors of *Nashe slovo* (*Our Word*), the Social Democratic newspaper. He was arrested by the French police in November 1916 and deported to Spain, from where he traveled to New York City, arriving in January 1917 to work with Nikolai BUKHARIN and Aleksandra KOLLONTAI on the revolutionary newspaper *Novy mir.* Trotsky's American sojourn was cut short by the FEBRUARY REVOLUTION in Russia. He arrived in Petrograd in May 1917 and, disapproving of the Menshevik support for the Provisional Government, joined the Bolsheviks in July. Trotsky was among those arrested by the Provisional Government in the aftermath of the JULY DAYS, an attempted Bolshevik insurrection. By late September, with the political pendulum again favoring the Bolsheviks, Trotsky was released and quickly named chairman of the Petrograd Soviet. As a member of the Petrograd Revolutionary Committee, Trotsky was instrumental in planning the Bolshevik takeover of October 25, 1917 (November 7 by the Western calendar).

As the first Soviet people's commissar of foreign affairs, Trotsky conducted negotiations with Germany to end Russia's involvement in World War I. He tried to delay a settlement, hoping for a socialist revolution in Germany, but with German troops marching toward Petrograd, Trotsky was ordered by Lenin to accept German terms and sign the Treaty of BREST-LITOVSK, surrendering large portions of Russian territory. Trotsky's accomplishments as commissar of war were more substantial. To fight the civil war, he built a Red Army, often with great ruthlessness, drafting former czarist officers for their expertise, much to the concern of many revolutionaries. Although the Bolshevik victory in the civil war validated Trotsky's organizational gamble, his other ideas, such as state control of trade unions and militarization of labor, engendered great resistance in the Communist Party.

Lenin's death in 1924 left Trotsky without a major ally and placed him in the middle of a fierce succession struggle. Resented by many colleagues for a brilliance that bordered on arrogance, Trotsky proved less nimble at political infighting than he had been at organizing armies and was quickly outmaneuvered by his rivals, especially Joseph STALIN. The clash with Stalin was personal and ideological, the product of a rivalry that went back to the civil war but also grounded in differing conceptions of the revolutionary process. While Trotsky supported the extension of revolution throughout the world as the best way to ensure the survival of the Russian Revolution, Stalin advocated the idea of "socialism in one country." Ironically, in the late 1920s Stalin co-opted Trotsky's ideas about rapid industrialization in drafting the system of five-year plans. In 1925, Trotsky was dismissed from his post as commissar of war, and the following year he was expelled from the ruling Politburo of the COMMUNIST PARTY. In 1927, after repeatedly denouncing Stalin, he was expelled from the party itself. After a year of internal exile in Alma-Ata (Almaty) in Central Asia, in 1929 he was ordered to leave the Soviet Union. Considered a dangerous revolutionary and pressured by the Soviet government, Trotsky was refused admission by several countries, and moved from

Turkey to France to Norway before accepting an offer of asylum from Mexico in 1936. He founded the Fourth International as a vehicle to oppose Stalinism and advance his views of world revolution. After 1929, his defeat and exile gave Trotsky the time to write extensively, and some of his longer-lasting works belong to this period, including the autobiography *My Life* (1930), a three-volume *History of the Russian Revolution* (1931–33), and *The Revolution Betrayed* (1937), a critical analysis of Stalinist Russia. In August 1940, after one unsuccessful attempt on his life, a Soviet agent infiltrated Trotsky's compound in the suburbs of Mexico City and assassinated him, the last of the Old Bolsheviks eliminated by Stalin.

Tsiolkovsky, Konstantin Eduardovich (1857–1935)
inventor

Considered the father of Soviet rocket design, Tsiolkovsky was a visionary pioneer in the study of aviation, rocketry, and the theory of cosmic travel. Born in the village of Izhevskoe in Ryazan oblast, Tsiolkovsky lost much of his hearing in a childhood accident. He largely educated himself during his early years, then took correspondence courses, gained certification as an instructor, and taught mathematics, physics, and geometry at the Borovsk District College in Kaluga province (1880–92). In 1892 he became an instructor at the Kaluga Gymnasium and the College of Kaluga Diocese. He began his scientific research with studies of design for metal dirigibles and improved aircraft, then turned to problems of jet flight and space travel. In 1903 he published a scientific paper in which he discussed the possibility of exploring space with jet-driven vehicles. In later papers he laid out the principles for constructing a jet engine, depicted multistage rockets, and argued for the possibility of launching earth satellites into orbit. Tsiolkovsky also studied the social problems that would be encountered by people living on artificial orbital islands. By the 1920s, with widespread popular interest in aviation and science fiction, Tsiolkovsky became a public figure. His work was extremely influential in shaping the practical research of the first generation of Soviet rocket scientists. He died on September 19, 1935. A two-volume edition of his collected writings was published in 1934, a second version in 1962.

Tsoi, Viktor Robertovich (1962–1990)
musician

An influential rock musician whose early death earned him a central place in the pantheon of Russian and Soviet youth. Tsoi was born in Leningrad. At the age of 12 he organized his first group, Palata no. 6, which was disbanded three years later. Another group, Garin i Giperboloidy, established in 1981, served as the predecessor to Kino, the group that would insure his reputation with Soviet youth in the 1980s. The first version of Kino was formed in 1982, and the group toured with the legendary Akvarium. In 1984, Kino released one of their best-known albums, *Nachalnik Kamchatki,* which solidified its cultish reputation among Soviet youth. Later that year a second version of Kino was formed, with Tsoi remaining the group's central presence. The group's popularity and Tsoi's own status as a genuine Soviet rock star grew with the relaxation of political control during the GORBACHEV years of the late 1980s; this translated into greater recording opportunities and record sales. In addition, Tsoi pursued an acting career, appearing in several films, including *Assa* (1986), a film that was considered controversial when released in the early years of Gorbachev's rule. In the late 1980s, Tsoi and Kino took advantage of new opportunities to record and travel, and the group embarked on tours of the United States and Japan. His tragic death on August 15, 1990, in a motorcycle crash deprived the Russian and Soviet music world of a highly creative musician, while cementing his iconic status among Russian and Soviet youth. Soon after his death a "Wall of Viktor Tsoi" appeared on the centrally located Arbat Street in Moscow, where fans could inscribe messages.

Tsushima, Battle of (1905)

The final and decisive naval battle of the RUSSO-JAPANESE WAR of 1904–5 in the course of which most of Russia's lumbering Baltic Sea Fleet was sunk or captured by a more mobile Japanese fleet led by Admiral Heihachiro Togo. The Baltic Sea Fleet, under the command of Admiral Zinovy Rozhdestvensky, had left St. Petersburg in October 1904 to relieve the Pacific Fleet that had been captured in Port Arthur in the initial stages of the war. The battle took place from May 27 to May 29, 1905, near Tsushima Island in the Sea of Japan between Japan and Korea. By the time the battle had ended with a Japanese victory, the Russian fleet had lost 20 of its warships and more than 4,000 sailors, while three admirals, including Rozhdestvensky, and more than 7,000 sailors were captured. In turn, Japan lost three torpedo boats and 116 sailors. After the Battle of Tsushima, even with Japan the clear victor, both sides were ready for an armistice. Japan requested that U.S. president Theodore Roosevelt serve as the mediator for a peace treaty, and negotiations were completed in Portsmouth, New Hampshire, in August 1905.

Tsvetaeva, Marina Ivanovna (1892–1941)

poet

An inventive and tempestuous poet, Tsvetaeva was born in Moscow and brought up in a cultured family that traveled frequently to western Europe. She began writing at the age of 10, and later joined a circle of young writers and playwrights that became the Third Studio of the Moscow Arts Theater. Her personal life was difficult. She married early and survived the Russian Revolution and civil war alone with her daughter in Moscow, while another daughter died. In 1922 she followed her husband, Sergei Efron, a former White officer, into emigration in Germany and Czechoslovakia, before settling in Paris in 1925, where they lived in poverty. Again following her husband, who by now had switched political sympathies and worked for the Soviet secret police, she returned with her son to Moscow in 1939. She briefly worked as a translator but was not allowed to publish her own work. Evacuated to the Tatar Autonomous Republic after the outbreak of World War II, with her husband and daughter arrested, and unable to find work of any kind, she took her own life on August 31, 1941, in the town of Elabuga, on the Kama River. Tsvetaeva was a writer of strong and simple fundamental ideas, all essentially romantic: the isolation and sanctity of the creative artist; the injustice and inhumanity of bourgeois society; the moral superiority of the individual over the mass; the impossibility of reciprocated sexual love; the sordid inadequacy of material reality. More personal is her passionate commitment to lost causes. She worked in cycles moving from romantic to classical dramas to longer poems, including her two masterpieces *Poema gory* (*Poem of the Mountain*) (Paris, 1926) and *Poema kontsa* (*Poem of the End*) (Prague, 1926). In the 1930s she turned to criticism and autobiography, at which she also excelled. Her work was not published in the Soviet Union until the 1960s, when she was hailed as one of the four great Russian poets of the 20th century, along with Anna AKHMATOVA, Osip MANDELSTAM, and Boris PASTERNAK.

Tukhachevsky, Mikhail Nikolaevich (1893–1937)

military commander

Tukhachevsky was the leading Soviet military strategist of his time and one of the principal victims of STALIN's 1937 purge of the officer corps. He was born to a noble family and grew up in Penza and Moscow. He received his military training first from the Moscow Cadet Corps and then the Alexandrov Military Academy, from which he graduated in 1914. At the time of World War I he was posted to the Imperial Guards. In 1915 he was captured and sent to Germany as a prisoner of war. After several attempts, he finally succeeded in escaping to Switzerland in October 1917. Back in Russia, he joined the BOLSHEVIK Party in April 1918 and volunteered for the Red Army. As a Red Army officer, his career was impressive. His first appointment was as military commissar of the Moscow district. As army commander in 1918–19, he fought successfully on several fronts: with the First Army he captured Simbirsk, in Siberia he routed KOLCHAK's troops, and in the south he captured Novorossiisk from DENIKIN. In early 1920 he was appointed commander of the Red Army in the Caucasus. Later that year he was transferred to the western front, where he led Soviet forces in the 1920 SOVIET-POLISH WAR. Tukhachevsky had been one of the leading advocates of using the Red Army to support the spread of socialist revolution, and the Soviet-Polish War provided a concrete opportunity to do so. Soviet forces came within striking distance of Warsaw, but at the Battle of the Vistula they were repelled by the Poles. Strained lines of communication and poor coordination with the First Cavalry, led by BUDENNY, contributed to the defeat. Although he may have gained the long-term enmity of Stalin, the defeat in Warsaw did not hinder Tukhachevsky's career. In 1921 he commanded the Soviet forces that suppressed the sailors' uprising at the Kronstadt naval base and the ANTONOV UPRISING in Tambov province, two final chapters of the Russian civil war. Then, in succession he became director of the Military Academy (1921), commander of the Western Front (1922), deputy chief of staff (1924), and chief of staff of the Red Army and member of the Revolutionary Military Council (RMC; 1925). In 1931, he became deputy commissar for military and naval affairs and deputy chairman of the RMC. Further proof of his preeminent status in the Soviet military world came in 1935, when he became one of the first marshals of the Red Army. Two years later, however, as part of a wide-ranging purge of the military that eventually took the lives of 35,000 officers, Tukhachevsky was charged with conspiracy,

secretly tried, and executed. Tukhachevsky was officially rehabilitated in 1958.

Tupolev, Andrei Nikolaevich (1888–1972)
aircraft designer

A brilliant aeronautical engineer of international standing, Tupolev was born in the Tver region, northwest of Moscow. He studied under Nikolai Zhukovsky at the Moscow Higher Technical School and went on to play a key role in the development of Russian and Soviet aviation. In 1916 he established the Aerodynamic Aircraft Design Bureau, renamed the Central Aerodynamics and Hydrodynamics Institute after the October Revolution. During the 1930s he helped develop heavy bombers such as the Ant-25, but he was arrested in 1937 on the fabricated charge of selling designs to Nazi Germany. Like other prominent arrested scientists, he was placed in a special labor camp (*sharaga*), where he continued to design airplanes. The success of the Tu-2 bomber facilitated his release and rehabilitation in 1943. After 1945 he contributed to the development of over 100 other dual-purpose civilian and military aircraft, including the passenger aircraft Tu-104 and the Tu-144. The latter was the Soviet version of the Franco-British Concorde supersonic airplane, which was a commercial failure. (According to Soviet practice the letters in an aircraft's name indicate the main designer and the number indicates the number of planes the designer has produced up to that point.) Tupolev attained the rank of lieutenant general and was elected to the USSR ACADEMY OF SCIENCES in 1953, but he never joined the COMMUNIST PARTY. His son Andrei continued in his footsteps, designing civil and military aircraft.

Turgenev, Ivan Sergeevich (1818–1883)
writer

Although one of the most prominent authors of the Golden Age of Russian literature in the 19th century, and the first to gain an international reputation, Turgenev was overshadowed in his lifetime by Lev TOLSTOY and Feodor DOSTOEVSKY. Turgenev was born in Orel in central Russia to a well-established aristocratic family and later educated in St. Petersburg and Berlin. His writer's education took place on his family's estates, where he witnessed the inequities of SERFDOM and the Russian social system, a recurrent theme in his major works. After a short stint as a civil servant in St. Petersburg, Turgenev devoted himself to his literary career. Beginning with his long poem *Parasha* (1843) and the short stories that established him as an important writer, he developed an elegantly crafted, lucid style with a relatively balanced point of view. Nevertheless, Turgenev could not avoid taking part in the debates that divided Russian intellectuals in the period between the 1840s and 1870s. In the protracted debate between Slavophiles, who championed Russian traditions, and Westernizers, who sought to make Russia more European, Turgenev sided with the latter (see SLAVOPHILES AND WESTERNERS). His first important work was *Sportman's Sketches,* published in 1852, whose vigorous attacks on serfdom found wide resonance in Russian educated society and helped shape the intellectual climate that provided the foundation for the emancipation of the serfs in 1861. During the 1850s, Turgenev continued to publish well-received novels such as *Rudin* (1856), *A House of Gentlefolk* (1859), and *On the Eve* (1860), which portrayed the fears and aspirations of Russian educated society in the midst of broader social and political changes. But it was *Fathers and Sons,* published in 1862, that made the deepest impact at the time of its publication and has lived on to become a classic of Russian and world literature. Considered to be his masterpiece, *Fathers and Sons* addressed the issues of how to bring change to Russia through the timeless vehicle of generational conflict. Through the main character, an idealistic young radical student named Bazarov, Turgenev captured the feelings of an impatient younger generation ready to embrace new ideologies and

Ivan Sergeevich Turgenev, ca. 1880 *(Library of Congress)*

tactics such as nihilism and revolution. Controversial at the time of its publication, the novel was criticized by both the older and younger generations portrayed in the book, even though Turgenev seemed to sympathize with Bazarov's outlook while preferring gradual to revolutionary change. Other important, though less influential, novels followed *Fathers and Sons,* such as *Smoke* (1867) and *Virgin Soil* (1877). After 1855, Turgenev gradually distanced himself from Russia, living first in Germany and after 1870 in Paris, where he was drawn by his love for the celebrated opera singer Pauline Viardot-Garcia. With the French translations of his works, Turgenev achieved international recognition. He died near Paris in September 1883.

Tvardovsky, Aleksandr Trofimovich (1910–1971)

poet and editor

An accomplished poet, Tvardovsky is perhaps best remembered as the editor of the influential literary journal *Novyi mir* (*New World*) during the period of cultural de-Stalinization. Tvardovsky was born to a peasant family in the Smolensk region that was later classified as KULAK and stripped of its possessions. He graduated from the Moscow Institute of Philosophy and Literature in 1939 and joined the COMMUNIST PARTY in 1940. During the 1930s his poetry lauded collectivization and he became the most popular poet in the country while a war correspondent from 1939 onward. Tvardovsky first reported on the collectivization of agriculture for local newspapers, and he was later a war correspondent during World War II. The rural themes of his youth inform his best poetry, as in *Muravia Country* (1936), and his masterpiece and most popular work, the long narrative poem *Vasilii Terkin (Tyorkin)*, a brilliant picture of the life and travails of a simple Russian private soldier. Appointed editor of *Novyi mir* in 1950, he was well positioned to help shape the post-Stalin cultural thaw once it became politically possible to do so. He published his poem *Far Distances*, a critique of the mechanisms that ensured literary conformity, as well as nonconformist articles by young critics. He was dismissed from the editorship in 1954 but reinstated in 1958 in a more favorable political climate. During his tenure as editor, *Novyi mir* became a hugely influential literary journal. In 1962, with KHRUSHCHEV's permission, he published Aleksandr SOLZHENITSYN's *One Day in the Life of Ivan Denisovich*, about the previously taboo topic of life in the slave labor camp system. With the consolidation of the BREZHNEV regime and a more conservative cultural climate, his influence waned. In 1966, his closeness to Solzhenitsyn cost him the status of candidate member of the Central Committee that he had received in 1961. A sequel to *Vasily Terkin* was bitter and morose. He was ousted as editor in 1970 and died the following year. He was buried in Novodevichy Cemetery. In 1988 Mikhail GORBACHEV decided to donate the royalties from his works to a foundation to erect a memorial to Tvardovsky.

Tver

A city in western Russia with a population of almost half a million, Tver was one of the ancient cities that competed unsuccessfully with MOSCOW in the 14th and 15th centuries. Tver was founded in 1135 at the confluence of the Volga and Tversa Rivers. In the early 14th century Tver emerged from a period of fluid political boundaries as a major competitor of the principalities of Moscow, Vladimir, and Rostov for political hegemony in the area. Some of the princes of Tver held the rank of grand prince, but they served at the mercy of the Mongol khans. In 1327 the Mongols sent a punitive expedition against Tver that devastated the town. In the mid-14th century Tver again challenged Moscow for supremacy but lost out, remaining an independent principality until 1485, when Muscovite troops annexed it during the reign of IVAN III. Much of the city was destroyed by fire in 1763. In the late 19th century members of the Tver gentry were known for their liberalism. In 1862 the provincial assembly of Tver gentry renounced their privileges and called for a constituent assembly. In 1878 the Tver gentry called for the establishment of a constitution along the lines of the one ALEXANDER II had granted to newly independent Bulgaria. From 1933 to 1990, during the Soviet era, Tver was known as Kalinin, in honor of Mikhail Kalinin, ceremonial head of state of the Soviet Union from 1919 to 1946. With a 1995 population of close to 480,000 Tver remains an important manufacturing center.

U

U-2 Incident

On May 1, 1960, an American U-2 high-altitude reconnaissance plane left Peshawar, Pakistan, and flew over Soviet territory on a spying mission. This was not the first U-2 plane to fly over the Soviet Union, leading the Soviet army to improve its antiaircraft weapons. The plane was shot down and its pilot, Gary Francis Powers, was captured. Powers survived against great odds, when his defective parachute opened and ejected him. When he landed unconscious, he was discovered by a Soviet farmer before he could take the cyanide capsule issued to him by his superiors. When U.S. President Dwight D. Eisenhower denied knowledge of such spy flights, the Soviets produced Powers, to the embarrassment of the U.S. government. The incident triggered an international diplomatic crisis between the two superpowers that undid improvements in diplomatic relations over the previous years, including the visit of Soviet leader Nikita KHRUSHCHEV to the United States in September 1959. Although Eisenhower eventually apologized for the incident and the United States suspended U-2 flights over the USSR, the Soviets were not appeased and a planned summit of the four powers—United States, Soviet Union, Great Britain, and France—was canceled.

Under Soviet questioning, Powers admitted to being an American spy and after a highly public trial, he was sentenced to three years in prison and seven years of hard labor. Twenty-one months into his sentence, the Soviet and U.S. governments worked out a deal to free Powers. On February 10, 1962, at the Glienicker Bridge separating East from West Berlin, Powers was released to American authorities in exchange for Colonel Rudolph Abel (Willie Fisher), a Soviet spy who had been imprisoned since 1957 on charges of atomic espionage.

Ugra River, Battle of the (1480)

A bloodless confrontation that took place between Muscovite and Mongol armies on the banks of the Ugra River, 150 miles southwest of Moscow, the Battle of the Ugra River traditionally marks the end of Mongol rule in Russia. The events that led to the confrontation were sparked by the grand prince of Moscow IVAN III's public declaration that he would no longer pay tribute to the khan of the GOLDEN HORDE at SARAI, ending a period of almost 240 years during which Russian princes had paid allegiance to the Mongols. Already concerned about Ivan III's prior policy of increasingly limiting his allegiance to the Mongols by sending token presents rather than paying tribute, the Mongol khan AKHMED had sent punitive expeditions against Moscow in 1465 and 1472 that failed to bring Ivan to heel. With Ivan's public renunciation of allegiance, the stage was set for a decisive showdown. In preparation, Akhmed had forged an alliance with Casimir IV of Lithuania, while Ivan had enlisted the help of Mengli-Gerai, khan of Crimea, which had formerly been part of the Golden Horde. On the eve of the battle, the Mongol and Muscovite armies aligned on opposite banks of the Ugra River, but no fighting occurred. Akhmed's Lithuanian allies never arrived because they were fighting a Crimean raid into Lithuania. Akhmed's own army retreated to Sarai upon news of a raid by allies of Ivan. Despite later attempts by Muscovite chroniclers to embellish the military aspects of

Ivan's victory, the importance of the Battle of the Ugra River was mostly symbolic. Mongol power had already been declining over the past century, but despite the Muscovite victory, the Mongols would continue to threaten Moscow through most of the 16th century.

Ulanova, Galina Sergeyevna (1910–1998)
ballet dancer

Praised as one of the greatest Russian dancers since Anna PAVLOVA, Ulanova was the prima ballerina of the Bolshoi Theater from 1944 until her retirement in 1962. Born in St. Petersburg, she was the daughter of Sergei Ulanov and Maria Romanova, two dancers at the Imperial, or Mariinskii, Theater (renamed Kirov in Soviet times) of St. Petersburg. After the OCTOBER REVOLUTION of 1917, she studied at the Petrograd School of Choreography, first with her mother and eventually with Agrippina Vaganova, an important influence on her career. In 1928, she made her debut with the Kirov Ballet in Leningrad (St. Petersburg), where she performed until 1944. Ulanova's lyrical and direct style, rooted in the best traditions of prerevolutionary ballet, had a great impact on the further development of Soviet ballet. Ulanova excelled in Soviet ballets such as *The Fountain of Bachkisarai* (1934), as well as classical works such as *Swan Lake* and *Giselle*. She also created the role of Juliet for Lavroski's version of *Romeo and Juliet* by Sergei PROKOFIEV. Ulanova first appeared at the Bolshoi Theater in 1935 and, almost a decade later, became prima ballerina. Relatively unknown outside the Soviet Union, her first foreign appearance was in Florence, Italy, in 1951. A tour of England in 1956 established her reputation as one of the best dancers in the world. After her official retirement in 1962, she taught at the Bolshoi Theater and became its mistress ballerina. She was also noted for her superb acting, which translated well into films such as *Giselle* and *Romeo and Juliet*. She received numerous prizes, including the Stalin Prize (four times), People's Artist of the USSR, and, in 1974, the Lenin Order.

Ulianov, Mikhail Aleksandrovich (1927–)
actor

One of the most popular and versatile actors of his generation, Ulianov also played an important role in the late 1980s advancing Mikhail GORBACHEV's agenda of glasnost (openness) and perestroika (restructuring) in the world of theater. Ulianov was born in Tara, a remote Siberian town, to a peasant family. In 1945 he left to study acting in Omsk, but after one year he transferred to the Shchukin School of Theater in Moscow. After graduation in 1952, he joined the repertory company of the prestigious Vakhtangov Theater. As an actor, Ulianov became best known to audiences of the Soviet era for his portrayals of LENIN and Marshal ZHUKOV on the stage and screen. His insightful and complex portrayal of Yegor Trubnikov, a disabled war veteran who returns to his village to serve as chairman of a collective farm in the acclaimed film *The Chairman* (1964), won him a LENIN PRIZE. A COMMUNIST PARTY member since 1951, Ulianov became a staunch supporter of Mikhail Gorbachev after 1985, and he joined the Central Committee of the Communist Party. When theater professionals followed the example of the Filmmakers' Union and formed a Russian Theater Workers Union in October 1986 to break the stranglehold of party bureaucrats on the Soviet theater, they elected Ulianov as its director. In 1987 he was appointed artistic director of the Vakhtangov Theater. In 1989, together with other prominent progressive Soviet cultural personages, he was elected to the groundbreaking Congress of People's Deputies.

Ungern-Sternberg, Baron Roman Feodorovich von (1885–1921)
military commander

Known as the "mad Baron," Ungern-Sternberg was with Grigorii SEMENOV, one of the anti-Bolshevik Cossack commanders who ruled vast stretches of the Lake Baikal region and Mongolia during the Russian civil war. Ungern-Sternberg was born into a noble Baltic German family in Livonia (present-day southern Estonia). Details about his early years are sketchy except that he became an officer in the Czarist army, and like Semenov, served as squadron commander of the Nerchinsk Cossacks under Petr WRANGEL's command. Nominally subordinate to Semenov, during the civil war Ungern-Sternberg took his division of Cossack cavalry into Mongolia in October 1920. He captured the Mongolian capital Nyslel Huree in February 1921, which he made his headquarters, and took the Mongolian ruler, the Bogd Khan, hostage. Ungern-Sternberg recruited a core of Mongol troops with promises of loot and restoring the glory of the era of Genghis Khan. He adopted Mongolian dress, which he complemented with his Russian badges and decorations, including the St. George's Cross. Ungern-Sternberg's personal cruelty stands out in a cruel period. Accounts coincide in painting a portrait of a bizarre, even deranged, "puny-looking" man who personally ordered the flogging, torture, shooting, and slaughter of his prisoners, men and women alike. By May 1921, Red Army troops were assisting the indigenous Mongolian Revolutionary Army in their struggle against Ungern-Sternberg. Defeated in an early encounter, Ungern-Sternberg turned westward and north into the present-day Buriat Republic, where he confronted the Red Army near Lake Gusinoye in August 1921. As he retreated back into Mongolia, he was captured on August 22. Accounts of his death vary in the details. Mongol sources state that Ungern-Sternberg was taken by the BOLSHEVIKS to Novonikolaevsk (now Novosibirsk), tried, and executed on September 15, 1921, while other sources place his execution a few days later, almost 1,000 miles away in Irkutsk.

Ustinov, Dmitrii Feodorovich
(1908–1984)
Soviet official

Dmitri Ustinov was a highly influential member of Leonid BREZHNEV's inner circle in the 1970s and 1980s who, as defense minister, succeeded in advancing the interests and status of the Soviet military to an unchallenged position inside the Soviet government. Born in the Volga River town of Samara, Ustinov studied engineering and received degrees from Moscow's Bauman Higher Technical School and the Leningrad Military Technical Institute in 1934. A party member since 1927, after graduation he directed the eponymously named Bolshevik arms factory in Leningrad. In 1941 at the outset of the war with Nazi Germany, he was appointed people's commissar for arms industry, a position he held until 1946. In this capacity he supervised the transfer of many Soviet industries eastward from the western regions to safety in the Urals and beyond. As minister of armaments (1946–53), Ustinov was actively involved in promoting Soviet rocketry by gathering information from captured German scientists. In 1953 he became minister of defense industry and again played an important role in developing space research. After serving as deputy chair of the USSR Council of Ministers from 1957, in 1963 he was promoted to first deputy chair with responsibility for the defense sector. Ustinov's career in the COMMUNIST PARTY ranks also progressed smoothly in the postwar period. In 1952 Ustinov became a member of the Central Committee. Closely allied to Brezhnev, in 1965 he was appointed Central Committee secretary with responsibility for the defense industry and made a candidate member to the Politburo. From 1976 until his death, he reached one of the pinnacles of Soviet power, joining the Politburo as a full member and succeeding Marshal Andrei Grechko as USSR minister of defense, the first civilian in Soviet history to hold that rank. Ustinov was promptly given the rank of marshal, allegedly to counter the reluctance of top military officers to follow orders from a civilian. With Brezhnev in poor health, Ustinov was, together with Mikhail SUSLOV and Andrei GROMYKO, one of the kingmakers in the Kremlin during the final years of Brezhnev's long rule, playing a key role in the decision to invade AFGHANISTAN in 1979 and in selecting Yuri ANDROPOV and then Konstantin CHERNENKO as successors to Brezhnev. He died in December 1984.

V

Vasili I (1371–1425)
(Vasilii Dmitrievich)
ruler

The second son of DMITRII DONSKOI, who defeated the Mongols at the Battle of KULIKOVO in 1380, Vasili was grand prince of MOSCOW from 1389 to 1425. Vasili was a cautious ruler, criticized by some as indecisive, who enlarged the territories of Moscow at the expense of its neighbors while balancing threats from Lithuania and the GOLDEN HORDE. Vasili also had to contend with Russian challenges to the growing supremacy of Moscow, particularly from Tver and Ryazan. In 1399, the princes of Tver and Ryazan agreed never to challenge for the throne of Moscow. Despite his father's victory at Kulikovo, Russian princes still had to pay tribute to the Tatars, and Vasili continued to journey to SARAI, the Tatar capital. During his reign, however, the power of the Golden Horde was considerably weakened by Tamerlane (Timur), who decisively defeated the Mongols, led by Toqtamish, in 1395. Nevertheless, the Tatars attacked Moscow in 1408 in punishment for its failure to pay tribute to the Tatar Khan Idiqu, forcing Vasili to flee to nearby Kostroma. The city of Moscow was not damaged, but the Tatars did extensive damage to the principality. Although he married Sofia, the daughter of the grand prince of Lithuania in 1391 and signed an alliance with her father, Vitvot (Vitold), Vasili witnessed continued tensions with Lithuania during his reign.

Vasili II (1415–1462)
(Vasili Vasilievich)
ruler

Also known as Vasili the Blind, Vasili was the fifth son of VASILI I and Sofia, daughter of the grand prince of Lithuania, who became grand prince of MOSCOW in 1425, at the age of 10. His four older brothers had all previously died. Vasili's reign witnessed a complicated political situation with three civil wars occurring almost simultaneously for the thrones of Moscow, Lithuania, and the Golden Horde, even as the three states continued their struggle for supremacy in the region. Of most lasting significance, the Golden Horde splintered into feuding khanates during Vasili's reign, to Moscow's great benefit. In 1444, the Tatar khan, Uleg Mahmed, began hostilities against Moscow, capturing Vasili in battle in July 1445. While in captivity, Vasili took advantage of divisions and resentments amongst the khan's sons, especially after one of them, Mahmudek, murdered his father and took control of the Mongol army. In the fall of 1445, he established the Khanate of KAZAN, the first of various territories to break off from the Golden Horde. Back in Moscow, Vasili was challenged in his claim to the throne by his cousin Dmitrii Shemiaka as well as Vasili the Squint-eyed. Dmitrii Shemiaka temporarily deposed Vasili, but by 1452 he had been defeated, often with the help of Tatar princes. In repayment, Vasili helped another of Uleg Mahmud's sons, Kasim, establish his own khanate.

Renamed the Khanate of Kasimov in 1471 after Kasim's death, this was the first Tatar state to accept Russian suzerainty, an important step in the ongoing struggle between Russians and Tatars. Although Tatar armies reached and burned the outskirts of Moscow in 1452, Vasili repealed their attack. In 1456, Vasili then attacked Novgorod, one of Moscow's historic rivals, which had sheltered Dmitrii Shemiaka after his defeat and forced it to sign a treaty that further limited its autonomy, a prelude to its full annexation by Muscovy after his death. Vasili was succeeded by his second son, Ivan, who reigned as IVAN III and completed the process of shaking off Tatar rule and consolidating Moscow as Russia's preeminent principality.

Vasili III (1479–1533)
(Vasilii Ivanovich)
ruler

Grand prince of Muscovy. Vasili was the son of IVAN III (the Great) by his second marriage to Sophia (Zoe) Paleologos, niece of the last Byzantine emperor, Constantine XI. Vasili was an active, energetic man who enjoyed hunting and religious pilgrimages. As grand prince, from 1505 to 1533, he continued the policy "of gathering of the lands" begun by his father, establishing control over Pskov in 1511 and Ryazan in 1517. War with Muscovy's neighbors, Lithuania, Crimea, and KAZAN, was an almost constant feature of Vasili's reign. Relations with the Crimean Khanate to the south were particularly troublesome as the Crimea broke off its previous alliance with Muscovy and, in 1512, joined Lithuania in making war on Muscovy. Crimean forces plundered the suburbs of MOSCOW in 1521 and, even though in the aftermath of these campaigns, Vasili organized a relatively effective frontier system, for the next two centuries Moscow's southern frontier witnessed many confrontations. To the east, the appointment of two pro-Muscovy khans in Kazan (Kasimov) in 1519 and 1532 testified to Muscovy's growing ascendancy over Kazan. Nevertheless, even though Muscovy built the fortress of Vasilsursk (Vasili's fortress) in 1523, the actual conquest of the city would have to wait until the reign of Vasili's son, IVAN IV, in 1552. Vasili's reign continued the emergence of Muscovy's importance begun by his father when he formally repudiated that Tatar yoke in 1480. Like Ivan III, Vasili was open to Western (particularly Italian) influences that are most evident in the Renaissance styles introduced in the Moscow Kremlin at this time. The foreign settlement in Moscow, known as the "German settlement," grew during this time. Vasili himself adopted the beardless look popular in the West, to the great consternation of traditional Orthodox authorities. He died on December 3, 1533, and was succeeded by his infant son, who reigned as Ivan IV and later generations would know as Ivan the Terrible.

Vasili IV (1552-1612)
(Vasili Shuisky)
emperor

A member of an ancient and prominent clan of boyar aristocrats, Vasili Shuisky briefly reigned as czar from 1606 to 1610 during the chaotic TIME OF TROUBLES (1598–1613) that developed when Czar FEODOR I died without issue in 1598. The Shuisky family had gained great influence throughout IVAN IV's reign, but in the power struggle to gain control of the regency following Ivan's death during the reign of the infirm Feodor I (1584–98), eventually lost out to Boris GODUNOV. With Boris Godunov as regent, Vasili Shuisky, along with his three younger brothers, was banished to internal exile, but by 1591 he had returned to Moscow and regained most of his previous posts. That same year he was appointed to chair the commission that officially investigated the mysterious death of Prince Dmitrii of Uglich, youngest son of Ivan IV and half brother of the czar. Although the commission asserted that Prince Dmitrii had died accidentally during an epileptic fit, the widespread suspicions that Boris Godunov had ordered his death never disappeared completely. Toward the end of Boris Godunov's reign (1598–1605), an impostor known as FALSE DMITRII emerged, claiming to be the true Prince Dmitrii who had escaped Boris Godunov's attempt on his life. In the confusion that followed Boris Godunov's death in April 1605, Vasili Shuisky played an important role in shaping the events that ultimately resulted in his election as czar one year later. First he publicly reversed the findings of the commission that had investigated Prince Dmitrii's death, thus lending credence to the claims of False Dmitrii and undermining the position of Godunov's infant son, Feodor, who reigned for a few months as FEODOR II. Feodor II was strangled in June 1605 in a conspiracy, as troops loyal to the impostor False Dmitrii marched on Moscow. With False Dmitrii crowned as czar, Vasily Shuisky reversed himself again, and claimed the throne for himself in his capacity as the senior member of a historic princely family. Captured and sentenced to death, Vasili Shuisky was pardoned by False Dmitrii, a decision he would soon regret since Vasili Shuisky organized the plot that led to his overthrow and assassination in May 1606. An assembly of the land (ZEMSKII SOBOR) named Vasily Shuisky czar, but his authority did not reach far beyond Moscow. His reign was marked by continued Polish and Swedish intrigue and a virtual state of civil war, first in the 1606–07 rebellion led by the COSSACK Ivan Bolotnikov, and then by the emergence of a second False Dmitrii, who established a rival camp in the Moscow suburb of Tushino. By July 1610, with Polish troops advancing on the capital, Vasili Shuisky lost all support and was forced to abdicate by his fellow boyars and take monastic vows. In November 1610, with Polish troops in the Kremlin, Vasili Shuisky was part of a delegation that also included his rival FILARET Romanov, father of the future czar Michael ROMANOV, which was sent to negotiate with the Polish king Sigismund III. They were arrested and held hostage, as Sigismund maneuvered to gain the Muscovite throne for himself. Vasili Shuisky died in exile two years later.

Vavilov, Nikolai Ivanovich (1885–1943)
botanist

After a private education in preparation for a commercial career, Vavilov attended the Timiriazev Academy in Moscow. He spent a year in England (1913–14) working at the newly established John Innes Horticultural Institute, where he engaged in pioneering research that examined the genetically based resistance of cereals to fungal-based diseases. Back in Russia, he began the work that would first establish his reputation, the origin of cultivated plants. A series of well-planned but physically daunting expeditions took him to Persia, Abyssinia, AFGHANISTAN, China, and Central and South America. These trips further contributed to his growing reputation as an original and productive scholar. In 1921, he was named president of the Lenin Academy of Agricultural Sciences and director of the Institute of Applied Botany. By 1934, he had established about 400 research institutes across the Soviet Union, and his journal, the *Bulletin of Applied Botany, Genetics and Plant Breeding,* was recognized as a leading international publication. His experimental station in Leningrad cultivated almost 26,000 varieties of wheat that unfortunately did not survive the German siege of Leningrad in 1941–44. At the peak of his career, Vavilov was recognized as an international authority on the origins of cultivated plants. To his great misfortune, however, this field of research was uncomfortably close to that of Trofim LYSENKO, an agronomist emerging as the dark eminence of Soviet agricultural sciences and advocating unconventional theories of inheritance based on Michurin's horticultural research. Although he had supported some of Lysenko's early experiments, Vavilov vocally opposed his most outrageous claims, but lost out in the political battle that ensued. As a result, Vavilov was removed from all executive positions, arrested in 1940, and after a five-minute trial in 1941, where he was accused of spying for England, he disappeared into the concentration camps. Many of his staff members suffered a similar fate. He is said to have died, in a cruel irony, of starvation in a labor camp near Saratov on January 26, 1943. News of his election as a foreign member of the Royal Society probably never reached him. His reputation was rehabilitated after STALIN's death.

Verbitskaia, Anastasia Alekseevna (1861–1928)
writer

One of the most popular and controversial women writers of her time, Verbitskaia was born Anastasia Ziablova into a gentry family, and began studies at the Moscow Conservatory. The economic position of gentry women in particularly deteriorated considerably after the emancipation of the serfs in 1861 and, like others of her background, in 1879 Ziablova was forced to suspend her studies and seek employment at the age of 18. For the next two decades, even after her marriage in 1882, she taught music. With the growth of a commercial book market, she found an outlet for her prolific writing and in time developed a large and devoted readership, although critics routinely dismissed her work as vulgar "boulevard" literature. Her best-known works, such as *Dreams of Life* (*Sny zhizni,* 1899) and *The Keys to Happiness* (*Kliuchi schastia,* 1909–13), centered on some basic themes: love and marriage, relationships, and the sexual emancipation of the "new woman." She also published a long novel about the 1905 Revolution, *The Spirit of the Time* (*Dukh vremeni,* 1907–8). Her three-volume autobiography, *To My Reader!* (1908–11), told the story of her female ancestors in the romantic style that gained her a wide readership. Her final novel, *The Yoke of Love* (*Igo liubvi*) (1914–1920), also in three volumes, recycled much of the autobiographical material about her mother's and grandmother's romances but now presented them in fictional form. Early Soviet critics used her work to epitomize the decadent, bourgeois ways of the Czarist regime. Wary of public criticism Verbitskaia retreated behind a male pseudonym and turned to children's literature until her death in 1928.

Vereshchagin, Vasilii Vasilievich (1842–1904)
artist

Vereshchagin became known as a painter of historical scenes and an ardent antiwar spokesman. He became a member of the Russian Academy of Arts but was stripped of his membership because of the harsh approach he took in depicting some of the victories won by Czarist troops. His well-known canvas, *Apotheosis of War* (1872), depicting the brutality of the Russian conquest of Turkestan, was particularly censured in Russia for its vivid portrayal of that campaign. It features a pyramid of skulls and is dedicated to "all great conquerors, past, present and future." Among his paintings devoted to the Russo-Turkish War of 1877–78, which was the occasion for great patriotic feeling among Russians, is *All Quiet on the Shipka,* featuring a soldier freezing to death. Vereshchagin visited Europe and the United States and arranged exhibitions in those countries, contributing several of his works to the Brooklyn Museum. During the early years of the 20th century, he completed his most ambitious paintings, depicting scenes from the Napoleonic campaign in Russia of 1812. During the RUSSO-JAPANESE WAR, he traveled to the east to gain subjects for paintings of the battles fought in that conflict. Aboard the Czarist battleship *Petropavlovsk,* when the Japanese attacked and sank it, Vereshchagin was killed along with most of its crew.

Vertov, Dziga (1896–1954)
film director and theoretician

One of the great innovators of early Soviet documentary film, Vertov was born Denis Arkadievich Kaufman in the town of Bialystok, now in Poland. Originally an experimental poet, Vertov had his first contact with the cinema in May

1918 as a volunteer at the Moscow Cinema Committee, in charge of editing the first newsreels sent from the AGIT-TRAINS in the countryside. He then traveled in propaganda trains and shot his first film, *Godovshchina revoliutsii* (*The Anniversary of the Revolution*) (1919). A member of the Kinoglaz (Cine-Eye) group, Vertov worked on its first manifesto, issued in August 1922. Entitled *We: Variant of a Manifesto,* the manifesto asserted that "future of cinema art lies in a rejection of its present," and extolled the virtues of the machine, and particularly the camera, in creating, new Soviet man and, new Soviet reality. Kinoglaz's second manifesto, *The Cine-Eyes: A Revolution* (1923), further developed the mechanical theme, stating "I am the Cine-Eye. I am the mechanical eye. I, the man-cine, show you the world as only I can see it." Vertov first developed his ideas on the construction of new reality through dynamic editing (montage) in a series of Kinopravda (Cine-truth) newsreels (1922–24). He also worked on a series of feature-length documentaries, *Shagai, Sovet!* (*Forward, Soviet!,* 1926), *Shestaia chast mira* (*A Sixth Part of the World,* 1926), *Odinnatsatyi* (*The Eleventh Year,* 1928), and *Chelovek s kinoapparatom* (*Man with the Movie Camera,* 1929), the latter perhaps his best-known work. Vertov experimented next with editing sound both in harmony with and in counterpoint to edited images: *Sinfoniia Donbassa* (*Symphony of the Donbass,* known also as *Enthusiasm,* 1930), *Tri pesni o Lenine* (*Three Songs of Lenin,* 1934), and *Kolybelnaya* (*Lullaby,* 1937). Vertov fell from favor in the 1930s as his films became increasingly inaccessible to mass audiences, but he remains perhaps the most important theoretician of documentary cinema. He was arrested during the Great Purge but later released and permitted to continue his career, although no further films appeared under his name.

Vesnin Brothers
architects

Three brothers, Leonid (1880–1933), Viktor (1882–1950), and Aleksandr (1883–1959), who were influential in developing constructivist avant-garde architecture in Russia and the Soviet Union. Leonid was educated at the Academy of Fine Arts in St. Petersburg (1901–9), while Viktor and Aleksandr graduated from the Institute of Civil Engineering in St. Petersburg. Of the three, Aleksandr stood out as the leader, not only in shaping their joint designs but also because of his work in the fields of design philosophy, theory, and criticism. Aleksandr was one of the main forces behind the creation of the architectural faculty of the seminal State Higher Art and Technical Workshops (Vkhutemas) in 1920. With Moisei GINSBURG, he founded the Society of Contemporary Architects in 1925 and edited its journal, *Sovremennaia arkhitektura* (*Contemporary Architecture*) from 1926 to 1930. Although a number of their constructions survive to this day, mainly in Moscow, the Vesnin brothers staked a claim in the history of Soviet architecture for designs that were either later torn down (the Karl Marx monument on Moscow's RED SQUARE) or never built (designs for the Palace of Labor competition, the Leningrad Pravda building). Their designs were often characterized by asymmetrical structures. The Vesnin brothers also contributed to town planning, applying the ideas of the "ribbon city" in designs for Stalingrad and Kuznetsk in 1930, which later formed the basis of Soviet town-planning principles. When the newly formed All-Union Academy of Architecture adopted the tenets of socialist realism in 1932, the Vesnin brothers remained true to their principles. No longer in the mainstream of Soviet architecture and town planning, they concentrated on industrial projects such as the Dneprostroi hydroelectric power dam on the Dnieper River in the Ukraine.

village prose

A literary movement that flourished from the 1950s through the 1970s, Russian "village prose." Its members were known as *derevenshchiki,* a term derived from the Russian word for village, *derevnya.* Among the leading *derevenshchiki* were authors such as Vasili SHUKSHIN (1929–74), Feodor ABRAMOV (1920–1983) and Valentin

Rasputin (b. 1937). In their works these and other writers evoked rural life, often writing with nostalgia about a world that they felt was disappearing under the onslaught of industrialization and agricultural collectivization. It was this sense of regret about the lost past in contrast to the celebration of industrialization or collectivism found in socialist realist novels that provided a slightly subversive subtext to the village prose movement. Among the classic works of the village movement is Rasputin's *Farewell to Matyora* (1976) Vasili Shukshin's untimely death in 1974 deprived the village prose movement of one of its leading members. By the mid-1980s, the leading representatives of the village prose movement had moved from the original rural settings of their works to more aggressively anti-urban themes. With the flowering political openness of the GORBACHEV years (1985–91), the village prose movement began to fragment, as many of its exemplars took more open political stands. With a few exceptions, they more commonly adopted conservative nationalist positions, which in some cases opened into thinly disguised anti-Semitism.

Vladimir I (the Great) (unknown–1015)
ruler

Best known as the ruler whose baptism in A.D. 988 made Orthodox Christianity the official religion of KIEVAN RUS and hence of Russia, Vladimir was the illegitimate son of Sviatoslav I, prince of Kiev. His birth date is unknown, but around 970 he was sent by his father to rule over the city of Novgorod, where he remained a decade. After his father's death in 972 and the accession of his half brother Yaropolk to the throne of Kiev, Vladimir was forced to flee to Scandinavia. He became prince of Kiev in 978 but had to fend off challenges to his rule from his father's legitimate children, Yaropolk and Oleg. Raised a pagan, he had many wives and was reputed to have had about 800 concubines in three different palaces. The traditional account of his conversion to Christianity states that Vladimir received Bolgar Muslims,

Roman Catholics, Jewish Khazars, and Byzantine Orthodox delegates, but was ultimately overwhelmed by the splendor and mystery of the Byzantine rite and chose Orthodox Christianity. As part of the negotiations that preceded his conversion, Vladimir campaigned in Byzantine territories in the Crimea and demanded the hand of the Byzantine emperor's sister, Anna Porphyrogenita. The emperor in turn demanded Vladimir's conversion to Christianity before agreeing to the marriage in 988. After his conversion, Vladimir ordered the destruction of most pagan works of art. In the latter part of his rule, Vladimir was concerned with the threat posed by the steppe-dwelling Pechenegs, whom he was still fighting at the time of his death. His death in 1015 triggered another struggle for succession among his many sons, with Yaroslav, latter known as "the Wise," emerging victorious in 1019 and leading Kievan Rus to its apogee during his reign.

Vlasov, Andrei Andreevich (1900–1946)
general

Organizer of the anti-Soviet Russian Liberation Army, Vlasov was the highest-ranking officer to defect to the Germans during World War II. A peasant by birth, Vlasov joined the Red Army in 1919. He served as a military adviser to Chinese leader Chiang Kai-shek in 1938–39. During the German invasion of the USSR, Vlasov distinguished himself in the defense of Kiev (August 1941) and Moscow (December 1941), and was promoted to lieutenant general in January 1942. Disillusioned with the army's high command, he refused to escape from SEVASTOPOL in the Crimea and was captured by the Germans when the city fell in May 1942. Although he quickly proposed the formation of an anti-Stalin army, the Germans preferred for him to confine himself to propaganda broadcasts. Hitler, in particular, was resistant to the idea of a Russian anti-Stalin army, and in October 1943, he ordered the transfer of all national units, including Russian, to the western front. The order was never fully implemented by some German commanders, and in November 1944 with the encouragement of Heinrich Himmler, head of the SS and minister of the interior, Vlasov was allowed to form the Committee for the Liberation of Russia and recruit Soviet troops from prisoner-of-war camps and hard-labor factories. Vlasov became commander in chief of the Russian Liberation Army (ROA) and in February 1945 its first division was formed, although Hitler was still reluctant to use it for more than propagandistic purposes. The ROA first fought the Red Army on the Oder front in April 1945 without much success and was then transferred to Czechoslovakia. During the Prague uprising of May 1945, the ROA assisted the Czechs in defeating the German SS. Vlasov's plans to hand over Czechoslovakia to the Americans was declined. He was captured by the Red Army later in May and, according to the Communist Party paper *Pravda,* tried and executed for treason with some of his officers sometime before August 1946.

Volga River

A river whose valley served as the cradle of medieval and early modern Russia, the Volga River is the largest river of European Russia and the European continent. The Volga rises in the Valdai hills to the northwest of MOSCOW and flows eastward toward NIZHNII NOVGOROD and KAZAN, where it turns sharply to the south and flows past Samara, Simbirsk (Ulianovsk) and Saratov, before reaching Volgograd (known as Tsaritsyn in pre-revolutionary times). At Volgograd the river turns to the southeast toward ASTRAKHAN, where it forms a delta that fans out into the Caspian Sea. In its course it flows for almost 2,300 miles and drains a vast area of about 530,000 square miles that contains about two-fifths of the population of Russia. Known to the ancient Greeks as the Rha River and to Arab cartographers, the Volga was part of medieval trade routes that linked northern Europe with Central Asia through the Caspian Sea and Persia. Its banks were site to various medieval states such as those of the Bulgars, the Khazars, the

GOLDEN HORDE and two of its successor states, the khanates of Kazan and Astrakhan, while the principality of MOSCOW developed farther upstream between the upper reaches of the Volga and the Oka River. During the 16th century, the Muscovite state captured most of the river valley between Kazan and Astrakhan. Scientific investigation of the river and its tributaries took place mostly between 1700 and the early twentieth century. The construction of artificial waterways such as the Volga-Baltic Canal (first built in 1810), the White Sea-Baltic Canal (built 1931–33), the Moscow-Volga Canal (built 1932–37), and the Volga-Don Canal (built 1947–52) have made the Volga the centerpiece of the world's largest network of commercial waterways linking the White, Baltic, Caspian, Azov and Black seas.

Vrubel, Mikhail Aleksandrovich
(1856–1910)
artist

Vrubel was the first important painter to break completely with the dominant ideas of the Peredvizhniki (WANDERERS). He first studied law at St. Petersburg University before turning to art and enrolling in the Society for the Encouragement of the Arts and at the Academy of Arts from 1880 to 1884. Rejecting the Wanderer's concern with art as a social service as "journalism," Vrubel advocated an art whose elements were significant in themselves rather than a means for communicating socially redeeming messages. Vrubel reintroduced religious, mythological, and mythical themes that had long been absent from Russian art, albeit through his own highly idiosyncratic prism. His interest in early Russian icons brought into vogue a venerable art form that had become neglected. He visited Venice and restored frescoes in the ancient church of St. Cyril in Kiev; he also designed murals on themes from Russian epics. He adapted themes from Greek mythology into a Russian context as in the case of Pan, whom he portrayed as a Slavic-looking god with the hands of a Russian peasant. His travels to Spain resulted in studies of Russian gypsies. Vrubel was much influenced by the theme of unfathomable despair in LERMONTOV'S "Demon," and painted a sequence of works that respond to that theme, including *Demon: Demon Seated* (1890), *Tamara's Dance* (1890), *Lilac* (1900), *Swan Princess* (1900), and *Demon Cast Down* (1902). He also painted the portraits of the wealthy art patron Savva Mamontov (1897) and the poet Valeri Briusov (1906). In 1905, Vrubel went mad and spent the last years of his life in an asylum. Vrubel forms an essential bridge between late-19th-century realism and the work of early-20th-century masters like KANDINSKY, MALEVICH, and CHAGALL.

Vyshinsky, Andrei Yanuaryevich
(1883–1954)
Soviet official

A midlevel Soviet politician who gained international notoriety for his role as chief prosecutor during the show trials of the 1930s, Vyshinsky was born in ODESSA to a family of Polish descent. He trained as a lawyer and joined the Russian Social Democratic Labor Party in 1902. When the party split into two factions—Bolshevik and Menshevik—in 1903, Vyshinsky sided with the latter. He played an active role in the 1905 Revolution. Vyshinsky spent the first years of the revolution as an official in the Commissariat of Food Supply and did not join the COMMUNIST PARTY until 1920. During the 1920s he joined the faculty of Moscow University as a lecturer and professor, before being appointed rector. From 1928 to 1931, he served as head of the department of higher education in the Commissariat of Enlightenment, as the entity overseeing education was known in the early decades of Soviet rule. In 1931, Vyshinsky was appointed procurator of the Russian Federal Republic of the Soviet Union, and made a name for himself as a shrill and vindictive prosecutor, most notably in the Metro-Vickers trial of alleged industrial saboteurs that took place in 1933. In 1935, he was appointed procurator of the USSR and served as prosecutor for the highly publicized trials of leading Soviet

officials and Old Bolsheviks such as Nikolai BUKHARIN, Grigory ZINOVIEV, and Lev KAMANEV that took place from 1936 to 1938. In 1939 he became deputy chairman of the Council of People's Commissar and the following year became deputy foreign minister to Vyacheslav MOLOTOV. After the annexation of the three Baltic republics in 1940, Vyshinsky was given responsibility for the "sovietization" of Latvia. After 1945, he also served as the Soviet delegate to the United Nations, where he contributed to the climate of conflict of the early cold war, with frequent condemnations of the United States and its Western allies. In 1949, with Molotov in temporary disfavor with STALIN, Vyshinsky was appointed foreign minister, a position he held until 1953, when Molotov regained his post following Stalin's death. He died in New York on November 22, 1954, while posted to the Soviet UN delegation.

Vysotsky, Vladimir Semeyonovich
(1938–1980)
musician and actor

Now widely recognized as the voice of protest of the BREZHNEV era, Vysotsky was one of the first Soviet performers to develop a widespread underground cult following. He was born in Moscow of a father who was a military officer briefly posted to East Germany, where Vysotsky spent some of his youth. He first pursued two careers, graduating from the Moscow Construction Engineering Institute and the Moscow Arts Theater (MkhAT) as an actor. In 1964 he joined Yuri LIUBIMOV's newly formed Taganka Theater, which became his artistic home as he pursued other creative interests in music and film. But he always returned to the theater. As an actor he was best known for his role as Hamlet. He also acted in numerous films of varying quality, sometimes with his wife, the French actress Marina Vlady. But it was as a singer that Vysotsky made his biggest contribution, becoming perhaps the greatest balladeer of his generation. Beginning in the 1960s, he began writing lyrics, which he performed to his own guitar accompaniment. The topics varied from the usual humorous critiques of Soviet bureaucratism and shortcomings that were permissible in the Brezhnev era to songs on taboo topics such as labor camps. Although authorities disapproved of the latter and disliked his nonconformism, Vysotsky managed to avoid official persecution. Like Bulat OKUDZHAVA and Aleksandr GALICH, the extent of Vysotsky's great popularity among Soviet audiences would not have been possible without the growing availability of tape recorders. His songs circulated clandestinely on tape (*magnitizdat*), and fans wrote down his lyrics and passed them on. A few official sanitized recordings were issued in his lifetime, especially toward the end of his career, when his popularity was impossible to ignore. A highly creative, tortured soul, Vysotsky died prematurely from alcoholism and drug abuse. He was mourned throughout the country, with many thousands turning up for his funeral. His death brought forth a wave of spontaneous unofficial mourning, especially in front of the Taganka Theater. Not since Sergei ESENIN in the 1920s had the tragic early death of a beloved bard touched Russians so deeply.

W

Wanderers

A group of artists whose aesthetic values dominated Russian painting between the 1870s and the 1890s. Known as the Peredvizhniki (Wanderers), they derived their name from the Society for Traveling Art Exhibitions (Tovarishchestvo peredvizhnikh khudozhestvennykh vystavok), which they formed in 1870. But the roots of the movement go back to 1863, when 13 artists resigned from the St. Petersburg Academy of Arts, protesting the topic that had been assigned for the yearly competition, "The Entrance of Odin into Valhalla," calling instead for art that reflected Russian reality. Strongly influenced by the populist political ideas of the time (see POPULISM), the artists believed that art should have a social purpose and show realistic paintings, and that it should be brought to the people in the provinces through traveling exhibitions. Implied in the dictum to represent Russian reality was a criticism of the Russian social order that was expressed by the artists in varying degrees of openness. As a formal society, the Wanderers also sought to provide its members the facilities for exhibiting and selling their work. Among the founding members of the society were Ivan Kramskoi, its original leader, Vasilii Perov, Nikolai GE, Grigorii Miasoedov, Ivan Shishkin, and Aleksei Savrasov. Ilia REPIN, Russia's most prominent realist painter, joined a year later and outlived most of his colleagues. By the 1890s, the MIR ISKUSSTVA (World of Art) movement was establishing its hegemony over the arts. The Wanderers soon lost all influence, even though their society nominally existed until the 1920s, and some of its representatives like Repin lived until the 1930s. The Wanderers found a strong patron in the Moscow businessman and art collector, P. M. Tretiakov (1832–98), founder of the Tretiakov Gallery, where many of their works are still displayed.

Warsaw Pact

A military alliance of European Communist nations headquartered in Moscow, the Warsaw Pact was signed on May 14, 1955, in Warsaw, Poland, as a Soviet response to the rearmament of West Germany (Federal Republic of Germany) and its admission to the U.S.-led military alliance, the North Atlantic Treaty Organization (NATO). Formally called the Warsaw Treaty of Friendship, Cooperation and Mutual Assistance, the pact's original members were Albania, Bulgaria, Czechoslovakia, East Germany (German Democratic Republic), Hungary, Poland, Romania, and the Soviet Union. In 1961, at the height of Nikita KHRUSHCHEV's de-Stalinization campaign, Albania broke off diplomatic relations with the Soviet Union and in 1968 officially withdrew from the pact. Yugoslavia, although Communist-ruled, was never a member. Politically, the pact was an extension of Soviet power in the region; militarily the supreme commander was from the Soviet army. The pact's only military action came in 1968 when members' forces invaded a member country, Czechoslovakia, to suppress the reformist movement led by Alexander Dubcek and install a pro-Soviet government. Despite Soviet hegemony, Romania refused to participate in the invasion, though it remained a member of the pact. Another military action against a Warsaw

Pact member, the 1956 invasion of Hungary to suppress a growing nationalist Communist revolution, was actually a unilateral maneuver by the Soviet Union that did not involve Warsaw Pact troops.

In 1985, the Warsaw Pact was officially renewed for another 20 years, but it lasted only until July 1991, in view of the revolutionary changes that swept Eastern Europe and the Soviet Union between 1989 and 1991. As part of the relaxation of tensions with the West that signaled the coming end of the cold war, the Soviet Union began to pull its troops from other War-

saw Pact countries in 1989. East Germany withdrew from the pact in October 1990 and joined West Germany in a unified German state. After ceasing joint military actions in March 1991, the remaining six nations dissolved the pact in July 1991. Within six months the Soviet Union itself dissolved, giving way to 15 independent nations.

Winter War (1939–1940)

A war fought between Finland and the Soviet Union between November 1939 and March 1940 that followed from the secret protocol in

A cartoon expressing outrage at the Soviet invasion of Finland shows Joseph Stalin about to kill a young woman (labeled "Finlandia") and her child with a hammer and sickle, ca. 1940 *(Library of Congress)*

the NAZI-SOVIET PACT of August 1939, which relegated Finland to the Soviet sphere of influence. Concerned that Finnish territory could serve as a staging area for a future German attack on Soviet territory, especially the city of Leningrad (now St. Petersburg), the Soviet Union pressed Finland to allow the construction of Soviet military bases on Finnish territory. When Finland refused, the Soviet Union revoked the 1932 nonaggression pact between the two countries and attacked Finland without a declaration of war on November 30, 1939. The Finns became legendary for their spirited resistance to Soviet troops against overwhelming odds and with little outside assistance and for their distinctive white uniforms.

The Soviet attack began with the bombardment of Helsinki and other cities and ports, while 20 Soviet divisions crossed the Finnish border at various points. Led by Baron Mannerheim, the Finnish army of three infantry divisions concentrated its resistance along the 70-mile-wide Karelian isthmus, establishing a series of fortifications known as the Mannerheim line, and at four other points north of the isthmus. By January 1940, the Finns had cut the Soviet army's communication and supply lines and in some cases forced the Soviets to retreat into Soviet territory. Faced with a very poor Soviet performance, Marshal Semyon K. Timoshenko was given command of the Soviet war effort and quickly produced more favorable results by concentrating on breaking the Mannerheim line. By February 1940, Finnish resistance was weakening in the face of a costly Soviet artillery offensive against the Mannerheim line. The Soviets captured the city of Summa on February 16 and Vyborg (Finnish, Viipuri) on March 11. The following day a truce was declared while arrangements for a peace treaty were finalized.

At a peace treaty signed in Moscow on March 13, 1940, Finland yielded 41,888 sq km (16,173 sq mi) of its southeastern lands to the Soviet Union, about 10 percent of its territory, including the Karelian isthmus. Other terms of the treaty included Finnish agreement to limit the size of its army, a 30-year rental of Hanko peninsula to serve as a Soviet base, and unrestricted transit privileges for Soviet troops across Pechenga province. Hostilities between the two countries resumed in June 1941, after Germany declared war on the Soviet Union and Finland joined the German war effort. By 1944, however, Finland sued for peace and agreed to pay $300 million in war reparations. Finland lost about 23,000 soldiers with another 55,000 wounded or permanently disabled. Estimates of Soviet war losses have varied, ranging from a Soviet estimate of 48,000 and a Finnish one of close to 200,000 Soviet losses.

Witte, Sergei Yulevich (1848–1915)
statesman

Widely recognized as the ablest minister to serve ALEXANDER III and NICHOLAS II, Witte left a legacy that is especially evident in the rapid industrial growth that Russia experienced in the 1890s. Of Baltic ascendance, Witte was born in Tbilisi, Georgia, and graduated with a degree in mathematics from Odessa University in 1870. Before entering government service in 1889, Witte developed a reputation as an excellent and innovative executive in railway management. His first post in government was as director of the Ministry of Finance's Department of Railway Affairs. He rose rapidly, becoming acting minister of finance in August 1892, and minister of finance in January 1893. As finance minister, he devised a program for economic growth centered on protectionist tariffs, foreign loans, and railway construction to promote national integration. He accelerated the construction of the TRANS-SIBERIAN RAILROAD and promoted the CHINESE EASTERN RAILWAY. By 1897 his sound financial management allowed Russia to join the gold standard. Witte argued, with increasing lack of success as the new century began, against Russia's imperialist policies in the Far East, favored by other ministers and, ultimately, the czar, preferring instead to spread Russian influence through economic penetration. By August 1903, his policy differences with Nicholas led to his dismissal, a fall from power that was aided by the intrigues of other ministers like Viacheslav von Plehve and Witte's own abrasive personality, which did not sit well with his colleagues or with Nicholas, who preferred less domineering subordinates. Witte returned from the political wilderness in June 1905 when Nicholas turned to him as a last-resort candidate to negotiate an end to the RUSSO-JAPANESE WAR in Portsmouth, New Hampshire. Given Russia's disastrous performance in the war, Witte acquitted himself admirably and Nicholas rewarded him with the title of count. In serious political trouble at the decisive moment of the 1905 Revolution, Nicholas again turned to Witte, who recommended the drafting of the October Manifesto, promising new civil liberties and a parliament (DUMA). Witte served, less admirably this time, as chairman of the Council of Ministers until April 1906, when, with the passing of the crisis, old animosities resurfaced and Nicholas accepted his resignation. Bitter at his latest downfall, Witte spent his last years drafting his memoirs and defending his record in public service.

Women's Battalion of Death

One of several "Death Battalions" or "Shock Battalions" formed by the Provisional Government during the summer of 1917, the Women's Battalion of Death gained worldwide recognition because it was composed of women. Formed under the initiative of War Minister, later Prime Minister, Alexander KERENSKY, the Death Battalions were generally composed of young men from well-to-do classes who were supposed to strengthen the morale and discipline of a reluctant army by their heroic example. In May 1917, Maria Bochkareva, a woman from Tomsk, in Siberia, who had successfully petitioned NICHOLAS II to serve in the army during World War I, convinced Kerensky to allow the formation of a women-only battalion. The battalion had early successes against the Germans in the southwest

front, capturing more than 2,000 soldiers in one instance. The Women's Battalion was initially composed of 2,000 women, but by August its numbers had dwindled to about 250. As support for the Provisional Government dissipated during September and October 1917, the Women's Battalion found itself among the government's few defenders. The battalion was at the Winter Palace when the BOLSHEVIK-led forces attacked it on October 25 (November 7), 1917. The Battalion was officially dissolved by the Bolshevik Military Revolutionary Committee on November 21, 1917, a few days after the still-functioning parliament (DUMA) had investigated charges of physical abuse by the Bolsheviks and concluded that three women had been raped and one had committed suicide. The investigation also absolved the Bolsheviks of the widely reported charge that many of the women in the battalion had been thrown out of the windows of the Winter Palace. Bochkareva was able to escape Russia, eventually reaching the United States, where she settled and lived in relative obscurity until her death.

Wrangel, Ferdinand Petrovich (1797–1870)
explorer

A naval officer and government administrator, Wrangel left an impressive legacy of exploration, especially along the Arctic Ocean coastline of Siberia. Wrangel was born in the ancient town of Pskov to a noble family of Baltic ancestry and held the title of baron. He graduated in 1815 from the Imperial Naval Academy in St. Petersburg and joined the expedition under the command of Vasili Golovnin that sailed around the world in 1817–19 in the sloop *Kamchatka*. Wrangel first made a lasting name for himself by mapping the polar regions of northeastern Siberia between 1820 and 1824. In 1825 he embarked on another expedition around the world, this time commanding his own sloop, the *Krotky*, from which he returned to Russia in 1827. In 1829 he was rewarded with an important administrative post, becoming the first governor of the Russian colonies in Alaska, a post he held until 1835. From 1840 to 1849 he was the director of the RUSSIAN AMERICAN COMPANY, the colonial trading company, first chartered in 1799, that had a monopoly on commerce with Alaska and the Aleutian Islands. In 1855 Wrangel was appointed minister of the navy, a post he held until 1857. After retiring from government service in 1864, he came out in strong opposition to the Russian government's plan to sell Alaska to the United States, a purchase that was completed in 1867. Wrangel was an active participant in the scholarly world of his time, both as a member of the Russian ACADEMY OF SCIENCES and as a founder of the Russian Geographical Society. He also published several books, including the *Narrative of an expedition to the polar sea in the years 1820, 1821, 1822 & 1823* (1841) and *Russian America: statistical and ethnographic information* (1839). His name also lives on in several geographical features: the Wrangel Mountains in Alaska, three different Wrangel islands, two capes and a volcano.

Wrangel, Baron Petr Nikolaevich (1878–1928)

military commander

The last and perhaps most skilled major commander of the White (anti-BOLSHEVIK) armies during the Russian civil war, Wrangel came from a Baltic noble family of Swedish origin. After service in the RUSSO-JAPANESE WAR, he graduated from the Academy of the General Staff in 1910. A cavalry commander during World War I, he joined General Aleksei Kaledin in his opposition to the Provisional Government's military reforms and was forced to resign in July 1917. He followed Kaledin to the Don area, and after Kaledin's suicide in February 1918, Wrangel attached himself to General Anton DENIKIN's anti-Bolshevik armies. Wrangel emerged as a talented commander when he reached the Kuban, in the north Caucasus, in late 1918, and more prominently with the capture of Tsaritsyn (now Volgograd) in July 1919. After the failure of the advance on Moscow, Wrangel briefly commanded the Volunteer Army, but his poor relations with Denikin led to his dismissal for conspiracy in early 1920. Exiled briefly to Constantinople, Wrangel was recalled to Crimea to command the White forces in April 1920, following Denikin's resignation. The most talented White officer had been given command when the cause was almost lost. He showed relative political sophistication, unlike his predecessors, initiating a modest land reform that passed land to peasants and proposing an alliance with Poland, then at war with Soviet Russia, but which the Polish leader Jozef Piłsudski rejected. By November 1920, cornered into the Crimean Peninsula, Wrangel organized the evacuation of more than 150,000 White troops, families, and sympathizers from Sevastopol across the Black Sea to Turkey. Settling in Belgium, Wrangel remained a leader of the Russian émigré movement until his death and organized the Russian Social Union, an association of White veterans. He died in Brussels but is buried in Belgrade.

Y

Yagoda, Genrikh Grigorevich (1891–1938)

Soviet official

Together with Lavrenty BERIA and Nikolai YEZHOV, Yagoda belongs to the troika of the bloodiest secret police chiefs of the Stalinist era. As commissar of the People's commissariat for internal affairs (NKVD), Yagoda prepared and conducted the early purges that followed the assassination of Sergei Kirov in December 1934, but in 1937 he himself fell victim to the executioner's bullet. He was born into a Jewish family and joined the Bolshevik Party in 1907. Exiled for his revolutionary activities from 1911 to 1913, he then served in the Russian army from 1915, and after the Russian Revolution of 1917 worked in the People's Commissariat for Foreign Trade, 1919–22, and joined the CHEKA in 1920. He advanced to deputy chairman of the GPU in 1924. STALIN made him people's commissar of internal affairs in 1934, and as such he carried out the early purges after the assassination of Kirov. In July 1936, Stalin dismissed him for alleged slackness and replaced him with Nikolai Yezhov. Toying with Yagoda while a case against him was prepared, Stalin appointed him people's commissar for posts and telegraph after his dismissal. In 1937 he was arrested and became one of the chief defendants at the Trial of the Anti-Soviet Bloc of Rightists and Troskyites, an ironic touch given Yagoda's past persecution of these groups. Rumor has it that Yagoda was personally executed by his successor, Yezhov, in the cellars of the Lubianka Prison in Moscow. The party commission that in 1988 rehabilitated the defendants of the 1938 trial pointedly excluded Yagoda from its list.

Yakovlev, Aleksandr Nikolaevich (1923–)

Soviet official

Yakovlev is often considered the father of glasnost (openness) and the intellectual mentor of Mikhail GORBACHEV during the latter's years in power. Yakovlev was born into a peasant family in Yaroslavl and joined the Red Army in 1941 in time for the war. Severely wounded in fighting in 1943, Yakovlev joined the COMMUNIST PARTY in 1944 and graduated from the Yaroslavl Pedagogical Institute in 1946. After a few years in the Yaroslavl party apparatus, Yakovlev was called to Moscow in 1953 to work in the party's Central Committee apparatus. While studying at the Academy of Social Sciences of the Central Committee, Yakovlev spent a year at New York City's Columbia University in 1959 as one of the first participants in the Soviet-American cultural exchanges, an experience that he later acknowledged shaped his future thinking about communism. From 1965 to 1973, Yakovlev occupied a top-level position in the Central Committee's department of propaganda, on his way to a solid career in the BREZHNEV-era Communist party. However, in 1973 he was shunted aside and appointed Soviet ambassador to Canada, after publishing an article that offended conservative party members by attacking what he saw as rising Soviet nationalism and chauvinism. During Mikhail Gorbachev's 1984 tour of Canada in his capacity as the Politburo's specialist on agriculture, Yakovlev impressed favorably the rising star of Soviet politics. In 1983, General Secretary Yuri ANDROPOV appointed Yakovlev director of the prestigious Institute of World Economy and International Relations (IMEMO) in Moscow. In

July 1985, Gorbachev, made him head of the Central Committee propaganda department, a key center from which Yakovlev promoted the agenda of perestroika (restructuring). Yakovlev played a central role in advancing Gorbachev's ideological agenda as a theorist of perestroika and glasnost. By June 1987, four years after returning from the political wilderness, Yakovlev had become a full member of the Party's Politburo. He battled Yegor Ligachev, an advocate of less far-reaching reform, until Ligachev's influence waned after the 19th Party Conference of June 1988. From 1988 to 1990, Yakovlev was an important voice shaping party policy on international affairs. He stepped down from the Central Committee and the Politburo in July 1990, but remained as Gorbachev's senior adviser. Although his influence declined in the last months of Gorbachev's rule, Yakovlev remained loyal to Gorbachev, and in 1992 he became vice president of the Gorbachev Foundation after Gorbachev left government service.

Yalta

A town in the Crimean Peninsula that has been a popular winter and health resort since the 19th century, Yalta was the site of the World War II YALTA CONFERENCE held on February 4–11, 1945, in the nearby Livadiya Palace. The modern town of Yalta, located on the Black Sea in southern Crimea, about 55 miles east of SEVASTOPOL, was founded in 1838 on the site of an ancient Greek colony. The region around Yalta was annexed by Russia in 1783. Within a few decades it had become an exclusive resort for members of the Russian royal family and nobility, who came to escape the winters of northern Russia and built palatial estates. As the main site of a network of health resorts that grew in southern Crimea after the 1880s, Yalta is associated with numerous members of Russia's political and literary elites who summered in the area. Among them was the playwright Anton CHEKHOV, and Yalta is the site of an important Chekhov Museum. In the 1950s, Yalta and the entire Crimean Penin-

sula became a part of the Ukrainian Soviet Socialist Republic, the present-day Republic of Ukraine. By the 1960s Yalta was receiving close to 300,000 visitors, either tourists or health resort patients. In the early 1990s, the year-round population was estimated at 89,000.

Yalta Conference

The second of three major wartime conferences held by the leaders of the United States, Great Britain, and the Soviet Union, the Yalta Conference was held at Livadiya Palace near the Black Sea resort of YALTA in Crimea, present-day Ukraine, from February 4–11, 1945. With U.S. president Franklin Roosevelt, British prime minister Winston Churchill, and Soviet premier and general secretary of the Communist Party Joseph STALIN in attendance, the Yalta Conference planned the final defeat and the postwar occupation of Nazi Germany.

A number of important decisions were made at Yalta by the three Allied leaders, as the end of the war against Germany approached. The Allies agreed to divide Germany into four postwar occupation zones and to give the Soviet Union one-half of a proposed $20 billion in war reparations to be paid by Germany. The conference also announced the establishment of a United Nations by calling for a conference to meet in San Francisco in April 1945 to lay the ground for its establishment. More controversial, and a portent of the future postwar tensions that would lead to the cold war, were the conference's decisions about the borders of Poland, partitioned by Germany and the Soviet Union in 1939. Faced with the presence of the Red Army on most of the prewar territory of Poland, Roosevelt and Churchill reluctantly confirmed the Soviet Union's occupation of the territories it had annexed from eastern Poland as part of the 1939 NAZI-SOVIET PACT. They agreed to compensate Poland with prewar German lands to the north and west and the Free City of Danzig (Gdansk). The postwar Polish-German border was essentially shifted 75–100 miles to the west of the prewar border. The conference's decisions were made public in a communiqué issued on February 11, 1945, and known subsequently as the Yalta Declaration. Other decisions, namely those that pertained to Japan, with which the Soviet Union was not officially at war, were kept secret. The three Allied leaders agreed that the Soviet Union would declare war on Japan within three months after the end of hostilities in Europe. In exchange, the Soviet Union was to receive the southern half of Sakhalin Island (lost to Japan after the RUSSO-JAPANESE WAR). As the cold war unfolded from the 1950s through the 1980s, the Yalta Conference was seen by Western observers as a conference where the Soviet Union made important territorial and diplomatic gains without surrendering much in return.

Yashin, Lev Ivanovich (1929–1990)
athlete

A legendary and innovative goalkeeper in the history of world soccer, Yashin was perhaps the greatest Russian soccer player of all time. Known around the world in his playing days as the Black Spider because of his all-black goalkeeping uniform and his remarkable agility and reflexes, Yashin also embodied the best qualities of sportsmanship. Born in Moscow, Yashin spent his entire career with the Moscow Dinamo team, one of the powerhouses of Soviet soccer. He was also a talented ice hockey player who almost chose hockey over soccer, but an injury to Dinamo's starting goalie opened a spot for him on the soccer squad. Between 1954 and 1971, Dinamo won the Soviet league championship five times and the USSR Cup three times. As the starting goalie of the Soviet national team, Yashin played in 78 international games with the Soviet national team and played in three successive World Cups (1958–66). With Yashin in goal, Soviet teams won an Olympic gold medal in 1956, the European Cup in 1960, and finished third in the 1966 World Cup. Criticized for his play in the 1962 World Cup, he excelled four years later. He was named as Europe's

player of the year in 1963 and was also awarded the Golden Ball for achievement, awards rarely given to goalkeepers. During his 408 games for Dinamo, he recorded 207 shutouts, a remarkable achievement that will not likely be broken. Like other top Soviet sports performers, Yashin was drawn into the Soviet establishment, joining the COMMUNIST PARTY in 1957, receiving an Order of Lenin in 1968, and graduating from the Higher Party School in 1972. His retirement in 1971 was marked with an honorary match played in front of 100,000 spectators at the Moscow Luzhniki stadium between his Dinamo team and an international team of all-stars. In October 1984 his right leg was amputated after complications from knee surgery. At the time of his death of stomach cancer in 1990, he was considered the most famous Soviet sportsman ever.

Yeltsin, Boris Nikolaevich (1931–   )
politician

A Communist politician who emerged as an advocate of reform in the late 1980s, Boris Yeltsin became the first popularly elected president of Russia after the breakup of the Soviet Union. Yeltsin was born in the region near Ekaterinburg (Sverdlovsk in Soviet times); his father was a construction worker and his mother a seamstress. Both his father and his grandfather, a well-off peasant, suffered from state repression in the early 1930s, with his father serving three years in the GULAG camps from 1934 to 1937. The Yeltsin family moved to the Perm region in the late 1930s, where Yeltsin graduated from high school. He then attended the Ural Polytechnic Institute in Sverdlovsk, graduating in 1955 as a construction engineer. Always fond of sports, Yeltsin played in the first division of the Soviet volleyball league while in college. In 1956, he married Naina Girina, and their two daughters were born in the next three years. Yeltsin found employment at a giant construction combine in the Sverdlovsk region, rapidly mastering various construction skills and advancing from foreman to chief engineer of an integrated plant by 1963. In 1961 he joined the COMMUNIST PARTY, and in 1968 moved into full-time party work in the Sverdlovsk oblast party committee (obkom), becoming chief of the Construction Department. By 1976 he had been appointed first secretary of the Sverdlovsk oblast committee, a significant milestone for a man in his mid-forties. In 1981 he was elected to the Central Committee of the Communist Party, and in 1984 to the Supreme Soviet (parliament) of the USSR. In 1977, during his tenure as first secretary in Sverdlovsk, he supervised the destruction of the house where Czar NICHOLAS II and his family were executed in 1918, an act he publicly regretted later. On the other hand, his concern for improving workers' housing made him popular with the rank and file and gave him reformist credentials. In 1985, Yeltsin was transferred to Moscow, and in December of that year he was appointed first secretary of the Moscow City Committee of the Communist Party, a highly prominent post in the party hierarchy. In 1986 he became a member of the party Politburo, in which he emerged as a voice for rapid reform, often clashing with Yegor Ligachev, a more cautious reformer. In October 1987, at the plenary meeting of the party's Central Committee, he criticized the Party Secretariat for moving too slowly on reforms, after which he was dismissed from the Politburo and the Moscow City Committee with Mikhail GORBACHEV's approval, the beginning of a highly personal quarrel between two former allies. Yeltsin was appointed to an obscure post on the State Committee of Construction, the apparent end to a promising career.

In March 1989, however, as the old Soviet system was beginning to crack under the momentum that Gorbachev's reforms had gathered, Yeltsin returned to the political stage as a member of the Congress of People's Deputies, convened by Gorbachev in an attempt to bypass the Communist Party's resistance to his reforms, in the first multiparty elections in Soviet history. He allied himself with the Interregional Group of deputies, the vehicle of liberals and democrats in the Con-

gress. In May 1990, he was elected speaker of the Supreme Soviet of the Russian Republic of the USSR, from where he continued to forcefully criticize Gorbachev. In July 1990, one month after the Russian Republic had declared itself sovereign in relation to the Soviet Union, Yeltsin resigned from the Communist Party, fully embracing the new political currents developing in Russia. In February 1991, he called for Gorbachev's resignation and the negotiation of a new Union Treaty for the constituent republics of the Soviet Union. In June 1991, Yeltsin was elected president of the Russian Republic, the first democratically elected leader of Russia. On August 18, 1991, on the eve of the signing of a new Union Treaty, the Soviet experiment with reform seemed to come to an end when a group of high-level conspirators launched a coup in Moscow. Yeltsin's courageous resistance, symbolized by his climbing on to a tank and delivering a rousing speech in front of the White House (Russian parliament), helped turn the tide, and three days later the AUGUST COUP collapsed. Six months later, with the Communist Party outlawed for the time being, Yeltsin played a central role in dissolving the Soviet Union.

As Russian president, Yeltsin faced a difficult transition toward a free-market economy. Admired for his political savvy but widely criticized for his economic incompetence, he oversaw the development of a ferocious crony capitalism that impoverished the bulk of the Russian population and benefited a small elite of insiders. His rule also witnessed the consolidation of democratic reforms, in spite of the opposition of the reborn Communist Party. In October 1993, he ruthlessly suppressed a rebellion led by Communists and his own vice president, shelling that same White House in front of which he had resisted the 1991 coup. In 1994, he launched a brutal war on the secessionist autonomous region of CHECHNYA, a conflict that still awaits resolution. Although in poor health, he ran for president again in 1996, winning a narrow victory over the Communist challenger, Gennadi Ziuganov. His second term was equally controversial, as his government presided over a series of economic crises including the collapse of the ruble in August 1998, charges of corruption, frequent ministerial changes, Chechen terrorist incursions into Russia, and continued questions about his health. On December 31, 1999, after having steered a parliamentary victory and appointed the previously obscure Vladimir PUTIN as prime minister, Yeltsin announced his resignation a few months before the end of his term. He was succeeded by Putin, who proceeded easily to win the 2000 presidential elections.

Yenisei River

One of the longest rivers in the world at an estimated 2,540 miles, the Yenisei forms in the Savan Mountains in the eastern part of Tuva and flows through central Siberia northward into the Yenisei Bay of the Kara Sea of the Arctic Ocean. It is first formed from the union of the Biv-Khem (Greater Yenisei) and the Ka-Khem (Little Yenisei) and flows through a deep gorge in the Savan Mountains. South of the large Siberian city of Krasnoyarsk, the Yenisei becomes navigable and remains so for most of its course to the Arctic Ocean, although it is usually frozen from November to May. As it flows north of Krasnoyarsk, it divides the western Siberian lowlands from the central Siberian plateau. Its main tributaries are the Angara, the Stony Tunguska, and the Lower Tunguska Rivers. Oceangoing vessels can sail into the river as far the port of Igarka, about 425 miles inland.

The Yenisei was first seen by Russian explorers in the 16th century, and in the following century its basin was gradually colonized. Like other parts of Siberia, it became a place of banishment and, during the STALIN years, the site of several labor camps, both in the region north of Krasnoyarsk and farther north near its mouth around the nickel-producing region of Norilsk. Since 1956, with the construction of the Krasnoyarsk and Yeniseisk hydroelectric stations, the river has become a great energy producer for Russia.

Yezhov, Nikolai Ivanovich (1895–1939)

Soviet official

One of the most sinister figures of the STALIN era, which certainly produced other worthy candidates for that dubious title, Yezhov prepared and conducted the Great Purge of 1936–38, as commissar of internal affairs. He joined the BOLSHEVIK Party in April 1917, worked as a political commissar in the Red Army during the civil war, then worked in relative obscurity until 1934, when he became a member of the COMMUNIST PARTY's Central Committee and its Organizational Bureau in 1934. He was soon appointed chairman of the Commission of Party Control (the Party's "intelligence service") and in 1936 replaced Genrikh YAGODA as people's commissar for internal affairs. In this capacity he organized the Great Purge, becoming so identified with it that the period is often known colloquially as the "Yezhovshchina" (the Yezhov era). In 1937 he became a member of the Politburo. He is said to have personally executed his predecessor, Yagoda, in 1938. Yet, he soon suffered the same fate as Yagoda. Dismissed by Stalin in December 1938, Yezhov was appointed commissar for river transport but was arrested in March 1939. He was probably executed soon after his arrest and succeeded by Lavrenty BERIA. At the peak of his tenure, the press referred to him as the Iron Commissar, but in the privacy of people's homes and thoughts, he was known more colloquially as the "bloody dwarf," in reference to his short stature. In his Secret Speech of 1956 at the 20th Party Congress, KHRUSHCHEV sharply denounced Yezhov as a criminal, drug addict, and degenerate whose fate was more than well deserved.

Yevtushenko, Yevgenii Aleksandrovich (1933–)

poet and writer

A Russian poet who came to prominence during the cultural "thaw" that followed Joseph STALIN's death in March 1953, Yevtushenko was part of a young generation of Soviet poets, including Bella

AKHMADULINA (his first wife) and Andrei Voznesensky, who captured the imagination of a poetry-loving public impatient with the straitjacket of Stalinist cultural policies. An international literary celebrity since the early 1960s, Yevtushenko was born in the Siberian town of Zima near the city of Irkutsk, where his Ukrainian ancestors had been exiled in the late 19th century. In 1944 he moved to Moscow with his mother, and in 1951 he enrolled in the Moscow Literary Institute, from which he graduated three years later. His first collection of poems, *Prospectors of the Future*, was published in 1952. In his first major narrative poem, "Zima Junction" (1956), Yevtushenko evoked the setting of his Siberian childhood in a clear, direct language that, after decades of stifling socialist realism, reminded audiences of early Soviet poets such as Vladimir MAYAKOVSKY and Sergei ESENIN. In seminal poems such as "Babi Yar" (1961) and "The Heirs of Stalin" (1963), Yevtushenko spoke out against highly politically sensitive topics such as Soviet ANIT-SEMITISM and the persistence of Stalinism, at a time when the Soviet political climate was beginning to change from the relative cultural liberalism of the middle KHRUSHCHEV period. The former poem, in particular, an attack on Soviet anti-Semitism as part of a tribute to the victims of the Nazi massacre of Ukrainian Jews at BABI YAR near Kiev, had great resonance in Soviet culture, inspiring, among others, Dmitrii SHOSTAKOVICH's Thirteenth Symphony. Politically charged poems, coupled with growing celebrity status in the West and the 1963 publication in Paris of *Precocious Autobiography,* contributed to greater official condemnation of his work, but by 1966 Yevtushenko had regained the favor of the literary establishment with the publication of *Bratsk Station*, a cycle of poems that presented Soviet industrial initiatives in Siberia in a favorable light. Criticized in some quarters for having more flash than substance, he nevertheless took courageous stands during the BREZHNEV years against the 1968 WARSAW PACT invasion of Czechoslovakia and the persecution of dissidents such as Andrei SAKHAROV. Yevtushenko

successfully negotiated the literary currents of the remainder of the Brezhnev years, emerging as a strong liberal voice in support of Mikhail GORBACHEV's reform policies in the late 1980s. He served in the Congress of People's Deputies from 1989 to 1991. During the AUGUST COUP of 1991 he showed his support of fledgling Russian democracy when he recited poetry to the crowds standing outside the Russian White House in defiance of the attempts to restore the old Soviet order. That same year, he published a novel, *Don't Die Before You Die*, depicting events in Soviet history from the end of World War II. In addition to the poems he is best known for, Yevtushenko has written novels, political essays, and popular songs and has directed two films. In the past decade Yevtushenko has divided his time between Russia and the United States, where he is a distinguished professor of literature at Queens College in New York City. He is a member of the European Academy of Arts and Sciences and has been awarded honorary membership in the American Academy of Arts.

Yudenich, Nikolai Nikolaevich (1862–1933)
general

The most consistently successful Russian general of World War I, Yudenich later joined the anti-Bolshevik White movement and almost captured the city of Petrograd (St. Petersburg) in 1919. A veteran of the RUSSO-JAPANESE WAR of 1904–5, Yudenich was appointed to the Caucasus Army in 1907 as deputy chief of staff. Five years later he became chief of staff of the Caucasian Military District. When World War I reached the Caucasus in November 1914 with the outbreak of war between Russia and Turkey, Yudenich quickly made a name for himself with a victory at Sarikamish in eastern Turkey in December 1914. He was promoted to commander in chief of the Caucasus army in January 1915, a position he retained even after Grand Duke Nikolai was transferred to the Caucasus in September 1915 as a face-saving maneuver following the disasters of the Russian army throughout 1915. For the next two years, Yudenich's armies won important victories in eastern Turkey, capturing Erzerum in February 1916, Trebizond in April, and Erzincan in July. Yudenich's career and reputation benefited from his distant posting in the Caucasus, far from the political intrigues and the defeats faced by the Russian army at the hands of the Germans. By late 1916, however, the Turkish army was beginning to regroup while the Russians were facing supply problems and declining discipline as the political crisis that brought down the government of NICHOLAS II was ripening. He was given command of the front after the FEBRUARY REVOLUTION of 1917, but

was faced with the rapid breakdown of the army through desertions and war weariness. The Provisional Government relieved him of his command in April 1917, after which he returned to Petrograd. Following the OCTOBER REVOLUTION later that year, he hid in Petrograd until he was able to escape to Finland in November 1918. Based in Estonia, he assumed command of the White armies in the Baltic region in September 1919. The following month he advanced on Petrograd, reaching the city suburbs before the better-equipped Red Army drove his troops back to Estonia. Defeated, he was briefly interned in Estonia before emigrating to France, where he died.

Z

Zamyatin, Yevgenii Ivanovich (1884–1937)
writer

Fiercely independent and nonconformist, Zamyatin wrote satire in the tradition of GOGOL and SALTYKOV-SHCHEDRIN and ran afoul of the Soviet literary authorities during the 1920s. Born in rural Tambov province, which he satirized in early works like *District Tales* (1913), Zamyatin was trained as a naval engineer. A sojourn in Great Britain during World War I provided material for *The Islanders* (1918), a highly critical collection about English life. An early BOLSHEVIK, Zamyatin left the party soon after the October Revolution of 1917. A member of the Union of Soviet Writers, Zamyatin took part in early Soviet literary politics. As a mentoring influence on the "Serapion Brothers," a group of mostly irreverent young writers who sympathized with Communist goals but rejected the subordination of literature to propaganda, he exercised considerable influence. His opposition to the regime became more pronounced during the 1920s, and he joined the "inner emigration" of intellectuals who remained in Russia but stood aloof from the postrevolutionary order, or actively opposed it. Zamyatin's most important work is the dystopian novel *We*, written in 1919–20, but first published in English in 1925, before a Russian-language edition came out in 1927. In it he portrays a world of regimented mechanization where characters are known by numbers and that stands in contrast to the optimistic views of technology in the work of the English writer H. G. Wells. An artistically richer forerunner of the genre later mined by George Orwell in *1984* and Aldous Huxley in *Brave New World*, the novel was widely perceived as a critique of the utopian promises of the new regime and contributed to its growing hostility toward Zamyatin. This hostility escalated after the Russian-language edition appeared in an émigré journal in Czechoslovakia, and Zamyatin's works were no longer staged or published in the Soviet Union. He withdrew from the Writers' Union and personally wrote to STALIN asking for permission to emigrate, which he did by moving to Paris in 1932. His last years were not happy, and the petty intrigues of the émigré movement only nourished his misanthropic tendencies.

zapovednik (pl. *zapovedniki*)

The term for a scientific nature preserve, *zapovedniki* are vast areas of land in the Russian Federation closed off to human activity, with the exception of ecological research. Scholars have maintained that the development of *zapovedniki* from the time of the OCTOBER REVOLUTION was testimony to the unlikely survival of a surprisingly persistent and independently minded nature conservancy movement in the face of increased Communist ideological orthodoxy. There are presently 95 *zapovedniki* across the Russian Federation, ranging in size from the 570-acre Galichia Gora natural preserve in Lipetskaya province in the Black Earth region south of Moscow to the 10.3-million-acre Great Arctic Zapovednik in the Krasnoyarsk region of Siberia. Altogether, the 95 nature preserves cover an area of about 110 million acres. The first *zapovednik*, the Barguzinsky Zapovednik in the present-day Buriat republic east of Lake Baikal, was established in 1916. *Zapovedniki* were established on a fairly consistent basis during the Soviet period and in the decade after the end of the Soviet Union. In the first revolutionary decade after 1917, nine more *zapovedniki* were established, in such provinces as Astrakhan, Cheliabinsk, Krasnodar, Voronezh, and Samara. Even during the height of the Soviet industrialization campaign and in the middle of propaganda campaigns promoting triumphing over nature, 16 *zapovedniki* were established between 1928 and 1945. Thirty more were added in the years between 1946 and 1985. The pace accelerated during the GORBACHEV years (1985–1991), with the creation of 15 more *zapovedniki*. Some of the largest *zapovedniki,* such as the Great Arctic *Zapovednik* and the 9-million-acre Komandorsky *Zapovednik* in the Kamchatka Peninsula, were created after 1992, during which time 21 new preserves were established. Since 1983, the *zapovedniki* have been supplemented by a network of national parks. From 1983 to 1996, 32 national parks covering about 19 million acres of land in the Russian Federation have been created. In size the parks range from the 11,800 acres of the Orlovskoe Polesie National Park in Orel province to the south of Moscow to the 4.7-million-acre Yugyd Va National Park, located in the Komi Republic, 1,200 miles to the northeast of Moscow.

Zasulich, Vera Ivanovna (1849–1919)
revolutionary

A populist revolutionary who later advocated Marxism, Zasulich made her mark on the revolutionary movement through a spectacular act of political violence. In January 1878, she shot and wounded the St. Petersburg governor, General F. F. Trepov, in retaliation for his illegal order to flog a revolutionary who had been imprisoned six months earlier. Although the revolutionary organization Land and Liberty had made plans to avenge the deed by assassinating Trepov, Zasulich took matters into her own hands. Under the provisions of the GREAT REFORMS instituted by ALEXANDER II, Zasulich was tried by a jury that, impressed by the apparent altruism of

her motives, acquitted her, to the dismay of the government. The verdict was widely seen as an indictment of autocracy. In 1879, when Land and Liberty split into two factions over the further use of terrorism, Zasulich joined the faction that had renounced terrorism, G. V. PLEKHANOV's Black Repartition (Chernyi Peredel). The other faction, PEOPLE'S WILL (Narodnaia Volia), went on to mastermind the assassination of Alexander II in March 1881. In 1883, four years after fleeing Russia for Switzerland, Zasulich joined Plekhanov and other revolutionary émigrés in founding the first Russian Marxist organization, Liberation of Labor (Osvobozhdenie truda). Although she wrote extensively, her main contribution to the movement was her moral leadership, in addition to the heroic mantle she had gained through her early activism. As the Social Democratic Party began to fragment into its two main factions, Menshevik and Bolshevik, she tried unsuccessfully to serve as a conciliator. After the 1903 Congress of the Russian Social Democratic Labor Party (RSDLP) that resulted in the formation of the BOLSHEVIK and Menshevik factions, she sided with the Menzheviks. Zasulich returned to Russia in 1905 but ceased to be politically active. During World War I, she supported the defensive position and later opposed the Bolshevik revolution.

zemskii sobor (pl. *zemskie sobory*)

A term generally translated as "assembly of the land," an assembly of representatives of various segments of Muscovite society that was called to decide on important matters of state. Initially its members were appointed, but over time they came to be elected. The first formal Zemskii Sobor, composed of titled aristocrats and gentry, convened in 1549 during the reign of IVAN IV "the Terrible," followed by others in 1566 and 1575, to deal with issues such as the czar's proposed reforms or the Livonian War that occupied most of his reign. The Zemskii Sobor of 1584 confirmed FEODOR I, Ivan's son, as czar. In 1598, another assembly of the land was called by Patriarch Iov to elect a successor to Feodor I, who had died childless. The assembly, composed of boyars, clergy, gentry, and some merchants, chose Boris GODUNOV as czar, an election that would usher in the TIME OF TROUBLES. In 1606, at the height of the Time of Troubles, a *zemskii sobor* was called by Moscow boyars to choose a new czar after they had assassinated Dmitrii I, known as the FALSE DMITRII, who had reigned briefly as czar. The assembly chose one of its own, a boyar named Vasili Shuiiskii, who reigned until 1610 as Vasili IV.

The *zemskii sobor* that is best remembered in history is the one that convened in January 1613 to put an end to the dynastic instability of the Time of Troubles, after a national army had driven out the Poles, who had seized MOSCOW in 1610. More representative than other assemblies, its delegates numbered about 800, with about 500 coming from the provinces of Russia. The assembly was dominated by gentry and merchant interests, who had come to the fore in the drive to liberate Moscow from foreign rule. After the assembly agreed not to consider foreign candidates to the throne, it chose MICHAEL ROMANOV, a sickly 16-year old, around whose candidacy most segments of Muscovite society could unite. Thus began the ROMANOV DYNASTY, which would rule Russia for the next 300 years. With Michael as czar, an assembly of the land met with great frequency, especially during the first decade of his reign, when it met almost continuously. His son ALEKSEI also convened *zemskie sobory* to deal with such matters as the Ulozhenie of 1649 and the annexation of Ukraine.

Historians have argued over the scope and importance of these assemblies within the context of Muscovite autocracy. Most have argued that the *zemskie sobory* assisted the czars in formulating policies but did not limit their powers. Even when its members were elected rather than appointed, membership in the *zemskii sobor* was seen in the light of service to the crown. Others have noted that, especially in the reigns of Michael and the first part of Aleksei's reign, the *zemskie sobory* decided on matters of vital importance to the state. Because they could possibly grow to challenge the power of the czar, Aleksei

began to call them less frequently and PETER I, perhaps the most absolutist of 17th-century autocrats, ultimately abolished the *zemskii sobor.*

zemstvo (pl. *zemstva*)

Named after a term for a 16th-century tax-collecting institution, the *zemstva* were institutions of local government established in 1864 as part of the GREAT REFORMS designed by the government of Czar ALEXANDER II. As initially established, the *zemstva* existed on two levels, district and provincial. Delegates to the district *zemstva* were chosen indirectly and represented both the landowning gentry and the village peasant communes. The district *zemstva* then chose delegates to the provincial *zemstva*. Both district and provincial *zemstva* appointed executive boards to carry out a series of activities, such as elementary education, road construction, and the provision of health care. The *zemstva*, however, were not established uniformly across the empire. They were mostly active in the provinces of European Russia. Only in 1911 did the czar allow their establishment in the Belorussian and western Ukrainian provinces of the empire, and they were never established in Siberia.

Even though they were under the formal supervision of provincial governors, the *zemstva* operated with considerable autonomy until 1890, when a new law gave the minister of the interior the right to approve the appointment of *zemstvo* directors. The law also restricted the proportion of peasant delegates to the *zemstvo* provincial assemblies. In 1895, NICHOLAS II quashed the long-standing hope of many *zemstvo* activists for greater participation in the government as "senseless dreams." *Zemstvo* leaders were involved in the Union of Liberation that contributed to the liberal pressures on the monarchy in the first years of the 20th century. The *zemstvo* congress that met in November 1904 in St. Petersburg articulated part of the agenda of civil rights that would help drive the events of the 1905 Revolution. During World War I, despite the government's suspicion of voluntary activism, the *zemstva*, joined under the umbrella of the Union of Zemstva, became the vehicle for civic participation in assisting the war effort, under the able leadership of Prince Georgii LVOV. The February Revolution of 1917 opened up greater possibilities for action for the *zemstva*, but this was short-lived, as the Bolshevik government abolished them by 1918.

Zhdanov, Andrei Aleksandrovich (1896–1948)

Soviet official

One of STALIN's chief lieutenants, Zhdanov enjoyed a prominence that rests mainly on his role in the post–World War II early period as cultural commissar promoting a campaign to cleanse Soviet culture from "alien," Western influences. Zhdanov first came into prominence as Sergei Kirov's successor as first secretary of the Leningrad party apparatus, after the latter's assassination in December 1934. He played a central role in conducting the Great Purge of the 1930s in Leningrad and became a full member of the Communist Party's Politburo in 1939. Zhdanov participated in the defense of Leningrad against the German invaders during World War II, setting up with Kliment Voroshilov, Commissar of war until 1940 and a member of the top-level State Defense Committee, a Military Soviet for the Defense of Leningrad without consulting Stalin. When it became clear they had failed, they were dismissed but both, especially Zhdanov, managed to bounce back into the dictator's good graces. By 1946, he had replaced MALENKOV as Stalin's right-hand man. For the next two years, as party Central Committee secretary for ideological affairs, Zhdanov conducted with zeal and ruthlessness the xenophobic campaign against Western influences in Russian culture and science, a campaign known as the Zhdanovshchina (the time of Zhdanov). It began with his attack on the satirist Mikhail ZOSHCHENKO and the poet Anna AKHMATOVA, which led to their expulsion from the Union of Soviet Writers, and spread to prominent figures in philosophy, theater, film, music, and science.

Andrei Zhdanov *(Library of Congress)*

Zhdanov died in 1948 of heart failure, but his anticosmopolitan campaign continued until Stalin's death in 1953, by which time it had acquired explicit anti-Semitic overtones. In 1949–50, Malenkov and BERIA took advantage of his death to purge the party of Zhdanov's protégés in an incident known as the LENINGRAD AFFAIR. Zhdanov's unexpected death was also used as a pretext to initiate charges, subsequently dropped, against a group of Jewish doctors in the DOCTOR'S PLOT of 1953.

Zhenotdel

The acronym for the Women's Section (Department) of the Central Committee Secretariat, Zhenotdel was the agency within the Soviet

COMMUNIST PARTY that concerned itself with the defense and advancement of women's issues. The Zhenotdel was established in 1919 after much internal debate in the party on whether women's issues merited a separate institutional representation. Prominent Bolshevik women such as Aleksandra KOLLONTAI and Inessa ARMAND played an active role in the early years of the Zhenotdel but were often frustrated by the deeply rooted stereotypes about the roles of women in society, even within a party that considered itself the vanguard of the revolution. Zhenotdel activists were also constrained by their status as party members subject to party discipline. In addition to working to advance causes seen as women's issues such as curbing sexual exploitation and discrimination in the factories, the Zhenotdel also involved itself in famine relief and the campaign against mass illiteracy. In 1930, STALIN closed Zhenotdel, ironically at a time when industrialization was integrating women into the workforce at a faster rate than ever before.

Zhukov, Georgii Konstantinovich (1896–1974)

military commander

The Soviet Union's most outstanding commander during World War II, Zhukov also played a crucial role in assisting Nikita KHRUSHCHEV's consolidation of power in the first five years after STALIN's death in March 1953. Born to a peasant family, Zhukov joined the Red Army in 1918 and the COMMUNIST PARTY in 1919. He first gained recognition for his successful operations against the Japanese on the Mongolian-Manchurian frontier in 1939. During World War II, he was at first chief of the General Staff and subsequently deputy commissar of defense and deputy supreme commander in chief of the Soviet armed forces. He was prominent in the planning of Soviet operations, often coordinating the actions of a number of army groups (the defense of MOSCOW against the Germans in 1941, the Battle of STALINGRAD in 1942–43, the

relief of Leningrad in 1943, and the Red Army's advance to the West in 1943–44. On occasion he took personal command of an army group, as in the final advance on Berlin in 1945. On May 8, 1945, he received the surrender of the German High Command in Berlin, and in 1945–46 he headed the Soviet Control Commission in Germany. In 1946 he was removed by STALIN, who resented his great popularity, and after a brief period as commander in chief of land forces and deputy minister of the armed forces, he was sent into a kind of honorable retirement as commander of a Russian military district. He again became a first deputy minister upon Stalin's death in 1953, and two years later minister of defense. He was the first professional soldier to enter the real seat of power in the USSR when he became a candidate member of the Presidium of the Communist Party's Central Committee in 1956. Zhukov sided with Khrushchev against Stalin's lieutenants MALENKOV, KAGANOVICH and MOLOTOV during the "ANTI-PARTY GROUP" crisis of June 1957 and provided crucial assistance by providing transport to Central Committee members to fly to Moscow for the party vote that maintained Khrushchev in power. Khrushchev rewarded Zhukov with a seat in the Presidium, but as he began to assert the army's autonomy, Khrushchev dismissed Zhukov as minister of defense and arranged for his expulsion from the Presidium and Central Committee in October 1957. In the 1960s, particularly, the official evaluation of Zhukov's role changed in inverse proportion to that of Stalin's, rising when Stalin's fell and falling when Stalin's rose. In 1995 a monument to Zhukov was placed behind the Historical Museum that stands at one end of RED SQUARE opposite St. Basil's Cathedral.

Zinoviev, Grigorii Yevseyevich (1883–1936)

revolutionary and Soviet official

One of LENIN's closest collaborators before the Russian Revolution of 1917, Zinoviev played an important role in the early 1920s as leader of the

Leningrad Communist Party organization. Zinoviev, the pseudonym of O. G. Radomylsky, was born to Jewish dairy farmers in the Kherson region of the Ukraine. He joined the Russian Social Democratic Party in 1901, and after meeting Lenin and PLEKHANOV in Switzerland, sided with the BOLSHEVIK faction after 1903. During the 1905 Revolution, Zinoviev gained prominence as a local Bolshevik leader in St. Petersburg. He was arrested in 1908, and after being released for ill health, he joined Lenin in Kraków, then a part of Austrian Poland, beginning a close partnership. He spent the war in Switzerland, and after the FEBRUARY REVOLUTION of 1917 returned to Petrograd (St. Petersburg) with Lenin aboard the "sealed train" that brought Lenin and his close advisers from Switzerland through Germany and Finland to Russia in April 1917 after the fall of the Russian monarchy. During 1917 he formed a common front with Lev KAMENEV in speaking out against a premature seizure of power, even after the party had adopted Lenin's proposals for a Bolshevik uprising on October 25. After resigning over the exclusion of non-Bolshevik socialists from the Soviet government, Zinoviev quickly reconciled himself to the new realities of power and rejoined the government. A superb though overly dramatic speaker, he became a highly visible member of the new regime as an original full member of the party's Politburo, leader of the Petrograd Communist Party, and chairman of the Communist International (Comintern). As Lenin's health deteriorated after 1922, Zinoviev joined STALIN and Kamenev in a triumvirate to block TROTSKY from emerging as Lenin's successor. By 1925, Stalin was ready to turn against his two allies, and in 1926 Zinoviev was removed from the Politburo and the Comintern, and in 1927 expelled from the party. Subsequently readmitted and twice expelled again, he was arrested in 1935, tried secretly with Kamenev as the alleged planners behind the assassination of Stalin's close adviser Sergei Kirov and condemned to 10 years' imprisonment. The following year in August 1936 he was retried in the first of the big purge trials staged by Stalin, found guilty on a fabricated charge of conspiracy, sentenced to death for treason, and executed on August 25, 1936.

Zoshchenko, Mikhail Mikhailovich (1895–1958)
writer

An enormously popular satirist who captured the contradictions of Soviet life in the 1920s with a gentle but humorous touch, Zoshchenko was the target of particularly vicious official criticism in the years following World War II. He was born in St. Petersburg to Ukrainian parents. While a law student at Petrograd University during World War I, he volunteered for the army, enroling at Pavlovskoe Military School. An infantry lieutenant in 1915, he was wounded and poisoned by gas at the front in July 1916. He retired from the army in March 1917 with the rank of captain. He lived in Petrograd during the February and October 1917 Revolutions. In 1918, he joined the Red Army but left after two years. In 1921, he joined the literary group Serapion Brothers, which featured another future writer of prominence, Evgenii ZAMYATIN. Zoshchenko attained the peak of his popularity as a humorist during the 1920s, the era of the New Economic Policy. His short stories deftly portrayed the often bewildered but resilient man in the street, caught in the midst of a grandiose political project. He also skewered the pretensions of an emerging new elite. Zoshchenko tried to adapt to the changing winds of Soviet politics in the 1930s by writing works that fit in with the new socialist realist cultural orthodoxy. Along with other writers, he spent the war years in Kazakhstan. After the war, in 1946, his work was singled out along with that of the poet Anna AKHMATOVA by the new cultural commissar, Andrei ZHDANOV, as targets in his campaign against "cosmopolitan" tendencies in Soviet culture that needed to be rooted out. A harsh public campaign followed, during which Zoshchenko and Akhmatova were expelled from the Writers' Union, in effect banishing them to the status of nonpersons, since they could not officially work as writers. Zoshchenko lived in obscurity until his death in Leningrad. After Stalin's death in 1953, his works appeared in print again, and he regained some of the great popularity among later Soviet readers that he had formerly enjoyed.

Zubatov, Sergei Vasilievich (1864–1917)

police official

Zubatov is best known to later generations as an innovative police official who was the force behind the unusual failed experiment known as "police socialism." Zubatov was born in Moscow, where his father was an apartment manager. Zubatov's early education was typical for a future member of the intelligentsia; he read progressive literature and soaked in the ideas of the revolutionary movement. A talented speaker, he soon formed his own study circle, which soon led to broader contacts with the revolutionary world. Perhaps pressured by his father, he briefly suspended his revolutionary contacts and worked at various jobs, including managing a bookstore. Around 1882, he renewed his activities, distributing banned literature and participating in revolutionary circles. The reasons behind his conversion from a budding revolutionary to a police agent remain unclear, but in 1883 he began cooperating with the police and in 1886 formally enlisted in the Moscow branch of the czarist police, the Okhrana. Specializing in political intelligence, he sponsored innovations that helped the police grapple with the challenge of a growing revolutionary movement: photographic files, registration of suspects, mobile squads to track down suspects quickly. By 1896, at the age of only 32, he was appointed chief of the Moscow Okhrana, a reward for an until-then brilliant career. Zubatov's idea of police socialism was to create docile trade unions that, by advancing workers' agendas, would dilute their enthusiasm for more extreme revolutionary organizations. In 1901, Zubatov sponsored the foundation of the Society of Mutual Help of Workers in Mechanical Production, the first legal trade union in Russia. Under police protection this society flourished, and the experiment was later imitated in Minsk, ODESSA, and, most famously, St. Petersburg under the leadership of Father Georgii GAPON. Zubatov was able to control the movement in Moscow, but elsewhere the police trade unions were infiltrated by Social Democrats and became unruly. His initial success sparked bureaucratic jealousies, and Zubatov was transferred to St. Petersburg, where he got caught in the feud between the minister of finance Sergei WITTE and the minister of the interior Viacheslav von Plehve, and was dismissed by the latter in 1903. Exiled to Vladimir, Zubatov turned to writing about his career, a long account of which was published posthumously in the journal *Byloe* (*Past*) in 1917. On hearing of the abdication of NICHOLAS II, he committed suicide.

CHRONOLOGY

sixth–eighth centuries
Slavs migrate from central Europe into the forest zone of Russia.

Kievan Rus
862–1240

862
Traditional date for arrival in Novgorod of semilegendary Varangian (Norse) prince Rurik and establishment of Rurikid dynasty, which will provide Russian rulers until 1598.

862–879
Rurik rules in Novgorod.

882–913
Reign of Oleg.

882
Legendary arrival of Oleg at Kiev; Novgorod and Kiev unified as one state; capital transferred to Kiev.

907
Oleg attacks Constantinople, signs treaty with Byzantine Empire.

911
Second trade treaty between Kiev and Constantinople.

913
Oleg's death.

913–945
Reign of Prince Igor in Kiev.

941–944
Igor leads expedition against Constantinople.

943
Kievan campaign in Persia.

945
Igor's treaty with Constantinople.
Derevlian rebellion and Igor's death.

945–962
Olga rules as regent for her son, Sviatoslav.

954 (955?)
Olga converts to Christianity. Olga visits Constantinople and is baptized.

962–972
Reign of Sviatoslav.

964–967
Sviatoslav leads campaign against Khazar state to the east.

967–971
Sviatoslav's campaigns in the Balkans (967–92).

968
Kiev attacked by the Pechenegs.

970–971
Sviatoslav conquers Bulgaria.

971
Kiev signs treaty with Constantinople; yields territories in the Balkans and the Crimean Peninsula.

972
Sviatoslav's death.

972–980
Reign of Yaropolk.

980–1015
Reign of Vladimir, grandson of Olga.

985
Vladimir wars against Volga Bulgars.

988

Baptism of Vladimir and adoption of Orthodox Christianity as the official religion of Kievan Rus; pagan beliefs continue among population.

1015

Death of Vladimir, followed by power struggle among his sons.

Murder of Boris and Gleb, sons of Vladimir; both are later canonized by Russian Orthodox Church.

1015–1019

Reign of Sviatopolk "the Damned."

1016

Russo-Byzantine force attacks Khazar state.

1019–1054

Reign of Yaroslav "the Wise"; considered peak of Kievan power.

1025

Traditional date of the founding of the town of Yaroslavl.

1026

Yaroslav founds Dorpat.

1027

Yaroslav defeats the Pechenegs.

1030

Yaroslav starts first school in Novgorod.

1031

Yaroslav attacks Poland.

1036

Yaroslav begins undivided rule.
Pechenegs attack Kiev.

1037

Yaroslav defeats the Pechenegs.
Saint Sophia Cathedral begun in Kiev.

1037–1056

Construction and decoration of Church of St. Sophia in Kiev.

1045–1052

Building of St. Sophia, Novgorod (1045–57?).

ca. 1050

Ilarion's "Sermon on Law and Grace."

1051

Ilarion consecrated as metropolitan of Kiev and all Rus.

Cave at Peshchersk Lavra, near Kiev, settled by Antonius of Chernigov.

1054

Death of Yaroslav "the Wise."
Polovtsians arrive at Kievan frontiers.
Schism between Eastern and Western Christian Churches.

1054–1073

Russkaya Pravda (Russian Justice), first Russian law code, prepared.

1054–1113

Period of frequent war among sons of Yaroslav, covers the reigns of Iziaslav (1054–78, passim), Sviatoslav (1073–76), and Vsevolod (1076–93, passim), and Iziaslav's son, Sviatopolk II (1093–1113).

1061

Polovtsians attack Kievan territory for first time.

1068–1069

Uprising in Kiev against Prince Izyaslav. Polovtsian invasion of Kiev.

1072

Canonization of Princes Boris and Gleb.

1095

First election of a prince in Novgorod.

1096

Polovtsy attack Kiev and burn Pecherskii Monastery.

1097

Grandsons of Yaroslav meet at Liubech Conference and attempt to settle territorial disputes and succession claims by partitioning Kievan Rus into patrimonial estates.

1108

Traditional date of the founding of the town of Vladimir.

1109

"Monk Nestor," possibly several authors in reality, completes the Primary Chronicle.

1111

Vladimir Monomakh defeats Polovtsians at Salnitsa.

1113

Rebellion in Kiev.

1113–1125

Reign of Vladimir Monomakh in Kiev as grand prince.

1116

Primary Chronicle composed.

1125

Second version of Russkaia Pravda begun; completed ca. 1200.

1125–1132

Reign of Mstislav, son of Vladimir Monomakh.

1126

First election of a mayor by the Novgorod veche (assembly).

1132–1136

Emergence of semiautonomous Novgorod.

1132–1139

Reign of Yaropolk, Vladimir Monomakh's second son.

1136

Novgorod expels its ruling prince.

1139–1146

Reign of Viacheslav, Vladimir Monomakh's sixth son.

1147

First reference to Moscow in a chronicle.

1148

First election of a bishop in Novgorod.

1149–1157

Reign of Yuri Dolgoruky, seventh son of Vladimir Monomakh.

1153–1187

Reign of Yaroslav Osmomysl as prince of Galicia.

1156

Construction of first Kremlin walls in Moscow.

1157

Death of Yuri Dolgorukii, prince of Suzdalia, considered the founder of Moscow.

1157–1174

Reign of Andrei Bogoliubsky, prince of Vladimir-Suzdal, first son of Yuri Dolgoruky.

1169

Andrei Bogoliubsky captures Kiev; city destroyed; capital transferred to Vladimir.

1174

Death of Andrei Bogoliubsky.

1176–1212

Reign of Vsevolod III "Big Nest," second son of Yuri Dolgoruky.

1185

Unsuccessful expedition of Prince Igor of Novgorod-Seversk against Polovtsians, basis of Tale of Igor's Campaign.

1191–1192

Novgorod signs commercial treaty with Scandinavians and Germans.

1196

Novgorod granted the right to select its own prince.

ca. 1200

Polovtsians cut the Kiev-Constantinople trading route.

1203

Kiev sacked by forces from Smolensk and Chernigov.

1204

Latin Crusaders capture and sack Constantinople, will rule until 1261.

1206

Chinggis (Genghis) Khan assumes command of the Mongols.

1209

First recorded reference to Tver.

1211

Mongols invade China.

1212

Death of Grand Duke Vsevolod III of Vladimir-Suzdal and partition of Vladimir-Suzdal principality.

1212–1237

Reign of Yuri II, third son of Vsevolod III.

1218–1221

Mongols conquer Central Asia.

1221

Founding of Nizhnii Novgorod on the Volga River.

1223

First Mongol raid of southern Russia; Mongols defeat Kievan forces at Battle of Kalka.

1227

Death of Chinggis Khan.

1237

Mongol invasion of Russia under Batu, Genghis Khan's grandson, begins.

1237–1238

Mongol attacks on northeastern Russia.

1237–1246

Reign of Yaroslav, fourth son of Vsevolod III.

1240

Mongols conquer southern Russia, fall of Kiev.

Mongol Rule and the Rise of Muscovy
1240–1598

1240

Alexander Nevsky, prince of Novgorod, defeats Swedes on the Neva River.

1240–1242

Mongols continue attacks in southern Russia, Poland, and Hungary before withdrawing to Mongolia to resolve succession crisis.

1242

Alexander Nevsky defeats Teutonic knights at "Battle on the Ice," at Lake Chud (Peipus).

Grand Prince Yaroslav confirmed in office by Mongols.

ca. 1243

Formation of the Mongol state known as the Golden Horde, with northeastern Russia and Novgorod as tributary states.

1252

Emergence of Moscow as an independent hereditary principality.

Alexander Nevsky of Novgorod made grand prince.

1252–1263

Reign of Alexander Nevsky, great prince of Vladimir.

1253

Founding of Sarai as capital of the Golden Horde.

1256–1259

Mongols conquer the Caucasus and Iran.

1257

Mongols conduct the first census of Russia.

1257–1259

Anti-Mongol uprisings throughout Kievan Rus.

1262

Rebellion in Suzdal.

1263

Death of Prince Alexander Nevsky.

1263–1304

Brothers and sons of Alexander Nevsky rule as grand princes of Vladimir.

1270

Novgorod negotiates a treaty with the Hanseatic League.

1275

Population of Russia estimated at 10 million.

ca. 1276

Appanage principality of Moscow carved out for Nevsky's son Daniil, who rules until 1303 as prince of Moscow.

1282–1283

Leaders of the Golden Horde adopt Islam.

1294

Death of Qubilai (Kublai) Khan; decline in unity of Mongol Empire.

First Russian icon dated and signed in Novgorod.

1300

Transfer of Metropolitan Office from Kiev to Vladimir.

1301

Moscow annexes Pereyaslavl, Kolomna, and Mozhaisk, beginning process of territorial expansion later known as the "gathering of the Russian lands."

1303–1325

Reign of Yuri Danilovich as prince of Moscow.

1316–1341

Reign of Gedymin of Lithuania.

1318

Prince Yuri Danilovich of Moscow becomes first Muscovite to be recognized as grand prince by the Mongols.

1322

Charter of the grand prince passes to Dmitrii of Tver.

1325

Metropolitan Peter moves to Moscow.

1325–1340

Ivan I (Kalita, or "Moneybags"), prince of Moscow.

1327

Anti-Mongol uprising in Tver, suppressed by Ivan I with Mongol help.

1328

Ivan I gains the title of grand prince.

Metropolitan moves his seat from Vladimir to Moscow.

1337

Founding of Holy Trinity Monastery by St. Sergius in Sergiev-Posad.

1341–1353

Reign of Simeon "the Proud," eldest son of Ivan I, in Moscow.

1348

By mutual agreement, Pskov separates itself from Novgorod and forms an independent city-state.

Swedish King Magnus marches against Novgorod.

1349

Galicia annexed by Poland.

1352

Black Death in Novgorod and Moscow.

1353–1359

Reign of Ivan II "the Meek," third son of Ivan I Kalita.

1359–1389

Rule of Dimitrii Donskoi, prince of Moscow (grand prince after 1362), son of Ivan II.

1360–1362

Struggle between Moscow and Suzdal for the title of grand prince.

1360s

Dynastic crises in Golden Horde.

1362

Kiev taken by Olgerd, grand duke of Lithuania.

1367–1368

First stone fortifications of the Moscow Kremlin laid.

1368

Olgerd of Lithuania attacks Moscow.

Collapse of Mongol power in China.

1371–1375

Heresy of Strigolniki (Shearers) in Novgorod.

1375

Tver acknowledges Moscow as a grand principality.

1377

Death of Olgerd of Lithuania, who controlled about half of the old Kievan Rus lands.

1378

Feofan Grek (Theophanes the Greek) paints first frescoes in Novgorod.

Dmitrii Donskoi defeats Mongols on the banks of the Vozha River.

1380

Dmitrii Donskoi defeats Khan Mamay at the Battle of Kulikovo.

1382

Moscow taken and burnt by Khan Tokhtamysh.

1386

Dynastic union of Lithuania with Poland and conversion of Lithuanian dynasty to Catholicism.

Volhynia annexed by Lithuania.

1389–1395

Timur (Tamerlane) attacks Golden Horde and sacks Sarai, its capital.

1389–1425

Reign of Vasili I, eldest son of Dmitrii Donskoi, in Moscow.

1390–1430

Active life of icon painter Andrei Rublev.

1392

Moscow absorbs Suzdal and Nizhnii Novgorod.

1395

Tamerlane begins march against Moscow but turns back near Oka River.

1408

Principality of Moscow devastated by the Golden Horde.

1425–1448

War of succession for Moscow's throne between Vasili II, son of Vasili I, and his uncle, Prince Igor, whose cause was later defended by his sons Vasili the Squint-eyed and Dimitrii Shemiaka.

1425–1462

Reign of Vasili II, the Blind

1427

Beginning of disintegration of Golden Horde and formation of the Crimean Khanate.

1436

Founding of Solovetsky Monastery.

1437

Formation of the Kazan Khanate.

1437–1439

Council of Florence attempts to reunite Eastern and Western Churches. Russian hierarchy rejects attempt.

1441

Metropolitan Isidore deposed in Moscow for acceptance of Council of Florence.

1447

Renewed union of Poland and Lithuania.

1448

Church of Moscow declared autocephalous; Council of Russian bishops chooses Bishop Iona of Ryazan as metropolitan, without approval of Constantinople.

1452

Mongol prince of Kasimov places himself under Muscovite authority; first Mongol ruler to accept Russian suzerainty.

1453

Ottoman Turks capture Constantinople; end of Byzantine Empire.

1458

Kievan metropolitan assumes independence from Moscow.

1459

Formation of the Astrakhan Khanate.

1462–1505

Reign of Ivan III the Great.

1463

Moscow annexes the principality of Yaroslavl.

1463–1468

First limitations upon freedom of peasant movement.

1470

The "Judaizer" heresy spreads throughout Novgorod.

1471

Moscow attacks Novgorod and defeats its armies.

1472

Moscow annexes the principality of Perm.
Ivan III marries Zoe (Sophia) Paleologos, niece of last Byzantine emperor.

1474

Moscow annexes Rostov.

1475–1479

Building of the Uspensky Sobor (Cathedral of Assumption) in the Moscow Kremlin by Fieravanti.

1476

Ambrosio Contarini, first Westerner to visit and write about Moscow.

1477
Moscow again attacks Novgorod and annexes it; introduction of conditional land tenure, known as *pomeste*.

1480
After Battle of Ugra, Ivan III declares formal independence of Moscow from Mongol control.

1484–1489
Muscovite massacres in Novgorod and inland deportation of its leading citizens.

1485
Moscow annexes Tver.

1485–1516
Building of the new Kremlin in Moscow.

1488
Uprising in Novgorod.

1489
Moscow annexes Viatka.

1493
Ivan III adopts title of "Sovereign of All Russia."

1494
Hanseatic League closes depot in Novgorod.
Treaty with Lithuania recognizes Moscovite territorial claims.

1497
Ivan III issues Sudebnik (Code of Laws), which contains first substantial limitation on peasant movement, a precursor of serfdom.

1500–1503
War with Lithuania. Muscovy conquers Lithuanian "Severian principalities" and Chernigov.

1503
Church Council condemns the heresy of Judaizers and rejects Nil Sorsky's appeal for voluntary renunciation of ecclesiastical properties.

1505–1509
Cathedral of Archangel (Arkhangelsk) Michael built in Moscow Kremlin by Alevisio Nuovi of Milan.

1505–1533
Reign of Vasilii III as grand prince of Moscow.

1510
Moscow annexes city-state of Pskov, followed by mass deportations of local population.

1512–1522
War with Lithuania.

1514
Moscow conquers Smolensk.
First Russian-language books printed in Prague.

1521
Vasili III deposes Metropolitan Varlaam.
Moscow annexes Ryazan, last independent principality in central Russia.
Crimean forces reach Moscow.

1524
Novodevichi Convent founded by Vasili III in Moscow.

1525
Metropolitan Daniil authorizes Vasili's divorce.
Maxim the Greek found guilty of heresy.

1533
Ivan IV inherits throne at age of three as grand prince of Moscow.

1533–1538
Regency of Ivan's mother, Elena Glinskaia

1533–1584
Reign of Ivan IV ("Grozny," or "the Terrible").

1535
Edicts against further monastic acquisitions of land.

1547

Marriage and coronation of Ivan IV, who becomes first Muscovite ruler to assume title of "Czar."

1549

First *zemskii sobor* (assembly of the land).

1550

New *sudebnik* (law code) issued by Ivan IV.
Streltsy (musketeer) regiments first organized.

1550–1551

Church proposes reforms at Council of Stoglav (Hundred Chapters).

1550s

First chancelleries formed and reforms of local administration.
Moscow constructs chain of stockades along southern border and Russian colonization of the steppe begins.

1551

Foundation of Sviiazhsk and incorporation into the Muscovite state of the part of the Khanate of Kazan on the right bank of the Volga.

1552

Capture and annexation of remaining part of Khanate of Kazan.

1553

Ivan's illness.
English merchants led by Richard Chancellor reach Russia through White Sea route.

1555

Formation of the Muscovy Company in London and extension of privileges to it for trade throughout the Moscow state.
Reform of local fiscal system.
St. Basil's Cathedral on Red Square begun.

1556

Conquest of the Khanate of Astrakhan.

1558

Stroganov family granted land along the Kama River.

1558–1583

Livonian War fought against Poland-Lithuania and Sweden. Initial Muscovite victories are followed by eventual failure to secure access to Baltic Sea coastline.

1560

Death of Ivan's first wife, Anastasia Romanova.

1560s

First edition of Domostroi, a book of principles of family life.

1561

The Livonian Order disbanded.

1563

Death of Metropolitan Macarius.
Russians capture Polotsk.

1564

Flight of Andrei Kurbsky to Lithuania.
Fearful of conspiracy in Moscow, Ivan IV retires to Aleksandrovsk.
First book printed in Moscow by Ivan Fedorov.

1565

Creation of Ivan IV's personal guard, the oprichnina, which will conduct reign of terror in Moscow and other towns until 1572.

1566

Zemskii Sobor (Assembly of the Land) convened to discuss Livonian War.

1568–1571

Famine and plague visit Muscovy.

1569

Union of Lublin leads to the merger of Poland and Lithuania and establishment of the Polish-Lithuanian Commonwealth.

1570

Ivan's oprichnina attacks Novgorod, razes city, and massacres inhabitants.

1571–1572

Crimean Tatars raid and burn Moscow.

1571–1600

Fortification of southern frontier; beginning of Don, Zaporozhe, and Ural Cossacks.

1572

Ivan IV disbands oprichnina and purges its leaders.

1575

Ivan abdicates temporarily in favor of Semyon Bekbulatovich.

1577

Establishment of commercial ties with Holland.

1580

First law forbidding peasants to change landlords.

1580s

Boris Godunov sends 18 Russians to study abroad; they do not return.

1581

Ivan kills his eldest son, Ivan.

1581–1584

Cheremis and Tatar uprisings against Muscovite rule.

1581–1592

New property books drawn up that serve as basis for serfdom.

1582

Yermak's initial conquest of khanate of western Siberia.

Privilege of St. George's Day (November 26), permitting peasant movement once a year, is abolished.

1584

Founding of Archangel (Arkhangelsk) on the White Sea.

Death of Ivan IV.

1584–1598

Reign of Feodor I, third son of Ivan IV.

1586

Founding of the fortress of Ufa in the Urals.

1586–1587

Founding of Tobolsk and Tiumen, the first Russian fortresses in Siberia.

1587–1598

Boris Godunov, Feodor's brother-in-law, acts as regent.

1588

Giles Fletcher visits Moscow.

1589

Law code (Sudebnik). Russian patriarchate established and office established in Moscow.

1590

Outbreak of war with Sweden.

1591

Murder of Prince Dmitrii, son of Ivan IV, at Uglich.

1595

Peace of Teusin ends war with Sweden.

1596

Creation of Uniate Church in Poland-Lithuania.

1597

Ukaz grants nobles five years to claim their fugitive peasants.

1598

Feodor dies childless, ending lineage of rulers who could trace their ancestry back to Rurik.

Time of Troubles
1598–1613

1598

Coronation of Boris Godunov, brother-in-law of Feodor III and virtual ruler since 1587.

Traditional date for beginning of Time of Troubles, a period of dynastic crises, foreign invasions, and internal social rebellions that will end with the accession of the Romanov dynasty in 1613.

1598–1605

Reign of Boris Godunov.

1601–1602

Edicts further restricting peasant mobility.

1601–1604

Years of famine.

1604

First invasion by Poles in support of First False Dmitrii.

1605

Death of Boris Godunov.

(April–June) Rule of Feodor II, Boris Godunov's son, killed in June 1605.

1605–1606

First False Dmitrii reigns as czar.

1606

Moscow uprising and murder of False Dimitrii.

1606–1607

Rebellion under Bolotnikov and Shakhovskoi.

1606–1610

Rule of Czar Vasili Shuisky, the "boyar czar."

1607–1610

Rebellion under Second False Dmitrii.

Poles intervene in support of Second False Dmitrii.

1609

Swedish intervention on behalf of Shuiskii.

1610

Shuisky deposed by Muscovite population.

Second False Dmitrii murdered.

Polish troops occupy Moscow; Prince Władysław, son of king of Poland, crowned czar.

1611

Poland-Lithuania conquers Smolensk.

National revival begins in Nizhnii Novgorod, led by Minin and Pozharsky.

1611–1617

Swedes occupy Novgorod.

1612

Russian troops led by Pozharsky capture Moscow from Poles.

1613

Zemskii Sobor elects Michael Romanov as czar. Beginning of Romanov dynasty, which will last until 1917.

Romanov Dynasty
1613–1917

1613–1645

Reign of Michael Romanov.

1617

Treaty of Stolbovo; Sweden evacuates Novgorod and Muscovy loses outlets to Baltic Sea.

1618

Treaty of Deulino: Muscovy cedes Smolensk and the "Severian" principalities to Poland-Lithuania.

1619

Filaret, Michael Romanov's father, consecrated as patriarch; coruler with Michael from 1619–33.

1619–1648

Russian explorers advance in Siberia beyond the Yenisei and Lena Rivers as far as the Pacific Ocean. Yakutsk is reached in 1632 and Okhotsk in 1648.

1631

Peter Mogila, metropolitan of Kiev, founds Kiev Academy.

1632

Winius and Marselis found Tula and Kashira iron foundries.

1632–1634

"Smolensk War" with Poland follows from Russian attempt to recapture Smolensk.

1634–1638

Adam Olearius visits Moscow.

1636

Patriarch orders all musical instruments burned.

1637

Don Cossacks conquer Azov.
Establishment of the Sibirskii Prikaz (Siberian Chancellery).

1639

Russian explorers first reach the Pacific Ocean.

1642

Michael Romanov calls the Assembly of the Land (Zemskii Sobor).

1643–1646

Peyarlov reaches the Sea of Okhotsk.

1645–1676

Reign of Aleksei Mikhailovich.

1648

Urban rebellions across Russia; tax revolt in Moscow.

Bogdan Khmelnitsky leads Dnieper Cossacks in rebellion against Poland-Lithuania.
Trading privileges of the Muscovy Company are withdrawn.

1649

Law Code fully establishes serfdom by strengthening provisions that lead to bondage of peasant population.

1650

Patriarch standardizes the five-domed church.
Novgorod and Pskov rebellions.

1650s

Moscow population estimated at about 200,000.

1652

Founding of the German settlement (Nemetskaia Sloboda) in Moscow as required residence for foreigners.
Nikon consecrated as patriarch of the Russian Orthodox Church.
Last full meeting of Zemskii Sobor.

1652–1658

Nikon as patriarch institutes reforms of liturgy and scripture that will eventually lead to schism in the Russian Orthodox Church.

1652–1661

Establishment of the fortress of Irkutsk near Lake Baikal in Siberia.

1654

Agreement of Pereiaslav and Moscow between the Dnieper Cossacks and the Muscovite czar. Cossacks recognize Muscovite suzerainty.
Russians conquer Smolensk.

1654–1657

(Second) Northern War with Sweden.

1654–1667

Thirteen Years' War between Russia and Poland over Ukraine.

1655

Muscovy establishes military alliance with Kalmyks near Caspian Sea area.

1656–1668

War with Sweden.

1660s

Moscow first linked with Amsterdam and Berlin by regular postal service.

1662

"Copper riots" in Moscow.

1663

Little Russian Chancellery established to deal with Ukrainian affairs.

1664

Russian official, Grigorii Kitoshikhin, flees to Sweden.

1666–1667

Establishment of postal service in Russia.

Church Council deposes Patriarch Nikon, but retains his reforms; issues anathema for those who reject reforms marks; beginning of schism (*raskol*) in Russian Orthodox Church. Schismatics will be known as Old Believers.

1667

Treaty of Andrusovo ends Thirteen Years' War; Poland cedes Kiev and Smolensk to Russia and Ukraine is divided between the two countries. Territorial changes are confirmed and made permanent by 1686 treaty of "eternal peace."

New Commercial Code promulgated.

1667–1676

Monks at Solovetsky Monastery on the White Sea revolt against church reforms.

1670–1671

Stenka Razin leads popular uprising of Cossacks and peasants.

1671

Archpriest Avvakum writes his *Life* in prison.

1672

Birth of Peter Alekseevich, the future Peter the Great.

Russians establish embassies in all major European states.

First theatrical performance, *Artakserova deistva*, given at Moscow court.

1674

Synopsis, first Russian history textbook, appears.

1676

Theater opens at Preobrazhenskoe.

Death of Czar Alexis and accession of Feodor III, half brother of Peter.

1676–1681

War with the Ottoman Empire (First Russo-Turkish War).

1676–1682

Reign of Feodor III.

1682

Abolition of *mestnichestvo*, precedence system that had regulated military and government appointments.

Feodor III's death is followed by *streltsy* rebellion in Moscow; Ivan V and Peter, half brothers, are installed as co-czars with their sister Sophia as regent.

Execution of Archpriest Avvakum.

1684

Institution of formal persecution of Old Believers.

1685

Office of the metropolitan of Kiev is placed under the jurisdiction of the Moscow Patriarchate.

1686

Treaty with Poland promises "eternal peace" between two nations and confirms territorial changes of 1667 Treaty of Andrusovo.

Russia joins anti-Turkish Holy League with Venice, Poland, and the Holy Roman Empire.

Slavic-Greek-Latin academy opens in Moscow.

Peter begins experiments in shipbuilding on Lake Pleshcheyev.

1687

Peter marries Evdokiia Lopukhina.

1687–1689

Vasilii Golitsyn's failed campaigns against the Tatar Khanate of Crimea.

1689

Treaty of Nerchinsk with China establishes boundaries between the two nations.

Sophia removed as regent, banished to Novodevichi Convent.

1689–1695

Second regency under Peter's mother; Ivan V and Peter I continue as co-czars.

1689–1725

Reign of Peter I the Great.

1690

Birth of Peter's son and heir, Alexis.

1693

Peter visits Archangel and sees ocean for the first time.

1696

Following Ivan V's death, Peter becomes sole czar.

Russians capture port of Azov on the Sea of Azov, near the Black Sea, after an unsuccessful attack in the previous year.

Building of a naval squadron begins at Azov.

1697

Preobrazhenskii Prikaz given exclusive authority over political crimes.

Conquest of Kamchatka peninsula.

1697–1698

Peter leads Great Embassy to Western Europe. He visits the Netherlands, England, and Austria but fails to secure help against the Ottoman Empire.

1698

Streltsy revolt breaks out in Moscow while Peter is in the West and is savagely suppressed.

1699

Beginning of metal production in the Ural Mountains region.

1700

Peace with Ottoman Empire.

Swedes defeat Russians at Narva.

Patriarch Adrian dies; no successor will be appointed until 1917.

Russia adopts Julian calendar.

1700–1721

Great Northern War between Russia and Sweden.

1701

Kiev College is transformed into an academy.

Monasteries required to turn over revenues to state.

School of Mathematics and Navigation founded.

1702

Peter issues manifesto welcoming foreigners to Russia.

First public theater opened in Moscow.

1703

Founding of St. Petersburg on the banks of the Neva River; construction of Peter and Paul fortress begins in St. Petersburg.

Publication of first Russian newspaper, *Vedomosti* (Gazette).

1704

Russians take Narva from Swedes.

1705

Systematic military conscription established.

1705–1706
Streltsy revolt at Astrakhan.

1707
Reform of provincial administration.
Swedes, led by King Charles XII, begin major advance against Russia.

1707–1708
Cossack revolt on lower Don River, led by Kondratii Bulavin.

1708
Swedes defeated at the battle of Lesnaya. Cossack ataman Mazepa joins their side.
Reformed Cyrillic alphabet adopted.

1708–1709
Sweden invades Russia.

1709
Battle of Poltava gives Russia a decisive victory over Sweden.

1710
First household and tax census.
Russians take Livonia and Estonia.

1711
War with Turkey; Russian troops defeated on the Prut River; Azov surrendered to the Turks.
Peter abolishes most trading monopolies.
Peter creates the Senate to replace the traditional Czar's Council (Boyar Duma).
Court and many administrative agencies transferred to St. Petersburg from Moscow.

1712
Peter's marriage to Catherine, his mistress.

1713
St. Petersburg becomes Russia's capital.
Peace treaty with the Ottoman Empire.

1713–1718
Measures taken against Muslim Tatar nobility.

1714
Decree requires that estates be handed down to a sole heir.
Practice of "feeding" (*kormleniia*) is abolished, and civil servants are placed on a salary.
Naval academy is opened.
Russians win naval victory over Swedes at Hangö.

1715–1717
First Russian expedition to Central Asia.

1716
Flight of Peter's son Alexis to Vienna and Naples.
Military Code is issued.

1716–1717
Construction of Peterhof (Petrodvorets) palace near St. Petersburg begins.

1716–1718
Founding of the fortresses of Omsk and Semipalatinsk.

1717
Peter's second journey to western Europe; he visits the Netherlands and Paris.
Alexis returns to Russia.
Establishment of government colleges to replace chancelleries.

1718
Investigation and trial of Alexis and others on charges of conspiracy. Alexis is executed after guilty verdict.

1718–1722
National census conducted.

1719
Provincial reform.

1720
Naval Code and General Regulation are issued to assist in efforts to systematize the government bureaucracy.

Publication of Ivan Pososhkov's book *On Poverty and Wealth*.

1721

Treaty of Nystadt ends Great Northern War with Sweden; Russia acquires Livonia, Estonia, Karelia, and Ingria.

Peter assumes title of emperor; Senate honors him with designation of Peter the Great.

Spiritual Regulation issued establishing office of Holy Synod to administer the Church; Patriarchate formally abolished.

Merchants allowed to purchase villages to attach serf laborers to industrial and mining enterprises.

Organization of state postal service.

1722

Table of Ranks promulgated.

Peter abolishes succession law and assumes right to choose his own successor.

Little Russian College founded to administer Ukranian affairs.

1722–1723

War with Persia; Russians campaign along Caspian Sea and conquer parts of Azerbaijan, which they will hold until 1735.

1722–1724

Completion of first universal (male) census; first collection of "soul tax."

1724

Catherine, Peter's second wife, is crowned as empress.

Founding of the Imperial Russian Academy of Sciences at St. Petersburg.

1725

Death of Peter and accession of Catherine.

1725–1727

Reign of Catherine I (hegemony of Alexander Menshikov).

1725–1729

First Arctic expedition of Vitus Bering.

1726

Supreme Privy Council created; it will dominate Russian politics until 1730.

Alliance between Russia and Austria established.

1727

Death of Catherine and accession of Peter II, son of Czarevich Alexis.

Downfall and exile of Alexander Menshikov.

1727–1730

Reign of Peter II, grandson of Peter the Great from his son Alexis.

1728

First issue of newspaper, *Sankt-Peterburgskie vedomosti*.

1730

Constitutional crisis results from Supreme Privy Council's unsuccessful attempt to impose limitations on Anna's power.

Peter's inheritance law of 1714 requiring inherited gentry estates to be handed down undivided is repealed.

Emergence of Ernst-Johann Biron as favorite in Anna's government.

1730–1740

Reign of Anna Ivanovna, second daughter of Ivan V, Peter the Great's half-brother.

1731

Establishment of Noble Cadet Corps, a cadet school for gentry children.

1731–1742

Kazakh khans swear oaths of loyalty to Russia.

1732–1741

Vitus Bering's Second Arctic expedition.

1733–1735
War of Polish Succession against France (Russia in alliance with Austria).

1734–1740
Final subjugation of the Bashkirs, who offer bitter resistance in full-blown colonial war.

1735
Orenburg founded on southeastern border and southern Urals to assist in campaign against Bashkirs.

1736
Changes in Peter's system limit compulsory state service for gentry to 25 years instead of lifetime service; service may begin at age 20. One son may remain at home to care for landed estates. "Possessional" serfs attached in perpetuity to factories and mines.

1736–1739
War against Turkey.

ca. 1740
Imperial Ballet School established at the Winter Palace.

1740–1741
Reign of infant Ivan VI (son of regent Anna Leopoldovna, Anna's niece).

1741
Bering's expedition reaches the coast of Alaska. Lomonosov appointed to the Academy of Sciences.

1741–1743
War against Sweden.

1741–1755
Aggressive missionary policy toward Muslims and other non-Christian subjects.

1741–1762
Reign of Elizabeth, daughter of Peter the Great from second marriage.

1743
Peace of Abo, new border with Finland.

1744
Sophie of Anhalt-Zerbst, the future Catherine the Great, arrives in Russia to marry Peter, Elizabeth's nephew, and designated heir to the throne.

1746
Ban of purchase of serfs by non-nobles.

1746–1748
Russia participates in War of Austrian Succession.

1750
First professional Russian theater founded in Yaroslavl by Feodor Volkov.

1753
Internal tariffs and tolls in Russian Empire abolished.

1754
Abolition of internal tariffs; establishment of Noble Bank.

1754–1762
Bartolomeo Rastrelli builds the Winter Palace.

1755
University of Moscow founded through efforts of Lomonosov.

1756–1762
Russian participates in Seven Years' War.

1760
Landowners granted right to exile serfs to Siberia.

1761–1762
Reign of Peter III.

1762
Manifesto on rights of nobility exempts gentry from all compulsory state service requirements.

Secularization of monastic lands sequesters church and monastic properties, beginning in 1764.

Most commercial and manufacturing monopolies abolished.

Law of 1721 allowing merchants to buy villages is revoked.

Peter III overthrown and murdered in palace coup. His wife assumes throne as Catherine II.

1762–1763

Catherine the Great (r. 1762–1796) issues manifesto inviting foreign colonists to Russia.

1762–1796

Reign of Catherine II, "the Great."

1764

Cossack office of ataman abolished.

Automatic promotion for certain categories of civil servants.

Death of Ivan VI, imprisoned since 1741.

Russo-Prussian alliance.

Final secularization of church lands.

1764–1767

Founding of German colonies along the lower Volga region.

1765

Establishment of Free Economic Society.

1766

Publication of Catherine's "Great Instruction."

1767

Automatic promotion rules for civil servants extended.

Peasants fobidden to submit complaints against their landowners.

1767–1768

Legislative Commission convoked to draft new code of laws.

1767–1773

Commission for new legal code.

1768

Greater Russian influence on Poland-Lithuania.

1768–1774

Russo-Turkish War. Russia acquires the areas to the north of the Black Sea.

1769

First Russian satirical journals published by Catherine.

Establishment of Imperial Council.

1771

Bubonic plague epidemic spreads through Russia with riots in Moscow.

Conquest of the Khanate of Crimea, which becomes Russian protectorate.

Massive Kalmyk emigration to Central Asia and abolition of Khanate of the Kalmyks.

1772

First partition of Poland (July)—Belorussia annexed to Russia.

1773–1774

Pugachev Rebellion, a popular uprising of peasants and Cossacks in the lower Volga region.

1774

Treaty of Kuchuk-Kainarji ends Russo-Turkish War and recognizes Russian protectorate over Christians in Ottoman Empire.

1775

Conquest, destruction, and dissolution of the Zaporozhian Cossacks; limits placed on Cossack autonomy.

Promulgation statute on provincial administration.

Manufacturing opened to all estates.

1780

Russia joins League of Armed Neutrality.

1780s

Construction of imperial palaces at Tsarskoe Selo, outside St. Petersburg.

1781
Alliance with Austria.

1781–1786
Administrative absorption of the Ukraine follows end of Ukrainian autonomy.

1782
Law on Provincial Police.

1782–1786
Giacomo Quarenghi builds the Hermitage Palace.

1783
Gentry allowed to operate private printing presses.
Russia establishes protectorate over east Georgian kingdom in Treaty of Georgievsk.
Annexation of the Khanate of the Crimean Tatars.

1783–1785
Russian administrative reforms applied to the Baltic provinces (partially revoked in 1796).

1784
Acquisition of Kodiak Island off Alaska; Grigorii Shelekov establishes first Russian colony in Alaska.
Foundation of fortress of Vladikavkaz.

1785
Charters to the nobility and towns.

1785–1791
Chechens and Dagestanis under Sheik Mansur wage guerilla war against Russia.

1787
Catherine's tour of "New Russia."

1787–1792
War with the Ottoman Empire.

1788
Establishment of Assembly of Muslim Clergy in Ufa.

1789
French Revolution begins.

1790
Publication of Aleksandr Radishchev's *Journey from St. Petersburg to Moscow,* followed by his arrest and banishment to Siberia.

1791
Polish Constitution of May 3.

1792
Novikov arrested.
Treaty of Jassy ends war with Turkey.

1793
Second Partition of Poland.
Russia breaks diplomatic relations with revolutionary France.

1794
Polish uprising under Tadeusz Kosciuszko.
Introduction of double taxation for Jews.

1795
Third Partition of Poland.

1796
Death of Catherine.
Alexander palace completed.

1796–1801
Reign of Paul I, son of Peter III and Catherine II.

1797
Paul issues new law of succession.
Serfdom extended to southern Russia.
Imperial edict restricts labor duty of serfdom to three days a week.

1798
Paul elected grand master of the Knights of Malta.
Russia forms the Second Coalition against France.
War with France.
Suvorov's campaigns in Italy and Switzerland.

1799

Founding of Russian American Company.

1800

Russia changes alliances, tie to France.

1801

With Napoleon's encouragement Paul plans Russian expedition to India.
Palace coup and assassination of Paul.
Annexation of Kingdom of Georgia.
Nongentry allowed to own land.
Formation of Unofficial Committee.

1801–1825

Reign of Alexander I, first son of Paul.

1802

Reorganization of senate and establishment of ministries to replace administrative colleges.
University of Dorpat reopened.

1803

Law on voluntary emancipation of serfs.

1803–1811

Russian protectorate over principalities of west Georgia (complete incorporation by 1857).

1804

Educational Reform; establishment of three additional universities in Vilna, Kazan, and Kharkov.
Statute on Jews establishes Pale of Settlement, restricting Jewish residency to the western provinces of the empire.

1804–1807

Russia joins alliance against Napoleon.

1804–1813

Russo-Persian War, conquest of khanates in northern Azerbaijan.

1805

War of Third Coalition.
Russians defeated by Napoleon at Austerlitz.

1806

Russians conquer Dagestan and Baku.

1806–1812

War with Turkey.

1806–1815

Construction of new Admiralty building in St. Petersburg by Zakharov.

1807

Abolition of serfdom in Duchy of Warsaw.
Russians defeated by Napoleon at Friedland.
Treaty of Tilsit with Napoleon.

1807–1811

Speransky reforms.

1808–1809

War with Sweden.

1809

Speransky's plan for a constitution presented.
Grand Duchy of Warsaw expanded.
Krylov publishes first fables.
Abortive attempt to introduce civil service examinations.
Conquest and annexation of Finland, which becomes an autonomous Grand Duchy within Russia.

1810

Annexation of Kingdom of Imeretia.
Council of State established.

1811

Forcible integration of autocephalous Georgian Church into Russian Orthodox Church.
Ministry of Police created; abolished in 1819.

1812

Population of Russian Empire estimated at 41 million, based on tax revisions.
Treaty of Bucharest with Turkey. Russia acquires Bessarabia, the northeastern part of the Principality of Moldavia.

Union of Old Finland, which had been Russian since 1721 and 1743, with Grand Duchy of Finland.

Fall of Speranskii.

Russians establish settlement at Fort Ross in northern California; it will remain until 1741.

(June–October) Napoleon's Russian campaign.

(June) Napoleon invades Russia.

(August) Battle of Borodino.

(September) Napoleon captures Moscow; Moscow burnt.

(October) Napoleon retreats from Moscow.

1813

Battle of Leipzig.

1813–1814

Russians drive French armies back to Paris.

1814

Napoleon defeated at Waterloo; Alexander I enters Paris triumphant.

1814–1815

Congress of Vienna, new partition of Poland, leads to formation of "Kingdom of Poland," with Alexander I as king, a constitution, and a large measure of autonomy within the Russian Empire.

1816

University of Warsaw opened (closed in 1831).

Union of Salvation founded; first secret organization of the future Decembrists.

1816–1819

Serfs emancipated without land in Estonia, Kurland, and Livonia.

1816–1821

Arakcheev's military colonies.

1817

Makarev Fair transferred to Nizhnii Novgorod.

1817–1857

Construction of St. Isaac's Cathedral in St. Petersburg.

1818

Bessarabia granted large measure of autonomy.

Alexander I opens the first *sejm* (parliament) of the Kingdom of Poland.

Karamzin publishes *History of the Russian State*.

1819

University of St. Petersburg founded.

1820

Constantine, Alexander's brother, renounces rights to the throne.

1821

Start of Greek revolt against Turkey.

1822

Mikhail Speranskii reforms Siberian administration. Statute on the administration of *inorodtsy*.

Annexation of the Middle Horde, and in 1824, of Small Horde of the Kazakhs.

1823

Nicholas designated heir apparent to childless Alexander.

1824

Founding of Latvian Literary Society.

1825

Novosiltsev's *Constitutional Charter* presented.

Griboedov's comedy *Woe from Wit*.

Pushkin's *Boris Godunov*.

Death of Alexander in Taganrog.

Decembrist revolt.

1825–1846

Kazakh uprising led by Kenisari Kasimov.

1825–1855

Reign of Nicholas I, younger brother of Alexander I.

1826

Execution of five Decembrist conspirators; others condemned to Siberian exile.

Organization of Third Section of Imperial Chancery, the government's political police.

Censorship Code.

1826–1828

War with Persia leads to Russian conquest of khanates of Erivan and Nakhichevan; ends with Treaty of Turkmanchai.

1827

Battle of Navarino.

1828

Resumption of Orthodox missionary activity in the east of the empire.

Autonomous status of Bessarabia curtailed.

1828–1829

War with Turkey; ends with Treaty of Adrianople.

1829–1864

Caucasian War.

1830

Publication of *The Complete Collection of Laws of the Russian Empire*, first codification of laws since 1649.

Cholera Riots.

Munchengratz agreement.

Mathematician Lobachevsky publishes first work.

1830–1831

Revolutions in France, Belgium, and German principalities.

November Insurrection in Poland; Polish constitution abrogated.

1831

Founding of Finnish Literary Society.

Pushkin completes *Eugene Onegin*.

Aleksandr Herzen, representative of emerging radical intelligentsia, banished to Vyatka.

1832

Uvarov enunciates ideological foundation of Nicholas I's government: "autocracy, orthodoxy, nationality."

Alexandrine theater in St. Petersburg opens.

"Organic Statute of Kingdom of Poland" abolishes Poland's previous legal status, abolishes its army, and dissolves its Sejm (parliament).

Reform of University Statutes.

Uprising in Georgia.

1833

First modern law code (Svod zakonov) is published; takes effect in 1835.

Doctrine of "Official Nationality" proclaimed.

Treaty of Unkiar Skelessi.

Convention of Berlin.

Uvarov becomes minister of education.

1834

Russian language is introduced in the administration, the courts, and schools in areas of Poland-Lithuania annexed in the previous century.

(Russian) University of Kiev opens in place of (Polish) University of Vilna, which was closed in 1832.

1834–1859

Shamil takes over anti-Russian resistance in Caucasus and founds a theocratic imamate.

1835

Population of Russian Empire estimated at 60 million, based on tax revisions.

1836

Independence and privileges of Armenian church are confirmed.

Peter Chaadaev's "First Philosophical Letter," highly critical of Russian culture, is published. Chaadaev is officially declared insane by the government.

First performance of Gogol's *The Government Inspector* and Ivan Glinka's *A Life for the Tsar*.

1837

Alexander Pushkin killed in a duel.

1837–1842

State peasant reforms under P. D. Kiselev.

1838

Founding of Estonian Scholarly Society.

First Russian railroad—St. Petersburg to Tsarskoe Selo (Pushkin).

1838–1847

Vissarion Belinsky works on *Notes of the Fatherland.*

1839

Incorporation of Uniate Church (with the exception of the Kingdom of Poland) into Russian Orthodox Church.

Failed Russian expedition against Khiva.

1840

Abolition of Lithuanian Statute in "Western provinces."

Lermontov's *Hero of Our Time* published.

Publication of *Kobzar,* a volume of poetry by the Ukrainian writer and patriot Taras Shevchenko.

Bakunin leaves Russia for Germany.

1841

Straits Convention.

Ban against individual sale of peasants.

Lermontov killed in a duel.

1842

Gogol publishes *Dead Souls.*

Glinka's opera *Ruslan and Liudmilla.*

1842–1851

Construction of first long-distance Russian railway line (St. Petersburg–Moscow).

1844

Agreement with Britain over partition of Turkey.

1845

Hereditary gentry status restricted to top five ranks of Table of Ranks.

Revised version of Criminal Code is issued.

Annexation of Kazakh Inner Horde, followed by 1848 annexation of Great Horde.

1845–1847

Movement to convert Latvians and Estonians to Orthodox Church.

1846

Founding of Ukrainian secret national society of St. Cyril and St. Methodius in Kiev.

Russians occupy Cracow.

Abolition of English Corn Laws; increase in Russian grain exports.

Dostoevsky publishes *Poor Folk.*

Turgenev publishes A Sportsman's Sketches.

1847

Exchange between Gogol and Belinsky ([Belinskii's *Letter to Gogol*]).

Herzen leaves Russia for western Europe and never returns.

1848

Revolutions in France, Austria, Italy, and Germany.

Publication of Marx's "Communist Manifesto."

Death of Vissarion Belinsky.

1849

Nicholas intervenes to help Austria put down Hungarian revolt.

Arrest of Petrashevsky Circle. Dostoevsky and other members sentenced to death, but reprieved on the scaffold, and sentenced to hard labor in Siberia.

Russia rediscovers mouth of Amur River.

1849–1860

Second stage of agrarian reform in Baltic provinces.

1850

Olmutz Agreement.

1852

Louis Napoleon proclaimed emperor of France.

Leo Tolstoy publishes *Childhood.*

Death of Gogol.

1853

Menshikov ultimatum to Turkey.

War with Turkey.

Russian naval battle over Turks at Sinope.

Ostrovsky's first play produced.

1854

Allies land in the Crimea.

Founding of fortress of Vernii (modern Almaty).

Founding of Khabarovsk.

1854–1856

Crimean War; Russia at war with Great Britain, France, and Ottoman Empire.

1855

Allies take Sevastopol.

Death of Nicholas I.

1855–1881

Reign of Alexander II.

1856

Peace of Paris, ending Crimean War.

Alexander's speech to the nobility of Moscow stresses the need to end serfdom "from above."

Hereditary gentry status restricted to top four ranks of Table of Ranks.

Relaxation of Russian policy toward Poland.

1857

(January) Secret committee for serf reform established.

(November) Nazimov Rescript invites nobility to collaborate in reforms; Chief Committee on Peasant Affairs under Rovstovtsev established to oversee emancipation.

Alexander Ivanov's painting *Christ's Appearance to the People.*

1857–1867

Herzen publishes *Kolokol* (*The Bell*) from London.

1858–1860

Russia accelerates penetration of northeast Asia, acquiring Amur-Ussuri and Maritime region from China.

1859

Shamil surrenders in north Caucasus; conquest of Caucasus complete except for Circassia (1864).

Goncharov's *Oblomov.*

1859–1860

Noble deputations come to St. Petersburg.

1860

Founding of Vladivostok.

Rural courts introduced.

State bank established.

China recognizes Russian expansion in Treaty of Peking.

1860–1873

First railway boom.

1861

Emancipation Manifesto of February 16 abolishes serfdom in Russia.

Discontent over terms of emancipation leads to peasant and student unrest and formation of first revolutionary groups.

Establishment of St. Petersburg Conservatory.

1862

Bismarck becomes chancellor of Prussia.

St. Petersburg Conservatory founded, with Anton Rubinstein as its first director.

The Mighty Handful (Balakerev, Cui, Borodin, Rimsky-Korsakov, and Mussorgsky) announce intention to create a school of national Russian music.

Publication of Turgenev's *Fathers and Sons.*

1863

Leo Tolstoy begins *War and Peace.*

University Statute increases faculty rights.

Publication of N. G. Chernyshevskii's *What Is to Be Done?*

Convocation of Finnish Diet (parliament).

Ban on teaching and printing of works in Ukrainian (with the exception of belles lettres) is followed by a ban on printing works in Belorussian and Lithuanian (using Latin script).

N. I. Ilminsky begins native-language schools as part of process of bringing Christianity to non-Christians in eastern part of the empire.

1863–1864

January uprising in Poland and Lithuania (and Belorussia).

1864

Reforms of local self-government (zemstvo), judiciary, and elementary schools.

Nikolai Chernyshevsky banished to Siberia.

Severe reprisals against participants in the January uprising in Poland, followed by measures against Polish Catholic Church, and use of Polish language in administration and schools.

Agrarian reform in Congress of Poland.

Conquest and eviction of west Caucasian Circassians.

Colonel Cherniaev's first campaign in middle Asia.

1864–1870

Agrarian reform in Transcaucasia.

1864–1885

Conquest of Central Asia (Turkestan).

1865

Conquest of Tashkent.

Reform of censorship system (Temporary Regulations).

1866

Prussia defeats Austria at Koniggratz.

First attempt on Alexanders's life.

Moscow Conservatory founded; Tchaikovsky becomes a professor.

Dostoevsky's *Crime and Punishment* published.

1867

Russia sells Alaska to United States.

Establishment of Governor-Generalship of Turkestan.

1867–1869

Church reforms.

1868

Conquest of Samarkand.

Russia establishes protectorate over Emirate of Bukhara.

1869

Publication of Peter Lavrov's *Historical Letters* and Tolstoy's *War and Peace*.

Compulsory military service introduced.

Kazakhs of the Small Horde begin uprising.

Founding of the (Russian) University of Warsaw.

Revolutionary Sergei Nechaev involved in the murder of a fellow revolutionary, the student Ignatiev.

Tchaikovsky's first opera, *The Voyevodya*, performed.

1870

Municipal reform.

Formation of artists' group Wanderers (Peredvizhniki)

Vladimir Ilich Ulianov (Lenin) born in provincial town of Simbirsk.

Mendeleyev's Principles of Chemistry.

Population of Russian Empire estimated at 86 million.

Russia renounces the Black Sea military restrictions imposed on it by the 1856 Treaty of Paris.

London Convention on the Straits.

1870–1871

Prussia defeats France. Bismarck unites Germany under William I.

1870–1874

Minister of War Dmitrii Miliutin issues military reforms.

1871

Abolition of special status of colonists.

1872

Russian publication of Marx's *Das Kapital*.

Carl Fabergé takes over his father's business.

1873

Three Emperor's League first formed with Russia, Germany and Austria-Hungary.

Russia establishes protectorate over Khanate of Khiva.

1873–1874

First Going to the People movement.

1874

Introduction of universal military service in Russian Empire, the final component of Miliutin's military reforms.

Mussorgsky's opera *Boris Godunov.*

1875

Sakhalin Island becomes Russian after Treaty of St. Petersburg with Japan.

1876

Annexation of Khanate of Kokand.

Formation of revolutionary group *Land and Liberty.*

1877

Introduction of Russian municipal order in the Baltic provinces.

Tchaikovsky's *Swan Lake.*

Tolstoy completes *Anna Karenina.*

1877–1878

Russo-Turkish War; areas of Kars, Ardahan, Batumi, and southern Bessarabia are ceded to Russia.

Mass trials of radicals and revolutionaries.

1878

Treaty of San Stefano in March 1878 between Russia and Turkey. Settlement seen as too favorable to Russia by other European powers. Congress of Berlin in June, presided over by Bismarck, amends previous treaty.

Grand Duchy of Finland receives a largely autonomous army.

Terrorist wave in St. Petersburg begins in August when Vera Zasulich shoots St. Petersburg police chief. Government issues temporary law allowing court-martialing of terrorists. It also issues secret circular permitting the arrest and exile of persons suspected of seditious intent.

Tchaikovsky's First Piano Concerto takes Paris by storm.

1878–1881

Terrorist activities continue. Winter Palace is dynamited; imperial trains attacked. Alexander II survives several assassination attempts.

1879

Land and Liberty divides into Black Repartition and People's Will.

Temporary Governors General created (April).

Tchaikovsky's *Eugene Onegin.*

Tekke Turkmen defeat Russians.

1880

Death of Empress Maria and remarriage of Alexander II.

Dostoevsky completes *Brothers Karamazov.*

Konstantin Pobedonostsev, conservative adviser, begins term as procurator of the Holy Synod. Will serve until 1905.

1880–1881

General Loris-Melikov's "dictatorship of the heart" to deal with terrorist threat.

1881

Conquest of Turkmen fortress of Gok Tepe, annexation of Turkmenistan.

Treaty of St. Petersburg with China; Russia returns territories in Chinese Sinkiang, seized in 1871.

Assassination of Czar Alexander II by members of People's Will.

1881–1882

Reaction against terrorism. Temporary Regulations give the police "extraordinary powers" in fighting the revolutionary movement.

Pogroms against Jews in the Ukraine and Warsaw.

Three Emperors' Alliance agreement signed by Russia, Germany and Austria; renewed for three years in 1884.

1881–1894
Reign of Alexander III.

1881–1899
Construction of Transcaspian Railway.

1882
Law prohibits factories from hiring children under 12 or from employing those aged 12 to 15 more than eight hours a day.
May Laws further anti-Jewish discrimination.

1882–1884
Period of counterreforms in censorship (1882), education (1884), and the church (1884).

1883
First Russian Marxist organization, Emancipation of Labor, established in Geneva by Russian exiles.
Ismail Bey Gasprali founds *Tercuman* (*Interpreter*), influential journal addressed to Muslims in the Russian Empire.

1884
Russia occupies Merv.
University Statutes curtail university autonomy.

1885
Introduction of Russian as teaching language in primary schools in the Kingdom of Poland.
Anglo-Russian crisis over Afghanistan leads to agreement over Russo-Afghan frontier.
New edition of Criminal Code.
Establishment of Gentry Land Bank.
Poll tax abolished.

1886
Special rules governing forced labor.

1887
Reinsurance Treaty between Russia and Germany.

Revolutionaries attempt to assassinate Alexander III. Among those captured and executed is Aleksandr Ulianov, Lenin's older brother.
Soul tax abolished.
Introduction of restrictions on the number of Jews in grammar schools and tertiary secondary educational institutions.

1888
Rimsky-Korsakov's *Scheherazade*.

1889
Russian judicial reform; Russian established as language of the courts in Baltic provinces.
Creation of the office of Land Captain.

1890
Decree on zemstvos strengthens government's power over them.
German government refuses to renew Reinsurance Treaty with Russia.
Founding of Revolutionary Armenian Federalist Party (Dashnaks).
Borodin's opera *Prince Igor*.
Tchaikovsky's ballet *Sleeping Beauty*.

1891
Statute on administration of steppe areas.
Jews expelled from Moscow.

1891–1892
Famine in European Russia.

1891–1903
Construction of Trans-Siberian Railway.

1891–1893
Franco-Russian alliance takes shape.

1892
Founding of Polish Socialist Party (PPS).
New restrictions on urban zemstvos.
Sergei Tretiakov donates his art collection to the city of Moscow.

1892–1903

As minister of finance, Sergei Witte revolutionizes industry, commerce, and transport.

1893

Clauses in Emancipation Act permitting the leaving of communes are abrogated.

German University of Dorpat is transformed into Russian university of Iurev.

1894

Formal ratification of Franco-Russian Alliance ratified.

Alexander III dies at the age of 49.

1894–1917

Reign of Nicholas II.

1895

Pamir Agreement with Great Britain determines border between Russian empire in Central Asia and British empire in India.

"Senseless dreams" speech of Nicholas II deflates reformist hopes of liberal nobility.

1896

Coronation ceremonies of Nicholas II in Moscow marred by accidental deaths among crowd gathered at Khodynka Field.

Disastrous production of Chekhov's *The Seagull* in St. Petersburg.

Closure of Armenian church schools.

Russian expansion into Manchuria and construction of Chinese Eastern railway.

Textile workers strike in St. Petersburg; St. Petersburg Union for the Liberation of Labor established.

1897

First general census of the Russian Empire records population of 129 million.

Founding of Moscow Art Theater (MkhAT).

Witte establishes the gold standard for the ruble.

Founding of the Bund (General Jewish Workers' Association) in Lithuania, Poland and Russia.

1898

Founding of Marxist Russian Social-Democratic Labor Party and first party congress, held in Minsk.

Andizhan insurrection.

Russia occupies Port Arthur in China.

Diaghilev founds influential journal *Mir isskustva* (World of Art).

1899

February Manifesto curtails Finnish autonomy.

Publication of Vladimir Lenin's first major work, *The Development of Capitalism in Russia.*

1899–1904

Russification in Finland.

1900

Boxer rebellion in China; Russia occupies Manchuria.

Founding of Revolutionary Ukrainian Party; renamed Ukrainian Social Democratic Workers' Party in 1905.

1901

Compulsive Military Service Law in Finland.

Chekhov's *Three Sisters* opens at MKhAT to poor reviews.

1901–1903

Moscow police chief Sergei Zubatov experiments with government-sponsored trade unions to undermine socialist influence on workers.

1902

Founding of Socialist Revolutionary Party (1901–2).

Assassination of D. S. Sipyagin, minister of the interior.

(March–April) Peasant disorders in Poltava and Kharkov.

Gorky's *Lower Depths* opens at MKhAT.

Lenin writes *What Is to be Done?*

Foundation of Belorussian Revolutionary Hramada.

1902–1904

Peasants' movement in left-bank Ukraine and in Georgian Guria.

1903

Establishment of Union of Liberation, a left-liberal political organization.

Second Congress of the Social Democratic Party in London results in internal division between Bolsheviks, led by Lenin, and Mensheviks, led by Martov.

Labor strikes in south Russia.

Anti-Semitic pogrom in Kishinev.

Property of Armenian Church confiscated.

1904

Assassination of V. I. Plehve, minister of the interior.

Corporal punishment abolished.

Zemstvo "banquet" campaign demanding constitution begins in November.

General strike in Tbilisi and Baku.

1904–1905

Russo-Japanese War.

1905

(January) Russia surrender Port Arthur to Japan.

Bloody Sunday. 1905 Revolution begins. Mass strikes and demonstrations in Poland, "western provinces," and Baltic provinces.

Grand Duke Sergei, second cousin to the czar and commander of the Moscow military region, is assassinated.

(February–March) Battle of Mukden.

(March) Founding of Association for Equal Rights for Jews.

(April–May) Tolerance edicts reduce discrimination against non-Christian faiths.

(May) Destruction of Russian fleet at Tsushima by Japanese.

(June) General strike and fighting on the barricades in Lodz, Poland.

Sailors mutiny on the battleship *Potemkin* on the Black Sea.

Disturbances in Odessa.

(August) Treaty of Portsmouth, New Hampshire, ends Russo-Japanese War.

First congress of Muslims in Nizhnii Novgorod.

Government offers "Bulygin Duma."

(October) General strike across Russia and Poland.

St. Petersburg Soviet formed.

October Manifesto issued promising civil liberties and representative institutions, including a parliament known as the State Duma.

Pogroms against Jews in western part of empire.

Restoration of Finland's autonomy.

(December) Moscow Uprising begins; violently repressed.

Third Congress of the Social Democratic Party.

1905–1907

Revolution of 1905, followed by peasant disturbances that last until 1907.

1906

(January) Second Congress of Muslims, St. Petersburg.

Founding of Union of Muslims of Russia (Ittifak).

(February) Nicholas calls for the meeting of the new State Duma.

(April–July) First Duma in session.

(May) Fundamental Laws (constitution) promulgated. First Duma opens.

(July) Petr Stolypin becomes prime minister; Vyborg Manifesto.

(November) Legislation enables peasants to leave their communes and consolidate their land holdings.

Fourth Congress of the Social Democratic Party.

1907

(March) Second Duma opens (February–June).

(June) Stolypin changes election law; introduces more restrictive franchise.

Redemption payments and arrears canceled.

Fifth Congress of the Social Democratic Party.

Emergence of Triple Entente (France, Britain, and Russia) against Triple Alliance (Germany, Austria-Hungary, and Italy).

1907–1912
Third Duma in session.

1908
Austria annexes Bosnia-Herzegovina, heightening tensions in the Balkans.

1909
Publication of *Vekhi* essays, symposium published by a group of politicians and philosophers.
(May) First performance of Diaghilev's Ballets Russes.

1910
Igor Stravinsky's *Firebird* ballet scandalizes Paris.
Lev (Leo) Tolstoy dies at Astapovo railroad station.

1910–1911
Stolypin land reform laws passed by Duma.

1911
Agadir crisis.
(January) Western zemstvo bill defeated.
(September) Assassination of Stolypin in Kiev Opera house.

1911–1913
Ritual murder case against a Jew, Beilis, in Kiev.

1912
(April) Massacre of workers in Lena goldfields, followed by strike wave.
First issue of *Pravda*, Bolshevik newspaper edited by Vyacheslav Molotov.
(November) Fourth Duma convenes; will last until March 1917, a few months short of completing its full term.

1912–1913
(October–May) First Balkan War.

1913
(July–August) Second Balkan War.
Stravinsky's *The Rite of Spring* creates an uproar in Paris.

1914
Demonstrations in the Ukraine marking centenary of Taras Shevchenko's birthday.
(June) Czar Nicholas II considers abolition of Duma.
Assassination of Austrian Archduke Franz Ferdinand in Sarajevo triggers crisis that leads to European war.
(July) Austria declares war on Serbia.
(August) Germany declares war on Russia; World War I begins with Russia fighting with France, Great Britain, and Serbia against Germany, Austria-Hungary, and, later, the Ottoman Empire.
Russian defeat at Tannenberg.
Prohibition decreed.
St. Petersburg renamed Petrograd.

1915
Formation of War Industries Committee.
German offensive leads to major territorial losses of Poland, Lithuania, Kurland, and western Belorussia.
Germans, Poles, and Jews deported from western border areas of Russian Empire.
(May) German-Austrian breakthrough at Gorlice-Tarnow.
(August) Formation of Progressive Bloc in Duma; political crisis.
(September) Nicholas II assumes personal command of troops in Mogilev.
International socialist antiwar conferences at Zimmerwald.

1916
(April) International socialist conference at Kienthal.
(June) Brusilov offensive.
Uprisings in various parts of Central Asia, protesting labor mobilizations of local residents.
(November) Miliukov's "Stupidity or Treason" speech in Duma.
(December) Rasputin assassinated in St. Petersburg.

Russian Revolutions and Union of Soviet Socialist Republics
1917–1991

1917

(February/March)

Bread riots, strikes, and demonstrations begin in Petrograd; garrison joins the protesters. February Revolution begins. (25 February–1 March).

Formation of the Provisional Government (March 1).

Formation of the Petrograd Soviet (March 1).

Nicholas II abdicates in favor of his brother Grand Prince Michael (March 2).

Grand Prince Michael refuses throne, transfers power to Provisional Government, composed of Duma members and led by Prince G. E. Lvov (March 2).

"Program" of the Provisional Government (March 8).

"Appeal to all Peoples of the World" by Petrograd Soviet (March 14).

Petrograd Soviet Order no. 1.

Formation of Central Ukrainian Rada in Kiev.

Provisional Government recognizes independence of Poland.

Revocation of discriminatory special powers, also against *inorodtsy* (non-Russians) and Jews.

(April) Lenin returns to Russia in "sealed train"; issues April Theses adopting an uncompromising line toward Provisional Government.

Petrograd crisis (April 23–24).

(May) Fall of Foreign Minister Pavel Miliukov; formation of the First Coalition government.

Trotsky returns to Russia.

First All-Russian Congress of Muslims in Moscow.

(June) Election of Constituent Assembly set for September 30.

First All-Russian Congress of Soviets.

(June–July) Kerensky offensive.

(July) July Days, unsuccessful Bolshevik-supported uprising against Provisional Government.

Lenin escapes to Finland.

Prince Lvov resigns, Kerensky becomes prime minister.

Finns declare autonomy.

Sixth Bolshevik Party Congress.

(August) Formation of the Second Coalition government.

Dates set for election of Constituent Assembly (postponed until November 25).

(September) Kornilov affair; Kornilov marches on Petrograd with his Wild Division.

Kerensky arms the Bolsheviks; puts down Kornilov mutiny.

Bolsheviks win control of Moscow and Petrograd soviets.

Publication of Lenin's *State and Revolution.*

(October) Lenin returns to Petrograd.

Lenin wins approval for coup in Bolshevik Politburo.

(November) Bolshevik Revolution (October 25).

Decree on Peace and Decree on Land.

Elections to Constituent Assembly (November 25).

Patriarchate reestablished.

(December) Kadet (Constitutional Democrats) Party outlawed.

Armistice with Germany.

Cheka organized to combat enemies of revolution.

Peace talks with Germany begin at Brest-Litovsk.

Creation of Supreme Council of the National Economy.

Left Socialist Revolutionaries enter coalition with Bolsheviks.

1918

(January) Constituent Assembly meets; dispersed by Bolsheviks.

Central Rada of Ukraine issues declaration of independence.

(February) Trotsky declares "no war, no peace" policy; German offensive follows and threatens to capture Petrograd.

Capital moved from Petrograd to Moscow.

Red Army established.

Separation of church and state proclaimed.

Lithuania and Estonia declare independence.

Russia moves to Gregorian calendar (Orthodox Church continues to use Julian calendar).

(March) Treaty of Brest-Litovsk signed between RSFSR and Central Powers.

Trotsky becomes commissar of war.

Bolshevik Party renamed Communist Party.

SRs leave the coalition government.

Allied troops land at Murmansk.

(April) Japanese land at Vladivostok.

(May) Food requisitioning begun in the countryside.

Revolt of Czech Legion.

Georgia, Armenia, and Azerbaijan declare independence.

(June) Committees of the Village Poor established.

Large-scale industry nationalized.

(July) Nicholas II and his family executed in Ekaterinburg.

Socialist Revolutionary revolt in Moscow.

First Soviet constitution.

(August) White forces capture Kazan.

Americans land in Vladivostok.

Assassination attempt on Lenin.

(September) Proclamation of "Red Terror".

Omsk Directorate formed.

Red Army captures Kazan.

Americans land at Arkhangelsk.

(October) Poland declares independence.

(November) Armistice ends World War I.

Soviets repudiate Treaty of Brest-Litovsk.

Latvia declares independence.

French troops land at Odessa.

Omsk Directorate overthrown.

Kolchak becomes Supreme White Commander.

(December) British troops land at Batum, on Black Sea.

1918–1921

Civil War and War Communism.

1919

(March) First Congress of the Communist International (Comintern).

Eighth Communist Party Congress.

Kolchak takes offensive in Siberia.

(April) French withdraw from Odessa.

Kolchak offensive halted.

(May) Denikin begins northward offensive.

(June) Kolchak begins to retreat.

Treaty of Versailles.

(October) White armies under Denikin and Yudenich threaten Moscow and Petrograd; height of White challenge to Bolsheviks.

Denikin retreats from Orel.

Yudenich retreats from Petrograd.

Allies withdraw from Arkhangelsk and Murmansk.

1920

(January) Allied blockade ends.

(February) Peace with Estonia.

Kolchak executed by Bolsheviks in Irkutsk.

(March) Ninth Party Congress.

(April) Soviets retake Azerbaijan.

Soviet-Polish War begins.

Wrangel succeeds Denikin as leader of Whites.

(May) Poles take Kiev.

(June) Wrangel offensive northward from the Crimea.

Polish retreat from Kiev.

(July) Second Comintern Congress.

(August) Battle of Warsaw.

(October) Peace negotiations with Poles at Riga.

(November) Wrangel evacuates the Crimea; civil war ends in Russia.

(December) Soviets retake Armenia.

1921

(February) Soviets retake Georgia.

(February–March) Kronstadt uprising.

(March) Tenth Communist Party Congress.

New Economic Policy (NEP) inaugurated.

Treaty of Riga.

1921–1922

Famine along the Volga and the southern Ukraine.

1922

New criminal code drawn up and promulgated.

Cheka replaced by OGPU.

(March) Eleventh Party Congress meets.

(April) Stalin assumes the Communist Party post of general secretary.

(April) Russia signs Treaty of Rapallo with Germany.

(May) Lenin suffers first stroke.

(October) Japan evacuates Vladivostok.

(December) Lenin suffers second stroke.

Formation of the Soviet Union.

1923

Lenin suffers third stroke. Comintern encourages uprising by German Communists.

(January) Lenin completes his "Testament," assessing strengths and weaknesses of five possible successors: Trotsky, Zinoviev, Kamenev, Bukharin, and Stalin.

Twelfth Party Congress.

1924

(January) Lenin dies.

USSR constitution approved.

(February) USSR officially recognized by Great Britain.

(October) Diplomatic relations with France established.

"Zinoviev letter" harms British-Soviet relations.

Thirteenth Party Congress.

Petrograd renamed Leningrad.

Bukhara and Khiva, people's republics since 1920, are incorporated into Soviet Union.

1925

Soviet Congress ratifies Soviet constitution.

Soviet Union and Germany sign commercial treaty.

Defensive alliance with Turkey.

Fourteenth Party Congress; Trotsky dismissed as war commissar.

1926

Census establishes population of Soviet Union at 147 million.

Zinoviev and Kamenev form a leftist alliance with Trotsky; all three are dismissed from Politburo.

New Russian Family Code makes it easier to obtain divorce.

Treaty of Berlin between USSR and Germany.

1927

New Soviet Criminal Code enacted.

(April) Chiang Kai-shek crushes Communist revolt; Soviet Union breaks diplomatic relations with China.

(May) Britain breaks diplomatic relations with Soviet Union; war scare in USSR.

(December) Fifteenth Party Congress; Trotsky expelled from Party.

1928

(January) First "emergency" grain confiscations from peasants.

(Fall) Crisis in food deliveries.

(October) First Five-Year Plan formulated; scheduled to run through 1933.

Trotsky exiled to Kazakhstan.

Shakhty trial of alleged industrial saboteurs.

1929

Trotsky expelled from Soviet Union.

USSR and Great Britain resume diplomatic relations.

Mikhail Sholokhov publishes *Quiet Flows the Don*.

(November) Party bureaucracy moves against Right Opposition and removes Bukharin from Politburo.

Beginning of forced collectivization of peasant households.

(December) Stalin authorizes liquidation of kulaks.

1929–1932

First Five-Year Plan inaugurates period of rapid industrialization. After four years government decides that quotas have been met.

1930

Trial of alleged conspirators known as the Industrial Party.

Sixteenth Party Congress.

(March) *Pravda* article "Dizzy with Success" by Stalin marks temporary retreat from forced collectivization.

(July) Litvinov replaces Chicherin as commissar of foreign affairs.

(Fall) Resumption of forced collectivization.

1931

Trial of Mensheviks.

Renewal of neutrality treaty with Lithuania, first signed in 1926.

(September) Manchuria invaded by Japan.

1932

Conspiracy led by M. N. Riutin uncovered.

Government introduces mandatory internal passports for urban dwellers.

USSR signs nonaggression pacts with China, Finland, Latvia, Estonia, Poland, and France.

Sergei Prokofiev returns from abroad.

Soviet Union establishes relations with Nationalist Chinese government.

Dissolution of Russian Association of Proletarian Writers (RAPP).

(December) Early conclusion of First Five-Year Plan.

1932–1933

Widespread famine in the Ukraine and other regions of Soviet Union.

1933

(January) Hitler assumes the post of German chancellor.

Ivan Bunin wins Russia's first Nobel Prize in literature.

(November) USSR officially recognized by the United States.

1933–1937

Second Five-Year Plan (adopted January 1934).

1934

Clauses added to Criminal Code sections dealing with antistate, or "counterrevolutionary," crimes.

Birobidzhan, a territory in eastern Siberia, becomes autonomous Jewish state.

(January–February) Seventeenth Party Congress, known as the "Congress of Victors," meets.

(January) Germany and Poland sign Non-Aggression Treaty.

(August) First Congress of the Union of Soviet Writers adopts policy of socialist realism.

(September) League of Nations admits Soviet Union.

(December) Sergei Kirov, Leningrad party boss, is assassinated; beginning of Stalinist purges.

1935

Chinese Eastern Railway sold to Manchukuo, Japanese puppet government in Manchuria.

Collective farm statute.

(May) Soviet treaties with France and Czechoslovakia.

(July–August) Seventh Congress of Comintern.

(August) Stakhanovite movement begins.

1936

Maxim Gorky dies.

(March) Hitler occupies Rhineland.

(June) Divorce made more difficult by new family law; abortions outlawed except when a mother's health endangered.

(July) Start of the Spanish civil war.

(August) First Moscow "show trial": Kamenev, Zinoviev, and other members of Left Opposition put on trial; prosecuted by Vyshinsky.

(September) Yezhov replaces Yagoda as head of secret police (NKVD).

(November) Anti-Comintern Pact among Germany, Italy, and Japan.

(December) New constitution—"Stalin Constitution"—adopted with 11 constituent republics.

1936–1938

Most intense phase of the Great Terror.

1937

(January) Second Moscow show trial: Piatakov, Radek, and others put on trial.

(June) Marshal Tukhachevsky secretly tried and executed together with half of the Red Army officer corps.

(August) Major purge of Ukrainian leaders begins.

Completion of collectivization.

1938

Publication of Stalin's *History of the All-Russian Communist Party: Short Course*.

Study of Russian made compulsory throughout Soviet Union.

Soviet and Japanese border clashes in Far East.

(March) Third Moscow show trial: Bukharin, Rykov, and Yagoda tried and executed.

(September) Munich conference opens door to dismemberment of Czechoslovakia.

(December) Yezhov succeeded by Beria as head of NKVD.

Eisenstein's film *Alexander Nevsky* completed.

1938–1941

Third Five-Year Plan; completion interrupted by World War II.

1939

(summer) Soviet-Japanese troops clash along Mongolian frontier with Soviets victorious.

(August) Soviet-German Non-Aggression Pact signed by Soviet Foreign Minister Molotov and German counterpart Ribbentrop.

(September) World War II in Europe begins with German invasion of Poland; Russia takes over eastern Polish territory; occupies Estonia, Latvia, and Lithuania; armistice with Japan.

Eighteenth Party Congress (first since 1934).

1939–1940

Russo-Finnish "Winter War" (November–March).

1940

Mikhail Bulgakov completes *Master and Margarita*.

Mikhail Sholokhov completes *Quiet Flows the Don*.

(June) Germany defeats France.

(July) Soviet Union annexes Baltic states, as well as Bessarabia and Bukovina (from Romania).

(November) Molotov's visit to Berlin.

Trotsky assassinated in Mexico.

1941

(April) Germany invades Yugoslavia.

Soviet Neutrality Treaty with Japan.

(June 22) Germany invades USSR.

Stalin names himself head of government.

(September) Kiev falls; 900-day siege of Leningrad begins.

Mass evacuation of Volga Germans.

(October) Moscow is threatened; some of the city is evacuated.

(December) Battle of Moscow; United States enters World War II after Japanese attack on Pearl Harbor.

Beginning of deportations of Germans, Kalmyks, Crimean Tatars, and several Caucasian ethnic groups to Soviet Central Asia; continues until 1944.

1941–1945

Soviet Great Patriotic War against Germany.

1942

(July) Germans capture the Crimea.

Churchill visits Moscow.

Lend-Lease in full operation.

1942–1943

Battle of Stalingrad, considered turning point of World War II. Battle begins in August 1942, Soviets counterattack in November 1942, and German Sixth Army surrenders in February 1943.

1943

(May) Comintern is abolished.

(July) Battle of Kursk, USSR victorious; Allied invasion of Sicily.

(September) Patriarchate is reestablished with Metropolitan Sergei as patriarch.

Moscow Conference.

(November–December) Tehran Conference.

1944

(January) Siege of Leningrad is lifted.

(May) Crimean Tatars banished to Siberia.

(June) Allied landings at Normandy Beach (D day) establishes "Second Front" in Europe.

(August–October) Warsaw Uprising.

1945

(January) Yalta Conference.

(April) Soviets attack Berlin.

(May) Germany surrenders to Soviet forces.

(July–August) Potsdam Conference.

(July 24) United States successfully tests atomic bomb.

(August) USSR enters war against Japan.

(September) Japan surrenders.

Eisenstein's *Ivan the Terrible*, part 1, wins Stalin Prize.

1946

(February) Stalin's remobilization speech to Supreme Soviet.

(March) Churchill's Iron Curtain speech in Fulton, Missouri.

(August) Zhdanov begins attack on Zoshchenko, Akhmatova, and other cultural figures.

First elections to Supreme Soviet since 1937.

First session of United Nations opens.

Communist government in Bulgaria.

1946–1950

Fourth Five-Year Plan.

1947

Soviet currency reform requires citizens to exchange old rubles for new rubles at a rate of 10:1; Cominform founded.

Wartime rationing abolished in USSR.

(March) Truman Doctrine and Marshall Plan announced in United States.

1948

(February) Communist takeover in Czechoslovakia.

Czechoslovakia joins Soviet bloc.

(June) Stalin-Tito split; Cominform expels Yugoslavia;

Berlin Blockade begins (lasts until May 1949).

(August) Zhdanov dies.

1949

Industry and agriculture restored to level of pre–World War II output.

Chinese Communists defeat Nationalists in Chinese civil war.

(April) NATO organized.

(August) Soviets explode atomic bomb.

1950

Sino-Soviet agreement between USSR and new China communist government.

1950–1953

Korean War (June 1950–July 1953).

1951–1955

Fifth Five-Year Plan.

1952

(October) Nineteenth Party Congress meets, first since 1939.

1953

(January) Alleged doctors' plot is uncovered and followed by arrests seen by many as a prelude to another campaign of mass terror.

(March) Stalin dies.

Malenkov appointed prime minister.

(June) Beria is arrested and executed later in the year.

Berlin uprising in East Germany.

(September) Nikita Khrushchev officially named first secretary of the Communist Party.

1954

(March) Khrushchev begins Virgin Lands campaign that will run through 1956.

(April) The Crimea transferred to the Ukraine.

(October) Khrushchev and Bulganin visit China; sign friendship treaty.

Ehrenburg's *The Thaw* published.

1955

Abortion relegalized.

(February) Malenkov, Khrushchev's rival, replaced by Bulganin as prime minister.

(May) West Germany joins NATO; Warsaw Pact established.

Khrushchev and Bulganin visit Yugoslavia.

(July) Geneva summit with U.S. President Dwight Eisenhower; agreement signed to end four-power occupation of Austria.

1956

(February) Twentieth Party Congress; Khrushchev's "Secret Speech" condemns Stalin "cult of personality."

(June–October) Reforms in Poland; return of Wladyslaw Gomulka to power.

(October–November) Soviet troops crush Hungarian revolt and support János Kádár as new Hungarian leader.

Molotov resigns as foreign minister.

1957

(June) Khrushchev defeats attempt of "anti-Party" group to remove him as first party secretary (Malenkov, Kaganovich, and Molotov ousted).

(September) Nuclear accident near Cheliabinsk.

(October) *Sputnik I* launched; Defense Minister Zhukov is dismissed.

Boris Pasternak's *Dr. Zhivago* is published outside the Soviet Union.

USSR successfully tests intercontinental ballistic missiles.

1957–1965

Regional economic councils established; decentralization of economic organization.

1958

(February) Khrushchev begins antireligious crusade.

(March) Bulganin ousted, Khrushchev becomes premier.

(October) Nobel Prize in literature awarded to Pasternak; government pressures him to decline the prize.

(December) Promulgation of school reforms and new criminal code.

U.S.-USSR cultural exchange agreement.

1958–1959

Berlin crisis (November 1958–March 1959).

1959

First post–World War II census establishes Soviet population at 212 million.

Russian spacecraft *Lunik III* photographs moon.

Galina Ulanova appointed ballet mistress of the Bolshoi Ballet.

(September) Khrushchev visits United States accompanied by Anastas Mikoyan and Frol Kozlov.

Khrushchev launches campaign to encourage Soviet citizens to plant and consume corn.

Twenty-first Party Congress.

USSR cancels economic and technical aid to China.

Sino-Soviet split becomes evident.

(May) U-2 incident, in which American spy plane is shot down over Soviet territory.

Paris conference.

1959–1965

Seven-Year Plan.

1960

Khrushchev at U.N. General Assembly in New York City.

Death of Boris Pasternak.

1961

(April) Yury Gagarin becomes first man to travel in space.

(June) Khrushchev and Kennedy hold summit in Geneva.

(August) Berlin Wall erected.

(October) Twenty-second Party Congress meets; Stalin's body is removed from Lenin mausoleum.

1962

(June) Demonstrators killed in Novocherkassk.

(October) Cuban Missile Crisis.

(November) *One Day in the Life of Ivan Denisovich* by Aleksandr Solzhenitsyn published.

1963

Bad harvest (food shortages in cities).

(July) Nuclear test-ban treaty among United States, USSR, and Britain.

U.S.-USSR "hot line" established.

Sino-Soviet split deepens.

Central Committee Conference on Ideology; Ehrenburg, Yevtushenko, and others attacked for nonconformity.

Founding of Taganka Theater (Moscow).

1964

(February) Poet Joseph Brodsky tried on charges of "parasitism."

(October) Nikita Khrushchev removed from power; replaced by collective leadership led by Leonid Brezhnev and Aleksei Kosygin.

1965

Soviet cosmonaut Aleksei Leonev becomes first man to walk in space.

Demonstrations in Moscow against U.S. air raids over North Vietnam.

Mikhail Sholokhov wins Nobel Prize in literature.

(September) Economic decentralization plan adopted by Communist Party Central Committee.

1966

Mikhail Bulgakov's *Master and Margarita*, written in 1940, finally published in Soviet Union.

Treaty of Friendship between USSR and Mongolia.

(January) Tashkent Conference.

(February) Sinyavsky-Daniel trial (for publishing abroad).

(March–April) Twenty-third Party Congress.

1966–1970

Eighth Five-Year Plan.

1967

(June) U.S.-Soviet summit conference at Glassboro, N.J.

Yuri Andropov becomes head of the KGB.

Outer Space Treaty.

Svetlana Allilueva, Stalin's daughter, defects to the West.

Fiftieth anniversary of the October Revolution.

1968

Censorship again tightened. Andrei Tarkovsky's film *Andrei Rublev* is not released because of its "negative" view of history.

"Prague Spring" begins in Czechoslovakia, with attempts to establish "communism with a human face."

Moscow-New York commercial airline service established.

(April) First appearance of *A Chronicle of Current Events*, journal of the emerging dissident movement.

(July) Renowned physicist Andrei Sakharov publishes *Thoughts on Progress, Peaceful Coexistence and Intellectual Freedom.*

Nuclear nonproliferation treaty signed by United States and USSR.

(August) Warsaw Pact invasion of Czechoslovakia, led by Soviet troops, ends "Prague Spring" experiment.

(November) Brezhnev Doctrine is proclaimed justifying Soviet Union's right to intervene in Soviet-bloc countries to defend socialism.

1969

(March) Soviet-Chinese skirmishes along Amur-Ussuri River border.

Preliminary round of SALT talks.

1970

Treaty of Friendship between USSR and Czechoslovakia.

Treaty of Friendship and Mutual Assistance with Finland extended for 20 years.

USSR and West Germany sign Treaty of Renunciation of Force.

(September) Soviet unmanned lunar landing.

U.S.-Soviet Nuclear Non-proliferation Treaty.

U.S.-USSR cultural exchange.

Celebration of centenary of Lenin's birth.

Nobel Prize in literature awarded to Aleksandr Solzhenitsyn.

1970–1971

SALT talks.

1971

(February) Khrushchev dies.

Mars 3 makes soft landing on moon.

(March–April) Twenty-fourth Party Congress.

1971–1975

Ninth Five-Year Plan.

1972

Renewed inflexibility with regard to policy on nationalities.

(May) Nixon-Brezhnev summit conference in Moscow; SALT treaties signed.

Restrictions on Jewish emigration; Jackson-Vanik amendment.

(June) Large-scale Soviet grain purchases from United States.

1973

Brezhnev-Nixon summit in the United States.

1974

(February) Aleksandr Solzhenitsyn expelled from USSR after publication of *Gulag Archipelago* in the West.

(June–July) Nixon and Brezhnev hold summit in Moscow.

First section of the Baikal-Amur Magistral railroad is completed.

(November) Ford-Brezhnev summit conference in Vladivostok.

1975

(July) Joint space project ("Soyuz") with United States.

(July–August) Helsinki Security Conference.

(December) Elena Bonner accepts the Nobel Peace Prize on behalf of her husband, physicist Andrei Sakharov.

1976

Helsinki Watch Groups formed in Russian Republic, Armenia, Georgia, Lithuania, and the Ukraine.

Twenty-fifth Party Congress.

1976–1980

Tenth Five-Year Plan.

1977

(June) Brezhnev elected president of USSR Supreme Soviet.

(October) "Brezhnev Constitution," fourth constitution in Soviet era, is approved.

Bulgakov's *Master and Margarita* staged at Taganka Theater.

1978

Demonstrations in the Caucasus over Kremlin attempts to weaken the use of native languages.

Solzhenitsyn's Harvard Speech.

1979

Census establishes Soviet population at 265 million.

(April) Formal cancellation of Soviet-Chinese alliance.

(June) SALT II signed by U.S. president Jimmy Carter and Brezhnev (not ratified).

(December) Soviet invasion of Afghanistan.

Gorbachev made candidate member of Politburo.

1980

(January) United States declares boycott of Summer Olympic Games in Moscow and imposes grain embargo.

(January) Sakharov exiled to Gorky (Nizhnii Novgorod), a closed city on the Volga.

(July–August) Summer Olympic Games in Moscow; 64 countries boycott to protest Soviet invasion of Afghanistan.

Gorbachev promoted to full member of Politburo.

Death of popular bard, Vladimir Vysotsky.

(August) Solidarity trade union legally established in Poland.

(October) Kosygin resigns as premier; dies a few months later.

1981

Twenty-sixth Party Congress.

(December) Martial law declared in Poland; Solidarity trade union banned.

1981–1985

Eleventh Five-Year Plan.

1982

(November) Brezhnev dies. Yuri Andropov elected general secretary of the Communist Party of the Soviet Union Central Committee and member of the Presidium.

1983

(January) Anticorruption drive begins.

Andropov elected president of the Presidium.

(September) Korean Airlines jetliner with 269 passengers shot down by Soviet air force off Sakhalin Island.

1984

(February) Andropov dies. Konstantin Chernenko elected general secretary of the Communist Party of the Soviet Union Central Committee.

Soviet Union withdraws from Summer Olympic Games in Los Angeles citing security concerns.

Filmmaker Andrei Tarkovsky emigrates to Italy.

1985

(March) Chernenko dies. Gorbachev succeeds Chernenko as party general secretary.

Antialcoholism program ("dry law") initiated by Gorbachev.

Gorbachev introduces policy of *perestroika* (restructuring).

(November) Geneva summit with U.S. President Reagan.

1986

(February–March) Twenty-seventh Party Congress.

(March) Boris Yeltsin becomes member of Politburo.

(April) Nuclear disaster at Chernobyl.

(October) Reykjavík, Iceland, summit with U.S. President Reagan.

(December) Sakharov released from internal exile in Gorky (Nizhnii Novgorod).

Ethnic riots in Kazakhstan.

Gorbachev's anticorruption campaign begins.

1986–1990

Twelfth Five-Year Plan.

1987

(February) Competitive elections for some local soviets.

(June) New enterprise law adopted, effective January 1988.

(October) Yeltsin removed from Politburo.

(November) Gorbachev publicly condemns Stalin's crimes.

(December) Washington summit conference between U.S. President Reagan and Gorbachev; INF treaty signed.

Moscow showing of Abuladze's bold film *Repentance*.

Joseph Brodsky awarded Nobel Prize in literature.

Mathias Rust, 19 years old, lands his Cessna 172 in Red Square; Air Defense Commander Koldunov removed.

Soviet diplomats visit Israel for first visit since 1967.

1988

National conflicts break out in Transcaucasia and in Baltic republics; national movements spread throughout Soviet Union.

(February) Ethnic violence breaks out in Armenia and Azerbaijan over contested Nagorno-

Karabakh territory; demonstrations in Armenia; anti-Armenian pogrom in Sumgait, a suburb of Baku, the capital of Azerbaijan.

(March) Nina Andreeva's anti-perestroika letter published in *Sovetskaia Rossiia*.

(May) Soviets begin pullout from Afghanistan.

(May–June) Moscow summit between U.S. President Reagan and Gorbachev.

Trial of Yuri Churbanov, Brezhnev's son-in-law, for bribery and extortion.

(June) Celebration of millennium of Christianity coming to Kiev.

Nineteenth Party Conference in Moscow.

Kremlin sends troops to Nagorno-Karabakh.

(October) Gorbachev becomes president of the Soviet Union, replacing former Foreign Minister Andrei Gromyko.

(November) New presidential system and Congress of People's Deputies adopted.

Estonian Communist Party declares supremacy of Estonian laws.

(December) Gorbachev offers unilateral Soviet military reductions.

Earthquake in Soviet Armenia.

Gorbachev and U.S. President Reagan meet in New York City.

Doctor Zhivago first published in Russia.

1988–1990

Various Soviet republics declare themselves to be sovereign.

1989

(February) Soviet troops complete withdrawal from Afghanistan.

(March) National elections for Congress of People's Deputies; first elections to permit multicandidates and nonparty candidates; Boris Yeltsin and Andrei Sakharov overwhelmingly elected to seats in new Congress of People's Deputies.

Gorbachev calls for dismantling of collective farm system.

(April) Troops shoot at pro-independence demonstrators in Tbilisi, Georgia.

Soviet-Chinese summit in Beijing.

Coal miners strike in Siberia, the Ukraine, and Central Asia.

Pro-independence demonstrations in Baltic republics.

RUKH (Popular Movement of Ukraine) demands independence.

(May–June) Congress of People's Deputies and reformed Supreme Soviet hold meetings, televised across Soviet Union; Gorbachev elected chairman of new Supreme Soviet (USSR president).

(June) Gorbachev abandons Brezhnev Doctrine.

(July) Coal miners strike in Vorkuta, Karaganda, Siberia, and the Ukraine.

(August–December) Collapse of Communist governments across Eastern Europe.

(October) Armenia and Azerbaijan engage in war.

(November) Berlin Wall comes down.

(December) Lithuanian parliament approves multiparty system.

Death of Andrei Sakharov.

1990

(February) Civil war in Azerbaijan; Soviet troops occupy Baku.

Massive pro-democracy rally in Moscow.

End of Communist Party's political monopoly; Central Committee votes to allow multiparty system.

(March–August) Various republics declare their independence and/or sovereignty.

(March) Free elections in East Germany.

Lithuania declares independence.

(April) Georgia declares independence.

(May–June) Gorbachev-Bush summit in Washington, D.C.

(June 12) RSFSR Congress of People's Deputies passes "Declaration of State Sovereignty of Russia" (Independence Day).

(July) Lithuania agrees to postpone independence.

Twenty-eighth Party Congress.

Yeltsin and other liberals resign from Communist Party.

Supreme Soviet passes law to lift press censorship.

(August) Gorbachev and Yeltsin agree on 500-day plan for transition to market economy.

(October) Gorbachev presents plan for more gradual economic reform.

Reunification of East and West Germany.

(November) Law on Peasant Farms allows collective farm members to own private farms.

(November) CFE treaty signed in Paris.

(December) Eduard Shevardnadze resigns as foreign minister, warning that dictatorship is approaching.

Gorbachev awarded Nobel Peace Prize.

1991

Population of Soviet Union estimated at 290 million.

(January) Soviet special forces attack communication centers in Vilnius, Lithuania, killing 14 people; Soviet troops also attack public buildings in Riga.

Gorbachev picks conservative Valentin Pavlov as Soviet prime minister.

(March) Major strike of miners begins.

(April) Georgia declares independence.

(May) Law passed permitting free travel and emigration for Soviet citizens by 1993.

(June) Yeltsin wins popular election to presidency of Russian Republic, becoming first democratically elected leader of Russia.

(July) Gorbachev-Bush summit and signing of START treaty in Moscow.

Bodies of Nicholas II and family exhumed.

(August) August Coup.

Vice president Gennadi Yanaev, Interior Minister Boris Pugo, and Defense Minister Dmitrii Yazov announce the formation of "emergency government." Gorbachev held under house arrest in Crimea. Yeltsin mobilizes Moscow population to resist coup, speaking to crowd from tank and barricades himself in parliament building. Gorbachev returns to Moscow, resigns as general secretary of Communist Party. Pugo commits suicide. Yeltsin closes *Pravda* and disbands CPSU. Activities of Communist Party suspended in most Soviet republics.

Unsuccessful coup is followed by declarations of independence by all 15 republics of the USSR.

(September) Soviet government recognizes independence of the three Baltic republics.

Leningrad renamed St. Petersburg.

Centralized government replaced by voluntary agreement among now sovereign republics.

Ten former Soviet republics agree to set up common market.

(October) Yeltsin presents radical plan for Russian Republic's transition to market economy.

(November) COMECON dissolves.

(December) Ukrainian referendum on independence receives 90 percent approval.

(December) Presidents of Russia, the Ukraine, and Belorussia meet to establish Commonwealth of Independent States and dissolve Soviet Union. Gorbachev resigns.

Russian Federation
December 1991

1992

Yeltsin's "shock therapy" stimulates inflation.

(January) Yeltsin's "shock therapy": Prime minister frees prices, ruble drops drastically, prices skyrocket.

(March) Russian government signs Federation Treaty with all autonomous republics inside Russian Federation except Chechnya and Tatarstan.

(April) Western nations announce $1 billion aid package for Russia.

Congress of People's Deputies begins its attack on the government.

(May) Russia, Armenia, Kazakhstan, Kyrgystan, Tajikistan, and Uzbekistan sign Treaty on Collective Security.

(June) Yegor Gaidar appointed acting prime minister.

(October) Voucher privatization begins.

(December) Viktor Chernomyrdin replaces Yegor Gaidar as prime minister.

1993

(January) START-2 Treaty signed in Moscow.

(March) Yeltsin declares emergency presidential rule after Congress of Peoples' Deputies limits the government's power to implement reform.

(March) Speaker of Congress Ruslan Khasbulatov calls for Yeltsin's impeachment.

(April) Yeltsin meets President Clinton at summit in Vancouver, Canada.

Referendum supports president and reforms.

(August) Russian troops withdraw from Lithuania but remain in Latvia and Estonia.

(September) Gaidar rejoins government as first deputy prime minister.

Yeltsin dissolves Russian parliament.

Parliament appoints Vice President Rutskoi as president.

(October) Troops loyal to Yeltsin fire on the Russian parliament building.

(December) New Russian constitution approved and new parliament called the Federal Assembly of Russia is elected; parliamentary elections make the Liberal Democratic Party, led by right-wing extremist Vladimir Zhirinovsky, the largest party in the Duma.

1994

(January) Federal Assembly begins its work.

(February) State Duma passes amnesty for political and economic crimes.

Moscow signs treaty with Tatarstan granting it considerable autonomy.

(June) Gaidar resigns as first deputy prime minister.

(July) Yeltsin meets G-7 leaders in Naples, Italy.

(October) Ruble crushes.

Aleksandr Solzhenitsyn addresses the State Duma.

(December) Russian invasion of Chechnya begins.

1995

(January) Federal Assembly bans loans from Central Bank to the government without its approval.

(May) Yeltsin-Clinton summit in Moscow.

(June) Russian-Ukrainian agreement on Black Sea Fleet.

(June) Chechens take hostages at Budennovsk.

(July) Yeltsin suffers first heart attack.

(October) Yeltsin-Clinton summit in Hyde Park, New York.

Yeltsin suffers second heart attack.

(December) New Duma elections make the Communist Party, led by Gennadi Ziuganov, the largest party in the Duma.

1996

(January) Evgenii Primakov replaces Andrei Kozyrev as Russian foreign minister.

(March) Russia, Belarus, Kazakhstan, and Kyrgystan sign integration accords in Moscow.

(April) G-7 leaders and Yeltsin meet in Moscow; Yeltsin visits China.

(June) Ukrainian Parliament adopts constitution.

(June–July) Yeltsin wins two-stage presidential election.

(August) Yeltsin inaugurated as first elected president of independent Russia.

Chechens retake Grozny; full-scale Russian operations end in Chechnya; special presidential envoy Aleksandr Lebed and Aslan Maskhadov sign peace accord in Chechnya.

(November) Yeltsin undergoes quintuple bypass surgery.

Belorussian President Aleksandr Lukashenko signs new constitution extending his powers and replaces parliament.

(December) Russian troops begin withdrawal from Chechnya.

1997

(January) New Criminal Code replaces 1960 Soviet code.

Chechen elections held; Maskhadov wins 65 percent of the vote.

(March) Yeltsin and U.S. President Clinton meet in Helsinki to discuss expansion of NATO.

(April) Union Treaty signed.

(May) Russian-Belarus Union Charter signed by Lukashenko and Yeltsin.

Yeltsin and Clinton sign "Founding Act on Mutual Relations, Cooperation and Security between NATO and the Russian Federation," which creates a permanent joint council including Russia in NATO decision making.

(June) Russian-Belarus Union Charter goes into effect.

Tajik Peace and National Reconciliation Accord signed in Moscow.

1998

(March) Yeltsin fires Prime Minister Viktor Chernomyrdin, reorganizes cabinet.

(April) Sergei Kirienko finally confirmed as prime minister.

(May) Massive sell-off of Russian bonds, securities, and rubles.

(July) Nicholas II and family interred in St. Petersburg.

(August) Russian financial crisis: Kirienko announces ruble devaluation; market paralyzed by liquidity shortages; share prices plunge; Russia defaults on foreign loans; Yeltsin sacks entire government and reappoints Chernomyrdin interim prime minister.

(September) Chernomyrdin steps aside as Duma rejects nomination twice.

Evgenii Primakov named prime minister and confirmed by Duma.

1999

(May) Yeltsin fires Primakov and cabinet.

Duma begins impeachment proceedings against Yeltsin, but final vote falls short of impeachment.

Duma approves Sergei Stepashin as new prime minister.

(August) Yeltsin dismisses Stepashin as prime minister.

Vladimir Putin confirmed as prime minister.

(September) Russian money-laundering scheme via Bank of New York is unveiled.

2000

(January) Former president Boris Yeltsin visits Israel and the sites of the Holy Land.

Acting President Putin temporarily suspends Russian bombardments in Chechnya in observance of Orthodox and Muslim religious holidays.

(March) Vladimir Putin elected president of the Russian Federation.

(May) Putin proposes reforms to recentralize Russian federal system.

First decree reorganizes 89 gubernatorial territories into seven administrative districts overseen by a regional official reporting to Putin. The second decree proposes to abolish the 89 guaranteed seats that regional governors had on the Federation Council, one of the two houses of the Russian legislature.

(August) The nuclear submarine *Kursk* sinks in the Arctic Ocean. One hundred eighteen sailors are killed.

2001

(July) Russia and China sign treaty of friendship and cooperation.

(September) Terrorist attacks in New York and Washington. Russia offers support to United States in worldwide struggle against terrorism.

(November) Putin travels to United States for first official visit and meets U.S. president George W. Bush in Crawford, Texas.

Russia signs agreement with Moldova pledging to cooperate against pro-Russia separatists in Transdnistria region of Moldova.

2002

(December) United States renounces from 1972 Antiballistic Missile Treaty.

(April) Aleksandr Lebed, former general, presidential candidate in 1996, and governor of Krasnoyarsk in Siberia, dies in helicopter crash.

(October) On October 23, terrorists attack the Dubrovka Theater Center in Moscow and hold audience hostage. Three days later, Russian security forces launch a rescue operation with nerve gas that results in more than 100 deaths.

2003

(March) Russia joins France and Germany in attempt to stop U. S.-led invasion of Iraq.

(October) Mikhail Khodorskovsky, chairman of Yukos Oil and one of Russia's most prominent business oligarchs, is arrested on charges of fraud and embezzlement.

(November) Georgian president Eduard Shevardnadze resigns.

(December) Russia fails to ratify Kyoto Protocol on global warming.

Suicide bomber kills five near parliament building in Moscow.

Putin's party, United Russia, wins a plurality of votes in parliamentary elections and gains a two-thirds majority in Russian Duma.

2004

(January) Russia and Kazakhstan agree to extend Russian lease on Baikonur Cosmodrome until 2050.

(February) Bomb explodes in Moscow subway and kills 41 passengers.

Nine imperial Fabergé eggs purchased from Malcolm Forbes's collection by Russian oligarch Viktor Vekselberg, who will take them back to Russia for display.

Putin dismisses Prime Minister Kasianov and appoints Mikhail Frydkov as his successor.

(March) Presidential elections held. Putin reelected to second four-year term.

APPENDIXES

Appendix I
Russian Rulers from 1462 to 2004
(including dates of rule)

Appendix II
Maps

APPENDIX I

RUSSIAN RULERS FROM 1462 TO 2004
(including dates of rule)

HOUSE OF RURIK	
Name	**Reign**
Ivan III (the Great)	1462–1505
Vasily III	1505–33
Ivan IV (the Terrible)	1533–84
Feodor I	1584–98

TIME OF TROUBLES	
Name	**Reign**
Boris Godunov	1598–1605
Feodor II	1605
False Dmitrii	1605–6
Vasili IV Shuisky	1606–10
Interregnum	1610–13

HOUSE OF ROMANOV	
Name	**Reign**
Michael	1613–45
Alexis	1645–76
Feodor III	1676–82
Ivan V and Peter I (the Great)	1682–96
Peter I (the Great)	1696–1725
Catherine I	1725–27
Peter II	1727–30
Anna	1730–40
Ivan VI	1740–41
Elizabeth	1741–62
Peter III	1762

HOUSE OF ROMANOV *(continued)*

Name	Reign
Catherine II (the Great)	1762–96
Paul I	1796–1801
Alexander I	1801–25
Nicholas I	1825–55
Alexander II	1855–81
Alexander III	1881–94
Nicholas II	1894–1917

PROVISIONAL GOVERNMENT

Name	Term
Prince Georgi Yevgenyevich Lvov	March 23, 1917–July 21, 1917
Aleksandr Fyodorovich Kerensky	July 21, 1917–November 8, 1917 (to November 18, 1917, in opposition)
Sergey Nikolayevich Prokopovich	November 18, 1917–December 2, 1917 (in opposition; acting for Kerensky)

SOVIET RUSSIA

Name	Term
Vladimir Ilyich Lenin, Chairman of Council of People's Commissars	1917–24
Joseph Stalin, general secretary	1922–53
Nikita Khrushchev, general secretary	1953–64
Leonid Brezhnev, general secretary	1964–82
Yuri Andropov, general secretary	1982–84
Konstantin Chernenko, general secretary	1984–85
Mikhail Gorbachev, general secretary	1985–91

RUSSIAN REPUBLIC

Name	Term
Boris Yeltsin, President	1991–99
Vladimir Putin, President	1999–

APPENDIX II

MAPS

Kievan Russia, 900–1054

Mongol Invasions of Russia, 12th–13th Centuries

Rise of the Principality of Moscow, 1300–1533

Growth of Russia, 1551–1700

Russia at the Time of Troubles, ca. 1600

Russia in the Reign of Czar Aleksei, 1645–1686

Peter I's Great Embassy and Northern War

Russia, 1700–1800

Social Composition of Russia, ca. 1800

Napoleonic Wars and Russia

Growth of Russia, 1801–1855

Crimean War, 1853–1855

Growth of Russia, 1855–1904

The Eastern Question

Growth of Russia, 1904–1955

Eastern Europe during World War I

Russian Civil War, 1918–1920

Revolution and Civil War

Petrograd on the Eve of the Revolution, 1917

Soviet Union, 1917–1922

Northeast Passage and the Trans-Siberian Railroad, 1891–Present

Russia in World War II

Soviet Bloc, ca. 1950

Comparative Soviet Nationalities by Republic, 1979

Breakup of the Soviet Union, 1991

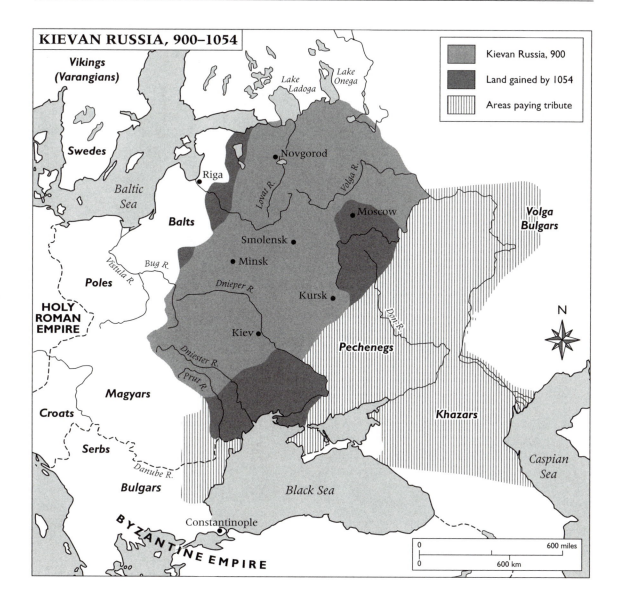

KIEVAN RUSSIA, 900–1054

Legend:
- Kievan Russia, 900
- Land gained by 1054
- Areas paying tribute

Vikings (Varangians)

Swedes

Lake Ladoga

Lake Onega

Baltic Sea

Balts

Riga

Novgorod

Lovat R.

Volga R.

Moscow

Smolensk

Volga Bulgars

Minsk

Kursk

Bug R.

Vistula R.

Poles

HOLY ROMAN EMPIRE

Dnieper R.

Kiev

Don R.

Pechenegs

N

Magyars

Dniester R.

Prut R.

Croats

Khazars

Serbs

Danube R.

Caspian Sea

Bulgars

Black Sea

Constantinople

BYZANTINE EMPIRE

0   600 miles

0   600 km

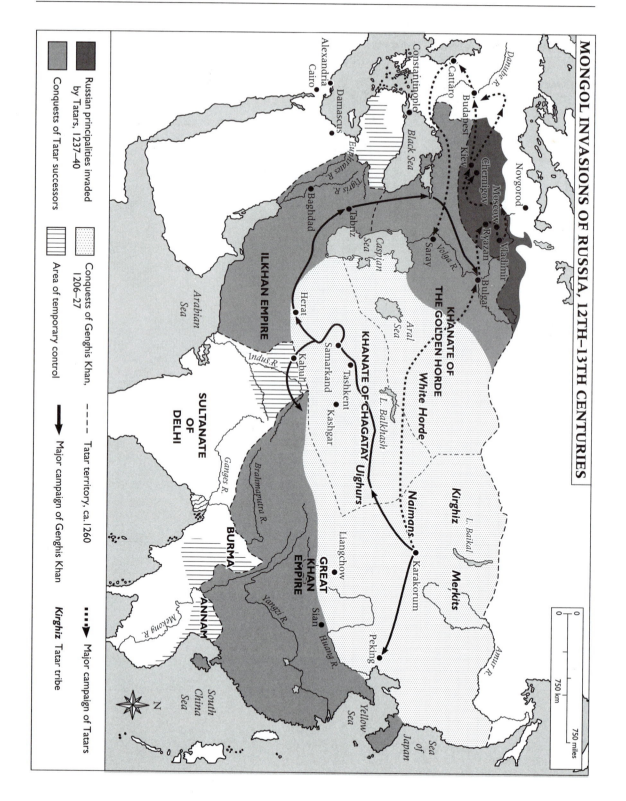

MONGOL INVASIONS OF RUSSIA, 12TH–13TH CENTURIES

Russian principalities invaded by Tatars, 1237–40

Conquests of Tatar successors

Conquests of Genghis Khan, 1206–27

Area of temporary control

Tatar territory, ca.1260

Major campaign of Genghis Khan

Major campaign of Tatars

Kirghiz Tatar tribe

Alexandria
Cairo
Damascus
Constantinople
Cattaro
Budapest
Kiev
Chernigov
Moscow
Novgorod
Ryazan
Vladimir
Bulgar
Danube R.
Black Sea
Euphrates R.
Tigris R.
Baghdad
Tabriz
Saray
Volga R.
Caspian Sea
ILKHAN EMPIRE
Arabian Sea
Herat
Aral Sea
KHANATE OF THE GOLDEN HORDE
White Horde
Kirghiz
Merkits
L. Balkhash
Kabul
Samarkand
Tashkent
Kashgar
KHANATE OF CHAGATAY Uighurs
Indus R.
SULTANATE OF DELHI
Ganges R.
Brahmaputra R.
BURMA
Naimans
Karakorum
Amur R.
L. Baikal
Liangchow
GREAT KHAN EMPIRE
Sian
Huang R.
Peking
Yellow Sea
Sea of Japan
Yangzi R.
Mekong R.
ANNAM
South China Sea
N
0   750 km
0   750 miles

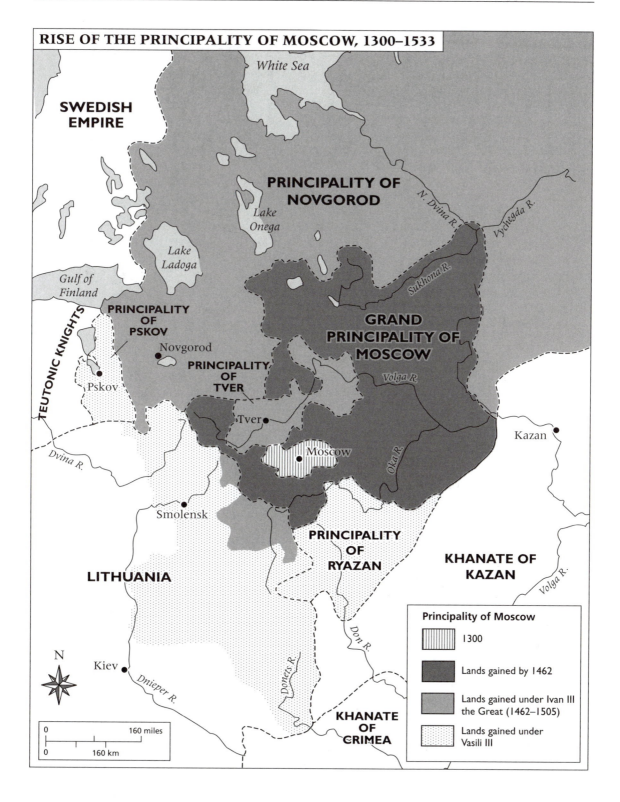

RISE OF THE PRINCIPALITY OF MOSCOW, 1300–1533

White Sea

SWEDISH EMPIRE

PRINCIPALITY OF NOVGOROD

Lake Onega

N. Dvina R.

Vychegda R.

Lake Ladoga

Sukhona R.

Gulf of Finland

TEUTONIC KNIGHTS

PRINCIPALITY OF PSKOV

Novgorod

GRAND PRINCIPALITY OF MOSCOW

PRINCIPALITY OF TVER

Pskov

Volga R.

Dvina R.

Tver

Moscow

Kazan

Oka R.

Smolensk

PRINCIPALITY OF RYAZAN

KHANATE OF KAZAN

LITHUANIA

Volga R.

N

Kiev

Don R.

Dnieper R.

Donets R.

KHANATE OF CRIMEA

Principality of Moscow	
	1300
	Lands gained by 1462
	Lands gained under Ivan III the Great (1462–1505)
	Lands gained under Vasili III

0 ——— 160 miles

0 ——— 160 km

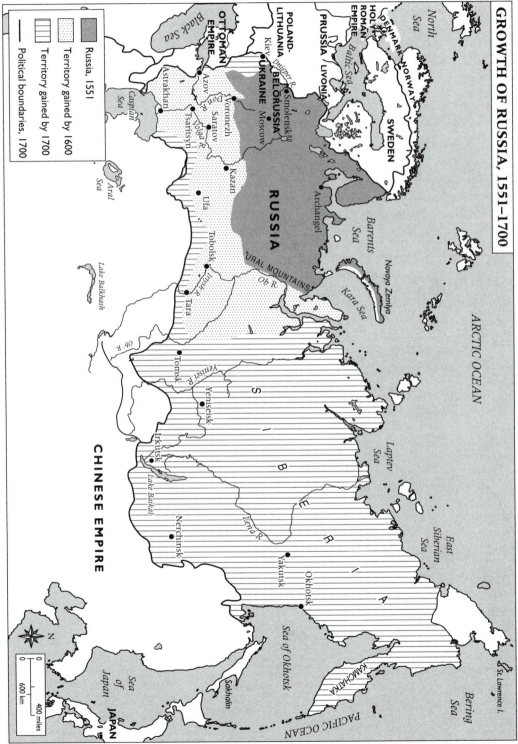

GROWTH OF RUSSIA, 1551–1700

Political boundaries, 1700
Territory gained by 1700
Territory gained by 1600
Russia, 1551

RUSSIA AT THE TIME OF TROUBLES, CA. 1600

Occupied by Poland, 1611–13	Russia, 1618	← Polish advance, 1610
Occupied by Sweden, 1613	Sweden, 1618	⇐ Swedish advance, 1610
Poland, 1618	⇐ Bolotnikov's march 1606–07	◄-- Russian counterattack under Minin and Pozharsky, 1611–12

Bolotnikov's rebellion, 1606–07

Uprising of non-Slav peoples, 1606–08

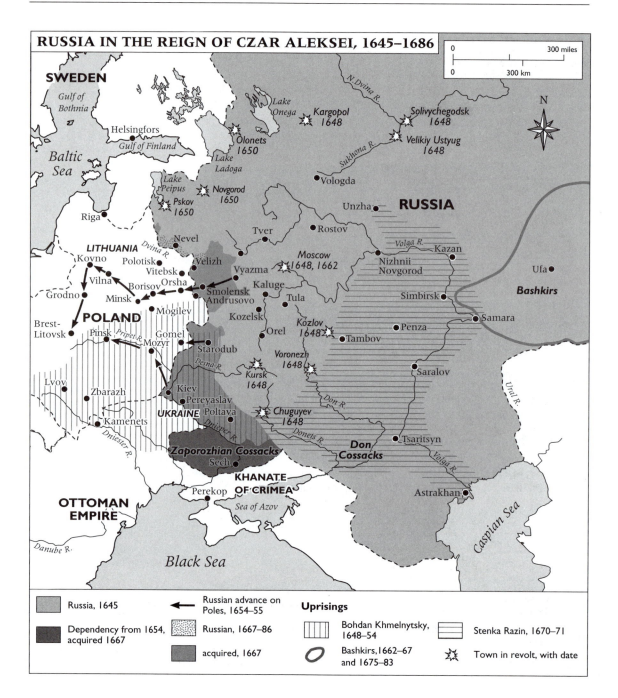

RUSSIA IN THE REIGN OF CZAR ALEKSEI, 1645–1686

SWEDEN

Gulf of Bothnia

Helsingfors

Gulf of Finland

Baltic Sea

Riga

Lake Onega

Kargopol 1648

Solivychegodsk 1648

Velikiy Ustyug 1648

Olonets 1650

Lake Ladoga

Lake Peipus

Novgorod 1650

Pskov 1650

Vologda

Unzha

RUSSIA

N. Dvina R.

Sukhona R.

Nevel

Tver

Rostov

Volga R.

Kazan

LITHUANIA

Dvina R.

Kovno

Polotisk

Vitebsk

Velizh

Vyazma

Moscow 1648, 1662

Nizhnii Novgorod

Ufa

Bashkirs

Vilna

Borisov

Orsha

Smolensk

Kaluge

Simbirsk

Samara

Grodno

Minsk

Andrusovo

Tula

POLAND

Mogilev

Kozelsk

Orel

Kozlov 1648

Penza

Brest-Litovsk

Pinsk

Pripet R.

Gomel

Mozyr

Starodub

Desna R.

Voronezh 1648

Tambov

Saralov

Lvov

Zbarazh

Kiev

Pereyaslav

UKRAINE

Poltava

Kursk 1648

Don R.

Kamenets

Dniester R.

Dnieper R.

Chuguyev 1648

Donets R.

Don Cossacks

Tsaritsyn

Volga R.

Zaporozhian Cossacks

Sech

KHANATE OF CRIMEA

OTTOMAN EMPIRE

Perekop

Sea of Azov

Astrakhan

Ural R.

Caspian Sea

Danube R.

Black Sea

	Russia, 1645	→	Russian advance on Poles, 1654–55	**Uprisings**			
	Dependency from 1654, acquired 1667		Russian, 1667–86	Bohdan Khmelnytsky, 1648–54		Stenka Razin, 1670–71	
			acquired, 1667	Bashkirs, 1662–67 and 1675–83		Town in revolt, with date	

0   300 miles
0   300 km

N

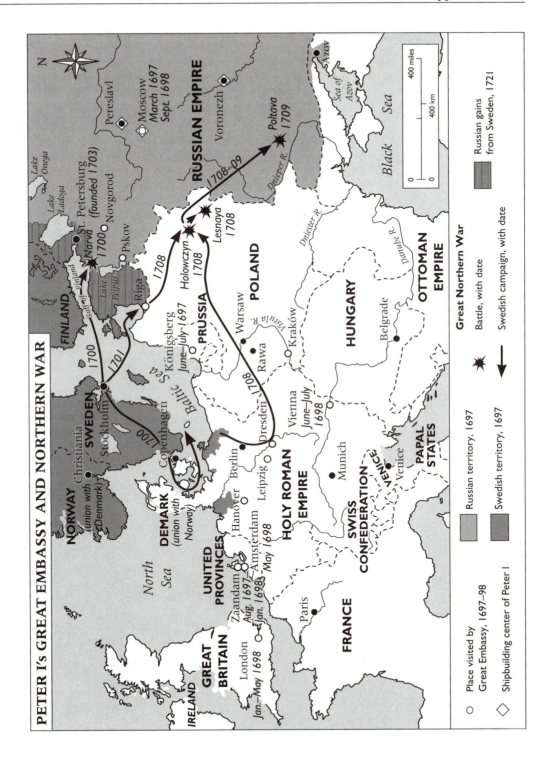

PETER I's GREAT EMBASSY AND NORTHERN WAR

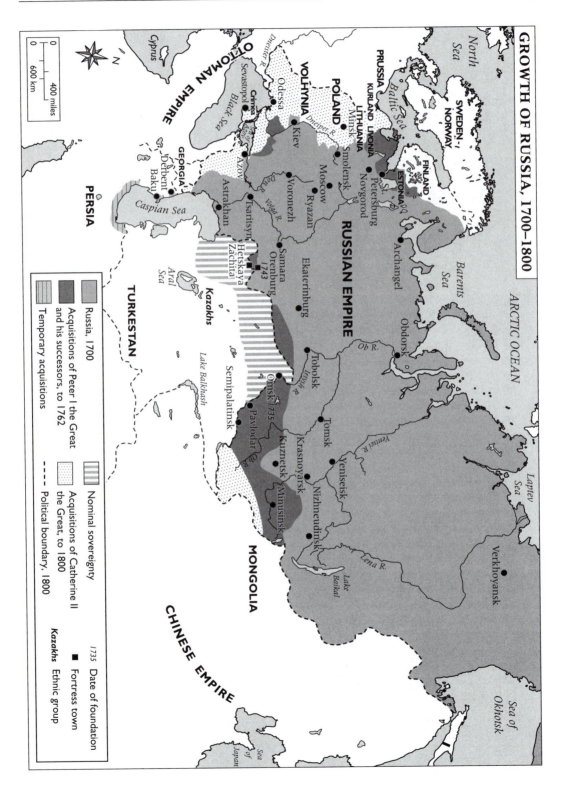

GROWTH OF RUSSIA, 1700–1800

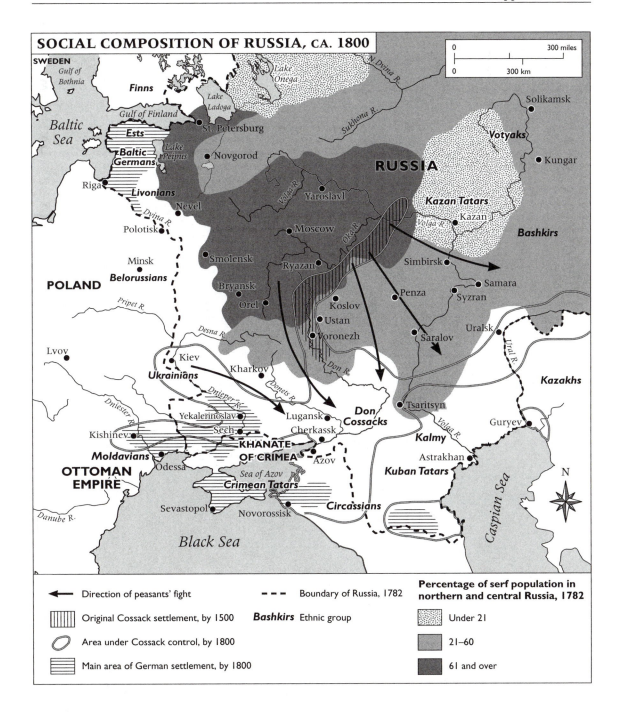

SOCIAL COMPOSITION OF RUSSIA, CA. 1800

0   300 miles
0   300 km

SWEDEN
Gulf of Bothnia
Finns
Baltic Sea
Gulf of Finland
Lake Onega
N. Dvina R.
Lake Ladoga
St. Petersburg
Sukhona R.
Solikamsk
Ests
Baltic Germans
Lake Peipus
Novgorod
RUSSIA
Votyaks
Kungar
Riga
Livonians
Dvina R.
Nevel
Volga R.
Yaroslavl
Kazan Tatars
Kazan
Bashkirs
Polotisk
Moscow
Oka R.
Volga R.
Minsk
POLAND
Belorussians
Smolensk
Ryazan
Simbirsk
Samara
Pripet R.
Bryansk
Penza
Syzran
Orel
Koslov
Ustan
Saralov
Uralsk
Desna R.
Voronezh
Ural R.
Lvov
Kiev
Kharkov
Don R.
Kazakhs
Ukrainians
Donets R.
Dnieper R.
Tsaritsyn
Dniester R.
Yekalerinoslav
Sech
Lugansk
Cherkassk
Don Cossacks
Kalmy
Volga R.
Guryev
Kishinev
KHANATE OF CRIMEA
Astrakhan
Moldavians
Odessa
Azov
Kuban Tatars
Caspian Sea
OTTOMAN EMPIRE
Sea of Azov
Crimean Tatars
N
Sevastopol
Novorossisk
Circassians
Danube R.
Black Sea

←   Direction of peasants' fight

||||| Original Cossack settlement, by 1500

⬭   Area under Cossack control, by 1800

≡   Main area of German settlement, by 1800

– – –   Boundary of Russia, 1782

Bashkirs   Ethnic group

Percentage of serf population in northern and central Russia, 1782

▒   Under 21

▓   21–60

█   61 and over

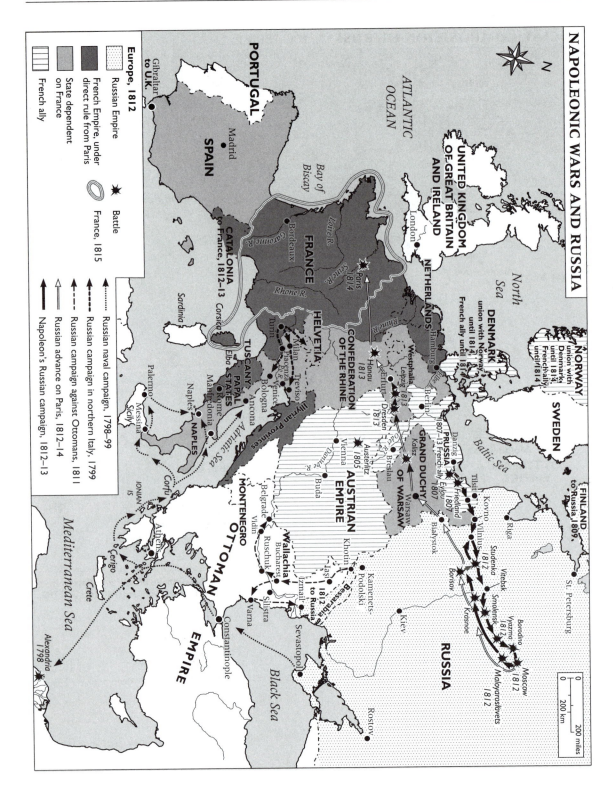

NAPOLEONIC WARS AND RUSSIA

Europe, 1812

Russian Empire

French Empire, under direct rule from Paris

State dependent on France

French ally

★ Battle

France, 1815

Russian naval campaign, 1798–99

Russian campaign in northern Italy, 1799

Russian campaign against Ottomans, 1811

Russian advance on Paris, 1812–14

Napoleon's Russian campaign, 1812–13

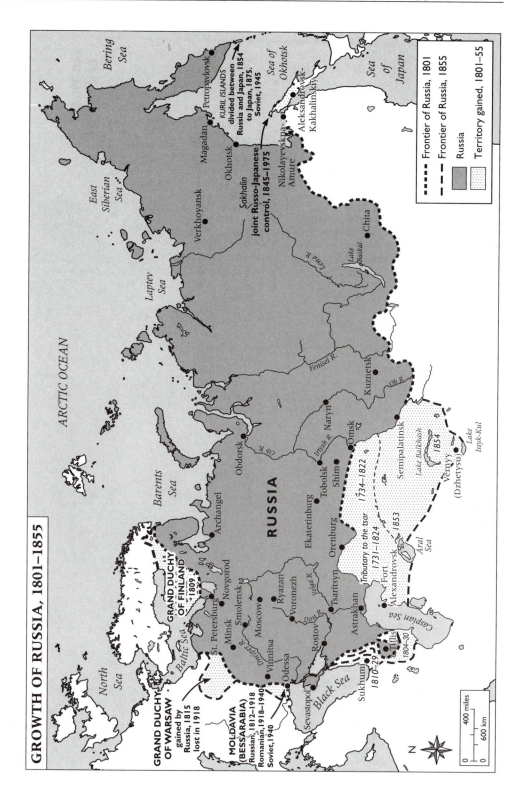

GROWTH OF RUSSIA, 1801–1855

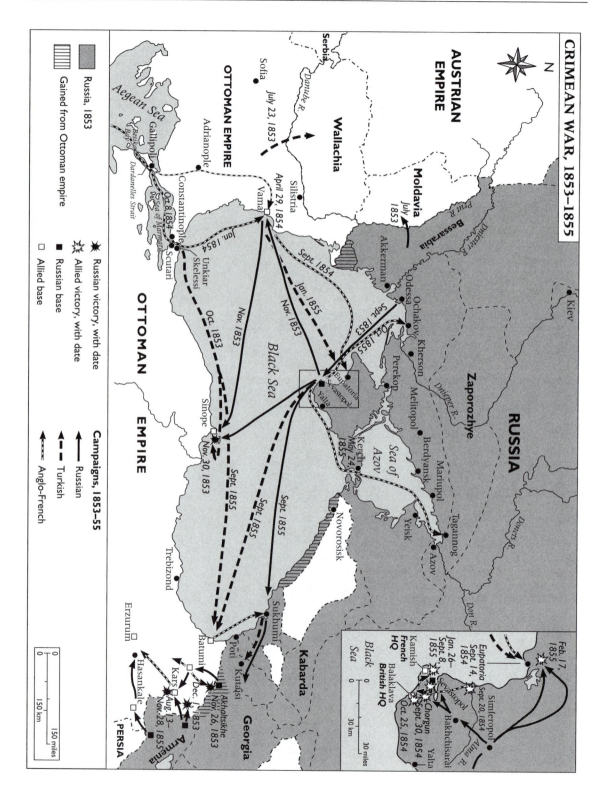

CRIMEAN WAR, 1853–1855

Russia, 1853

Gained from Ottoman empire

★ Russian victory, with date

✺ Allied victory, with date

■ Russian base

□ Allied base

Campaigns, 1853–55

→ Russian

---→ Turkish

→ Anglo-French

AUSTRIAN EMPIRE

Serbia

OTTOMAN EMPIRE

Sofia

July 23, 1853

Danube R.

Wallachia

Moldavia

July 1853

Bessarabia

Prut R.

Dniester R.

Akkerman

RUSSIA

Kiev

Silistria

April 29, 1854

Varna

Sept. 1854

Odessa

Ochakov

Kherson

Sept. 1853

Oct. 1853

Zaporozhye

Dnieper R.

Adrianople

Jan. 1854

Jan. 1855

Nov. 1853

Perekop

Melitopol

Constantinople

Scutari

Unkiar Skelessi

Oct. 8, 1854

Sea of Marmara

Dardanelles Strait

Gallipoli

Besika Bay

Aegean Sea

Oct. 1853

Nov. 1853

Black Sea

Eupatoria

Sevastopol

Yalta

Berdyansk

Sea of Azov

Kerch

May 24, 1855

Mariupol

Taganrog

Azov

Don R.

OTTOMAN EMPIRE

Sinope

Nov. 30, 1853

Sept. 1855

Sept. 1855

Sept. 1855

Novorosisk

Yeisk

Trebizond

Sukhumi

Kabarda

Erzurum

Batumi

Poti

Kutaisi

Georgia

Hasankale

Kars

Dec. 1853

Akhaltsikhe

Nov. 26, 1853

Aug. 1, 1855

Nov. 28, 1855

Armenia

Nov. 13, 1853

PERSIA

0 ——— 150 miles

0 ——— 150 km

Black Sea

Eupatoria

Sept. 14, 1855

Jan. 26–Sept. 8, 1854

Kamish

French HQ

Balaklava

British HQ

Sept. 20, 1854

Sevastopol

Oct. 25, 1854

Chorgun

Sept. 30, 1854

Simferopol

Bakhchisarai

Yalta

Alma R.

Feb. 17, 1855

0 ——— 30 miles

0 ——— 30 km

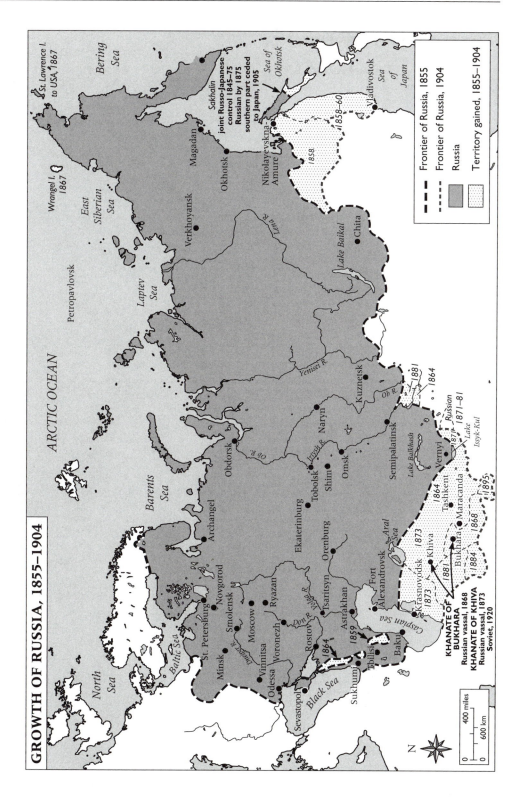

GROWTH OF RUSSIA, 1855–1904

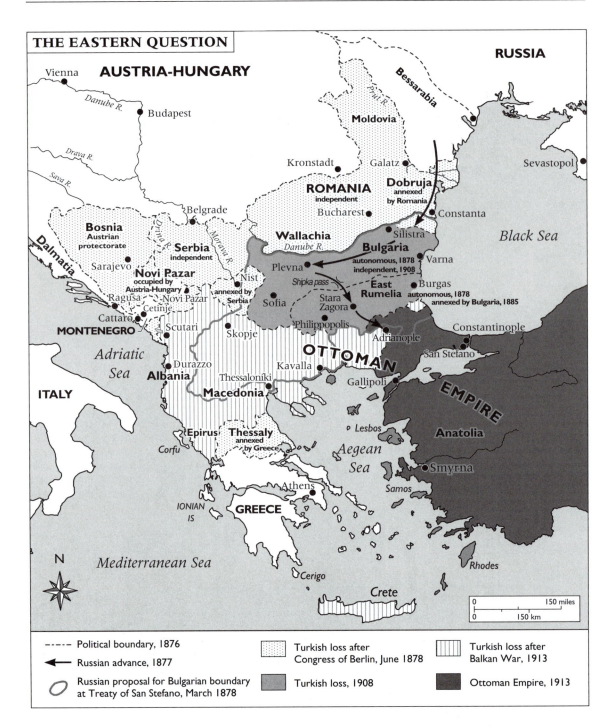

THE EASTERN QUESTION

RUSSIA

AUSTRIA-HUNGARY

Vienna

Danube R.

Budapest

Drava R.

Sava R.

Kronstadt

Galatz

Sevastopol

Bessarabia

Prut R.

MOLDOVIA

ROMANIA
independent

Dobruja
annexed
by Romania

Constanta

Bucharest

Belgrade

Bosnia
Austrian
protectorate

Drina R.

Serbia
independent

Morava R.

Wallachia
Danube R.

Silistra

Bulgaria
autonomous, 1878
independent, 1908

Varna

Black Sea

Dalmatia

Sarajevo

Novi Pazar
occupied by
Austria-Hungary

Nist

annexed by
Serbia

Plevna

Shipka pass

**East
Rumelia** autonomous, 1878
annexed by Bulgaria, 1885

Burgas

Ragusa

Novi Pazar

Sofia

Stara
Zagora

Cetinje

Scutari

Philippopolis

Adrianople

Constantinople

MONTENEGRO

Cattaro

Skopje

San Stefano

*Adriatic
Sea*

Durazzo

Kavalla

OTTOMAN

ITALY

Albania

Thessaloniki

Gallipoli

Macedonia

EMPIRE

Lesbos

Anatolia

Epirus

Thessaly
annexed
by Greece

Corfu

*Aegean
Sea*

Smyrna

Athens

Samos

*IONIAN
IS*

GREECE

Rhodes

Mediterranean Sea

N

Cerigo

Crete

0   150 miles

0   150 km

- – – – Political boundary, 1876

⟶ Russian advance, 1877

◯ Russian proposal for Bulgarian boundary
at Treaty of San Stefano, March 1878

Turkish loss after
Congress of Berlin, June 1878

Turkish loss, 1908

Turkish loss after
Balkan War, 1913

Ottoman Empire, 1913

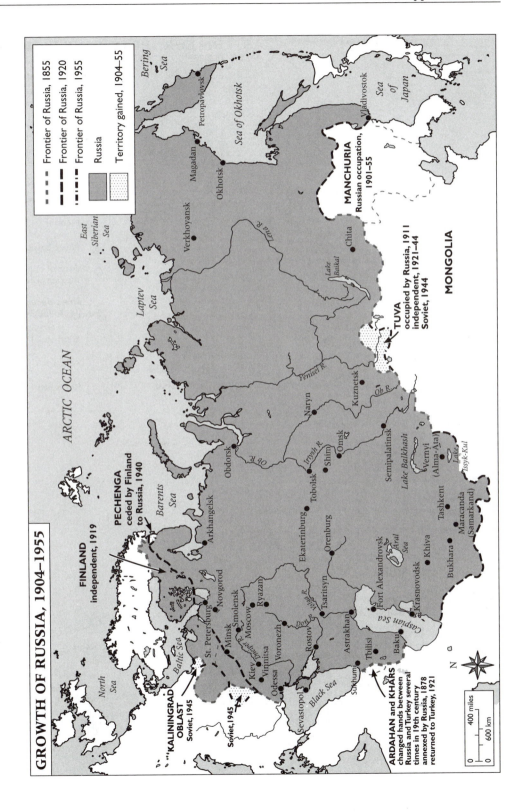

GROWTH OF RUSSIA, 1904–1955

EASTERN EUROPE DURING WORLD WAR I

Russian frontier, 1914
Front lines
December 1914
November 1915
December 1916
December 1917

Entente power

Central power

Neutral

Major battle

Area of mutiny by Russian army, July 1917

Area occupied by foreign force, March 1918

German   Turkish

Austrian   British, American, and other Allies

Romanian

0   200 miles
0   200 km

Barents Sea

Murmansk

White Sea

Archangel

NORWAY

Gulf of Bothnia

FINLAND

Shenkursk

SWEDEN

Helsinki

Lake Ladoga

Stockholm

Gulf of Finland

Petrograd
Tallinn   Kronstadt
Estonia

Baltic Sea

Riga
Livonia

RUSSIAN EMPIRE

Moscow

Memel
Königsberg   **Kourland**
Gumbinnen   **Lithuania**   Dvinsk
Danzig   Kovno
Berlin   Masuran Lakes   Vilnius
Tannenberg   Kievo   Smorgon
GERMANY   Plotsk   Białystok   Minsk
Kalisz   Mogilev
Piotrków   Lodz   **Poland**
Warsaw
Brest-Litovsk   Pinsk
Kraków   Krasnik   Lublin
Tarnow   Komarov
Galicia   Lemberg
Tarnopol

Smolensk

Belorussia

Orel

Voronezh

Volga R.   *Ural R.*

Vienna   *Danube R.*   Budapest
Stanislau
Czernowitz

Kiev

Dnieper R.

Kharkov

AUSTRIA-HUNGARY

Ukraine

Dniester R.
Iasi   **Bessarabia**
Moldavia   Izmail   Odessa

Nikolayev

Rostov

Astrakhan

Belgrade
Sarajevo
SERBIA
MONTENEGRO
ALBANIA   Skopje

ROMANIA
Bucharest

Sevastopol   Simferopol

Sea of Azov

Novorossisk

Caspian Sea

BULGARIA
Sofia

Black Sea

CAUCASUS MTS.

Georgia   Tbilisi
Batumi
Kars   **Azerbaijan**   Baku
Armenia

Constantinople

GREECE
Athens

Aegean Sea

Gallipoli

Ankara

Trebizond
Erzurum

OTTOMAN EMPIRE

Izmir

Tabriz

PERSIA

N

Mediterranean Sea

RUSSIAN CIVIL WAR, 1918–1920

Barents Sea

0 _____ 600 miles
0 _____ 600 km

N

SWEDEN

FINLAND
1921

Baltic
Sea

1921
ESTONIA

LITHUANIA

LATVIA
1921
1921

GERMANY

GERMANY
(Danzig)

● Warsaw

POLAND
1920

Minsk

CZECHOSLOVAKIA

HUNGARY

ROMANIA

BULGARIA

Aegean
Sea

TURKEY

● Petrograd
February Revolution, 1917–
Czar Nicholas II abdicates;
provisional government established
October Revolution,–1917
Bolsheviks under Vladimir Lenin seize power

● Moscow
Bolsheviks move government
from St. Petersburg, January 1918

BOLSHEVIK RUSSIA

Kiev

UKRAINE

Black Sea

GEORGIA
ARMENIA
AZERBAIJAN

PERSIA

Ekaterinburg ●
Czar Nicholas II and family
executed by Bolsheviks, July 1918

Omsk

Orenburg ●

Caspian
Sea

———— Boundary of Russian Empire, 1914

Area controlled by the Bolshevik
(Communist) government by
October 1919

– – – – Boundary of Soviet Union, 1922

1921   Date of independence recognized
        by the Soviet Union

✷ Fighting between Red (Bolshevik)
and White (anti-Bolshevik) armies

REVOLUTION AND CIVIL WAR

Legend:

–·–· Boundary of Russian Empire, 1914

⊙ Center of Bolshevik influence, July–September 1917

⊗ Principal town where Bolsheviks seized power, November– December 1917

– – Boundary of territory occupied by German and Turkish forces after Treaty of Brest-Litovsk, March 1918

▨ Area controlled by Bolsheviks, August 1918

← Advance of anti-Bolsheviks

- - - Boundary of Boshevik territory, October 1919

— Front line of anti-Bolshevik armies, May 1920

▨ Soviet territory, March 1921

–·–· Other political boundary, 1921

Entente fleet 1918–20

Petsamo

Murmansk

Barents Sea

White Sea

Arkhangelsk

Entente forces

Shenkursk

FINLAND *Finns*

Helsinki

Lake Ladoga

Lake Onega

Gulf of Bothnia

Stockholm

Gulf of Finland

Narva Petrograd

Tallinn Kronstadt

Estonia

Dorpat

Riga Valka Pskov

Latvia

Konigsberg

Lithuania Dvinsk

Kaunas

Danzig Vilnius

Maloya Vishera

Vologda

Czechs

Glasov ⊗ Perm

BOLSHEVIK RUSSIA

Kolchak 1918–19

Tver Ivanovo

Kazan

Ekaterinburg (Sverdlovsk) **Czar Nicholas II and family assassinated by Bolsheviks, July 1918**

Ufa

Moscow **Government moves from Petrograd, March 1918**

Nizhni Novgorod

Simbirsk

Vitebsk

Smolensk

Mogilev Kaluga Tula

Penza

Samara

Białystok Minsk

POLAND **Poles**

Warsaw Pinsk

Comel

Tambov

Orenburg

Brest-Litovsk

Łódź Lublin

Orel

Voronezh

Saratov

Volga R.

Ural R.

Lvov

Galicia

Zhitomir

Tarnopol

Kiev

Khartov

Denikin 1919

Sommer 1919

Tsaritsyn

Cossacks 1918–20

Aral Sea

Romanians

Dniester R.

Bessarabia

Dnieper R.

Kharkov

Donets R.

Don R.

Ukraine

Yekaterinoslav

Poltava

Nikolayev

Taganrog

Novocherkassk

Astrakhan

Odessa

Mariupol Rostov

ROMANIA

Bucharest

Izmail

Sea of Azov

French

Ukrainians, Cossacks, White Russians

Vladikavkaz

Caspian Sea

BULGARIA

Sofia

Sevastopol Simferopol

Novorosslysk

British

CAUCASUS MTS.

Krasnovodsk

British

Constantinople

Black Sea

Entente fleet 1918–20

Sochi

British Georgia Batumi Tbilisi

Baku

British

Ankara

Kars

Armenia

British

GREECE

Aegean Sea

Izmir

TURKEY

Tabriz

Mediterranean Sea

Crete

N

Gallipoli

PERSIA

0	200 miles
0	200 km

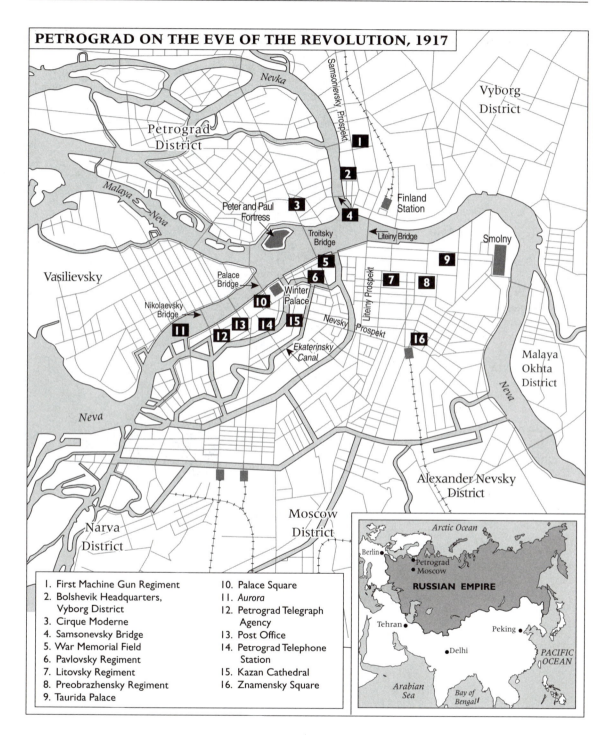

PETROGRAD ON THE EVE OF THE REVOLUTION, 1917

Vyborg District

Petrograd District

Nevka

Samsonievsky Prospekt

1

2

Finland Station

Malaya Neva

Peter and Paul Fortress

3

4

Troitsky Bridge

Liteiny Bridge

Smolny

Vasilievsky

Palace Bridge

5

6

9

Liteiny Prospekt

7

8

Nikolaevsky Bridge

10

Winter Palace

11

13

14

15

Nevsky Prospekt

12

Ekaterinsky Canal

16

Malaya Okhta District

Neva

Alexander Nevsky District

Narva District

Moscow District

1. First Machine Gun Regiment
2. Bolshevik Headquarters, Vyborg District
3. Cirque Moderne
4. Samsonevsky Bridge
5. War Memorial Field
6. Pavlovsky Regiment
7. Litovsky Regiment
8. Preobrazhensky Regiment
9. Taurida Palace
10. Palace Square
11. *Aurora*
12. Petrograd Telegraph Agency
13. Post Office
14. Petrograd Telephone Station
15. Kazan Cathedral
16. Znamensky Square

Arctic Ocean

Berlin

Petrograd
Moscow

RUSSIAN EMPIRE

Tehran

Peking

Delhi

PACIFIC OCEAN

Arabian Sea

Bay of Bengal

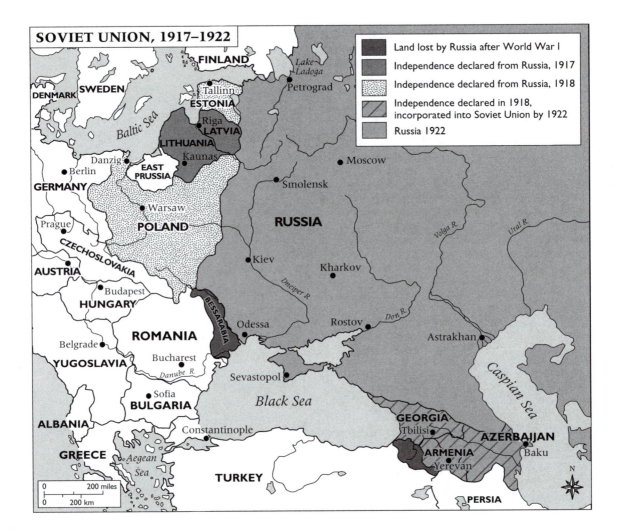

SOVIET UNION, 1917–1922

Legend:
- Land lost by Russia after World War I
- Independence declared from Russia, 1917
- Independence declared from Russia, 1918
- Independence declared in 1918, incorporated into Soviet Union by 1922
- Russia 1922

DENMARK
SWEDEN
FINLAND
Lake Ladoga
Petrograd
Tallinn
ESTONIA
Riga
LATVIA
LITHUANIA
Kaunas
Moscow
Danzig
Berlin
EAST PRUSSIA
Smolensk
GERMANY
Prague
Warsaw
POLAND
RUSSIA
CZECHOSLOVAKIA
Volga R.
Ural R.
AUSTRIA
Kiev
Kharkov
Budapest
HUNGARY
BESSARABIA
Dnieper R.
ROMANIA
Odessa
Rostov
Don R.
Astrakhan
Belgrade
Bucharest
YUGOSLAVIA
Danube R.
Sevastopol
Caspian Sea
Sofia
BULGARIA
Black Sea
GEORGIA
Tbilisi
ALBANIA
AZERBAIJAN
Constantinople
Baku
GREECE
ARMENIA
Aegean Sea
Yerevan
TURKEY
PERSIA

0   200 miles
0   200 km

N

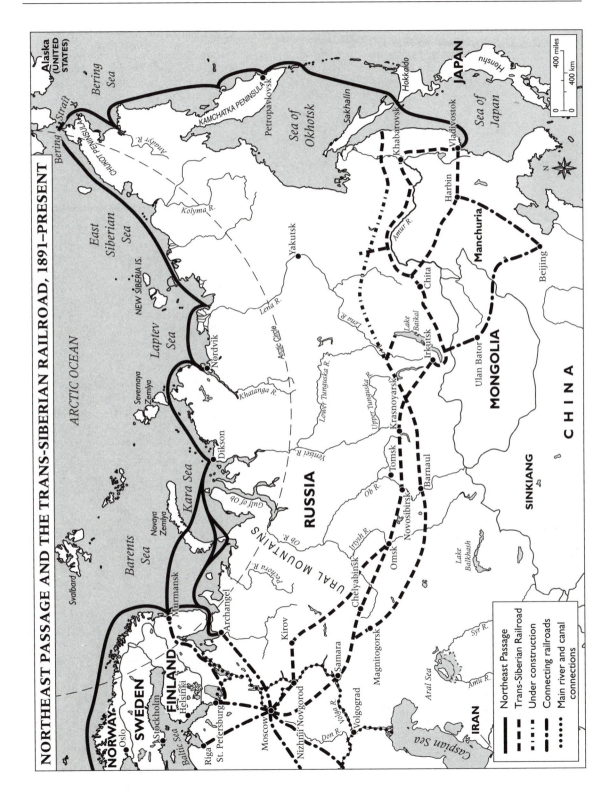

NORTHEAST PASSAGE AND THE TRANS-SIBERIAN RAILROAD, 1891–PRESENT

RUSSIA IN WORLD WAR II

Scale: 0 — 200 miles / 0 — 200 km

Legend:

- ■ Industrial center
- Russia, 1939
- Land gained by USSR, 1939–40
- Germany and Axis-controlled area, 1940
- –·–·– Political boundary, 1940
- ⊢⊢⊢ Major railroad behind front line
- ▬▬▬ Front line, December 1941
- ═══ Front line, November 1942

Population movement
- ◄···· Before German occupation
- ◄──── During German occupation

Labels on map:

Barents Sea, Murmansk, Allied supply route, White Sea, Archangel, NORWAY, SWEDEN, Stockholm, Gulf of Bothnia, FINLAND, Helsinki, Lake Ladoga, Gulf of Finland, Tallinn, Leningrad, Estonia, Novgorod, Vologda, Kirov, Molotov (Perm), Baltic Sea, Riga, Pskov, Yaroslavl, Latvia, Velikiye Luki, Gorki, Kazan, Ufa, Lithuania, Danzig, Vitebsk, Moscow, Ulyanovsk, Berlin, GERMANY, Białystok, Minsk, Kuibyshev, Oder R., Warsaw, Pinsk, Bryansk, Gomel, RUSSIA, Kraków, POLAND, Kursk, Voronezh, Saratov, Volga R., Ural R., Vienna, SLOVAKIA, Lvov, Tarnopol, Ukraine, Kiev, Dnieper R., Danube R., Stanislau, Dnepropetrovsk, Kharkov, Stalingrad, Budapest, HUNGARY, Bessarabia, Dniester R., Krivoy Rog, Voroshilovgrad, CROATIA, ROMANIA, Nikolayev, Zaporozhye, Rostov, Astrakhan, Sarajevo, Belgrade, Bucharest, Odessa, Kherson, Sea of Azov, SERBIA, Crimea, Novorosslysk, CAUCASUS MTS., Caspian Sea, ALBANIA, Sofia, BULGARIA, Sevastopol, Yalta, Black Sea, Grozny, Tbilisi, Baku, Allied supply route, Istanbul, Trebizond, GREECE, Athens, Aegean Sea, Ankara, TURKEY, Erzurum, Izmir, Tabriz, PERSIA, Mediterranean Sea, SYRIA, IRAQ

SOVIET BLOC, CA. 1950

USSR, 1939

Pre-1945 territory regained

New territory

Western boundary of Soviet sphere of influence, 1945

Iron curtain, 1948

Communist-governed country, with date

NATO country, 1949

Barents Sea

Pechenga
Murmansk
Kuplayavi

SWEDEN

NORWAY
Oslo

FINLAND

Stockholm
Helsinki
Vyborg
Leningrad

N

North Sea

DENMARK

Copenhagen

Baltic Sea

Estonia
Riga
Pskov

Latvia

Klaipėda
Kaliningrad
Lithuania

Volga R.

Moscow

NETHERLANDS **WEST GERMANY**

Berlin
Gdańsk
East Prussia

Vilnius
Belorussia

Smolensk

Bonn
EAST 1949 **GERMANY**
Erfurt
Dresden

Białystok
Warsaw
Minsk

POLAND
1947

Pinsk

FRANCE Nuremberg
Prague

Vistula R.

UNION OF SOVIET SOCIALIST REPUBLICS

Munich
CZECHOSLOVAKIA
Kraków
Przemysl

Ukraine

Volga R.

SWITZ.
Vienna
1948

Uzhgorod
Lvov

Kiev

AUSTRIA
Bratislava
Carpatho-Ukraine
Chernovtsy

Trieste
Budapest
Dniester R.

ITALY
HUNGARY
1947

Iaşi
Moldavia
Kishinev
Odessa

Rome
YUGOSLAVIA
1945
regime breaks with USSR, 1948

Belgrade

ROMANIA
1947

Bucharest

Adriatic Sea

Niš

Constanta

Sofia

ALBANIA
1945

BULGARIA
1945

Black Sea

GEORGIA

ARMENIA

Istanbul

Mediterranean Sea

Athens
Aegean Sea

Ankara

TURKEY

0   300 miles
0   300 km

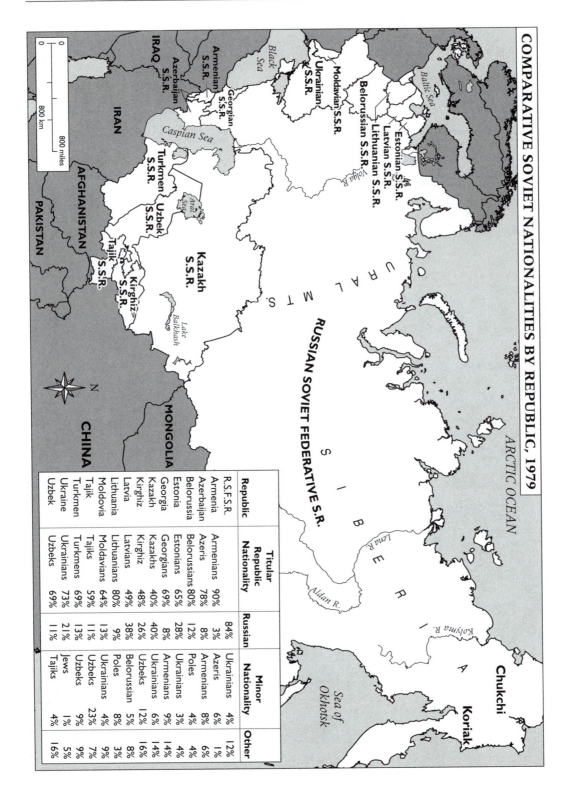

COMPARATIVE SOVIET NATIONALITIES BY REPUBLIC, 1979

Republic	Titular Republic Nationality		Russian	Minor Nationality		Other
R.S.F.S.R.				Ukrainians	4%	12%
Armenia	Armenians	90%	3%	Azeris	6%	1%
Azerbaijan	Azeris	78%	8%	Armenians	8%	6%
Belorussia	Belorussians	80%	12%	Poles	4%	4%
Estonia	Estonians	65%	28%	Ukrainians	3%	4%
Georgia	Georgians	69%	8%	Armenians	9%	14%
Kazakh	Kazakhs	40%	40%	Ukrainians	6%	14%
Kirghiz	Kirghiz	48%	26%	Uzbeks	12%	16%
Latvia	Latvians	49%	38%	Belorussian	5%	8%
Lithuania	Lithuanians	80%	9%	Poles	8%	3%
Moldovia	Moldavians	64%	13%	Ukrainians	4%	9%
Tajik	Tajiks	59%	11%	Uzbeks	23%	7%
Turkmen	Turkmens	69%	13%	Uzbeks	9%	9%
Ukraine	Ukrainians	73%	21%	Jews	1%	5%
Uzbek	Uzbeks	69%	11%	Tajiks	4%	16%

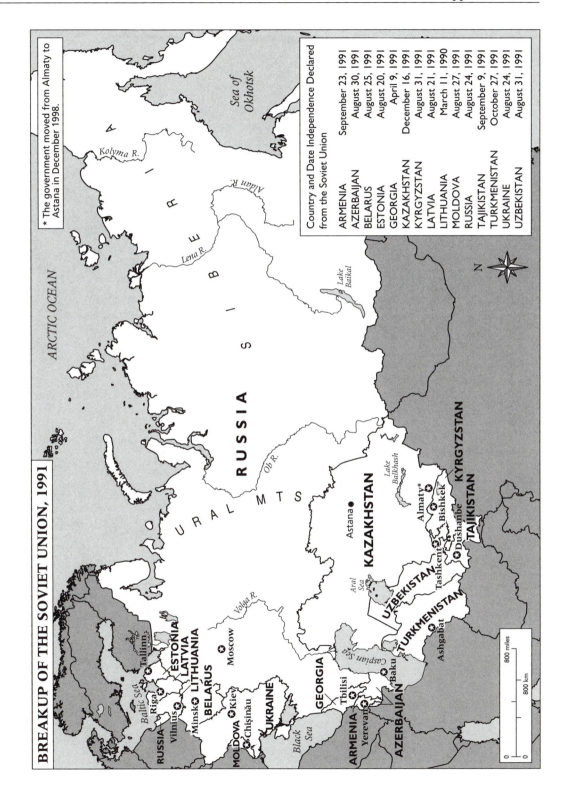

BREAKUP OF THE SOVIET UNION, 1991

* The government moved from Almaty to Astana in December 1998.

Country and Date Independence Declared from the Soviet Union

ARMENIA	September 23, 1991
AZERBAIJAN	August 30, 1991
BELARUS	August 25, 1991
ESTONIA	August 20, 1991
GEORGIA	April 9, 1991
KAZAKHSTAN	December 16, 1991
KYRGYZSTAN	August 31, 1991
LATVIA	August 21, 1991
LITHUANIA	March 11, 1990
MOLDOVA	August 27, 1991
RUSSIA	August 24, 1991
TAJIKISTAN	September 9, 1991
TURKMENISTAN	October 27, 1991
UKRAINE	August 24, 1991
UZBEKISTAN	August 31, 1991

SELECTED BIBLIOGRAPHY

The following selected bibliography focuses primarily on recently published English-language sources that are available in most general reference libraries. Older works that have become classics in the field of Russian and Soviet history are also included. The sources are divided chronologically rather than thematically, according to the major categories used in the study of Russian history.

GENERAL HISTORIES AND MONOGRAPHS

Auty, R., and D. Obolensky, eds. *An Introduction to Russian History.* Cambridge: Cambridge University Press, 1976.

Blum, J. *Lord and Peasant in Russia.* Princeton, N.J.: Princeton University Press, 1969.

Florinsky, M. T. *Russia: A History and Interpretation,* 2 vols. New York: Macmillan, 1953.

Freeze, G., ed. *Russia: A History.* Oxford: Oxford University Press, 1997.

Glants, M., and J. Toomre, eds. *Food in Russian History and Culture.* Bloomington: Indiana University Press, 1997.

Kappeler, A. *The Russian Empire: A Multiethnic History.* New York: Longman, 2001.

Keep, J. L. H. *Soldiers of the Tsar.* Oxford: Clarendon Press, 1985.

Kliuchevskii, V. O. *History of Russia,* 5 vols. New York: E. P. Dutton, 1911–31.

Liashchenko, P. I. *History of the National Economy of Russia to the 1917 Revolution.* New York: Macmillan, 1949.

Levin, E. *Sex and Society in the World of the Orthodox Slavs, 900–1700.* Ithaca, N.Y.: Cornell University Press, 1989.

Moss, W. *A History of Russia,* 2 vols. New York: McGraw-Hill, 1997.

Riasanovsky, N. V. *A History of Russia,* 5th ed. New York: Oxford University Press, 1993.

Vernadsky, G. *A History of Russia,* 5 vols. New Haven, Conn.: Yale University Press, 1943–69.

FROM KIEVAN RUS TO THE RISE OF MUSCOVY

Cross, S., and O. P. Sherbowitz-Werzor, eds. and trans. *The Primary Russian Chronicle: Laurentian text,* 3d ed. Cambridge: Cambridge University Press, 1973.

Crummey, R. O. *The Formation of Muscovy, 1304–1613.* London: Longman, 1987.

Kaiser, D. H. *The Growth of the Law in Medieval Russia.* Princeton, N.J.: Princeton University Press, 1980.

Martin, J. *Medieval Russia, 980–1584.* Cambridge: Cambridge University Press, 1995.

Fennell, J. *The Emergence of Moscow, 1304–1359.* London: Secker & Warburg, 1968.

———. *The Crisis of Medieval Russia, 1200–1304.* London: Longman, 1983.

———. *A History of the Russian Church to 1448.* London: Longman, 1995.

Halperin, C. J. *Russia and the Golden Horde.* Bloomington: Indiana University Press, 1987.

Martin, J. *Treasury of the Land of Darkness.* Cambridge: Cambridge University Press, 1986.

Rybakov, B. A. *Kievan Rus.* Moscow: Nauka, 1989.

Shchapov, Ya. N. *State and Church in Early Russia.* New Rochelle, N.Y.: Melissa Media, 1993.

MUSCOVITE RUSSIA, 1480–1689

Alef, G. *Rulers and Nobles in Fifteenth-Century Muscovy.* London: Various Reprints, 1983.

Baron, S. H., and N. S. Kollmann, eds. *Religion and Culture in Early Modern Russia and Ukraine.* DeKalb: Northern Illinois University Press, 1997.

Bushkovitch, P. *Religion and Society in Russia.* Oxford: Oxford University Press, 1992.

Bussow, C. *The Disturbed State of the Russian Realm.* Montreal: McGill's-Queens University Press, 1994.

Crummey, R. O. *Aristocrats and Servitors: The Boyar Elite in Russia, 1613–1689.* Princeton, N.J.: Princeton University Press, 1983.

Dunning, C. *Russia's First Civil War: The Time of Troubles and the Founding of the Romanov Dynasty.* University Park: Pennsylvania State University Press, 2001.

Fennell, J. L. I. *Ivan the Great of Moscow.* London: Macmillan, 1963.

Hartley, J. *A Social History of the Russian Empire.* London: Longman, 1998.

Hellie, R. *The Economy and Material Culture of Russia, 1600–1725.* Chicago: University of Chicago Press, 1999.

———. *Enserfment and Military Change in Muscovy* Chicago: University of Chicago Press, 1971.

———. *Slavery in Russia, 1450–1725.* Chicago: University of Chicago Press, 1982.

Hughes, L. *Sophia: Regent of Russia, 1657–1704.* New Haven, Conn.: Yale University Press, 1990.

Keenan, E. L., Jr. *The Kurbskii-Groznyi Apocrypha: The Seventeenth-Century Genesis of the 'Correspondence' Attributed to Prince A. M. Kurbskii and Tsar Ivan IV.* Cambridge, Mass.: Harvard University Press, 1971.

Kollmann, N. S. *Kinship and Politics.* Stanford, Calif.: Stanford University Press, 1987.

Longworth, P. *Alexis, Tsar of All the Russias.* New York: Franklin Watts, 1984.

Platonov, S. F. *Boris Godunov.* Gulf Breeze, Fla.: Academic International Press, 1973.

———. *Ivan the Terrible.* Gulf Breeze, Fla.: Academic International Press, 1974.

———. *The Time of Troubles.* Lawrence, University Press of Kansas, 1970.

Presniakov, A. E. *The Tsardom of Muscovy.* Gulf Breeze, Fla.: Academic International Press, 1978.

Skrynnikov, R. G. *Ivan the Terrible.* Gulf Breeze, Fla.: Academic International Press, 1981.

———. *The Time of Troubles.* Gulf Breeze, Fla.: Academic International Press, 1988.

Stevens, C. *Soldiers in the Steppe.* DeKalb: Northern Illinois University Press, 1995.

IMPERIAL RUSSIA, 1689–1917

Alexander, J. T. *Catherine the Great.* New York: Oxford University Press, 1989.

Anderson, M. S. *Peter the Great.* London: Thames and Hudson, 1978.

Anisimov, E. V. *The Reforms of Peter the Great.* Armonk, N.Y.: M. E. Sharpe, 1993.

———. *Empress Elizabeth.* Gulf Breeze, Fla.: Academic International Press, 1995.

Ascher, A. *The Russian Revolution of 1905,* 2 vols. Stanford, Calif.: Stanford University Press, 1988–92.

Avrich, P. *Russian Rebels, 1600–1800.* New York: W. W. Norton, 1976.

Barany, G. *The Anglo-Russian Entente Cordiale of 1697–1698.* Boulder, Colo.: East European Monographs, 1986.

Barrett, T. *At the Edge of the Empire: The Terek Cossacks and the North Caucasus Frontier, 1700–1860.* Boulder, Colo.: Westview Press, 1999.

Bassin, M. *Imperial Visions: Nationalist Imagination and Geographical Expansion in the Russian Far East, 1840–1865.* Cambridge: Cambridge University Press, 1999.

Bernstein, L. *Sonia's Daughters: Prostitutes and Their Regulation in Imperial Russia.* Berkeley: University of California Press, 1995.

Blackwell, W. L. *The Beginnings of Russian Industrialization, 1800–1860.* Princeton, N.J.: Princeton University Press, 1968.

Bonnell, V. E. *Roots of Rebellion.* Berkeley: University of California Press, 1983.

Bradley, J. *Muzhik and Muscovite.* Berkeley: University of California Press, 1985.

Brooks, J. *When Russia Learned to Read.* Princeton, N.J.: Princeton University Press, 1985.

Brower, D. R. *The Russian City between Tradition and Modernity, 1850–1900.* Berkeley: University of California Press, 1990.

Burbank, J., and D. Ransel, eds. *Imperial Russia: New Histories for the Empire.* Bloomington: Indiana University Press, 1998.

Burds, J. *Peasant Dreams and Market Politics: Labor Migration and the Russian Village, 1861–1905.* Pittsburgh, Pa.: University of Pittsburgh Press, 1998.

Bushnell, J. *Mutiny and Repression.* Bloomington: Indiana University Press, 1985.

Byrnes, R. F. *V. O. Kliuchevskii: Historian of Russia*. Bloomington: Indiana University Press, 1995.

Clements, B. E., et al., ed. *Russia's Women*. Berkeley: University of California Press, 1991.

Clowes, E. W., et al., eds. *Between Tsar and People*. Princeton, N.J.: Princeton University Press, 1991.

Cracraft, J. *The Petrine Revolution in Russian Architecture*. Chicago: University of Chicago Press, 1988.

———. *The Petrine Revolution in Russian Imagery*. Chicago: University of Chicago Press, 1998.

———, ed. *Peter the Great Transforms Russia*, 3d ed. Lexington, Ky.: D.C. Heath, 1991.

Crisp, O., and L. H. Edmondson, eds. *Civil Rights in Imperial Russia*. Oxford: Clarendon Press, 1989.

Crummey, R. O. *The Old Believers and the World of Antichrist*. Madison: University of Wisconsin Press, 1970.

Curtiss, M. *A Forgotten Empress*. New York: Ungar, 1974.

Daly, J. *Autocracy Under Siege: Security Police and Opposition in Russia, 1866–1905*. DeKalb: Northern Illinois University Press, 1998.

Madariaga, I. de. *Politics and Culture in Eighteenth-Century Russia: Collected Essays*. London: Longman, 1998.

———. *Russia in the Age of Catherine the Great*. New Haven, Conn.: Yale University Press, 1981.

Eklof, B. *Russian Peasant Schools*. Berkeley: University of California Press, 1986.

———, and J. Bushnell, eds. *Russia's Great Reforms, 1855–1881*. Bloomington: Indiana University Press, 1994.

Emmons, T. *Formation of Political Parties and the First National Elections in Russia*. Cambridge, Mass.: Harvard University Press, 1983.

Emmons, T. E., and W. Vucinich, eds. *The Zemstvo in Russia: An Experiment in Local Self-Government*. Cambridge: Cambridge University Press, 1982.

Engelstein, L. *The Keys to Happiness*. Ithaca, N.Y.: Cornell University Press, 1992.

———. *Castration and the Heavenly Kingdom: A Russian Folktale*. Ithaca, N.Y.: Cornell University Press, 1999.

———, and S. Sandler, eds. *Self and Story in Russian History*. Ithaca, N.Y.: Cornell University Press, 2000.

Field, D. *The End of Serfdom*. Cambridge, Mass.: Harvard University Press, 1976.

———. *Rebels in the Name of the Tsar*. Boston: Unwin Hyman, 1989.

Frank, S. *Crime, Cultural Conflict and Justice in Rural Russia, 1856–1914*. Berkeley: University of California Press, 1999.

Freeze, G. L. *The Parish Clergy in Nineteenth-Century Russia*. Princeton, N.J.: Princeton University Press, 1983.

Freeze, G. L. *The Russian Levites: Parish Clergy in the Eighteenth-Century*. Cambridge, Mass.: Harvard University Press, 1977.

Fuller, W. C., Jr. *Civil Military Conflict in Imperial Russia, 1881–1914*. Princeton, N.J.: Princeton University Press, 1985.

Fuller, W. C., Jr. *Strategy and Power in Russia, 1600–1914*. New York: Free Press, 1992.

Gammer, M. *Muslim Resistance to the Tsar: Shamil and the Conquest of Chechnia and Daghestan*. London: Frank Cass and Co., 1994.

Gatrell, P. *The Tsarist Economy, 1850–1917*. New York: Palgrave Macmillan, 1986.

Geifman, A. *Entangled in Terror: The Azef Affair and the Russian Revolution*. Wilmington, Del.: Scholarly Resources, 2000.

Geraci, R. *Window on the East: National and Imperial Identities in Late Tsarist Russia*. Ithaca, N.Y.: Cornell University Press, 2001.

Geyer, D. *Russian Imperialism*. New Haven, Conn.: Yale University Press, 1987.

Hamm, M. F., ed. *The City in Late Imperial Russia*. Bloomington: Indiana University Press, 1986.

Haxthausen, A. von. *Studies on the Interior of Russia*. Chicago: University of Chicago Press, 1972.

Hoch, S. L. *Serfdom and Social Control in Russia*. Chicago: University of Chicago Press, 1986.

Hughes, L. *Russia in the Age of Peter the Great*. New Haven, Conn.: Yale University Press, 1998.

Hutchinson, J. F. *Politics and Public Health in Revolutionary Russia, 1890–1913*. Baltimore: Johns Hopkins University Press, 1990.

Jahn, H. *Patriotic Culture in Russia During World War I*. Ithaca, N.Y.: Cornell University Press, 1995.

Jelavich, B. *A Century of Russian Foreign Policy, 1814–1914*. Philadelphia: Lippincott, 1964.

Johanson, C. *Women's Struggle for Higher Education in Russia, 1855–1900*. Kingston: McGill-Queen's University Press, 1987.

Jones, R. E. *The Emancipation of the Russian Nobility, 1762–1785.* Princeton, N.J.: Princeton University Press, 1973.

———. *Provincial Development in Russia.* New Brunswick, N.J.: Rutgers University Press, 1984.

Jones, W. G. *Nikolay Novikov.* Cambridge: Cambridge University Press, 1984.

Kagan, F. *The Military Reforms of Nicholas I: The Origins of the Modern Russian Army.* New York: St. Martin's Press, 1999.

Kan, S. *Memory Eternal: Tingit Culture and Russian Orthodox Christianity through Two Centuries.* Seattle: University of Washington Press, 1999.

Khalid, A. *The Politics of Muslim Cultural Reform: Jadidism in Central Asia.* Berkeley: University of California Press, 1999.

Kingston-Mann, E. *In Search of the True West: Culture, Economics and Problems of Russian Development.* Princeton, N.J.: Princeton University Press, 1999.

Kizenko, N. *A Prodigal Saint: Father John of Kronstadt and the Russian People.* University Park: Pennsylvania State University Press, 2000.

Klier, J. D. *Russia Gathers Her Jews.* DeKalb: Northern Illinois University Press, 1986.

Kollmann, N. S. *By Honor Bound: State and Society in Early Modern Russia.* Ithaca, N.Y.: Cornell University Press, 1999.

Kotsonis, Y. *Making Peasants Backward: Agricultural Cooperatives and the Agrarian Question in Russia, 1861–1914.* New York: St. Martin's Press, 1999.

LeDonne, J. P. *Ruling Russia.* Princeton, N.J.: Princeton University Press, 1984.

Lieven, D. C. B. *Russia and the Origins of the First World War.* New York: St. Martin's Press, 1983.

———. *Russia's Rulers under the Old Regime.* New Haven, Conn.: Yale University Press, 1989.

Lincoln, W. B. *In the Vanguard of Reform.* DeKalb: Northern Illinois University Press, 1982.

———. *Nicholas I, Emperor and Autocrat of all the Russias.* DeKalb: Northern Illinois University Press, 1989.

———. *The Great Reforms.* DeKalb: Northern Illinois University Press, 1990.

Lowe, H. D. *Tsar and Jews.* Chur, Switzerland: Harwood Academic Publishers, 1993.

Malia, M. *Alexander Herzen and the Birth of Russian Socialism, 1812–1855.* New York: Grosset and Dunlap, 1965.

Manning, R. T. *The Crisis of the Old Order in Russia.* Princeton, N.J.: Princeton University Press, 1982.

Marker, G. *Publishing, Printing, and the Origins of Intellectual Life in Russia, 1700–1800.* Princeton, N.J.: Princeton University Press, 1985.

McReynolds, L. *The News under Russia's Old Regime.* Princeton, N.J.: Princeton University Press, 1991.

Moon, D. *Russian Peasants and Tsarist Legislation on the Eve of Reform.* Houndmills, Basingstoke, 1992.

Neuberger, J. *Hooliganism.* Berkeley: University of California Press, 1993.

Owen, T. C. *The Corporation under Russian Law, 1800–1917.* Cambridge: Cambridge University Press, 1991.

Pintner, W. M., and D. K. Rowney, eds. *The Bureaucratization of Russian Society from the Seventeenth to the Twentieth Century.* Chapel Hill: University of North Carolina Press, 1980.

Phillips, E. J. *The Founding of Russia's Navy.* Westport, Conn.: Greenwood Press, 1995.

Pososhkov, I. *The Book of Poverty and Wealth.* Stanford, Calif.: Stanford University Press, 1987.

Raeff, M. *Understanding Imperial Russia: State and Society in the Old Regime.* New York: Columbia University Press, 1983.

———. *Origins of the Russian Intelligentsia.* New York: Harcourt, Brace & Jovanovich, 1966.

———. *The Well-Ordered Police State.* New Haven, Conn.: Yale University Press, 1983.

———. *Michael Speransky.* The Hague: Martinus Nijhoff, 1957.

Ransel, D. L. *The Politics of Catherinean Russia.* New Haven, Conn.: Yale University Press, 1975.

Ransel, D. *Mothers of Misery.* Princeton, N.J.: Princeton University Press, 1988.

Reiber, A. J. *Merchants and Entrepreneurs in Imperial Russia.* Chapel Hill: University of North Carolina Press, 1982.

Riasanovsky, N. V. *The Image of Peter the Great in Russian History and Thought.* New York: Oxford University Press, 1985.

Robbins, R. G. *The Tsar's Viceroys.* Ithaca, N.Y.: Cornell University Press, 1987.

Rogger, H. *Jewish Policies and Right-Wing Politics in Imperial Russia.* Berkeley: University of California Press, 1986.

Seton-Watson, H. *The Russian Empire, 1801–1917.* Oxford: Clarendon Press, 1967.

Stanislawski, M. *Tsar Nicholas I and the Jews.* Philadelphia: Jewish Publication Society of America, 1983.

Starr, S. F. *Decentralization and Self-Government in Russia, 1830–1870.* Princeton, N.J.: Princeton University Press, 1972.

Stites, R. *The Women's Liberation Movement in Russia,* 2d ed. Princeton, N.J.: Princeton University Press, 1991.

Thaden, E. C., ed. *Russification in the Baltic Provinces and Finland, 1855–1914.* Princeton, N.J.: Princeton University Press, 1981.

Venturi, F. *Roots of Revolution.* Chicago: University of Chicago Press, 1983.

Verner, A. M. *The Crisis of Autocracy.* Princeton, N.J.: Princeton University Press, 1990.

Von Laue, T. H. *Sergei Witte and the Industrialization of Russia.* New York: Columbia University Press, 1963.

Weissman, N. B. *Reform in Tsarist Russia.* New Brunswick, N.J.: Rutgers University Press, 1981.

Wildman, A. L. *The Making of a Workers' Revolution: Russian Social Democracy, 1891–1903.* Chicago: University of Chicago Press, 1967.

Wirtschafter, E. K. *From Serf to Russian Soldier.* Princeton, N.J.: Princeton University Press, 1990.

Wortman, R. S. *Scenarios of Power,* vol. 1. Princeton, N.J.: Princeton University Press, 1995.

Zaionchkovskii, P. A. *The Russian Autocracy under Alexander III.* Gulf Breeze, Fla.: Academic International Press, 1976.

———. *The Russian Autocracy in Crisis, 1878–1882.* Gulf Breeze, Fla.: Academic International Press, 1979.

Zelnik, R. E. *Labor and Society in Tsarist Russia.* Stanford, Calif.: Stanford University Press, 1971.

FROM THE RUSSIAN REVOLUTION TO POST-SOVIET RUSSIA

1917–1941

Abraham, R. *Alexander Kerensky: The First Love of the Revolution.* New York: Columbia University Press, 1987.

Acton, E. *Rethinking the Russian Revolution.* London: Edward Arnold, 1990.

Anderle, V. *Workers in Stalin's Russia.* New York: Palgrave Macmillan, 1988.

Andreev-Khomiakov, G. *Bitter Waters: Life and Work in Stalin's Russia.* Boulder, Colo.: Westview Press, 1997.

Avrich, P. *Kronstadt, 1921.* Princeton, N.J.: Princeton University Press, 1991.

Bailes, K. E. *Technology and Society Under Lenin and Stalin.* Princeton, N.J.: Princeton University Press, 1978.

Ball, A. M. *The Nepmen: Russia's Last Capitalists.* Berkeley: University of California Press, 1987.

———. *And Now My Soul Has Hardened.* Berkeley: University of California Press, 1994.

Benvenuti, F. *The Bolsheviks and the Red Army 1918–22.* Cambridge: Cambridge University Press, 1988.

Brovkin, V., ed. *The Bolsheviks in Russian Society: The Revolution and Civil Wars.* New Haven, Conn.: Yale University Press, 1997.

Browder, R. P., and A. Kerensky, eds. *The Russian Provisional Government, 1917. Documents,* 3 vols. Stanford, Calif.: Stanford University Press, 1961.

Burdzhalov, E. N. *Russia's Second Revolution: The February 1917 Uprising in Petrograd.* Bloomington: Indiana University Press, 1987.

Carr, E. H. *The Bolshevik Revolution, 1917–1923,* 3 vols. London: Macmillan, 1985.

———. *The Interregnum, 1923–1924.* Harmondsworth, U.K.: Penguin, 1969.

———. *Socialism in One Country, 1924–1926,* 3 vols. Harmondsworth, U.K.: Penguin, 1970.

———, with R. W. Davies. *Foundations of a Planned Economy, 1926–1929,* 2 vols. New York: Macmillan, 1971–74.

Carrere d'Encausse, H. *The Great Challenge.* New York: Holmes & Meier, 1992.

Chamberlin, W. H. *The Russian Revolution, 1917–1921,* 2 vols. Princeton, N.J.: Princeton University Press, 1987.

Chase, W. J. *Workers, Society, and the Soviet State.* Urbana: University of Illinois Press, 1987.

Clements, B. E. *Bolshevik Women.* Cambridge: Cambridge University Press, 1997.

Cohen, S. F. *Bukharin and the Bolshevik Revolution.* Oxford: Oxford University Press, 1980.

Conquest, R. *The Great Terror: A Reassessment.* New York: Oxford University Press, 1990.

Curtiss, J. S. *The Russian Church and the Soviet State, 1917–50.* Boston: Little, Brown, 1953.

Daniels, Robert. *Red October: The Bolshevik Revolution of 1917.* New York: Scribner, 1967.

Danilov, V. P. *Rural Russia under the New Regime.* Bloomington: Indiana University Press, 1988.

Davies, R. W. *The Industrialization of Soviet Russia,* 3 vols. Cambridge, Mass.: Harvard University Press, 1980–91.

———, et al., eds. *The Economic Transformation of the Soviet Union, 1913–1945.* Cambridge: Cambridge University Press, 1994.

Davies, S. *Popular Opinion in Stalin's Russia: Terror, Propaganda and Dissent, 1934–1941.* Cambridge: Cambridge University Press, 1997.

Degras, J., ed. *Soviet Documents on Foreign Policy, 1917–41,* 3 vols. New York: Octagon Books, 1978.

Elleman, B. *Diplomacy and Deception: The Secret History of Sino-Soviet Diplomatic Relations, 1917–1927.* Armonk, N.Y.: M. E. Sharpe, 1997.

Etkind, A. *Eros of the Impossible: The History of Psychoanalysis in Russia.* Boulder, Colo.: Westview Press, 1997.

Fainsod, M. *How Russia Is Ruled,* 2d ed. Cambridge, Mass.: Harvard University Press, 1965.

———. *Smolensk under Soviet Rule.* Cambridge, Mass.: Harvard University Press, 1958.

Farnsworth, B. *Alexandra Kollontai: Socialism, Feminism, and the Bolshevik Revolution.* Stanford, Calif.: Stanford University Press, 1980.

Ferro, M. *October 1917: A Social History of the Russian Revolution.* London: Routledge & Kegan Paul, 1980.

———. *The Russian Revolution of February, 1917.* Englewood Cliffs, N.J.: Prentice-Hall, 1972.

Figes, O. *Peasant Russia, Civil War: The Volga Countryside.* Oxford: Oxford University Press, 1989.

———. *A People's Tragedy: A History of the Russian Revolution.* New York: Viking, 1997.

———, and B. Kolonitskii. *Interpreting the Russian Revolution: The Language and Symbols of 1917.* New Haven, Conn.: Yale University Press, 1999.

Fitzpatrick, S. *Everyday Stalinism: Ordinary Life in Extraordinary Times: Soviet Russia in the 1930s.* New York: Oxford University Press, 1999.

———, ed. *Stalinism: New Directions.* London: Routledge, 2000.

———. *The Commissariat of the Enlightenment: Soviet Organization of Education and the Arts under Lunacharsky.* Cambridge: Cambridge University Press, 1970.

———. *Education and Social Mobility in the Soviet Union, 1921–1934.* Cambridge: Cambridge University Press, 1979.

———, ed. *Cultural Revolution in Russia, 1928–1931.* Bloomington: Indiana University Press, 1979.

———. *The Cultural Front.* Ithaca, N.Y.: Cornell University Press, 1992.

———. *Stalin's Peasants.* Oxford: Oxford University Press, 1994.

———, A. Rabinowitch, and R. Stites, eds. *Russia in the Era of NEP.* Bloomington: Indiana University Press, 1991.

Filtzer, D. *Soviet Workers and Stalinist Industrialization.* Armonk, N.Y.: M. E. Sharpe, 1986.

Gaddis, J. L. *Russia, the Soviet Union, and the United States,* 2d ed. New York: McGraw-Hill, 1990.

Garros, V., N. Korenevskaya, and T. Lahusen, eds. *Intimacy and Terror.* New York: New Press, 1995.

Getty, J. A. *Origins of the Great Purges.* Cambridge: Cambridge University Press, 1985.

———, and R. T. Manning, eds. *Stalinist Terror: New Perspectives.* Cambridge: Cambridge University Press, 1993.

Gill, G. *The Origins of the Stalinist Political System.* Cambridge: Cambridge University Press, 1990.

———. *Peasants and Government in the Russian Revolution.* New York: Barnes & Noble Books, 1979.

Gleason, A., P. Kenez, and R. Stites, eds. *Bolshevik Culture: Experiment and Order in the Russian Revolution.* Bloomington: Indiana University Press, 1985.

Goldman, W. Z. *Women, the State, and Revolution.* Cambridge: Cambridge University Press, 1993.

Gorsuch, A. E. *Youth in Revolutionary Russia: Enthusiasts, Bohemians and Delinquents.* Bloomington: Indiana University Press, 2000.

Graham, L. R. *Science, Philosophy, and Human Behavior in the Soviet Union.* New York: Columbia University Press, 1987.

Gray, C. *The Russian Experiment in Art, 1863–1922.* New York: Thames & Hudson, 1986.

Groys, B. *The Total Art of Stalinism.* Princeton, N.J.: Princeton University Press, 1992.

Hasegawa, T. *The February Revolution: Petrograd, 1917.* Seattle: University of Washington Press, 1972.

Geller, M., and A. Nekrich. *Utopia in Power: The History of the Soviet Union from 1917 to the Present.* New York: Hutchinson, 1992.

Hindus, M. *Red Bread.* Bloomington: Indiana University Press, 1988.

Holmes, L. E. *The Kremlin and the Schoolhouse.* Bloomington: Indiana University Press, 1991.

Hoffmann, D. *Peasant Metropolis: Social Identities in Moscow, 1929–1941.* Ithaca, N.Y.: Cornell University Press, 1994.

Hosking, G. A. *The First Socialist Society: A History of the Soviet Union from Within,* 2d ed. Cambridge, Mass.: Harvard University Press, 1990.

Hughes, J. *Stalin, Siberia, and the Crisis of the New Economic Policy.* Cambridge: Cambridge University Press, 1991.

Hughes, J. *Stalinism in a Russian Province.* New York: St. Martin's Press, 1996.

Husband, W. *"Godless Communists": Atheism and Society in Soviet Russia, 1917–1932.* DeKalb: Northern Illinois University Press, 2000.

Keep, J. L. H. *The Russian Revolution: A Study in Mass Mobilization.* New York: W. W. Norton, 1976.

Kenez, P. *The Birth of the Propaganda State.* Cambridge: Cambridge University Press, 1985.

———. *Cinema and Soviet Society, 1917–1953.* Cambridge: Cambridge University Press, 1992.

King, D. *The Commissar Vanishes: The Falsification of Photographs and Art in Stalin's Russia.* New York: Metropolitan Books, 1997.

Knight, A. *Who Killed Kirov? The Kremlin's Greatest Mystery.* New York: Hill and Wang, 1999.

Koenker, D. P., and W. G. Rosenberg. *Strikes and Revolution in Russia, 1917.* Princeton, N.J.: Princeton University Press, 1989.

———, and R. G. Suny, eds. *Party, State, and Society in the Russian Civil War: Explorations in Social History.* Bloomington: Indiana University Press, 1989.

Kotkin, S. *Magnetic Mountain.* Berkeley: University of California Press, 1995.

Lewin, M. *Russian Peasants and Soviet Power.* New York: W. W. Norton, 1975.

———. *The Making of the Soviet System.* New York: Pantheon, 1985.

McAuley, M. *Soviet Politics, 1917–1991,* rev. ed. Oxford: Oxford University Press, 1992.

McAuley, M. *Bread and Justice.* New York: Oxford University Press, 1991.

———, ed. *The Russian Revolution and the Soviet State, 1917–1921.* London: Longman, 1988.

McNeal, R., et al., eds. *Resolutions and Decisions of the Communist Party of the Soviet Union,* 5 vols. Toronto: University of Toronto Press, 1974–82.

Malia, M. E. *The Soviet Tragedy: A History of Socialism in Russia, 1917–1991.* New York: Free Press, 1994.

Mandelshtam, N. *Hope against Hope.* New York: Atheneum, 1970.

Medvedev, R. A. *Let History Judge,* 2d ed. New York: Columbia University Press, 1989.

Nogee, J. L., and R. H. Donaldson. *Soviet Foreign Policy since World War II,* 4th ed. New York: Macmillan, 1992.

Nove, A. *An Economic History of the USSR, 1917–91,* 3d ed. New York: Penguin, 1992.

Pethybridge, R. *The Social Prelude to Stalinism.* New York: St. Martin's Press, 1974.

Pipes, R. *The Russian Revolution.* New York: Knopf, 1991.

———. *Russia under the New Regime.* New York: Knopf, 1994.

Rabinowitch, A. *Prelude to Revolution.* Bloomington: Indiana University Press, 1968.

———. *The Bolsheviks Come to Power.* New York: W. W. Norton, 1978.

Raleigh, D. J. *Revolution on the Volga.* Ithaca, N.Y.: Cornell University Press, 1986.

Thomas F. Remington, *Building Socialism in Bolshevik Russia.* Pittsburgh, Pa.: University of Pittsburgh, 1984.

Rittersporn, G. T. *Stalinist Simplifications and Soviet Complications.* New York: Harwood Academic Publishers, 1991.

Rosenberg, W. G., and L. H. Siegelbaum, eds. *Social Dimensions of Soviet Industrialization.* Bloomington: Indiana University Press, 1993.

Rosenberg, W. G., ed. *Bolshevik Visions,* 2 vols. Ann Arbor: University of Michigan Press, 1990.

Scott, J. *Behind the Urals.* Bloomington: Indiana University Press, 1966.

Siegelbaum, L. H. *Soviet State and Society Between Revolutions, 1918–1929.* Cambridge: Cambridge University Press, 1992.

———. *Stakhanovism and the Politics of Productivity in the USSR, 1935–41.* Cambridge: Cambridge University Press, 1986.

Simon, G. *Nationalism and Policy towards the Nationalities in the Soviet Union.* Boulder, Colo.: Westview Press, 1991.

Smith, S. A. *Red Petrograd: Revolution in the Factories, 1917–18.* Cambridge: Cambridge University Press, 1983.

Solomon, P. *Soviet Criminal Justice under Stalin.* Cambridge: Cambridge University Press, 1996.

Stites, R. *Revolutionary Dreams.* New York: Oxford University Press, 1991.

Thorniley, D. *The Rise and Fall of the Soviet Rural Communist Party, 1927–39.* New York: Palgrave Macmillan, 1988.

Tucker, R. C. *Stalin as Revolutionary, 1879–1929.* New York, 1973.

———. *Stalin in Power.* New York: W. W. Norton, 1990.

———, ed. *Stalinism.* New York: W. W. Norton, 1977.

Viola, L. *Peasant Rebels under Stalin.* New York: Oxford University Press, 1996.

Volkogonov, D. *Stalin: Triumph and Tragedy.* New York: Grove Weidenfeld, 1991.

Hagen, M. von. *Soldiers in the Proletarian Dictatorship.* Ithaca, N.Y.: Cornell University Press, 1990.

Ward, C. *Russia's Cotton Workers and the New Economic Policy.* Cambridge: Cambridge University Press, 1990.

White, S. *The Bolshevik Poster.* New Haven, Conn.: Yale University Press, 1988.

Wildman, A. K. *The End of the Russian Imperial Army,* 2 vols. Princeton, N.J.: Princeton University Press, 1980–87.

Youngblood, D. J. *Movies for the Masses.* Cambridge: Cambridge University Press, 1992.

1941 to the Present

Andreyev, C. *Vlasov and the Russian Liberation Movement.* Cambridge: Cambridge University Press, 1987.

Christopher, Andrew, and Vasili Mitrokhin. *The Sword and the Shield: The Mitrokhin Archive and the Secret History of the KGB.* New York: Basic Books, 1999.

Armstrong, J. A. *Ukrainian Nationalism,* 3d ed. Englewood Cliffs, N.J.: Prentice-Hall, 1990.

Aslund, A. *Gorbachev's Struggle for Economic Reform,* 2d ed. Ithaca, N.Y.: Cornell University Press, 1991.

Barber, J., and M. Harrison. *The Soviet Home Front, 1941–45.* London: Longman, 1991.

Belov, F. *The History of A Collective Farm.* New York: Praeger, 1955.

Bialer, S. *Stalin's Successors.* Cambridge: Cambridge University Press, 1980.

Boshyk, Y., ed. *Ukraine during World War II.* Edmonton: Canada Institute for Ukrainian Studies, University of Alberta, 1986.

Breslauer, G. W. *Khrushchev and Brezhnev as Leaders.* London: Allen & Unwin, 1982.

Brody, R. *Ideology and Political Mobilization.* Pittsburgh, Pa.: University of Pittsburgh Press, 1994.

Brown, A. *The Gorbachev Factor in Soviet Politics,* 2d ed. New York: Oxford University Press, 1992.

Buckley, M., ed. *Perestroika and Soviet Women.* Cambridge: Cambridge University Press, 1992.

Anatoli, Cherniaev. *My Six Years with Gorbachev.* University Park: Pennsylvania State University Press, 2000.

Davies, R. W. *Soviet History in the Gorbachev Revolution.* Bloomington: Indiana University Press, 1989.

Divine, R. A., ed. *The Cuban Missile Crisis,* 2d ed. New York: M. Wiener, 1988.

Djilas, M. *Conversations with Stalin.* New York: Harcourt, Brace & Jovanovich, 1962.

Dunmore, T. *Soviet Politics, 1945–53.* New York: St. Martin's Press, 1984.

Gerald, Easter. *Reconstructing the State: Personal Networks and Elite Identity in Soviet Russia.* Cambridge: Cambridge University Press, 2000.

Ellis, J. *The Russian Orthodox Church: A Contemporary History.* Bloomington: Indiana University Press, 1986.

English, Robert D. *Russia and the Idea of the West: Gorbachev, Intellectuals and the End of the Cold War.* New York: Columbia University Press, 2000.

Erickson, J. *The Road to Stalingrad.* New York: Harper & Row, 1975.

———. *The Road to Berlin.* Boulder, Colo.: Westview Press, 1983.

Fireside, H. *Icon and Swastika.* Cambridge, Mass.: Harvard University Press, 1971.

Gaiduk, Ilya. *The Soviet Union and the Vietnam War.* Chicago: Ivan R. Dee, 1996.

Gall, Carlotta and Thomas de Waal. *Chechnya: Calamity in the Caucasus.* New York: New York University Press, 1998.

Garrard, J., and C. Garrard, eds. *World War II and the Soviet People*. London: Westview Press, 1993.

Gill, G. J. *Collapse of a Single-Party System*. Cambridge: Cambridge University Press, 1994.

Glantz, David. *Stumbling Colossus: The Red Army on the Eve of World War II*. Lawrence: University Press of Kansas, 1998.

———, and J. House. *When Titans Clashed*. Lawrence: University Press of Kansas, 1995.

Gorbachev, M. S. *Perestroika,* rev. ed. Nottingham, U.K.: Spokesman, 1988.

Gustafson, Thane. *Capitalism Russian Style*. Cambridge: Cambridge University Press, 2000.

Hosking, G. A. *The Awakening of the Soviet Union,* rev. ed. Cambridge, Mass.: Harvard University Press, 1991.

Harrison, M. *Soviet Planning in Peace and War, 1938–45*. Cambridge: Cambridge University Press, 1985.

Herspring, Dale. *Russian Civil-Military Relations*. Bloomington: Indiana University Press, 1996.

Holloway, D. *Stalin and the Bomb*. New Haven, Conn.: Yale University Press, 1994.

Hosking, G. A. *Beyond Socialist Realism*. New York: Holmes & Meier, 1980.

Hough, Jerry F. *Democratization and Revolution in the USSR, 1985–1991*. Washington, D.C.: Brookings Institution, 1997.

Ivanova, Galina M. *Labor Camp Socialism: The Gulag in the Soviet Totalitarian System*. Armonk, N.Y.: M. E. Sharpe, 2000.

Kaiser, Robert J. *The Geography of Nationalism in Russia and the USSR*. Princeton, N.J.: Princeton University Press, 1995.

Keep, J. L. H. *Last of the Empires*. Oxford: Oxford University Press, 1995.

Khrushchev, N. S. *Khrushchev Remembers,* 2 vols. Boston: Little Brown, 1970–74.

———. *Khrushchev on Khrushchevism*. Boston: Little Brown, 1990.

Lubin, N. *Labour and Nationality in Soviet Central Asia*. Princeton, N.J.: Princeton University Press, 1984.

McAuley, A. *Economic Welfare in the Soviet Union*. Madison: University of Wisconsin Press, 1979.

McCauley, M., ed. *Khrushchev and Khrushchevism*. Bloomington: Indiana University Press, 1987.

Medvedev, R. *Khrushchev*. Garden City, N.Y.: Anchor Press/Doubleday, 1984.

Millar, J., ed. *Politics, Work, and Daily Life in the U.S.S.R.: A Survey of Former Soviet Citizens*. New York: Cambridge University Press, 1987.

Moskoff, W. *The Bread of Affliction*. Cambridge: Cambridge University Press, 1990.

Nekrich, A. M. *The Punished Peoples*. New York: W. W. Norton, 1978.

Porter, C., and M. Jones. *Moscow in World War II*. London: Chatto & Windus, 1987.

Resis, A., ed. *Molotov Remembers*. Chicago: Ivan R. Dee, 1994.

Reynolds, D., ed. *The Origins of the Cold War in Europe*. New Haven, Conn.: Yale University Press, 1994.

Sakwa, R. *Gorbachev and His Reforms, 1985–1990*. New York: Philip Allan, 1991.

Shatz, M. *Soviet Dissent in Historical Perspective*. New York: Cambridge University Press, 1980.

Shukman, H., ed. *Stalin's Generals*. New York: Grove Press, 1993.

Smith, G., ed. *The Nationalities Question in the Soviet Union*. London: Longman, 1990.

Sodaro, M. J. *Moscow, Germany, and the West from Khrushchev to Gorbachev*. Ithaca, N.Y.: Cornell University Press, 1990.

Suny, R. G. *The Revenge of the Past*. Stanford, Calif.: Stanford University Press, 1994.

Van Goudoever, A. P. *The Limits of Destalinization in the Soviet Union*. London: Macmillan, 1986.

Weinberg, G. L. *A World at Arms*. Cambridge: Cambridge University Press, 1994.

White, S. *Gorbachev and After,* 3d ed. Cambridge: Cambridge University Press, 1992.

Yeltsin, B. *Against the Grain*. New York: Summit Books, 1990.

INDEX

Note: **Boldface** page numbers indicate primary discussions of a topic. *Italic* page numbers indicate illustrations.

A

Abel, Rudolph 351
Abkhazia **45**
Abramov, Feodor Aleksandrovich **45–46,** 318, 359
Abramtsevo **46,** 52
Academy of Sciences **46**
   Chekhov and 112
   Lomonosov in 46, 219, 405
   Siberian branch of 50
Acmeist movement 50, 51, 171, 227
Adashev, Aleksei Feodorovich **46–47**
Adashev, Daniil Feodorovich 47
Adrian, Patriarch 402
Adrianople, Treaty of **47,** 304, 410
Afanasiev, Alexander Nikolaevich **47**
Afghanistan **48–49**
   Borovik's accounts of war in 94
   Soviet invasion of 38, 48–49, 97, 170, 307, 353
   Soviet withdrawal from 40, 49, 165, 429
Aganbegyan, Abel 50
"agit-films" 49, 207
"agit-trains" **49,** 359

agriculture
   of Kievan Rus 5
   Lysenko's experiments in 357
   of Soviet Union. *See* collectivization of agriculture
Aigun, Treaty of 62, 226, 249
Ainu people 70
aircraft design 318–319, 348
Aitmatov, Chingiz Torekulovich **49–50**
Akademgorodok **50**
Akhmadulina, Bella Akhatovna **50,** 375–376
Akhmat (Mongol khan). *See* Akhmed
Akhmatova, Anna Andreevna **50–51**
   and Brodsky 98
   campaign against 51, 384
   Chukovskaya on 117
   and Gumilev 51, 171
Akhmed (Mongol khan) **51,** 351
Aksakov, Ivan Sergeevich 52, 322
Aksakov, Konstantin Sergeevich 52, 322
Aksakov, Sergei Timofeevich 46, 51–52, *52*
Aksakov family **51–52**
Akselrod, Pavel 109
Aksenov, Vasili Petrovich **52–53,** 160
Alaska **53–54**
   exploration and colonization of 65, 79, 80, 87, 106, 407
   first governor of 369

   Russian American Company in 53, 80, **299–300,** 369
   sale of 54, 369, 413
Albania 365
Aleichem, Sholem **54**
Alekhine, Aleksandr Aleksandrovich **54–55,** 94
Aleksandr. *See* Alexander
Aleksandrov, Grigorii Vasilievich **55–56,** 138, 261
Alekseev, Mikhail Vasilievich 56
Aleksei (son of Nicholas II) 61, 251, 290
Aleksei, Metropolitan of Moscow 10, **56–57,** 130, 178
Aleksei I (Aleksei Mikhailovich) (czar of Russia) 16, 17, 18, **57,** 297, 400
   and Avvakum 72
   discontent during rule of 119–120
   foreign policy under 301–302
   and Nikon 252, 253
   wives and heirs of 19
Aleksei II, Patriarch 268
Alexander I (czar of Russia) 28, **57–58,** 408
   and Arakcheev 68
   foreign policy under 302, 409
   meeting with Napoleon 337
   serfdom under 58, 408
Alexander II (czar of Russia) 28–29, **58–59,** 412
   assassination of 29, 59, 109, 193, 271, 282, 414